D0793815

Conquest and Pestilence in the Early Spanish Philippines

Published with the support of the
School of Pacific and Asian Studies,
University of Hawai'i

Conquest and Pestilence in the Early Spanish Philippines

Linda A. Newson

University of Hawai'i Press
Honolulu

Printed in the United States of America

14 13 12 11 10 09 6 5 4 3 2 1

Library of Congress Cataloging-in-Publication Data

Newson, Linda A.

Conquest and pestilence in the early Spanish Philippines / Linda A. Newson.

p. cm.

Includes bibliographical references and index.

ISBN 978-0-8248-3272-8 (hard cover : alk. paper)

1. Philippines—Population—History. 2. Philippines—Colonization—History. 3. Disease—Philippines—History. 4. Spain—Foreign relations—Philippines—History. 5. Philippines—Foreign relations—Philippines—History. I. Title.

HB3649.N48 2009

304.609599'0903—dc22

2008048662

University of Hawai'i Press books are printed on acid-free paper and meet the guidelines for permanence and durability of the Council on Library Resources.

Designed by Paul Herr, University of Hawai'i Press production staff
Printed by The Maple-Vail Book Manufacturing Group

Contents

Illustrations and Tables

Figures

Maps

Tables

Preface

Having worked for some years on the demographic impact of Spanish colonial rule in various parts of Latin America, I became increasingly curious about an oft-repeated statement that the population of the Philippines did not suffer the same demographic disaster that afflicted Native American populations following European contact because it had acquired immunity to Old World diseases through trading contacts with Asia prior to Spanish arrival. My curiosity was aroused, not so much because at the time I thought this assumption was wrong, though this book suggests that to be partly so, but because no one had presented any evidence to support it. I therefore began to research the topic, believing I would write just one journal article looking at the Philippines experience in the context of the demographic impact of Spanish colonial rule more widely. As has now become familiar in my research, this small idea ended up as a long book.

Research on this topic meant not only engaging with areas that were hitherto unfamiliar to me, such as the nature of trading contacts in the South China Sea in pre-Spanish times, but also undertaking an in-depth analysis of the scattered, fragmentary sources that exist beyond those available in Emma Blair and James Robertson's fifty-five-volume *The Philippine Islands, 1493–1803* (Cleveland: A. H. Clark, 1903–1909). As a geographer, I was also concerned that the study should make a concerted effort to study all regions of Luzon and the Visayas, for experience has taught me that processes are seldom uniform over large areas and that regional study can often reveal the complexity of the factors at work. For many regions of the Philippines only sketchy accounts of their early histories existed, which sometimes meant constructing them from scratch in order to provide some context. So there was more to do than I anticipated, and the book was delayed further by several other writing projects and service as head of the School of Humanities at King's College between 1997 and 2000, when it proved impossible to snatch even a short period for sustained writing.

To support this research, I have been fortunate to receive grants for archival research in the Philippines, Spain, and Italy from a number of bodies, including the British Academy, the Central Research Fund of the University of London, and the School of Humanities at King's College, London, to all of whom I am most grateful. I have also been privileged to be awarded two Fellowships at the Newberry Library, Chicago. The Philippine collections of this library, including some manuscripts and many rare books, are excellent and underused, and its wonderful facilities greatly facilitated the writing of this book.

Sources for the study of the Spanish colonial Philippines are scattered. In Manila, research was conducted in the Philippines National Archive, the Archdiocesan Archives of Manila, and the Dominican archives at the University of Santo Tomas. I am grateful to the late Cardinal Jaime Sin and Father Pablo Fernandez for access to the latter archives and to the staffs of all these archives for their very helpful assistance. In the Philippines I also had the good fortune to meet the late William Henry Scott. Scotty kindly allowed me to use his unique library at Sagada, where we also spent many hours enthusiastically exchanging notes and ideas on various aspects of Philippine history. The Archivo General de Indias in Seville has an unparalleled collection of documents on the Philippines, many of which have probably never been consulted, particularly those dating from the eighteenth century. Many of the early Philippine documents are extremely fragile and for conservation reasons were unavailable, awaiting digitalization for significant periods of this research. This necessitated several not unwelcome research trips to Seville. Unfortunately, research in the Archivio Generale dell'Ordine dei Frati Minori in Rome failed to yield any significant materials, but sources in the Archivum Romanum Societatis Iesu proved invaluable. Thanks are due to Father Charles O'Neill for allowing me access to the library of the Jesuit Instititum Historicum in Rome.

During the extended period of research I was fortunate to draw on the expertise of some formidable scholars. At the beginning of the project, the late Paul Wheatley introduced me to the nature of trading contacts in the South China Sea and pointed me to research questions he thought I should follow up in the context of the Philippines. Discussions with Ann Jannetta about her research on epidemics in Japan deepened my understanding of epidemiology and the nature of immunity to acute infections. While researching in the Philippine National Archive, I also benefitted from discussions with fellow archival researchers Bruce Cruikshank and James Warren, and I have been encouraged to keep going with the project by the interest shown by Norman Owen, Dan Doeppers, Peter Boomgaard, and Raquel Reyes.

I would like to give particular thanks to the assessors of this manuscript. The nature of the detailed, insightful comments of one assessor were quite exceptional and the revisions he or she recommended have, I believe, resulted in a much better book. Any views expressed, however, remain my responsibility. I am also grateful to the Archivo General de Indias for permission to reproduce their maps and illustrations, and to Roma Beaumont and Lester Jones for producing such excellent maps from my very rough sketches. Finally, I would like to thank Pamela Kelley at the University of Hawai'i Press for her belief in the book and her patience while I was bringing it altogether.

Finally, I would like to dedicate this book to my only three uncles, Al, Bill, and Stephen, who all in their eighties or nineties have died within the past two years. They have always taken an interest in my work and had they been born in later times would have relished the educational opportunities and extensive travel I have been so lucky to enjoy in my academic career.

PART I

Introduction

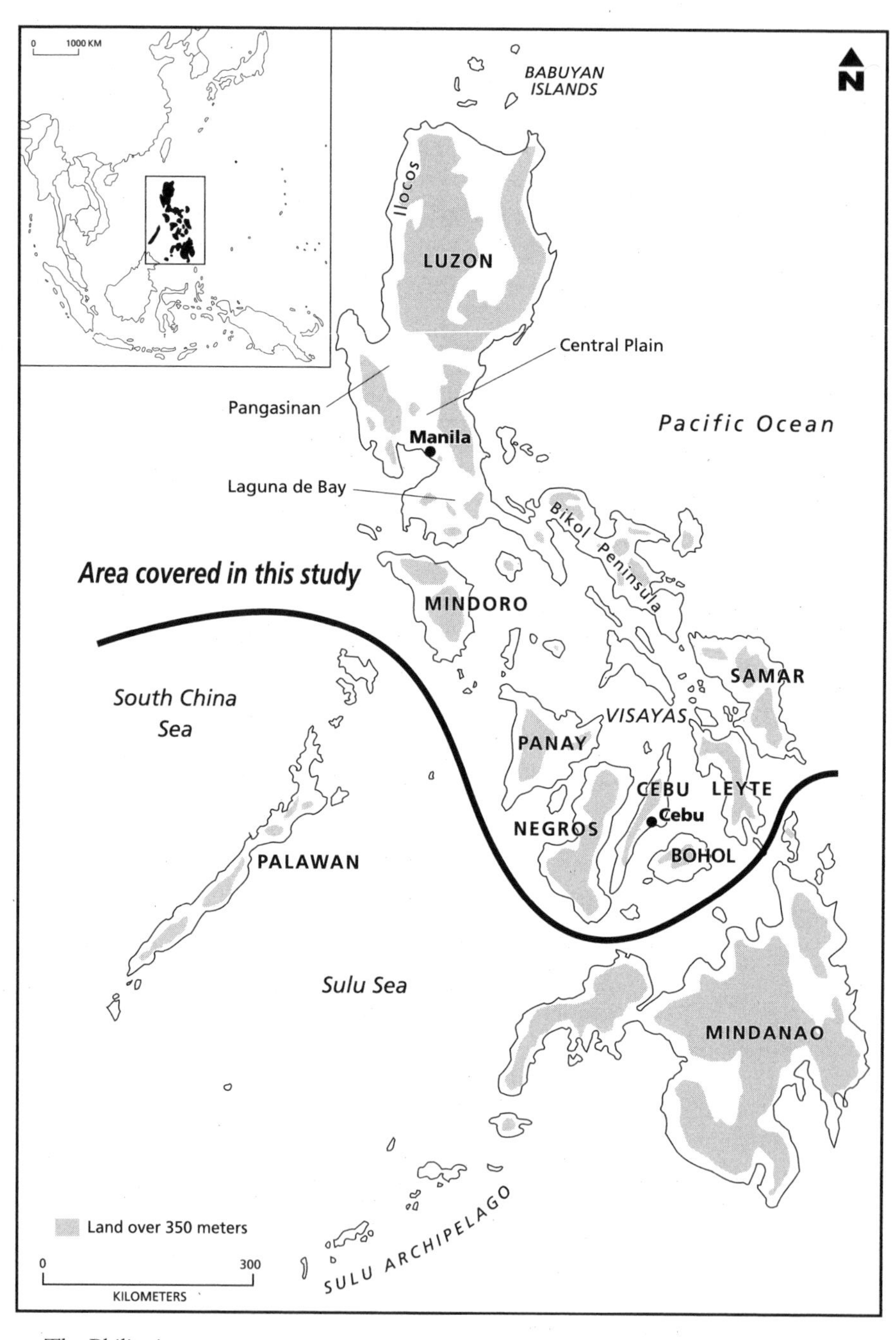

The Philippines

CHAPTER 1

A World Apart?

Spanish conquest and colonization of the Philippines brought fundamental changes to the political, economic, social, and cultural life of the islands. Scholarly studies of the early colonial period, such as those by John Phelan, Nicholas Cushner, and Martin Noone have focused on the initial conquest of the islands and Spanish attempts to set up an effective administration,[1] while others, such as Horacio de la Costa, Pablo Fernández, and Vicente Rafael, have examined the role of the missionary orders and the process of Christian conversion.[2] While these dimensions are critical to understanding the history of the early Spanish Philippines, the demographic decline that accompanied Spanish conquest and early colonial rule has not received such focused attention. This is partly because it is generally assumed that the Filipino population did not suffer a demographic collapse on the same scale as the native population of the Americas, where within the first 150 years of European contact it may have declined by as much as 90 percent, from about 50 to 60 million to only 6.5 million.[3] Comparing the colonial experiences of Mexico and the Philippines, John Phelan concluded that "conquest did not unleash a sharp decline of the Filipino population."[4] Inasmuch as attention has been paid to demographic decline in the early colonial Philippines, it has been attributed to the impact of the Hispano-Dutch War between 1609 and 1648, which generated extraordinary demands for labor and supplies.[5] Meanwhile the initial impact of conquest itself has often been overlooked.

While recognizing the demographic impact of the Hispano-Dutch War, this study aims to fill this gap in the literature and will argue that the Filipino population suffered a greater decline in the early Spanish period than has previously been thought and that the prolonged decline brought significant changes to Filipino society even in regions that were distant from Manila. Even though demographic trends in the Spanish Philippines were similar to those in other parts of the Southeast Asian archipelago, this study will argue that the factors underpinning them were different.

Disease or Conquest?

In attempting to explain why demographic decline in the Philippines was not as great as in the Americas, two explanations have commonly been suggested: first, that the Filipino population possessed immunity to the Old World diseases that devastated American populations, and second, that conquest in the Philippines was more benign. Before exploring these propositions in more detail, it is necessary to note that any analysis of demographic trends is dependent on an accurate assessment of the size of the initial population.

One reason why scholars may believe that population decline in the Philippines was limited in the early Spanish period is because the size of the pre-Spanish population has been underestimated. Current estimates for the population in 1565 range from 1 to 1.25 million.[6] These figures generally exclude Mindanao, as will this study, because most of the island did not come under effective Spanish administration in the early colonial period. These proposed estimates are not derived from a detailed analysis of documentary evidence, but are best guesses based on a limited range of sources. The extent of any decline during the colonial period has not been investigated for the Philippines as a whole, though a few in-depth studies exist for some islands, such as Cebu and Negros.[7] This study will undertake a detailed analysis of the population in each island and region in 1565 and will suggest that the pre-Spanish population probably exceeded 1.5 million. Despite the higher estimate, it will show that like other islands in the Southeast Asian archipelago,[8] population densities were low.

Differences in the scale of depopulation in the Philippines and the Americas in the early colonial period are usually explained by differences in the level of immunity that native peoples had acquired to Old World diseases in pre-Spanish times. In the Americas, the lack of immunity meant that in the early colonial period it was common for a single epidemic of smallpox, measles, plague, typhus, or influenza to result in the death of one-quarter, one-third, or even one-half of the population of a region.[9] Filipinos on the other hand are thought to have acquired some immunity to Old World diseases in pre-Spanish times as a result of frequent contacts with regions in Asia where they had become endemic.[10] The latter assertion has not been investigated directly, but rather inferred from the allegedly low level of population decline in the early colonial period. Since the issue of immunity and the impact of Old World diseases are so central to understanding the level of depopulation in the Philippines, particularly compared to the Americas, they will be considered separately in chapter 2.

Apart from the issue of immunity to Old World diseases, several other factors are generally thought to have moderated levels of demographic decline in the Philippines. First, it is often argued that compared to the Americas, the conquest of the Philippines was a relatively peaceful affair. This is sometimes attributed to the late settlement of the islands, which meant that the Spanish Crown could draw on seventy years' experience of conquest in the Americas. The devastating impact of conquest on native peoples there prompted theological and legal debates in Spain over the treatment of indigenous peoples and the policies that should be pursued in the acquisition of new territories. As a concerned monarch and devout Catholic, Philip II was determined that the demographic disaster that had occurred in the Americas should not be repeated in his newly acquired colony. Second, it is suggested that the absence of significant mineral deposits and dense native populations from which tribute and labor might be exacted left little to fire the imagination of would-be conquistadors and colonists.[11] Although trade with China and other parts of Asia constituted an attraction for some, the long distance from Spain and Mexico and the early reputation of the islands as being unhealthy for Europeans limited the number of settlers. Those who came to the islands were attracted by opportunities for trade rather than the development of agricultural or mining enterprises, and thus they remained concentrated in and around Manila. The alienation of native lands therefore proceeded more slowly in the Philippines, and the large-scale labor drafts that were often associated with mining in Spanish America were absent.[12] As a consequence, it is argued, Filipino societies did not experience such extensive restructuring as occurred among many groups in Spanish America.

The lack of productive enterprises in the Philippines also meant that it produced insufficient profits to cover the maintenance of the colony and had to be subsidized by the royal exchequer.[13] As a result, the administration was minimal and most Filipinos rarely came into contact with Spanish officials. In many regions, parish priests, who were often members of the missionary orders, were the main representatives of Spanish authority. John Phelan has therefore described the occupation of the Philippines as "essentially a missionary enterprise."[14] In 1588 there were just over 700 Spaniards in the Philippines and of these about 150 were priests.[15] For this reason, colonial rule in the islands is often considered to have been more benign. These propositions are worthy of further discussion.

A New Beginning?

Following Ferdinand Magellan's death at Mactan in Cebu in 1521, Spain sponsored several unsuccessful expeditions to the Philippines under Juan García Jofre de Loaysa, Alvaro de Saavedra, and Ruy López de Villalobos.[16] Spain's continuing interest in the islands lay in establishing a foothold in the Southeast Asian spice trade, which at that time was dominated by the Portuguese. The instructions issued to Miguel López de Legazpi in 1564 stipulated that his expedition was to bring back samples of spices, discover a return route to New Spain, and not settle in the Maluku (Moluccas) that the Crown had ceded to the Portuguese in 1529.[17] Unusual in the context of Spanish exploratory expeditions, Legazpi's instructions contained no precise directives over the settlement of any newly discovered lands or the rewards that might be bestowed on those who had taken part. Legazpi was permitted to barter with the natives, and if there proved to be items of economic interest such as spices or gold, he was to establish a settlement, report back to New Spain, and await further orders. With these instructions he set forth for the Philippines.

At this time new conquests often employed the *requerimiento*.[18] This was a document that was read to newly encountered native peoples and called upon them to recognize the superior authority of the Crown and Church, and if they did not they could be subjugated by force of arms and their goods could be confiscated. Patricia Seed argues that this proclamation had Islamic antecedents.[19] At the launch of a *jihad* (or struggle), subjugated peoples would be called upon to recognize the superior authority of Islam through the payment of tribute, the refusal of which provided justification for war. Nevertheless, under Islam subjugated peoples were not required to convert to the new religion, as was the case when the same procedure was adopted during the Christian Reconquest of the Iberian Peninsula.

Unease with the *requerimiento's* credentials, and the seemingly farcical manner in which natives who had no knowledge of Christianity, let alone the Spanish language, were called upon to submit to the authority of the Catholic Church and Spanish rule, provoked an early debate over Spain's dominion in the Indies and the basis on which "just war" might be conducted. During debates in the 1530s and 1540s, Francisco de Vitoria questioned the right of any temporal power to usurp the rights of non-Christian communities that belonged to them by virtue of reason and natural law, but he conceded that under the law of nations Spaniards had the right to trade with them and preach Christianity, while those being approached were required to accept them peacefully. If they did not, he argued, then this might form the basis of "just war." The culmination of these discussions, held after conquest was largely a *fait accompli* in the Americas, was the great debate between the Dominican friar Bartolomé de las Casas and the Aristotelian scholar Ginés de Sepúlveda at Valladolid between 1550 and 1551.[20]

Although there was no decisive outcome to the debate, Las Casas' insistence on the capacity of all peoples to become Christians and on their peaceful conversion had a significant influence on Philip II. Persistent criticism of the *requerimiento*, which came to symbolize the worst excesses of Spanish rule in the Americas, eventually led in 1573 to the introduction of new ordinances that indicated the procedures to be followed in undertaking new conquests. In these ordinances the term "conquest" was officially replaced by *pacificación*: "they are not to be called conquests; because they have to be undertaken in peace and charity as we wish."[21] The new ordinances reflected Philip II's genuine concern for the treatment of his subjects that had been foreshadowed in his instructions to Legazpi. The Philippines would effectively be the testing ground for this more enlightened colonial policy. Circumstances within the islands meant that it was doomed to fail.

Although Legazpi tried to follow the Crown's instructions, the first five years of the Spanish settlement in the islands proved particularly difficult due to shortages of provisions and threats of attack from the Portuguese. Soldiers sacked native villages, seizing food and other goods and enslaving the inhabitants. Hence the nature and impact of Spanish conquest differed little from events in the Caribbean more than half a century earlier. The Augustinian fathers Martín de Rada and Diego de Herrera, who accompanied Legazpi's expedition, were outspoken critics of the actions of the soldiers; their criticism even extended to Legazpi himself for his failure to condemn the atrocities. In fact Legazpi did try to restrain the activities of the soldiers, but he stressed the great hardship they had endured and the need to grant them some favors.[22] The Crown was slow to respond, but in 1568 relented and allowed the allocation of *encomiendas*.[23]

An *encomienda* was an allocation of native peoples to an individual that gave the *encomendero* the right to exact tribute, and up to 1549 also labor, in return for which he or she was supposed to see to their protection and instruction in the Catholic faith. In the Americas the *encomienda* contributed significantly to the dramatic decline in the native population, particularly in the Caribbean, and from an early date the Crown attempted to abolish it. However, it was clear that such privileges were essential if Spain were to maintain its tenuous foothold in the Philippines; any moral objections Philip II may have had about the *encomienda* were overshadowed by practical considerations. The *encomienda* gave legal license to private individuals to continue their hitherto illegal exactions, and the opportunity to initiate a less oppressive form of colonial rule was therefore lost. Although governors were at times reprimanded for not abiding by the new ordinances, the ideal of peaceful subjugation that permeated debates in Spain and Philip II's colonial policy had little impact on the course of conquest in the Philippines.[24]

Philip II tried to reinforce his new policy by appointing to episcopal office ecclesiastics, such as the Dominicans Domingo de Salazar and Miguel de Benavides, who espoused the doctrines of Vitoria and Las Casas.[25] These high church officials were actively involved in continuing debates over the treatment of native peoples and came into frequent and bitter conflict with the secular authorities.[26] The great debate between Las Casas and Sepúlveda had not really resolved the issue of "just war" or established whether it was right to exact tribute from those who had not received Christian instruction.

In the Philippines the ban on slavery also continued to be hotly debated because of its prevalence in the islands. At an early stage it was recognized that it was impossible to prohibit native slavery or debt servitude since it was so deeply embedded in Philippine society. Debates therefore revolved around whether the Spanish should be allowed to acquire slaves on the grounds that it was better for them to be slaves under a Christian owner. While at times the Crown permitted the enslavement of Moros, the term applied to Muslims, it reaffirmed the general prohibition on Spaniards owning slaves in 1574, 1580, and 1589.[27] Meanwhile native slavery persisted, though it gradually declined through the seventeenth century. The presence of Muslims, particularly in the southern Philippines, also brought another dimension to the issue of "just war" that had not featured in debates concerning the treatment of Indians in the Americas. Theological debates therefore continued and played a significant role in the course of events in the Philippines. It was not until 1692 that the transference of dependents through inheritance or purchase was effectively banned and the children of slaves born after that date were free.[28]

Economic Priorities and Philippine Realities

The economic imperative that initially drove the Spanish across the Pacific was to obtain a share in the spice trade that was controlled by the Portuguese. However, the resources they encountered in the islands failed to impress, and the Crown was frequently asked to consider abandoning the islands. In the 1620s the Council of the Indies recommended that Spain relinquish the islands or swap them for Brazil.[29] Cinnamon was found in Mindanao and at an early date identified as a potential export commodity,[30] but Mindanao's inhabitants were judged to be hostile. Throughout the islands the Spanish also encountered natives with gold jewelry, and during the conquest of Ilocos and Pangasinan exacted large quantities of gold.[31] Despite expeditions in search of gold, the deposits they found did not appear to be extensive, particularly compared to the silver found in Mexico and Peru, and the Spanish therefore did not become heavily involved in mining and probably never knew the extent of gold deposits in the islands.[32]

Both spices and gold soon appeared to offer few opportunities for profit compared to trade with China and other Asian regions. This trade revolved primarily around the exchange of Chinese silks for Mexican silver, but Manila was also well-located to develop as a major entrepôt where traders from all over Southeast Asia could exchange commodities such as spices from Maluku, pepper from Sumatra and the Malay Peninsula, and cotton cloth from India, as well as a range of fine goods such as porcelain, ivory, precious stones, and forest products such as resins, sandalwood, and deerskins.[33] In the 1580s there was growing resentment of Chinese domination of much of this trade, and Spanish gaze began to turn to China itself.[34]

Governor Sande was particularly enthusiastic about the conquest of China,[35] and the religious orders saw the conversion of the Chinese as part of their evangelical mission; indeed many had gone to the Philippines precisely because they saw the islands as a stepping-stone to China. The ambitious Jesuit Father Alonso Sánchez even advocated a "just war" against the Chinese for their reluctance to receive foreigners and for their ill treatment and persecution of Christians.[36] Apart from the fact that the conquest of China was unrealistic given the Philippines's weak financial position and limited military capability, Philip II remained unenthusiastic about further conquests and more concerned about the threat from the Dutch and Protestantism.[37] While trade with China made some individuals wealthy, the Philippines were only maintained as a Spanish colony by a royal subsidy from the Viceroyalty of Mexico known as the *situado*.[38] It averaged about 250,000 pesos a year, though it was considerably higher during the Hispano-Dutch War and when the Spanish had control of their outposts in Maluku.[39] The Philippines were also regarded as a drain on the Spanish economy, because silver produced in the Americas often found its way to Asia illegally through the hands of private traders.[40] By the end of the sixteenth century this illegal trade amounted to about five million pesos a year.[41] Merchants in Seville supported the proposal that Spain should abandon the islands since they saw the galleon trade as a threat to their control of trade with the American colonies.[42] Nevertheless, religious and imperial considerations prevailed and the Philippines remained a Spanish colony despite the significant cost it represented.[43]

The nature of Spanish rule in the Philippines was therefore to some extent different from that in most parts of Spanish America. However, through an examination of the early history of individual regions, this study will show that the conquest

itself was a bloodier affair than generally supposed and resulted in significant depopulation. It will also show that even though the Philippines might have lacked the large-scale mining and agricultural enterprises found in the Americas, its population was not spared persistent demands for tribute, labor, and supplies, on which the survival of the colony depended, even in times of peace. These demands, which will be elaborated upon in chapter 3, persisted throughout the colonial period, bringing significant restructuring to Filipino economies and societies.

While it will be suggested in this study that the demographic impact of Spanish colonial rule in the Philippines may have been different from that in America, it will also compare population trends following the arrival of Europeans with those elsewhere in the Southeast Asian archipelago. Due to the paucity of quantitative evidence, the demographic change in Southeast Asia prior to 1800 can be sketched only in broad terms. In fact for this period, apart from parts of Indonesia, the Philippines may be the best-documented region in the archipelago. Nevertheless, the broad trends suggest that at the time Europeans arrived Southeast Asia was characterized by low population densities that prevailed until the eighteenth and nineteenth centuries, when population growth exceeded 1 percent a year. While the latter growth is well-documented, much less is known about the sixteenth and seventeenth centuries. The shortage of evidence has led to considerable speculation on the causes of low population densities in pre-European times, such as interpolity conflict, birth and marriage practices, limitations on agricultural production, and nutrition.[44] Meanwhile, Anthony Reid has argued that the seventeenth century was one of economic and demographic crisis in Southeast Asia as a whole. He has suggested that an increase in military conflict and harsh conditions imposed by colonial rule in certain export-producing regions were responsible for population decline between 1500 and 1630. He also raises the question of whether climate change may have played a role.[45] This study will show that while demographic change in the Philippines followed these broad trends, the importance of factors underlying them were somewhat different, at least in emphasis.

CHAPTER 2
The Role of Disease

Southeast Asia is generally considered to have been part of the Eurasian disease pool, with Old World diseases spreading to the islands as trading contacts with the mainland developed in the Christian Era.[1] Hence, the lower level of depopulation in the early colonial Philippines compared to the Americas is often attributed to its populations having acquired some immunity to Old World diseases, such as smallpox and measles, prior to Spanish arrival. However, the issue of whether or not Filipinos had acquired such immunity has not been investigated directly. Rather it is has generally been inferred from the relatively low level of depopulation in the early colonial period. The issue is important because if Filipinos lacked immunity it could be argued that population decline in the early colonial period could be attributed to Old World diseases rather than other causes, such as conflict or colonial rule. This chapter will show that any immunity to acute infections the Filipinos had in pre-Spanish times was very limited because the population of the Philippines was small and dispersed. But that low population density may have been a product, at least in part, of the presence of chronic infections, which took a regular toll of the population. This factor has not been considered in explaining low population densities in Southeast Asia in general, for which warfare and low fertility are usually held responsible.[2] This chapter will therefore examine what diseases were present in the Philippines when the Spanish arrived and explore their demographic implications.

Some Key Concepts

Critical to an understanding of the demographic impact of Old World diseases is the distinction between chronic and acute infections.[3] Chronic diseases do not kill their hosts or provoke an immune response that results in the death of the disease organisms, which means they can persist for long periods even in small populations. Diseases such as dysentery and typhoid are often related to sanitary or environmental conditions, while others, such as such as leishmaniasis, malaria, filariasis, and schistosomiasis, are spread by non-human vectors.[4] Among the few diseases that are spread by human contact and that can persist in small populations are tuberculosis, leprosy, and treponemal infections. While these infections may affect individuals, the parasites do not threaten the survival of the population as a whole and their persistence is not contingent on the presence of a large population. They remain in the population indefinitely, though they may occasionally erupt as epidemics.

Acute infections, such as measles, rubella, and smallpox, on the other hand, require the presence of a large population before they can become endemic. These infections are spread from human to human and are characterized by short periods of infection that result in high mortality. They normally confer lifelong immunity on survivors and are characterized by short periods of communicability, generally less than two weeks. As a consequence, they only become endemic where human populations are of sufficient size to generate enough susceptibles, generally children, to maintain the disease indefinitely, hence they are often termed "crowd infections." Maurice Bartlett has estimated that for measles to become endemic in U.S. and U.K. cities it is necessary to have a population of between 250,000 and 300,000 or one where there are more than 4,000 to 5,000 new cases a year.[5] However, for densely settled island populations Francis Black suggests a higher figure of 500,000.[6] Frank Fenner and others have estimated that since smallpox spreads less rapidly than measles,[7] to sustain the disease a smaller population of between 100,000 and 200,000 is required.[8] Below these thresholds and where the population is dispersed the spread of disease is slow and "fade outs" are common.[9] This is especially true in pre-industrial societies, where the rate of natural increase is too low to generate a sufficiently large pool of susceptibles to sustain the disease indefinitely. Indeed the birth rate may be critical in determining whether or not an acute infection can become endemic.[10] Small communities may therefore remain relatively disease-free for long periods, but their lack of exposure to infection leads to a build-up of susceptibles, so when a disease is re-introduced it is associated with high mortality that affects adults as well as children. The fact that adults are affected may have significant implications for the economic and social functioning of the group.

In small, dispersed populations contacts are fewer and there are frequent "fade outs," so in a single epidemic some communities may escape infection. In modeling measles epidemics in Iceland, Andrew Cliff and Peter Haggett found that districts with more than two thousand people were generally affected, but below that threshold the probability of a community escaping infection increased with its remoteness.[11]

While some individuals may have innate immunity to a particular disease that derives from their genetic, biochemical, or physiological makeup, most acquire it through contact with the infection.[12] Most acute infections bestow lifelong immunity on survivors, a notable exception being influenza.[13] At the community level populations may acquire immunity to such infections through constant exposure as those who are more resistant reproduce and those who are not die in childhood. Immunity can only be acquired in large populations that are constantly exposed to a disease because the infection has become endemic or, less likely, in smaller populations where there are very intense contacts with a distant area where the disease is sustained in endemic form. Historical experience suggests that at least a century of constant exposure is required for a disease to become endemic.[14] However, once acquired, the level of immunity does not remain constant, but may vary over time according to population dynamics and size.

The Influence of Philippine Geography

Given the significance of the size and distribution of the population to the spread of diseases and their ability to become endemic, it is worth commenting briefly on the physical and human geography of the Philippines. The hot and humid tropical climate would have generally favored the propagation of many diseases, especially water-borne infections, though there might be regional or seasonal variations in climate that might affect the incidence of some diseases. In general, however, the fact that the Philippines comprise some seven thousand islands, some of which are uninhabited even today, would have discouraged the spread of infections, as would the low population density.

Characteristically, the basic social unit was the *barangay*, which comprised a group of perhaps twenty to a hundred families linked together by blood ties, marriage, and ritual kinship. The *barangays*, which formed small communities subsisting primarily on rice and fish, were located in narrow river valleys or on small discontinuous strips of coastal plain, often backed by steep mountains. Communications between communities were therefore primarily by water rather than overland, and contacts with interior groups were limited. In the interior mountain regions, settlements were even smaller, perhaps averaging 150 to 200 persons, and since they practiced shifting cultivation and exploited wild food resources, the population was dispersed and groups were sometimes seminomadic or nomadic. Some trade took place between the highlands and lowlands,[15] but relations were often hostile and most highland groups remained relatively isolated. Foreign trade, notably with Arabs and the Chinese, appears to have stimulated the emergence of a few larger coastal settlements,[16] and just prior to Spanish arrival Muslim missionaries, traders, and settlers from Brunei had established settlements at Pasig and Tondo in Manila Bay. Nevertheless, even in the most densely settled regions such the Central Plain of Luzon, around Manila Bay, and in Laguna de Bay, which were inhabited by Tagalogs and Pampangans, few settlements exceeded several thousand in population and most were much smaller.

The low population density in pre-Spanish times had a significant influence on the spread and impact of diseases. The absence of large permanent nucleated settlements would have discouraged the build-up of wastes and parasites and hindered the spread of those acute infections dependent on face-to-face contact. Chronic diseases that become endemic in small populations and take a regular toll of the population may have played a critical role in limiting population growth and density. This would have meant that in pre-Spanish times the population would not have been able to reach the thresholds necessary to enable acute infections to become endemic and for the population to acquire immunity to them. The presence of chronic infections is therefore important to any discussion of the influence of disease on demographic trends both before and after Spanish conquest.

Sources of Evidence

It is difficult to investigate what diseases may have been present in the Philippines in pre-Spanish times. Paleopathological studies of Filipino populations are few, and in any case skeletal remains can provide only limited insight into the incidence of diseases, particularly acute infections, which tend to kill their hosts before they can leave a mark on the skeleton.[17] In order to address this question it is therefore necessary to rely on historical evidence and what is known of the epidemiology of particular diseases from modern scientific research. Of particular importance is evidence for the presence of diseases on the Asian mainland and in Japan and for the existence of trading contacts between them and the Southeast Asian archipelago that might have facilitated their introduction. Evidence for the familiarity of native populations with different diseases at the time of Spanish arrival can be gleaned from Filipino dictionaries compiled by Spanish friars in the early colonial period.[18] Finally, colonial accounts of the nature, spread, and impact of Old World diseases in the sixteenth and seventeenth centuries can provide insights into the level of immunity acquired by Filipino populations in pre-Spanish times.

Chronic Infections in the Philippines in Pre-Spanish Times

There is circumstantial evidence that many infections found in small populations would have been present in Southeast Asia, including the Philippines, from an early date. Indeed William McNeill has argued that the well-watered environment of Southeast Asia was particularly favorable for the spread of malaria, dengue fever, and water-borne enteric infections, to the extent that they posed a formidable obstacle to population expansion on the scale experienced in China and India.[19]

Enteric diseases such as dysentery and typhoid fever emerged with the beginnings of agriculture and were probably widespread in Asia before the arrival of Europeans.[20] The existence of terms for severe and bloody diarrhea and for intestinal worms in early colonial Tagalog, Visayan, Iloko, and Bikol dictionaries suggests that they were also common in the Philippines.[21] Nevertheless, compared to the mainland, their prevalence was probably moderated by the dispersed settlement pattern that would have limited the build-up of refuse and hence the contamination of food and water. The Filipino habit of frequent washing would also have created more hygienic conditions that discouraged the spread of some infections.[22]

According to McNeill, malaria, dengue, and schistosomiasis had become endemic in southern China by the first two centuries of the Christian Era.[23] They are also likely to have become established in the Philippines in pre-Spanish times, though they would only have been found where the non-human vectors necessary for their transmission occurred. The malarial parasites *Plasmodium falciparum* and

P. vivax are both found in the islands, and the main vector for their propagation, except in Mindoro, is *Anopheles minimus flavirostris*, which is found in the foothills between about 800 to 2,000 feet.[24] The spread of malaria is often positively correlated with forest clearance and the establishment of wet-rice cultivation.[25] There is archaeological evidence for domesticated rice from Andarayan in northern Luzon dated 1700 BC,[26] but intensive wet-rice cultivation does not appear to have spread to Southeast Asia until the Christian Era,[27] and in the early colonial period it was still quite localized.[28]

It is not clear when malaria became established, but the limited genetic resistance to the disease possessed by Filipinos suggests a relatively recent origin.[29] However, the limited resistance could reflect the lack of coincidence in the distribution of malaria and human populations, the ineffectiveness of *A. flavirostris* as a transmitter of malaria, and/or the presence of alternative hosts, rather than its recent appearance. While it is not possible to date the appearance of malaria in the Philippines, the fact that early Spanish expeditions attempting to extend colonial control into the interior mountain regions often succumbed to fevers suggests that by the sixteenth century at least it was well-established in the foothills.[30] Many early dictionaries contain terms for different varieties of mosquito and all have words for fever, the most common being *lagnat* in Tagalog and *hilanat* in Visayan, and some have several. The Tagalog dictionary compiled by Miguel Ruiz in the late sixteenth or early seventeenth century distinguishes six kinds of fever—daily, tertian, quartan, continual, weak and prolonged, and severe and intense. The reference to tertian and quartan fevers is particularly significant given their association with malaria.[31]

Dengue, which is spread by *Aedes aegypti*, and also *Ae. albopictus* and *Ae. polynesiensis*, has only been clinically known for two hundred years and historically was probably not distinguished from malaria. It probably has a long history in the Philippines, for at the beginning of the twentieth century it was not considered a serious infection and, with the exception of some mountain regions or isolated islands, populations had acquired a high level of immunity to it.[32] Today it is most prevalent in urban areas where water collects in discarded cans and containers, creating ideal breeding grounds for the mosquitoes. In the past, limited urban development and lower population densities would have created less favorable environments for its spread. Finally, schistosomiasis, which is dependent on the presence of snail hosts, was probably localized in areas of wet-rice cultivation. Even today it is found only in some islands, notably Mindoro, Samar, Leyte, and northern Mindanao, and is most prevalent in densely populated rice-growing districts.[33]

Among the diseases spread by human contact that may have been present in pre-Spanish times were leprosy, tuberculosis, and treponemal infections. Leprosy was not a major killer, but it appears to have been an ancient disease in China, Japan, and Korea.[34] It probably has a long history in the Philippines, and as early as 1578 the Franciscans had established a hospital for lepers at Naga in the Bikol Peninsula and later another in Manila.[35] Numerous words for *lepra* exist in the early dictionaries, especially from the Visayas, but this may reflect Spanish concern about the disease or a failure to distinguish it from yaws, which was probably widespread in the islands.

Yaws can survive in small isolated populations and is endemic in most hot, humid tropical climates where limited clothing is worn and there is poor hygiene.[36] Yaws can be debilitating, but it is rarely fatal. Yaws and syphilis are closely related and have similar clinical manifestations, so it is unlikely that they would have been distinguished in the early colonial period. Syphilis is generally considered to have been introduced by the Portuguese and therefore to have been absent in China, Japan, and Korea prior to the arrival of Europeans.[37] In 1582 Miguel de Loarca reported that the inhabitants of Cebu in the Visayas were afflicted with itchy lesions and "bubas" and that in Panay "bubas" had been unknown until islanders fleeing from raiders from Maluku introduced the disease from Bohol.[38] This suggests that the disease was new in the Philippines. By the 1590s it was said that an additional hospital was required in Manila to treat "bubas" by sweating and unctions of mercury, often used to treat syphilis,[39] but also noted that the disease afflicted many people because the "land" was suitable for its spread, which is suggestive of yaws rather than syphilis.

Bubas are defined in all the early dictionaries with different terms being used according to their severity and where they were located on the body. Only the Tagalog dictionary compiled by Domingo de los Santos in 1703 refers to a type of *bubas* (*cati* t.) as "mal francés,"[40] or venereal syphilis. It may be significant that his dictionary is the latest of the three Tagalog dictionaries considered here, but it is worth noting that the term *cati* is found in Miguel Ruiz's earlier dictionary, where it is defined as *lepra* or leprosy.[41] Most likely many of the local names for *bubas* referred to yaws, and, as in Indonesia, the spread of venereal syphilis was inhibited by the prior presence of yaws, which provides strong cross-protection from the disease.[42] In the 1660s the Jesuit father Francisco Ignacio Alcina described the symptoms of a disease in which tumors the size of large nuts or hazelnuts developed all over the body, but especially on the face, hands, and joints, which if not properly treated could leave disfiguring scars. He described the disease as "general," affecting children and adults, who were so debilitated they were often unable to leave the house for several months.[43] Although he refers to the disease as *buti*, which the compilers of the Visayan dictionaries define as *viruelas* (smallpox), in the text he clearly distinguishes it from smallpox, and the symptoms he describes are suggestive of yaws.

The presence of tuberculosis in the pre-Spanish Philippines is less certain. The first description of tuberculosis in China may date back to 2700 BC, but texts from 400 BC clearly describe the symptoms.[44] Tuberculosis is commonly associated with poverty, malnutrition, and crowded, unhygienic living conditions found in cities. There is little evidence for the disease in the early colonial period. Early Filipino dictionaries give local names for asthma, coughs, colds, and catarrh, and, perhaps surprisingly, Father Alcina placed respiratory infections at the top of his list of diseases afflicting Visayans, attributing their prevalence to frequent changes of climate.[45] However, the dictionaries contain no reference to coughs being associated with blood, which might suggest tuberculosis. Nevertheless, tuberculosis can survive in small populations, and in the nineteenth century it was a major cause of death in the Philippines, where it had become endemic in many areas and occasionally erupted as epidemics.[46] While the incidence of tuberculosis is likely to have increased significantly during the nineteenth century, when accelerated population growth against a background of deteriorating economic conditions promoted rapid urbanization, its presence in pre-Spanish times cannot be ruled out. Paleopathological studies of pre-Spanish skeletal remains might throw light on this issue.

Evidence that some of the aforementioned infections had become endemic in the Philippines is attested by the early experience of Spaniards in the region. As will be shown in the regional chapters, Spaniards often described the environment as salubrious and Filipinos as healthy with people living to an old age, while they themselves suffered high mortality and had low life expectancy.[47] In the mid-seventeenth century the diseases identified as causing them to "take to their beds and carry them off to their graves" were severe and malignant fevers, dysentery, beriberi, *bubas*, and St. Lazarus' disease (leprosy).[48] In addition it has already been noted that Spanish expeditions that penetrated the foothills often fell victim to malaria. Spaniards appear to have been most at risk from at least some of these infections, though reports could reflect in part the Eurocentric bias of the documentary sources; it also suggests that local populations had already acquired some immunity to them, though in particular cases it may have been quite limited and localized.

In many cases the incidence of disease would have expanded with changing environmental and social conditions. For example, the expansion of wet-rice cultivation during the colonial period is likely to have encouraged the spread of malaria and schistosomiasis. Also, it is known that the incidence of malaria increased in the nineteenth century with the colonization of the foothills where it was endemic, while its distribution today may reflect in part attempts to control the disease.[49] Finally, population increase, urban growth, and malnutrition, particularly from the nineteenth century, would have enhanced the spread of other infections such as tuberculosis. Most likely the incidence of some chronic infections in pre-Spanish times would have been moderated by the low population density, which reduced the likelihood of unhygienic conditions developing and limited opportunities for vectors to spread diseases. While enteric diseases, dengue fever, and malaria may have contributed to low levels of population density in the islands, as will be shown below the lack of agricultural intensification, interpolity warfare, and low fertility also played significant roles.

Acute Infections in the Philippines in Pre-Spanish Times

It seems likely that Filipinos were afflicted by acute infections in pre-Spanish times, but it is less certain that they developed immunity to them. As noted above, immunity can only be acquired in large populations where infections have become endemic or in smaller populations where there is constant contact with an external region where infections have become endemic. Population densities in the Philippines, and most of Southeast Asia, were so low that even in the most densely settled regions populations failed to reach the thresholds necessary to sustain acute infections. Although the island of Luzon as whole possessed a sufficiently large population, it was scattered in small clusters on the coast and in narrow river valleys between which communications were often difficult, while there were few contacts between the highlands and lowlands. This limited, dispersed population would have been unable to sustain acute infections indefinitely, and therefore the ability of communities to acquire some immunity to them would have depended on their re-introduction from outside regions where they had become endemic.

Archaeological and early colonial sources suggest there were some contacts between the Philippines and Thailand and Vietnam in pre-Spanish times,[50] but most epidemics probably originated in China, Japan, or India, where large populations enabled many acute infections to become endemic at an early date.[51] In 1500 China had a population of between 110 and 130 million, India about 100 million, and in 1600 Japan had about 10 million.[52] Due to the proximity of China to the Philippines and growing trading contacts between the two regions in the centuries prior to Spanish contact, the epidemic history of China is of particular significance to that of the Philippines, while Japan, with whom contacts appear to have been increasing in the sixteenth century, was most likely a secondary source of infection. While China and Japan were the most important sources of infection, some diseases may have arrived via islands in the Southeast Asian archipelago.[53]

Fortunately a number of detailed epidemic chronologies exist for China and Japan for the Christian Era.[54] The first millennium of the Christian Era saw the disease pools of Europe and Asia merge as contacts between the continents were established on a regular basis.[55] Acute infections first arrived overland along the Silk Road and later by sea through the ports of Chekiang and Fukien on the south China coast, from whence they were later transmitted to Japan and Korea.[56] Smallpox first arrived in China in the fourth century, and by the eleventh century pediatricians were writing treatises on smallpox, which indicates it had become an endemic disease of childhood.[57] In AD 735–737 a major epidemic of smallpox occurred in Japan that caused 25 to 35 percent mortality, but by the thirteenth century the disease was afflicting only young children.[58] Measles probably arrived in China about the same time as smallpox,[59] but since larger populations are needed to sustain it, it probably became endemic in China after smallpox. Ann Jannetta doubts that it was established in Japan prior to the arrival of Europeans.[60] Other acute infections spread by human contact that had afflicted China, Japan, and Korea by 1500 included influenza, mumps, and chicken pox.[61] Yet to arrive were probably scarlet fever, diphtheria, and cholera, all of which probably failed to reach China until the eighteenth or nineteenth centuries.[62]

Before examining the trading links that existed between the Philippines and other Asian regions, it is worth noting briefly that two diseases, plague and typhus, which were probably established on the Asian mainland in pre-Spanish times, are unlikely to have reached the Philippines. The introduction of bubonic plague would probably have been dependent on the introduction of the black or brown rat and their fleas, which act as the main vectors for the disease. Caravans that traveled the Silk Road could have carried suitable rats to China, or they may have been introduced by sea from the south.[63] Whether or not there was an early outbreak of plague in the seventh century, a serious epidemic occurred in AD 762. The disease does not appear to have spread to Japan, perhaps because few goods that might attract rats, such as rice or grain, were traded between China and Japan.[64] Meanwhile epidemics of plague continued to afflict China, with the outbreak in AD 1331 possibly being the origin of the Black Death that devastated Europe in the fourteenth century.[65]

Porcelain, metals, and textiles dominated imports from China,[66] but provisions that were needed to support crew and passengers might have attracted rats and enabled the disease to be carried over short distances. Also, within the Philippines there was an active long-distance bulk trade in rice within the islands that could have facilitated their spread.[67] However, they were probably not the rats that carried plague. Father Alcina's mid-seventeenth-century compendium of animals found in the Visayas lists rats that he likened to those in Spain. He described them as infesting rice fields and noted that local populations sought protection from them through special sacrifices.[68] This was probably the local Philippine field rat (*Rattus mindanensis mindanensis* (Mearns)) that currently infests rice fields; the rats that act as vectors for plague are less common. The black rat is absent from the islands and the brown rat (*Rattus norvegicus norvegicus* (Berkenhaut)) is found only in the larger islands and mainly in the ports and towns.[69] The latter is regarded as an introduced species, and while small numbers may have existed in the main trading centers from pre-Spanish times, there is no evidence for outbreaks of bubonic plague in early colonial sources.

The introduction of epidemic typhus, which is spread by the human body louse, is even more problematic. It is thought to have developed from murine typhus, which is a disease of rats and other rodents. Typhus is generally regarded as a relatively new disease that was first identified in Europe in the fifteenth century and was often associated with crowded, unsanitary conditions that prevailed on large-scale military campaigns.[70] It is particularly prevalent in cold, dry climates that discourage the frequent washing of clothing. In the Philippines the hot climate, dispersed population and the habit of frequent bathing would have militated against its spread.

Contacts between Mainland Asia and the Southeast Asian Archipelago

In the pre-Christian Era, contacts between Asia, the Middle East, and India were predominantly overland, and sailing patterns within the South China Sea favored coastal mainland routes. Direct contacts across the South China Sea were infrequent and often accidental[71] and any diseases that reached the islands would have failed to become endemic because of the low population density.[72] In the first centuries of the Christian Era trade within Southeast Asia was being integrated into a pattern of trade that extended from the Red Sea to South China,[73] but it was not until the fifth century AD that voyages from Indonesia directly to China occurred on a regular basis. Chinese interest in Southeast Asia was stimulated by the loss of an overland route to west Asia through northern China. Many products sought in the islands were substitutes for those they had previously obtained overland. Particularly interesting was the substitution of Arabian resins and frankincense by pine resin from Sumatra. This was used as a remedy for ulcers and eruptions from Greek times, and Chinese interest may have been stimulated by the arrival of new diseases, notably smallpox.[74]

Once trade became organized on a regular basis and China emerged as a new and constant source of infection, the opportunities for the introduction of diseases greatly expanded. Due to its large population, sophisticated market, and contacts with the rest of the world, China became a major focus of Southeast Asian trade.[75] Indeed foreign envoys were actively encouraged to undertake tribute missions to China; in return they received prestigious gifts and titles. The first tribute missions from the Philippines date from the eleventh century.[76] In addition, in the twelfth century pirates from the Visayas were conducting raids on the South China coast.[77] From that date China displayed a growing interest in the Southeast Asian archipelago, but by the beginning of the fourteenth century it had become alarmed at the outflow of metallic currency and in response imposed import duties at Chinese ports and prohibited private trading in gold, silver, copper currency, ironware, and slaves.[78] While Chinese trade with the archipelago generally languished and Muslim traders began penetrating established maritime trading routes,[79] the Philippines remained an important focus of Chinese trade. This is attested by the large quantities of porcelain from the Yuan and early Ming periods recovered from archaeological sites throughout the Philippines.[80] Hence when Europeans arrived in the South China Sea, foreign trade still appears to have been dominated by trade with China, although trade with Melaka through Sulu and Brunei had also become significant, some of it conducted by traders based in the Philippines.[81] It has been suggested that diseases may have been introduced to the Philippines through the latter route, with populations in the Southeast Asian archipelago acting as "boosters" in maintaining the chain of infection.[82]

The expansion of trade was facilitated by improvements in nautical engineering, which included the development of the maritime compass and the oceangoing "junk."[83] Junks not only made trade possible, but they also carried sufficient crew and passengers to maintain a chain of infection over the relatively short distance to the Philippines. The journey from China to the Philippines could be as short as six to eight days, from Japan seven or eight days, and to Brunei only ten days.[84] According to Marco Polo, Chinese trading vessels commonly had sixty cabins for merchants and their families and between forty and one hundred sailors.[85] It is significant that merchants traveled with their families, because children could have maintained infections when most adults who came from regions where diseases were endemic would have been immune. In 1572 twelve to fifteen ships were coming from mainland China annually,[86] though there were probably fewer in pre-Spanish times because the Chinese were quick to respond to the new opportunities for trade afforded by the establishment of a permanent Spanish presence in the islands. However, only a few Japanese traded annually in the islands, mainly on the coasts of Ilocos and Pangasinan, and many were pirates who indulged in trade or raiding as the opportunity offered.[87]

The Spread of Disease within the Philippine Archipelago

While opportunities existed for the introduction of acute infections to the Philippines, their spread through the islands was more problematic. There is considerable documentary evidence to indicate that foreign trade in the Philippines focused on a limited number of locations, notably Manila, Mindoro, Cebu, Mindanao, and Jolo, from which Muslim traders distributed Chinese goods to other islands in the archipelago, collecting in return products they traded with the Chinese and in Melaka.[88] Apart from cotton and marine products (coral, pearls, and tortoiseshell), the Chinese were interested in obtaining forest products, such as beeswax, betel, animal hides, civet, and rattans, which were found in interior regions.[89] Forest products, particularly deerskins, were also a major focus of Japanese trade.[90] It is clear from the porcelain and other trade items found in interior parts of the islands among the Igorot, Ifugao, and Kalinga of upland Luzon[91] that the acquisition of forest products effectively established a network of trading contacts that extended to remote locations beyond the limits of kinship ties.[92]

While the existence of trading networks enabled the spread of disease, communications within the islands were slow and the population dispersed. Interisland trade was conducted in boats known as *barangays* and *caracoas*, which were smaller and slower than trading junks.[93] When in 1571 Miguel López de Legazpi transferred the Spanish base in the Philippines from the island of Panay to Manila, it was said that the journey took one month because the expeditionary force had to stop at regular intervals to enable the accompanying native boats to catch up.[94] Progress overland was even slower, and since the population was dispersed, many diseases would have died out before they reached a new group of people to infect. Hence many communities might escape individual outbreaks, but as a consequence, once acute infections struck they suffered high mortality. The inability of small populations to sustain acute infections indefinitely, coupled with the fact that any subsequent introduction of the same infection would have been unlikely to have followed the same trajectory, particularly in remote locations,[95] makes it doubtful that Filipino populations could have acquired a high level of immunity to acute Old World infections in pre-Spanish times. Only in the more populated trading centers that were regularly visited by foreign traders is it possible that Filipinos acquired a degree of immunity to such diseases in pre-Spanish times.

Early Filipino dictionaries indicate some familiarity with smallpox, measles, and mumps.[96] In the Visayas and Bikol different types of smallpox were distinguished.

Honga in Bikol was described as "fatal" and *pinarurcan* in Visayan was defined as "the virulent kind." These terms suggests that certain strains of the diseases at least had been associated with high mortality and that local populations possessed only limited immunity to them. The general absence of lexical borrowings of Chinese terms for diseases, drugs, and medical treatments in Tagalog[97] also suggests a limited acquaintance with acute infections introduced from China.

The circumstantial evidence presented here, together with that from early Filipino dictionaries, suggests that while acute infections may have been introduced from China or neighboring islands, the low population density in the Philippines did not enable them to become endemic. Further evidence to support this conclusion can be found in the pattern of mortality produced by epidemics of smallpox and measles in the early colonial period.

Old World Diseases in the Early Colonial Period

During the sixteenth century there were major epidemics in 1574, 1591, and 1595 and several other more local outbreaks that resulted in significant population losses (Appendix A). Prior to 1571, when the Spanish were based in the island of Panay, there was said to have been "a great famine among the natives of this island and pestilence" in which half the population died.[98] The "pestilence" was not specified, but it is unlikely to have been smallpox, which struck the islands in 1574. The latter epidemic was described as a "gran enfermedad de viruela" from which many died.[99] The Augustinian father Martín de Rada elaborated that the epidemic had spared "neither child, nor youth, nor old person."[100] The fact that able-bodied adults were not specified suggests that smallpox had struck the islands before, but since youths were affected it was probably at least a decade before.

In 1591 Manila and its surrounding region was also struck by another epidemic that was referred to as an outbreak of contagious malignant fever.[101] It has been suggested that it was malaria,[102] but this seems unlikely given that malaria is not contagious. Could this have been influenza? The same year also saw an outbreak of smallpox in the *doctrina* of Balayan in Batangas, which was referred to as *bolotong* and which Father Pedro Chirino reported was "killing off children and old men, although of greater danger to adults than to the young."[103] The fact that adult mortality was experienced suggests that here, unlike the Manila region, the population may not have experienced it recently. Although it is possible that the two outbreaks in 1591 were the same disease, this seems unlikely given that the symptoms of the disease in Manila appear different from those associated with smallpox.[104]

Only a few years later another disease referred to only as "peste" was devastating the islands. In 1595 it was reported that it had caused high mortality and there were fears that the population would become extinct "as in Santo Domingo."[105] The comparison with Santo Domingo is particularly noteworthy, for it indicates that disease mortality was comparable to that in the Americas. It was probably the same disease that the following year spread to Jesuit *doctrinas* near Manila, causing high mortality.[106] In 1595 there was also a "gran peste de viruelas" in Cagayan that devastated children.[107] This could have been the same disease, but the patterns of mortality seem to have been distinct and if the former were smallpox, it would probably have been referred to specifically.

From these observations it would appear that when a disease struck in the Philippines it resulted in high mortality, though this depended in part on the length of time that had elapsed since the population had previously been infected. However, the scale of epidemics appears to have been limited by the Philippines' relatively small population and dispersed settlement pattern, and acute infections continued to cause exceptionally high levels of disease mortality into the nineteenth century.[108] In remote regions the introduction of new infections was often associated with missionary activity. However, the population of Manila and possibly some other ports, where there were frequent trading contacts with regions where acute infections had become endemic, may have been able to acquire a degree of immunity to them at an early date. However, from the seventeenth century trade with China declined as a result of political upheavals, and Japan pursued a policy of isolation.[109] At the same time, their introduction from the Americas is unlikely since the small number of crew and passengers on ships from Mexico were insufficient to maintain the chain of infection during the three-month-long journey across the Pacific Ocean.[110]

For much of Luzon and the Visayas, acute infections continued to take a regular toll of the population through the early colonial period, and they occasionally erupted into moderate epidemics. The periodicity of these epidemics depended on the frequency of contact and the birth rate, which determined the speed with which a new susceptible population could emerge. The Augustinian Casimiro Díaz, writing on smallpox, said, "These epidemics and plagues are very frequent in these islands, but smallpox is very punctual in causing general devastation every twenty years."[111] In Indonesia the frequency was between seven and eight years,[112] suggesting that the region had a higher population and fertility rate. Despite the introduction of vaccination into the Philippines after 1805, it took almost a century for it to be fully effective.[113] Therefore, as late as the nineteenth century smallpox mortality was still seen as a major factor holding back the growth of the Philippine population.[114]

Conclusion

This chapter has suggested that the impact of disease in pre-Spanish times was twofold. First, it has shown that chronic infections, such as enteric diseases, malaria, dengue, leprosy, yaws, and possibly schistosomiasis and tuberculosis, were probably endemic in the islands and that acute infections, such as smallpox and measles, also visited the islands from China or indirectly through other islands in the Southeast Asian archipelago. Together these diseases probably contributed to the low population densities in the islands in pre-Spanish times, though other factors such as interpolity conflict and low fertility, to be discussed in chapter 5, also played significant roles.

Second, the low population density in turn meant that acute infections were unable to become endemic in the islands, which makes it doubtful that Filipino populations could have acquired high levels of immunity to acute infections from the Old World in pre-Spanish times. This is supported by the high mortality rates associated with epidemics in the early colonial period that involved adults as well as children. Old World diseases made a greater contribution to the decline in the Filipino population in the early colonial period than generally thought, but because of the low population density their impact was moderate compared to that in much of the Americas. Relatively low levels of depopulation in the colonial period owed more to Philippine geography than to any immunity that Filipinos had acquired to acute infections in pre-Spanish times.

CHAPTER 3

Colonial Realities and Population Decline

Despite the Crown's intention that the "pacification" of the Philippines should be brought about peacefully and its subjects well treated, the conquest and establishment of Spanish rule in the islands was characterized by conflict and bloodshed, which in some regions was prolonged throughout the colonial period. Conflict arose initially because the Spanish experienced shortages of food and resorted to seizing provisions by force, while in their desperate search for gold they devastated native communities and conscripted local people to serve on exploratory expeditions.

Once the Spanish had established a permanent foothold in the islands, their retention of the colony continued to depend on Filipino tribute and labor. Native tribute constituted one of the two main sources of Crown revenue in the Philippines, the other being taxes derived from the galleon trade.[1] Since the defense and administration of the islands depended to a large extent on Filipino tribute and labor, it was essential that effective systems be put in place to facilitate their exaction. Faced with a small Spanish population and insufficient royal officials to administer these levies, the task had to be devolved to local representatives, very often priests, and native leaders.[2] The cooption of native leaders into the Spanish administration system brought significant transformations to native political and social structures, while excessive demands for commodities and labor destabilized native communities, precipitating flight and demographic decline long after regions had been pacified. As will be shown in detail in parts II through IV, the extent of these transformations and their demographic impact varied spatially according to Spanish aims for each region and the character of native societies and environments they encountered. However, these regional variations can be best understood in the context of Spain's overall objectives in the Philippines and the common administrative structures it set up to achieve them.

Spain had two main aims overseas: to generate wealth for the Crown and its subjects and to bring about the Christian conversion and "civilization" of any native peoples that were encountered. These aims differed somewhat from those of other European powers, whose prime focus in Southeast Asia was trade and who never made transformation of native societies a state policy or a goal in itself, even though trade alone might indirectly bring significant economic, social, and political changes.[3] The reality was that the Philippines were too far from Spain and lacked the natural resources and dense populations to enable Spain to achieve its economic objective. However, the other aim of Christianizing and "civilizing" native Filipinos remained, and the methods employed brought important changes to native societies and beliefs, which had significant implications for demographic trends.

Filipinos were required to pay tribute in recognition of Spanish overlordship and the temporal and secular benefits that Spanish rule was thought to confer.[4] At the same time, resettlement programs were undertaken to enable more effective administration and, as the Spanish saw it, create more civilized citizens and communities. Meanwhile the imposition of Christianity heralded major changes to social practices, such as marriage customs and slavery, while the need for the Spanish to work through native intermediaries altered the distribution of power within native societies. An equally important factor affecting demographic trends was the position of the Philippines within the wider geopolitical context of rivalry with the Dutch and conflicts with Muslim groups. Not all regions were affected by all these factors; rather there were significant spatial and temporal variations in their impact.

Administration, Authority and Incorporation

In the Philippines Spain could apply a bureaucratic system and body of legislation that had already been worked out in the Americas. This served to minimize the type of political disorder and loss of life that had characterized the early years of colonial rule in Spanish America. However, the failure of the Philippines to generate sufficient revenue to support the colony, let alone profits for the Crown, meant that for reasons of economy its administration was basic and the number of Spanish officials in the islands small.[5] Not only were there relatively few officials, but because few Spanish towns were founded, municipal government in the Philippines was also limited.[6] The creation of the Audiencia in 1583 resulted in a small influx of bureaucrats,[7] but by 1588 there were still only about forty Spanish officials in the islands, and most resided in Manila.[8] This concentration of administration in Manila was to remain a feature of Spanish colonial government in the islands,[9] as was the degree of autonomy with which it was conducted due to its distance from the Viceroyalty of New Spain and Spain itself. In 1597 Antonio de Morga reported that royal decrees issued by the Crown were mostly suspended or not observed.[10]

Since the Spanish bureaucracy remained skeletal, the administration of the islands depended to a large extent on the cooption of elites. Administration in the provinces was largely conducted by *alcaldes mayores* or *corregidores*, who had political and judicial authority over jurisdictions of which they were also military commandants.[11] The first *alcaldes mayores* and *corregidores* were appointed sometime in the 1570s.[12] For much of the colonial period there were twelve *alcaldías* and eight *corregimientos* in the Philippines as a whole, but there were often suggestions that they should be reduced in number.[13] Although these officials were charged with bringing law and order to the provinces and seeing to the welfare of the inhabitants of their jurisdictions, they soon became their worst oppressors. In 1619 Hernando Rios Coronel wrote to the Crown that "the multiplication of these offices [of *alcaldes* and *corregidores*] means the multiplication of those who destroy the Indians and inflict innumerable injuries upon them."[14]

Alcaldes mayores were paid annual salaries of only 300 pesos and *corregidores* between 150 to 250 pesos,[15] so the posts attracted only poor quality incumbents who sought to enhance their meager incomes through various forms of fraud and corruption, often at the expense of the native population. They bought up large quantities of produce, especially rice, which they purchased when prices were low and later sold at considerable profit. They also drafted labor for cutting timber, rowing boats, building houses, and providing many other services, for which they often did not pay.[16] Sometimes they appointed *alguaciles* who brought charges against the natives for the slightest offenses, such as, it was claimed, "for walking in the sun."[17] Initially *alcaldes mayores* were also involved in the collection of tribute from Crown *encomiendas*, but because of the abuses they committed, in 1598 this task was entrusted to collectors appointed by the royal exchequer.[18]

Charged with the administration of districts containing tens of thousands of Filipinos, *alcaldes mayores* and *corregidores* necessarily had to work through local elites, which thereby modified pre-Spanish political and social structures. The Spanish recognized the authority of pre-Spanish *datus* who became known as *cabezas de barangay*. In pre-Spanish times these positions might be hereditary, but the power exercised by *datus* also depended on performance and popular support. In colonial times, however, their authority depended on selection by the colonial authorities. Initially within any town or village all the adult males participated in the nomination of three candidates for the post of *gobernadorcillo*, but from the mid-seventeenth century the right of nomination was restricted to the senior *cabezas de barangay*. Of the three nominees, the governor or an *alcalde mayor* selected one for a year's term of office. The duties of both *cabezas* and *gobernadorcillos* were similar, but those of the latter were more extensive. The *cabezas* were responsible for the collection of tribute and organizing labor services within their *barangays*, as well as for maintaining peace and order. The *gobernadorcillo* supervised these activities and had judicial authority over minor civil and criminal cases.[19] Together previous and incumbent *cabezas* and *gobernadorcillos* formed the local elite, referred to by the Spanish as the *principalia*. This class also included the *gobernadorcillo*'s deputy, a constable, an inspector of palm trees, an inspector of rice fields, and a notary, together with church officials, the *fiscales* and *cantores*. Despite the introduction of the principles of election and rotation of office, the local administration was essentially oligarchic rather than democratic.[20]

The existence of a class of administrative intermediaries meant that Spanish colonial rule in the Philippines was to a significant degree indirect. Nevertheless, it did not mean that Filipinos escaped the exactions made by Spanish officials. Native elites were often caught between the demands of the Spanish administration and serving their subjects. While some tried to defend their communities, many saw opportunities for improving their social position.[21] The phenomenon of native leaders as social climbers has been well-documented in Spanish America,[22] and in the Philippines the greater dependence of the Spanish on local elites probably created greater opportunities for economic and social advancement. Certainly by the nineteenth century land was concentrated in the hands of the *principalia*, who also controlled many other commercial activities.[23] It could be argued that this indirect form of administration, where the native elites often used their position to serve their own economic and political ends rather than moderate Spanish demands, both extended and increased those demands.[24]

Since most bureaucrats, *encomenderos*, and merchants resided in Manila, most Filipinos did not come into frequent contact with Spaniards. In most communities, the parish priest, whose post was often filled by a member of one of the religious orders, was often the main representative of Spanish authority. Oskar Spate has described the parish priests in the Philippines as "forming a network for cultural impregnation and social control."[25] Although the clergy were not beyond reproach,[26] their exploitative activities were probably not as persistent or pervasive as those of secular officials. Indeed, the priests achieved considerable success in converting Filipinos to Christianity in part because of the support they provided local communities, especially in the Visayas, where they played an important role in mobilizing local populations for defense against Moro raids.[27]

To enable their effective administration and Christian instruction, the Spanish sought to congregate Filipinos into nucleated settlements of several thousand people. While settlements of this size existed in some regions, for example in Manila Bay, in many regions families either needed or preferred to remain near their lands. The early missionary experience in the Philippines, which was also the case in New Spain, was that it was counterproductive to force them to move. As such a *cabecera-visita* organization developed that represented a compromise between the Filipinos' preference to remain on their lands and the missionaries' desire to convert them.[28] Each parish or mission consisted of a permanently staffed *cabecera* possessing a church that was the focus of worship for a number of surrounding communities. More distant villages contained chapels, which were visited periodically by priests from the *cabecera* and were attended by scattered populations that sometimes lacked formal settlements. Geographically, *cabeceras* were often located adjacent to the coast or rivers, whereas *visitas* were often found upvalley or in the foothills. Even given this organization, the shortage of clergy meant that many communities were visited only a few times a year and converts often needed to travel to attend church. According to the availability of clergy, the status of a mission might fluctuate between being a *cabecera* and a *visita*.

Beyond the *visitas*, especially in Luzon, attempts would be made to push back or hold the frontier. Here missionary activities were often supported by small garrisons of soldiers that together formed a buffer zone protecting lowland populations from attacks by hostile highlands groups.[29] Missions in these areas were often ephemeral and native contact with missionaries or soldiers fleeting.[30] The lack of personnel meant that missionary activities on the frontier were often suspended,[31] with the result that within a short time the neophytes had returned to their way of life, "just like a bow which when strung is bent; but when unstrung at once straightens and regains its former position."[32] This instability in mission settlements creates considerable difficulties in tracing their demographic histories.

Tribute, *Vandalas*, and *Polos*

The Spanish introduced a system of tribute payments to the Philippines so that Filipinos would recognize Spanish authority, *encomenderos* would be rewarded, and revenue generated that could cover the costs of administration, including the salaries of priests. Its introduction proved problematic because Filipinos were not familiar with paying tribute and there were no pre-existing mechanisms to exact it. Filipinos not only objected to the amount of tribute levied and the way in which it was collected, which they often expressed in fugitivism and revolts, but also to the payment of tribute in principle. Since converts were required to pay tribute, it became a significant obstacle to Christian conversion and the settlement of Filipinos in formal villages. Although the requirement for Filipinos to pay tribute generated some of the most valuable records for the demographic historian, it also provoked temporary or permanent migration that exacerbates efforts to track populations over time.

Initially each tributary was required to pay two *fanegas* of rice and a piece of cotton cloth, or else three *maes*[33] in gold or their equivalent in commodities produced by the community. Governor Lavezaris regarded this levy as moderate since Filipinos were such excellent farmers and traders that they could easily pay it through working only four days. He also noted that three *maes* was only half the value of tribute paid in Mexico, when the Spanish cost of living in the Philippines was twice that of New Spain.[34] However, Father Martín de Rada regarded the levy as excessive, arguing that agriculture was not very productive and that Filipinos had great difficulty surviving such that for part of the year they were forced to live on root crops and could scarcely afford a *manta* with which to clothe themselves.[35] In the early 1580s Filipinos were commonly paying the equivalent of eight reals, but in 1589 this was increased to ten reals for a married man and half that for a single person, of which one and a half reals of the two-real increase went to support soldiers in the region and the other half real went to pay for the cathedral chapter.[36]

The late sixteenth century witnessed a prolonged debate about the level of tribute levied and whether it should be paid in cash or kind.[37] In other Spanish colonies, cash payments forced workers into the labor market, thereby meeting labor demands in developing mining and agricultural enterprises, but this was not the main concern in the Philippines. Here, in the early colonial period agricultural production remained largely in native hands and the priority was to ensure sufficient provisions to support the colony. The issue was finally resolved in 1604 when the levy was set at four reals in cash, one real for a chicken, and four reals payable in either cash or kind, the type and value of the commodities varying according to the nature of agricultural production in different provinces.[38] This level of taxation and the balance between commodities and cash seems to have remained fairly constant until the early eighteenth century, but it was often exceeded illegally, and in reality the goods levied were often worth considerably more.

On top of tribute demands, in times of crisis or exceptional need, such as for war or construction projects, additional levies were made in the form of *vandalas* (forced sales to the government), often of rice, and *polos* (forced labor). These exactions, which were at their height during the Hispano-Dutch War, did not affect all regions equally but where imposed they were particularly onerous and at the time regarded as a major cause of population decline.

Rice was the dominant crop requisitioned, but other agricultural products, such as chickens, eggs, and pigs, were also levied. Provinces were assigned quotas that were distributed by the *alcalde mayor* to communities under his jurisdiction, and their *cabezas de barangay* were responsible for meeting them.[39] This was backed by the inspection of rice fields to ensure that communities were planting and could meet their quotas. Although communities were supposed to be paid for the products they supplied, often the royal treasury lacked the necessary funds or payments remained in the hands of the *cabezas de barangay* and failed to reach the producers.[40] Those Filipinos who did not have access to land or were wage laborers were forced to purchase rice to meet the quotas, often at high prices, and many fell into debt, while others opted to flee.[41]

In addition to tribute payments and *vandalas*, Filipinos were also required to work as forced laborers under the *polo*. The earliest demands for forced labor were associated with the construction of Manila, including its fortifications, churches, monasteries, and private houses.[42] Later the main call for *polo* labor came for the extraction of timber and work in the shipyards. This system of forced labor was loosely based on the Mexican *repartimiento* and required males between sixteen and sixty to work on government projects for forty days. Although the levy was not supposed to exceed eleven persons out of each five hundred *tributos enteros*, a significant number of people were exempt and the proportion was often higher.[43] Unlike the Mexican *repartimiento* or Peruvian *mita*, the Filipino *polo* does not appear to have been a fixed quota; rather levies were made as the need arose. Like food producers under the *vandala*, *polo* workers seldom received wages, and the conditions of work were poor. In 1609 the Crown attempted to regulate the *polo*, ordering that Filipinos should not be drafted for private or public purposes where Chinese labor was available. Where it was not, then Filipinos were to be persuaded to work voluntarily and were not to be forced to travel over long distances from different climates. They were also to have fixed hours of work and be paid personally at the end of the week.[44]

It was envisaged that the *polo* would be organized so that all participated and the burden on particular individuals would be light. However, the beginning of the Hispano-Dutch War heralded a massive increase in the demand for *polo* labor. Conditions of work were harsh, particularly in the extraction of timber, and rations were skimpy. Moreover, the levies drew labor from subsistence activities, which resulted in food shortages and financial hardship for workers.[45] To ameliorate conditions it was frequently suggested that ships should be constructed outside the islands, in places such as Bengal or Cochin, as indeed some were.[46] However, only with the end of the Hispano-Dutch War did the burden of providing labor for the shipyards become lighter. Because of the hard labor associated with the *polo*, workers often tried to gain exemption, or they fled, placing even greater burdens of meeting the quotas on the communities they had left.

Friar Estates

In the Philippines there were few economic enterprises that could be profitably developed. Gold deposits were limited and in the context of Spanish mercantilism, which only allowed trade within the empire, the islands were too distant from large markets to stimulate an export trade in agricultural produce; much higher profits could be made in trade and commerce. Hence although land grants were distributed at the time of conquest, Spaniards showed little interest in developing agricultural enterprises. Nevertheless, there was a local market in Manila that did stimulate the commercialization of agricultural production in its hinterland. Here landed estates, many established by the missionary orders, fundamentally altered the nature of agricultural production and landholding and generated demands for labor.

Spanish principles of access to land were based on private property, which allowed the alienation of land by individuals. As such they recognized the legal rights of colonial subjects to lands they owned in pre-Spanish times, but lands exceeding a small amount for communal pasturing were liable to alienation.[47] In the Philippines some *datus* had possessed private holdings, but the predominant form of land tenure was one of communal holdings, where the *datu* controlled the allocation of land as well as rights to common land.[48] Lands where Filipinos exercised only usufruct rights, including those lands that appeared uncultivated during fallow periods in the cycle of shifting cultivation, were not recognized in Spanish law and were therefore particularly at risk of appropriation. The alienation of communal lands was encouraged by some *datus* who in colonial times assumed ownership of the lands they controlled on behalf of the community, often selling them for personal gain. In other cases communal lands were distributed to individual *barangay* members who then sold it, sometimes remaining on the land as tenants or *inquilinos*.[49] Even in those areas where permanent cultivation was practiced, the absence of any supra-*barangay* political organization made it difficult for communities to resist land encroachment.

Most estates had their origins in Spanish donation or purchase, but they were expanded piecemeal,[50] generally by usurping or purchasing Filipino lands.[51] Since private individuals showed little interest in developing agricultural enterprises, much of the land was acquired by the missionary orders. Although at an early date the religious orders were forbidden to acquire land from native owners, they often did so through third parties.[52]

The alienation of native lands contributed to the growth of a landless labor force. Some Filipinos without access to land, as well as some Chinese, became tenants, sharecroppers, or wage laborers on nearby estates. In addition to those who lived on the estates, significant numbers were employed as wage laborers. From an early date most landowners sought to employ Filipinos designated as *casas de reservas*, who unlike other workers were exempt from the *polo* and other services and thus could be employed throughout the year. It was envisaged that the *casas de reservas* would be *vagamundos* rather than registered tribute payers, since the former were already de facto exempt from forced labor. The designation of *vagamundos* as *casas de reservas* received official support since it was recognized that agricultural labor was essential to ensure a supply of provisions for Manila, and it had the additional benefit of adding new names to the tribute rolls. Although some recruits were vagabonds, the term was generally interpreted to mean any person who had left his or her place of birth.[53] In fact the stipulation that the *casas de reservas* should be vagabonds was generally ignored, and the religious orders increasingly used promises of exemption from forced labor to attract workers or to retain valued tenants.[54] Even though work on the estates was onerous and not well-remunerated, it was regarded as preferable to being conscripted to serve as a forced laborer in wood cutting or shipbuilding, so many attempted to get themselves designated as *casas de reservas*, in some cases by bribing their *gobernadorcillo*.[55] As early as the beginning of the seventeenth century towns were springing up around estates comprised of *casas de reservas*, and by the eighteenth century estates were employing several hundred of them.[56] The result was that the burden of meeting *polo* and *vandala* demands fell on those who remained in their native communities.[57]

The absence of extensive mineral deposits, the spatially limited development of commercial agricultural enterprises, the low levels of Spanish immigration, and the skeletal bureaucracy generally favored the survival of the population of the Philippines to a greater extent than in many parts of Spanish America. However, two factors affected demographic trends in the Philippines that were absent in the Americas, namely the presence of Muslim groups primarily in Mindanao and the Sulu archipelago who conducted raids on the Visayas and Bikol in particular, and the Hispano-Dutch War.

Confrontation with Islam

Islam arrived in the Philippines in the late fourteenth and early fifteenth centuries. Its arrival was part of the wider process of Islamization of Southeast Asia that began in the ninth century and spread through Sumatra, east Java, Melaka, the east coast of Malaya, Champa, and Borneo.[58] The judge-cum-scholar Makdum first introduced it to Sulu, but it was not until the second half of the fifteenth century that the sultanate of Sulu was established. By the time the Spanish arrived it had spread to Zamboanga on the coast of Mindanao.[59] Meanwhile in the early sixteenth century the sultanate of Magindanao had emerged in the Pulangui River and become the most powerful in Mindanao.[60] These sultanates possessed a more centralized form of government than that found among the Tagalogs and Visayans.[61] In addition to the sultanates established in the southern islands, from the early sixteenth century traders from Brunei began settling in Manila Bay, where they intermarried with local Filipinos.[62]

It was inevitable that Spanish arrival in the Philippines would result in conflicts with Muslim groups established there. Part of Spain's hostility toward Muslim rule in the south was based on long-standing religious differences it had with Moors in Spain, which had recently been reinforced during the Reconquest.[63] Apart from these religious differences, Spanish intrusion into Philippine waters threatened flourishing commercial activities and effectively thwarted the further expansion of Islam through the archipelago.[64] Open conflicts in the early years of conquest contributed to a hardening of attitudes on both sides as Moro raids were countered by retaliatory expeditions that in turn provoked further raids. Both groups considered themselves to be defenders rather than aggressors: the Spanish as defenders of their subjects in the Visayas who were prey to Moro raids; the Moros as defenders of their peoples from Spanish incursions and retaliatory expeditions.

Philip II's instructions to Legazpi insisted that the natives should not be enslaved, except those who were already slaves in their own societies, but should be converted to Christianity by peaceful means.[65] However, in 1568 he permitted Muslims to be enslaved if they actively continued to spread the Islamic faith or to make war on Spaniards or their subjects. This did not extend to Filipinos who had recently been converted to Islam, who were to be persuaded to become Christians.[66] By 1570 the rhetoric had changed and Philip II granted permission for Spaniards to enslave Mindanaos on the grounds that they were Muslims and Spain's traditional enemies.[67] The Spanish found further justification for the subjugation of Muslim groups in the Muslims' unwillingness to accept Spanish sovereignty, in rumors of an imminent Brunei attack, and in the continued arrival of Muslim preachers in Luzon.[68] Although the Spanish initially succeeded in subjugating Moro groups in Manila Bay in 1571 and in Brunei in 1578, later attempts, such as Estebán de Rodríguez' expedition to Mindanao in 1596, were failures.[69] It was clear that Spain lacked the resources to conduct major campaigns and subsequently retain control of any conquered territories, and in addition the islands occupied by Moros appeared to offer limited opportunities for trade compared to China and Japan. As a result, Spanish policy became essentially defensive.[70] Nevertheless, the authorities did not demur from supporting major retaliatory expeditions against Magindanao and Sulu when it was considered necessary.

Moro raids aimed to acquire captives for sale elsewhere in Southeast Asia, a practice that existed in pre-Spanish times. For Southeast Asia as a whole this trade involved a general movement of slaves from east to west, with slaves being acquired through raids on weaker polities and on non-Muslim groups. Since Islamic law forbade the enslavement of Muslims, as the Islamization of Southeast Asia proceeded, the places from which slaves could be obtained became more limited. So when the Spanish arrived, the Philippines were becoming increasingly important as a source of slaves. Laura Lee Junker has suggested that at the same time there was an increase in raiding within the Philippines due to expanding opportunities for external trade, especially with China. This created a demand for labor to produce or assemble items for export, and led to competition between emerging trading centers, which encouraged raiding aimed at eliminating potential rivals.[71]

The extent to which Moro groups were involved in slave raiding in pre-Spanish times is not clear. Cesar Majul argues that it was limited and that it only developed on a major scale in response to Spanish aggression, and in the latter part of the seventeenth century from growing European demands for labor.[72] Whether or not this was the case, in pre-Spanish times rivalries do not appear to have been polarized between Muslims groups and others, and most scholars agree that the frequency of slave raids increased in the colonial period, and particularly from the second half of the eighteenth century.

Nicholas Tarling has argued that increased Moro raiding was a response to the intrusion of Europeans into Southeast Asian waters, which reduced commercial opportunities, thwarted Moro political aspirations, and led the "decaying" sultanates to turn to increased slave raiding and piracy.[73] For Tarling, therefore, increased raiding was born out of economic and political decline. Others see increased slave raiding as a positive response to economic opportunities. In the seventeenth century, European markets for slaves emerged in the Dutch-dominated spice plantations of Maluku[74] and in the cities of Batavia and Makassar. From Makassar slaves were often re-exported to Sumatra and southern Borneo to work on pepper plantations.[75] For the late eighteenth century, James Warren argues that the acquisition of slaves was driven by an expansion in trade between Sulu and China that focused on marine and forest products—*tripang* (sea cucumber), bird's nest, wax, camphor, mother of pearl, and tortoiseshell—whose collection and redistribution was labor-intensive and created an internal demand for labor.[76]

Moro raids continued throughout the colonial period, though their frequency and intensity varied over time, mainly in response to political and economic changes occurring in the broader Southeast Asian region. Following Spanish attempts to subjugate Magindanao and Sulu, the Moros went on the offensive, and between 1599 and 1604 they conducted major raids on the Visayas. Preoccupied with preventing the expansion of the Dutch into the Maluku, Governor Pedro de Acuña tried unsuccessfully to make peace with Magindanao. Even so, between 1604 and 1634 Moro raids appear to have declined in scale,[77] possibly because the erection of a permanent garrison at Caraga in 1609 effectively cut off the Magindanaos' escape route and/or because of internal political reorganization in Mindanao.[78] During this apparent lull in Magindanao activity, the Sulus emerged to become the main scourge of the Visayas. In addition, largely non-Muslim Camucones from Palawan began raiding the Visayas.[79] These were independent groups who at different times operated under the protection of the sultans of Brunei or Sulu.[80] They often followed in the wake of Magindanao and Sulu raids and took booty for themselves,[81] ruthlessly decapitating those they captured.[82]

The Spanish were generally unable to defend the Visayas. A naval squadron was based at Cebu and another at Iloilo in Panay, but their roles were often reduced to the ineffective pursuit of the raiders. The establishment of the fort at Zamboanga in 1635 and attempts at conciliation seem to have had some effect in limiting raids through the mid-seventeenth century, although in 1660 Father Ignacio Alcina was still writing that there was not a year when Moros from Mindanao and Jolo and the Camucones failed to take captives.[83] Nevertheless, the situation is unlikely to have improved after 1663, when fear of a Chinese invasion resulted in troops both there and in Maluku being withdrawn to defend Manila.[84] As soon as the Chinese threat had waned, the Crown ordered the garrison at Zamboanga to be re-established, but it was not reoccupied until 1719 and subsequently seems to have been increasingly ineffective in limiting the number of raids.[85] Meanwhile, in the early eighteenth century the Spanish tried to negotiate peace since they sensed that the Sulus were keen to trade.[86] However, this strategy changed in 1753 when the Spanish suspected the Sulus of treachery and declared all-out war on them. The Sulus immediately responded by widespread attacks on the Visayas, making 1753 the bloodiest year in Moro piracy.[87] From the late eighteenth century, therefore, the frequency and scale of Moro raids expanded significantly.[88]

As will be shown in subsequent chapters, the impact of Moro raids was far-reaching. They not only resulted in considerable loss of life and the enslavement of large numbers of Filipinos, but they generated demands for labor and provisions for expeditions and garrisons, which severely disrupted subsistence activities and family life. Communities in the Visayas and Bikol were most directly affected, but other regions were not immune since the presence of raiding vessels in Philippine waters made travel hazardous, paralyzed trade, and made administration less effective.

The Dutch and the Hispano-Dutch War

While Moro raids varied in intensity through the colonial period, one significant factor that was confined to the seventeenth century and is generally recognized by scholars as having caused severe depopulation was the Hispano-Dutch War.

During the late sixteenth century the Dutch developed an interest in the East Indies. They first appeared in Philippine waters in the late sixteenth century; indeed Olivier van Noort engaged the Spanish in their first major naval battle in Manila Bay in 1600.[89] In 1602 the Vereenigde Oostindische Compagnie (VOC or the United East India Company) was established and given the monopoly of trade east of the Cape of Good Hope.[90] The VOC was empowered to build fortresses, wage defensive wars, and conclude peace treaties and alliances. Its formation marked the beginning of a more aggressive Dutch stance in the East Indies that was directed at gaining control of the spice trade and striking a blow at its archenemy, Spain. The initial aim of the Dutch was to seize Maluku, which until 1606 was under the Portuguese, but ultimately the goal was to occupy the Philippines itself. Dutch strategy was to cut off supplies to the Spanish garrisons in Maluku and to disrupt trade and communications with New Spain by blockading Manila. The island of Panay became a prime target of Dutch attack because troops and supplies were gathered there for transfer to Maluku. Although the Dutch and Moros did not generally mount expeditions together, the Dutch encouraged them to undertake raids to coincide with their offensives.

The first attack on Panay occurred in 1609 when François de Wittert, with a force of three thousand men, unsuccessfully attacked the port of Iloilo. Wittert went on to blockade Manila for five months before being defeated in a major naval battle off Playa Honda in Zambales.[91] Subsequently in 1614 the Dutch returned to sack and burn Iloilo,[92] and two years later Joris van Speilbergen attempted to occupy the town with about five hundred men. In anticipation of an attack, troops had been dispatched to Iloilo, and the Dutch were repelled and sustained heavy losses.[93]

The Dutch continued to infest Spanish waters, but their singular lack of success in cutting off Malukan supplies in Panay seems to have persuaded them to change tactics and focus on disrupting Spanish trade.[94] Once in control of the spice trade and having seized Melaka in 1641, the Dutch sought to control the trade in Chinese silks, and in the 1640s they stepped up their offensive against the Spanish at Manila and Cavite. The last Dutch attack on Panay occurred in 1647,[95] and after the Treaty of Westphalia in 1648, in which Spain recognized Dutch independence, the Dutch ceased their aggression against the Philippines.[96]

While lives were lost in the sacking of the main towns in Panay, and more generally in the large naval battles, many authors have noted that the indirect effects of the Hispano-Dutch War were far greater through the demands that expeditions and garrisons generated for provisions, soldiers, sailors, and ships. *Polo* and *vandala* obligations were highest during this period. Pedro de Acuña's expedition that drove the Dutch from Tidore and established a fortified settlement at Ternate in 1606 was launched from Iloilo and consisted of more than three thousand people, not counting those involved in supplying provisions or constructing ships.[97] John Phelan has judged the burdens imposed by the *polo* and *vandala* during the Hispano-Dutch War to be a major cause of the decline of the Filipino population in the first half of the seventeenth century.[98]

Climatic Change and Demographic Trends

Conquest, exploitation, and conflict were underlying demographic trends in the islands in the early colonial period. While recognizing their impact, Anthony Reid suggests that climatic change may also have contributed to population decline in the seventeenth century.[99] There is some evidence, notably from tree-ring data from Java, that during the seventeenth century some countries in Southeast Asia experienced unstable climatic conditions, perhaps linked to the "Little Ice Age" in Europe, that included frequent dry periods that resulted in food shortages and famines.[100] However, Peter Boomgaard suggests that climatic conditions were probably not so anomalous as to constitute a climatic crisis equivalent to the "Little Ice Age" in

Europe.[101] On the other hand, he suggests that a variety of natural hazards, including typhoons, floods, volcanic eruptions, and earthquakes, may have contributed to mortality indirectly by destroying crops, livestock, and boats, which affected subsistence and nutrition and raised mortality amongst infants and the aged. Whether or not such episodes characterized the Philippines will be revealed through an examination of the climatic regimes and agricultural practices of individual regions.

Conclusion

This chapter has argued that despite the Crown's intention to incorporate the Philippines into the Spanish empire by peaceful means, the dependence on the native population for the survival of the colony often led to exploitation, continuing conflict, and depopulation, processes that will be elaborated upon in parts II through IV. Commercial economic activities remained concentrated in and around Manila, which was the focus of the galleon trade and where landed estates emerged to support the urban population. It might be expected that the impact of colonial rule was more devastating there, but this chapter has argued that the reliance on native leaders for the delivery of tribute, labor, and supplies, and on parish priests for general administration beyond conversion, extended the reach of colonial rule into distant regions and brought transformations to native economies and societies that were often disproportionate to the number of Spaniards living there. Even outside Spanish administration, where contacts were often hostile, conflict might still destabilize communities and result in migration, if not depopulation.

However, the islands did not exist in isolation. Moro raids and the Hispano-Dutch War significantly affected the nature and impact of colonial rule, though they did not affect all regions equally. The Visayas, for example, were largely unaffected by the establishment of commercial enterprises, but they suffered most from Moro raids. Not only were there geographical variations in the nature of Spanish-Filipino relations, but also changes over time. It is generally recognized that the Hispano-Dutch War took a heavy toll of the Filipino population, but Moro raids also varied in intensity over time, and climatic changes may also have affected economic production and population levels in the seventeenth century. This study will therefore adopt a regional approach to illuminate these differences, but before proceeding it is necessary to be aware of the strengths and limitations of the evidence on which the analysis is based. It is to this subject that the next chapter turns.

CHAPTER 4
Interpreting the Evidence

No one will ever know exactly how many people there were in the Philippines when the Spanish arrived or the extent to which the Filipino population declined in the subsequent two centuries. However, through a careful analysis of the evidence available, the demographic history of the Philippines can be discerned in sufficient detail to enable an assessment of the impact of Spanish colonial rule and to make comparisons between population trends in the islands with other parts of the Southeast Asian archipelago. Unfortunately there are no Filipino written records dating from pre-Spanish times, while Chinese sources, which have been used so effectively by William Henry Scott to throw light on pre-Spanish Filipino society and its contacts with China,[1] have so far yielded little information of direct demographic value. By far the most important sources for the early demographic history of the Philippines are Spanish colonial documents, which are diverse and relatively abundant but pose considerable difficulties of interpretation.[2] However, it can be aided by corroborative evidence drawn from colonial ethnographic accounts and archaeology.

Early Spanish Colonial Sources

Spanish colonial sources for the demographic history of the Philippines range from letters and memorials written by the first explorers, conquistadors, and priests, to later administrative reports by secular and ecclesiastical officials, including fiscal materials and censuses, as well as records of vital events kept by parish priests. Much of the evidence for the pre-Spanish population of the Philippines and for demographic change in the early colonial period is drawn from the observations of the first conquistadors, missionaries, and officials, as well as from attempts to establish effective control of the islands through the *encomienda* and the extension of missionary activity. Available evidence from before about 1750 is fragmentary, giving rise to difficulties of interpretation and debate. Although documentary evidence generally increases over time, thereby enabling greater cross-checking of evidence, estimates must still be regarded as having a margin of error.

Eyewitness evidence for the pre-Spanish population of the Philippines often consists of passing comments on the numbers of people living in particular islands or villages. Such estimates often reflected the course of exploration and therefore did not take account of populations off the expeditionary track, or it included best guesses at the numbers living there. In about 1567 Legazpi reported that the Spanish had only explored inland regions that were accessible by water because there were too few Spaniards and they lacked horses.[3] This partial knowledge was reflected in the distribution of the first *encomiendas*, where individual communities were often not specified but were defined by river valleys or described as being "en los tingues" or in the mountains. Even toward the end of the sixteenth century large areas had still not been explored and significant numbers remained outside Spanish control and were not paying tribute.[4] For some interior regions of Luzon, this remained true into the nineteenth century.

Even where early numerical estimates exist there are significant difficulties in assessing their validity. Early eyewitness accounts have often been judged as unreliable and exaggerated.[5] It is suggested by some scholars that early observers inflated populations in order to magnify their achievements and obtain privileges from the Crown such as honorific titles and *encomiendas*. They might also have exaggerated numbers to stimulate the Crown to take some required action, such as sending more missionaries or military reinforcements, or, in the context of rapid depopulation, to condemn the activities of certain individuals. Other reasoning claims that in the early colonial period, people were not experienced in visualizing large numbers and lacked statistical sophistication. This claim may be overgeneralized, for while soldiers in the heat of battle might not be good judges of the numbers involved, Spanish administrative accounts show they were clearly capable of handling complex numerical data.[6]

In some cases the Spanish estimates might be based on native testimony, but the latter would have been no less subjective. Native witnesses might exaggerate or minimize populations according to context. They might inflate numbers to impress Spaniards that conquest would be difficult or depress them to avoid being enrolled as tribute payers. We should not be surprised at such manipulation of numbers, for it has occurred throughout history. To dismiss all early estimates as exaggerated would, as Woodrow Borah notes, imply some sort of conspiracy.[7] Some figures are undoubtedly more reliable than others, but it is the historian's craft to subject them to critical analysis in the light of other available evidence.

Apart from the questionable reliability of numerical estimates, further difficulties exist in estimating what proportion of the population they represented. The question of varying population categories and the use of multipliers to assess total populations will be discussed more fully below in the context of tribute data, but the same problem applies to converting figures for the numbers of warriors or those baptized to total populations. The number of baptisms might vary due to differences in policy between the missionary orders toward baptism. The millenarian vision of the Franciscans meant they generally undertook mass baptisms and followed with Christian instruction, whereas other orders believed that individuals should have some understanding of Christian beliefs before they were baptized.[8] This might lead to differences in the proportion of the population recorded as baptized or converted in different missionary provinces. Aside from any manipulation of the figures, however, such accounts might at least suggest a minimum population.

Civil Records

Although the Crown would have liked to abolish the *encomienda*, which had been so disastrous for Spanish American populations, it was forced to permit its introduction into the Philippines in order to establish Spanish control of the colony. *Encomiendas* were allocated as soon as territories were explored and communities made liable to pay tribute. Because of the importance of tribute income, records of the number of persons liable for tribute or the amount they paid are the most systematically kept of civil records. Because of this, reports by other secular and church officials, particularly in the early colonial period, often depended on them, referring to populations in terms of tributary numbers. Inspections to assess the numbers of persons liable for tribute were supposed to be undertaken at regular intervals by Audiencia officials, but even in Spanish America they were irregular and schedules were normally out of date. In the Philippines inspections were rare and the authorities came to rely on parish records to determine the number of tribute payers. While *cabezas de barangay* and *gobernadorcillos* were responsible for maintaining tribute registers, priests oversaw and verified their returns, which were supposed to be made annually.[9]

Very few registers for individual municipalities have survived; indeed Michael Cullinane speculates that *cabezas de barangay* and *gobernadorcillos* simply used the annual accounts of parish priests known as *estados de almas*. However, for the early colonial period it is not known how regularly these accounts were drawn up. These returns might later be combined to produce an overall *padrón general* for a civil jurisdiction, often an *alcaldía mayor*. Unfortunately, very few *padrones generales* appear to have been compiled and then only from the late eighteenth century onwards.

Fiscal Sources for the Early Colonial Period

Due to their wide geographical coverage, estimates of the population of the Philippines in the sixteenth century have placed much reliance on tribute records and particularly on a list of *encomiendas* drawn up in 1591.[10] Indeed the figures included in this list are often assumed to be indicative of and sometimes even the same as the population in 1565, even though the account was drawn up twenty to twenty-five years after first contact. Also it is clear from the rounded estimates it contains, as well as comments in other sources, that the inhabitants of large areas had not been pacified and were still not paying tribute.[11] This source is therefore an inadequate guide to the total population in 1591, let alone at first contact.

Prior to 1591 only a few sources provide overviews of the population of the islands and most include only rounded figures with some regions covered in more detail than others. The first fairly detailed and comprehensive report by a royal official, Hernando Riquel, consists of lists of *encomiendas* allocated between 1571 and 1576.[12] This document has many limitations, but it is valuable because of its early date. For some regions it contains figures in terms of "indios" for individual communities or islands, which can be aggregated to give an account of the population of whole islands or provinces. However, the figures are rounded to thousands and in most instances were not derived from systematic counts. Rather they were based on expectations that certain numbers would be present, which might have been obtained from native informants but more likely were intelligent guesses.[13] Often, subsequent inspections found fewer people than anticipated. This might suggest that any difference in estimates was an artifact of the sources rather than indicative of a real difference in population levels, but this should not be assumed.

Isolated figures for the number of tributaries in individual communities or regions are scattered throughout late-sixteenth-century documents and these will be commented upon in the regional chapters, but several accounts from the pre-1591 period provide more comprehensive information that seems to have been based, at least in part, on official sources. One such account was that of Miguel López de Loarca. Loarca accompanied Legazpi's expedition and later became a *vecino* of Arévalo and *encomendero* of the town of Otón. Because of his long residence in the islands and his interest in native customs, the *Relación de las Yslas Filipinas* that he compiled in 1582 is generally regarded as one of the more reliable accounts for the period.[14] However, the value of this source for reconstructing the population of the islands as a whole is reduced by the fact that his figures are inconsistently recorded as "indios" and "hombres." The amount of detail available for each region also varies widely, being notably stronger for the Visayas, for which it is one of the most reliable accounts written in the sixteenth century.

The Dominican friar Domingo de Salazar, who arrived in Manila as bishop in 1582, compiled another report. In 1588 he drew up a memorial aimed at securing more priests for the islands, in which he included figures for the number of tributaries in most provinces in the islands. The greater part of the memorial was not written by the bishop himself but was a copy of a report compiled by the *cabildo* of Manila for the *procurador* Alonso Sánchez in 1586, presumably based on secular records, most likely fiscal accounts. Bishop Salazar had good reason to exaggerate the size of the population in order to secure more priests, but he stressed that he had included the most accurate figures available and even attached some supplementary information for some islands not included in the 1586 report. He commented, "Many of the islands I have named, I have been to in person and the rest I have been informed about by people who are knowledgeable, and although it is not possible to know the truth precisely, I have tried to ascertain it."[15] Unfortunately the account only provides summary figures for ten secular provinces and they are rounded to hundreds or thousands. Nevertheless, they are useful for those regions where the population was under effective administration and they provide some guide to the numbers still to be converted. The report estimated there were a total of 146,700 "tributarios pacíficos," but it suggested if all were pacified the number would be about 200,000. It noted that there were indications of large populations in Cagayan, Mindoro, Cebu, Panay, and other islands, and in his supplementary comments the bishop provided detail on some 30,000 of them, mainly in Leyte, Samar, the Catanduanes, and Mindoro. In the text he uses a multiplier of four to convert *tributarios* to the total population, and his account suggests a total population of about 800,000 for Luzon and the Visayas.

To complete the review of estimates of tributary populations in the early colonial period, reference should also be made to the list of *encomiendas* drawn up in 1606.[16] This is a detailed list giving information on the name of each *encomendero*, the location of the *encomienda*, and the number of *tributos*. A significant problem in using these records, particularly for the Visayas, is that many *encomiendas* comprised communities in different islands and provinces, so obtaining a figure for a single island or province often requires adjustments to make them comparable with other lists; furthermore it is not always clear where the communities were located.[17]

Through the seventeenth century there are occasional reports of the tributary population,[18] though few give a breakdown by province. Notable exceptions are those for 1618 and 1655,[19] which provide information on the number of tributaries in Crown and private *encomiendas*. Few details exist of the context of these reports. The 1618 report was drawn up for Governor Pedro de Bivero, probably by a secular official, and gives an account of the inhabitants, government, and agricultural products in the islands.

Later Civil Records

This study focuses on population trends prior to 1700, but because information for the eighteenth century is considerably more abundant, it has been used to aid analysis, particularly for remote regions where significant numbers remained outside Spanish administration in the early colonial period. For the eighteenth century, fiscal accounts remain the main source of evidence. For the eighteenth century there exists an almost continuous set of accounts by officials of the royal exchequer that give summaries of the number of *tributos* and *almas* in different civil jurisdictions. These are to be found in the Contaduría section of Archivo General de Indias. These records have been used by Angel Martínez Cuesta in his *History of Negros* but otherwise have not been subject to scholarly examination. Given that the emphasis of this study is on the early colonial period, no detailed analysis was undertaken of these eighteenth-century accounts. However, the figures for 1700, 1735, and 1750 have been used to provide a brief overview of population levels in Luzon and the Visayas. The date of 1735 was chosen to enable comparison with the figures presented by San Antonio, which have been judged by some authors as too low.[20] San Antonio based his figures on information solicited from the clergy, and he challenged people to compare them with those provided by officials of the royal exchequer. In fact, a comparison of his figures for Luzon with those contained in treasury accounts shows that San Antonio's figures are fairly similar, being just over 1,800 higher.[21] If his figures appear low, it is because he had not received returns for some regions or because large numbers were not under effective administration. However, where this is the case it is indicated in the text. While recording that the total native

Christian population was 837,182, he estimated that the total population was more than one million.[22] The similarity of the figures suggests that royal officials were also using parish registers as the basis of their records. However, it became clear in reviewing the fiscal accounts for this study that figures for individual towns were similar over long periods, which suggests that reassessments were irregular. This means that they can only be regarded as rough estimates of the population at any particular time. The failure of fiscal accounts to keep up with demographic changes was probably also a feature of the early colonial period.

While fiscal accounts continue to be the most important civil records available for the demographic historian of the colonial period, toward the end of the eighteenth century the first censuses become available. The first census of the Philippines was initiated as part of the Crown's aim to draw up censuses for all of its overseas territories in 1776.[23] Censuses were to cover all persons, whatever age, sex, or race. Instructions were sent to both civil and church authorities, and in the case of the Philippines both authorities responded to the request. The archbishop of Manila and the bishops of Cebu and Nueva Caceres all drew up returns, while the governor initiated censuses using *alcaldes*, *corregidores*, and military commanders.[24] These censuses vary somewhat in the amount of detail they contain, though they generally give figures for all parishes, whether or not they were under the secular or regular clergy. What is not known is whether the information was drawn up specifically for the census or used pre-existing information gathered for some other unspecified purpose. Some data from these censuses are contained in the regional tables. As far as I am aware, the censuses, which are extremely rich, have not been subject to scholarly analysis. Following this initial project, it was the Crown's intention that censuses be drawn up annually, but the effort involved meant that this rarely occurred. It remained the case that many returns drawn up in the eighteenth century did not constitute comprehensive accounts, but often referred only to one region.

The Limitations of Tribute Records

Perhaps the most important drawback in using tribute records to estimate total populations is that for many provinces a significant proportion of the population was not under effective Spanish administration. Moreover, the proportion might fluctuate over time. Registration is likely to have been more effective closer to centers of Spanish administration, but even here, for example around Manila, migration meant that keeping track of the population was not easy. For outlying areas the numbers included on tribute rolls would vary with the intensity of missionary activity. This issue will be discussed more fully below. Further difficulties exist in converting the number of tributaries to total populations and in using them to track demographic trends. These difficulties applied through the colonial period, but were probably most acute in the early colonial period.

One difficulty is the lack of consistency in the terms for tributaries, but more significantly how they were defined. The initial allocation of *encomiendas* in 1571 referred only to "indios." It is assumed by comparison with other figures available at about the same time that this referred to able-bodied male heads of household and was comparable with the category of "tributos." Unmarried adults were calculated as a fraction of a *tributo*, while native leaders were exempt, as were children, the sick, the disabled, and the aged. The term "indios" might have been more embracing, including male heads of household who were exempt from tribute and counting single persons as whole rather than half tributaries. It is the most commonly used term in the earliest accounts and for regions where the population had not been pacified and possibly not formally registered on tribute rolls. On the other hand, later accounts often refer to *tributantes*, with two *tributantes* equivalent to one *tributo*.

Not only did the terms vary, but the precise definition of these categories did not remain constant over time. In the sixteenth century there was some debate over who should be liable for tribute payment, both in terms of age and whether or not they had been baptized or recognized Spanish authority. In the Spanish empire a person was generally liable to pay tribute between the ages of eighteen and fifty, but Patricio Hidalgo Nuchera's study of the *encomienda* in the Philippines shows that in the late sixteenth century there was considerable debate over the age of liability. This was not resolved definitively until 1604, when the upper limit of liability was set at sixty and the lower limit for single persons between sixteen and twenty-five, depending on sex and whether or not the individual was still under the legal authority of parents; all married persons were liable to pay tribute.[25] In theory such changes in definition should have affected the numbers of tributaries reported, but the lack of effective accounting, particularly in the early colonial period, probably means that ages would have been imperfectly known and any changes in administrative guidelines would probably have had a minimal effect on the numbers recorded, especially in regions remote from Manila.

Another factor, particularly in tracing the native Filipino population as opposed to other ethnic groups, is that it is not known whether the Chinese and *mestizos*, who also paid tribute, were included in the number of tributaries reported. Eighteenth-century fiscal accounts often separate them out because they paid a different level of tribute, but for the early colonial period they may have been included.[26] Apart from Manila and its hinterland, where the numbers in these ethnic categories fluctuated significantly, this is not a major problem since elsewhere the numbers were quite small.

Lack of consistency in the definitions of recorded categories not only urges caution in making comparisons over time, but also in converting tributary numbers to total populations. The 1591 list of *encomiendas* uses a multiplier of four, but there are likely to have been regional differences in family size stemming from differences in social organization and the extent to which societies had felt the impact of conquest and colonial rule. There is evidence from Spanish America that in the immediate postconquest period fertility and household size fell.[27] In the Philippines the multiplier applied by different authorities to the islands as a whole seems to have varied over time, dropping to three in the early seventeenth century but rising to four and a half or five toward the end of the eighteenth century.[28] The multipliers included in the documentary sources may have had some validity for the particular time and place, so in the absence of any contradictory evidence, they are used here rather than applying a common factor throughout the colonial period, even though this approach might appear inconsistent. Parish records might provide some check on the validity of multipliers, but these are not generally available before the latter part of the eighteenth century and in any case would not include evidence for the numbers who were exempt from tribute payment that could affect the multiplier.

Ecclesiastical Records

As described above, the administration of the islands relied to a large degree on the clergy and in particular on the missionary orders to provide or verify the numbers liable for tribute and *polo* labor. However, priests also collected information for their own purposes, some of which is of value to demographic historians. Parish priests were required by canon law to record all baptisms, marriages, confirmations, and burials.[29] The earliest known parish registers for the Philippines date from the 1620s, but very few dating from before the late eighteenth century have survived.[30] Although many parish registers are not available today, they formed the basis of the *estado de almas* that priests were required to draw up on an annual basis. Since parish priests were required to record all vital events, these summary accounts covered the whole population or souls within a parish regardless of age or ethnicity. Very few of the *estados de almas* compiled at the parish or municipal level appear to have survived, though a few annual series exist in the Archivo de la Provincia del Santísimo Rosario at the University of Santo Tomas in Manila for the Dominican missions of Cagayan and Pangasinan for the late eighteenth century. The amount of detail they contain varies. Some of the *estados de almas* specify that the figures included those who were not of an age to confess, normally taken to be aged seven, but in other cases they are recorded as just "almas" rather than "almas de confesión y communion." Also in some cases other groups, such as Spaniards, *mestizos*, or Negritos, are listed separately and in others they are included. The lack of consistency needs to be noted, though for most regions the numbers were small and would probably not have affected total populations significantly.[31]

A more important problem was the extent to which priests succeeded in recording people within their parishes, because despite attempts at congregating them into nucleated settlements, within a single parish the population might be quite dispersed. Moreover, people often migrated or fled. Norman Owen has suggested that in nineteenth-century Bikol perhaps 10 to 20 percent of all births and deaths were not registered, and the figure might be higher in more remote areas, with under-recording being most acute among children.[32]

The *estados de almas* for individual parishes might be combined at a diocesan level or in the case of the missionary orders at a provincial or district level. One of the earliest attempts to summarize the population of the Philippines based on church records was by the Archbishop of Manila, Miguel García Serrano, in

1622.[33] His account provides figures by region and religious order, but the figures are generally rounded to thousands and inconsistently recorded as *almas* or *almas de confesión*. Apart from the eighteenth-century account by San Antonio, discussed above, which was based on church records, the next *planes de almas* at the level of the archbishopric or bishopric appear to have been drawn up by the Bishop of Nueva Segovia in 1800 and the Archbishop of Manila in 1812.[34] More common before the nineteenth century are summary lists of *almas* drawn up by missionary orders for their own provinces. Where they exist, these diocesan or provincial reports contain valuable demographic data, but a significant drawback in using them to track change over time is that the administration of parishes within any given island or region often did not remain constant. From the beginning parishes associated with the main towns were placed under the secular clergy, but piecemeal secularization occurred through the colonial period. Since the missionary orders were generally better record keepers than the secular clergy, this generally resulted in a decline in the quantity and quality of information available. Also, parishes often changed hands between different missionary orders or were abandoned due to lack of priests or to Moro raids. Hence the number of parishes and missions administered by different groups of clergy did not remain constant over time, even assuming that parish boundaries remained fixed, which is not certain. Since these reports by different groups of clergy were not generally drawn up at the same time, getting an overview of just a single island or region at a single point in time from ecclesiastical sources is difficult.

Corroborative Evidence

Given the fragmentary nature of the documentary record, corroborative evidence derived from records of native traditions and from archaeology may aid interpretation. Both sources cannot in general provide precise numbers, but they can provide insight into the nature of Filipino subsistence and society and thereby be used as a check on numerical estimates generated by documentary sources, as well as contribute to understanding demographic trends. Observations on the nature of native subsistence and society, including birth and marriages practices, are often included in early eyewitness reports, including those written by members of the missionary orders, but there are also a number of detailed accounts that focus specifically on the character of native societies. Such descriptions have all been refracted through Spanish eyes and as such often contain moral judgments on Filipino social practices that served to justify colonial domination and missionary enterprise. However, if this is kept in mind, they can still provide insight into practices, such as infanticide or marriage customs, that have demographic implications.

Among the most important missionary accounts written from an ethnographic perspective are those compiled by the Franciscan father Juan de Plasencia and the Jesuit fathers Pedro Chirino and Francisco Ignacio Alcina. Juan de Plasencia was based at Nagcarlan in Laguna de Bay and in the 1580s wrote in some detail on the law, social customs, and religion of the Tagalogs.[35] Pedro Chirino served in Jesuit missions in the hinterland of Manila and in 1595 was assigned to the Jesuit College in Cebu in 1595, from whence he visited Mindoro, Marinduque, Samar, Bohol, and Mindanao. He therefore covered both regions in his *Relación de las islas Filipinas*, published in 1604. Exceptionally detailed is Francisco Ignacio Alcina's four-volume *Historia de las islas e indios de Bisayas*, which is particularly strong on Leyte and Samar. Alcina arrived in the Philippines in 1632 and shortly afterwards moved to the Visayas, where he lived for at least thirty-five years until his death in 1674.[36] Although his account postdates conquest by a century, he attempted to reconstruct native culture in pre-Spanish times by interviewing elderly residents. Although not written until the late colonial period, the reports written by the Dominican Francisco Antolín, who spent nearly twenty years as a missionary in the province of Ituy and Paniqui and served as the order's archivist, are exceptional in the amount of ethnographic material they contain.[37] As will be described in chapter 13, Antolín showed a particular interest in the demographic history of the region, on which he wrote a special account titled *Discurso sobre el gentió y población de esta misión de Ituy y Paniqui* in 1787.[38] Apart from these major sources, many descriptions of native peoples are contained in missionary letters. In his book *Barangay*, William Henry Scott has imaginatively used early Filipino dictionaries, which were generally compiled by members of the religious orders, to throw light on Filipino society at the time of Spanish conquest.[39]

But it was not only missionaries who took an intelligent and active interest in the islands' inhabitants, but also laymen and secular officials. Mention has already been made of the *encomendero* Miguel López de Loarca, who included ethnographic information in his *Relación*, while chapter 8 of Governor Antonio de Morga's history of the Philippines gives an account of native customs.[40] The Boxer Codex may have been based on some of these sources, notably those of Loarca and Plasencia, but it is the first to include a substantial account of the province of Cagayan. Charles Boxer has surmised that it may have been compiled or commissioned by Governor Gómez Pérez Dasmariñas or his son Luis Pérez Dasmariñas.[41]

So far archaeological evidence has not played a significant role in estimating the size of populations at the time of Spanish conquest or even later. Unfortunately, large-scale excavations have been rare and there has been virtually no archaeological work in large parts of the Philippines. The research that exists has drawn on excavations of individual burials or cemetery sites aimed at providing descriptive historical and cultural accounts. Only a few studies, such as that of Tanjay in Negros, have attempted to understand the political and economic dynamics of sites or sought to integrate historical and ethnographic evidence in the analysis.[42] However, archaeology can be informative about settlement patterns, subsistence, and diet, which can have implications for population levels.

Archaeological excavations of settlements can give some indication of population size, though it is not always clear whether all houses were occupied contemporaneously and extrapolation from limited sites to wider regions can be quite problematic. Other indirect evidence may come in the form of plant and animal remains or agricultural techniques or implements that can provide insight into the nature of subsistence and diets. Archaeological evidence for intensive forms of production, such as irrigation that would allow continuous cropping, would suggest larger populations than could be supported by shifting cultivation. In the Philippine context, the antiquity of irrigation and terracing in Ilocos and interior Luzon is important to the debate on population levels in those regions. Certain staples also have greater potential to support larger populations than others. Maize, by providing a more balanced diet than many root crops, can release societies from dependence for protein on wild food resources such as game or fish, allowing higher population densities to be supported. Demographic growth in Cebu, particularly in the nineteenth century, has been linked to a switch from the cultivation of millet to maize.[43] At present, documentary sources are probably a better source of evidence for dietary changes than archaeology, but in the future the greater use of stable isotope analysis of human skeletal remains should provide more precise information on the composition of the pre-Spanish diets. Nevertheless, the difficulty of assessing the implications of diets for population levels would remain.

Paleopathology can also contribute to an understanding of population dynamics by providing evidence for age structure, age at death, sex ratios, health, and nutrition.[44] However, estimating fertility and mortality is not easy; even the basic aging of skeletal remains is not an exact science. As noted in chapter 2, paleopathology can provide good evidence for the presence of chronic infections, but not as yet for acute infections. As far as I am aware there have been no analyses of skeletal remains in the Philippines from the perspective of nutrition or paleopathology.

Population Trends: Real or Imaginary?

Apart from the normal difficulties associated with the use of early Spanish colonial sources for demographic analysis, a problem that appears to be particularly acute for the Philippines is determining whether population trends were real or were a function of the effectiveness of administrative control. At a general level there are arguments that the Filipino population did not decline significantly in the early colonial period, but rather that many fled to evade tribute payments, the *vandala*, and *polo*. It is an argument that is made particularly for Luzon, but also for some Visayan islands such as Cebu. Conversely, the rapid growth in the Filipino population in the nineteenth century is seen as a function of more effective administration,[45] changes in agricultural production and trade that resulted in more stable communities, and in some regions due to the cessation of Moro raids. In fact, administrative reforms may have increased the registered population earlier in the late eighteenth century. Following the English invasion in 1762 and the Silang insurrection in Pangasinan, the zealous *fiscal* of the Audiencia, Francisco Leandro Viana, sought to improve defense by raising revenue through an overhaul of the tribute system. More concerted efforts were made to settle Filipinos "under the bells," and parish priests and *alcaldes mayores* rather than *cabezas de barangay*, who he claimed each hid ten *tributarios*, became responsible for compiling lists of tributaries.[46]

That some migration to escape Spanish rule occurred seems irrefutable; the problem is judging its scale and how far it affected overall demographic trends. The impression is that most evasion took place over short distances, with peripheral regions suffering a constant hemorrhaging of population despite missionary efforts. While the missionary orders constantly sought to extend their mission fields, their ability to do so depended on available personnel. It was not uncommon for a new mission field to be opened up, only to be closed a few years later, with the neophytes returning to their former way of life and the few remaining converts transferred to well-established parishes. Although the Spanish aimed to congregate people in nucleated settlements, either in *pueblos* or missions, due to subsistence imperatives or lifestyle preferences populations often remained dispersed over wide areas and were visited only irregularly.[47] Moro raids often reinforced such centrifugal tendencies. The lack of effective administration meant that there are fluctuations in recorded mission populations that are largely independent of demographic trends.

In coming to a judgment on the proportion of the population that may have been outside Spanish administration, it is necessary to consider the likelihood that migration could have occurred on a scale that could account for any recorded population losses. Within any one region a few thousand might be credible, but tens of thousands less likely.

Population Losses and Racial Mixing

In the Americas racial mixing was a significant factor holding back population growth, especially in the eighteenth century. The Spanish Crown generally discouraged contact between the races, partly to protect native peoples from ill treatment and abuse and partly to clearly separate the races for the purposes of assessing and levying tribute and labor. It thus pursued a policy of residential segregation that envisaged the creation of two republics—a *república de indios* composed of Indians, who resided in the countryside, and a *república de españoles* composed of all other racial groups who were to be confined to the towns.[48] In Spanish America this policy proved impracticable since native labor was essential to the functioning of the empire. The towns, mines, and haciendas that attracted both Indian and African slave labor soon emerged as racial melting pots. The situation in the Philippines was different. Relatively few Europeans made it to the islands, so the number of Spanish *mestizos* was always small. Also, there were no highly profitable enterprises that required the importation of labor on a large scale. On the other hand, the presence of Spaniards in the islands encouraged traders from China and created a demand for skilled urban and agricultural labor that was filled by the Chinese. At different times the Chinese were massacred or expelled from the islands, but over time their numbers increased and they intermarried with native Filipinos. By the end of the eighteenth century about 4 to 5 percent of the Philippine tributary population was

Chinese *mestizo*, though it was significantly higher in Manila and its hinterland.[49] The growth in the Chinese *mestizo* population is only considered in this study to the extent that it affects estimates of the Filipino population. Where the numbers of Chinese *mestizos* are distinguished, they have not been incorporated in such estimates, but for many regions the numbers would probably have been too small to warrant separate accounts of them. Perhaps more significant to the demographic analysis here is that racial mixing led to a reclassification of Filipinos as Chinese *mestizo*s, with wives and children being classified for tribute purposes according to the ethnicity of the husband or father respectively.[50] This process of intermarriage was encouraged because even though *mestizos* paid a higher rate of tax, there were social status advantages in being classified as one.[51] Changing numbers in different ethnic categories may therefore reflect reclassification rather than demographic processes.

A Regional Approach

Very little research has been conducted on the early demographic history of the Spanish Philippines, and that which exists tends to rely on tribute records or other official accounts that cover all major provinces.[52] As has been demonstrated, such sources are few for the early colonial period and they require careful interpretation. Reliance must therefore be placed on fragments of information found in letters or accounts written by secular and church officials, as well as by private individuals, including conquistadors, missionaries, and settlers. The best and perhaps the only way to build a general picture of demographic trends for this period is to construct it from the bottom up through a critical analysis of the evidence for each island and region. In this way, small pieces of information, not only of a quantitative nature and each perhaps insignificant in itself, can be brought together to form a significant body of persuasive evidence on which tentative conclusions can be made about demographic trends. An advantage of a regional approach is that it can draw out differences in population trends across regions and enable more complex analyses that can take account of differences in local cultures, environments, and histories. So far there have been only a few studies of the early demographic history of individual regions, the most notable being by Canute VanderMeer and by Michael Cullinane and Peter Xenos of the island of Cebu, and by Angel Martínez Cuesta of the island of Negros.[53]

Conclusion

This study aims to analyze the evidence for demographic trends for each major island and region in the Visayas and Luzon, broadly following the trajectory of Spanish conquest. The emphasis is on the period up to 1700, but it also draws on evidence from later periods. The study is concerned not only with numbers *per se*, but with demographic trends as a barometer of and formative influence on economic, social, and political changes. It will demonstrate that Spanish conquest and early colonial rule in the Philippines resulted in significant population decline that was more pervasive and prolonged than generally envisaged, but that it varied regionally. These regional demographic trends reflected in part the specific objectives the Spanish had for different regions, notably in terms of the development of commercial enterprises and the demand for tribute and labor. Less often recognized is that they were also influenced by the ability of native societies in different parts of the Philippines to respond to the changed circumstances of colonial rule. Some societies were better able to meet the extracommunal demands imposed on them or had marriage practices and population policies that favored population growth and enabled them to recover more easily from demographic crises. Once the overall pattern of demographic change in the early colonial Philippines has been established, the study will explore the question of how far these demographic trends and the factors that underlay them differed from the early colonial experience of native societies in the Americas and from other islands in the Southeast Asian archipelago.

PART II

The Visayas

CHAPTER 5

Conquest and Depopulation before 1600

Miguel López de Legazpi's expedition to the Philippines dropped anchor in Gamay Bay off Samar on 13 February 1565 (see Map 5.1).[1] Preoccupied with finding provisions, the expedition skirted the coasts of Samar and Leyte and finally encountered the relatively large settlement of Cabalian on the east coast of Leyte. There it seized supplies of rice, *camotes*, and chickens, for which, on departing south, it left behind barter goods as a form of payment. Provisions proved even more difficult to acquire in Limasawa and Bohol since the natives fled fearing further attacks by the Portuguese who had preceded the Spanish. In the search for a permanent base in the islands, Legazpi dispatched a number of exploratory expeditions to Mindanao, one of which, by accident rather than design, passed the islands of Negros and Cebu. On hearing news of dense populations and good food supplies in Cebu, Legazpi directed the expedition to the island, where it arrived on 27 April 1565. After a brief skirmish with "almost two thousand warriors," Legazpi founded the town of San Miguel.[2] Spanish sojourn in the Visayas was to be relatively short. The large populations and abundant food supplies proved a chimera and it was not long before the islands were abandoned for Luzon. However, in the brief period from 1565 to 1571, when the Spanish were confined to the Visayas, they wrought havoc among local populations in their desperate search for provisions and wealth.

While the Visayan Islands have some environmental and cultural features in common, there are also some important differences between them. In terms of their physical geography, the islands typically have interior mountain regions ranging from 1,000 to 8,000 feet, while their lowlands are limited to narrow coastal strips; only in the Leyte Valley, the Iloilo Plain in Panay, and northern and western Negros are there more extensive lowlands.[3] Climatically the islands receive between about 50 to 80 inches of rain a year and experience a short but marked dry season between January and March. The eastern Visayas, particularly Samar, are afflicted by frequent typhoons between October and December, which have discouraged settlement of the most exposed coasts. Rainfall is lower in the central Visayas, where the porous soils make the region susceptible to drought. Here in pre-Spanish times emphasis was placed on the cultivation of millet and root crops. The soils of the western Visayas are more fertile. The lowlands of Panay are covered with recent alluvial deposits, while those of western Negros are of volcanic origin and fairly

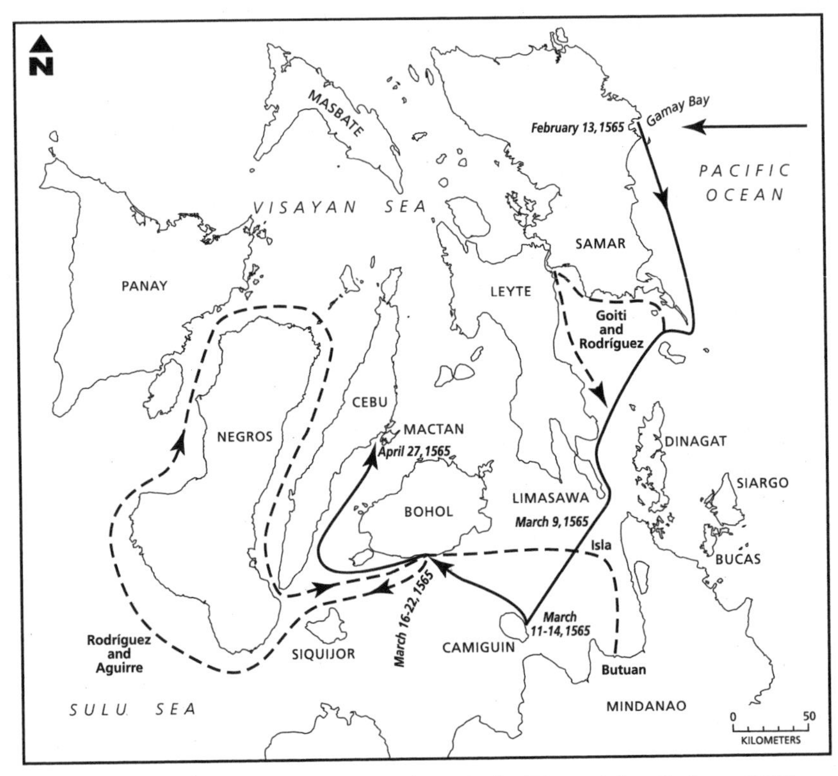

Map 5.1. Miguel López de Legazpi's expedition in the Visayas (after Cushner, 1971)

deep, though poorly drained. In colonial times Panay became the breadbasket for the Visayas and the source of supplies for garrisons and expeditions.

Most inhabitants of the Visayan Islands were Austronesian in origin and were distinguished by their tattoos and distinct language, though they spoke different dialects.[4] Good evidence exists for Visayan culture in the late sixteenth and early seventeenth centuries. The Jesuit fathers Pedro Chirino and Francisco Ignacio Alcina compiled the most detailed accounts,[5] but a number of Jesuit letters also make reference to native customs.[6] The detailed writings of Chirino and Alcina postdate a number of early secular accounts, such as those of Miguel López de Loarca and the Boxer Codex, which includes a description of the *Costumbres y usos serimonias y rritos de Bisayas*.[7] Even earlier fragments of information can be gleaned from accounts of Magellan's expedition in 1521, notably that of Antonio Pigafetta,[8] and from letters written by Spaniards prior to their move to Manila in 1571. In his book *Barangay*, William Henry Scott provides a succinct description of Visayan culture based on these sources as well as on early Visayan dictionaries.[9] It is not the intention here to duplicate this work, but to highlight those aspects of native society that had implications for the nature of Spanish rule and demographic trends in the islands.

Before proceeding, it is necessary to note that Negros and Panay also contained Negritos who were the descendants of the original Australoid inhabitants of the Philippines, who had been displaced or absorbed by Austronesian migrants who began arriving about five to six thousand years ago.[10] Negritos were observed by Magellan's expedition in 1521,[11] and Esteban Rodríguez encountered them in the island of Negros in 1565.[12] He observed them half a league from the shore but reported that there were many "Negros" in the hills, on account of which the island received its name.[13] The Negritos were probably more numerous than they are at present, but colonial accounts provide few estimates of their numbers. They were still numerous at the beginning of the eighteenth century,[14] and in the 1870s were said to number about 8,900 in northern Negros alone, though this number probably included other unconverted groups, such as the Bukidnon;[15] at the beginning of the twentieth century about 1,000 Negritos existed in northern Negros.[16] Negritos seem to have been less numerous in Panay. In 1728 the Augustinians formed three villages among Negritos at Bosoc in Otón,[17] and in the nineteenth century Rafael Díaz Arenas recorded that there were 500 in the province of Iloilo and about 1,200 in Antique.[18] In the 1970s about 450 were living in two groups, one in the Bais Forest Reserve in Negros Oriental and the other in northern Negros.[19] The Negritos lived in small groups of twenty to thirty persons, subsisting on hunting and fishing, with some secondary root cultivation. They traded and continue to trade with lowland peoples, exchanging forests products, such as wax, honey, and rattans, for rice, marine products, and manufactures.[20] According to the Augustinian father Gaspar de San Agustín, the Negritos of Panay lived "without king, lord or settlement."[21]

Subsistence and Settlement Patterns in the Visayas

Subsistence in the Visayas was based on the cultivation of rice, millet, taro, yams, bananas, and plantains. Rice was the preferred food, but in many islands production was insufficient to meet subsistence needs throughout the year and heavy dependence was placed on the cultivation of root crops.[22] In some islands, notably Cebu and Bantayan, drier conditions favored the cultivation of millet, known as *dawa*, rather than rice.[23] Coconuts were widely raised for palm wine and the flesh used as bread, particularly when rice was short.[24]

Despite the availability of a wide range of crops and wild plants, early colonial observers noted that the basic diet was one of rice and fish.[25] Extensive fisheries were noted in some islands, including Bohol, where there were many "corrals" and salt fish was an important item of trade.[26] Game, especially deer and wild pigs, were also commonly hunted. The Jesuit Diego Sánchez recorded that game was so abundant in Bohol that it was possible to purchase twenty-five deer or pigs for a *tostón*.[27] Animals were hunted not only for food, but also for their skins, which were often exported.[28] In addition, domesticated animals, notably pigs, goats, and chickens, were widely raised. Pigs were important in feasting and, along with goats and chickens, were frequently offered to Legazpi, suggesting their high status.[29]

Differences in the fertility of the islands and in the timing of the monsoon regularly produced differences in supply and demand, while swarms of locusts or browsing animals also created shortages.[30] Sometimes, as occurred at Palapag in Samar in 1611, a drought might be so great as to destroy not only the rice crop, but also root crops on which reliance was placed in times of shortage.[31] These variations in production encouraged a trade in rice. Leyte and Panay were important suppliers of food to other islands, though much of the trade passed through Cebu, which itself produced little rice.[32] The fertility of Panay was evident to the Spanish at an early date and was crucial in their decision to move there from Cebu.[33] Leyte's pivotal role in supplying other Visayan islands was observed by Legazpi, who at Cabalian encountered a *parao* that had come from another island to obtain rice and roots. Later in Bohol he met another boat from Leyte laden with rice and yams.[34] Despite this trade in provisions even the most productive islands might experience severe shortages.[35] In times of famine, people resorted to other islands to acquire provisions in exchange for gold, slaves, and other valuable items.[36] Famine and harvest failure were frequently cited as reasons why families and individuals became indebted.[37]

Swidden cultivation or *caingin* was the dominant form of agriculture practiced in the Visayas. Although chiefs may have had exclusive rights to certain lands and resources, such as fisheries, land was not alienable, but access was open to all. Hence farmers only had rights to the product of cultivation, not to the land, though they retained ownership of any tree crops they planted.[38] This meant that chiefs with more dependents could effectively control larger stretches of land. Although Spanish observers considered the land to be abundant and able to support much larger populations, fertile cultivable lands were not extensive. The Jesuit Alejo López observed that unlike Luzon, where there were large stretches of fertile land, in the Visayas "a quarter or a half a league of good land is separated by much poor land," so the population was dispersed.[39] As argued by David Henley for Southeast Asia in general, the shortage of fertile land and the land-extensive form of cultivation probably limited overall population densities.[40]

Esther Boserup has argued that population pressure acts as a stimulus to agricultural intensification, for example through irrigation or terracing, so the absence of such techniques in the Visayas might suggest a lack of population pressure on resources.[41] On the other hand, the occurrence of severe food shortages suggests otherwise. However, the development of intensive techniques would not have been a viable proposition in the Visayas due to the relative shortage of labor and indeed may not have been necessary since provisions could be acquired through trade.[42]

There was not only an interisland trade in provisions, but within individual islands symbiotic relations existed between highland and lowland groups.[43] Highland groups acquired rice, pottery, salt, and marine products from the lowlands in return for wax, honey, hardwoods, gold, and cotton.[44] As foreign trade increased, products reaching the interior included more high-status goods such as locally manufactured decorated pottery, metal weapons, and gold jewelry, as well as imported goods such as Chinese porcelain. Meanwhile, the goods demanded by foreign traders led to an increased emphasis on forest products, such as wax, resins, animal skins, civet, medicinal plants, and rattans.[45] As noted in chapter 2, these highland-lowland contacts acted as important channels through which infections could be spread.

Gold, iron, and textiles were the most important items produced for export and for furthering alliances and controlling interior trade. Early lists of gold deposits found in the Philippines indicate that only small, scattered deposits were present in the Visayas.[46] Antonio de Morga recorded that gold was mined at Taribon in Cebu and the natives of Bohol told Magellan's expedition that although gold was as abundant "as the hairs of their heads," it was not mined because of the lack of iron tools with which to extract it.[47] Recent scholars have suggested that shortages of labor, the peripheral location of the islands with respect to main trading centers, and competition from the major gold-exporting regions of Sumatra, the Malay Peninsula, and Champa may also have discouraged production.[48] Iron was in high demand not only for tools, but also increasingly for weapons. Early encounters with the Spanish revealed an exceptional native interest in iron goods. An anonymous account of Legazpi's expedition noted that when they saw "the nails they desired nothing else and paid for them in gold dust."[49] Archaeological evidence indicates that some local deposits of iron were exploited and smelted in Cebu,[50] but the difficulties of extraction meant most iron and iron goods were imported from China and Borneo.[51] The control that elites had over the manufacture or trade in iron[52] also gave them command over the production of weapons that might enhance their military power and gave them access to prestige tools that could be used to promote alliances. Finally, cotton and cotton textiles, as well as *medriñaque* made from abaca, were highly sought after by foreign traders.[53] Households produced cloth for their own needs,[54] but specialized centers of cotton production existed in Cebu[55] and in Iloilo in Panay.[56]

This pattern of economic activities was reflected in the settlement pattern of the islands. While the population was generally dispersed and communities small, archaeological and ethnohistorical evidence suggests that a small number of larger centers had emerged on the coast, often at the mouths of rivers, where they were strategically located to control exchange between interior groups and foreign traders.[57] A major trading center existed at Cebu, but it owed its importance to its strategic location in the central Visayas rather than its ability to control trade between the highlands and lowlands.[58] Other significant population clusters existed at Otón near Arévalo in Panay,[59] and at Dauis at the crossing point between the islands of Panglao and Bohol.[60] Leyte possessed fourteen significant settlements, of which Ogmuc (Ormoc) was the largest.[61]

Most communities or *barangays* comprised fewer than a few thousand people. About 1567 Legazpi reported that "the settlements in this land are not cities or even towns, but they are communities of thirty to one hundred houses or less, and others are scattered in the form of *caserías*, in twos, sixes or tens."[62] Within a community a *datu*'s house was distinguished by its larger size and the presence of function rooms and storehouses, while most people lived in small single-family houses, built on stilts,[63] which the eighteenth-century traveler Monsieur de Pagès likened to "bird cages."[64] Houses and villages were constructed on riverbanks or near other sources of water to enable frequent bathing.[65]

Visayan Polities and Social Practices

By now it will be apparent that at the time the Spanish arrived, Visayan society was undergoing a process of significant change. Like much of Southeast Asia, the political landscape of the Visayas was one of scattered small polities headed by *datus*. Although the position of a *datu* was apparently hereditary, his power seems to have depended on the number of subjects and slaves he could attract or acquire, which in turn derived from his charisma, military prowess, or wealth, which enabled him to distribute goods, sponsor elaborate feasts and rituals, and support politically advantageous marriage alliances.[66] Chiefs acquired their wealth through controlling the production of prestige goods or foreign trade, for which the acquisition of labor was critical. This was needed not only to produce goods but also to conduct military raids and expeditions, which might not only increase the number of slaves and disrupt rival commercial activities, but if successful could attract more followers. In such circumstances a paramount chief might emerge out of a loose federation of *datus*.

Apart from the *datus*, Visayan society included two other social groups: *timaguas* and *oripun*. The *timaguas* were freemen who could live where they wished and could attach themselves to any *datu*. The *datu* would provide them with protection or avenge wrongs committed against them in return for service at feasts and on expeditions.[67] They were a relatively privileged group, who unlike *oripun* did not perform agricultural labor.[68] The Spanish often referred to the *oripun* as slaves, though most were probably indebted dependents who fell into debt as a result of poverty for social reasons, such as to acquire marriage gifts, or in time of crises, such as famines.[69] William Henry Scott has shown that this group, which comprised the majority of Visayans, consisted of individuals of varying levels of economic and social standing, ranging from those who lived independently and only worked for their masters for a few days a week, to those who were chattel slaves.

Sixteenth-century observations and archaeological evidence suggest that when the Spanish arrived, interpolity conflict was increasing in scale and intensity. Raids were conducted for the slightest reason, to avenge an attack, treachery, or robbery, to capture wives, or to extract a debt.[70] The Spanish generally regarded the people of the Visayans as more warlike than those of Luzon,[71] and inter-*barangay* conflict probably constrained population growth in the region. However, since a *datu*'s wealth, social position, and military power depended on the number of people in his service, it was in his interest to protect his dependents. Therefore those captured in raids were not killed, and the few slaves who were put to death were those who were buried with chiefs for which "foreign" slaves were chosen.[72] An esteemed *datu* might possess one to two hundred dependents and his wife slightly fewer, but even ordinary *datus* commonly had fifty to sixty.[73] Dependents were so essential to the economic and political power of *datus* that Spanish attempts to abolish "slavery" became an obstacle to their Christian conversion in the early colonial period.[74]

Marriages were often contracted before birth or during childhood, but there is little evidence for the age at which marriage took place. From a survey of marriage patterns in Southeast Asia as a whole, Anthony Reid inclines to the view that marriage before or at puberty was probably uncommon and restricted to elites.[75] However, Father Alcina recorded that many women married at twelve, though the marriage might not be consummated until later.[76] Child marriages are still common in central Panay today.[77] These observations are consistent with general findings that correlate low age at marriage with ease of access to land.[78]

Marriages between people without property only involved a few simple gifts,[79] but the marriage of a *datu* was accompanied by the payment of bridewealth, usually in the form of slaves, gold, or other valuable items, of which slaves were the most esteemed.[80] In the sixteenth century Loarca claimed that bridewealth for a chief might amount to one hundred pesos, when a single slave cost between six and twelve pesos.[81] There seems to have been some difference in the payment of bridewealth within the Visayas. Father Alcina noted that in Leyte, Samar, and Ibabao[82] bridewealth was given to the girl's father, who distributed it among his closest relatives, whereas in other islands such as Bohol and Cebu bridewealth had to be sufficient to provide for all the relatives, which meant it was higher and as such acted as a constraint on marriage.[83] This difference might partially account for the slightly lower population densities in the latter islands compared to the eastern Visayas. Any bridewealth had to be returned to the husband's family in case of divorce, so there was some incentive for the wife's family to preserve the marriage.[84] Nevertheless, a number of observers reported that couples separated for the slightest reason, and it was common for individuals to have been married several times.[85] There was no cultural or legal barrier to polygamy, but because of the financial burden it imposed it was relatively uncommon, and where practiced only involved two or three wives.[86] Father Chirino claimed polygamy existed in Leyte and Ibabao, but that he had not observed it in Panay. He also stated specifically that it was not found in Bohol.[87] However, the fact that Loarca, being most familiar with Panay, makes reference to polygamy and that it is a contemporary custom in the island suggests that it was practiced, but probably on a small scale.[88]

A distinctive feature of sexual relations in Southeast Asia, which drew frequent comment from early observers in the Visayas, was the practice of penis piercing.[89] This was done with a pin or ring of metal, ivory, or bone that often had wheels, spurs, or other protrusions attached. It was said to provide the women with greater stimulation and give them great pleasure and that men who did not possess them were scorned. This practice has generally been interpreted as a reflection of the greater autonomy and equality of women in Southeast Asian societies, which was also evident in property rights, marriage practices, and high divorce rates.[90] In order to accommodate the pierced penises it was said that women had their vaginas opened from the age of six, a practice that may well have affected fecundity. Father Alcina estimated that nineteen out of twenty women suffered from pains in the abdomen and "ahogamiento de la madre" (a nervous illness affecting reproductive functioning), which were said to be impediments to procreation. This could have derived from the use of penis inserts, although Alcina attributed it to frequent bathing.[91] Antonio de Morga reported that penis inserts resulted in women's shedding a lot of blood and sustaining other injuries,[92] which together with the infections that might follow might have induced infecundity, or even death. Men might also die through penis pins' causing virulent ulcers.[93] An early seventeenth-century observer, Francesco Carletti, also claimed it reduced the frequency of sexual intercourse and was used as a form of birth control,[94] though this appears contrary to other evidence that suggests women enjoyed it. Whatever the reason for the use of penis pins, most likely they would have had a negative impact on fertility. In Borneo today the Iban, who use penis pins, produce less offspring per mating that the Rungus, who do not.[95]

Whether or not penis piercing contributed to low birth rates, population growth was affected by abortion and infanticide.[96] Loarca recorded that the Visayans regarded it as a disgrace to have many children, because the family's property would have to be divided and they would be poor. They believed it was better to have one child since this would enable them to pay higher bridewealth and thereby acquire higher-status women. Though probably overgeneralizing, Loarca noted that nobody married beneath his or her station.[97] Similarly, the Boxer Codex recounts how the Visayans regarded those who had many children as "pigs," presumably because they would be poor, so that once a woman had borne two or three children, she practiced abortion. Abortions were also common for unmarried women for whom it was a disgrace to become pregnant.[98]

Infanticide also contributed to small families. Infanticide seems to have been routinely practiced for infants who were born blind or with deformities, but also where families were too poor to raise more children.[99] Father Alcina recorded that abortion and infanticide were widespread and held back population growth,[100] while another observer noted that these practices were more widespread in the Visayas than in Luzon.[101] Anthony Reid argues that birth control, and hence smaller families, was more common among swidden cultivators than among more sedentary groups due to greater labor demands and hence less time for pregnancy and child rearing, as well as the greater insecurity with which this form of subsistence is associated.[102] In these societies people are also more mobile due to the need to tend distant plots, acquire food supplements from forest products, game and fishing, or trade, and due to their involvement in intercommunity raiding. This greater mobility can restrict family life, encourage child spacing due to the difficulty of carrying more than one infant, and encourage smaller families. Certainly in the Visayas women were heavily involved in cultivation as well as domestic duties. Although this was attributed to the laziness of men, it probably reflected a division of labor where men were involved in fishing, trading, and raiding. The absence of men may have reduced the frequency of intercourse, while the heavy labor undertaken by women may have encouraged miscarriages, but whether there were deliberate attempts to control fertility for economic reasons is less clear. The impression from the early colonial sources is that abortion and infanticide were aimed at avoiding poverty and achieving social advancement, and because of this the Spanish regarded the Visayans as selfish.[103] On the other hand, Visayan beliefs reveal a concern for maternal and infant well-being. Pregnant women abstained from certain foods such as turtles, tortoises, certain fish, venison, or plantains, and after birth other taboos and practices were observed to strengthen the infant.[104] Children, once born, were cherished and indulged.[105]

In conclusion, the population density of the Visayas was low. Societies were based on extensive forms of cultivation, labor was in short supply, and marriage customs and sexual practices functioned to control population growth. These features of Visayan societies were to have important implications for population trends in the colonial period, among other things through their influence on the Visayans' ability to recover from demographic crises.

Population Estimates for the Visayas in 1565

Estimates of the native population of the Visayas in 1565 are best understood in the context of the early settlement of the islands. As previously noted, the Spanish established their first permanent settlement in the Philippines at Cebu in 1565. This colony of some three hundred Spaniards[106] was beset by shortages of food and threat of attack by the Portuguese. Given the island's low agricultural productivity and the local inhabitants' reluctance to sell them, provisions were not readily available, so the Spanish resorted to seizing them by force, often conducting *entradas* inland and to neighboring islands. Although some supplies arrived from New Spain in 1567 and 1568, they did little to alleviate the shortages since the expeditions also brought additional mouths to feed.[107] This, coupled with persistent threats of attack from the Portuguese, who in 1568 blockaded Cebu for three months, encouraged the Spanish to move their base to Panay, where they had already ascertained that there were abundant supplies of rice and where it was thought the Spanish colony could be better protected from the Portuguese.[108]

Despite the relative abundance of supplies in Panay, the Spanish continued to seize provisions, which led to increasing conflicts with the Augustinian friars, who became outspoken critics of their activities.[109] Father Juan de Alva reported that morale among the soldiers was low and that because they had no other means of support, their only occupation had been to "rob in order to eat."[110] Accounts describe how they seized food and mistreated, enslaved, or killed those who resisted. According to Father Martín de Rada, the atrocities had not been punished or remedied because the crimes were so widespread that Legazpi had said that all the soldiers would have to be hung.[111] Reports of dense populations and good food supplies in Manila Bay, coupled with the prospect of developing trade with China, were critical in determining the move to Luzon in the spring of 1571. Before shifting the center of Spanish operations in the Philippines north, Legazpi first sought to consolidate Spain's claim to the Visayas by returning to Cebu with fifty married couples recently arrived from Spain and refounding the city of Santísimo Nombre de Jesús de Cebú in November 1570.[112] In 1568 Legazpi had been given the authority to allocate *encomiendas*, which he did in January 1571 before returning to Panay.[113]

When the center of Spanish operations moved north, so did most of the soldiers and missionaries. In 1582 there were fifty to sixty Spaniards living in the city of Cebu, of whom about thirty were *encomenderos* and the rest soldiers, while in 1588 about the same number of Spaniards were to be found in Arévalo in Panay.[114] In 1603 the Jesuit Mateo Sánchez reported that there were about three hundred Spaniards in the Visayas as a whole.[115] While the number of resident Spaniards remained few, it is clear that *encomenderos* or their agents visited the islands at harvest time to exact tribute; the collection of tribute from Crown *encomiendas* was charged to *alcaldes mayores*.[116] In the late sixteenth century there were widespread abuses in the collection of tribute that stimulated extensive unrest and resulted in the murder of a number *encomenderos* and other Spaniards in the Visayas.[117] The unrest prompted *encomenderos* to seek the presence of missionaries,[118] while the authorities sought to quell it by transferring the collection of tribute to appointed officials.[119] However, the latter did little to moderate abuses, and in 1603 Father Mateo Sánchez noted the "justices are not justices, but injustices."[120]

Just as the soldiers departed for Luzon, so did most of the priests. An Augustinian monastery was established when the town of San Miguel was founded in Cebu in 1565 and others were built at Otón in Panay in 1572 and at Binalbagan in Negros in 1575.[121] However, the number of priests in these monasteries was small, and as late as 1588 Bishop Salazar reported that both Leyte and Samar had never been visited.[122] In 1578 the shortage of priests persuaded the Augustinians to limit their activities by abandoning their missions in Mindoro, Balayan, Lubao, Araut, and all their islands in the Visayas except Cebu and Panay.[123] By 1590 the order had closed eight residences including three in Panay and two in Negros,[124] and the following year there were only twenty priests working in the whole of the Visayas.[125]

The shortage of priests applied not only to the Visayas, but also to the Philippines as a whole. In 1594 Bishop Ortega estimated that 230 more priests were needed, of which about 70 were required for the Visayas.[126] In response, the Crown agreed to send 100 (40 Augustinians, 24 Dominicans, 18 Franciscans, and 18 Jesuits) and ordered that the areas administered by the different missionary orders be grouped into distinct contiguous provinces.[127] Over time some changes occurred in the parishes administered by different orders, but the islands basically comprised eastern and western groups. The eastern Visayas, which had been the least visited prior to 1595, became the responsibility of the Jesuits.[128] Initially they were assigned the islands of Leyte and Samar, but at the request of an *encomendera* also began working in Bohol.[129] In the western Visayas the island of Panay remained primarily an Augustinian province, though secular clergy resided in a number of parishes, while the latter predominated in Negros, and the Recollects later worked in the Calamianes. All the religious orders had a presence in Cebu, but their activities were confined to the monasteries and hinterland of the city.

The Population of the Visayas 1565 to 1600

Between Magellan's expedition in 1521 and 1565, three other Spanish expeditions visited the Visayas, but their presence was fleeting and their demographic impact probably minimal. The date of 1565 is therefore chosen as the baseline for estimating the pre-Spanish population of the Philippines. Given the fragmentary and partial nature of the evidence for the period of initial contact, evidence will be drawn from the subsequent few decades. As far as possible, sixteenth-century sources will be used, because population levels thereafter were affected by Moro raids and the Hispano-Dutch War. However, the period between 1565 and 1600 was also one of major change, so it is essential to be clear about the precise dates of the observations. The nature, problems of interpretation, and limitations of the evidence available, including the fiscal accounts on which scholars have placed much reliance, have been reviewed in chapter 4. This chapter follows the course of Spanish expeditions reviewing population estimates for the six major Visayan Islands in 1565 and examining the decline to 1600. Chapter 5 will analyze later demographic trends, where the discussion will be framed around the nature of Spanish activities in the islands and particularly those of the missionary orders.

Leyte

Prior to 1565 Spanish expeditions to the Philippines often stopped at Leyte, but accounts of their voyages provide few insights into the nature of native societies or the size of their populations. Magellan visited the island at Limasawa off the south coast of Leyte, where he remained for seven days before sailing on to Cebu,[130] but it was only in 1543 that the main island of Leyte was visited by the Ruy López de Villalobos expedition. This stopped at Abuyog and Tandaya to acquire provisions, and here Father Gerónimo de Santisteban observed that the inhabitants formed *behetrías*, or communities without a hereditary leader, reporting "they do not recognize anyone as leader, they rob each other, are heathens, I did not see a temple or place dedicated to their gods . . . their food is rice and yams, of which there are many kinds, and a little fruit and chickens and a few pigs and goats."[131]

Legazpi's expedition also made contact with the inhabitants of Leyte. Unable to obtain sufficient provisions in Samar, where the natives appeared hostile, Esteban Rodríguez and Martín de Goiti sailed down the west coast of the island, passing Tandaya, the San Juanico Strait, and Abuyog on the east coast of Leyte. On this journey the inhabitants told them of many settlements inland that were not visible from the coast. They eventually reached Cabalian, which they estimated had two hundred houses and where six hundred people came to meet them.[132] Able to secure only limited provisions, the expedition headed south to Limasawa, which it found depopulated because of attacks by the Portuguese. At first Leyte failed to impress, but the Spanish soon became aware that it was one of the best-provisioned islands in the Visayas. It is not clear how much contact Spaniards had with Leyte before the

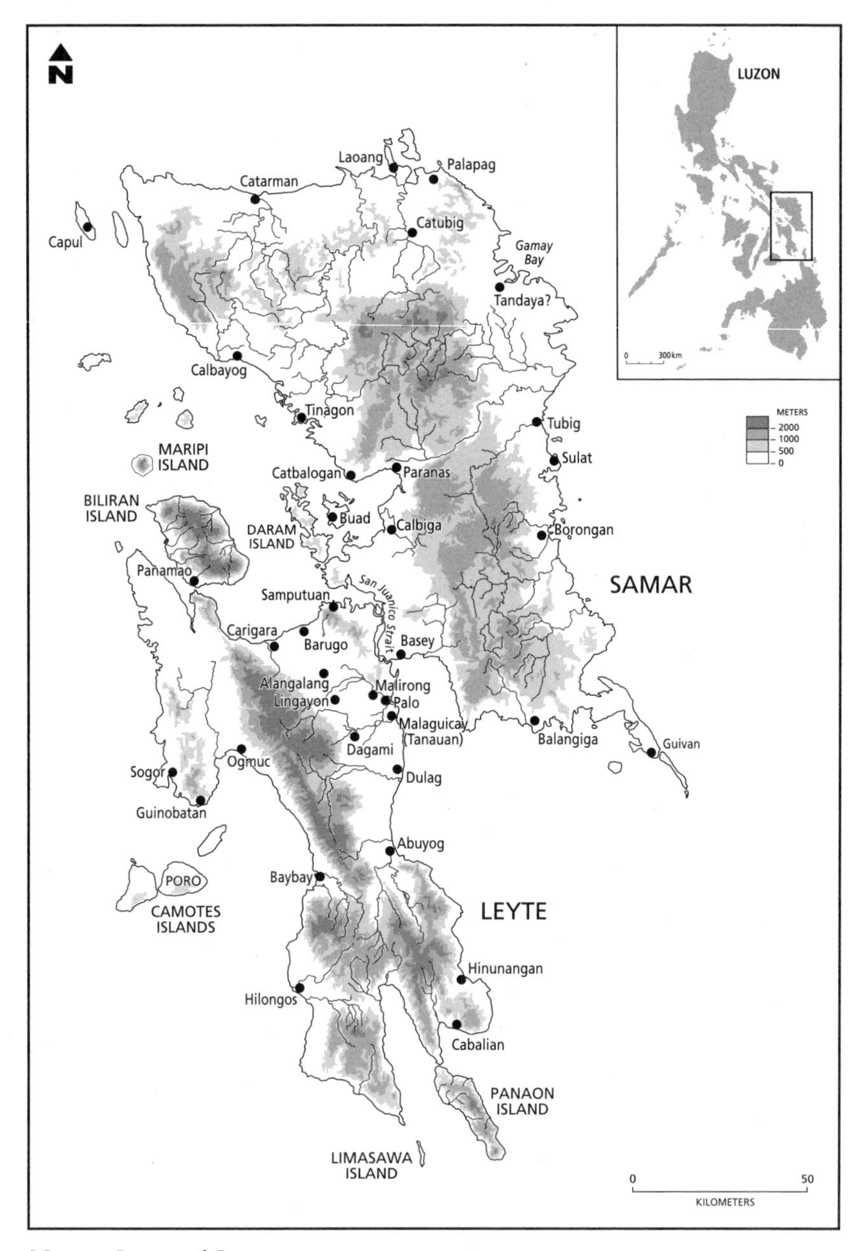

Map 5.2. Leyte and Samar

first *encomiendas* were allocated by Legazpi in 1571, but as early as 1567 Spaniards based in Cebu were sending expeditions there to obtain rice.[133]

On 25 January 1571, Legazpi, while in Cebu, allocated twelve *encomiendas* in Leyte, half of 2,000 "indios" and half of 1,500 "indios." The following September the location of the *encomiendas* was specified by river valley, and an additional *encomienda* of 2,000 "indios" was assigned, giving a total of 23,000.[134] In many areas the numbers of "indios" initially allocated appears to have been exaggerated, and in 1574, possibly to make up the shortfall, six *encomenderos* were given additional communities, although their size was not indicated. In 1582 Loarca reported that Leyte was "highly populated" and had twelve *encomenderos*, who together held between 14,000 and 15,000 "indios," though only 10,000 were paying tribute.[135] Bishop Salazar reported a similar figure of 15,000 to 16,000 *tributantes* in 1588, describing the island as one of the best in the bishopric.[136] The term *tributantes* refers to all tributary adults, including women. As such it is not as inconsistent with the figures of 6,597 *tributos* and 25,432 *almas* recorded in the 1591 list of *encomiendas* as might at first appear, though it suggests a continuing decline.[137] A few years later Bishop Ortega reported the island had eight *encomiendas* with about 5,000 *indios tributantes* who were paying tribute but had not seen a priest.[138]

It is unlikely that there was as significant a population decline as these figures suggest, since later missionary accounts indicate the presence of much larger populations that could not have been achieved by natural increase during the intervening period. In their request to extend jurisdiction over the island of Leyte, the Jesuit Superior, Antonio Sedeño, suggested the island possessed 70,000 *almas*.[139] While this figure might have been exaggerated in order to stimulate a positive response from the Crown, when the Jesuits arrived they reported that it was "the best and most highly populated island" they possessed in the Philippines.[140] Moreover, the first *cartas anuas* at the end of the sixteenth century reported that the island had about 30,000 *almas*.[141] The papal visitor Diego García in 1600 suggested an even higher figure of 24,500 *almas*, not counting 11,000 to 12,000 who had not received Christian instruction.[142] These figures are surprisingly high given that an epidemic accompanied Jesuit arrival.[143] However, because they were based on firsthand observations they are probably more reliable than earlier official reports.

It seems reasonable to take the Jesuit figure of about 35,000 as the best estimate for the total population in 1600, though this might be conservative. The extent to which the additional 11,000 to 12,000 who had not received instruction took account of all the island's inhabitants is not known. Most evidence suggests that Leyte was more densely settled than Samar and that it is likely to have suffered a sharper decline due to more intense contacts with Spaniards who resorted there for provisions. By comparison with Samar, therefore, a total contact population of 60,000 might be suggested, a figure that is consistent with early estimates of the number of tributaries, notably that of Loarca.

Samar

Magellan's first landfall in the Philippines was the island of Suluan off the southeast coast of Samar, but no details exist on the settlements or populations he encountered. Similarly, Legazpi's expedition in 1565 traveled down the east coast, but due to native hostility it did not land; instead Esteban Rodríguez and Martín de Gioti were sent further afield to search for provisions. They reconnoitered the west coast of Samar but encountered no settlement worthy of note before reaching Cabalian in Leyte.

Few references to Samar exist for the first few years following Spanish settlement in the Visayas. In fact in the early colonial period Samar was referred to as Ibabao, though later this name was used for the eastern part of the island only. On 25 January 1571, twelve *encomiendas* containing 19,000 "indios" were distributed in the islands of Ibabao and Paita.[144] Due to conflicts between *encomenderos* over which villages they had been assigned, in 1572 an interim allocation was made; between then and 1574 further knowledge was acquired and additional communities were allocated. By 1582 the Spanish had found 5,000 "indios" in twenty-five villages and valleys in Ibabao and a further 1,150 in neighboring islands, but the island had still not been fully explored.[145] About that time Bishop Salazar judged that the island of Ibabao was "large and not highly populated.[146]

When the list of *encomiendas* was drawn up in 1591, a number of *encomenderos* who had been assigned communities in the island of Samar also possessed some in other islands, so it is not known how many they possessed in Samar alone. In 1606, however, there were 5,186 *tributos* recorded in *encomiendas* in the island as a whole, a figure that is consistent with those above for the 1570s and 1580s.[147] In 1597 the Jesuits assumed responsibility for Samar and opened up a mission field based on Tinagon on the west coast. In 1600 this mission field comprised ten villages with 8,430 *personas*; another 14,000 to 15,000 *almas* were said to be living in Ibabao.[148] This was after swarms of locusts in 1596 and 1597 and an epidemic that in the latter year killed 1,000 converts at Tinagon. It seems, therefore, that a sizeable population still existed in Samar at the beginning of the seventeenth century. Indeed, Father Chirino described the island as "large and highly populated."[149]

On the basis of this fragmentary evidence, it is difficult to estimate the population of Samar in 1565. Compared to later accounts the figure of 19,000 "indios" for 1571, if taken to be adult males, would appear to be an overestimate since it would represent a total population of about 76,000. Taking the Jesuit figure of about 23,000 souls in 1600, another one-third might be added for those outside Spanish control, which would give a total of about 30,000.[150] Although epidemic disease and ill treatment by soldiers and *encomenderos* took their toll, few Spaniards ventured to the island, which reduced the opportunities for the introduction of infections and moderated the disruptive effects of colonial rule. It seems unlikely therefore that between 1565 and 1600 the population fell by 46,000, or 60 percent. Probably the figure of 19,000 "indios" in 1571 was little more than an educated guess in the absence of more detailed knowledge. I doubt the total population of Samar in 1565 was more than 40,000.

Bohol

Magellan's expedition visited the island of Panglao off Bohol in 1521, where, according to Antonio Pigafetta, Negritos were observed.[151] The next time Spaniards visited Bohol was in the spring of 1565 when Legazpi's expedition was blown off course on the voyage to Butuan and spent more than a month there. The expedition dropped anchor at a bay where there was a settlement of twenty houses and many palm trees and fish traps.[152] On arrival the natives fled to the hills, fearing a repeat of the Portuguese attack which two years previously had reputedly resulted in the death or capture of about a thousand people.[153] Father Alcina also described an attack by Ternatans from Maluku that destroyed the settlement at Dauis on the island of Panglao, causing some to flee to Dapitan on the island of Mindanao and others to found the town of Baclayon on Bohol.[154] Whether or not this was the same attack is not clear. Apart from losses associated with these assaults, they also caused the inhabitants to retreat to the interior, where they were still living when Jesuits began working there at the turn of the century.[155] Hence, when *encomiendas* were assigned in Bohol in 1571, the Spanish had very little knowledge of the island's population. In fact only one *encomienda* was assigned in Bohol consisting of an unspecified number of tributaries there and in the island of Bantayan.[156] In 1582 Loarca estimated the island possessed 2,000 "indios,"[157] but a number of other sixteenth-century observers refer to the island as possessing about 1,000 tributaries or fewer.

As Jesuit endeavors later revealed, these numbers represented only a small proportion of the total population. Within eight months of arriving in Bohol in 1596, the Jesuits claimed to have baptized 3,500 *almas* in the Loboc Valley alone,[158] and in 1600 the papal visitor, Diego García, estimated that there were 9,500 *personas* on the island, but they were not living in formal settlements and only 700 had been converted.[159] By 1605 the Jesuits were ministering to 8,500 souls located in nine settlements, seven of which were on the island of Bohol and the others on the islands of Baslao and Siquijor.[160] By then the population had sustained losses in Moro raids and in 1596 had been afflicted by an epidemic that caused pains in the stomach and head and resulted in the depopulation of whole villages.[161] In the mid-seventeenth century Father Colin wrote that the island had once ("antiguamente") possessed 10,000 *moradores* or families, which would imply 40,000 persons, but this seems high even given the significant losses sustained in the early colonial period.[162] Unfortunately Father Colin does not cite his source. In the absence of other evidence, the Jesuit estimate of 9,500 *personas* for 1600 might be reasonable, if a little conservative, and a population in 1565 of 20,000 to 30,000 possible.

Cebu

Although Cebu was the focus of Spanish settlement in the early years of conquest, evidence for its native population is relatively scant and requires particularly careful interpretation. A significant problem is that figures for Cebu often relate to the whole secular or ecclesiastical jurisdiction, not just to the island of Cebu. In addition, many *encomenderos* of Cebu had communities in other Visayan Islands and

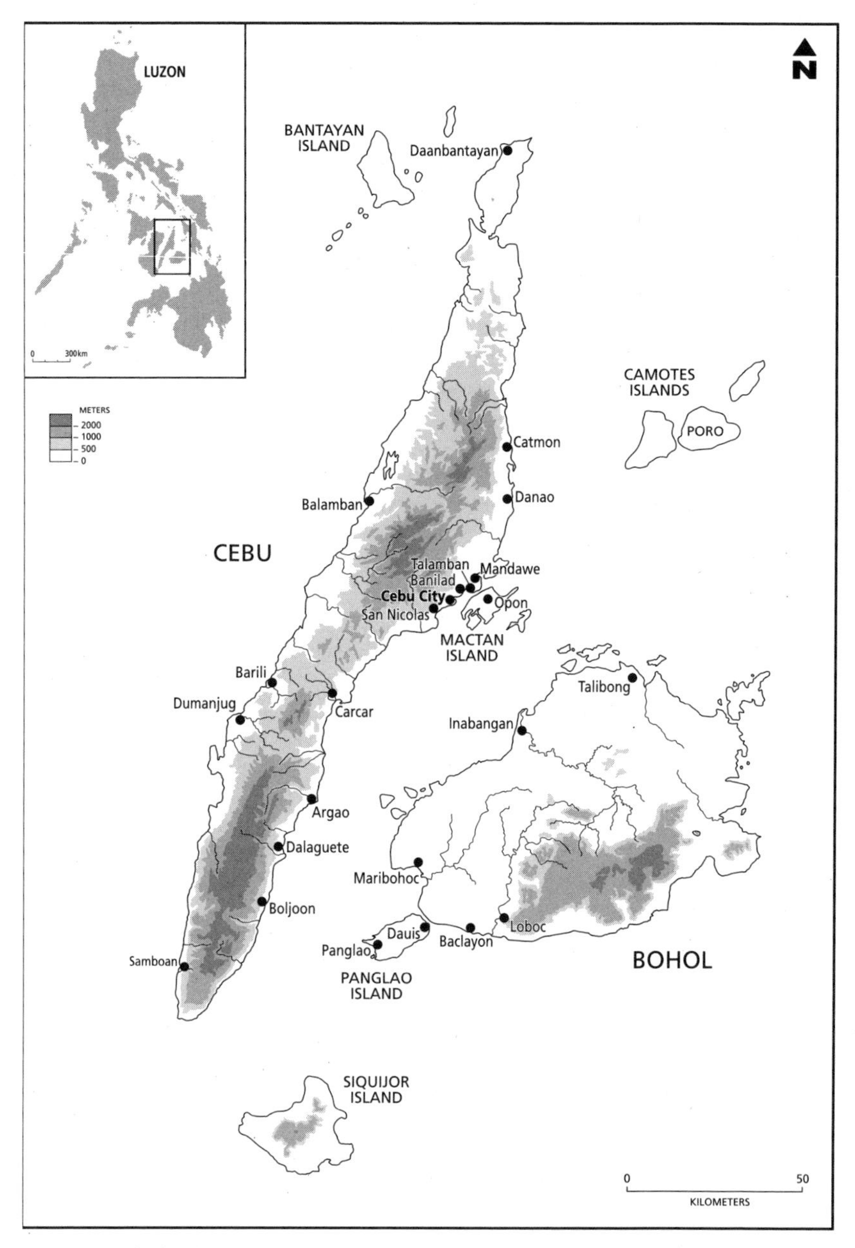

Map 5.3. Bohol and Cebu

information is lacking on the numbers they held in separate islands. Also, Spanish observers had different perceptions of how densely settled the island was, partly due to the timing and different trajectories taken by expeditions. The Spanish initially considered the island of Cebu to be highly populated, but once they had surveyed the island more thoroughly and the expected abundance of provisions failed to materialize, a different image emerged as to the extent of settlement on the island.

First contacts with Cebuanos suggested that Cebu was highly populated. On Magellan's expedition, Antonio Pigafetta recorded that they entered the port of Cebu "passing by many villages, where we saw many houses built on stilts," and he later reported that they had baptized 800 souls, including men, women, and children.[163] Sent by Legazpi in search of food, Juan de Aguirre and Esteban Rodríguez returned in 1565 from Negros along the west coast of Cebu, where for thirty leagues they observed "many people, towns and *sementeras* [cultivated lands]."[164] Rodríguez elaborated that they had found fourteen or fifteen villages, and although they needed provisions, they did not to go ashore until they found a place where there were only four or five houses.[165] Once established in Cebu, between 1566 and 1567 Mateo de Saz and Martín de Goiti undertook an expedition to the west coast, where they were received in fifteen or sixteen previously pacified communities which were described as "small of fifteen and twenty and thirty houses, some less, some more; but for the most part each principal, his children, debtors and slaves live by themselves not having dealings with or respecting anyone else."[166] While the west coast appears to have been characterized by small and dispersed settlements, on the east coast settlements were larger. The soldiers sent by Legazpi to ascertain why Aguirre and Rodríguez had not returned also described Cebu as possessing abundant provisions and being highly populated with one town containing three hundred houses and more than six hundred "indios."[167]

It was not until 1571 that Legazpi distributed three *encomiendas* in Cebu totaling 6,000 "indios" and reserved another unspecified number for the Crown.[168] Later accounts suggest that the Crown *encomienda* exceeded a thousand tributaries. The following year Legazpi commented that when *encomiendas* had been allocated in the Visayas the number of villages and people were unknown, with the result that many *encomenderos* found they had been allocated fewer than they thought, in some parts not one-sixth.[169] Whether or not this precise fraction applied to Cebu, by then the island was considered to be "sparsely settled."[170] Clearly disappointed with the size of settlements found in the Visayas, one anonymous observer compared them unfavorably to Aztec towns, reporting that there was "no Tlaxcala, Cholula, Tepeaca or Texcoco."[171] The largest town was Cebu, which had previously contained one thousand houses, but by the early 1570s had been reduced to only two hundred. When Loarca compiled his *Relación* in 1582, he recorded that there were 3,500 "indios" on the island as a whole. These included 800 around the city of Cebu who were paying tribute to the Crown and the towns of Jaro, Dalaguete, Peñol, Temanduc, Barili, and Candaya, which each had more than 200 "indios," while other communities comprised only eight or ten houses. There were a further 1,600 tributaries in the islands of Bantayan, Camotes, and Mactan.[172] Although Loarca refers to the population as "indios," it is clear by comparison with other accounts that he was referring to tributaries, not total populations. A conversion factor of four was commonly used to estimate total populations from tributary numbers, which suggests a total population of about 14,000 in 1582, with a further 6,400 in neighboring islands.

Canute VanderMeer has estimated that in 1500 the island of Cebu had between 35,000 and 40,000 inhabitants.[173] This figure excludes Bantayan and other adjacent islands. He calculates this on the basis that each of the thirteen *encomiendas* distributed in Cebu contained 2,000 people, to which he adds a further 10,000 to 15,000 for those who were living in the hills and were not paying tribute. In fact, VanderMeer's figure of thirteen *encomiendas* refers to 1574, when the island's *encomiendas* were reassigned, for as noted above there were only four in the initial allocation. Many of the reassigned *encomiendas* comprised a large number of villages. More than seventy villages were listed in the reassignment, including a significant number of communities in the hills ("en los tingues"). Even though many *encomiendas* comprised six to nine villages, each village averaged only eight to ten houses and so contained several hundred tributaries rather than the 2,000 assumed by VanderMeer.

VanderMeer supports his estimate by arguing that the island had been largely deforested by extensive swidden cultivation prior to Spanish arrival, which he attributed to its high population density.[174] He bases this judgment on archaeological evidence for iron tools, which indicate an ability to undertake significant land clearance, and on the widespread distribution of Chinese and other Southeast Asian porcelains that suggest that the island was extensively settled. However, as Michael Cullinane and Peter Xenos have argued, the only area that has been subject to scientific archaeological investigation is around the port of Cebu, and as yet these and other finds there cannot be linked to widespread deforestation or large populations. In support of his thesis VanderMeer also cites a few colonial sources to indicate that when the Spanish arrived the land was almost "barren of forests" and poor. However, the sources he cites do not specifically mention the absence of forest, but only refer to the land as "rugged and mountainous" or as being poor and infertile.[175] Indeed Legazpi commented that because trade was important to them, almost all Cebuanos lived on the coast and rivers and there were few settlements in the interior.[176] Furthermore, other sources indicate that throughout the Spanish period the island was an important source of wood for construction and fuel, and that extensive settlement of the interior hills did not occur until the nineteenth century.[177]

Cullinane and Xenos argue that the total population of the island was lower than that suggested by VanderMeer, but they do not provide an alternative estimate. However, they suggest that Loarca's figure is more reliable because of his long residence in the Visayas, albeit primarily in Panay. His figure of 3,500 tributaries for the island of Cebu is slightly lower than some later accounts, but it probably did not cover the whole island.[178] In 1594 Father Francisco de Ortega reported that there were 4,000 *tributos* under eight *encomenderos*, but he noted that this figure did not include the southern part of the island, which had not been visited and was not well-known.[179]

By then it was claimed that the Augustinians had baptized 6,000 "personas chicos y grandes" in Cebu and a further 3,000 "almas" in Bantayan, though it is not clear over what time period. Other evidence for the relatively low population of Cebu is seen in Father Ortega's petition for more missionaries for the Philippines in 1594. At that time Cebu had only one monastery in charge of one village, and he estimated that a further six priests were needed, whereas for Panay, which already had fourteen, he requested thirty-six, and for Leyte and Negros ten each.[180] Since there was a fictive ratio between the number of priests and the number of potential converts it suggests that Cebu was less populated than neighboring islands.

While Cebu may have been less densely settled than other islands, its pre-Spanish population is likely to have been higher than that recorded by Loarca, for the region around the port of Cebu at least suffered significant population losses during the initial Spanish occupation of the island. In early 1574 it was said the "greater part of that island of Cebu was destroyed and the natives died of hunger and many villages were depopulated, because as their food, goods, wives and children were seized, they went about restless not daring to live in their houses or to sow."[181] Over time many of those who had fled drifted back to their homes, but some probably remained in the hills outside Spanish control. These, and the small numbers that normally inhabited the interior, would not have been included in the early accounts and, as noted above, the southern part of the island was still largely unknown. It will be shown that in the eighteenth century more than 40 percent of the population of the island was living in the south of the island, which was more densely settled than other regions.[182] While the proportion in the eighteenth century may have been boosted by population decline elsewhere, it may also have reflected higher precolonial densities in the south that were associated with more fertile soils.[183] Taking Loarca's figure of 3,500 tributaries for the island of Cebu, it might be possible to add a conservative 20 percent, or 700, for those in the south. On top of this it would seem reasonable to add a further 20 percent to account for losses in the early contact period, though they would have been highly localized around Cebu. This would give a figure for the tributary population of 5,040, or a total of 20,160, which might be increased to about 7,000 to take account of those in the neighboring islands that in 1582 possessed 1,600 "indios." By the end of the sixteenth century the population of Cebu was estimated at about 4,000 *tributos* with about 750 in Bantayan.[184] However, the population in the south was still unknown, so applying the same estimate of 20 percent to the former figure would give an overall total of 5,550 *tributos* or 22,200 people. These figures suggest a slight increase over those provided by Loarca, and this is credible given that the population may well have achieved a level of recovery after most Spaniards left the island for Luzon and their influence became confined to the immediate hinterland of the city of Cebu.

Panay

There is no doubt that when the Spanish arrived Panay was the most densely settled island in the Visayas. There also seems little doubt that it experienced considerable depopulation in the sixteenth century, particularly prior to the Spanish

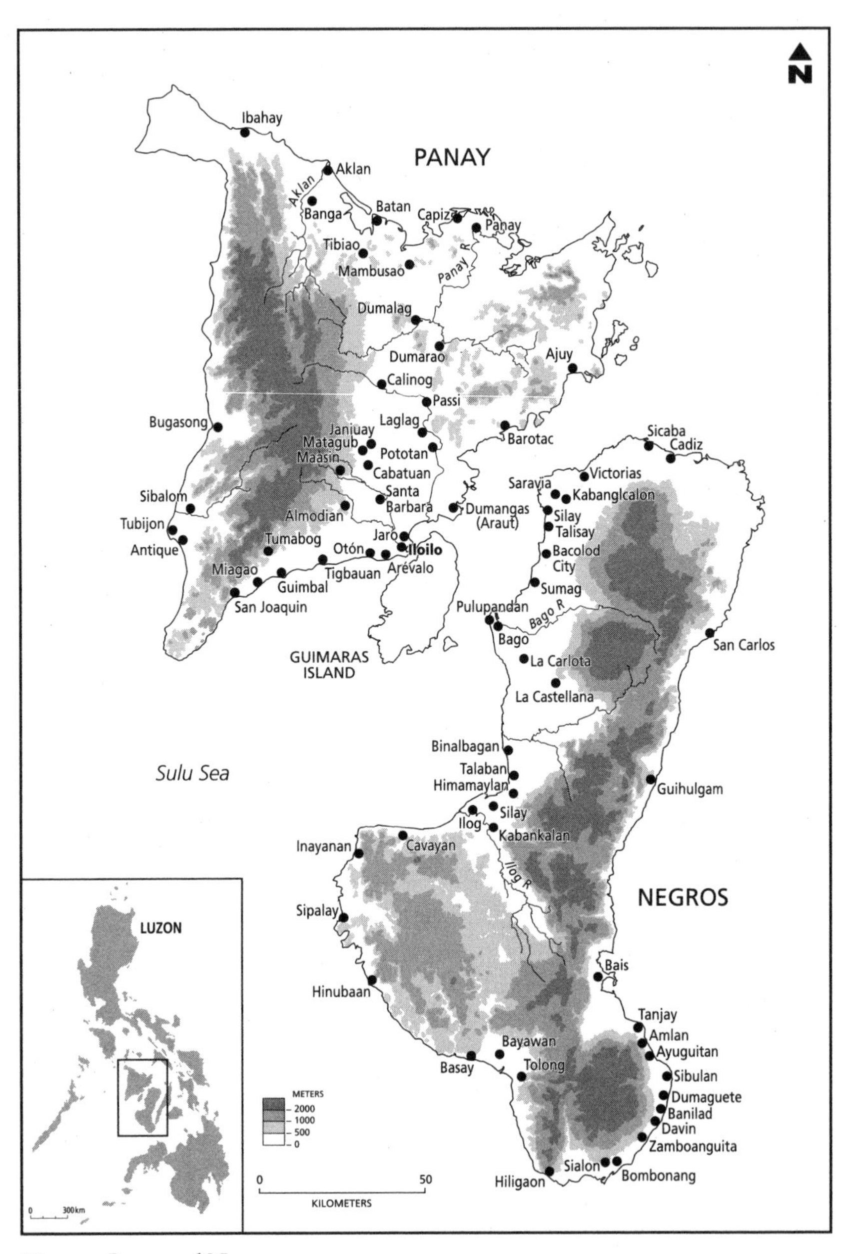

Map 5.4. Panay and Negros

move to Luzon in 1571. The Augustinian chronicler Gaspar de San Agustín claimed that when the Spanish arrived in 1566 the island had possessed 50,000 families, but subsequently their number had fallen significantly due to a famine caused by two successive years of locusts.[185] Shortages of food were exacerbated by Spanish exactions and depredations. From the earliest years of their establishment in Cebu, the Spanish regularly visited Panay to exact tribute in the form of rice, as did friendly natives who attempted to acquire provisions on their behalf.[186] Hence as early as 1570 Father Martín de Rada reported how three years previously Panay had possessed fifty villages and a great abundance of food, which was the reason the Spanish had moved there, but at that time none could survive, except in the River Araut (Dumangas) and the Bay of Ibalon (in Bikol), because the population always fled inland for fear of Spanish seizures.[187] In fact the Panayanos tried to drive the Spanish out by refusing to cultivate, but this was counterproductive because the Spanish found food elsewhere, while the Panayanos experienced a severe famine during which it was said they were forced to sell their slaves for rice.[188] In 1572 half of the inhabitants of Panay were said to have died because of a great famine and "pestilence."[189] By 1574 the population in the River Panay had reportedly fallen from 50,000 to 3,000 *ánimas* and in another unnamed valley from 7,000 to only 500.[190] As outspoken critics of Spanish activities, the Augustinians most likely exaggerated the level of depopulation, but there seems little doubt that the famine, epidemic, and ill treatment resulted in significant population losses.[191]

By the time that *encomiendas* were allocated in Panay in 1571, the native population had clearly suffered major losses. Between January 1571 and October 1572 Legazpi allocated sixteen *encomiendas* and reserved for the Crown an additional *encomienda* of the town and valley of Panay. Unfortunately, the numbers allocated are only known for eight private *encomiendas* and they total 28,000. In 1591 these eight *encomiendas* contained 8,700 tributaries and they comprised just under 40 percent of those registered in the twenty *encomiendas* at that time.[192] Adding 60 percent to the figure of 28,000 for 1571 would give 70,000 for the island as a whole. This would assume that all *encomiendas* were equally large and that the communities they comprised had declined to the same degree, which may not have been the case. Also, an anonymous account written in 1572 throws some doubt on the numbers initially assigned. The author complained that the reports sent to the Crown had exaggerated the numbers because the authors were uninformed or wished to impress the Crown. Hence, he reported that there was no *encomienda* in Panay with more than 1,000 "indios," even though *encomenderos* had received *cédulas* for 1,500 and 2,000. He gave the example of Pedro de Sarmiento, who had been given an *encomienda* of seven inhabited islands and more than thirty leagues of land in Panay, but which only comprised 600 "indios." He also claimed that another captain had informed him that in the River Araut there had been 15,000 "indios" and that he had been given an *encomienda* of 6,000, but in fact there were only 1,030 houses.[193] From these accounts it is difficult to judge whether the figures had been exaggerated in the initial allocation or reflect a real decline. If in reality the twenty *encomiendas* in 1591 only had about 1,000 *tributos* when first allocated, then this would give a total tributary population of 20,000. However, losses had already been sustained when the initial allocation was made. Nevertheless the figure of 70,000 tributaries seems high. The lower estimate of 50,000 families in Panay by Gaspar de San Agustín might have been possible, though if anything is likely an overestimate.

In the 1580s and 1590s bishops and the secular authorities consistently recorded about 25,000 tributaries and between 90,000 and 100,000 souls in Panay. Loarca, a long-term resident of Panay, recorded that it had 20,000 "indios" who had been pacified and were paying tribute and that there were a further 3,340 in neighboring islands.[194] These figures are given credence by the fact that Father Ortega requested thirty-six additional priests for Panay, bringing their total number to fifty, which, calculated at one priest for 500 *tributos*, again suggests there were about 25,000.[195] Despite the devastation wrought in the early years, therefore, Panay was still the most densely settled island in the Visayas.

Negros

The Spanish did not establish an early presence in the island of Negros, so the evidence for the size of its population in the sixteenth century comes primarily from observations by occasional visitors. In 1565 Esteban Rodríguez recorded that there were many houses about a league from the sea, including one "medium-sized" village of fifty houses;[196] the coast between the Himamaylan River and present-day Saravia was also highly populated. He concluded that the island was "poblada" and had abundant provisions, but because of the absence of a suitable port, the Spanish determined to move to Cebu rather than Negros. Nevertheless, the Spanish continued to visit Negros for provisions, especially prior to the move to Luzon in 1571.[197]

Despite Spanish expeditions to Negros, when the first *encomiendas* were allocated in 1571, the Spanish still did not have a detailed knowledge of the island. They clearly considered the island to be highly populated because Legazpi allocated 32,000 tributaries in eighteen *encomiendas*, ten of 2,000 "indios" each.[198] However, since their locations were not specified, conflicts soon arose between *encomenderos*. Therefore in September the same year Legazpi indicated their location in the valleys of the Tanjay, Hilo, Inavagan, Bago, and Caracol rivers, reflecting the concentration of population in the west and south of the island.[199] Conflicts continued, however, since there were fewer inhabitants than anticipated and each valley was shared by several *encomenderos*. Judging by later accounts, the figure of 32,000 "indios" allocated was exceedingly optimistic, as was a report in 1572 that suggested that the whole island had been pacified and had 20,000 *hombres*.[200]

In 1582 Loarca estimated that Negros had only 6,000 to 7,000 "indios," excluding the Negritos, whose numbers he said could not be ascertained because of their hostility.[201] It is difficult to assess the demographic impact of early contacts in the island while the Spanish were based in Cebu. Initially, expeditions frequently visited Negros for provisions, but contacts subsequently declined and no permanent

Spanish town was established there. Although Negros contained fairly large populations, it produced few products of Spanish interest and had few ports, so it featured less prominently in interisland trade. In the 1580s the Augustinians, experiencing a shortage of personnel, gave priority to other islands and closed the two residences they had in Negros.[202] There is no evidence that epidemics afflicted Negros in the sixteenth century. This could reflect more limited opportunities for the introduction of disease, though epidemics were reported in neighboring islands, or that there were fewer visitors to the island to record their occurrence. It is known, however, that the island was the focus of some Moro raids at the end of the sixteenth century (see Appendix B). Since limited contacts are likely to have moderated the level of depopulation during the sixteenth century, the pre-Spanish population is unlikely to have been significantly higher than the 6,000 to 7,000 tributaries reported in the 1580s. Hence it is suggested that they may have numbered about 7,500 in 1565, which would imply a total population of about 30,000.

Some insight into the size of the population can be gained from ecclesiastical accounts at the end of the century. It was generally recognized that Negros was larger than Panay, though not as highly populated.[203] Father Ortega's request for priests for the Philippines included only nine or ten for Negros, whereas for Panay he asked for an additional thirty-six, bringing the total number there to fifty.[204] This suggests that there were about 5,000 *tributos* and 20,000 *almas* in Negros and that the population there was only one-fifth of that in Panay. This figure is higher than the 12,120 *almas* recorded in the 1591 list of *encomiendas*, but a significant proportion of the population was outside effective Spanish administration. Indeed, most of the north and northeast of the island had virtually no Spanish contact until the nineteenth century.[205] Even in areas visited more regularly by Spaniards, there appear to have been larger populations than those recorded in the lists of tributaries. Hence, in 1591, 2,920 *almas* were recorded in *encomiendas* around Tanjay,[206] but when Jesuits from Bohol began undertaking regular visits there in 1600, they estimated there were 8,000 *almas*.[207] The areas to which the figures refer are unlikely to have been strictly comparable, but they do suggest larger numbers than appear in the fiscal accounts. It seems reasonable, therefore, to increase the estimate of 20,000 *almas* for the end of the sixteenth century to 25,000 to take account of those outside administration. This figure would include the Negritos, who probably numbered not less than 1,000.[208]

Population Levels in 1565

The preceding account has suggested that the pre-Spanish population of the Visayas might have been about 383,000, or probably nearer 400,000 if account is taken of the small islands whose populations are not recorded in the documentary sources (see Table 5.1). This is somewhat higher than often assumed, but it may be explained by the fact that most previous population estimates rely on lists of *encomiendas* drawn up at the end of the sixteenth century after the islands had experienced a

TABLE 5.1 Estimated Native Populations in the Visayas in 1565

	Number of *tributos*	Total population	Area in square kilometers	Persons per square kilometer
Leyte	15,000	60,000	7,791	7.7
Samar	10,000	40,000	13,665	2.9
Bohol	6,250	25,000	3,913	6.4
Cebu	7,000	28,000	5,022	5.6
Panay	50,000	200,000	12,717	15.7
Negros	7,500	30,000	12,934	2.3
TOTAL	95,750	383,000	56,042	6.8

Note: See the text for the sources of the population estimates. Areas are taken from *Census of the Philippines* 2: 28.

level of demographic decline. For the same reason, the average population density of the Visayas calculated here at 6.8 persons per square kilometer is higher than the 4.0 estimated by Anthony Reid for the Philippines in 1600,[209] though it generally confirms his observation of low population densities in Southeast Asia at the time of European arrival. Nevertheless, it is worth noting that population densities were higher in Panay and to a lesser extent Leyte and that there were some pockets of dense settlement associated with the major trading ports at Cebu, Tanjay, Dauis, Otón, and Ogmuc.

Anthony Reid has reviewed the factors that might account for low population densities in Southeast Asia in the sixteenth century, among which he includes health and nutrition, age at marriage, family size, polygamy, abortion, and infanticide, but he concludes that these were less significant than interpolity warfare.[210] He recognizes that warfare in Southeast Asian societies was not conducted with the aim of killing captives but acquiring them as sources of labor. However, he argues with some justification that warfare could have played a significant role in holding back population growth by drawing off labor, undermining subsistence production, disrupting marital relations, and causing stress-induced infertility. Observers noted that Visayans were more warlike than the inhabitants of other islands, and interpolity conflict appears to have been increasing in scale and intensity when the Spanish arrived. It seems likely, therefore, that warfare contributed to low population densities, but other factors were also involved.

Early observers recorded that Visayans were healthy and lived to an old age.[211] They also noted the lack of deformities, though this may have been disguised by the practice of infanticide. As indicated in chapter 2, the warm, humid climate meant they probably suffered from enteric infections such as diarrhea and typhoid fever, which would have taken a toll of infants and children in particular, though compared to other regions, their dispersed settlement pattern and the habit of frequent bathing would have moderated the impact of these infections.[212] A number of diseases found in small populations, notably schistosomiasis and malaria, were also likely to have been limited in the Visayas. Today schistosomiasis is only found in Leyte and Samar and even there it is localized in densely settled rice-growing areas.[213] Early Spanish accounts and Visayan dictionaries suggest that malaria was present in the islands in pre-Spanish times,[214] but that it too was quite localized. Today the main Visayan islands afflicted by malaria are Samar and southern Negros.[215] VanderMeer attributes the more rapid expansion of the Cebuano population during the colonial period to the relative absence of malaria.[216] Yaws, which is closely related to syphilis and has similar symptoms, is likely to have been present, but syphilis was probably not introduced until colonial times.[217] In fact, Father Alcina put respiratory infections at the top of his list of diseases afflicting Visayans, which he attributed to frequent changes of climate.[218] Overall, the Visayas were generally considered to be healthier for Spaniards than was Luzon.[219]

In addition to chronic infections, the Visayas were occasionally devastated by epidemics of smallpox and measles; most likely plague and epidemic typhus did not arrive until late colonial times, if at all. However, due to the slow transport and dispersed settlement pattern, not every island or community would have been afflicted on every occasion. The high mortality experienced when acute infections arrived suggests that there were extended intervals between outbreaks. It seems unlikely therefore that epidemics contributed significantly to low population densities overall, though they might result in high losses in particular places at particular times.

Food shortages and famines may also have had some impact on demographic trends. Reid argues that nutrition in Southeast Asia as a whole was good and that large-scale famines occurred only as a result of warfare.[220] However, this may not apply to the Visayas. There were variations in the extent of fertile, cultivable land both between and within the islands, and there were frequent food shortages and famines that might encourage people to become slaves or dependents. While warfare may have contributed to food shortages, many shortages more likely reflected local limitations on agricultural productivity that were exacerbated by natural disasters, such as the lack of rain or swarms of locusts. This was particularly true in Cebu. Due to the variety of climatic conditions within the Visayas, however, shortages might be overcome through interisland trade. There is little evidence for chronic food shortages, but rather occasional severe ones that might have temporary effects on mortality, particularly among infants and children, and on fertility levels. Shortages of food might encourage abortion and infanticide, but this was generally not the rationale given; more often reference was made to social or ideological reasons.

Age at marriage is generally regarded as having the greatest cumulative effect on fertility in societies practicing little or no contraception,[221] but unfortunately, little information is available for the Philippines. That which exists often describes a postcontact situation where social practices might have been modified by attempts to encourage early marriage, both to prevent "immoral" behavior and to expand the numbers of tribute payers, even though the marriage of minors was expressly forbidden.[222] Nevertheless, there is some evidence, noted above, that marriage was contracted at an early age. Although this should have promoted larger families, abortion and infanticide were widely practiced and there was a clear preference for smaller families, perhaps encouraged by high bridewealth. David Henley has collected evidence from Sulawesi and elsewhere to suggest that slaves had lower birth rates.[223] The prevalence of slavery and debt servitude in the Visayas in pre-Spanish times may also have contributed to low population densities. In addition, the practice of penis piercing may have affected fecundity. These birth and marriage practices would not only have functioned to limit population growth and promote low fertility, but also made it difficult for communities to recover from major demographic crises associated with epidemics or famines. Low fertility may have been a more important factor behind low population densities in the Visayas than elsewhere in Southeast Asia.

Population Decline 1565 to 1600

It has been estimated that in 1600 the native population of the Visayas was about 221,700, which represents a decline of just over 40 percent from 1565 (see Table 5.2). There are some perceptible differences in the level of decline between the islands, although these figures must be regarded as having a wide margin of error. Built into these figures are judgments about the brutality of conquest and the intensity of Spanish contact in different islands, so in analyzing trends there is the danger of constructing circular arguments. While the numerical estimates themselves may be open to question, the qualitative evidence that supports them remains. Hence the population seems to have declined the least in the islands, such as Samar and Negros, where there were few Spanish settlers, while those that became important sources of

TABLE 5.2 Estimated Native Populations in the Visayas in 1600

	Number of *tributos*	Total population	Percent decline 1565–1600
Leyte	8,750	35,000	41.7
Samar	7,500	30,000	25.0
Bohol	2,375	9,500	62.0
Cebu	5,550	22,200	20.7
Panay	25,000	100,000	50.0
Negros	6,250	25,000	16.7
TOTAL	55,425	221,700	42.1

Note: See the text for sources of the estimates.

provisions, such as Panay and Leyte, probably suffered higher losses. The high losses in Bohol were associated with fugitivism following Portuguese raids coupled with a devastating epidemic in 1596. For Cebu the quantitative evidence suggests a lower level of decline than might be expected given the significant losses in conflict in the first years of Spanish rule. However, unlike Leyte and Panay, it was not a source of provisions, so that once the Spanish had moved to Panay, contacts were far fewer.

At first glance the level of decline proposed for the Visayas may be considered too high. However, the ravages wrought by Spanish soldiers in their desperate search for provisions were highly destructive of life and property and disrupted subsistence activities and family life, while the prolonged unrest that occurred after the majority of Spaniards had moved to Luzon was testimony to continuing demands made on native communities in the islands. In addition to which, as outlined in chapter 2, there were occasional epidemics, often combined with food shortages, which resulted in high mortality. However, a significant factor in the decline in the population was the inability of Visayan societies to recover rapidly from mortality crises due to birth and marriage practices that functioned to produce small families and keep population levels low.

CHAPTER 6

Wars and Missionaries in the Seventeenth-Century Visayas

After the Spanish shifted their base in the Philippines to Luzon in 1571, the Visayas became an economic backwater. However, the islands were not abandoned totally, for they were of strategic importance in the Hispano-Dutch War and in holding the frontier against Moro incursions. Particularly important were Panay and Cebu, the former because it was the main source of provisions, labor, and ships to support expeditions and garrisons in the Philippines and Maluku, and the latter because of its strategic location.

On account of the abundant supplies of rice, timber, and labor in Panay, economic activities in the Visayas were concentrated there. Even so, its Spanish civilian population remained small and was clustered in the southeast of the island. Arévalo was founded in 1581, but in 1637 its inhabitants were moved to Iloilo where a fort had been built in 1602.[1] In 1760 there were only forty Spaniards living in the jurisdictions of Iloilo and Panay.[2] Nevertheless, from an early date the demands for provisions led to the commercial production of rice and livestock, and a shipbuilding industry emerged based on the island's abundant supplies of timber and labor. These activities were to bring some fundamental changes to landholding, settlement patterns, and family life in Panay.

Although economic activities focused on Panay, Cebu, because of its central location, remained the political and religious capital of the Visayas, becoming the seat of the bishopric of the Visayas in 1595.[3] Nevertheless, in the late seventeenth century Cebu City was described as "a small village," while in the eighteenth century the French scientist Le Gentil claimed it did not merit the title of city since it was "an assemblage of a few miserable huts" and its magnificent monasteries were inhabited by only two or three people.[4] By 1751 the *cabildo* had been disbanded due to the lack of suitable people to fill its offices.[5]

As for other islands, the number of resident Spaniards was even smaller and many were priests. Apart from a small detachment of soldiers, there were only ten legitimate Spaniards in Leyte in 1785 and none in Samar, which had only a few Chinese *mestizos* in Catbalogan and one or two in other villages.[6] These islands were therefore less affected by the early commercialization of agricultural production that elsewhere brought changes to landholding and labor systems. Hence in the late eighteenth century, communal land ownership and shifting cultivation were still prevalent in these islands and in the late nineteenth century about 70 percent of Samar and Leyte was still forested.[7] Commercial activities were more developed in Bohol, where there was an active trade in salt fish and some two thousand weavers produced cotton and abaca cloth for export.[8] Nevertheless, apart from the shipbuilding industry established at Panamao off the north coast of Leyte, the Spanish authorities were generally content to profit from the eastern Visayas by extracting tribute, and occasionally labor, while entrusting the inhabitants to the Jesuits for their Christian conversion. The eastern Visayas were not totally isolated from external influences, however, since Moro raids, which were particularly intense in the late eighteenth century, had a major impact on demographic trends there. Different Visayan Islands thus followed distinct demographic trajectories that reflected the uneven impact of economic activities, missionary endeavors, and Moro raids.

Garrisons, Shipbuilding, and Provisions

Commercial economic activities in the western Visayas, especially Panay, were largely driven by the needs of defense. Provisions and labor were required to maintain the garrisons established in the Visayas, Maluku, and Mindanao and to support naval expeditions, particularly during the Hispano-Dutch War. When the Spanish first arrived they established forts at Cebu and at Otón in Panay.[9] With the increase in Moro incursions toward the end of the sixteenth century, Spanish defenses in the Visayas were strengthened by the construction of a fort at Iloilo staffed by two companies of soldiers[10] and by the establishment of a garrison at Caraga in northeast Mindanao in 1609. Subsequently other forts were built in Mindanao at Zamboanga and Iligan in 1636 and 1639 respectively. Apart from these garrisons, support was also needed to maintain the forts on the islands of Ternate and Tidore following their seizure from the Dutch in 1606. However, all forts in Maluku and Mindanao were abandoned in 1662 when, fearing a Chinese attack, the troops were withdrawn to concentrate their defensive efforts further north. Up to that date, however, the needs of defense placed a considerable burden on local communities.

Regular Spanish soldiers and Pampangans rather than Visayans staffed the garrisons at Cebu and Otón, as well as the forts at Ternate and on Mindanao, and the naval squadrons commonly employed native and Chinese convicts, though some Visayans were drafted in times of crisis.[11] Even though Visayans were not commonly employed in the navy, labor was needed in the shipyard at Otón and to serve on ships that carried supplies to outlying garrisons. The demands generated by the garrisons were sometimes considerable. In the 1630s, about 612 Spaniards and 200 Pampangans were stationed in Ternate, where the garrison was totally dependent on outside supplies.[12] Here food shortages were common and conditions harsh enough to persuade some soldiers to desert to the Dutch or to flee when ordered to serve there. In the early 1660s the garrison at Zamboanga, which was one of the most important in the archipelago, possessed 800 to 1,000 military personnel, and there were another 100 soldiers at Iligan. During the first half of the seventeenth century therefore, there were about 2,000 soldiers and other personnel based in garrisons who needed to be supported.[13] No less a burden, particularly in the early seventeenth century, were the demands generated by expeditions. One of the most notable was Pedro de Acuña's expedition to Maluku in 1606 that involved more than 3,000 soldiers and seamen and was accompanied by four storeships.[14] In 1627 the rations specified for common seamen or shipyard workers were between twenty and thirty *gantas* a month,[15] which was equivalent to the per capita annual tribute in rice. While some of the provisions for the forts were acquired locally, significant amounts were imported from the Visayas or even further afield. In 1738 the Visayas were supplying Zamboanga alone with nearly 30,000 *gantas* of rice a year, of which about 55 percent came from Panay.[16]

The Hispano-Dutch War and the needs of defense also encouraged the development of a shipbuilding industry. Shipbuilding required an abundance of timber, a safe harbor, and a large labor force. These requirements were seldom found together in the Visayas, so most large vessels were constructed elsewhere, notably at Cavite, and to a lesser extent in Bikol.[17] Nevertheless, six galleons were constructed on the island of Panamao (Biliran) off the north coast of Leyte,[18] and a shipyard was established at Otón.[19] Although Negros did not have a shipbuilding industry, it produced black cord that was used for ships' cables.[20] Compared to Luzon, forced labor demands for the shipyards were generally low and localized. With the exception of Otón in Panay, and in particular the town of Dumangas, where the inhabitants were regarded as the best sailors and expert rowers, the same was true of labor drafts for service on ships and *caracoas*.[21] The hazardous nature of this form of labor is suggested by the introduction of legislation requiring *caracoas* to be constructed to prevent injury and to protect sailors from the inclement weather.[22] Many involved in expeditions died at sea or were captured or killed in Moro raids. Those who returned often received no wages, while their several-month-long tours of duty left lands uncultivated, tribute unpaid, and women exposed to abuse.[23]

The demand for provisions was met through the development of agricultural estates and tribute levies. The *vandala* does not appear to have been imposed in the seventeenth century, but in the eighteenth century additional levies were made to support the garrison at Zamboanga. Agricultural production in the Visayas centered on the cultivation of rice and the raising of livestock; sugar production that became so important in the nineteenth century, especially in Negros, was of minor importance.

Despite the devastation of the early years, Panay remained the main source of provisions in the Visayas. As early as 1582 it was providing Manila and other areas with large quantities of rice and meat,[24] and in the early seventeenth century it was said to produce more rice and provisions than any other province in the Philippines except Manila.[25] Rice was also produced in large quantities in Negros, but exports seem to have been limited by the absence of ports, though some was shipped to Cebu and to Iligan in Mindanao.[26] Despite these exports, rice remained relatively cheap.[27] Panay and Negros were well-supplied with food, and food shortages were uncommon, but Cebu was a rice-deficit region that depended on imports from other islands. Although over time the introduction of maize improved food supplies in Cebu, it did not become the dominant staple until the nineteenth century.[28] In 1634, 1651, 1668, and 1675 there were severe famines in Cebu that were caused by drought or locusts, the first so acute that even animals died.[29]

Livestock raising also expanded rapidly to meet the demand for provisions. In the early seventeenth century it was said that the Augustinian residence of Dumangas had once possessed more than 30,000 cattle and that they were so abundant in Panay as to be of no value; one head cost only four reals.[30] Whether or not this was an exaggeration, some large ranches emerged in the island. Another ranch bequeathed to the Jesuits in 1596 apparently had 14,000 cattle.[31] Horses were also raised in Panay, with those around Iloilo regarded as the best in the islands.[32] In Cebu cattle raising expanded rapidly, but as early as 1630 some ranches were already in decline, with one near the city that had originally had 2,000 cattle containing only 500, while others that had owned 1,000 no longer existed.[33] These estates later turned to the production of rice and sugar.[34]

The development of rice and livestock production led to changes in landholding and agricultural practices. There is little evidence for these changes, but only in Cebu did the religious orders effectively monopolize the most fertile lands. Legazpi granted the Augustinians an *estancia* at Banilad, and when most Spaniards abandoned the island for Manila they gradually acquired lands to the north and south of the port.[35] The Jesuits also established an estate north of the city at Mandawe. By purchase and donation these orders gradually came to control most of the fertile coastal plain in the hinterland of Cebu City.[36] The extent of non-ecclesiastical landholding in the Visayas is difficult to gauge, but it may have been relatively limited, for only a few land grants were made to Spaniards in the early colonial period.[37] Nevertheless, access to land changed. With their power over native labor weakened by colonial attempts to eliminate slavery and reduce dependency, opportunistic or needy *datus* sought to retain their status through controlling land and hence indirectly labor. *Datus* thus began alienating community lands, reducing their former dependents to the status of tenant farmers or sharecroppers.[38]

The alienation of native lands and the demands for labor affected subsistence production and the ability of local populations to produce sufficient food to meet their own needs and tribute demands. The early history of tribute assessments in the Visayas follows that outlined in chapter 3 for the Philippines as a whole. Following the debate over whether Filipinos should be required to pay tribute in cash or in kind, Governor Acuña set the level of payment at four reals in kind, one chicken (*gallina*), with the rest payable in cash or kind.[39] Under this *tasación* most Visayans were required to pay in rice, cloth, and chickens, but wax was levied in Negros and Ibabao, coconut oil in Aklan, palm wine in Negros and the River Panay, and gold in the island of Ymaras (probably Guimaras). These *tasaciones* appear to have remained in force throughout the seventeenth century.[40] Although they took some account of the diversity of goods produced by Visayans, the level of tribute demanded in the islands was equivalent to that in other Philippine provinces, when commentators thought they should pay less than what was paid in Manila and Pampanga[41] because "they are not such hard workers or farmers," a comment that probably referred to the less intensive nature of agricultural production in the Visayas.

As predicted, Visayans found it difficult to meet official tribute demands. Intensive forms of agricultural production were not practiced even though in pre-Spanish times some islands, notably Panay and Leyte, produced significant surpluses that were traded. There were, however, considerable variations in levels of production, from island to island, from year to year, and from season to season. The ability of individual communities to meet extracommunal demands thus varied considerably and might be problematic in times of Moro raids or other crises. However, the levy in rice was judged necessary to encourage the natives to plant.[42] Temporary shortages might not only lead to excessive coercion, but they might enhance opportunities for officials, *encomenderos*, and priests to make profits at their expense. In order to ensure that tribute payments could be met, *alcaldes mayores* were required to inspect native communities and fine those failing to cultivate the land or raise chickens.[43] These inspections seem to have had little effect other than open up another channel by which officials could profit from their positions.

At the same time as demands for rice increased, the ability of communities to meet the tribute levies declined. In the early conquest years, declining production was blamed on population losses from ill treatment and the employment of Filipinos on expeditions.[44] Declining populations continued to be a factor through the seventeenth century, but food shortages were generally attributed to the inability of Visayans to farm their lands as a result of labor drafts.[45] The impact of these drafts was greatest in Panay, but in the eastern Visayas, Moro raids diverted labor from subsistence into defense, while the raids themselves often devastated lands and destroyed harvests, making it difficult to meet external demands.

Resistance to demands for tribute and labor was reflected in unrest that resulted in the death of several officials and *encomenderos* and led the Jesuits to act cautiously in their initial establishment in the islands. In Leyte and Samar, resistance was also reflected in fugitivism and in a reluctance to produce goods other than those for their own subsistence. In the 1660s Father Alcina commented that only 5 or 10 percent of tribute payers would anticipate their tribute demands, and only when pressed would they weave some cloth or collect some beeswax.[46] Resistance might erupt into revolts. In 1621 there was an uprising in Bohol inspired by a *diwata*, a spirit, which allegedly encouraged significant numbers to flee with promises of food in abundance and escape from the burdens of tribute and forced labor.[47] It was brutally suppressed by a force of fifty Spaniards and a thousand troops from Cebu. The harsh treatment meted out was intended to deter other potential rebels, but in 1622 six villages in Leyte rebelled. Widespread opposition to labor drafts occurred in 1649 when attempts were made to draft Visayans to serve in the shipyards at Cavite. Revolts, collectively known as the Sumoroy rebellion, occurred in Palapag, Bacor, Catubig, and other towns in Samar, and then spread to other parts of the Visayas and Camarines.[48]

Moro Raids and Their Impact

The needs of defense were greatest during the Hispano-Dutch War in the early seventeenth century, but Moro raids, which were concentrated in the eastern Visayas, occurred intermittently throughout the early colonial period. The background to Moro raids has already been discussed in chapter 3, so the discussion here focuses on their impact.

Raiding from Mindanao and the Sulu islands followed an annual cycle (Map 6.1). During the southwest monsoon, Moros would sweep up through the Visayas to Bikol, either striking islands and towns on the western peninsula or sailing through the San Bernardino Strait to attack the island of Catanduanes and the Pacific coast, before returning south during the northeast monsoon to attack settlements on the coasts of Leyte and Samar.[49] In the late eighteenth century, the construction of coastal defenses on northern Mindanao forced raiding groups to take a more westerly route via Palawan, from whence they entered the Visayas via the Cuyo islands, but even so, Leyte and Samar remained the worst affected. The frequency of raids and the devastation they caused prompted many communities, especially in the larger coastal towns, to erect watchtowers, construct fortifications, and acquire cannons and weapons.[50] In response the raids shifted to more vulnerable scattered settlements and lone trading vessels.[51] During these raids towns were looted and burned, and significant numbers were killed or captured.

In the early phase of the Moro wars the Magindanao and Sulu used *caracoas*, but later they employed larger *joangas*.[52] When raids took place, the whole crew participated, and each vessel might carry off about twenty slaves.[53] During the late sixteenth and early seventeenth centuries major expeditions by the Magindanao might seize 700 to 800 people.[54] A report by the Jesuit Father Gregorio López in 1607 estimated that in the previous five years Moros had taken more than 4,000 captives,[55] and the following year Juan Manuel de la Vega estimated that in the previous two years at least 1,600 people had been seized in the Visayas.[56] When the latter led an expedition to Mindanao in 1609, he is said to have released 1,500 Christians held captive by the Caraga at Tandag.[57] This number probably represented only a small proportion of those held in Mindanao as a whole. In 1621 it was thought that there were about 10,000 Christian captives in the island,[58] but many others would have been sold outside the region. About 1658 Father Domingo Navarrete observed that in Makassar there were "4,000 Indians of Manila in slavery" and noted they were in every island of the Southeast Asian archipelago, because "there is not a ship that sails from Manila, whether it belongs to Siam, to Camboxa, or the Portugueses [*sic*], etc., but it carries Indians [native Filipinos] away out of those Islands."[59] Governor Hurtado de Corcuera estimated that up to 1635, 25,000 to 30,000 Crown subjects had been captured,[60] a figure similar to that reported by the Bishop of Manila, who estimated that in the previous thirty years Moros had seized 20,000 Filipinos.[61] Hence between 700 and 1,000 captives were being taken annually, and there was a fear, though exaggerated, that the Visayas would be totally destroyed.[62]

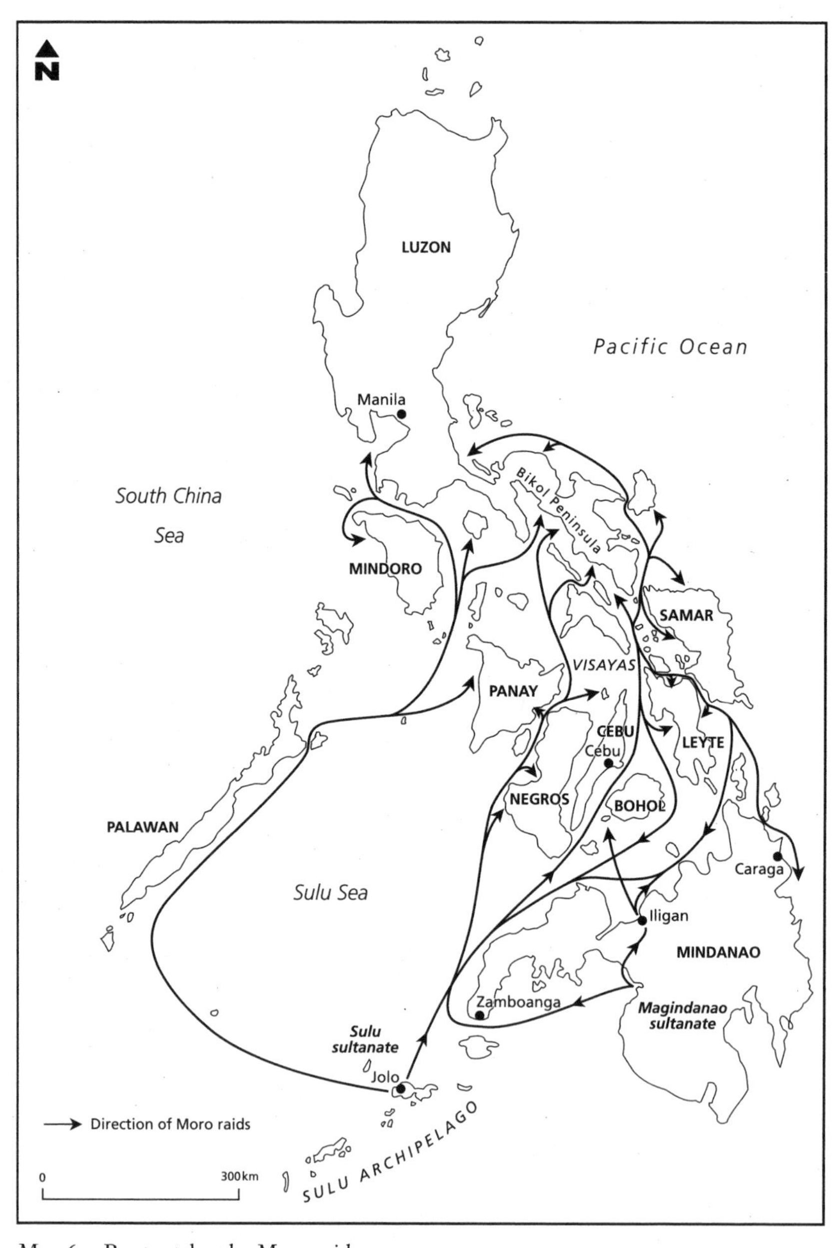

Map 6.1. Routes taken by Moro raiders

Up until the mid-eighteenth century, Moro raids declined in intensity, but losses were still sustained. The provincial of the Recollects claimed that between 1719 and 1751, 10,000 *almas* were captured or killed in the town of Paragua in Palawan alone.[63] For the last quarter of the eighteenth century, when raids by the Iranun and Balangingi increased, James Warren has suggested that the Sulu sultanate was importing between 2,000 and 3,000 slaves a year.[64] Other authors give lower annual estimates of between 400 and 500.[65] According to Thomas Forrest, an agent of the East India Company who visited the Sulu islands and Mindanao in the 1770s, the Sulus purchased Visayan slaves from Iranun and Magindanao cruisers, sometimes in whole boatloads, for sale at Passir in Borneo or, if they were handsome females, in Batavia.[66] José Montero y Vidal has calculated that on average more than 1,000 captives or slaves were being sold annually in Jolo, Borneo, Makassar, and Batavia.[67] Some captives would have come from beyond the Visayas, but this region suffered the heaviest losses. In the early 1770s, two hundred raiding vessels were harrying the islands of Leyte and Samar. Between 1768 and 1772, 2,000 captives were taken from Leyte alone,[68] while Samar was losing about 100 a year.[69] Overall losses were so great that Spain appealed to the Netherlands to stop the sale of captives in Batavia.[70]

Losses were not uniformly spread throughout the islands. Leyte and Samar suffered most, but within these islands certain coasts and communities were more vulnerable to attack. Located on the return route through the Visayas, the west and north coasts of Samar and the west and south coasts of Leyte were the worst-affected. The uneven demographic impact of Moro raids is not readily apparent from the population statistics available in mission records. Raids might provoke flight that would result in an apparent rather than real loss in population. On the other hand, as Bruce Cruikshank has observed, the effect might be to encourage the population to cluster in larger and better-fortified settlements for defense, attracting inhabitants who had formerly been outside Spanish administration.[71] The most vulnerable communities might therefore register the largest increases in population; the opposite of what might be expected. As indicated in Appendix B, certain communities, notably Ogmuc, Baybay, and Sogor, were the focus of regular raids, during which a significant proportion of the community might be seized. For example, in the early seventeenth century a Caraga attack on Leyte resulted in 60 being captured in Baybay, 90 in Ogmuc, and 160 in the island of Poro, where Moros were said to have hunted the natives down like "deer."[72] About that time the mission of Ogmuc, which comprised three settlements, had 4,000 inhabitants.[73] Although losses such as this, which generally involved adults, were important in the case of particular towns, for most communities the most significant demographic effects of Moro raids were indirect through bringing changes to settlement patterns and disrupting subsistence activities and family life.

Fear of attack forced many to flee their settlements or to shift their communities as a whole. The new sites were often less favorably located for subsistence purposes, while the needs of defense and adult losses in raids might create shortages of labor that affected subsistence production. The rice harvest itself was often a target of raids, leaving local populations to survive on roots or wild plants.[74] Food shortages might in turn affect nutrition and susceptibility to disease, while heightened stress might impact on fertility.[75] Even more indirect was that Moro raids paralyzed trade and rendered administration more difficult.[76] In the 1770s, trade between Manila and Leyte and Samar totally ceased for ten years.[77] While a reduced Spanish presence might be beneficial to local communities, the inability to travel between the islands had a negative impact on economic activities. Hence in the 1780s Boholanos were complaining that they were unable to trade their salt fish, cloth, and coconuts where they could obtain the best prices;[78] it also meant that food shortages could not be overcome by importing food from other islands as had been the custom from pre-Spanish times.

Ecclesiastical Administration and Missionary Activities

Most economic activities described above were quite localized, and for large parts of the Visayas the clergy were the only Spaniards living there. Even so, the intensity of contacts with priests varied significantly between and within the islands. While the Jesuits were given charge of the eastern Visayas, the western islands came under the jurisdiction of the Augustinians or secular clergy. The Augustinians assumed control of much of Panay, but had two parishes in Cebu at San Nicolás and Carcar, while the secular clergy administered most of the rest of the region. The Jesuits had residences in Cebu and Arévalo, but only administered the parish of Mandawe in Cebu. Although they visited Negros in the early seventeenth century, it was not until 1630 that they established a mission at Ilog. Since much of the evidence for demographic changes in the colonial period derives from missionary accounts, this chapter proceeds with a brief account of the activities of the religious orders in different parts of the Visayas, noting observations made on population levels, not only by them but also by the secular authorities. Since most is known about the activities of the Jesuits, the analysis begins with the eastern Visayas and Bohol.

The Eastern Visayas and Bohol

As a consequence of the royal decree in 1594 sanctioning more priests for the Philippines, eight Jesuit fathers and one lay brother arrived in Manila.[79] In 1595 they established a residence in Cebu and from there moved on to found the missions of Carigara and Dulag in Leyte. By the end of the year they were ministering to "5,400 and as many catechumens,"[80] and within two years they had founded further missions at Palo, Alangalang, and Ogmuc.[81] By 1597 Father Francisco de Encinas claimed to have baptized two-thirds of those in the Carigara mission, while two years later the Dulag mission comprised eight pueblos and 10,000 souls.[82]

In Samar, Francisco de Otazo founded the first Jesuit mission at Tinagon in 1597. Initially progress was slow due to a locust-induced famine and epidemic that also afflicted Palo. After a year and a half the Jesuits had baptized 2,500 people, but 1,000 had died.[83] A chapel was also established at Catubig, but because of the shortage of priests it was not developed into a mission at that time even though it was in a densely settled area of sixteen *rancherías*.[84] Finally, in 1596 Jesuits began working in Bohol at the request of an *encomendera*, Doña Catalina de Bolaños. After founding Baclayon they established missions at Talibong and Loboc, where they baptized more than 3,000 souls.[85]

Commissioned from Rome to undertake a visitation of the Philippine vice-province, in 1600 Diego García personally inspected parishes in the Visayas. He reported that the Jesuits were ministering to more than 50,000 Visayans, though less than 20 percent were judged to be Christians (see Table 6.1). In addition, there were said to be 11,000 or 12,000 *almas* in Leyte and 14,000 to 15,000 in Ibabao in Samar who had never received Christian instruction.[86] The Jesuits faced significant obstacles to their work. The initial establishment of the missions in 1596 and 1597 was delayed by a major epidemic and in Leyte by the need to proceed slowly due to native unrest provoked by ill treatment by *encomenderos*. Other more persistent constraints on missionary advance were the dispersed settlement pattern, Moro raids, and the existence of polygamy and slavery.

TABLE 6.1 Jesuit Missions in the Visayas in 1600

Residence	Number of towns	Number of fathers	Number of brothers	Number of souls	Number of Christians
Carigara	4	1	1	2500	1100
Dulag	8	2	1	8000	1400
Palo	5	1	1	6000	1200
Ogmuc	3	1	1	4000	646
Alangalang	5	1	1	4000	600
LEYTE TOTAL	25	6	5	24500	4946
SAMAR (Tinagon)	10	3	3	8430	2600
BOHOL	4 being formed	2	1	9500	700
NEGROS (Tanjay)	Not yet established			8000	600–700
GRAND TOTAL		11	9	50430	8896

Source: ARSI Phil 10 fols. 26–27 Diego García 7 July 1600.
Note: In addition, the Jesuits based in Cebu ministered to the community of Mandawe with 400 souls.

A major obstacle to the progress of the missions, particularly given the shortage of priests, was the dispersed settlement pattern. The Jesuits found that in contrast to the Tagalog region, where villages were located close together, in the Visayas they were small and scattered.[87] Congregating dispersed populations was not practicable because they needed to live close to their swiddens and be able to supplement their diets by hunting and fishing.[88] Initially the threat of Moro raids also encouraged population dispersal, though this tendency was reversed in the eighteenth century when the missions developed more effective defenses.

During their first four years in the Visayas the Jesuits established a relatively large number of missions from which the one or two resident priests periodically visited four to six outlying towns. This meant that they often spent long periods alone without the moral support of other priests, when it was said that they were exposed to many dangers and temptations.[89] Therefore, when Diego García visited the Visayas in 1600 he recommended that no new missions be founded and that the number of permanently staffed missions be reduced so that each should have more than six priests. Under this scheme, towns without missions would be visited at regular intervals from these central residences. Hence on the island of Leyte, the five missions were reduced to two, while on Samar the closure of the Catubig residence had already left only one mission at Tinagon. Bohol was to be administered from Cebu by two priests who served on a rotating basis, while the newly acquired town of Tanjay (Tanay) on the east coast of Negros was also to be visited by Jesuits from Cebu.[90]

This new strategy did not really succeed. Outlying settlements were generally visited only four or five times a year for eight to ten days and then often by only one priest.[91] The Jesuits judged that their influence had declined compared to when the missions had been permanently staffed and they complained that much time was spent traveling, which took a toll on missionary health and which could be better used in evangelization. As a result, in 1615 the former missions were re-activated, but as subordinate rather than separate missions.[92] When Father Ignacio Alcina reported in 1660, the situation differed little from what had prevailed at the beginning of the century.[93] Priests were constantly on the move with their "house on their shoulders like a snail" and on return often found that their work had been undone.

During the seventeenth century, the total number of priests working in Bohol, Leyte, and Samar fluctuated between about twenty-five and thirty.[94] Despite their small number and the dispersed population, the number of converts gradually increased. The Jesuits seem to have found the Visayans receptive to their teaching, which was often conducted in the native language.[95] Their initial strategy was to convert native leaders. In 1597 when Father Alonso Rodríguez established the mission of Ogmuc, he was greatly helped by the conversion of one of the leaders, "because he was so important and rich and had more than one hundred slaves."[96] From the earliest days the Jesuits also established a number of boarding schools for the sons of native leaders. The first, which catered to sixty sons of *datus*, was founded at Dulag in 1595, and by the early seventeenth century others had been established at Tinagon in Samar and Loboc in Bohol.[97] The most loyal and knowledgeable in Christian doctrine later became teachers in outlying towns, where they taught the catechism and attempted to impose Christian values. Not all conversions proceeded peacefully, however. In 1610 in Bohol, the Jesuits had destroyed seventy idols and were encouraging the natives to settle in the lowlands "partly by exercise of their authority, partly by persuasion."[98] About the same time, soldiers stationed in Leyte for defense against Moro raids were "assisting" the Jesuits in the establishment of Dulag.[99]

Obstacles to initial conversion derived not so much from differences in religious beliefs but from changes to social practices and the requirement to pay tribute. The strategy to convert *datus* first was not always successful since they were reluctant to abandon polygamy and slavery.[100] Father Chirino suggested that the reluctance to abandon polygamy was related more to the loss of property that might ensue than their desire to keep several wives.[101] Similarly the abandonment of slavery might threaten their economic and political power.[102] However, the basis of *datu* authority shifted in the colonial period. In the 1660s it was said that *datus* who had previously had one hundred or more slaves by then had ten, and those who had had fifty or sixty had only two. Alcina commented that *datus* greatly regretted the loss of their slaves since they had been a source of pride.[103]

Jesuit statistics for slaves, called *manicipia*, found in missions in the eastern Visayas are shown in Table 6.2. Unfortunately they are inconsistently recorded between census periods, and the numbers in individual towns fluctuate considerably over time. No slaves at all are recorded for 1675, but they are included in all other five censuses. Most likely the figures reflect differences in the definitions being used by individual priests, with some including indebted dependents as part of the general population rather than as slaves. It is possible, however, that part of the variation reflected success in acquiring captives through conflict with Moros or inter-*barangay* warfare.

While early attempts at conversion often met with resistance, later the willingness of the Jesuits to provide practical and moral support in the face of Moro raids encouraged voluntary settlement in the missions. During the early colonial period, priests were the only Spaniards in most native pueblos and they often organized defenses against Moro depredations, sometimes dispensing weapons and allowing the church to be used as a defensive site.[104] The fact that the priests suffered equally from Moro raids—indeed they were particularly sought after for ransom—may have also encouraged sympathy for their cause.[105] The effect of Moro raids was therefore to encourage Visayans to settle "under the bells," rather than, as might be expected, to disperse. In a brilliant analysis of the demographic impact of Moro raids on Samar in the late eighteenth century, Bruce Cruikshank shows how the population became more concentrated on the west coast, where raids were more frequent, and the Franciscans, who assumed control of the missions after the Jesuits were expelled in 1768, could provide more effective defense, whereas on the east coast missionary efforts were less successful.[106]

Table 6.2 Populations Administered by Jesuits in the Eastern Visayas, 1659 to 1755

	Married persons UXORATI	Single persons SOLUTI	Male youths EPHEBI	Female youths VIRGINES	Boys PUERI	Girls PUELLAE	Total excluding slaves	Slaves MANICIPIA	Total including slaves
Leyte									
1659	4,441	1,983	650	777	1,873	2,207	11,931	161	12,092
1675	7,615	1,911	764	988	1,721	2,122	15,121		15,121
1696	9,162	3,157	747	705	3,870	3,591	21,232	235	21,467
1737	15,324	5,816	2,232	2,194	7,073	7,176	39,815		39,815
1743	15,955	7,299	3,270	2,885	5,974	6,022	41,405		41,405
1755	16,381	8,284	3,426	2,981	8,025	8,358	47,455	7	47,462
Samar									
1659	3,661	2,243	538	710	2,136	2,214	11,502	450	11,952
1675	9,268	3,475	1,933	1,988	2,761	3,231	22,656		22,656
1696	10,410	4,566	3,100	3,157	4,516	4,528	30,277	1718	31,995
1737	18,470	8,010	4,677	4,763	5,907	5,623	47,450	29	47,479

1743	15,889	6,685	3,554	3,169	7,455	7,566	44,318	20	44,338
1755	19,819	9,221	2,339	2,497	11,948	11,779	57,603		57,603
Bohol									
1659	1,100	510	368	430	612	708	3,728	396	4,124
1675	2,160	773	721	1,017	1,330	1,419	7,420		7,420
1696	4,209	1,738	748	905	1,581	1,673	10,854	237	11,091
1737	11,256	4,265	2,223	2,248	5,185	4,686	29,863	35	29,898
1743	10,446	3,332	1,181	956	6,074	6,155	28,144		28,144
1755	14,046	5,329	4,738	5,492	5,977	5,646	41,228	11	41,239

Sources: ARSI Phil 2 I fols. 412–415, II fols. 314–317, Phil 14 fols. 106–117 Catologus christianorum quos colit societas in Philippinis.
Note: These Figures are total populations calculated from figures for individual pueblos in each island. There are significant problems with the quality of the data in these sources. Some errors were made by the scribe. It is clear that the category of slaves was inconsistently recorded. In addition, there appear to be significant arithmetic errors in the calculation of the totals included in the manuscripts. The extent of the summation errors is difficult to judge given the difficulty of deciphering many of the figures. The author first read these figures on the microfilm held at Saint Louis University, but since parts proved difficult to decipher, the six censuses were checked with the originals in ARSI. This enabled some corrections to be made, but the handwriting in the manuscripts, particularly in the censuses for 1737 and 1743, makes it difficult to be certain about some of the figures. The balance of errors attributable to the scribe and the researcher are difficult to assess. The maximum deviation of my calculations from the totals given was about 3 percent higher, but at the village level they were often more significant. The percentage deviations of my totals from those given in the manuscripts were 1659 +1.16, 1675 +2.25, 1696 -0.04, 1737 -1.13, 1743 +3.17, 1755 +0.23.

In Bohol and Samar, resistance was more prolonged. The Boholanos were generally regarded as warlike and the island described as not being for the faint-hearted.[107] In 1785, forty years after a revolt in Talibong, there were still said to be 4,000 rebels; the unrest, known as the Dagohoy rebellion, was to continue until 1829, when it was finally suppressed by military force.[108] At its peak the rebels numbered 8,000 *tributos enteros*.[109] Although sparked by the actions of an overzealous priest, the rebellion occurred against a background of resistance to missionization. Similarly, the rugged, forested central part of Samar was a refuge for many apostates and criminals, and as late as 1849 one quarter of the population still remained outside effective Spanish administration.[110]

Although the Jesuits left more abundant records of their activities than other missionary orders, tracking demographic trends for the eastern Visayas, particularly for the seventeenth century, is in many respects more difficult, since the population data available generally relate to the missions only and often reflect the presence or non-presence of missionaries. Jesuit accounts from the early seventeenth century suggest the native population was increasing. The number of converts rose from 7,546 in Leyte and Samar together in 1600 to 14,300 in 1620.[111] However, the growth was not sustained and was not typical of the islands as a whole. In the mid-seventeenth century Father Colin claimed that the population of Leyte and Samar had fallen from 20,000 *tributarios* when the Jesuits first entered to between 6,000 and 7,000.[112] He attributed the decline to Moro raids, epidemics, and forced labor in the construction of galleons, though some losses may have been due to fugitivism. Subsequently, between 1659 and 1755 the Visayan population under Jesuit control increased from 28,168 to 146,304, an increase of more than 2 percent per year. A natural increase of this magnitude is not realistic for pre-industrial societies based on non-intensive agriculture, so it must reflect in part Jesuit success bringing converts into the missions or more effective record keeping.[113] During the second half of the eighteenth century the total population of Leyte varied between about 38,000 and 47,000 and of Samar between 41,000 and 57,000 (see Appendix D), with the fluctuations reflecting the impact of Moro raids and epidemics, as well as differences in the sources used by different authors. The tributary population of Leyte and Samar together declined by about 0.2 percent a year between 1750 and 1792.[114] Where growth occurred, it was due to the success of the Franciscans in bringing more people under effective administration and in Samar by immigration from Leyte.[115]

In Bohol the missions failed to expand significantly during the seventeenth century due in part to Moro raids, but also because of continuing unrest. Much of the population kept its distance from Spaniards and preferred to live in the hills, while the missions remained concentrated on the southern coast around Loboc, Baclayon, and Panglao.[116] Progress was also slow because initially the missions were not permanently staffed but visited on a rotational basis from Cebu.[117] In 1660 Father Colin claimed that when the Spanish arrived there were 10,000 families in Bohol, but at the time of writing there were only 1,200 *tributarios*.[118] The situation changed dramatically in the first half of the eighteenth century, when the population of Bohol nearly quadrupled (see Appendix D). This expansion was confirmed by the Franciscan friar San Antonio, who in the 1730s commented that there was no more room on the island.[119] The rapid increase in the population of Bohol was in marked contrast to the trend in Leyte and Samar and is surprising given the continued unrest. It will be suggested below that the earlier increase there may reflect the absence of Moro raids and possibly changing marriage practices.

Panay

In 1588 the Augustinians in Panay had a monastery at Arévalo and four residences at Otón, Araut (Dumangas), Panay, and Tigbauan, but a shortage of priests had forced the abandonment of those at Aklan and Antique.[120] By 1610 new missionaries had arrived and twenty-nine were ministering to 15,500 *tributos* from twelve residences.[121] However, by 1626 there were only eighteen Augustinians who had charge of 10,300 *tributos*, while the secular clergy catered to another 2,400.[122]

Augustinian attempts at conversion were hampered by demands for forced labor and tribute that drove many coastal Panayanos into the interior. Fugitivism was encouraged by *babaylanes*, or shamans, who attributed many of the calamities they were experiencing to the arrival of Christians.[123] One notable *babaylan*, Tapar, based in Malonor, founded a sect that in 1663 promoted an uprising in the province of Otón.[124] The fugitives became known as *mundos*, taking their name from *mundos*, or wild bananas, that became an essential feature of their diet.[125] Efforts to draw the *mundos* from the interior were also retarded by a jurisdictional conflict between the Jesuits and Augustinians that was not settled until 1696.[126] The conflict generated an extensive memorial that identified three distinct groups of *mundos*, each with a number of *principales*. To the north between Ibahay, Aklan, and Bugasong there were three *principales* with 1,380 families, and in the "montes" between Panay, Passi, Laglag, Jaro, and Dumangas there were eleven *principales* with 1,145 families. Finally, in the "montes" between Damisdan and Bogol there were 1,913 families under ten *principales*.[127] The memorial also includes a twenty-two-page *padrón* of 2,407 adults who were predisposed to come down from the mountains and settle at Tumabog (Tumagboc) and Tanguian but were reluctant to return to Augustinian administration because they would be required to settle away from their lands. In 1696 it was resolved that the *mundos* should be allowed to return to their homes, but the numbers resettling in the lowlands were small, and significant numbers remained in the interior until the nineteenth century.[128] Nevertheless, by 1714 the number of tributaries administered by the Augustinians had risen to 13,635.5 (Table 6.3).[129]

Although most parishes in Panay remained under the Augustinians throughout the early colonial period, due in part to secularization the proportion of the population they administered fell from about 80 percent in the early seventeenth century to about 65 percent in the early nineteenth century.[130] It is therefore difficult to compare Augustinian figures over time. Population estimates in Appendix D suggest that the population of Panay reached its nadir in the mid- to late seventeenth

Table 6.3 Tributary Populations under the Augustinians in Panay, 1610 to 1778

	1610	1626	1714	1765	1778
Antique	600	1,000	1,000	2,904	2,800
Ibahay	2,000	Secularized (600)	Secularized	Secularized	Secularized
Aklan (Capiz)	1,200	Secularized (1,000)	500	927.5	890
Batan	800	Not given	933	Secularized	Secularized
Mambusao	1,500	1,000	930	Under the Recollects	Secularized
Panay	1,200	1,000	930	1,500	1,075
Dumalag		800	350	2,667	2,501
Dumarao		800	287.5	1,238.5	900
Dumangas	900	500	1,000	1,910	1,721
Baong	800	500			
Salog (Jaro)	1,500	1,000	1,900	1,200	1,208
Otón	1,000	1,000	1,300	1,415	2,255.5
Guimbal			1,400	2,875	3,092.5
Tigbauan		1,000	1,400	2,262.5	2,294.5
Santa Barbara				512	595.5
Cabatuan				1,439.5	1,461

Passi	3,000	1,000	925	772	745
Laglag	1,000	700	780	2,126.5	1,686
Matagub				1,082.5	460
Axui		Secularized (800)	Secularized	Secularized	Secularized
TOTAL under Augustinians	15,500	10,300	13,635.5	24,832	23,685
TOTAL under the secular clergy		2,400			
TOTAL	15,500	12,700	13,635.5	24,832	23,685

Sources: 1610 AGI AF 67-6-20 Memoria de los conventos y ministerios de la orden de nuestro padre San Agustín 1610.
1626 Rodríguez, *Historia*, 2: 72–74, Pedro de Arce, July 1626. Excludes 1400 in Calamianes and 1000 in Balayan.
1714 Rodríguez, *Historia*, 2: 391, Sebastián de Foronda 1714.
1765 BL Additional Mss. 13,976 Lista de los conventos y ministerios que tiene esta provincia del santísimo nombre de jesús destas islas . . . Valladolid 1765. Figures for individual parishes have been aggregated to make them comparable to earlier figures.
1778 Redondo y Sendino, *Breve reseña* , 139–141, Extracto tomado del plan de almas 1778. Figures given as *tributantes* are divided by two to obtain the number of *tributos*.

century, coinciding with the Hispano-Dutch War, when demands for labor and supplies were at their peak. As noted above, its impact was felt particularly on the southeast coast. Although unreliable, Augustinian figures for the towns of Dumangas, Jaro, Otón, and Guimbal follow this trend, revealing a decline from 4,200 *tributos* in 1610 to 2,500 in 1626, but recovering to 5,600 in 1714.[131] Some of the losses were due to migration to the interior; it has already been noted above that in 1696 there were 4,438 *mundo* families living in the hills,[132] and there were undoubtedly others who escaped official notice. Thus, Casimiro Díaz was probably not far wrong when in 1718 he estimated that the whole island had about 20,000 *tributos*, not counting those living in the interior.[133] The latter may be roughly estimated at 5,000 families, of whom Negritos made up about a quarter.

In the eighteenth century more concerted evangelization by the Augustinians resulted in some interior populations being settled in the lowlands. The number of *tributos* thus rose from about 14,000 in 1698 to nearly 26,000 in 1735.[134] Subsequently the number under Augustinian administration remained fairly constant, fluctuating between 22,500 and 26,000 (Appendix D). The population of Augustinian parishes grew slowly partly due to the secularization of some parishes, but also because the population was probably not replacing itself. In 1760 the ratio of women to children in these parishes in Panay and Iloilo was 1:1.35 and 1:1.59 respectively, and in 1765 it was 1:1.55 and 1:1.71.[135] Apart from the impact of Moro raids, disruption of conjugal relations caused by labor drafts that caused the prolonged absence of men is also likely to have affected fertility. It was also noted that excessive labor at the rice harvest caused women to miscarry, give birth, or even die in the fields.[136]

In the second half of the eighteenth century, Moro raids threatened the coast of Antique and the north and east coast of Panay.[137] Although there was a raid on Miagao in 1754, the presence of a garrison generally protected the southern coast from attack. Montero y Vidal calculates that between 1750 and 1757 the towns of Panay, Banton (Batan?), Kalibo, Banga, Ibahay, Tibiao, and the island of Romblon lost more than 2,620 *tributantes* primarily due to Moro raids. While these raids are well-documented, it was suggested at the time that their impact was exaggerated and that those perpetrating them were often not Moros but "bad Christians."[138] It was claimed that *cabezas de barangay* inflated the losses to pocket the tribute of fugitives or those captured in raids, while others suggested that the *alcalde mayor* exaggerated the numbers because he wished to emphasize the need for defense in order to obtain more support for *entradas* against the *mundos* who were raiding lowland villages.[139] Whatever the truth, the impact of these raids is not apparent in the official statistics.

Apart from Moro raids, other crises served to destabilize the population. In 1787 there was an earthquake in Iloilo and the following year an outbreak of smallpox. While the earthquake probably caused little loss of life, calamities such as this played into the hands of *babaylanes*, who fomented unrest and encouraged some to flee to the hills.[140] In the mid-nineteenth century Rafael Díaz Arenas estimated that there were 12,900 unconverted people living in Antique and Iloilo, of whom 10,405 were living in the interior.[141] Of the latter about 15 percent were Negritos and the rest, approximately 8,700, were referred to as *mundos*, almost double the number estimated at the beginning of the century.

External factors seem to have been the most important in determining demographic trends in Panay. The island was generally well-supplied with provisions and even in the nineteenth century was regarded as healthy, with death rates lower than the Philippines in general.[142] After the sixteenth century, few epidemics were recorded in Panay, perhaps because its population had acquired some immunity to acute infections as a result of constant re-infection by troops and travelers through the port of Iloilo. Smallpox was probably a fairly regular visitor to the island, occasionally erupting into an epidemic, such as occurred in 1788. In the nineteenth century, smallpox was affecting children and adolescents in Iloilo but was not causing high mortality.[143] This may have been helped by vaccination programs, though they were not very effective.[144] In any case the most important causes of death at that time were considered to be enteric diseases and tuberculosis.

The population in Panay thus experienced a sharp decline in the sixteenth century that was prolonged by forced labor drafts and exactions during the Hispano-Dutch War. By the end of the seventeenth century, the population had only just recovered to its level in 1600. Subsequently, in the eighteenth century it began to grow, though the increase reflected in part more effective missionization. Growth in the Augustinian parishes seems to have reached a plateau in the second half of the century, but the population as a whole continued to increase. By 1800 there were about 50,000 *tributos* on the island and perhaps another 2,000 living in the hills. At the time, officials commonly employed a multiplication of five rather than four to arrive at the total population.[145] However, Augustinian figures for 1760 and 1765, which indicate both tributary and total populations, suggest lower ratios of 4.6 and 4.2 respectively. Using a multiplier of 4.5 would give a total population in 1800 of about 235,000. Based on Casimiro Díaz's figures, the population in 1700 may have been about 100,000, which implies a rate of increase during the eighteenth century of about 0.85 percent per annum, slightly lower than in Cebu. Whether this reflected a real increase or more effective administration is difficult to judge. Most likely it was a combination of both.

Cebu

Although Cebu was the capital of the Visayas, the conversion of its native population proceeded slowly. The Jesuits, Augustinians, and Recollects all had monasteries in Cebu and administered some of its parishes, but their main interests lay elsewhere. The missions were not staffed permanently and Moro raids sometimes prompted their relocation inland or their abandonment.[146] By the 1660s there were only seven parishes or missions in the island, four of which were near Cebu City and the other three at Carcar, Barili, and the island of Bantayan.[147] Until the late eighteenth century many of the island's inhabitants thus had limited contact with priests or indeed any Spaniard,[148] and Spanish was not widely spoken.[149] Since the religious orders administered only a few parishes and for relatively short periods, the evidence for demographic trends in the island is scant. Also, many figures for Cebu refer to the whole bishopric or secular jurisdiction, from which it is difficult to extract numbers for the island of Cebu alone.

Michael Cullinane and Peter Xenos have undertaken the most detailed analysis of demographic trends for the island of Cebu.[150] For the early colonial period they rely, as does this study, on the history of the establishment of parishes in Cebu and project back from more reliable figures from the late eighteenth century. They estimate there were about 41,480 people on the island in the 1770s. Unfortunately they do not provide a detailed account of how they arrived at the figures for the constituent subregions, though some are derived from the 1818 census. What their analysis shows is that population growth in the eighteenth century was relatively slow compared to the nineteenth century, when the increase was dramatic. The latter increase has been attributed to a switch from millet to maize as the main staple, to an expansion in domestic trade, to the establishment of more formal settlements and parishes, and to an improvement in defense against Moro raids. Canute VanderMeer similarly sees the demographic growth occurring primarily in the nineteenth century and for similar reasons.[151]

Although these studies provide different population estimates for 1600 and 1800, they suggest similar rates of population growth during this period. VanderMeer assumes a constant upward trend, estimating that the population grew by 0.46 percent per annum during this period, while Cullinane and Xenos, though not specifically referring to Cebu, appear to accept an increase of 0.5 percent for the lowland Philippines.[152] My own estimates of 23,000 in 1600 and of 60,000 in 1800 suggest a broadly similar growth rate of 0.48 percent per annum.[153]

This overall demographic trend masks significant variations over time and space. There is little doubt that populations in the vicinity of the port of Cebu experienced a sharp decline in the early colonial period as a result of Spanish depredations, Moro raids, and the displacement of local populations by estates. However, subsequently raids declined in frequency and pressure on native communities moderated as Spanish commercial activities shifted to Luzon. Even when Moro raids resumed in the mid-eighteenth century, the east coast was largely spared since it was well-defended by a garrison and naval squadron; the north and west coasts, however, remained vulnerable to attack. The island of Bantayan never really recovered from the Moro raid of 1600, when 800 were captured, and despite being largely depopulated it suffered another devastating raid in 1627 (see Appendix B).[154] The Moro raids of the 1750s that inflicted widespread damage on the Visayas also resulted in the destruction of Bantayan, Potat, and Balamban and the seizure of many captives.[155] The southeast coast also suffered intermittently from Moro raids, but in 1815 it was densely settled with the four parishes of Carcar, Argao, Boljoon, and Dalaguete together possessing 3,825 *tributos*, a larger population than the eight parishes in the hinterland of Cebu City (see Table 6.4).[156] This population concentration may have dated from pre-Spanish times,[157] but the region's ability to retain its demographic prominence may have also been due to the absence of Spanish enterprises that around Cebu displaced communities from their lands.

VanderMeer recognizes there may have been an initial fall in the population of Cebu after the Spanish arrived and that the decline may have continued in the early seventeenth century due to forced labor associated with the Hispano-Dutch War and Moro raids. One might also add epidemics that included an outbreak of smallpox in 1652 when "many people died."[158] However, he generally sees the colonial period as one of continuous growth, albeit initially at a low level. He attributes growth in the seventeenth-century Philippines as a whole to increased food production resulting from the effective enforcement of planting quotas by government inspectors.[159] However, he provides no evidence for this argument. Indeed, as noted above, in the seventeenth century Cebu was periodically afflicted by severe food shortages and needed to import rice on a regular basis. VanderMeer also suggests that in the eighteenth century food supplies were aided by the adoption of maize and possibly the absence of malaria. However, in both cases the benefits these brought were probably not apparent until the late eighteenth and nineteenth centuries. The 1818 census indicates that by then the population had increased markedly to 79,755 *almas*.[160] While this figure might be exaggerated, it is consistent with a report by the Bishop of Cebu in 1815 that the population had doubled in forty years.[161]

TABLE 6.4 Tributary Populations under the Augustinians in Cebu, 1760 to 1818

	1760	1765	1778	1815	1818
San Nicolás	700	559	1,547	690.5	1,210
Boljoon	650	680	543	1,097.5	1,210
Opon	790	210.5	356	821	1,415
Talamban		465		383.5	
Carcar	500	311	171	565	included in Argao
Argao	225	925	1,260	1,083	1,625
Dalaguete				1,079.5	1,278
TOTAL	2,865	3,150.5	3,877	5,720	6,738

Sources: 1760 NL Ayer Ms. 1449 (Box) Razón de los pueblos, tributos . . . cargo de la religión de Nuestro Padre San Agustín, Pedro de Velasco 16 Apr. 1760.

1765 BL Additional Mss. 13,976 Lista de los conventos y ministerios . . . provincia del santísimo nombre de jesús destas islas . . . Valladolid 1765. Figures for individual parishes aggregated to make them comparable to earlier figures.

1778 Redondo y Sendino, *Breve reseña*, 139, Extracto tomado del plan de almas 1778. Figures given as *tributantes* are divided by two to obtain the number of *tributos*.

1815 AUST Libro 229 Censo del archipelago 1815.

1818 Buzeta and Bravo, *Diccionario geográfico*.

The evidence presented here suggests there was a significant decline in Cebu's population during the initial occupation of the island and, although there may have been a slight recovery in the late sixteenth century as Spaniards moved to Luzon, Moro raids in the early seventeenth century delayed any significant increase. While an annual growth of 0.46 percent between 1600 and 1800 has been posited, it masks two periods of distinct demographic trends: estimates here suggest a decline by about 0.14 percent in the seventeenth century and an increase of about 1.10 percent in the eighteenth century, though with the increase concentrated in the latter part of the century.

Negros

The Augustinians began work at Binalbagan and Tanjay, whose jurisdictions covered the west and east coasts of Negros respectively,[162] but by 1588 they had closed these residences because of a shortage of priests.[163] Bishop Ortega's request for more missionaries for the Visayas in 1594 included nine or ten for Negros, but none of those that arrived at the end of the century were assigned to the island.[164] Instead, Jesuits began undertaking regular visits to Tanjay from Bohol and by 1600 had managed to baptize 600 people.[165] However, it was not until 1630 that they established a permanent presence on the island. Meanwhile, in the early seventeenth century other parishes were established at Binalbagan, Ilog, and Dumaguete.[166] The first was administered for a short time by the Recollects,[167] and in 1630 the Jesuits assumed responsibility for the town of Ilog. In 1626 these four parishes together possessed 3,000 *tributos*. The Jesuit mission of Ilog made steady progress through the seventeenth century, increasing in population from 1,962 in 1659 to 3,150 in 1696,[168] and in the early eighteenth century Jesuit efforts in western Negros were consolidated with the arrival three German and Czech missionaries.[169] In 1755 the Jesuits were ministering to a total of 3,932 persons in the island.[170] When the Jesuits were expelled in 1768 their missions passed to Dominican administration, and in 1770 the missions contained 6,488 souls, 728 in a newly established mission of Boyanan.[171] As for Dumaguete, it remained in the hands of the secular clergy.

Similar problems beset missionaries working in Negros as in Leyte and Samar, particularly in their attempts to congregate populations into larger settlements. Their efforts were also hampered by the vast expanse of territory and the limited number of priests who only worked there for short periods. At the beginning of the eighteenth century, Casimiro Díaz maintained that only 1,600 families were paying tribute and the rest were living like "brutes," taking advantage of the island's rugged and forested terrain.[172] In 1850, Díaz Arenas estimated that there were 8,545 people in Negros who had not been converted, of whom only 735 were living in formal communities.[173]

Evidence for demographic change on the island of Negros is fragmentary because the island was a colonial backwater and there was no permanent missionary presence. The most extensive records are for the Jesuit missions, but the 1818 census of Yldefonso de Aragón suggests that the region formerly administered by the Jesuits covered only about 30 percent of the island's population.[174] For Negros, therefore, greater reliance must be placed on fiscal records. However, this evidence is unreliable due to extended periods between reassessments, fraud, and because many potential tributaries remained outside Spanish administration.[175] Another problem is that the collection of tribute from the island was split between the *alcalde mayor* of Iloilo, who had responsibility for towns on the west coast, and his counterpart in Cebu, who collected from those on the east.[176] This makes it difficult to obtain a single figure for the island as a whole at any one point in time.

Angel Martínez Cuesta has undertaken a detailed analysis of demographic trends in Negros during the colonial period based primarily on fiscal data. He suggests that the population declined by about 10 percent during the first half of the seventeenth century.[177] However, this decline was not constant, for the number of tribute payers actually increased between 1606 and 1635 largely as a result of the evangelizing efforts of Jesuits and Recollects, but then declined to 2,166 *tributos* in 1660. More active evangelization was also responsible for the increase in population in Jesuit parishes from 2,073 in 1659 to 3,182 in 1696.[178] In 1701 the number of *almas* registered in fiscal accounts was 9,607.[179] If one-third extra is added to take account of those outside Spanish administration, which might be conservative, the total population in 1700 may have been about 12,800.

During the early eighteenth century, mission populations fluctuated, but in the 1740s and 1750s they showed a marked increase with the establishment of separate settlements at Himamaylan and Hilhongan. That these figures reflect increased missionary activity rather than population increase is suggested by declining ratios of women to children. In the seventeenth century the ratio was quite high, ranging from 1:2.51 in 1659 to 1:4.16 in 1696, but in the eighteenth century it was consistently below 1:2.[180]

While Jesuit parishes may have increased in population during the early eighteenth century, albeit by attracting new converts, the fiscal records suggest that the number of tribute payers declined to 1,367 *tributos* in 1713. However, by mid-century the number had increased and remained fairly stable at around 4,000 to 5,000 *tributos* or about 24,000 to 28,000 souls in the second half of the century.[181] Negros does not appear to have participated in the significant population increase that characterized many other islands and regions at that time.

Certain factors militated against a significant increase in the population in the eighteenth century. The island of Negros did not suffer from Moro raids on the same scale as the eastern Visayas, but it was affected by the first wave of Moro incursions at the end of the sixteenth century, and in the eighteenth century raids became a regular occurrence (Appendix B). In 1722, 1754, and 1785 the island suffered significant attacks that had lingering demographic impacts on particular towns. Fear of Moro raids caused people to flee to the hills and join the already significant numbers of *cimarrones* and Negritos. Epidemics might have had the same effect, but there is little evidence for them. The only mention is an epidemic of "petite variole" that attacked children and their households in 1734.[182] However, the island may have been struck by the smallpox epidemics that hit the Visayas in 1760–1762 and 1789. In the nineteenth century the island was regarded as quite healthy, with the main afflictions being enteric and skin diseases.[183]

By the end of the eighteenth century, a significant proportion of the population was living outside Spanish administration, which Martínez Cuesta judges may have been as high as one-sixth.[184] This fraction would add about 4,000 to the numbers registered in the fiscal records and would suggest a total population of between 28,000 and 32,000. The figure of 4,000 is lower than the 8,545 people living in the mountains of Negros about 1850.[185] What this broad analysis suggests is that the population of Negros had not changed significantly since the time the Spanish arrived, although there were some losses in the initial contact period and fluctuations throughout the seventeenth century that reflected Moro raids and other crises. The level of decline may not have been as great as suggested in Table 6.5 since it is likely that the figure of 12,800 *almas* for 1700 has been underestimated. Assuming an estimate of the total population in 1600 of about 25,000 and of about 30,000 in 1800, the rate of increase was very low at 0.09 percent per annum. This minimal level of change is not surprising given that the island was a colonial backwater.[186] Few Spaniards settled in Negros and few commercial activities were established there; therefore there were fewer demands for labor and less significant changes to systems of agricultural production, although the inhabitants were still subject to tribute payments and the *vandala*. In addition, efforts at evangelization were less intense and limited to only part of the island. Indeed, the inhabitants of most of the north and northeast of the island had virtually no contact with Spaniards until the nineteenth century.

Mortality

It is generally acknowledged that the seventeenth century was a demographic low point in Southeast Asia as a whole and that subsequently the population increased significantly. Anthony Reid has attributed the rapid expansion in Southeast Asian populations, especially after the eighteenth century, to the suppression of interpolity warfare that had raised mortality and indirectly affected subsistence activities and marital life. Colonial sources contain very few comments on inter-*barangay* conflict in the Visayas after the sixteenth century.[187] Most likely it declined under missionary influence and as *barangays* focused more on the external threat posed by Moro raiders. The impact of Moro raids, on the other hand, can be detected in the populations of individual towns and islands. The numbers lost in raids in Samar and Leyte in the late eighteenth century averaged about one or two hundred a year. These numbers might not seem particularly high, but since they often involved only a few pueblos at a time, they were disastrous for those communities affected; the indirect demographic effects of Moro raids were probably greater. Adult losses and the needs of defense disrupted subsistence activities, trade, and family life and retarded population expansion. It is significant that in contrast to the western Visayas and most parts

Table 6.5 Estimated Total Native Populations of the Visayas, 1565 to 1800

	1565	**1600**	**1700**	**1800**	**Annual rate of change 1600 to 1700**	**Annual rate of change 1700 to 1800**	**Population nadir**
Cebu	28,000	23,000	20,000	60,000	-0.14	1.10	Early 18th century
Panay	200,000	100,000	100,000	235,000	0.00	0.85	Mid to late 17th century
Negros	30,000	25,000	12,800	30,000	-0.67	0.85	Late 17th /early 18th century
Bohol	25,000	9,500	15,000	55,000	0.46	1.30	Late 17th century
Leyte	60,000	35,000	25,000	40,000	-0.34	0.47	Late 17th century
Samar	40,000	30,000	37,000	50,000	0.21	0.30	Late 17th century
TOTAL	383,000	222,500	207,800	470,000	-0.06	0.81	Late 17th century

Sources: 1565 and 1600 see Tables 5.1 and 5.2.

1700 figures estimated from the following:
Cebu: AGI AF 82-57 Bishop of Cebu 25 Feb. 1667 gives 5,000 *tributos*.
Panay: Díaz, *Conquistas*, 35, gives 20,000 *tributos*, plus 5,000 families in the hills.
Negros: Martínez Cuesta, *History of Negros*, 108, gives 9,607 *almas*. One-third added for those outside Spanish administration.
Bohol: ARSI Phil 14 fols. 106–109 Catologus christianorum 1696 gives 11,091 *almas*. 4,000 added for those in the hills.
Leyte: ARSI Phil 14 fols. 106–109 Catologus christianorum 1696 gives 21,467 *almas*. 3,500 added for those outside Jesuit administration.
Samar: ARSI Phil 14 fols. 106–109 Catologus christianorum 1696 gives 31,995 *almas*. 5,000 added for those outside Jesuit administration.

1800: For the western Visayas, see chapter 6. For the eastern Visayas, because of the marked fluctuations in population, the figures for Leyte and Samar are very rough estimates based on figures provided by different sources for the late eighteenth and early nineteenth centuries. For Bohol the figure is interpolated from figures for *tributos* for 1785 and 1815 (see Appendix D).

of Luzon, the populations of Leyte and Samar show no clear upward trend in the late eighteenth century; indeed for some periods they seem to have declined. On the other hand, the fact that Bohol escaped Moro raids at this time may have enabled its population to expand rapidly despite ongoing political unrest.

While it is clear that in the early colonial period major epidemics periodically afflicted the Philippines, there is relatively little evidence for their spread or impact in the Visayas. The best-documented epidemic is one that arrived with the Jesuits in the eastern Visayas between 1596 and 1597, the impact of which was heightened by harvest failure and famine caused by plagues of locusts.[188] Commentators generally did not specify the disease, though Pedro Chirino, describing its impact in Bohol, referred to it as "a pestilence that caused pain in the head and stomach" that resulted in death and the depopulation of entire villages.[189] The epidemic was described as "serious and widespread," and in Samar as worse among children and old persons, although some adults also died.[190] This pattern of infection suggests that the same disease had previously infected the area within a few decades. Nevertheless its impact was considerable, for within the space of one and half years the mission of Tinagon in Samar lost 1,000 of its 2,500 converts.

In the mid-seventeenth century Father Colin recorded that the Visayas were visited periodically by epidemics that were a significant factor in the decline of the native population, along with losses inflicted by Moro raids and forced labor.[191] However, there is scant and often only circumstantial evidence for acute infections on the islands. In 1626 the inhabitants of Catbalogan in Samar were suffering from smallpox when the town was attacked by Camucones.[192] It also possible that the islands were affected by the general epidemics of smallpox in 1656[193] and by a "peste general" in 1668, which both caused high mortality, the latter reportedly resulting in the death of 50,000 in the Philippines as a whole.[194] However, it was not always the case that outbreaks in Luzon spread to the Visayas.[195] On the other hand there were probably some localized epidemics, many of which went unrecorded. For example, in 1652 there was a smallpox epidemic in Cebu in which many died,[196] and in 1692 many died in Dagami in Leyte as a result of "a malignant epidemic of shivers and fevers accompanied by bloody diarrhea," but neither outbreak is mentioned elsewhere.[197] These occurred against a background of enteric diseases, respiratory infections, and fevers, including malaria, that were regarded as the most frequent infections in the nineteenth century.[198]

Famines, which often followed in the wake of epidemics, also regularly contributed to high mortality. The alienation of native lands by private individuals, the missionary orders, and *datus* affected access to land in some regions, though it was relatively localized, particularly in the eastern Visayas and Negros. However, the need to meet tribute and *vandala* obligations imposed new burdens on native production, while labor was regularly withdrawn, primarily for defense. In addition to these external threats to production, droughts, heavy rains, and locusts continued to cause significant food shortages and famines. Recorded famines occurred in the Visayas in 1601, 1611, 1623, and 1656.[199] While few people would have starved to death, food shortages may have impacted on levels of infant and child mortality and increased disease susceptibility.

Fertility

Anthony Reid argues that increased fertility contributed to the expansion of Southeast Asian populations in the eighteenth century. However, he attributes the increase not to changes in social practices, but to the cessation of hostilities that had caused conjugal relationships to break down as partners were seized, fled, or were drafted to serve in raids or for defense. The stress caused by living in a climate of warfare may also have induced amenorrhea and promoted lower fertility. However, other social changes independent of warfare may also have encouraged an increase in fertility in early colonial times. Peter Boomgaard has stressed the importance of bridewealth payments, birth control practices, and slavery in limiting population densities.[200] The evidence for such changes to social practices that might influence fertility is very limited for the Philippines, so the following discussion necessarily relies on reasoned argument and is therefore to some extent speculative.

Age at marriage is one of the most important factors affecting fertility in non-contracepting societies. In seems likely that officials and priests in the Philippines would have encouraged early marriage to increase the number of tribute payers and prevent what they perceived to be "immoral" behavior. From the beginning of the seventeenth century married men were liable for tribute payment at age sixteen and women from age twenty, but single men only paid from age twenty and single women from age twenty-five.[201] Hence, although officials may have encouraged early marriage, there was some incentive for marriages to be delayed. Unfortunately there is little evidence for age at marriage in the early colonial period, and, even if age at marriage fell, it is unlikely to have had a significant effect on fertility since premarital intercourse was common in the Visayas. Similarly, the suppression of polygamy, which generally leads to an increase in fertility,[202] would have had only a minor impact since it was not widespread and where practiced involved only two or three wives.

Perhaps more significant in influencing fertility were bridewealth payments, which contemporary observers considered to be an obstacle to marriage. In pre-Spanish times bridewealth was often paid in the form of slaves, and it functioned to control labor and build political support. In colonial times the Spanish sought to suppress slavery, while the political and economic power of *datus* became more dependent on land ownership and the hereditary authority invested in *cabezas de barangay* and *gobernadorcillos* by the colonial state. These processes should have reduced the role bridewealth played in economic and political relations and moderated the amount demanded. Certainly as slavery was abolished bridewealth payments were more often paid in gold, bells, and china plates or increasingly in cash. However, in the 1660s Father Alcina noted even though Visayans had greater freedom to pursue their own livelihoods and acquire wealth than they did in pre-Spanish times, in reality many were still too poor to accumulate the bridewealth necessary for marriage; indeed *principales*, rather than acquire several wives, often had concubines for whom they did not have to pay bridewealth.[203] Even in 1815 the Bishop of Cebu was claiming that bridewealth was an obstacle to marriage and that as a result many people lived together for years without getting married.[204] At that time bridewealth could be as high as forty pesos and not less than ten pesos. While this was lower than in the sixteenth century when Loarca claimed that bridewealth for a chief might amount to one hundred pesos,[205] these figures may be compared to an annual tribute payment of one and a quarter pesos (ten reals).[206] If bridewealth did decline, then it would have not only have encouraged earlier marriage but also allowed families to have more children since the level of bridewealth required for each son was lower. Any reduction in bridewealth payments may have had a greater impact in Bohol, where in pre-Spanish times the amount paid was higher than in Leyte and Samar. There are suggestions that the marriage rate was slightly higher in Bohol (see Table 6.6), but how far this was related to changes in bridewealth is not clear.

Jesuit efforts to suppress abortion, infanticide, and the use of penis inserts are likely to have had a more direct impact on fertility. It is clear that both abortion and infanticide continued to be practiced quite widely, and in the mid-seventeenth century were deemed to be important in holding back population growth.[207] By then, however, according to Father Alcina, the use of penis inserts had largely died out.[208] The reasons for this are unknown. Although it might be suspected that the practice continued in secret, there seems little reason to doubt the veracity of Alcina's account. Penis inserts are not mentioned after this date and are not used in the Visayas today, whereas they are still used in some other Southeast Asian islands, notably Borneo. Since modern accounts suggest that the practice has a negative influence on fertility, it might be expected that its abandonment in the Visayas might have facilitated population growth.

The suppression of slavery is also likely to have encouraged higher fertility. David Henley has collected evidence from Sulawesi and elsewhere to suggest that slave-owning societies and the slaves themselves had lower birth rates, since in both cases there was little incentive for women to have children.[209] It has been noted above that by the mid-seventeenth century the numbers of slaves held by *datus* had been significantly reduced. Although precise evidence is lacking, it may therefore be speculated that the reduction in the prevalence of slavery and debt servitude would have facilitated higher fertility.

Father Alcina also claimed that unbalanced sex ratios contributed to low fertility. Referring to the Visayas, he reported that most pueblos had twice as many women as men and that many women were not marrying.[210] He attributed this imbalance to men being drafted to serve in the navy, gun factories, and other public works. Although his observation may have been valid for particular towns in the seventeenth century, it was clearly an exaggeration. However, there is some evidence for unbalanced sex ratios in the missions. The demographic data available only distinguish

TABLE 6.6 Demographic Characteristics of Populations under Jesuit Administration in the Eastern Visayas

	Youths Number of males to 100 females	**Children Number of males to 100 females**	**Woman:child ratio Calculated using all adult females**	**Percent of adults married**
Leyte				
1659	84	85	1:1.71	55
1675	77	81	1:1.17	68
1696	106	108	1:1.45	65
1737	102	99	1:1.77	67
1743	113	99	1:1.56	64
1755	115	96	1:1.85	62
Samar				
1659	76	96	1:1.90	62
1675	97	85	1:1.56	73
1696	98	100	1:2.04	70
1737	98	105	1:1.58	70
1743	112	99	1:1.93	70
1755	94	101	1:1.97	68
Bohol				
1659	86	86	1:2.63	68
1675	71	94	1:3.06	74
1696	83	95	1:1.65	71
1737	99	111	1:1.85	73
1743	124	99	1:2.09	76
1755	86	106	1:2.26	72

Sources: ARSI Phil 2 I fols. 412–415, II fols. 314–317, Phil 14 fols. 106–117 Catologus christianorum quos colit societas in Philippinis.

Note: The source gives the population in four categories: married persons, single persons, youths, and boys and girls. Unfortunately it does not give the age at which people were categorized as single, youths, or children. Neither does it indicate the age for married persons. The calculation of the woman-to-child ratios is necessarily based on the assumption of balanced sex ratios. Hence the figures for married persons (uxorati) and single persons (soluti) indicated in Appendix D have been divided by two. For reasons indicated in the text, this procedure may underestimate the number of women.

adults as married or single. However, the sex ratios for youths and children suggest that there were generally fewer males than females, with the imbalance being greater in Bohol where the number of male youths ranged from 71 to 86 for every 100 females. In all three islands the difference is more marked for youths, but the imbalance extends to children, suggesting it was not related to labor drafts.[211] The dominance of females could be a function of differential infanticide, since girls were more valued for the bridewealth they could attract, whereas boys were perceived as being a greater financial burden.[212]

Despite some changes to social practices, the woman-to-child ratios calculated for the Jesuit missions in the three islands do not reveal any consistent pattern over time, though there are significant differences between individual villages that reflect the impact of Moro raids and epidemics. The woman-to-child ratios in Leyte and Samar were generally below 1:2, which suggests that their populations were not replacing themselves.[213] It must be stressed that these are extremely crude calculations based on the broad categories of married and single adults, youths, and children that are undefined in terms of age. Furthermore, they assume balanced sex ratios when in fact there were significantly more women. In reality, the woman-to-child ratios are likely to have been even lower. What is interesting, however, is that for most dates the woman-to-child ratio for Bohol is higher than for the other two islands.[214] This is consistent with contemporary observations that the population was increasing rapidly.[215]

Conclusion

The evidence presented suggests that the population of the Visayas continued to decline in the seventeenth century. In 1655, 38,294 *tributos* were registered, which, assuming a multiplication factor of four, suggests a total population of about 150,000.[216] To this might be added another 20,000 for those who were outside Spanish administration. In 1667 the Bishop of Cebu claimed that 32,000 *tributos* had been counted in twenty-nine islands, though he had been informed that there were in fact 36,000, not including Spaniards and those who were exempt or were serving in the army.[217] In the first half of the century, the Hispano-Dutch Wars and Moro raids contributed significantly to population decline, but part of the decrease was probably due to Visayans disappearing from the official view. As discussed in chapter 3, the population in Southeast Asia as a whole appears to have stagnated in the seventeenth century due to economic decline perhaps associated with climatic deterioration that affected agricultural production, particularly between 1660 and 1685.[218] There were indeed some severe famines in the Visayas in the seventeenth century. While their dates coincide to some extent with years of crisis elsewhere in Southeast Asia, they are not recorded during the most significant dry periods in the second half of the seventeenth century.[219] Whether or not agricultural production in the Visayas was affected by climate change, the islands were less integrated into the international economy and are less likely to have been affected by the economic downturn and decline in trade that affected the Philippines in the seventeenth century.

Anthony Reid believes the population growth in the Philippines was the most precocious in Southeast Asia. He sees the demographic recovery beginning in the 1680s with the population increasing at "well over 1 percent per year" after 1735.[220] Norman Owen suggests a slightly lower figure of nearly 1 percent a year.[221] The estimates calculated for the Visayas generally support an increase after the late seventeenth century, but not to this level and with differences between the islands. While the growth rate for the Visayas as a whole during the eighteenth century may be calculated at 0.81 percent per annum, the increase appears to have been more sluggish in Leyte and Samar. While the population of these two islands appears to have increased in the early part of the eighteenth century, subsequently it tailed off in part due to Moro raids that were felt most acutely in those islands. Between 1696 and 1755 the mission populations of Leyte and Samar grew by 1.35 and 1.00 percent per annum respectively. Part of this growth probably reflected the success of the missionary orders in bringing Filipinos under their administration and possibly in the suppression of abortion, infanticide, the use of penis inserts, and slavery, which would have encouraged higher fertility. As noted in chapter 5, low birth rates generally prevail among swidden cultivators, and the transition to a more sedentary existence, often associated with wet-rice cultivation, would have favored population increase, as would the imposition of Christianity, which led to the suppression of practices that operated to control population growth. By the end of the eighteenth century, missionary activity seems to have brought some adjustments to marriage and birth customs in Leyte and Samar, but agricultural practices there had seen few changes. Communities in those islands would therefore not have experienced the full demographic benefits associated with sedentary wet-rice cultivation. The relatively low rate of increase there of less than 0.5 percent per annum during the eighteenth century as a whole compared to other Visayan islands may thus reflect not only the impact of Moro raids but also more limited cultural change. This argument might also be applied to the island of Negros, where the population grew at 0.85 percent a year in the eighteenth century (see Table 6.5). While the higher rate of increase might be attributed to fewer Moro raids, it might also reflect more effective enumeration and tribute collection.

In the eighteenth century, increases in the population appear to have been highest in Bohol and Cebu, with the former achieving the highest growth rate in the Visayas of 1.30 percent. As early as the 1730s contemporary observers also noted that the population was growing rapidly, suggesting that the increase was real rather than an artifact of record keeping.[222] The reasons for this exceptional growth are not clear. Bohol seems to have largely escaped the Moro raids of the late eighteenth century, but it was characterized by continual internal unrest that destabilized communities and created an environment that would have discouraged population increase. Part of the early increase in the population would have been due to Jesuit success in settling the population in lowland communities, but they generally found the Boholanos resistant to conversion. There are suggestions that marriage rates and woman-to-child ratios were highest in Bohol, but the reasons that might explain them remain obscure. Toward the end of the eighteenth century the population of the western Visayas was also beginning to show signs of significant increase associated with changes in the character and scale of agricultural production and trade, but the real expansion was yet to come.[223]

PART III

Southern Luzon

CHAPTER 7

Manila and Tondo

Dissatisfied with the island of Panay as the center of Spanish rule in the Philippines, Legazpi sought a location that had better food supplies, a more secure port, and preferably regular trade with China. Having heard rumors through traders of the existence of a settlement at Pasig River, in 1570 Legazpi dispatched the first of three expeditions to Luzon.[1] The first expedition headed by Juan de Salcedo only skirted Mindoro and Lubang, but the second, in May 1570 led by Martín de Goiti, resulted in skirmishes with 10,000 to 12,000 Moros under Ladyang Matanda and his nephew, Raja Soliman, at a fort at the mouth of the Pasig River.[2] Here at what became the site of Manila, they also encountered forty Chinese and twenty Japanese traders. The expedition returned to Panay with enthusiastic accounts of the region's fertility, its dense populations, and the presence of foreign traders.[3] Legazpi therefore decided to transfer the base of Spanish operation in the Philippines to Luzon. In spring 1571 the expedition set sail and after tense negotiations and resistance from the Pampangan inhabitants of Macabebe, who were allies of Rajah Lakandula, a nephew of Ladyang Matanda, the city of Manila was formally established on 24 June 1571.[4] This did not mark the end of hostilities; the inhabitants of Taytay and Cainta, who were able to muster a fighting force of 3,000 from surrounding villages and possessed well-fortified settlements, continued to offer resistance. Juan de Salcedo was dispatched to pacify them and in the ensuing battles about 300 "Moros" were killed.[5]

The establishment of Manila heralded radical transformations to the way of life of the Tagalog inhabitants of what became the jurisdiction of Tondo. Manila became the secular and ecclesiastical capital of the Philippines and the terminus of the Manila galleon from Mexico on which the colony depended. As a result, the region was the main focus of immigration by bureaucrats, priests, and traders. Among the last were large numbers of Chinese, and to a lesser extent Japanese, who together greatly exceeded the number of Spanish residents. The Chinese were known as Sangleyes, a term that Gaspar de San Agustín claimed derived from the Chinese "xian-glay" meaning "traders who come."[6] The influx of foreign settlers, whether permanent or temporary, and the maintenance of the galleons that plied the Pacific Ocean created new demands for food, supplies, and labor. To these were added the needs of a non-productive military that was required to safeguard this trade and defend Spain's only foothold in Asia.

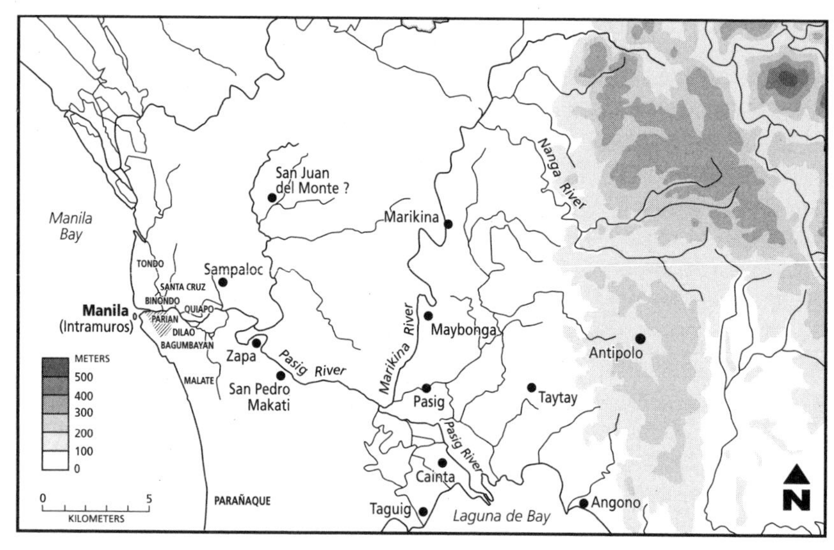

Map 7.1. Manila Bay and Tondo

As in other parts of the Philippines, the natives of Tondo were allocated in *encomiendas* and required to perform labor services, for which there was a high demand due to the large urban population and high level of commercial activity associated with the city and its port. There was also a large demand for food that encouraged the rapid development of commercial agricultural enterprises, but since most Spaniards showed little interest in agricultural production, it was left primarily to the missionary orders. Hence, the local population became rapidly integrated into the cash economy and from an early date paid tribute in cash rather than commodities.[7] The burden of providing labor increased during the Hispano-Dutch War when communities near Manila were required to supply workers to extract timber, work in the shipyards and munitions factories, and man vessels that participated in naval campaigns.

Initially the city of Manila was confined within city walls, known as the Intramuros. In the sixteenth century its jurisdiction was known as the province of Manila and it broadly corresponded to what later became the province of Tondo.[8] The region's ecclesiastical administration was more complex. While there were secular benefices in Manila and at Cavite and Bagumbayan,[9] all four missionary orders possessed monasteries in Manila and administered a number of parishes within the jurisdiction of Tondo. The Augustinians had charge of Pasig, Taguig, and coastal settlements that included Tondo, Malate, and Parañaque, while the Dominicans assumed responsibility for the Chinese population in the Parian and at Binondo. Meanwhile the Franciscans worked primarily in the more southerly region of Laguna de Bay. The Jesuits, who arrived later, began working in the Marikina Valley in 1591. This complex division of ecclesiastical administration severely complicates efforts to determine demographic trends in what was the island's most dynamic region.

Pre-Conquest Society

The city of Manila was founded on the narrow strip of land that links the Central Plain of Luzon to the volcanic lowlands of southwest Luzon. Bounded by Manila Bay to the west and the Eastern Cordillera to the east, this lowland is drained by the Pasig River and its tributaries. Here rainfall averages about 80 inches a year, but falls mainly between June and October, when heavy showers, often associated with typhoons, cause widespread flooding.[10] Father Chirino described how at Taytay rice had to be harvested from boats because from August to October or November the land was flooded to the height of a person.[11] While these annual floods might cause damage to crops, they helped to maintain the soil fertility. Although the seasonality of the climate meant only one crop of rice a year was possible, Miguel de Loarca considered the strip of land where Manila was founded to be the most fertile in the Philippines.[12]

At the beginning of the seventeenth century, Antonio de Morga succinctly described life in the province of Manila as follows: "The natives generally gather in districts and settlements where they sow their rice, grow their palm trees, their groves of *nipa*, banana, and other trees, and where they keep their fishing tackle and sailing-gear."[13] Rice was the main staple, of which more than twenty varieties were known, and the Tagalogs had a sophisticated vocabulary associated with its cultivation and processing.[14] In addition, they had kitchen gardens where they cultivated a wide range of tropical fruits and vegetables, and they also had extensive stands of *nipa* palms, which they used for wine and thatch.[15] They also raised trees producing areca nuts, known as *bonga*, which were wrapped in betel leaves and chewed.[16] Fish were vital to the Tagalog diet;[17] indeed the name Tagalog derives from "taga ilog," meaning river dweller.[18] Apart from fishing in Manila Bay and Laguna de Bay, freshwater fish were abundant in the Pasig River and its tributaries, as well as in the flooded rice fields.[19] Some domesticated animals such as chickens, ducks, goats, and buffaloes were raised, but Islamic influences in this region meant that pork was not eaten.[20]

In addition to these subsistence activities, Tondo was an entrepôt where goods were delivered by merchants from China, Japan, Borneo, Siam, and the Malay Peninsula and subsequently distributed throughout the islands. Although some foreign traders settled at Tondo, in pre-Spanish times the scale of international trade was relatively limited because Manila Bay was off the main trade route to the spice-producing islands to the south. However, the Spanish move to Manila resulted in a rapid expansion of foreign trade encouraged by the alleged "fondness" of the Tagalogs for trading and bargaining.[21]

Early eyewitnesses were effusive about the dense populations around Manila Bay. They claimed that Raja Soliman had given them the names of forty towns situated along the shore not counting those inland.[22] Settlements were located on coasts or on the banks of rivers to facilitate transport, fishing, and frequent bathing. Individual family houses were built on stilts and were reputedly arranged with greater order and neatness than in the Visayas.[23] The chief's house was generally larger and used for public meetings and ceremonies.[24] Not all parts of the jurisdiction of

Tondo were so densely settled. Inland toward the foothills of the Central Cordillera, shifting cultivation was practiced and, as the Jesuits found when they began working around Antipolo, the population there lived in widely scattered *rancherías*.[25]

The character of Tagalog social structure and beliefs are discussed in chapter 8, which is devoted to southwest Luzon, since a major source of evidence for Tagalog culture is the writings of the Franciscan Juan de Plasencia, who was based at Nagcarlan in Laguna de Bay. However, it is worth noting here the presence of Muslim groups that were particular to the Tondo region. The Islamization of Luzon only began in the early sixteenth century when Brunei traders settled in the Manila area. When the Spanish arrived, the most important leaders were the old rajah, Ladyang Matanda, and his nephew, Soliman, who resided at Manila, and the former's cousin, Banaw Lakandula, who lived at Tondo and who appears to have had the monopoly of trade with two or three junks that arrived annually from China.[26] These Muslim settlers had intermarried with local Filipinos but had maintained kinship and trade links with Brunei and thereby with Muslim centers elsewhere in Southeast Asia.[27] Since initial Spanish contacts in this region were with Muslims,[28] the Spanish assumed that Muslims occupied the whole coast, and the inhabitants of Luzon as a whole were often referred to as Moros.[29] However, there is no evidence that Islam had become a major religious and political force in the region. Indeed, in 1570 Father Herrera observed that Moros were found only in certain villages near the coast and were Muslim only in name and in their abstinence from eating pork; they did not possess mosques or religious leaders.[30] Furthermore, attempts by Raja Soliman to extend control over the coast were being opposed by local communities who complained that Moros had plundered their towns and killed many inhabitants.[31]

The Population of Tondo in 1570

In 1572 one anonymous observer reported that the reconnaissance expedition of 1570 had suggested that Manila had 80,000 Moros, but in reality there were only 2,000 excluding women and children.[32] The latter estimate probably referred to the city of Manila only, but the region to which the former refers is not known. Contemporary observers were generally clear that the region was densely settled, but despite the large Spanish presence in Tondo there is little evidence for its population in the first two decades following the city's foundation. The size of *encomiendas* allocated in 1571 is not known. The first summary figure available is for 1588, when it was suggested that there were 7,500 "indios" within five leagues of Manila.[33] This figure would not have included those living toward the foothills, where in 1591 there were said to be 2,000 *tributos*, who although they had been pacified were not paying tribute.[34] As will be shown below, by that date conflict, epidemics, and labor drafts for the construction and servicing of the city would have taken a toll on the population. Assuming the contemporary multiplication factor of four and that perhaps 10 percent had been lost in conflict and epidemics, this may represent a population of about 33,000. To this figure should be added an estimate for those in the hills who were not yet under Spanish administration, which in the late sixteenth century probably numbered about 10,000. This would suggest a total estimated population of about 43,000 in 1570.

The Urban Transformation of Manila Bay

From a population of several thousand at the time the Spanish arrived, within fifty years the city of Manila, including the built-up area beyond the Intramuros, had expanded to house a multiracial population of about 40,000.[35] Throughout the colonial period the Spanish always accounted for a small percentage of the city's total population. Although the number grew during the late sixteenth and early seventeenth centuries, subsequently it declined. The initial Spanish population comprised about 250 soldier-settlers.[36] In 1588 Bishop Domingo de Salazar reported that Manila was home to about thirty bureaucrats and nearly fifty priests, most of whom belonged to the religious orders. It also had eighty *vecinos*, some of whom had intermarried with Filipinas, and in addition there were normally 200 soldiers.[37] By the last decade of the sixteenth century the city had 300 to 400 *vecinos*.[38] Most of these Spaniards would have lived in the Intramuros.

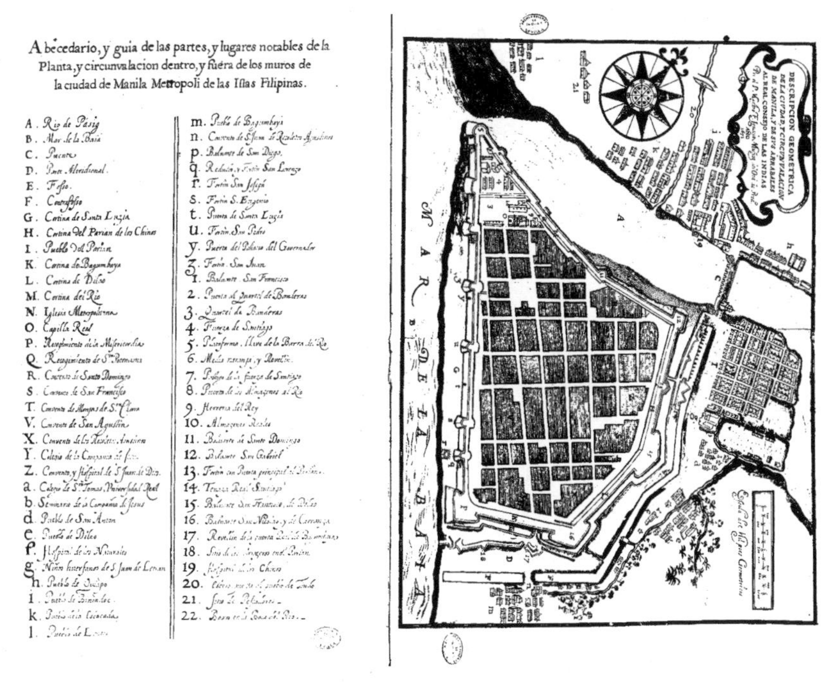

FIGURE 7.1. Manila in 1671. AGI Mapas y Planos Filipinas 10 Descripción geométrica de la ciudad y cirumvalación de Manila y de sus arrabales, F. Ignacio Múñoz.

Part of the growth in the Spanish population was due to immigration from Spain and Mexico, some of which was associated with the establishment of the colonial bureaucracy, particularly the foundation of the Audiencia in 1583.[39] Because the Spanish experienced high mortality and fertility was low because of the imbalanced sex ratio, as early as 1573 immigration was regarded as essential to maintaining the Spanish population and defend the islands.[40] Although it was estimated that 400 Spanish immigrants were needed each year,[41] attracting them to the islands proved difficult. Governor Santiago de Vera, having overseen the construction of the city of Manila in 1589, lamented the lack of population and described the city as "an empty purse or an inn without guests."[42]

There were several reasons why the islands failed to attract immigrants. Communications with Mexico were limited to two ships a year, and in the early seventeenth century sailings became irregular due to natural disasters and trading vessels being diverted into wars against the Dutch.[43] Although significant profits could be made in trade, many merchants only stayed a few years and there were few other profitable activities to attract permanent settlers.[44] In addition, the islands soon earned the reputation of being unhealthy, and officials and settlers were reluctant to undertake the long journey to the Philippines, and those stationed there constantly petitioned to return to Spain or Mexico. Those arriving included criminals or vagabonds sent from New Spain,[45] or soldiers who commonly outnumbered the civilian population and were particularly numerous during the Hispano-Dutch War. A census of Manila in 1634 indicates that, excluding church officials and priests, about 60 percent of the 238 Spanish *vecinos* were soldiers and only 10 percent were Audiencia or *cabildo* officials.[46]

While small numbers of Spaniards arrived periodically, in the early colonial period Manila grew as a result of Spanish migration from outlying islands and regions. Many of those who had been allocated *encomiendas* and lands in other regions abandoned them to seek more immediate profits in trade. Hence in the latter part of the sixteenth century Manila grew while the Spanish populations of Cebu, Nueva Cáceres, and Arévalo declined by one-half or one-third.[47] The early growth in the Spanish population of Manila was not sustained. Although initially the islands as a whole were regarded as healthy, as early as the 1570s it was said that the Spanish were losing about a hundred men a year, "because the land is unhealthy and a veritable glass furnace."[48] Soldiers were also lost in early expeditions aimed at pacifying other regions of the Philippines or countering external threats. In 1580 Gonzalo Ronquillo reported that many of the 460 soldiers and sailors that had accompanied him to the Philippines had died, including more than 200 who had been lost in a disastrous expedition to Borneo.[49] To these significant losses need to be added the many casualties sustained on smaller expeditions. In addition to the high mortality, the fertility rate was low. Even though the initial imbalance in the sex ratio later improved slightly, a census of Manila in 1634 reveals that nearly 60 percent of married couples were childless.[50] Despite the small Spanish population in Manila, the demands it generated for tribute, supplies, and labor were substantial, while despite its lack of interest in developing commercial agricultural enterprises, the alienation of Filipino lands proceeded rapidly.

Tribute, *Vandala*, and *Polo*

While the introduction of the *encomienda* to the Visayas was delayed for several years, the first allocation in the island of Luzon was made prior to the expedition that culminated in the foundation of Manila. Following the Crown's stipulation that the major cities and ports should be reserved for the Crown, in January 1571 Legazpi made Manila, Cavite, and settlements on the coast tributary to the Crown.[51] Only three *encomiendas* were allocated to private individuals. These were located in the "río de Manila," that is, up the Pasig and Taguig rivers.[52] In 1588 the Crown possessed 4,000 of the 7,500 "indios" within five leagues of the city.[53]

From the earliest days, there were complaints about tribute exactions. The Spanish deemed the inhabitants of Luzon to be relatively wealthy because they were merchants and had slaves to cultivate their lands.[54] Initially communities around Manila Bay were required to pay two *fanegas* of unhusked rice and one *manta*, or alternatively three *maes* in gold. As early as 1582 the *principales* of Tondo, Zapa, and Misilo were complaining that *alcaldes mayores* were levying rice at any price they thought fit, while at the same time forcing them to act as rowers, serve on expeditions for a month at a time, and often not paying them. These and other abuses caused many to flee. At that time one-third of Tondo's tributaries were reportedly absent.[55]

As described in chapter 3, abuses of the tributary system resulted in some modifications toward the end of the sixteenth century. The *tasaciones* drawn up by Luis Pérez Dasmariñas for Manila in 1594 required Filipinos to pay nine *reals* in cash and one *gallina*, whereas those in Pasig, Bulacan, and Malolos were to pay eighty *gantas* of rice, one *gallina*, and five reals in silver.[56] Among other things, this indicates the extent that those living in the immediate hinterland of Manila no longer derived their livelihoods from agriculture. Although by 1600 the needs of the colony had persuaded the Crown of the desirability of payments in kind,[57] when in 1604 Governor Acuña drew up the new *tasación* for the Philippines as a whole, the inhabitants of Tondo were not obliged to pay commodities, except for one *gallina*.[58]

In addition to regular tribute payments, Tagalog communities were also subject to exceptional levies known as the *vandala*, which were particularly high during the Hispano-Dutch War. In 1629 it was estimated that 50,000 *fanegas* of rice were needed to support Cavite and other parts. Officials recognized that this was a considerable burden and suggested that renting Crown lands to 2,000 Chinese, who were regarded as better farmers, might increase rice production.[59] Communities were supposed to receive payments for the goods they delivered, but between 1610 and 1616 alone those in the province of Manila were owed 70,000 pesos.[60]

Tagalogs in the hinterland of Manila were also subject to forced labor drafts. The earliest demands were associated with the construction of Manila, including its fortifications, churches, monasteries, and private houses, for which timber had to be hauled from fifteen to twenty leagues away.[61] The city was initially constructed of wood, but there were frequent fires, and following a particularly serious one in 1583, the authorities sought to replace the buildings with stone, bricks, and tiles, creating, according to Robert Reed, one of the most well-planned, well-fortified, and imposing cities in Asia.[62] The reconstruction required a substantial workforce not only for building work, but also for extracting stone from quarries at San Pedro Makati and clay for the manufacture of tiles and bricks. Thereafter *polo* labor was used primarily in the extraction of timber and for work in the shipyards, particularly during the Hispano-Dutch War.

The nature of *polo* and *vandala* demands is examined more fully in chapter 8, where activities associated with the port of Cavite are discussed, but it is worth noting here that tasks such as extracting timber, constructing ships, and serving on naval expeditions were arduous, hazardous, and poorly paid, and tours of duty increased in frequency as communities found it difficult to meet their quotas with declining populations. In 1719 the community of Taytay complained that although it had only 190 tributaries, each month seven, ten, or twenty were drafted to serve in Cavite and the same person might therefore serve two or three times a year. Some sought to gain exemption as *casas de reservas*, while others opted to flee. Others recruited substitutes, sometimes falling into debt or servitude in the process. Some from Taytay paid vagabonds six to eight reals to take their place or more commonly gave it to officials so that they could draft a substitute.[63] At the beginning of the eighteenth century, it was claimed that of the 1,200 drafted from Tondo, Bulacan, Balayan, and Tayabas to build a galleon, only 400 to 500 went; the rest bought their exemption.[64] These processes encouraged fraud and corruption and prolonged the dependent status of workers.

Missionary Activities in Manila's Hinterland

The Spanish were not only interested in profiting from the tribute and labor of Filipinos, but they also wished to bring about their Christian conversion. The Jesuits arrived in 1591 and began working in the Marikina Valley. Here they drew converts from the hills, congregating them at Taytay, Antipolo, and Cainta.[65] Despite "pestes y enfermedades," by 1599 they had baptized about 3,500 people, including some Negritos, and by 1600 another 1,500 converts had been baptized.[66] The Tagalogs proved receptive to Christianity and by the end of the sixteenth century these three towns had 6,000 to 7,000 Christians, and it was judged that few *infieles* remained.[67] Missionary efforts were considered to be more fruitful here than in the Visayas because the population was more settled, agriculture more productive, and travel easier between the missions and headquarters in Manila.[68] The missions soon became indistinguishable from secular parishes, but the Jesuits continued to administer them until their expulsion in 1768.

The Development of Agricultural Estates and the Evolving Urban Economy

The general process of land alienation was accelerated in the Manila region by the expansion of the city itself and by the high demand for provisions. The commercial estates that were established in response to this demand altered the Tagalog land-holding structure and generated significant demands for labor.[69]

Since Spanish law respected the right of Filipinos to the land they owned, the dense native settlement at Tondo meant that initially land grants there were fewer and smaller than in other Tagalog areas. Many grants were made to private individuals, but the lack of civilian interest in agriculture meant that from an early date the missionary orders, led by the Jesuits and Augustinians, became actively involved in the development of agricultural estates;[70] the Chinese also began buying up gardens, *estancias*, and other rural properties.[71] Hence in 1606 Fiscal Díaz Guiral reported that twenty-four livestock ranches had been established around Manila, some of which had more than 4,000 head of cattle.[72] Friar estates came to account for about 20 percent of the land in Tondo, much of which was the most fertile in the region, but unlike in Bulacan and Laguna de Bay they did not form such compact contiguous blocks.[73] By the end of the seventeenth century most Tondo communities were petitioning to pay tribute in cash rather than kind because they lacked lands to cultivate;[74] others cultivated lands some distance away. In the 1680s some Tondo residents were farming lands in Bulacan and some from Dilao at Taytay and Maybonga, while others from Quiapo and San Sebastián were forced to rent land from local haciendas owned by the Dominicans or Augustinians. A royal land commission in 1723 reported that most towns around Manila no longer possessed communal lands.[75]

As the estates expanded so did their need for labor. The alienation of native lands contributed to the growth of a landless labor force. Some without access to land became tenants, sharecroppers, or wage laborers on nearby estates, and sometimes the tenants rented lands they had formerly owned.[76] Others worked as wage laborers, for even though agricultural labor was not well-remunerated, as indicated in chapter 3, through being designated as *casas de reservas* the workers gained exemption from the *polo* and other services. Tenants were generally better off than wage laborers, but conditions for them, particularly in the early colonial period, were far from good. The plots of land they rented were often very small, so that once they had paid their rent and for any tools, seeds, and animals, their yield was scarcely sufficient to live on, even when there was no drought or harvest failure.[77] Nicholas Cushner has calculated that lands rented from the Augustinians by members of the community of Maybonga could yield sufficient rice for only 240 meals a year, thus requiring them to undertake other subsistence activities in order to survive.[78] In other cases, such as on the Augustinian hacienda of Pasig in the mid-eighteenth century, *casas de reservas* might lose their crops because estate demands for labor coincided with critical periods in the agricultural calendar.[79] In times of crisis, estate owners often advanced loans that might tie workers to estates.[80] Meanwhile native communities were left with fewer workers to fulfill their tribute and forced labor obligations.[81]

Harsh rural conditions encouraged many Filipinos around Manila to abandon farming altogether and support themselves by trading.[82] This may partially explain the early dependence of estates on Chinese labor. Conditions of poverty in China encouraged many Chinese to move to the islands, where they were willing to work for moderate wages and were highly esteemed as farmers.[83] In the mid-seventeenth century Father Colin recorded that "along both banks of the Pasig all the way down to Laguna de Bay there are many orchards, rice fields and large Spanish estates with more than 2,000 Chinese gardeners and farmers."[84] In fact, they had become "the feet and hands of this land as far as its sustenance is concerned."[85]

But the impact of Chinese immigration was felt beyond agricultural production. The Chinese, who were particularly interested in acquiring Mexican silver, were quick to exploit the new opportunities for trade afforded by the establishment of a permanent Spanish presence in Luzon. Whereas in 1572 only twelve to fifteen ships were arriving from China, by the end of the century the number had increased to forty or fifty per year.[86] Although initially attracted by trade, the Chinese began settling at Tondo and in Manila, where in 1581 they were confined to a distinct quarter, the Parian. Writing in 1590, Bishop Salazar estimated there were about 6,000 to 7,000 Chinese in and around the city, of whom 3,000 to 4,000 resided in the Parian, while others were to be found at Tondo and serving as fishermen and gardeners in the environs of the city.[87] The Chinese soon became indispensable to the urban economy. At that time they had two hundred shops in the Parian and provided all kinds of goods and services.[88] Father Chirino observed that "they have supplied skilled practitioners in every craft and trade, all of them experienced, proficient and cheap, from physicians and barbers to porters and carriers. Consequently, the Chinese are now the tailors, the shoemakers, the blacksmiths, silversmiths, sculptors, locksmiths, painters, masons, weavers, and in short all the craftsmen of the country."[89] In essence, the city depended for its functioning on the presence of a substantial Chinese population.[90] By 1595 the number had risen to between 10,000 and 12,000, and by 1603 to 16,000, and when the fleet was in town there might be 20,000.[91]

Manila depended on the Chinese for its supply of goods and services, but there were increasing complaints about the high prices they charged for goods and the pressure that their large numbers put on food supplies, which caused prices to rise.[92] They were also accused of monopolistic practices and criminal activities, and it was feared their presence might retard native conversion to Christianity.[93] Although some argued that they should be expelled and only be allowed to come and trade, in reality the Spanish were so dependent on the Chinese that this was not a practical policy. It was estimated that 3,000 to 4,000 were necessary to support the city.[94] However, the Spanish increasingly sought to confine them, particularly the non-Christian Chinese, to the Parian and Binondo and thereby minimize their contact with native Filipinos.[95]

The numbers of Chinese fluctuated significantly as discrimination often provoked uprisings that were followed by massacres, such as those that occurred in 1603, 1639, 1662, 1686, and 1762.[96] These periodically reduced the Chinese population to a fraction of its size, but it soon recovered. Hence the rebellion and subsequent massacre in 1639 resulted in the deaths of between 22,000 and 24,000 Chinese, but by 1649 the number in Manila had rebounded to about 15,000.[97] Despite the obvious risks incurred in settling in the Philippines, the Chinese continued to come, and the authorities seem to have been either powerless or unwilling to restrict their numbers. After the 1603 uprising, Antonio de Morga commented that "the city found itself in distress, for since there were no Sangleyes there was nothing to eat and no shoes to wear, no matter how exorbitant a price was offered."[98] Moreover, the *cabildo* and Audiencia derived considerable income from the taxes and rents the Chinese paid.[99]

Contemporary commentators held different views on the implications of the growth of the Chinese population. The consensus was that the Chinese had displaced the Filipinos from trade and crafts and had formed the middle class. Many, such as the late seventeenth-century Italian traveler Gemelli Careri, attributed this to Chinese industry and condemned the laziness of the natives.[100] He observed that the Chinese were found in all trades but that this was "the fault of Spaniards and Indians who apply themselves to nothing."[101] On the other hand, in the early eighteenth century the Archbishop of Manila, Bermúdez de Castro, believed that Filipinos had the skills, but because the Chinese had monopolized trade and the crafts from which they made considerable profit, Filipinos could only work as general laborers.[102] It was also commonly asserted that the Chinese made vagabonds of the Filipinos either because the Chinese were preferred as workers or because they had usurped the Filipinos' lands.[103] Chinese imports and production were also said to have undermined native manufactures. In 1591 Filipinos were forbidden to wear Chinese silk or clothing since competition from cheap textiles from China had resulted in a decline in cotton production and caused prices to rise.[104] Later, cheap Chinese imports from other parts of Asia, such as India, provided further competition for local products, as did Chinese manufactures that imitated native products but were cheaper.[105] Chinese immigration clearly had a significant impact on the economic changes experienced by Tagalogs in the Manila region, but it also offered opportunities for racial mixing and maintained open channels to China through which diseases could be introduced.

The number of Japanese settling in the Philippines was significantly smaller. In pre-Spanish times the Japanese used Manila as an entrepôt where they exchanged their own silver for Chinese silks and Southeast Asian sugar, spices, and deerskins; at the beginning of the seventeenth century they were also bringing provisions, such as wheat flour and salted meats, that could not be produced in the Philippines, as well as goods for sale in Mexico.[106] The number of Japanese ships trading in Manila was always small, rising from only one a year in the 1580s to about thirteen a year in the early seventeenth century.[107] Some of the traders remained in Manila and were assigned land outside the city walls at Dilao. By 1595 there were about 1,000

Japanese in the city.[108] Because of Japanese rebellions in 1606 and 1607 and the lack of profitability of trade with Japan, in 1609 the Spanish authorities tried to ban the Japanese from trading in the islands. But this proved ineffective, particularly after 1611, when the religious persecution of Christians in Japan provided added incentive for some to settle in the Philippines.[109] By the early 1620s their number had risen to between 2,000 and 3,000.[110] However, from the 1620s, fears that they might ally with the Dutch, together with strained relations with Japan, resulted in fewer Japanese arriving in the islands. Japan's increasing isolation culminated in the Tokugawa government's ban on Japanese travel overseas on pain of death and ultimately in 1639 to its self-imposed isolation.[111]

Demographic Trends in Manila and Tondo

Although Manila was the center of Spanish administration in the islands, demographic trends in the province of Manila and the jurisdiction of Tondo are difficult to track. This is partly due to the considerable population turnover. Mortality appears to have been high in the city of Manila, but high losses were partially disguised by immigration from other Philippine regions driven by migrants seeking to profit from trade, or escape tribute and labor demands, or from being assigned there as forced laborers. An additional problem for the eighteenth century is that the data available for total populations include an increasing but unspecified number of Chinese and Chinese *mestizos*. These problems add to the fundamental problem of the shortage of documentary evidence. Despite the concentration of Audiencia officials in Manila, there are relatively few secular accounts of the population in its jurisdiction. It is possible to glean a few figures from *cabildo* records, but even the fiscal accounts often refer only to those who paid tribute to the Crown. Another difficulty is that unlike many other Philippines regions that were entrusted to a single religious order, the administration of parishes in the jurisdiction of Manila and Tondo was split between the secular clergy and four missionary orders. Hence, although the bishops of Manila sometimes reported figures for the total population of the city and its hinterland, the information available from different groups of clergy differs in date and content, making it difficult to obtain a comprehensive view of the population at any one point in time.

The overall trend in the tributary population of Tondo suggests a pattern familiar in most Philippine regions, namely a decline to the mid-seventeenth century and thereafter an increase that accelerated toward the end of the eighteenth century. Spanish arrival brought military conflict that may have cost perhaps 1,000 lives, but pacification was not as prolonged as in some other regions. More disruptive were early demands for labor for the construction of the city and to provide food for its growing population. In the face of demands for labor and the alienation of their lands, local communities were increasingly unable to meet tribute levies and provide for their own subsistence. Food shortages and high food prices were exacerbated by epidemics that caused high mortality and reduced supply.

As described in chapter 2, in 1574 there was a widespread outbreak of smallpox that was said to have spared nobody and from which many died,[112] and in 1591 Manila and its surrounding region was also struck by "malignant and contagious fevers,"[113] which affected both Spaniards and Filipinos.[114] Further epidemics occurred in 1595 and 1599, with the latter spreading through the province as far as Antipolo and San Juan del Monte.[115] Little is known of their impact in Manila, but epidemics took a heavy toll of those recently established in Jesuit missions at Taytay and Antipolo.[116]

Epidemics were frequent in Manila in the sixteenth century, but subsequently there is only limited evidence for further outbreaks. Major epidemics of smallpox struck Manila in 1656 and 1705,[117] and the region was probably struck by the unspecified epidemic in 1668, which was widespread and caused high mortality.[118] Another two epidemics struck the region in 1786, one of "fever with vomiting and a cough" and the other of measles.[119] How far the local population was acquiring immunity to acute infections is difficult to gauge. The high mortality suggests that it was limited, but this may be related to the continuous arrival of migrants from other regions who had not experienced frequent exposure to acute infections and therefore had less immunity.

While epidemics took a periodic toll of the population, perhaps more significant in demographic terms were the unsanitary conditions that prevailed in the city. Conditions were worst for the poor, who were particularly affected by the shortage of fresh water.[120] Recognition of the health problems in the city can be seen in the early establishment of hospitals and the frequent correspondence with the Crown on the issue. Part of the concern was due to the high mortality among Spaniards, who quickly succumbed to tropical diseases and whose life expectancy in the islands was short.[121] In addition, the various expeditions and wars conducted in the early colonial period resulted in large numbers of sick and wounded. As early as 1574 the Crown ordered hospitals to be built for both Spaniards and Filipinos and by the end of the century Manila had four hospitals.[122]

As soon as the Spanish arrived in Manila, they established a makeshift hospital initially for Spanish soldiers, but following a fire in 1584 a new Hospital Real was built that received Crown support.[123] It was always short of funds and inadequate to deal with the large numbers of soldiers and settlers.[124] Meanwhile, in 1578 the Franciscans had established a hospital for native Filipinos, called Santa Ana. It was destroyed by a fire in 1583 and subsequently rebuilt. In the sixteenth century it normally housed about one hundred patients and had an extensive pharmacy.[125] After a fire in 1603 it was moved outside the city walls to near Dilao, where it became a hospital for patients with contagious diseases.[126] At the same time the Hospital de San Lázaro was established at Balete between Dilao and Malosac for those suffering from leprosy.[127]

On arrival in the Philippines in 1587, the Dominicans assumed responsibility for the Chinese population and immediately established a hospital in the Parian, known as the Hospital de San Pedro Mártir.[128] It was burned down several times and in 1598 was reconstructed at Binondo, where it became known as the Hospital de San Gabriel.[129] The hospital catered to both Chinese residents and traders[130] and in the 1630s was caring for 250 to 450 patients a year, of whom about 30 percent recovered.[131] By 1673, 24,000 Chinese had died in the hospital.[132] Finally, in 1597 the hospital of the Santa Hermandad de Misericordia was established, which provided medical care for African slaves and other groups that had previously been cared for by the Franciscans in the Hospital de Naturales.[133] When the latter was moved outside the city walls in 1603, the Santa Hermandad de Misericordia was given the former site. Here it constructed a hospital for patients with non-contagious diseases and also assumed responsibility for women who had also been cared for in the Hospital de Naturales.[134] In 1656 the hospital passed to the Order of San Juan de Dios, who operated it as a non-contagious hospital.[135]

Compared to European cities at the time, this level of medical care was exceptional, but the hospitals were still too few and ineffective given the health problems the colony faced with its continual wars and the unhealthy climate.[136] Also, the medical care provided was probably not very effective, though this largely reflected the state of medical knowledge of the time. At the end of the sixteenth century, the Hospital Real possessed a physician, apothecary, and surgeons, and there were three Franciscans who were of "great assistance to the sick both medically and spiritually."[137] Meanwhile, the hospital for native Filipinos, Santa Ana, was under three Franciscans and four lay brothers who acted as physicians, surgeons, and apothecaries and performed "marvelous cures in medicine and surgery." Although the Franciscans acted as "doctors," they mainly provided nursing care and used simple herbal remedies.[138] They practiced some phlebotomy and minor surgery, but mainly on soldiers. Apart from the Hospital Real there were few licensed medical practitioners in the Philippines, and even there posts were often vacant.[139]

Despite the negative impact of conflict, heavy demands for labor, and epidemics, the population of the Tondo region did not decline significantly during the late sixteenth century. This was primarily due to immigration, with forced laborers often remaining there once their duties had ended. In 1598 the tributary population of Tondo was about 6,700 or a total population of 26,800,[140] and in addition, by the end of the century the Jesuits had converted between 6,000 and 7,000 souls.[141] At that time small numbers still remained outside Spanish administration, and the region's total population in 1600 may be estimated at about 36,000, a decline of 16 percent from 43,000 in 1570.

During the first quarter of the seventeenth century the population of the Tondo region continued to decline. By 1630 there were only 5,031 *tributos*, including 781 vagabonds, in twenty-eight villages in the "costa de Manila."[142] Demands for labor and provisions were particularly high during the Hispano-Dutch War, and bureaucrats and priests alike recognized their negative demographic impact.[143] The shipyards were regarded as the "total ruin and death of the natives" due to the hard labor, poor food, and ill treatment to which workers were subjected, and because the drafts undermined subsistence. Flight to escape labor drafts was reflected in

Table 7.1 Demographic Characteristics of Jesuit Towns in Tondo, 1659 to 1755

	Married persons	Single persons	Male youths	Female youths	Boys	Girls	Total	Woman: child ratio	Percent of adults married	Number of males to every 100 females
1659	587	245	196	137	257	241	1,663	2.0	71	120
1675	722	418	169	104	272	292	1,977	1.47	63	111
1696	1,470	589	215	184	295	320	3,073	0.98	71	101
1737	2,264	976	439	348	1,207	1,092	6,326	1.90	70	114
1743	2,466	1,331	325	431	1,182	985	6,720	1.54	65	106
1755	2,414	1,600	336	459	1,435	1,140	7,384	1.68	60	111

Sources: ARSI Phil 2 I fols. 412–415, II fols. 314–317, Phil 14 fols. 106–117 Catologus christianorum quos colit societas in Philippinis.
Note: Figures exclude manicipia (slaves) whose sex and status are not recorded.

increasing numbers of vagabonds, who were likened to the gypsies of Spain.[144] *Polo* demands did not cease with the end of the Hispano-Dutch War since workers were still required to construct galleons and extract wood for various types of construction, including the repair of the city's walls and buildings. Nevertheless, during the second half of the century the tributary population grew to 7,224 in 1700, an increase of 0.52 percent per annum from 1630. It is possible that the increase was greater than this since in the 1740s it was supposedly an "ancient custom" in the provinces contiguous to Manila to exclude from tribute lists those who lived outside their natal communities who were registered as *vagamundos*.[145] When these were included under a new form of enumeration in the 1740s, the number of tributaries increased by 65 percent. It is not clear how far back the "ancient custom" dated, but some allowance should be made for those outside administration. Judging by the numbers later brought under Jesuit and Franciscan control, they may be estimated at about 3,000 souls. This would suggest a total population of 32,000 in 1700.

Ineffective registration probably accounted for the fall in the number of registered *tributos* in Tondo to 6,293.5 in 1735, but by 1750 the number had risen significantly to 13,914.[146] Two factors may have contributed significantly to this increase: increased missionary activity, notably by the Franciscans and Jesuits, and the new method of accounting. The numbers under the Franciscans rose from about 2,800 souls in 1649 to 7,900 in 1735,[147] and those under the Jesuits from 1,663 souls in 1659 to 7,384 in 1755.[148] The Jesuit towns had a relatively high ratio of men to women and a low woman-to-child ratio, which suggests that their populations were failing to replace themselves by natural increase (Table 7.1).[149] The two missionary orders may have been incorporating migrants from areas close to the city and dockyards who were attempting to escape the *polo*. In the second half of the eighteenth century, the parishes they administered grew rapidly. Between 1735 and 1798 the five Franciscan parishes grew from 7,900 to 15,791 *almas*.[150] Meanwhile, between 1760 to 1818 those parishes administered by the Augustinians experienced nearly a threefold increase from 25,808 to 73,296 *almas*.[151]

The rapid expansion in the registered population in the late eighteenth century was almost certainly due in part to more effective administration. Following the English invasion in 1762 and the Silang insurrection in Pangasinan, the zealous *fiscal* of the Audiencia, Francisco Leandro Viana, sought to improve defense by raising revenue through an overhaul of the tribute system. More concerted efforts were made to settle Filipinos "under the bells," and parish priests and *alcaldes mayores* rather than *cabezas de barangay*, who he claimed each hid ten *tributarios*, became responsible for compiling lists of tributaries.[152] It is not known how much of the increase can be attributed to this change of administration, but it was not wholly effective and there were other factors at work. By the early nineteenth century, baptisms far exceeded the number of burials so that by then the population was growing through natural increase as well as through immigration and more effective registration. In 1805 the total population, including all ethnic groups, in all parishes in Tondo was about 110,000 (Table 7.2).

TABLE 7.2 Total Populations of Manila and Tondo about 1805

Town	Ecclesiastical administration	Figures given in documentary source	Estimated total population
Tondo	Augustinian	Over 2,000 *tributos enteros*	10,000
Malate	Augustinian	5,607 *almas*	5,607
Parañaque	Augustinian	5,191 *almas*	5,191
Tambobong	Augustinian	15,179 *almas*	15,179
Pasig	Augustinian	15,111 *almas*	15,111
Taguig[1]	Augustinian	Not given	7,550
Las Pinas	Augustinian Recollect	663 *almas*	663
Binondo	Secular	Over 2,000 *tributos enteros*	10,000
San Gabriel[2]	Secular	807 *tributantes* Sangleyes, 129 *personas de naturales y mestizos*	2,147
Santa Cruz	Secular	1,600 *tributos*	8,000
Quiapo	Secular	3,737 *almas*	3,737
San Pedro Makati	Secular	1,200 *almas*	1,200
Sampaloc*	Franciscan	2,555 *almas*	2,555
San Miguel*	Franciscan	1,861 *almas*	1,861
Santa Ana*	Franciscan	4,151 *almas*	4,151
Dilao*	Franciscan	5,237 *almas*	5,237
Pandacan*	Franciscan	1,987 *almas*	1,987
Marikina	Secular – ex Jesuit	1,989 *almas*	1,989
San Mateo	Secular – ex Jesuit	3,214 *almas*	3,214
Cainta	Secular – ex Jesuit	1,345 *almas*	1,345
Taytay	Secular – ex Jesuit	2,472 *almas*	2,472
Antipolo	Secular – ex Jesuit	1,152 *almas*	1,152
Angono	Secular	Over 900 *almas*	Over 900
TOTAL			111,248

Sources: AAM Santa Visita de las Iglesias 9a (1751–1817) Testimonio de la visita diocesana . . . Juan Antonio Zulaybar 1805.

*1798 PNA Patronatos 1720–1799 Resumen del estado que actualmente tiene la provincia de San Gregorio 4 July 1798.

Notes:

[1] Figure for Taguig estimated at half that of Pasig. This proportion was consistent in 1760 and 1815 (NL Ayer MS 1449 (Box) Razón de los pueblos . . . Pedro de Velasco, 16 Apr. 1760; AUST Libro 229 no.1 Estatística [*sic*] de las islas Filipinas 1815).

[2] Total calculated by dividing 807 *tributantes* by two to obtain the number of *tributos* and multiplying by five to estimate the total Sangley population. 129 were then added to this figure.

While the total population grew significantly in the second half of the eighteenth century, the native tributary population of the Manila region remained virtually the same at about 13,000 *tributos*.[153] Given the expansion of the population, the number of *tributos* may have been underestimated, but more likely the growth in the native population was retarded by the parallel increase in the *mestizo* population, most of which was Chinese *mestizo*. Racial mixing was encouraged by the presence of foreign traders and immigrants "from all four parts of the world,"[154] and Father San Antonio described the province as containing "the confusion of Babylon."[155] While the city of Manila was the prime focus of foreign immigration, since the Chinese were also involved in agricultural production, the opportunities for racial mixing extended beyond the city. By the end of eighteenth century Chinese *mestizos* accounted for about 20 percent of Tondo's tributary population.[156] An anonymous account from about 1825 recorded that the population of Manila was between 115,000 and 120,000, of whom between 2,500 and 3,000 were whites, 25,000 to 30,000 Chinese *mestizos*, 10,000 to 12,000 Chinese residents and transients, and 70,000 to 75,000 "indios naturales."[157] It is not unreasonable to suggest that the native Filipino population in 1800 may have been about 70,000. If the figure of 32,000 for 1700 included those who resided outside their natal communities, then the increase during the eighteenth century was about 0.78 percent per annum. However, it would be significantly lower if the total population in 1700 were nearer 50,000. Hence, although the population of the Manila region grew in the eighteenth century, the increase was not on the scale experienced in some other regions, such as Ilocos, Pampanga, and southwest Luzon.

CHAPTER 8

Southwest Luzon

For the purposes of this study, southwest Luzon comprises the administrative jurisdictions of Laguna de Bay and Cavite, together with regions on the south coast variously known as Balayan, Bonbón, Batangas, Calilaya, and Tayabas, as well as the island of Mindoro.[1] The history of southwest Luzon was closely tied to that of Manila. The friar estates that developed in the west of the region became major suppliers of provisions for the city and gave it a distinct economic and social structure. Also located in the west were the shipbuilding industry and naval dockyards at Cavite. Elsewhere the imprint of colonial rule was weaker. Indeed, remoter parts of the region emerged as zones of refuge for large numbers of vagabonds, whose activities earned them a reputation for banditry. Mindoro was a significant trading center in pre-Spanish times, but it was soon eclipsed by the growth of Manila, although beeswax and honey remained significant items of trade throughout the colonial period.[2] Gold deposits were found in Mindoro and gold figured among early Spanish exactions, but there is no evidence that the deposits were worked in colonial times.[3] Mindoro therefore became an economic backwater where the missionary orders worked intermittently. Moro raids from Sulu and Mindanao occasionally afflicted the southern coast, Cavite, and Mindoro, but they were not as frequent as in the Visayas.

Spanish contacts with the region were initiated by Juan de Salcedo early in 1570 when on an exploratory expedition from Panay he touched the island of Ilin, sacked the town of Mamburao in Mindoro, and destroyed some settlements on the island of Lubang.[4] The expedition that returned in May 1570 under Martín de Goiti also explored Mindoro and had skirmishes with Filipinos in the province of Taal.[5] Landing at Cavite, this expedition was well-received because the local inhabitants hoped to gain Spanish support against Raja Soliman. Nevertheless, a permanent settlement was not established at that time. It was only after the founding of Manila and the defeat of the Moro strongholds at Taytay and Cainta that Juan de Salcedo was ordered by Legazpi to proceed with the pacification of Laguna de Bay. Accompanied by the Augustinian father Alonso de Alvarado, he headed for Bay, which was the largest settlement in the region, and, having persuaded the inhabitants to recognize Spanish authority, moved on with a small contingent to pacify hostile communities in the hills. Here it was claimed he brought more than two hundred villages under Spanish rule without shedding a drop of blood.[6] Prior to pacification, in January 1571 the coastal towns between Manila and Cavite, including Cavite itself, had been made tributary to the Crown, and Martín de Goiti had assigned 8,000 tributaries in Laguna de Bay and the River Bonbón.[7] In November a further eleven *encomiendas* were distributed, and the following year several others were assigned. In total more than 130 villages were allocated.

Once pacification had been achieved, the religious orders rapidly established a permanent presence in Laguna de Bay. An Augustinian father accompanied Juan de Salcedo on his expedition in 1571, and some attempts were made to suppress devil worship and sacrifice in the vicinity of Mahayhay, Lilio, and Nagcarlan before the Augustinians established a monastery at Bay in 1578.[8] It was apparently a populous town whose inhabitants produced silk and cotton stockings.[9] The Augustinians also founded residences at San Pablo de los Montes and Los Baños in 1586 and 1602 respectively.[10] By then the Franciscans had established a monastery and hospital for Spaniards at Los Baños and were exploiting its medicinal waters.[11] They had arrived in Laguna de Bay in 1578 and had immediately begun to learn Tagalog.[12] By the 1590s they had established residences at Pila, Lumban, Mahayhay, Nagcarlan, Panguil, Paete, Siniloan, and Morón, where they were ministering to 7,620 *tributos* and 22,903 Christians.[13] In fact, southwest Luzon became a predominantly Franciscan province. The Augustinians retained only two residences at Bay and San Pablo, which in 1610 together had 3,000 *tributos* and 9,000 "indios de confesión."[14] However, they founded others in the province of Taal at Batangas, Tabuco, Tanauan, and Lipa (San Sebastián), where in 1610 they were administering 4,100 *tributos* or 12,300 "indios."[15] Meanwhile, early Franciscan work in the province of Cavite was later assumed by the Jesuits, who founded a monastery at Silang in 1599.[16]

Southwest Luzon in 1570

Geographically, southwest Luzon is an extension of the sedimentary basin that forms the Central Luzon Plain (Map 8.1). The northern part of the region comprises the extensive Laguna de Bay that is fringed by alluvial plains. To the south and west the landscape is more volcanic, with some volcanoes, such as Mount Banahao, reaching over 7,000 feet.[17] Only short rivers flow to the south coast, where there are only small stretches of coastal plain. Cultivation is favored in southwest Luzon because the soils, being either alluvial deposits or derived from volcanic materials, are fertile and the dry season is shorter and less severe than in other regions. Rainfall is relatively heavy, varying from 70 inches a year to the west of Laguna de Bay to more than 100 inches in the Eastern Cordillera. Although the fringes of Laguna de Bay may be inundated during the rainy season, the soils are generally light and well-drained. In contrast, in Mindoro, lowlands suitable for cultivation are limited and most of the island consists of densely forested mountains that rise to about 8,200 feet.

The Tagalog inhabitants of southwest Luzon were farmers and fishers. It is thought that in pre-Spanish times, permanent wet-rice cultivation was practiced

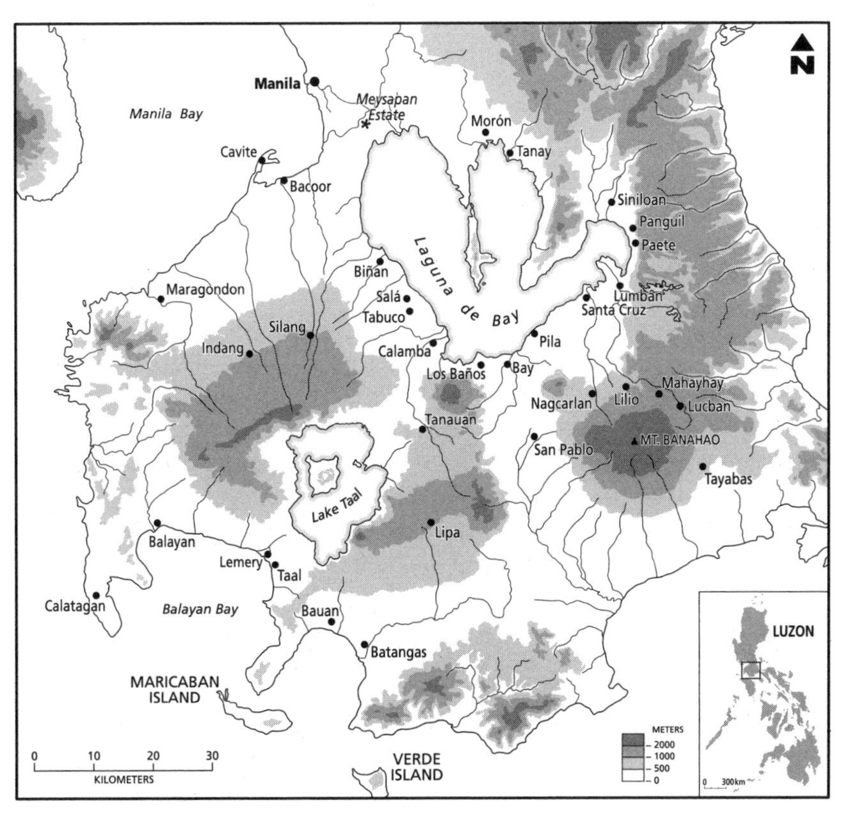

Map 8.1. Southwest Luzon

around Manila Bay to the north of Cavite and on the western shores of Laguna de Bay, while elsewhere a form of shifting cultivation dominated.[18] In the irrigated areas, *barangays* claimed exclusive control of the land, which the *datu* allocated to its members, whereas in upland areas any *barangay* member could use the land. As in the Visayas, a *barangay* probably claimed as much land as it could exploit and defend; in other words ownership derived from use of the land, and wooded areas that provided game and firewood were considered communal property. *Datus* appear to have had privileged access to certain lands and fisheries, and they also controlled markets. *Datus* could also alienate land either on behalf of the community or for private gain. For example, in the 1580s the *datu* of Pila in Laguna de Bay purchased land from another *datu* with gold and rented it out for one hundred *gantas* of rice a year.[19] The extent of private land ownership in pre-Spanish times is unclear, but sources generally suggest that most land was communally owned or worked under usufruct rights.[20]

Apart from rice, a wide variety of tropical fruits and palms were cultivated, and substantial quantities of cotton were produced, especially in Batangas.[21] Early accounts recorded the cultivation of *camotes* (sweet potatoes) (*Ipomoea batatas* (L.) Poir), which as an Amerindian crop must have been adopted rapidly after Spanish conquest.[22] Root crops were widely grown and were particularly important in times of shortage. While the inhabitants cultivated a wide variety of crops, it is clear that fish was a major component of their diets. Fishing was particularly important on the coast and around Laguna de Bay and Lake Taal, but freshwater fish were also exploited in streams, pools, and rice fields.[23] Given the importance of fishing, settlements were located on rivers and coastal plains, especially southeast of Manila and in and around Laguna de Bay, and the bays of Batangas and Tayabas on the south coast.[24] The presence of Chinese, Vietnamese, and Siamese pottery in burials at Calatagan in Batangas also indicates extensive trading contacts with Asia just prior to Spanish arrival. Indeed, Robert Fox suggests that direct Chinese trade may have centered at Balong Bato in Calatagan and that trade and intensive cultivation may have underpinned high population densities there.[25]

Native society in this region was described in detail by a number of contemporary observers.[26] Particularly noteworthy for southwest Luzon are the accounts of Juan de Plasencia, a Franciscan missionary who resided at Nagcarlan and had twelve years' experience in the region. He was regarded as particularly knowledgeable in the Tagalog language and was commissioned by the Franciscan order to compile a Tagalog grammar and dictionary and to translate the Christian doctrine into Tagalog.[27] Unfortunately, early contemporary accounts are sometimes contradictory and difficult to interpret because they often describe native society in terms of the framework of the Spanish "estate" system, where social status was based on Roman law and European feudalism. Hence they generally distinguished three social groups—the rulers, the ruled, and slaves—within which a number of subgroups were often identified. The following account will use these social categories, but it is recognized that they have their limitations in reflecting Tagalog social structure.[28]

Tagalog social organization and structure differed in detail from that found in the Visayas and Pampanga, but it was similar in its lack of an overarching political structure. First observations suggested that each village had its leader and there were very few whose power extended over two or three villages.[29] The basic unit of political and social organization was the *barangay*, whose composition was based on kinship, friendship, and common interest and might comprise a community of thirty to one hundred households. Relations between *barangays* were often hostile and conflict could break out over minor issues. Conflict occurred more frequently between kin groups of different communities than between whole communities.[30] Legazpi observed that it was quite common that in two neighboring villages half would be at peace and the other half at war.[31] Skeletal evidence for conflict and head taking has been found in burial excavations at Calatagan.[32] The authority of leaders or *datus*, referred to by the Spanish as *principales*, was based on their ability to command popular support through demonstrated success in raiding, trading, and regulating outside contacts. In their positions they also administered justice, though this was not their exclusive preserve, and they were involved in many other social and religious activities. Nevertheless, their authority appears to have derived essentially from their military prowess and increasingly from their economic status that was based, at least in part, on the number of slaves they owned. When the Spanish arrived, some chiefs owned 100, 200, and 300 slaves.[33] According to Legazpi, "he who has the most slaves and is most powerful can obtain anything he wishes."[34] There is no evidence to suggest that the social structure was defined by reference to a natural or cosmological order.[35] Thus the position of *datu* ultimately depended on his ability to command respect, so that a non-elite person could assume the post through popular support, though in practice the position was often inherited. The *datu* and his family comprised the village elite or *maginoo*.

In acknowledgment of a *datu's* superior status, commoners rendered a limited amount of goods and labor, such as constructing his house, working his fields, and accompanying him on military and trading expeditions.[36] Two kinds of commoners were distinguished.[37] First, there were *timawa*, who were defined by the fact that they were not slaves or members of the elite. Second there were *maharlikas*, who are noted only in Laguna. Technically they were less free than *timawa* since they could only transfer their allegiance when they married or through the payment of a fee. However, they were viewed as being of higher status than other commoners and were referred to by Plasencia as "hidalgos."[38] The origin of *maharlikas* is unknown, but they may have been a military aristocracy who had experienced a fall in status.[39] At the time the Spanish arrived they appear to have been reduced to renting land from *datus*.

Tagalog society also possessed serfs (*aliping namamahay*) and slaves (*aliping sagigilid*). Often the Spanish erroneously referred to both groups as slaves. The serfs lived by themselves, owned their own property, and had access to land controlled by the *barangay*, but they had to pay a proportion of the harvest as a form of tribute. In addition they were required to work the land of their masters and provide other services without pay. The level of "tribute" and services they rendered was highly variable and reflected their level of indebtedness.[40] Although Plasencia regarded the serfs as commoners rather than slaves, other Spaniards wishing to assume control of native labor labeled them as slaves. The *aliping sagigilid* or "hearth slaves," on the other hand, were inherited, acquired in war, obtained as payment for crimes, or became slaves through falling into debt.[41] They did not own property but belonged to their master's household and could be bought and sold. Conditions for slaves were highly variable. Legazpi noted that slaves were not under great subjection but only served their masters under certain conditions and "when and how they pleased."[42] Also, they might change their status by marriage or buying their freedom; Tagalog society was characterized by a fairly high level of social mobility.

Although many questions remain concerning the origin, status, and role of different social groups, it would appear that Tagalog society was in the process of differentiation, with two types of both commoners and slaves being distinguished. Also, the services rendered by commoners appear to have been more extensive than in other regions. William Henry Scott suggests that these changes in Tagalog society reflected the growing intensification of agricultural production, a decline of slave raiding, and an increase in the power of native elites.[43]

Of particular relevance to understanding pre-Spanish Tagalog demography are their marriages and birth practices, which in certain aspects differed significantly from those of Visayans. In general, Tagalog practices and beliefs functioned to promote large families, whereas in the Visayas small families were favored. Thus Tagalogs were described as more "depraved in matters of the flesh and indulge in it more than Visayans."[44] As in the Visayas, bridewealth was paid to the bride's parents, but it might be returned in the case of divorce unless the husband was responsible for the breakdown of the marriage.[45] The Boxer Codex suggests that a person could marry anyone except a brother or sister.[46] Polygamy was not practiced, but Tagalog men could have concubines, and sexual relations with a prospective wife's relatives were common.[47] As in Visayan society, marriages were contracted at an early date. In the eighteenth century the French traveler Monsieur de Pagès noted that his hostess in Manila had entered her "matrimonial career" at the age of thirteen.[48] Antonio de Morga also observed that from their earliest years girls and boys had sexual relations and mixed freely with little modesty. As in the Visayas, there were specialists whose occupation was to take the virginity of women because virginity was thought to be an impediment to marriage. However, it was considered dishonorable for an unmarried woman to bear children, and if an unmarried woman became pregnant infanticide was practiced.[49] However, infanticide was not such a routine practice as in the Visayas, since Tagalogs considered it desirable to have large families. Neither did they use penis inserts. The exception were some groups in the highlands around Laguna de Bay, where they inserted small balls of tar the size of chickpeas under the skin of the penis.[50] That large families were favored is seen in superstitions that encouraged fertility and the survival of infants. For example, women who wished to become pregnant raised pigs that were fed with the best foods, and once the child was born they abstained from milling rice under the houses because it was thought that if the rice fell from the mortar and was subsequently consumed by a chicken, the infant would die.[51] However, multiple births were considered undesirable and so pregnant women abstained from eating any foods that were joined together, such as two bananas.[52] Prayers were said for successful childbirth and it was thought that any woman or child who died in childbirth would be punished in the afterlife.[53] Since children were highly valued, they were pampered, indulged, and rarely punished.[54]

When the Spanish first arrived in Mindoro they made a clear distinction between the inhabitants of the ports and coastal towns, whom they referred to as "Moros," and those who lived inland, whom they called "chichimecos" after the hostile nomadic hunter-gatherer groups the Spanish encountered in northern Mexico. The town of Mindoro, which may have been located at Minolo about three miles to the northwest of Puerto Galera,[55] was referred to as an "excellent though poorly sheltered seaport" and was heavily defended.[56] Its port was one of a small number in the Philippines that were frequented by Chinese and other Southeast Asian traders. Contacts with China dated back to the tenth century when traders from Ma-yi,

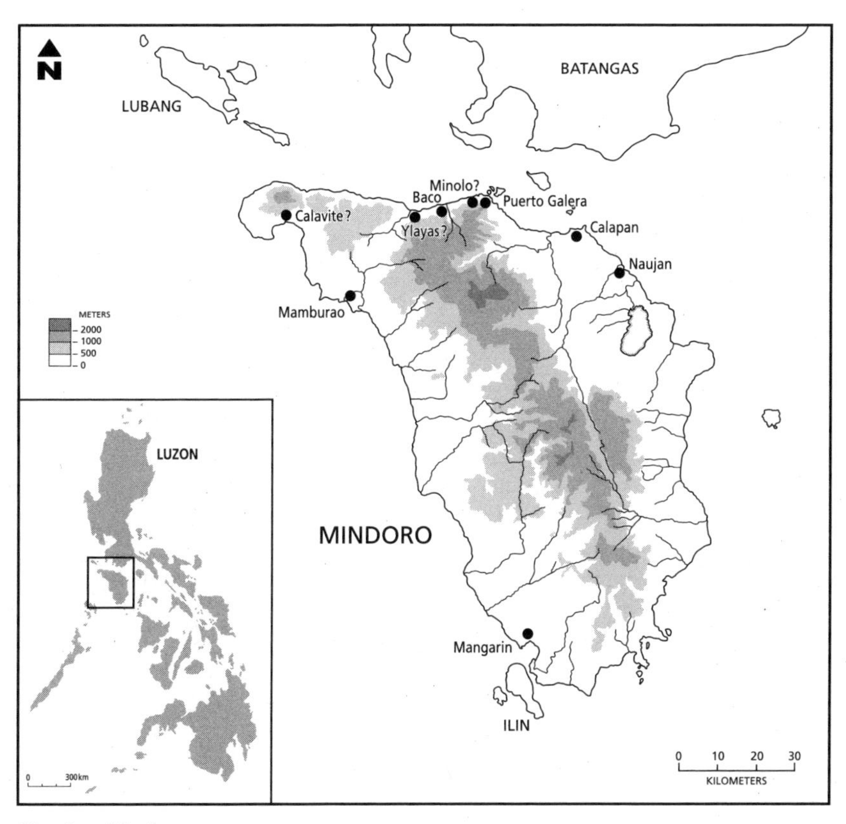

Map 8.2. Mindoro

probably northern Mindoro, were sailing to China; subsequently Sung trading vessels commonly visited the island from whence their merchandise was distributed throughout the islands.[57] Goiti's expedition in 1570 attacked two Chinese vessels trading silks and porcelain in Mindoro. These items, together with iron and copper, figured among the goods imported, in return for which the traders obtained beeswax, tortoiseshell, kapok, betel, and textiles.[58]

In colonial times the inhabitants of interior Mindoro were generally referred to as Mangyans, though some mention was made of Negritos, who are found mainly in the north of the island.[59] The Mangyans comprise a number of distinct cultural-linguistic groups, some of which are of mixed ethnic origin resulting from contact with Tagalogs or Visayans.[60] Spanish accounts generally describe them as nomadic and subsisting on wild roots, fruits, and some boiled rice.[61] Population density among the Mangyans would have been low. In the early twentieth century, infanticide was widely practiced, with 15 to 25 percent of infants being killed at birth. Also, early marriage, often at age twelve, thirteen, or fourteen for girls, resulted in low birth weights and high infant mortality.[62] Not all groups in Mindoro were nomadic. The

Hanunóo in the south of the island were swidden cultivators who lived in permanent, scattered settlements of five or six nuclear family households.[63] Here too, population density would have been low since many women died in childbirth, infant mortality was high, and few survived to age fifty.[64] Today population density among the Hanunóo averages only about ten persons per square kilometer, or about seven per square mile.

The Population of Southwest Luzon in 1570

Numerical estimates of the population of southwest Luzon are not available until a decade after conquest, but it is clear from early accounts that most of the region was densely settled in pre-Spanish times, particularly the coast of Manila Bay and the margins of Lake Taal and Laguna de Bay. In the 1580s the *alcaldía mayor* of Laguna de Bay was regarded as one of the most important in the Philippines and demographically equivalent to Pampanga in possessing some 30,000 "indios"; a further 20,000 were reputedly living in the provinces of Bonbón, Balayan, and Mindoro together.[65] About the same time, Miguel de Loarca estimated that *encomiendas* in southwest Luzon contained 18,400 men, though his figure did not include all the coastal settlements south of Manila.[66] In the late 1580s there were between 1,700 and 1,850 tributaries on the coast and in Cavite, though these numbers may have included some towns that fell under the jurisdiction of Tondo.[67] Of the total of 18,400 men, about half were in Laguna de Bay, while the three *encomiendas* of Balayan, Bonbón, and Batangas had total of 5,000 men and Calilaya 3,650.[68] Slightly more tributaries, some 23,170, were recorded in southwest Luzon in 1591, with the balance shifting from Laguna to regions to the south,[69] perhaps due to migration to escape tribute and labor demands. Communities in southwest Luzon were rapidly brought under Spanish administration with little bloodshed so that by the early seventeenth century *infieles* were only noted around Siniloan.[70] The figures appearing in official reports, although postdating the initial arrival of Spaniards, are therefore likely to have been a reasonable reflection of the numbers that existed in 1570. Taking into account the less disruptive impact of conquest and the number of tributaries registered at the end of the sixteenth century, the tributary population in 1570 was probably about 30,000, though it may have been nearer 40,000 as one account suggests.

The population of coastal Mindoro was once quite considerable. With more than 400 houses, the town of Mindoro itself was one of the largest in the Philippines.[71] Toward the end of the sixteenth century it possessed between 200 and 300 *tributos*.[72] An anonymous account in 1572 reported that most people thought that the whole island possessed only 8,000 "hombres," but the author, having been there, was sure there were 15,000.[73] In 1588 there were said to be 5,000 households in the island, of which only 2,000 had been pacified and were paying tribute, while there were another 500 *tributantes* in Lubang.[74] The rest were heathen. In the 1630s Mangyans in the interior mountains numbered more than 6,000 *almas*, though this was after some inhabitants had begun to move inland.[75] The figure of 15,000 men and hence a total population of 60,000 would therefore seem to be too high, particularly given that in the 1580s there were 20,000 "indios" in Bonbón, Balayan, and Mindoro together.[76] Given that initial skirmishes with the Spanish resulted in some casualties, but that the interior was not well-known, the potential tributary population might be estimated at about 10,000.

The Development of Friar Estates

In the colonial period the economy of southwest Luzon focused on supplying provisions and labor for Manila and the naval dockyard and port at Cavite. Tribute levies, *vandalas*, and *polos* became heavy burdens, particularly during the Hispano-Dutch War. Meanwhile conditions in rural areas deteriorated as the development of estates undermined native production and altered labor relations. Hence, the impact of colonial rule was sharply felt, particularly in the early seventeenth century.

Initially the Spanish secured food supplies through the tribute system, but this failed to satisfy the growing demand, and at the end of the sixteenth century food shortages were commonly being experienced in Manila. As a result, *alcaldes mayores* from surrounding regions were ordered to supply 300 egg-laying hens, 2,000 eggs, and as many pigs as necessary each month, with Laguna de Bay supplying them in September and October and Balayan and Mindoro in November and December.[77] The burden imposed by such levies and tribute demands was often increased by fugitivism and corruption. When in 1689 a *cédula* was issued against excessive exactions by *alcaldes mayores*, the *alcalde mayor* of Laguna de Bay was singled out for particular criticism and described as having exacted even the rice they had to sow.[78] In this instance the blame was placed at the door of the zealous governor who, seeing that communities in Cavite and Laguna were failing to meet tribute demands because of the large number of absentees, had required the *alcalde mayor* to impose an additional levy where producers were paid only half the market price for their produce.[79] It was noted that in Silang, 120 of the 227.5 registered tributaries were absent and that many other villages recorded 70, 80, or more absentees. However, this was not an isolated instance. Excessive exactions were a major source of complaint throughout the seventeenth century and did much to destabilize communities within the region.[80]

While such levies were clearly critical to the survival of the colony, provisions were increasingly produced commercially on estates, many of which were owned by the religious orders. The processes by which the missionary orders acquired land have been outlined in chapter 3. Dennis Roth estimates that during the greater part of the colonial period the religious orders controlled about 40 percent of the land in the four Tagalog provinces of Bulacan, Tondo, Cavite, and Laguna de Bay. In the last two regions most of the land appears to have been acquired from Spanish rather than Filipino owners. These haciendas were so extensive that they formed compact contiguous blocks that encompassed existing Tagalog towns. The Dominicans possessed six of the eleven large estates in Cavite and Laguna de Bay, while the Augustinians and Augustinian Recollects owned the rest.[81] Large estates were not developed on the same scale in other parts of southwest Luzon, but the Jesuits owned some lands in Batangas.[82]

In order to make their haciendas viable, the religious orders needed labor. First, they tried to encourage Filipinos to become tenants on their estates by offering them cash advances that were repayable at harvest. However, these *inquilinos* were subject to the *polo* and therefore were not available for labor throughout the year. As described in chapter 3, estate owners came to depend on the government to support exemptions from the *polo* for those who worked on estates, who were known as *casas de reservas*. In the early seventeenth century the number of exemptions allocated to each estate ranged from 15 to 40, but over time the religious orders negotiated larger numbers. For example, in the 1620s the number ceded to the Dominican hacienda of Biñan was between 20 and 30, but by 1731 it had risen to 213.[83] Later, many larger haciendas were given exemptions for all those they employed and they became totally dependent on this system of labor.[84] Hence by 1752 the same hacienda of Biñan was housing 1,639 Filipinos and 256 Chinese

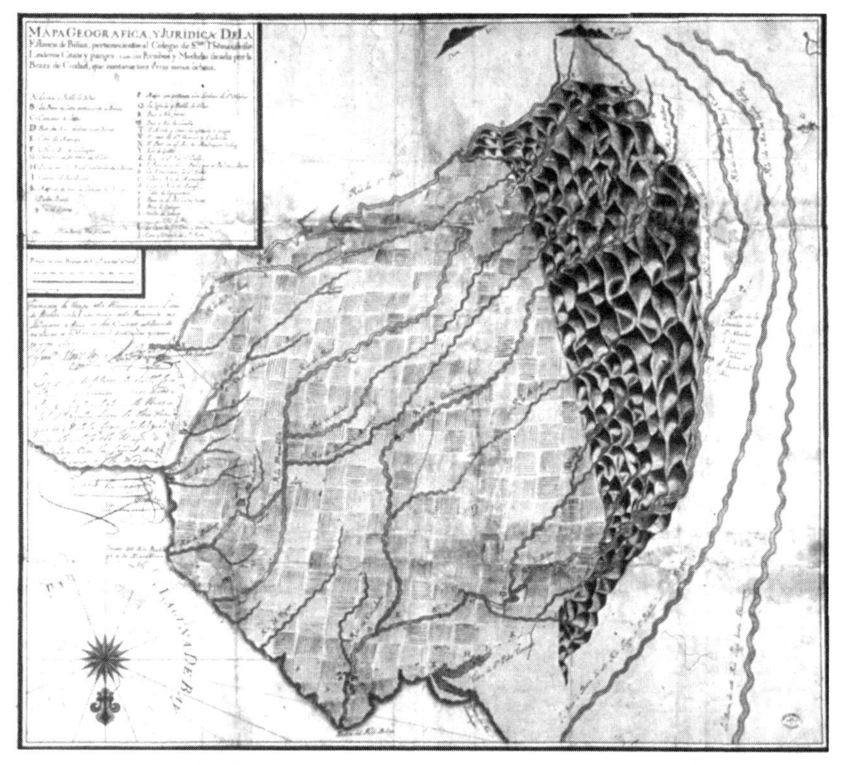

Figure 8.1. Hacienda of Biñan. AGI Mapas y Planos Filpinas 30(1) Mapa geográfica y juridical de la estancia de Biñan 1743.

mestizos.[85] Even though work on haciendas was onerous and not well-remunerated, it was more attractive than being drafted to serve as forced laborers in cutting wood or shipbuilding.[86] While individuals may have benefited from this system, it meant that the burden of meeting *polo* and *vandala* demands fell on those who remained in their natal communities.[87]

As the friar estates developed, they effectively displaced the native population from its communal lands to become tenant farmers on estates or fugitives in the towns or the interior. The process was accelerated in the hinterland of Manila, where land was fertile and provisions were in high demand. In pre-Spanish times social cohesion was largely based on mutual interest and respect. As the ability of native leaders to defend community interests was compromised and their control over slaves was weakened by legislation, their power and prestige declined. Many Tagalogs sought alternative lifestyles and social allegiances. Southwest Luzon gained a reputation for lawlessness and rebellion as many landless persons turned to crime[88] and as rural poverty drove many to seek restitution of their lands and the improvement of conditions on the estates.[89] The most important revolt, which began on the Augustinian estate of Meysapan in 1745, involved 6,000 armed men in Cavite, Laguna de Bay, Tondo, and Bulacan.

Some of those who became agricultural tenants and laborers were Chinese or Chinese *mestizos*. The religious orders considered the Chinese to be better workers than Filipinos and recruited them as *casas de reservas*.[90] Other Chinese were also forced by the Spanish authorities to work as agricultural laborers. In 1639 a major revolt broke out among some Chinese assigned to work in rice production at Calamba. The revolt began with the assassination of a number of Spaniards, including the *alcalde mayor* of Laguna de Bay. In response, the authorities executed some 300 Chinese in Cavite, which provoked a general uprising that spread to Tondo, Pampanga, Bulacan, and Batangas. About 1,300 were killed in the port of Cavite alone and a further 450 at Silang and Maragondon.[91] Altogether about 22,000 to 24,000 died, while nearly 8,000 surrendered and remained. Continuing distrust of the Chinese resulted in orders for their expulsion in 1755 and 1766, after which Chinese *mestizos* acted as middlemen between peasant cultivators and merchants in Manila.[92] In 1792 about 20 percent of the registered Chinese *mestizos* of the Philippines were in Cavite and Laguna de Bay.[93]

Shipbuilding, *Polos*, and Fugitivism

The alienation of native lands was not the only cause of deteriorating rural conditions. Another destabilizing force was the demand for labor in the shipyards both for the construction of ships and the extraction of timber. The Cavite peninsula shelters a spacious harbor that was used as a port from beginning of the colonial period. Although overshadowed by Manila as a port of trade, it became one of the country's main shipbuilding and naval centers.[94] Manila galleons were built and fitted out in Cavite, as were naval vessels used in military campaigns. For its defense,

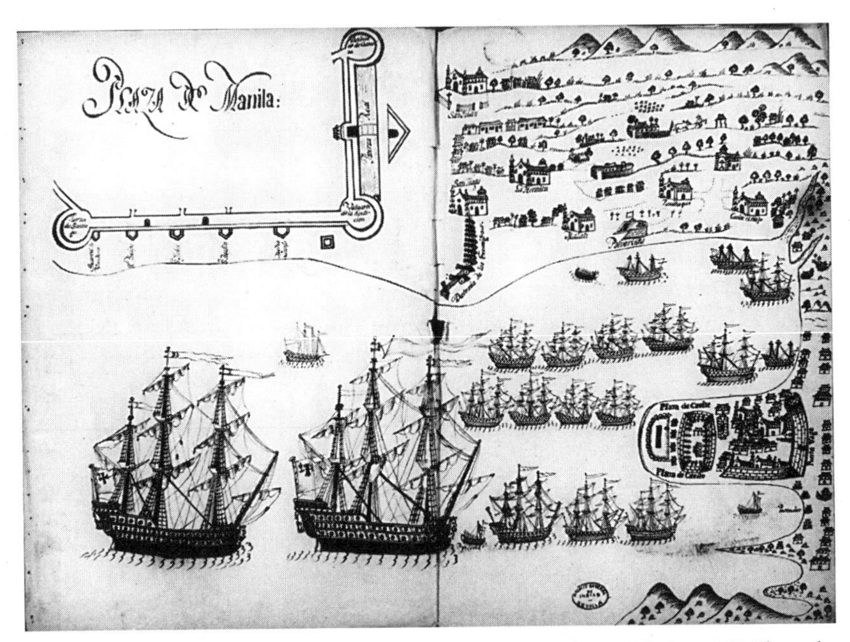

FIGURE 8.2. Manila Bay and Cavite in 1764. AGI Mapas y Planos Filipinas 153 Plano de la Bahia de Manila con la 'plaza de Manila', la 'plaza de Cavite', y los alrededores y la situación del enemigo inglés por mar y tierra 1764.

Fort San Felipe was constructed in 1610.[95] The port, fort, and shipbuilding industry employed a large number of workers from diverse backgrounds, while food and lodging were required for many transient officials, priests, traders, and sailors.[96] In 1622 the parish priest of Cavite was ministering not only to 2,400 Filipinos and slaves, who were presumably working in the shipyard or as sailors, but also to 430 Spaniards, including 50 soldiers stationed in the fort and 50 women, as well as 400 persons of diverse nationalities including some Japanese.[97] As time went on, the town attracted many footloose people, and in 1688 a new parish was established at San Roque.[98] A detailed account of the 347 people who were employed in the "rivera de Cavite" as shipwrights, foundry workers, spinners, and dyers indicates that two-thirds came from outside Cavite, mostly from Pampanga.

Labor demands for the construction and repair of galleons, which included the extraction of timber, were largely met through the *polo*. The wages paid to shipyard workers were paid partially in kind. Carpenters, turners, smiths, and rope makers were paid between twenty and thirty *gantas* of rice a month and four reals for fish; overseers received several times these amounts.[99] However, a reform of wages and rations in 1635 shifted the balance toward wages, with workers receiving an annual salary of between forty-eight and sixty pesos and only fifteen *gantas* of rice a month.[100] Work in the shipyards involved long hours of arduous work on skimpy rations. The rigging was made in surrounding villages, for which workers were given a ration and eight reals a month. This work was regarded as equally hard labor.[101] The most arduous and poorly paid work was the extraction of timber. In 1619 the wages paid to those involved in cutting wood were only seven or eight reals a month and a ration of half a *celemín* of rice, whereas more skilled workers received ten to twelve reals a month.[102] At that time it was judged that five pesos a month were needed to support a family.

The construction of individual ships required the mobilization of several thousand workers. This became more difficult as the population declined and others fled.[103] In 1618 a naval officer, Sebastián de Pineda, estimated that 1,400 were needed to prepare a fleet, but only 200 could be mustered since 600 had been captured or killed by Moros and others had died of hard labor or fled. On other occasions, the friars, whether to protect their own interests or those of their workers, resisted government attempts to recruit their charges for the shipyards.[104] While labor was drawn from the immediate hinterland of Cavite, the vastly increased demands generated by the Hispano-Dutch War meant that workers had to be drafted from more distant provinces, such as Pampanga and Laguna de Bay.[105] In 1649 Governor Diego Fajardo attempted to relieve the burden of the *polo* falling on Tagalog and Pampangan communities by extending it to the island of Leyte, but this did little more than provoke a revolt in Palapag.[106] By 1650, shortages of labor and the lack of capital meant that it was becoming impossible to build ships at Cavite.[107]

Even more burdensome were demands for labor to extract timber, most of which came from forests in Laguna de Bay. It was estimated that to acquire timber to build one galleon, 6,000 workers were needed for three months.[108] Often workers received no rations or wages and might suffer food shortages if they were employed at harvest time.[109] In 1621, those involved in extracting timber were owed more than one million pesos in wages.[110] The hard labor and ill treatment suffered by workers contributed to high mortality and stimulated others to evade the draft by selling themselves into slavery or fleeing into the interior; the more desperate committed suicide.[111] Contemporary observers considered the *polo* to be a major factor in population decline,[112] noting that in Laguna de Bay *encomiendas* that had originally possessed 2,000 "indios de tributo" now had only 500.[113] Nevertheless, the needs of defense and trade demanded that galleons be constructed. It was frequently suggested that ships should be built outside the islands, in places such as Bengal or Cochin, as indeed some were.[114] Others advocated that the Chinese should be employed.[115] Only with the end of the Hispano-Dutch War did the burden of providing labor for the shipyards moderate.

The *polo* not only raised mortality rates, but it also encouraged fugitivism on a wide scale. Some stayed on Cavite once their tour of duty had finished,[116] while others became *vagamundos* or turned to crime. Some tried to find others to take their place, offering them five, six, or even ten pesos, for which they often had to sell their possessions or submit themselves to bondage or slavery. In practice, those seeking replacements did not recruit them themselves, but paid a fee to the *alcalde mayor*, who hired *vagamundos*. It was therefore common practice for *alcaldes mayores* to inflate the number of workers required for private gain.[117] Flight was recognized at the time as being a major factor in the decline in the registered population and in the inability of communities to meet tribute and *polo* demands. *Alcaldes mayores* were therefore periodically ordered to force the fugitives to return.[118]

Missionary Progress

Not all regions felt the heavy hand of colonial rule, especially Mindoro, where contacts were primarily with the missionary orders and even these were not sustained. The early evangelization of Mindoro is obscure. While the conversion of coastal populations was relatively easy, interior groups were more resistant. Apart from their nomadic existence, those living in the interior were discouraged from settling in the missions by the requirement to pay tribute and the fear of becoming "slaves" on lands owned by those on the coast.[119] Coastal groups, who benefited from trading beeswax and honey with them, also encouraged their resistance. In 1636 the Jesuit provincial Juan de Bueras claimed that in fifty years it had not been possible to convert a single family.[120] The limited number of potential converts, the dispersed settlement pattern, the rugged terrain, and the unhealthy climate also acted as deterrents to missionary work. Many priests who worked there suffered from ill health attributed to the "poor disposition of the land."[121] This probably referred to malaria, for today Mindoro is one of the most malarial islands in the Philippines.

Progress with conversions was also slow because of constant changes in administration between the secular and regular clergy. An Augustinian convent was established in 1572 and the Augustinians worked in Baco, Calavite, Naujan, Calapan, and Lubang until 1578, when they decided to concentrate their efforts elsewhere.[122] The Franciscans replaced them, but by 1588 they had also left.[123] Because coastal populations had been easy to convert, it was believed they could be entrusted to the secular clergy,[124] but there were never enough parish priests, so the religious orders sometimes assisted. In 1626 the parish priest of Naujan invited a Jesuit father, Domingo de Peñalver, from Marinduque. He was so successful that in 1631 the Jesuits were invited to stay on a permanent basis, though their work was confined to the interior.[125] By 1636 the Jesuits had established seven *reducciones*, but for reasons unknown they ceased working in Mindoro about 1666,[126] though they continued to administer the island of Marinduque until their expulsion.

Other secular parishes were taken over by Augustinian Recollects who arrived in 1679. They gave up their missions in Zambales for four ministries, three in Mindoro and one in Lubang, and they established two new reductions at Mangarin and at Ylayas in the River Ylo or Ylog near Baco.[127] San Francisco de Assis recorded that when the Recollects took over the island it had only 4,000 Christians, but by 1692 their number had doubled to 8,000, and by 1716 to 12,000. Subsequently as Moro incursions increased in frequency, particularly on the west coast, the numbers they administered declined; in 1738 they were ministering to 7,552 souls.[128] The Recollects worked there until 1776 when they were replaced by two secular priests.[129]

Moro Raids

In addition to the dislocation of the native population by friar estates and forced labor, southwest Luzon continually suffered from Moro raids from Sulu and Mindanao. While these were not as devastating as in the Visayas, they afflicted the southern coast of Luzon and there were some bold raids on Cavite itself. The first major raid on the coast of Luzon occurred in 1602, when Magindanao and Buayan Moros from Mindanao, with the help of those from Sulu, raided Balayan and reputedly took 1,400 captives.[130] In response, forts were built along the coast at Lemery, Taal, Bauan, and Batangas.[131] While raids from Mindanao lapsed in the early seventeenth century, the Dutch presence in Philippine waters encouraged a bold attack on Cavite by Sulu in 1617 in which some 200 people were killed and 400 workers were taken captive, including some Spaniards for ransom.[132] Moro raids from Jolo and Brunei on southern Luzon continued during the 1620s.[133] In 1635 a new *padrón* was ordered for the province of Calilaya after Moros burned and robbed the village of Tayabas, capturing and killing 187 people and causing 400 to flee.[134] In 1675 Moros captured Balayan.[135] Fearing such raids, many inhabitants of Tayabas retreated inland, often permanently.[136] By 1701 the whole coast of Tayabas, which had previously been densely settled, was described as consisting of *rancherías* where the inhabitants subsisted by exploiting wild products such as wax, skins, and pitch.[137] Moro raids appear to have increased in intensity in the second half of the eighteenth century when the inhabitants of southern Luzon began to construct stockaded settlements in the mountains.[138] All of Tayabas was reputedly destroyed by a Moro invasion in 1758.[139] Attacks on this region continued in the late eighteenth century[140] and by 1790 Balayan had been raided three times.[141] Such regular losses were a drain on the population of the region. Apart from raising mortality, they disrupted food production and often drove the inhabitants to rely on wild food resources. In 1787 maternal malnutrition was identified as the cause of high infant mortality in Tayabas.[142]

Moro raids also afflicted the island of Mindoro intermittently through the colonial period. In 1602 a major raid led by Datu Bwisan resulted in many captives, including the local parish priest, being taken in the main town of Mindoro,[143] and in 1636 Mindanaos remained in the islands of Mindoro, Cuyo, and Calamianes for eight months, taking captives and robbing and destroying homes.[144] However, their greatest impact was in the eighteenth century, when raids on Mindoro occurred in 1726, 1734, 1736, 1739, and 1742.[145] However, the worst was in 1754, when a large number of villages in Mindoro and Marinduque were sacked, fields destroyed, and more than 600 people taken captive or killed.[146] During this period the Moros even established bases on the island itself from which they attacked vessels passing through the strait separating Mindoro from Batangas. Spanish expeditions in 1762 and 1778 achieved some success in rooting out the Moro pirates, but these raids destroyed many coastal towns, whose inhabitants either fled or were taken captive.[147]

Demographic Trends in Southwest Luzon

The conquest of southwest Luzon was achieved with relatively little bloodshed, but the population began its inexorable decline in the sixteenth century. By 1591 the population of southwest Luzon under Spanish administration had already fallen from an estimated 30,000 tributaries in 1570 to about 23,170, and this decline continued until at least the mid-seventeenth century (Table 8.1). Official tribute returns indicate that by 1655 the region possessed only 11,000 *tributos*, though this figure excluded the town and hinterland of Cavite. Jesuits records suggest that in 1659 Cavite had an adult population of nearly 2,700,[148] but this would have included many foreigners.[149] The population of southwest Luzon had therefore fallen by about half during the first half of the seventeenth century, though much of the decline was due to fugitivism.

The coast of Cavite apart, the population of southwest Luzon appears to have suffered one of the highest levels of decline during the colonial period. In the mid-seventeenth century, *alcaldes mayores* were frequently ordered to undertake new enumerations because many people were absent from their villages or had died in epidemics or Moro raids.[150] In 1642 the town of Morón had possessed 112.5 *tributos*, but by 1659, 32.5 had died and 14.5 were absent working on haciendas. During the second half of the seventeenth century, however, there was a slight increase in the total tributary population of about 0.27 percent a year to 12,425 *tributos enteros* in 1700.[151] This suggests a total population of about 50,000, but with a significant number escaping enumeration. Calculations working back from estimates of the total and tributary populations in the early eighteenth century produce a total population of about 65,000 in 1700.[152]

Like other Philippine regions, the population of southwest Luzon grew rapidly in the eighteenth century. Despite epidemics, volcanic eruptions, and Moro raids, between 1700 and 1792 the tributary population, excluding Cavite, grew by an average of 1.1 percent per annum. In 1800 the total number of *almas* was about 212,600, but this figure included other racial groups.[153] The native Filipino population may therefore have been about 195,000. However, these overall trends mask considerable variations in the causes, timing, and extent of demographic change.

Demographic trends in Mindoro are difficult to ascertain because of instability in the administration of mission settlements and the migration of coastal populations into the interior. Figures available from missionary accounts suggest that the tributary population of the island changed little up to the mid-eighteenth century, fluctuating between about 1,500 and 2,000 *tributos* (Appendix D), with the lowest numbers recorded in the early to mid-seventeenth century. However, these figures represent only a small proportion of those living in Mindoro. In the 1630s Mangyans were said to number 6,000 souls in the interior mountains.[154] This was probably an underestimate. In the mid-eighteenth century there was said to be enough work in interior Mindoro for thirty missionaries.[155] Normally the Crown supported the provision of priests at one for every 500 *tributos*, but because settlements in Mindoro

Table 8.1 The Tributary Population of Southwest Luzon, 1582–1792

	1582	**1591**	**1606**	**1655**	**1700**	**1735**	**1750**	**1792**
Laguna de Bay	9,300	9,600	8,742	5,931.5	6,722.5	7,790	10,034.5	11,076.5
Balayan (Batangas)	5,000	6,600	4,478	2,162.5	2,654.5	3,208	5,823	12,690
Tayabas (Calilaya)	3,650	6,200	5,493.5	2,905.5	1,631.5	1,817.5	4,386	6,732.5
Cavite	450	570	1,057		1,416.5	1,198.5	4,421.75	5,426
TOTAL	18,400	22,970	19,770.5	10,999.5	12,425	14,014	24,665.25	35,925

Sources: 1582 AGI PAT 23-9 and BR 5: 91–93 Miguel de Loarca [1582]. Figures are for the number of men.
1591 AGI PAT 25-28 fols. 14–15 and BR 8: 115–117 Relación punctual de las encomiendas 31 May 1591.
1606 AGI AF 29-87 Memoria y lista de las encomiendas 1606.
1655 AGI AF 22-7-20 fol. 11 Jueces oficiales de la real hacienda 16 June 1655.
1700 AGI CO 1253 Oficiales reales 1700.
1735 AGI CO 1266 Oficiales reales 1735.
1750 AGI CO 1276B Oficiales reales 1750.
1792 AUST Libro 229 no. 1 Estatística [*sic*] de las Yslas 1815.

were so scattered they were given charge of only 300 each.[156] Using the latter figure would give a tributary population of 9,000, which if multiplied by four would give a total population for the interior of the island of 36,000. This would seem to be an overestimate given the number present at the end of the eighteenth century.

Late eighteenth-century censuses suggest the total population of Mindoro in 1800 was about 15,000, but others remained outside Spanish administration. It is possible therefore that the total population at that time might have been nearer 20,000. In 1903, after further evangelization by the Recollects, who returned in 1802,[157] about 18 percent of the population was still classified as "wild."[158] Later, in the 1930s, Mindoro was said to have some 50,000 Christians and 10,000 Mangyans,[159] but the generally reliable Philippine census of 1939 suggested nearly double that number.[160]

Most observers attributed demographic decline in the seventeenth century in southwest Luzon, excluding Mindoro, to the high demand for labor in hazardous activities, which not only caused high mortality but also stimulated wide-scale fugitivism that in turn affected agricultural production. The greater part of the decline was concentrated in the first half of the seventeenth century, when between 1622 and 1649 towns under Franciscan administration lost an average of 45 percent of their populations.[161] However, some towns—Bay, Pila, Siniloan, and Tanay—located on the southern side of the lake or to the northeast of the lake near Manila and were nearest the regions of greatest labor demand, lost 65 percent. Perhaps surprisingly, those settlements on the east of Laguna de Bay furthest away from Cavite and Manila did not experience an influx of fugitives. Rather, the main zone of refuge appears to have been the interior between Manila Bay, Laguna de Bay, and the Batangas coast.[162] Others moved to Cavite, which as Table 8.1 indicates grew in population throughout the colonial period. It might be expected that the populations of Batangas and Tayabas, which are more remote, would have declined less than that of Laguna, since they would not have been so adversely affected by the *polo*. However, both the former regions suffered to a greater degree from Moro raids.

Epidemics were also a significant factor that contributed to the decline of populations in southwest Luzon. Due to Cavite's role as a port, the region was particularly exposed to the introduction of new diseases from overseas. Although the constant exposure to disease probably enabled the population to develop a level of immunity to acute infections, periodically the region suffered from epidemics with mortality rates comparable to those experienced in the Americas. Laguna de Bay and Tayabas were afflicted by the general epidemic of smallpox in the 1650s,[163] and in 1705 another similar epidemic that began in Manila struck adults and children in Cavite, where shortages of food heightened its impact. This outbreak reduced the combined populations of Silang and Indang from 2,300 to only 1,100 families. One group in the hills around San Isidro that had not previously experienced smallpox fled and stockaded itself until the epidemic had passed.[164] Another major outbreak of smallpox occurred in 1754. This coincided with the eruption of the Taal volcano, the ash from which clothed much of the region and caused poor harvests and food shortages.[165] The impact of this epidemic was so great that the authorities ordered a special report to be compiled, which found that 7,142 persons had died in Laguna de Bay, of whom about 46 percent were tributaries. This was about 14 percent of the total population of the region, though there were wide variations in mortality between communities, with losses ranging from 1 to 30 percent.[166]

Little is known about the spread of epidemics in Mindoro, but in the early twentieth century Mangyans still had little immunity to acute infections, for it was recorded that "when sickness comes upon us, even though small, we always die."[167] At that time they were particularly fearful of smallpox and in an outbreak often abandoned the sick, including children, to their fate.[168] Although acute infections were not unknown in the interior, their impact would have been moderated by the dispersed population and rugged terrain. The Mangyans generally regarded themselves as healthy, with skin infections the most important diseases that afflicted them.

Though epidemics periodically took a heavy toll of the population, health conditions in southwest Luzon seem to have been better than in regions further north.[169] In 1591 the Franciscans established a hospital at Los Baños, where they used the local thermal waters;[170] they also had an infirmary at Pila.[171] However, the region's main health problems were associated with the port of Cavite, where many suffered work-related illnesses and injuries and large numbers of sick travelers and soldiers required medical care. In 1591 the Franciscans established the hospital of Espíritu Santo exclusively for sailors and those employed in the port of Cavite.[172] In 1642 it was transferred to the administration of hospitalers of San Juan de Dios.[173]

High mortality was also associated with Moro raids, which mainly affected Batangas and Tayabas in the seventeenth and second half of the eighteenth centuries. The coast of Tayabas suffered so much that the region's population continued to decline in the second half of the seventeenth century when most other regions in the Philippines were beginning to show signs of demographic recovery after the Hispano-Dutch War. The population of Batangas was also badly hit by the eruption of the Taal volcano in 1754, which José Montero y Vidal exaggeratedly claimed killed 40,000 people and destroyed the villages of Taal, Tanauan, Salá, and Lipa.[174] Given the impact of these major events it is perhaps surprising that the population in Batangas and Tayabas grew at more than 1.5 percent per annum during the eighteenth century, although it was more sluggish in Tayabas during the second half of the century. It is possible that population growth on the south coast was sustained in part by immigration from Laguna, which grew at the much slower rate of about 0.5 percent per annum.

For southwest Luzon there is more information on the causes of mortality than on fertility, but it is clear that in the eighteenth century the population increased. In pre-Spanish times, social practices, including low age at marriage and the absence of infanticide, functioned to promote large families. These conditions would have helped the population rebound from major mortality crises. In the seventeenth century, however, the impact of labor drafts not only raised mortality rates, but also delayed marriages and disrupted sexual relations. Reduced access to land may also have brought changes to marriage practices that favored later marriage. Thus, even though the clergy encouraged early marriage, in the early nineteenth century the average age at marriage for women at Nagcarlan was twenty-two years, and a significant proportion did not marry.[175] Age at marriage may therefore have risen, but it is not known how typical this was of other communities. Since these socioeconomic changes were more advanced in Laguna, it might be speculated that higher age at marriage could partially account for slower population growth there compared to Batangas and Tayabas. However, migration probably played a more significant role in changing the balance of population within southwest Luzon as whole.

CHAPTER 9

Bikol

Bikol is a geographically fragmented region composed of an elongated peninsula and four islands. In colonial times overland travel was hampered by the rugged terrain, while the frequency of tropical storms and the lack of deep, well-sheltered harbors, especially on the western coast, made communications by sea difficult. The only passage between the west and east coasts was through the hazardous San Bernardino Strait.[1] Nevertheless, Bikol was unified by its history and to a large degree by its culture. Its distinctive character derived in part from its isolation from the rest of the island of Luzon. During the colonial period it remained a predominantly self-sufficient agricultural region largely under the administration of Franciscans. It was drawn into the wider political arena by its strategic location on the San Bernardino Strait, through which the Manila galleons passed. It was therefore prey to raids by Moros and foreign corsairs. Most of its ports were shallow, but they provided some protection from tropical storms, and an early shipbuilding industry developed there based on abundant supplies of timber.

The Bikol region was first visited in 1567 by Martín de Goiti and Mateo de Saz, who had been dispatched by Legazpi to pacify the islands of Leyte, Panay, and Masbate.[2] They explored the islands of Masbate and Ticao and reached Ibalon, probably Sorsogón, but made little contact with the inhabitants, who fled to the hills. Two years later Legazpi dispatched another expedition led by Captain Luis Enríquez de Guzman and the Augustinian friar Alonso Jiménez. This expedition visited Masbate, Ticao, and Burias, and then proceeded to Sorsogón, penetrating inland as far as Camalig in Albay.[3] It may have been from Camalig that the Spanish derived the name for the province of Camarines.[4] In 1570 a second expedition under Andrés de Ibarra, again with Father Jiménez, was dispatched to Luzon in search of provisions. The expedition followed the same route but pushed further inland to Kalilingo (Bato) and Buá (Nabua) in Camarines Sur. Father Jiménez remained in Masbate with a small occupation force.[5] Critics of the expedition reported that in the Bay of Ibalon it had "sacked and destroyed, killed and depopulated many villages."[6] Meanwhile the island of Masbate failed to impress. Although the expedition found gold, because there were few inhabitants and there was little trade, the deposits were judged to be of little value.[7] On the southern Bikol Peninsula, however, the Spanish found dense populations and an abundance of gold and provisions.[8] In 1572 three private *encomiendas* comprising thirty-five villages

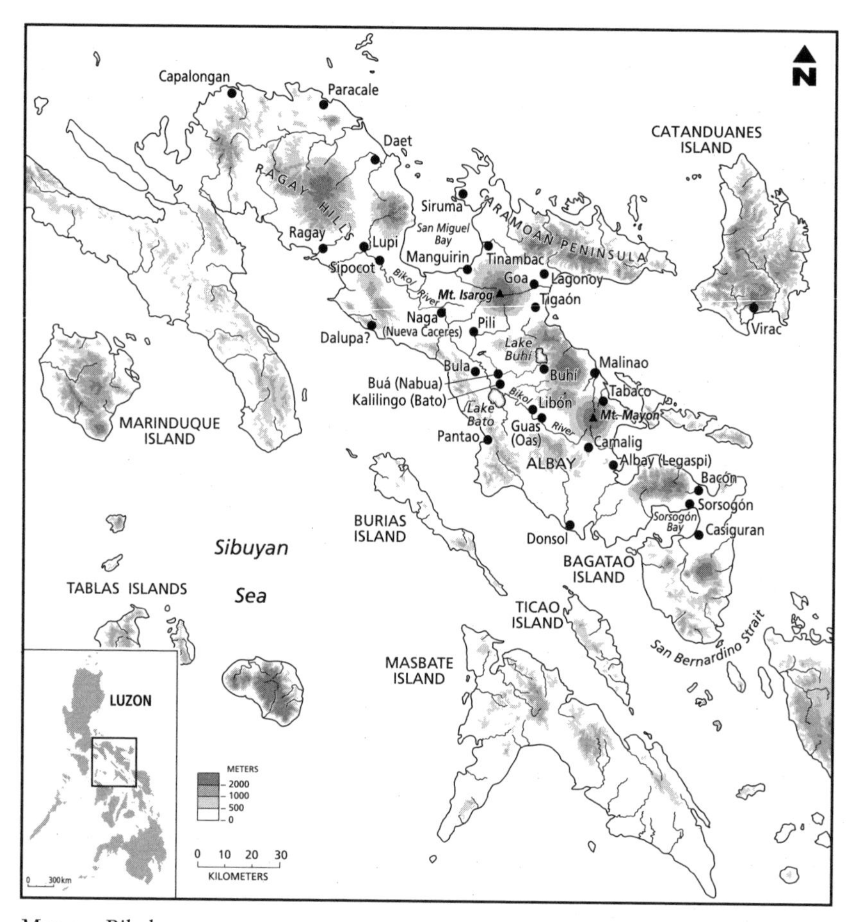

Map 9.1. Bikol

in the Bay of Ibalon were distributed, while another two were made tributary to the Crown.[9]

Meanwhile another Spanish expedition had arrived overland from the north.[10] After Juan de Salcedo had pacified Laguna de Bay, he petitioned for license to search for the mines of Paracale. He mustered eighty men and succeeded in locating the mines, but the natives fled and he was forced to retreat due to sickness and a shortage of supplies, and no permanent settlement was established.[11] However, Salcedo had learned that near Paracale there was a densely settled valley called Bikol that had more than 100,000 men capable of bearing arms, excluding those who were farmers and traders.[12] This news was sufficient to stimulate a second overland expedition in 1573.

The second expedition, which comprised 120 Spaniards, was accompanied by the Augustinian friar Francisco Merino in order to "avoid offences to God by the

Spaniards and harm to the natives," an indication that abuses had probably occurred on the previous expeditions.[13] The expedition proceeded beyond Paracale to San Miguel Bay and subsequently followed the Bikol River as far as Lake Bato, where the town of Santiago de Libón was established. Due to the rugged terrain and native hostility the expedition lasted five months. On returning, Salcedo left Captain Pedro de Chaves at Naga with an occupation force of eighty soldiers.[14] After various skirmishes with the inhabitants of Naga, Libón, and Bula, he established the city of Nueva Cáceres at Naga, naming it after the birthplace of the current governor, Francisco de Sande.[15] It was claimed that despite native hostility he had subjugated 20,000 "hombres" in the Bikol Valley and Camarines with as little injury as possible.[16] In 1574 further *encomiendas* were distributed, which included fourteen *encomiendas* in Camarines, Bikol, and Lagonoy, one in the island of Catanduanes and four in the *contracosta*.[17] By then a total of twenty-four *encomiendas* had been assigned to private individuals and a further three had been made tributary to the Crown. Excluding six *encomiendas* for which the number of villages was not specified, 206 villages had been allocated.[18] The number of *encomiendas* broadly corresponds to those recorded by Miguel de Loarca in 1582, though by then some had already changed hands and the *encomienda* of Catanduanes had been split between four *encomenderos*.[19] Some *encomiendas* included unpacified villages; for example, in 1575 Captain Pedro de Chaves was given an unspecified number of villages in the "tingues" of Guas, today Oas, and Santiago de Libón.[20] The number of Bikolanos distributed in *encomiendas* thus represented only a proportion of the total population. While in 1591 it was claimed that Camarines had been pacified, not all were receiving Christian instruction and some were only paying one-half or one-third of the tribute due.[21]

The pacification of the Bikol Peninsula was protracted. Although the inhabitants were initially judged as hostile,[22] later missionary accounts describe the Bikolanos as docile, obedient, and easy to convert.[23] Their hostile stance was probably a response to the treatment meted out to them by the Spanish. In 1574 the Augustinian friar Martín de Rada claimed that more people had died there than in any other region that had been pacified hitherto.[24] An anonymous report also noted that in the Bay of Ibalon many had died since soldiers had been given "wide license" and had enslaved many inhabitants and burned their villages.[25] This was a foretaste of what Bikolanos were to experience; since they were distant from Manila they were subject to particularly onerous exactions and enslavement.

Bikol in 1570

The Bikol Peninsula forms part of the Samar Arch or Eastern Bikol Cordillera that extends south through the eastern Visayas.[26] The western flank of the arch comprises the Ragay Hills, which constitute a narrow upland range rising to about 1,000 feet that in pre-Spanish and colonial times was sparsely populated. With the exception of Sorsogón Bay, there are only limited stretches of lowland on the west coast, and its shallow ports were exposed to inclement weather and Moro raids. The eastern flank of the Samar Arch is characterized by a series of volcanoes, notably Mounts Isarog and Mayon, which rise to between 6,000 and 8,000 feet, while a non-volcanic arm of the eastern range branches off to form the Caramoan Peninsula and the island of Catanduanes.

The peninsular highlands are separated by the structural trough of the Bikol River Basin, which was the most densely settled part of the peninsula. Other lowland areas were limited to the hinterland of Daet in northern Camarines and the major bays of San Miguel, Lagonoy, Sorsogón, and Albay. Although with the exception of the Bikol River Basin, the lowland plains are not extensive, the volcanic soils are fertile and well-drained, and it was here that the population was concentrated. In contrast, the surrounding hills supported a cloak of tropical rain forest. Although they were sparsely settled, they constituted an important source of timber and natural resources such as medicinal plants, wax, game, rattan, and bamboo. The Bikol Peninsula is not only blessed with fertile soils, but is also well-watered all year round. However, it suffers badly from frequent and destructive typhoons, particularly from September to December, when crops are often destroyed and shipping disrupted.[27] The neighboring islands of Catanduanes, Burias, and Ticao are characterized by forested mountains and only limited cultivable flatlands. Although the lowlands are more extensive in Masbate, like the other islands it was sparsely settled.

In pre-Spanish times Bikol was one of the most densely settled regions of the Philippines. In the nineteenth century the Franciscan José Castaño classified the inhabitants of Bikol into three "races" on the basis of differences in their character, language, and culture—Agta, Dumágat, and Cimarrón.[28] The Agta were to be found mainly in the interior mountains from Asog to Masagara. These Negritos were nomadic hunters, fishers, and gatherers who exploited honey, wax, and rattan, which they traded in the lowlands.[29] Like Negritos elsewhere, they were representatives of the first inhabitants of the region, who had been conquered and displaced from the lowlands by more recent Malay peoples, the Dumágat. The Cimarrones inhabited the slopes of Mount Isarog and the forested hills of Siruma and Caramoan. These groups were cultivators and hunters but were most renowned for the raids they conducted on those in the lowlands.[30] As their name suggests, they were probably fugitives from Spanish control,[31] and as such emerged as a distinct group only in colonial times. By the end of Spanish rule the Negritos and Cimarrones, among whom there was some intermarriage, probably accounted for 1 percent of the region's population.[32] By then some had been incorporated into communities in the lowlands, so in pre-Spanish times they probably accounted for a slightly higher proportion.

Most Bikolanos lived in the lowlands and were farmers, fishers, and traders. The Spanish were unanimously impressed by the fertility and abundance of provisions in the region, especially the Bikol Valley.[33] Bikol was one of the few regions in the Philippines where in pre-Spanish times rain-fed or stream-fed wet-rice cultivation was practiced using simple localized systems of drainage and water retention rather than large-scale irrigation works.[34] Dry-rice cultivation was also practiced in the highlands. Large surpluses of rice were produced and traded over long distances,[35] and under colonial rule rice became a major item of tribute along with gold. Although documentary sources contain few references to fishing, it was undoubtedly an important activity not only on the coast, but also on the major inland lakes and rivers. Apart from these subsistence activities, the Bikolanos made fine gold jewelry[36] using gold from Paracale and the islands of Catanduanes and Masbate.[37]

The importance of trade to the economy can be seen in the variety of Bikol terms for trading, which cover all forms of exchange from barter to big business.[38] Rice was not only traded within the Philippines, but also exported. In 1570 the inhabitants of Ibalon possessed silk and silk cloth, which they may have obtained through trade with China.[39] However, it is possible that these Chinese goods did not arrive directly from China but through Mindoro, which acted as an entrepôt for foreign imports.

The Population of Bikol in 1570

It is clear that when the Spanish first arrived in Bikol it was a densely settled region. As noted above, Gaspar de San Agustín's account of Juan de Salcedo's first expedition to Paracale claimed that the Bikol River and Camarines possessed 100,000 armed men, excluding farmers and traders.[40] The source of this figure is unknown, but if it came from Salcedo, it may have been inflated to get backing for another expedition. An anonymous account written in 1572 claimed that in general the numbers of inhabitants reported to the Crown were exaggerated because the soldiers were inexperienced and captains wished to magnify their achievements. To back his case the author gave the example of one captain who reported that there were 70,000 "indios" in the Bay of Ibalon when in fact there were only 4,000.[41] Given records of about 20,000 to 30,000 tributaries only a few years later, the figure of more than 100,000 men seems highly improbable, though it might be more credible if it referred to the total population.

In 1574 Governor Lavezaris reported that 20,000 men had been subjugated in the Bikol Valley and Camarines alone, and in the 1580s Miguel de Loarca recorded that there were about 28,000 tributary males in *encomiendas* in the region.[42] Loarca's figures are generally regarded as fairly reliable due to his long residence in the Philippines. Taking the figure of 28,000 tributary males and using the contemporary multiplication factor of four suggests a total population of not less than 112,000 for the region. To this should be added an estimate for those who remained outside Spanish control. In 1622 there were large numbers of unconverted people in the hinterlands of Daet in Camarines and Bacón in Albay, and there were many Negritos around Nabua and Buhi.[43] It is doubtful they numbered more than 10,000 at that time. Norman Owen estimates that in the nineteenth century only about 1 percent of the population lived in the hills, while 90 percent were to be found in settled communities and 9 percent in the missions.[44] The proportion living in the hills would have differed in 1570, since in the nineteenth century it is likely to have been inflated by fugitives from the lowlands, though on the other hand some highland converts would have been absorbed into lowland missions and towns. Whether the proportion was higher or lower in 1570, those living in the hills accounted for only a very minor share of the total population. If the particularly brutal conquest of Bikol is also taken into account, a contact figure of about 150,000 might be reasonable. Certainly qualitative accounts converge in reporting that the region was densely settled, even though the population was confined to a number of major valleys and the coast.[45] Captain Esteban Rodríguez de Figueroa was described as one of the most highly rewarded conquistadors in the Philippines since he possessed two *encomiendas*, one of which comprised the towns of Guas and Libón in Camarines which together had 1,174 *tributos* or 4,696 souls.[46]

An Economic Backwater

Prior to the nineteenth century the Bikol Peninsula was an economic backwater.[47] Relatively few Spaniards settled in Camarines; in 1588 the city of Nueva Cáceres possessed thirty *vecinos* and thirty soldiers, and during the early colonial period the number of Spanish householders probably never exceeded one hundred.[48] In 1768 there were only 464 "Spaniards," of whom many were Spanish *mestizos*, in the entire diocese of Nueva Cáceres, which included Tayabas and the island of Masbate.[49] In 1738 there was a small Parian at Naga,[50] but the numbers of Chinese and *mestizos* also remained small compared to other regions. In 1792, its 300 *mestizos* represented only 1 percent of those paying tribute.[51] Toward the end of the eighteenth century the city of Nueva Cáceres did not even possess a *cabildo*.[52] Spaniards who lived in Bikol were involved in gold mining, shipbuilding, and abaca production.

Gold was found in many parts of the Bikol Peninsula and its neighboring islands. It was mined in pre-Spanish times and by the end of the sixteenth century Spaniards were working deposits at Paracale, the Bay of Caporaguay in the island of Catanduanes, and Masbate.[53] With the exception of Camarines Norte, most gold was found in placer deposits that were not extensive enough to attract Spanish investment, at least until the late eighteenth century.[54] In 1618 it was reported that in Camarines they used to mine a lot of gold, which suggests that mining had ceased or declined.[55] In fact, mining occurred only intermittently since the mines quickly became flooded and yielded little profit.[56] It probably took place more continuously at Paracale, where the deposits were more extensive, but even there operations were small-scale. From time to time Spanish entrepreneurs, including priests, worked gold using local labor.[57] Some laborers were coerced into mining by the *alcalde mayor*,[58] but others appear to have worked as free laborers, probably because they earned higher wages than in other activities. In 1688 miners at Paracale who extracted ore received more than three reals a week plus food, whereas all other mine workers, including some women, received two reals plus food.[59] However, mine owners were often indebted and sometimes wages went unpaid. Once deposits had been exhausted, operations would be abandoned and workers would return to farming.[60] In the second half of the eighteenth century there was renewed interest in the gold mines, but techniques remained primitive.[61] Overall, gold production made only a small contribution to the Philippine colonial economy and it affected the lives of only a small proportion of the region's inhabitants.

The Bikol Peninsula and its neighboring islands had sheltered ports and good supplies of hardwood timber and abaca fiber for cordage. The region was located on the route taken by the Manila galleons and the local population was skilled in ship construction. Important shipyards were established at Bagatao and Pantao in Albay, Dalupa in Camarines, and in Masbate and Catanduanes.[62] Due to shortages of labor, the ports in Ticao and Burias did not develop as major shipbuilding centers, but they were used as stopping points for shelter, supplies, and repairs.[63] Some of the largest galleons constructed in the Philippines were built in the Bikol shipyards,[64] which soon became targets of Moro raids. Possibly for this reason, in the eighteenth century these shipyards were closed in favor of Cavite, though local shipbuilding continued.[65] There are no figures for the numbers employed in the shipyards, but numerous Moro raids on the shipyards succeeded in taking several hundred captives.[66] In the seventeenth century, wages were lower than in mining. Those involved in the extraction of timber were paid one and a half reals a week plus food, while master carpenters received two reals plus food.[67] In the early colonial period the abaca industry was small-scale and the fiber was collected as tribute by *alcaldes mayores*,[68] but in 1722 the Crown established a royal cordage works or *cordonería* at Sorsogón and later another at Nueva Cáceres. Here wage laborers were employed at the weekly rate of two reals plus food, though some forced labor may also have been used.[69] Conditions in the factories were harsh; in 1759 the Bishop of Nueva Cáceres, Manuel de Matos, found it necessary to order that workers should not work before sunrise or after sunset and be allowed two hours rest at midday.[70]

Relatively few people were involved in mining and shipbuilding, but like other Filipinos, Bikolanos were required to pay tribute, mainly in gold and rice, both of which were judged to be abundant in the region.[71] During the greater part of the colonial period the tribute levy in Bikol was set at ten or eleven reals, payable in the form of one chicken, and the rest in cash and rice,[72] but often the goods exacted were worth considerably more. Exactions in Camarines were such that some *principales* were beaten to death for failure to deliver the goods demanded by *encomenderos*, which were often not those specified in the *tasación*, but those on which *encomenderos* could make a profit.[73] Hence, some *encomenderos* preferred to levy tribute in slaves, to which *principales* objected since it deprived them of the opportunity to sell them elsewhere at double the price.[74]

As elsewhere in the islands, the greater part of the population of Bikol was brought under Spanish administration by the missionary orders that collected scattered populations into towns, where they could be more effectively instructed in the Catholic faith and their tribute collected. Although Augustinians accompanied the earliest expeditions, in 1578 two Franciscan fathers, Pablo de Jesús and Bartolomé Ruiz, were assigned to the region,[75] and when the Crown redefined the areas to be administered by the different religious orders in 1594, most of Camarines became a

Franciscan province.[76] In the 1620s the Franciscans had charge of 45,000 *almas* out of a total of 56,800.[77] In 1649 they possessed twenty-one residences in Camarines and Albay, but in 1696 the province of Albay was ceded to secular priests.[78]

Until the end of the seventeenth century, Franciscan efforts were concentrated in the lowlands, but from about 1684 they began converting Negritos and other Bikolanos in the hills. They focused on three main areas—Mount Isarog, the forests of Camarines Norte and west Bikol, and finally on the sparsely populated northeast coast along San Miguel Bay and the Caramoan Peninsula.[79] Apart from the Negritos, who had traditionally inhabited these interior regions, many had fled to the hills to escape tribute and labor demands.[80] In Camarines in particular it became the practice to conduct *entradas* into the hills to capture the fugitives for sale. So many were enslaved that when the Crown ordered all slaves to be released in 1679 there were vigorous protests from slave owners as the emancipated slaves fled to the hills.[81]

In 1709 the Franciscans had three mission fields centered on Ragay, Manguirin, and Matalavan that together had 1,165 *almas*.[82] By the 1730s only the first two were still operative, though the number of souls they ministered to had risen to 2,900.[83] The resistance of the Negritos and the existence of large numbers of *cimarrones*, especially at Mount Isarog, led the authorities in 1738 to provide military support for *entradas* aimed at forcing them to settle away from their homes. As a result, 3,000 people were settled at Santa Cruz, Salog, and Santa Clara.[84] In 1780 there were three missions on the slopes of Mount Isarog (Manguirin, Goa de Salog, and Tigaón), which contained 1,490 Negritos and 2,822 *almas*,[85] but Manguirin was described as "almost a ruin." Although the Franciscans achieved limited success in settling converts in the missions, in the 1780s they were ministering to another 10,000 *almas* living in scattered *rancherías* who were described as "all Christians."[86] At that time the mission in the Ragay Hills, even though it had been attacked by Moros, had 660 tributaries and 2,355 *almas*.

Moro Raids

For many Bikol communities, Moro raids had the greatest impact on their daily lives. The background to Moro raids has already been described in chapter 3. While the Visayas bore the brunt of these raids, Camarines also suffered heavy losses. In the early colonial period, raids focused on the shipyards in an attempt to destroy Spanish naval power, though at the same time large numbers of workers were captured as slaves, and persons of rank, especially priests, were captured for ransom.[87] After the shipyards were closed in the eighteenth century the raids focused on vulnerable towns and villages.[88]

Raids by Moro pirates had been a fact of life in pre-Spanish times. Father Diego de Herrera reported that each year a corsair named Carabie used to devastate Samar and Masbate, while Moros from Jolo carried out attacks throughout the Visayas and Camarines.[89] In 1616 the shipyard at Pantao was attacked by eighty *caracoas* from Mindanao, which destroyed a number of ships, sacked the town, and caused damage estimated at more than one million pesos. At the same time 200 people were killed and 400 were taken captive.[90] The same year, Magindanaos attacked a settlement called Calaguimit, which was probably located on the island of Bagatao.[91]

While subsequently there was a lapse in raids by Magindinaos, raids by other Moro groups continued. In 1627 about 2,000 Moros from Sulu attacked Bikol and captured two vessels, burning and looting the refitted shipyard at Pantao and carrying off about 300 captives.[92] Two years later, coastal settlements in Camarines, Samar, and Leyte were burned and looted and the captives sold as far afield as Melaka.[93] Moro raids continued in the 1630s, with Iguey being destroyed in 1636 and the shipyard at Pantao being assaulted in 1638.[94] In 1646 the shipyard at Bagatao was attacked, and throughout the 1640s there were frequent raids on Franciscan missions along the Albay coast and even on the town of Albay itself. A Franciscan account in 1649 noted that the previous year the Dutch, allied with Camucones and Moros from Mindanao, had burned churches in Albay, Tanaco (Tabaco), Capalongan, Paracale, and Bacón.[95] Oral history records many smaller raids, though they seem to have declined in frequency in the second half of the seventeenth century.

Despite the closure of the Bikol shipyards, in the mid-eighteenth century Moro raids began to increase once again, but the targets shifted to towns and villages on the islands of Ticao, Tablas, and Masbate, as well as Sorsogón and Albay. The raids of the 1750s were probably the most destructive.[96] As Moros shifted their targets from the shipyards to population centers, they used *joangas* rather than *caracoas* so they could carry off more captives.[97] The bishop of Nueva Cáceres reported that raids in 1757 had destroyed ten towns, including two missions, and resulted in 8,000 natives being captured or killed, with the provinces of Camarines and Albay being the worst affected.[98] For the last quarter of the eighteenth century, Najeeb Saleeby estimates that Moros were taking 500 captives a year.[99] A significant proportion of these were captured in the Visayas, but he suggests that Camarines, Batangas, and Albay also suffered badly.

During the late eighteenth century, Moro raids became a dominant feature of life in the region. During the southwest monsoon the Moros would sweep up through the Visayas to Bikol, striking islands and towns on the western peninsula or sailing through the San Bernardino Strait to attack the island of Catanduanes and the Pacific coast as far as Camarines Norte. They not only burned and looted the towns, but also timed their arrival to coincide with the rice harvest, which they seized together with other crops. Fear of attack forced many to flee their settlements or even shift their entire communities.[100] The new sites were often less favorably located for subsistence purposes, while the needs of defense, losses in raids, and the seizure of captives created shortages of labor that affected subsistence production. Government attempts to counteract the raids by fortifying towns and providing naval patrols, particularly in the San Bernardino Strait, seem to have been partially successful. Whether for this reason or due to internal political conflicts or changes within the sultanates, the Moro threat gradually waned.

Demographic Trends in Bikol

Demographic trends in Bikol are difficult to establish with any certainty. Bikol was remote from Manila, so fewer official accounts exist of either its population or Spanish activities there. Furthermore, many reports refer only to part of the region; this is particularly true after parishes in Albay were secularized in 1696. Also, throughout the colonial period, a fluctuating proportion of the population resided in the mountains outside Spanish administration.

It has been estimated in this study that in 1570 the total population of Bikol, including Catanduanes, Masbate, and other neighboring islands, may have about 150,000, or 37,500 male tributaries. As described above, the conquest of Bikol was particularly brutal, so that by the end of the century the population had fallen to about 22,160 *tributos* (see Appendix D). There is no evidence of epidemics in Bikol at this time, but there were outbreaks elsewhere in Luzon, and infections may have been carried by soldiers involved in pacifying the region or by ships that stopped at its ports. Neither were there any major Moro raids until the early seventeenth century. It seems likely, therefore, that the rapid decline in the number of tributaries was largely due to the brutal conquest of the area and the flight it precipitated. In 1622 large numbers of *infieles* were living in the hinterlands of Daet in Camarines and Bacón in Albay, though some probably lived there in pre-Spanish times.[101]

The decline continued during the first half of the seventeenth century. Taking Camarines and Albay together, but excluding the islands, between 1591 and 1649 the total population fell by about 47 percent, with some towns such as Iguey being totally destroyed (see Table 9.1). The only places that appear to have increased in population were the provincial capitals of Naga and Albay, perhaps encouraged by the needs of defense or possibly drawing laborers from the interior for service. Fiscal records for the second half of the seventeenth century indicate a continuing

Table 9.1 Total Populations of Camarines and Albay, 1591 to 1649

	1591	1622	1649	Percent decline 1591–1649	Percente decline 1622–1649	Percent decline 1591–1649
Camarines	32,880	24,800	17,700	-24.6	-28.6	-46.2
Albay	33,640	34,400	17,710	+2.3	-48.5	-47.4
TOTAL	66,520	59,200	35,410	-11.0	-40.2	-46.8

Sources: 1591 AGI PAT 25-38 Relación punctual de las encomiendas 31 May 1591. Figures exclude the islands which are not included in 1622 and 1649.
1622 Alonso de Montemayor 16 July 1622 in Abad, "Los franciscanos," 416–421.
1649 Retana, *Archivo bibliófilo filipino*, 1: 1–13, Entrada de la seráfica religión 1649.

decline of about 0.83 percent a year in the number of tributaries, to about 7,000 in 1700. This decline was one of the highest in Luzon, exceeded only by the province of Tayabas. Losses appear to have been significantly higher in Albay than in Camarines, with the former losing 55 percent of its tributary population and the latter 16 percent.[102] Higher losses in Albay might be explained by the higher demand for labor in the shipyards and the region's greater exposure to Moro raids, though a proportion might also be attributed to fugitivism or migration, particularly to Manila.[103] In the early eighteenth century, migration from Bikol to Manila was occurring on such a scale as to cause an imbalance in the sex ratio.[104] This trend is supported by figures for youths in parishes administered by the Franciscans in 1709 where there were only 90 men for every 100 women.[105] Such an imbalance is likely to have had a negative impact on fertility and delayed a demographic recovery once the Moro raids of the early seventeenth century decreased in intensity.

The population of Bikol was certainly higher than the numbers registered, but in the eighteenth century both Franciscan accounts and fiscal records indicate the population was increasing rapidly (Table 9.2). The tributary population appears to have quadrupled between 1700 and 1800, with growth being more marked in the second half of the century when it was growing at 2.01 percent a year. A growth rate of this magnitude is unlikely and is surprising given continuing out-migration and the greater impact of Moro raids at that time. Undoubtedly a significant part of the increase was due to government-backed efforts at settling fugitives and other remote groups in the lowlands. By 1800 the total population of Bikol and the surrounding islands was probably over 165,000 (see Appendix D).

The ability of the population to recover from the devastating impact of Moro raids was aided by abundant food supplies and relatively limited demands for labor. Gold mining and shipbuilding were conducted only intermittently and no major economic enterprises were established in the region; even the economic reforms of the late eighteenth century had little impact on Bikol.[106] The region was also consistently described as healthy. In fact, in 1601 the Franciscan chronicler Marcelo de Ribadeneyra claimed that the climate of Camarines was the best and healthiest in the Philippines and because of that its inhabitants lived to an old age.[107] Health problems seem to have been worse for Spaniards, who often fell victim to malaria as they penetrated the foothills. Juan de Salcedo's expedition was afflicted by "fevers,"[108] and in the early eighteenth century many Franciscans involved in *entradas* in the foothills of Mount Isarog died of fevers.[109] It may have been a concern for the health of Spaniards in the region that the Franciscans established an early infirmary at Camalig in 1583 and three years later founded the hospital of San Diego at Nueva Cáceres.[110] In addition, many communities under Franciscan administration possessed special buildings that were used as "hospitals" where the poor and sick were cared for.[111] The main illnesses to afflict Bikolanos were unspecified fevers, probably malaria, gastrointestinal infections, and respiratory diseases.[112] Bikol was remote from the rest of Luzon and there are no references to individual epidemics there in the early colonial period, though opportunities existed for the introduction

Table 9.2 Total Populations of Franciscan Towns in Bikol, 1622–1751

	1622	1649	1709	1751	Percent change 1622–1649	Percent change 1649–1709	Percent change 1709–1751
Bikol	10,200	7,800	9,242	20,170	-23.5	18.5	54.2
Camarines Norte	8,300	4,200			-49.4		
Iraya	12,300	8,100	10,032	22,714	-34.1	23.9	55.8
Rinconada	6,300	5,700	5,066	8,425	-9.5	-11.1	39.9
TOTAL	37,100	25,800	24,340	51,309	-30.5	-5.7	52.6

Sources: 1622 Abad, "Los franciscanos," 418–419 Alonso de Montemayor 16 July 1622.
1649 Retana, *Archivo bibliófilo filipino*, 1: 1–13 Entrada de la seráfica religión 1649.
1709 AGI AF 296 Razón de la gente adminstrada en esta provincia de San Gregorio 1709.
1751 AGI AF 323 Tabla y noticia, 1 May 1751 in Sánchez Fuertes, "Estado de las misiones," 146–151.

Note:
Bikol: Calabanga, Canaman, Libmanan, Magarao, Milaor, Minalabag, Naga, Quipayo.
Camarines Norte: Daet, Capalongan, Indan, Paracale, Tagboan.
Iraya: Camarines (Camalig), Cagsaua, Guinobatan, Ligao, Libón, Oas, Polangui.
Ricnonada: Baao, Buhi, Bula, Iriga, Nabua.

of infections by ships that stopped at its ports for supplies and shelter. By the nineteenth century, smallpox had become a largely childhood disease, which suggests that it was a fairly common visitor to the region. The familiarity of Bikolanos with smallpox is also implied by the statement by the chronicler Fray Juan Francisco de San Antonio that in Catanduanes "nature marks them permanently because of the disease which is common in those islands."[113] While recorded mortality rates were relatively low, they might be raised by typhoons that destroyed the rice harvest. Norman Owen has calculated that maybe 11,000 people died as a result of typhoon-induced famine in 1845.[114] In such crises, mortality levels might rise to over 35 deaths per 1,000, but normally they were around 22 per 1,000, which was lower than most regions in Luzon.[115] Also, there were no apparent attempts to control fertility, and illegitimacy was common, so that communities could rebound more easily from mortality crises than in some other regions, such as the Visayas.[116]

CHAPTER 10
Pampanga and Bulacan

Pampanga and Bulacan were among the most fertile and densely settled provinces that the Spanish encountered in the Philippines. However, in the colonial period their natural and human assets worked to their disadvantage as they became vital sources of provisions and timber, as well as labor to support the city of Manila and the extension and maintenance of Spanish rule in the islands. Pampanga suffered more than any other province from *vandalas* and *polos*, especially during the Hispano-Dutch War.[1]

Before the city of Manila was founded, more than 2,000 Pampangans from the towns of Haganoy and Macabebe arrived in Tondo and declared their resistance to Spanish rule.[2] Martín de Goiti was dispatched to pacify them, and in the process 300 "Moros" were killed and many others captured. Subsequently many towns in Pampanga rendered obedience, but Goiti was unable to proceed to Betis because of the difficulty of conducting a military campaign in the rainy season. About six or seven months later he returned to pacify Betis and Lubao, where he reported 10,000 to 20,000 people had fortified themselves. The Augustinians were critical of the pillage and enslavement that occurred, which they claimed had been undertaken under the pretext that the Pampangans had rebelled when they had offered no resistance.[3] Once pacified, on 5 April 1572 the towns of Macabebe, Calumpit, Batan, and Malolos were assigned in *encomiendas*, followed on 5 September by Betis, Lubao, and Bulacan.[4] By 1582, twelve *encomiendas* had been distributed, three of which were made tributary to the Crown. The population was judged to be sufficiently large to justify the establishment of four *alcaldías mayores* centered on Lubao, Calumpit, Candaba, and Bulacan.[5]

Pampanga and Bulacan in 1570

Pampanga comprises the southern part of the fertile Central Luzon Plain that extends from the Lingayen Gulf to Manila Bay. The region is dominated by the Pampanga River, which in its southern stretches is joined by several major tributaries before emptying into Manila Bay through a number of distributaries that form a delta fringed by mangrove and nipa swamps. To the east of the Pampanga River lies the Candaba Swamp, which in flood may extend for twenty miles and was once more extensive.[6] Although in the past these swamplands were of limited agricultural

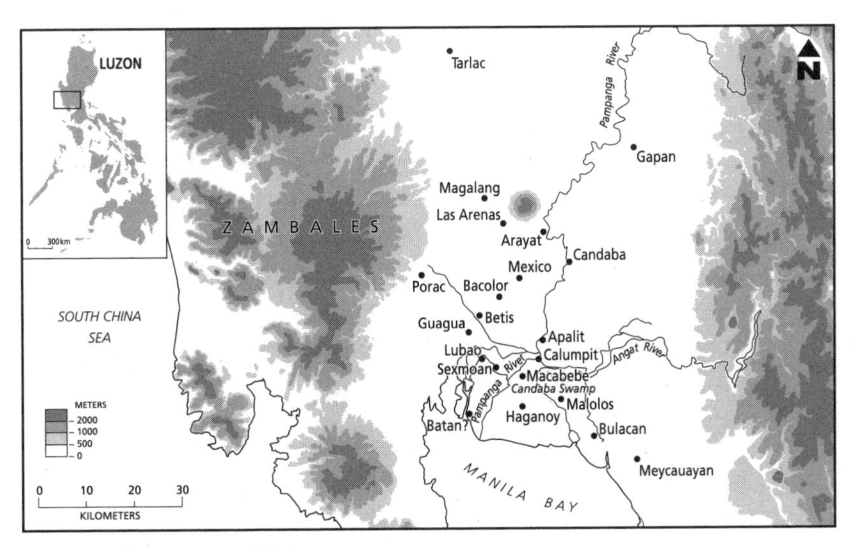

Map 10.1. Pampanga and Bulacan

value, they were an important source of fish. John Larkin draws an important distinction between the well-watered low-lying deltaic lands near Manila, which were suitable for the cultivation of rice, and the slightly higher, drier, sandier soils further north, which in the late eighteenth century were developed for the commercial production of sugar.[7] An important feature of the physical geography of the region is the strongly seasonal nature of the rainfall, 80 percent of which falls between May and October.

Under Spanish colonial rule, the southern part of the Central Luzon Plain was shared by Pampangans, who lived to the west of the Pampanga River, and Tagalogs, who lived to the east. The nature of Tagalog society in pre-Spanish times has been discussed in chapter 8, so only Pampangan society will be discussed here. The population of the Central Luzon Plain was concentrated around Manila Bay. Settlements were strung out along the rivers, with the houses of one village extending to that of another. The rivers facilitated access to fields and made communication easier; indeed Pampangans hardly ever traveled over land.[8] Some settlements were fortified, but even the largest probably did not exceed several thousand inhabitants. In 1576 Governor Sande reported that there were about 3,500 "Moros," all farmers, living on the banks of the Betis and Lubao Rivers.[9] In the drier interior plain, shifting cultivation and hunting were practiced and population density was correspondingly lower, with large stretches being forested and "unpopulated."[10] Hostile raids by Zambals and Negritos also discouraged population expansion into the interior.

Pampanga was said to consist wholly of rice fields and from an early date the region was reputed to produce the most rice in Luzon. Rice was grown on naturally irrigated swamplands along the major rivers and around Manila Bay, though a limited form of water control was probably also practiced. The area around Bacolor was regarded as the most fertile and its *principales* the richest. Downriver from Bacolor the Spanish established a granary at Sexmoan for the collection of foodstuffs for transshipment to Manila.[11] Pampanga was also abundant in fruit, fish, and meat.[12] Pigs, *gallinas*, some goats, and *búfanos* were raised, and fishing made a significant contribution to the local diet, particularly on the coast and areas of wet-rice cultivation.[13] *Aguardiente* was produced from sugar cane and wine from nipa palms.[14]

Pampangan society comprised three social classes: *datus*, *timaguas*, and slaves. The class of warrior nobles or *maharlika* found in Tagalog society seems to have been absent in Pampanga.[15] The position of a *datu* was apparently hereditary, though a more powerful leader might assume the position if he better served community interests. The authority of leaders seldom extended beyond their villages, and intervillage conflict was common.[16] Although Pampangans owned their own property, agricultural land was communally held. The *datu* supervised its cultivation while a small council of *principales* resolved conflicts over land.[17] In pre-Spanish times part of a *datu*'s economic status depended on the number of slaves or dependents he controlled, and in Pampanga slavery and debt peonage were extensive. John Larkin suggests that this may have been related to the region's strongly seasonal climate and hence agricultural production, which encouraged debt relationships.[18]

The Population of Pampanga and Bulacan in 1570

The dense population on the coast impressed early observers even though settlements there do not appear to have exceeded a few thousand people. Unfortunately there are no figures for the original size of *encomiendas* allocated in 1572. The first accounts date from the 1580s, a decade after conquest and after an epidemic of smallpox in 1574. The earliest estimate, probably in the early 1580s, suggests there were 30,000 "indios," assumed here to be of tributary status, under the *alcalde mayor* of Pampanga, whose jurisdiction at that time also embraced Bulacan.[19] This figure is higher than several accounts from the 1580s and 1590s that suggest a tributary population of about 19,000, although those of Bishops Salazar and Ortega suggest higher figures of between 22,000 and 23,500 (see Appendix D). Since most of the coastal plain was rapidly brought under Spanish control, these figures probably accounted for the majority of the Pampangans. Between Pampanga and Pangasinan there were another 3,000 in the mountains who were unpacified.[20] By the 1590s Father Ortega claimed that Pampanga possessed 90,000 *almas*, of whom few had not been baptized.[21] Taking account of the estimates for the 1580s and 1590s and of losses in conquest and the smallpox epidemic, it is not unreasonable to accept the figure of 30,000 tributaries, and thus about 120,000 souls, in 1570.

Tribute, *Vandala*, and *Polo*

The natural fertility of Pampanga and its proximity to Manila made it inevitable that the region would emerge as a major source of provisions. Most of the rice was supplied through tribute payments or *vandalas*. In 1594 tribute payments were regulated at two *fanegas* of rice, one *gallina*, and five reals, but unlike other regions where the produce could be commuted to a cash payment, in Pampanga it was specifically stated that tribute had to be paid in kind.[22] One-sixteenth of a *celemín* was regarded as sufficient for a meal for a male adult, so assuming two meals a day the levy of two *fanegas* represented sufficient rice for about a month.[23] Tribute payments were a particular burden in times of population decline, since adjustments were irregular and communities were often left paying for those who were absent or dead.[24]

Probably more onerous were the *vandalas*. In 1582 Pampanga was ordered to supply 12,000 *fanegas* of rice at the price of one *tostón* for 300 *gantas*, although it was judged at the time to be worth twice as much. Those unable to meet the levy, perhaps because they were involved in *polos* or wage labor, had to obtain rice elsewhere, frequently from local officials or *cabezas de barangay*, to whom they became indebted; instead many opted to flee.[25] Pampanga was also required to supply Manila with *gallinas*, eggs, and pigs during the months of April to June and Bulacan between July and August.[26] Commonly these goods were not paid for. As early as 1616 Pampangans were owed 71,705 pesos for rice, wood, and other goods.[27] The levies did not end with the Hispano-Dutch War,[28] and by 1660 they were owed more than 200,000 pesos for *vandalas* and *polos*.[29] The *vandala* was reduced following a major rebellion in 1660, and nominally abolished in 1679.[30] It continued sometime afterwards, but complaints gradually declined and it was imposed mainly in times of emergency.

Some surplus rice was probably traded in pre-Spanish times,[31] but tribute payments and *vandalas* constituted a marked increase in the demands made on agricultural production. Some efforts were made to expand irrigation and to introduce the plow, but they probably had little impact on production.[32] On the other hand, the alienation of native lands to create Spanish haciendas proceeded slowly in Pampanga. Even at the beginning of the eighteenth century it was judged that there was no hacienda "of consideration" in Pampanga, only some small-scale sugar mills, none worth more than forty pesos.[33] In Bulacan, however, the religious orders possessed some extensive haciendas, such as the Hacienda de Buenavista, which covered 74,000 acres.[34] As in southwest Luzon, in Bulacan the alienation of native lands and demands for labor threatened subsistence production and in 1745 provoked a revolt.[35] The main issue seems to have been one of labor shortage, particularly at critical periods in the highly seasonal agricultural calendar. Although laws were enacted stipulating that labor should not be drawn from agriculture at times of sowing and harvest,[36] in practice it was not adhered to, and work often had to be left to women and children.[37]

Demands for forced labor or *polos* in Pampanga were among the highest in the Philippines. Particularly onerous were those associated with the extraction of timber and military service, which increased during the Hispano-Dutch War. However, in the sixteenth century *polos* were imposed for the construction of Manila and for the production of charcoal for foundries making weapons and artillery at Candaba; others were levied for expeditions aimed at consolidating Spanish control in the islands.[38] Of all the demands for *polo* labor, the extraction of timber was the most onerous and arduous, though service on military campaigns might be equally hazardous. The presence of good sources of timber close to Manila and Cavite meant that Pampanga became a major source of molave wood that was used for ships and buildings. When demand required, the *alcalde mayor*, in consultation with the local priest, would specify the numbers of workers required. The construction of a ship might require the mobilization of 6,000 to 8,000 workers.[39] Exemptions were few, but *principales* who were liable for service could send a slave in their place.[40] Up to half of those liable for service might be drafted at any one time, so that for a specific project several hundred might be sent from one community. Those employed in cutting wood were to be paid seven to eight reals a month and a daily ration of half a *celemín* of rice, but there were constant complaints about low wages and poor food.[41] Many were ill-treated and died. It is significant that the 1660 uprising in Pampanga began at the end of an eight-month period when workers had been involved in extracting timber for the construction of three ships at Cavite.[42] Forced labor under the *polo* was not supposed to exceed four months, but in this case the period had been doubled, making workers unable to sow their rice. During the uprising 330 fled, and they inspired others to rebel and seek recompense for the goods and services they had provided. The uprising was ended by negotiation when the rebels were granted a general amnesty and received 14,000 pesos they were owed.[43]

Despite the lessons of the rebellion and the cessation of Hispano-Dutch War, Pampangans continued to be employed to extract timber.[44] The task was associated with high mortality, while it disrupted subsistence activities and family life and caused many to flee.[45] Some fled into the interior, but others went to Manila or became permanent workers in the shipyards of Cavite. By 1685 the parish of San Roque, adjacent to Cavite, had grown to such an extent that a petition was made to divide it into two.[46] Accompanying the petition was a list of 347 persons who were working in the shipyards, of whom 45 percent were from Pampanga, with the largest number coming from Bacolor and Guagua, followed by Lubao and Macabebe. This percentage exceeded that of people from Cavite itself, who accounted for 31 percent. Only 2 percent came from Bulacan. Most likely the proportion of workers from different regions reflected the areas from which *polo* labor was recruited, with workers staying on after their tours of duty had ended. Other Pampangans migrated to Manila,[47] while in the late seventeenth century some were living as fugitives in the hills around Gapan and were attacking native and Spanish settlements and lands.[48]

Another activity that generated significant demands for labor was military service. Soldiers and sailors were needed for campaigns against the Dutch and

Moros and to pacify hostile native groups. The Pampangans were renowned for military prowess and formed distinct companies within the Spanish militia. In 1574 the Pampangans aided the Spanish against the notorious Chinese corsair Lin [Ah] Feng (Limahon), and subsequently in 1603, 1,500 Tagalogs and Pampangans were involved in the suppression and massacre of the Chinese during the uprising in Manila.[49] During the Hispano-Dutch War large numbers of Pampangans were involved in naval campaigns. In 1606 Pedro de Acuña's expedition that aimed to drive the Dutch from Tidore and establish a fortified settlement at Ternate involved 1,300 Spaniards and 400 Tagalogs and Pampangans.[50] Ten years later, Juan de Silva's expedition to Singapore, which was the largest Spanish fleet ever mustered in Asia, employed sixteen ships and 3,000 Filipinos, of whom 700 died,[51] many of them Pampangans. The following year Pampangans were involved in repelling the Dutch off Playa Honda,[52] and in 1647, 240 out of the 400 Pampangans who drove the Dutch from Abucay and Samal were killed or captured.[53]

Although Pampanga was not a target of Moro raids, conscripts were frequently required for retaliatory and punitive expeditions; for example, Hurtado de Corcuera's expedition against Jolo between 1637 and 1638 involved 1,000 Filipinos. They were also required to staff distant permanent garrisons, such as those at Zamboanga and Ternate.[54] In 1654 the *cabezas de barangay* of Bacolor and Mexico complained that agricultural production and tribute payments were being adversely affected because 200 Pampangans were serving in the infantry.[55] Finally, in 1739 about 580 Pampangan soldiers were stationed at Manila, Cavite, Cebu, Zamboanga, and different points in Cagayan.[56]

Other demands for labor preceded and extended beyond the Hispano-Dutch War. Pampangans were drafted to serve on expeditions aimed at finding gold and pacifying mountain groups. In fact, few expeditions into unpacified territory did not involve at least small numbers of Pampangans. An early expedition to Ituy in 1591 by Luis Pérez Dasmariñas involved more than 1,400 Pampangans as soldiers or bearers.[57]

Pampangans were also used to pacify the Zambals and Negritos, and indeed were often keen to participate to avenge the raids these groups had committed. In Pampanga, the term Zambal was applied to all neighboring mountain groups, including Negritos. The Negritos lived mainly in the uplands and conducted headhunting raids on lowland villages and travelers, but they also foraged in the forested hills between the Agno and Pampanga rivers.[58] In 1592, between 500 and 600 Pampangans participated in an expedition that resulted in the capture or death of 2,500 Zambals.[59] This major expedition and the establishment of two forts at Tarlac and Las Arenas failed to stem the raids, which continued throughout the colonial period. In 1665, four forts were constructed and a garrison was established with 150 soldiers,[60] and two years later Pedro Durán de Monforte mounted an expedition aimed at bringing about the final conquest of the troublesome highlanders.[61] This disastrous expedition lasted nearly two years and involved some 2,000 native soldiers from Ilocos, Pampanga, as well as some friendly Zambals, some of whom were killed by hostile inhabitants while others died of illness and the cold. On the western side of the Central Luzon Plain, an expedition into the Zambales Mountains in 1680 involved 300 Pampangans and resulted in some Zambals settling at Alalan (Paynaoven), Balacbac, and Baubuen.[62]

Raids by small bands of Zambals and Negritos took a continual toll of the population of the mountain foothills and interior plain. Pampangans regularly petitioned for permission to enslave the Zambals on the grounds that their raids were unprovoked. The Crown never ceded to their request, though it did allow those captured in wars to be employed on galleys.[63] However, when slavery among Filipinos began to be abolished in 1679, the Audiencia conceded that in past times *alcaldes mayores* had conducted *entradas* among the Negritos to acquire slaves for sale and that Pampangans were also keen to enslave them to work their lands. Even so, it appears that most slaves in Pampanga were debt peons rather than captives.[64]

Given the extraordinary demands made on Pampangans, why did they remain so loyal? Even in the sixteenth century the Spanish regarded the Pampangans, together with the Tagalogs, as "truly our friends."[65] Phelan has suggested that fear of Zambal raids was an important factor encouraging their loyalty, but Larkin doubts that the Zambals ever constituted a major threat.[66] Political and economic motives may have played a significant role. *Cabezas de barangay* were quick to realize the benefits that cooperation with the new rulers could bring. Not only could they consolidate their positions as leaders, but they could benefit economically. The various levies imposed on Pampangans created opportunities for fraud and corruption that were greater than in many other areas, and because the Spanish depended so much on the cooperation of *cabezas de barangay*, they were reluctant to control their activities. However, at times the level of the demand placed upon Pampangans strained their loyalty, and during the Hispano-Dutch War the Spanish were aware that they were pushing them to the limit and feared a revolt.[67] In fact revolts did occur in Pampanga in 1585, 1614, and 1660, and in Bulacan in 1745.[68]

Ecclesiastical Administration

Pampanga's dense population and proximity to Manila not only led to the early establishment of a secular administration, but it also encouraged the Augustinians to take effective charge of the region. Hence by 1572 they had founded residences at Calumpit, Betis, and Lubao,[69] and by 1610 possessed ten residences in Pampanga and six among the neighboring Tagalogs.[70] Each was said to possess two priests who were ministering to between 2,500 and 3,000 *tributantes*.[71] Given the nucleated settlement pattern, a program of *congregación* was unnecessary except on the interior plain, where the missions of Porac and Magalang were founded in the hope of attracting Negritos and Zambals.[72] The administration of Pampangans was relatively easy and their apparent receptiveness to conversion made this a rewarding mission field.[73] Although the Augustinians relinquished some of their mission fields elsewhere in the Philippines to other religious orders, they retained control of Pampanga until 1773, when they were dispossessed following a dispute with the bishop.[74] While Augustinians dominated on the southern Central Luzon Plain, the Franciscans founded a number of missions in southern Bulacan, the first at Meycauayan in 1578.[75]

The Augustinian mission field did not expand significantly until the eighteenth century, when missions were established in the headwaters of the Pampanga River on the edges of the plain and in intermontane basins of the Caraballo Sur Mountains. In 1701 the Augustinians began working among the Abaca and Italon at Pantabangan and Caranglan (see Map 13.1) and by 1712 had converted about 700 families.[76] At that time the Italon comprised fifty-six to sixty small villages and the Abaca ten or twelve, each of which had between 100 and 150 families.[77] The conversion of these scattered groups of shifting cultivators posed greater difficulties for the Augustinians. Although in 1725 they were administering twenty small settlements and *visitas* in the region,[78] progress was slow and in 1759 they ceded the residences of Pantabangan and Caranglan to the Franciscans, who had been approaching the area from Baler on the east coast.[79] Meanwhile, population growth on the plain enabled some *visitas* to become separate parishes.[80] Some expansion also occurred in the forested interior, with missions among Zambals established at Magalang and Tarlac and among Igorrots at Tayug.[81] However, attempts to establish permanent settlements on the fringes of the plain were often resisted or ultimately unsuccessful.

Demographic Trends in Pampanga and Bulacan

Given the importance of the provinces of Pampanga and Bulacan to the survival of the colony and the general stability of the region's settlement pattern and secular and ecclesiastical administration, it is surprising how little quantitative information is available from which to determine demographic trends. Nevertheless, there is abundant qualitative evidence of official concern about population decline, particularly, though not exclusively, in the seventeenth century.

Conquest was not without bloodshed, and once pacified Pampangans were subject to a variety of exactions by *encomenderos*, Spanish officials, and priests. At the time Pampanga was judged to have suffered more in conquest than other regions, with many being killed and others being captured and sold as slaves.[82] Many of the tasks for which Pampangans were conscripted were hazardous and arduous and were associated with high mortality. When Pampangans were drafted to work in the gold mines of Ilocos in the early 1580s, they were unable to farm and were forced to live on palms and bananas, and it was said that 1,000 died in Lubao alone. Bishop Salazar noted that labor demands left them no time to rest, so that "they sow little and harvest less,"[83] and some were forced to sell themselves into slavery in order to survive.[84] Even in the sixteenth century, therefore, the adverse impact of labor service drew more comments than did epidemics, even though it is clear that epidemics also took a regular toll. Major epidemics afflicted Luzon in 1574,

1591–1592, and 1595 (see Appendix A), and it is unlikely that Pampangans escaped these epidemics given their proximity to Manila and Cavite, which were particularly exposed to the introduction of infections. By the early seventeenth century the population of 30,000 "indios" may have fallen by about half. The 1606 list of *encomiendas* indicates there were only 13,600 *tributos* in Pampanga and Bulacan.[85] Since this figure excluded those outside Spanish administration, a total of 15,000 adult males may be suggested.

Labor demands for shipbuilding and military service increased during the Hispano-Dutch War, and there seems little doubt that they contributed significantly to the population decline through the seventeenth century. Juan de Medina's observations on individual towns in Pampanga in 1630 are repetitive in their comments that towns such as Calumpit, Malolos, and Apalit, once large towns, were much reduced in size.[86] Observers generally attributed population decline to high mortality rather than low fertility. In the sixteenth century Father Ortega recorded that Pampangans were "people who multiplied a lot,"[87] and in the early eighteenth century, the Augustinian Casimiro Díaz noted that they were "very fertile,"[88] but it is clear that labor demands impacted on marital life and resulted in falling birth rates. The extended periods that Pampangans were employed away from their homes disrupted sexual relations[89] to the extent that at the end of the seventeenth century labor drafts were recognized as holding back population growth.[90] The inability of Pampangans to meet tribute or *vandala* demands drove some to seek contract work with Spaniards or *principales*, who often forced them to remain in their service after their contracts had ended "almost as slaves." The result was that spouses often ended up working for different employers.[91] The adverse demographic impact of the separation of spouses was recognized by the authorities, who in 1743 ordered that workers should not be absent from their home villages for more than forty days and that no woman should be employed in service unless her husband accompanied her.[92] Such official measures indicate the extent of the problem, though it is unlikely that they had much effect. The number of registered tribute payers in Pampanga and Bulacan fell from 13,600 in 1606 to a low point of 11,004 in 1655, after which it recovered to 12,304.5 in 1700.[93] While the decline in the early seventeenth century is not unexpected, the low rate of increase, averaging 0.25 percent per year after the end of the Hispano-Dutch War, is more surprising. Since mortality is likely to have declined, it suggests that the birth rate remained low. In 1700 the total population may have been about 52,000.[94]

Only in the eighteenth century did the population under Spanish control begin to grow, partly due to increased missionary activity. However this process was retarded by outbreaks of smallpox, which were most devastating in the neighboring mountains, where they struck either for the first time or after extended intervals. Fear of smallpox hampered missionary efforts in the highlands,[95] and some missions in the foothills failed to prosper because they were located in malarial areas and attempted to draw converts from non-malarial regions who lacked immunity.[96] Malaria does not appear to have been a problem on the plain, which was generally considered to be healthy, even though mosquitoes were present in swampy areas.[97] Pampanga, perhaps protected by the thinly populated interior plain, was also spared the major epidemic that struck Ilocos and Pangasinan in 1756.

Comparing the figure of 12,304.5 tributaries in 1700 with 31,783.5 in 1792 suggests an annual growth rate of about 1.08 percent per year, with the rate being higher in the second half of the century. By 1800 the total population in Pampanga, Bulacan, and Mariveles (in Bataan), excluding the Chinese and Chinese *mestizos*, was about 183,000.[98] As indicated in chapter 7, part of the increase is likely to have been due to more effective enumeration. Since native Filipinos made up about 86 percent of the total population of the Archbishopric of Manila in 1785,[99] there may have been about 155,550 in 1800. This exceeded the population that had existed in 1570.

PART IV

Northern Luzon

CHAPTER 11

Ilocos and Pangasinan

During colonial times travel to Pangasinan was generally conducted by sea since the Central Plain of Luzon was more heavily forested than at present and Zambal attacks made overland travel hazardous. Hence, although Pangasinan comprised part of the Central Plain of Luzon, its colonial history was more closely tied to that of Ilocos. The two regions along with Cagayan formed the bishopric of Nueva Segovia that was established in 1595. However, some geographical and cultural differences between the two regions were recognized by the appointment of separate *alcaldes mayores* and by the assignment of Dominicans to Pangasinan and the Augustinians to Ilocos.[1]

On his initial exploration of the west coast of Luzon, Juan de Salcedo found gold among its inhabitants. The amount proved limited, but the Spanish continued to search for the source of the gold and mounted many expeditions into the highlands, for which they conscripted auxiliaries from the lowlands, particularly from Ilocos. Meanwhile Pangasinan became a colonial backwater. It has been suggested that this was due to native hostility, the lack of suitable harbors, or the absence of large population centers, but these factors proved to have little foundation.[2] Because of the lack of Spanish interest in the region and native resistance, the pacification of Pangasinan was protracted and a significant proportion of the population remained outside effective administration through to the nineteenth century. Nevertheless, unlike their neighbors to the north, those who came under Spanish control were subject to labor drafts to extract timber and for work in the shipyards.

Despite Antonio de Morga's assertion that Miguel López de Legazpi conquered Ilocos and Pangasinan,[3] it is generally recognized that his grandson Juan de Salcedo first explored these regions.[4] Stimulated by rumors of gold, his expedition left Manila in May 1572 and stopped at several places on the coast, where although it was not always well-received, it did not meet the same resistance it encountered inland.[5] In Ilocos there were said to be towns of 200 to 400 houses, though Vigan had 800, and nearby there was reportedly an unspecified settlement of 3,000 houses.[6] Salcedo left his *alférez*, Antonio Hurtado, at Vigan before circumnavigating the island and arriving in Manila the following August.[7] During the journey Salcedo exacted 800 *taes* of gold and Hurtado returned to Manila with another 1,000 *taes*.[8]

In December, the new governor, Guido de Lavezaris, envious of Salcedo's feat and fearing that he might be a political threat, sent his field marshal Martín de

TABLE 11.1 Tribute Exacted on Martín de Goiti's Second Expedition to Ilocos, 1572–1573

	Number of villages	Number of houses	Average number of houses	*Taes* exacted	Average number of *taes* per house
Burinao [Bolinao]	1	30	30.0	28	.93
Pangasinan	29	2,805	96.7	945	.34
Purao	22	1,802	81.9	675	.37
Baratao	5	910	182.0	302.5	.32
Dumaquaque	20	1,240	62.0	385	.31
Candon	6	216	36.0	120.5	.56
Total	83	7,003	84.4	*2,456	.35

Source: AGI PAT 24-21 Martín de Goiti 3 Mar. 1573.
* There are minor differences in the total given in the document (2,462) and that derived from the figures for individual villages.

Goiti, accompanied by his quartermaster Andrés de Mirandola and captain Lorenzo Chacón, with an unusually large force of 130 soldiers and 800 native conscripts to survey the area prior to the allocation of *encomiendas*. Goiti's report included a detailed list of the settlements it visited, indicating that it exacted 2,456 gold *taes* from more than 7,000 households in eighty-three villages (see Table 11.1).[9]

The manner in which the exactions were made drew harsh criticism from the Augustinians. Father Francisco de Ortega claimed the expedition had entered villages demanding tribute without any attempt to preach to the natives or offer them gifts. When some attempted to flee, the soldiers had pursued and killed as many as they could, and then returned to their villages and destroyed their homes, animals, and provisions. He claimed the expedition had resulted in 4,000 houses burned and more than 500 people killed, and he estimated it would take six years or possibly a lifetime to recover from the devastation caused.[10] The Augustinian father, Martín de Rada, similarly reported the Spanish had made war on those who had refused to pay tribute, burning their houses and causing them to flee to the hills.[11] Members of the religious orders claimed that 6,000 *taes* had been collected, and that although similar raids and exactions had been conducted elsewhere in the islands, they judged that they had not been on the same scale.[12] In Pangasinan the exactions fueled native hostility to the extent that when the Chinese corsair Limahon took refuge at Lingayen in 1574, the inhabitants accepted him as their ruler in the hope they might free themselves from Spanish rule and benefit from increased trade with China.[13] Attempts to dislodge Limahon resulted in further casualties and promoted continued unrest, so that despite an attempt in 1583 to suppress the disorder by

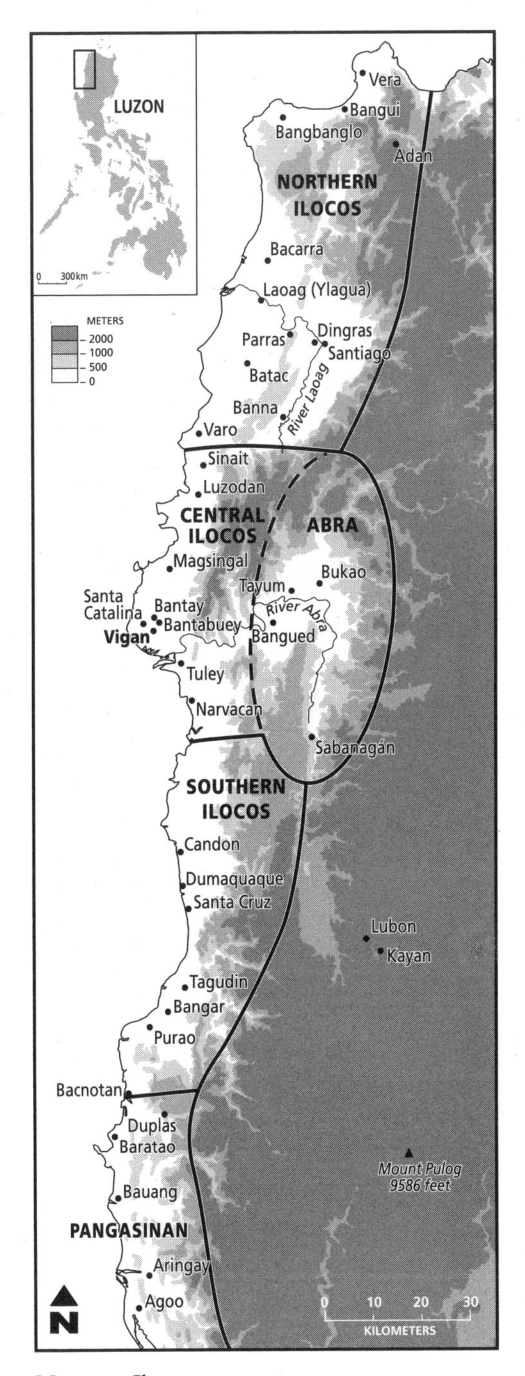

Map 11.1. Ilocos

the interim governor, Diego Ronquillo,[14] three years later the region was still regarded as unpacified.[15]

Eventually Governor Lavezaris became reconciled to Salcedo and commissioned him to establish a town on the River Vigan in Ilocos, naming it Fernandina after Phillip II's first-born son.[16] At the beginning of 1574 Salcedo embarked with eighty soldiers, some of whom had already been allocated *encomiendas* by Lavezaris.[17] In 1572 Salcedo had been assigned an *encomienda* of 4,000 "indios" and the following year Martín de Goiti was allocated 2,000 in the Naluacan [Narvacan] Valley, while villages in the Purao Valley were assigned to the Crown.[18] Details of the other *encomiendas* are lacking but, as will be elaborated below, most appear to have been formally assigned in April 1574. Salcedo not only established the town of Vigan, but also pacified the "provinces" of Varo [Badoc], Luzodan, and Magsingal, leaving Goiti to subjugate communities in the valleys of Vigan and Naluacan. Goiti noted that all the villages were within four leagues of the coast and that from them he had exacted nearly 3,000 *taes* of gold (see Table 11.2).[19] Altogether the three expeditions, none of which extended to northern Ilocos, levied a minimum of about 10,000 *taes*.

Table 11.2 Tribute Exacted by Juan de Salcedo and Martín de Goiti on their Third Expedition in 1574

	Number of villages	Number of houses	Average number of houses	*Taes* exacted	Average number of *taes* per house
Valle de Vigan	12	1,015	84.6	615	.61
Valle de Naluacan [Narvacan]	14	1,047	100.5	1,014	.97
Bantay and Bantabuey	3	400	133.3	136	.34
Varo [Badoc]	10 to12	600	54.5	100	.17
Sinay [Sinait], Luzodan, Caluntian	9 to10	950	100.0	535	.56
Province of Magsingal and Sanguian	14 to 15	1,005	69.3	341	.34
TOTAL	62 to 66	5,017	78.4	2,741	.55

Source: AGI PAT 24-21 fols. 10–12 Martín de Goiti no date [1570s].

Ilocos and Pangasinan in 1570

Ilocos and Pangasinan comprise distinct cultural and geographical regions.[20] Miguel de Loarca drew the boundary between the Pangasinans and Ilocanos between Aringay and Purao.[21] He observed that although the two groups were similar in behavior and customs, they spoke different languages and the former practiced infanticide. He considered the Pangasinans to be similar in dress and language to the Zambals, but were "more civilized" because of their trading contacts with the China, Japan, and Borneo. He also noted that unlike the Zambals the Pangasinans were peaceable and great farmers, whereas the former only cultivated small stretches of land.

Ilocos and Pangasinan were also distinct in their physical geography. Pangasinan forms part of the Central Plain of Luzon and is separated from Pampanga by a low drainage divide between the Agno and Pampanga rivers. Indeed, in colonial times there was a depopulated stretch about a day's journey in length between Pangasinan and Pampanga.[22] This relatively fertile plain is watered by rivers originating in mountains to the northeast that break up into numerous channels near the coast and create a landscape of small islands and inlets.[23] The presence of coastal swamps and the absence of natural harbors meant that settlements were concentrated inland along the major rivers rather than on the coast;[24] the interior was forested and sparsely settled.

In contrast, Ilocos mainly comprises a narrow coastal strip more than 150 miles long but only about 25 miles wide, from which the land rises rapidly to about 5,000 feet in the interior mountains.[25] The flood plains of the Abra and Laoag rivers constitute the most extensive lowlands, but the short rivers and steep gradients mean there is little accumulation of sediment from the interior mountains, which in any case is of relatively poor fertility. The annual rainfall in both regions exceeds 80 inches per year, being wetter in Ilocos, but due to the changing direction of the monsoon winds, it is highly seasonal, with 90 percent falling between May and October. The heavy rainfall provides abundant water for irrigation, but its seasonality means that some form of artificial water control is required to maintain production all the year round.

Even after the brutal conquest of Ilocos, Miguel de Loarca regarded it as being densely populated and possessing larger settlements than other regions.[26] However, most early observers clearly distinguished the densely settled coast from the sparsely populated and hostile interior. On the coast most settlements had several hundred houses or fewer, which according to the Augustinian, Francisco de Ortega, were more nucleated and better-ordered than in other regions.[27]

In Pangasinan, settlements seem to have been smaller. The lack of good anchorage points in the Lingayen Gulf may have restricted the opportunities for foreign trade to a small number of ports, such as Agoo, Bolinao, and the bar of Pangasinan (probably Lingayen) (Map 11.2).[28] Instead the thirty settlements visited by Martín de Goiti were described as being on river inlets[29] to enable easy communication and

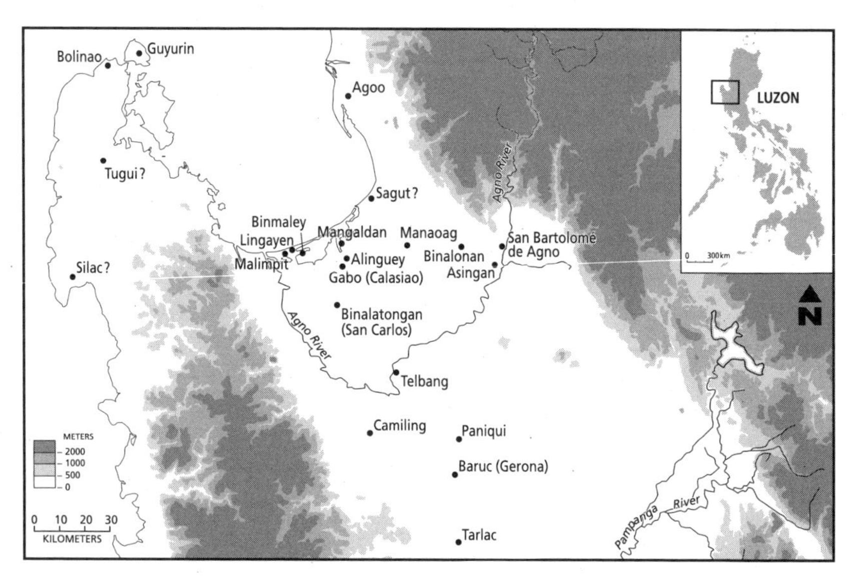

MAP 11.2. Pangasinan

access to good sources of fish.[30] Most had only thirty to fifty houses, and the largest, that of Gabo(n) (Calasiao), contained only six hundred houses.[31]

The basic unit of social organization appears to have been the nuclear family, as it is today.[32] Families may have been slightly larger in Ilocos than Pangasinan, because Ilocanos did not practice infanticide, whereas according to Loarca the Pangasinans performed it to avoid impoverishment.[33] Neither Ilocanos nor Pangasinans recognized a king or lord.[34] Nevertheless, the fact that Pangasinans organized tribute missions to China suggests a degree of political organization, and Rosario Mendoza Cortes argues that organized resistance in the region may reflect the strength of native leadership.[35] Unlike many groups in the islands, however, both were described as peaceful and having an aversion to war.[36]

Coastal Ilocanos were farmers, and the dense rural population suggests that wet-rice cultivation may have been practiced.[37] However, there are no references to irrigation techniques in the early colonial period, when rice cultivation was probably rain-fed. Today, artificial irrigation systems known as *zangjeras* are found only in Ilocos Norte, which experiences a longer dry season.[38] Various types of rice were grown including a forty-day rice and others that matured in two, three, and five months.[39] However, double cropping was probably only possible in the wetter areas, notably the Abra Valley.[40] In the late twentieth century very little rice was grown in Pangasinan in the dry season except under irrigation.[41] Pangasinan's emergence as one of the Philippines' major rice-producing regions dates mainly from the nineteenth century, when production intensified with the construction of dams and irrigation systems and migration from Ilocos made labor more readily available.

Despite the relatively limited stretches of arable land, poor soils, and strongly seasonal rainfall, in the early colonial period Ilocos was often described as fertile and abundant in provisions, rice, chickens, pigs, goats, *búfanos*, deer, and many kinds of water birds.[42] Such positive descriptions of the region's fertility contrast with its limited agricultural potential today. It is possible that deforestation of upland slopes has not only caused soil erosion there, but also resulted in gravelly stream wash being deposited in the lowlands, rendering large expanses of land uncultivable.[43] However, not all colonial accounts were so fulsome about the region's potential. In 1574 Father Martín de Rada observed that inhabitants scarcely produced enough to feed themselves and for part of the year had to live off roots.[44] This was attributed to the poor soils and the lack of efficient tools.[45] However, other common threats to production were floods and droughts caused by the highly seasonal climate and infestations by rats or locusts.[46] The fact that Ilocanos were said to esteem their provisions more than gold suggests that food security may have been a problem.[47]

Inland from the middle Ilocos coast was the broad Abra Valley that was reached through a narrow gorge called the Banauang Gap. The inhabitants here were known as Tinguians. There are few early accounts of subsistence activities in this region, but recent ethnographic studies suggest that root crop cultivation may have dominated and been displaced in colonial times by dry-rice cultivation spreading from the lowlands; wet-rice cultivation may only date from the last century.[48] When the Augustinian Father Juan Pareja was working there in the early seventeenth century he apparently ate nothing but roots.[49]

Apart from the cultivation of rice and roots, other subsistence activities receive scant attention in the early colonial record. Given the exposed conditions on the coast, fishing would probably have been confined to inshore waters and river estuaries. Freshwater fishing in rivers and rice fields using nets and various forms of traps was probably an important subsistence activity as it is today.[50] Pigs, *carabaos*, and goats were raised in both regions,[51] the first two being traded for gold with upland groups.[52] In addition, the inhabitants of Pangasinan exploited deer in the forested interior and developed an extensive trade in deerskins, particularly with the Japanese.[53] In fact the Pangasinans had long-standing contacts with mainland Asia and had sent tribute missions to China from the fifteenth century, if not earlier.[54] Miguel de Loarca characterized the Pangasinans as traders.[55] In Ilocos an item that attracted considerable attention was cotton, which was produced in large quantities and woven into cloth.[56] In colonial times it became an important item of tribute and illegal trade.

The Population of Pangasinan and Ilocos in 1570

Estimating the population of Pangasinan in 1570 is particularly difficult since such a large proportion of the population remained outside effective administration. The earliest evidence comes from Goiti's expedition that counted 2,835 households in Burinao (Bolinao) and Pangasinan. This figure was reportedly based on a comprehensive survey commissioned prior to the allocation of *encomiendas*, but 10,000 "indios" were eventually distributed in *encomiendas* by Guido de Lavezaris in 1574.[57] They included five *encomiendas* of 1,000 tributaries each in the Bay of Pangasinan, while the port of Japan (Agoo) and 1,000 "indios" in the villages of Sagut, Malonpot, Silac, and neighboring villages were assigned to the Crown. A further 4,000 were allocated in Zambales. The lack of specification of the villages, except those reserved for the Crown, suggests a limited knowledge of the region, while the 10,000 tributaries clearly represented only a proportion of the region's population.

Bishop Salazar's report in 1588 included a similar total figure but gave a different breakdown. He reported that there were 5,000 *tributos pacíficos*, of whom 1,500 paid tribute to the Crown, and that in the interior between the Pampanga and Pangasinan there were 3,000 "indios" in two *encomiendas*, who were cannibals but generally peaceful, and another 3,000 who had not been converted who were living in the mountains.[58] However, the list of *encomiendas* drawn up in 1591 includes only five *encomiendas*, with only two paying tribute to the Crown.[59] At that time it was judged that five more priests were needed to administer the total of 5,900 tributaries, of which about 1,000 in Tugui and Bolinao had not been pacified. Elsewhere in the report the figures are rounded to 6,000 *tributos enteros* and 24,000 *personas*, and these have generally been taken to represent the size of the population at the time of Spanish arrival.

Notwithstanding this early documentary evidence, Cortes suggests that in pre-Spanish times more likely the population of Pangasinan was between 30,000 and 40,000, or even 50,000.[60] She notes that many villages that were later converted by the Dominicans were not included in the early tribute lists and that at the end of the Spanish period the populations of Pampanga and Pangasinan were comparable and hence most likely would have contained similar populations in the past. While the population of Pangasinan was probably considerably higher than the number registered, the argument contains a number of assumptions that appear untenable. Although it is clear that a significant proportion of the population in 1570 was not included in early estimates, interior populations are unlikely to have existed on the scale found on the coast at that time, nor in numbers that were later living in the interior, when their numbers are likely to have been inflated by fugitivism. Furthermore, Cortes assumes that demographic trends in the two regions were similar, which is debatable given differences in the nature and intensity of Spanish contact. Nevertheless, some adjustment is needed to the recorded tributary figures to take account of interior populations, the likely impact of epidemics, and the protracted nature of conquest in Pangasinan. Hence, given the initial number allocated in *encomiendas* in 1574, the figure of 40,000 for the total population suggested by Cortes is not unreasonable, though not wholly for the reasons she gives.

In 1573 Father Francisco de Ortega made the first estimate of populations further north. Critical of the exactions made by the early expeditions, he claimed that when Salcedo first pacified "the province of Ilocos and the other three [provinces] that were discovered in the contracosta [opposite coast]," they had possessed 400,000 men, but by then no more than 40,000 remained.[61] These figures may have been exaggerated to condemn the activities of Salcedo and Goiti, but if they included Cagayan, the *contracosta*, and possibly Bikol, then the figure of 400,000 becomes more credible. However, the estimate of 40,000 tributaries in 1573 appears to have been for Ilocos alone. In April 1574 Lavezaris allocated 31,800 Ilocanos in thirty *encomiendas*, of which six of 1,000 each were distributed without the villages being specified because their names were unknown or they had not been pacified. A further 6,000 were reserved for the Crown.[62] The list of towns included in these *encomiendas* extends to Dingras in northern Ilocos, but 4,000 previously assigned to Salcedo and 2,000 in the Naluacan Valley allocated to Goiti need to be added to these figures. It is also necessary to add villages in the Purao Valley that were assigned to the Crown and which in 1573 possessed 1,800 houses.[63] This would give a minimum figure of about 45,600 tributaries. This figure is considerably larger than the 9,185 houses in Ilocos from which Goiti levied tribute, although his account only extended as far north as Sinait and Varo and during his relatively short period on the coast he would have been unable to visit every town or village. On the other hand, it was said that those who received *encomiendas* generally found fewer people than expected because of the soldiers' inexperience and their desire to magnify their achievements.[64]

Miguel de Loarca's list of *encomiendas* in 1582 included 27,100 tributaries in Ilocos, but it noted that there were other unknown and unpacified communities in the north between the valley of Vicagua and the Cagayan Valley.[65] Similarly, in 1588 Bishop Salazar reported that Ilocos possessed 27,000 tributaries, but also noted there were many in the hills that had not been allocated in *encomiendas*.[66] Thus while some observers believed the numbers allocated in *encomiendas* had been exaggerated, the figure of about 40,000 in 1570 seems credible, particularly given the record of decline prior to the 1580s.

It is clear that between 1570 and 1582 the population of Ilocos suffered a significant decline, mainly due to conquest and forced exactions, which not only caused high mortality but also caused many to flee inland. In addition to the Salcedo and Goiti expeditions, another headed by Don Luis Sahajosa to Cagayan in the mid-1570s was said to have caused more devastation than the corsair Limahon. On the return journey through Ilocos this expedition reputedly destroyed the province of Ylagua, which had once possessed 12,000 men, reducing one village from 4,000 houses to 50.[67] Some observers singled out Ilocos as the region most affected by Spanish expeditions of conquest.[68] Accepting that there may have been some exaggeration in the figures when the initial allocation of *encomiendas* was made and that there were about 30,000 in the early 1580s,[69] an estimate of 40,000 *tributos* for 1570 appears credible. To this number needs to be added those in Abra with whom the Spanish probably had only fleeting contact during the sixteenth century. In 1600 they may have totaled between 10,000 and 15,000, which, using the contemporary multiplier of four, would suggest an additional 2,500 to 3,750 *tributos*.[70] Hence, the total number of *tributos* in Ilocos in 1570 may be estimated at between 42,500 and 43,750.

The Search for Gold

Spanish interest in Ilocos was sustained in the early colonial period by the possibility of finding gold. When the Spanish failed to find gold deposits in the lowlands, they mounted expeditions into the highlands into Igorot territory. Nevertheless, the resident Spanish population of Ilocos remained small since the coast gained an early reputation for being unhealthy and was exposed to attacks by pirates; it also had relatively little to offer economically compared to the trading opportunities that existed in Manila. Similarly, no significant economic enterprises developed in Pangasinan, but its location closer to Manila meant that the burden of *vandalas* and *polos* was greater than in Ilocos. Nevertheless, the main contacts between Spaniards and Filipinos in both regions were with members of the missionary orders.

The Augustinian chronicler Gaspar de San Agustín claimed that gold had been worked in Ilocos in pre-Spanish times and was an important item of trade with China,[71] while in 1574 Andrés de Mirandola claimed that rich gold mines existed at Baratao, Turney, Aringay, and Dingras.[72] Some gold may have been extracted from these mines, but most was probably acquired by trade with Zambals and Igorots, in whose territories the richest gold mines were located.[73] It was not long before attempts were made to locate gold deposits in the interior highlands. In 1576 Sergeant Major Juan de Morón located some mines at an unspecified location "twenty leagues inland" and returned with samples that were sent to Mexico for testing.[74] During the 1580s two other expeditions headed by Juan Pacheco Maldonado and the chief of Candaba in Pampanga, Dionisio Capolo, penetrated the headwaters of the Pampanga and Cagayan rivers, and in 1591 Governor Dasmariñas commissioned a further three expeditions led by his son, Luis Pérez Dasmariñas, Francisco de Mendoza, and Pedro Sid.[75] Accounts of these expeditions and the groups they encountered are discussed in chapter 13. They are worthy of mention here due to the demands they made on lowland communities for provisions and auxiliaries. These expeditions often brought the conscripts into conflict with highland groups and exposed them to malarial infection as they penetrated the interior.

During the first few decades of the seventeenth century, the difficulties of mining in the remote, rugged, and hostile interior discouraged further expeditions. William Henry Scott suggests that from the 1580s Spanish interest in gold waned as Mexican silver proved an effective substitute for gold in its trade with China.[76] However, the advent of the Thirty Years War provoked the Crown to seek new sources of revenue, and in 1618 it pressed the authorities in the Philippines to develop the islands' gold mines.[77] As a result, in the 1620s three sizable expeditions were mounted that drew forces from Ilocos and Pangasinan.[78] In 1620 Captain García de Aldana y Cabrera led an expedition of some 1,700 men and managed to return with samples of ore.[79] In 1623 Sergeant Major Antonio Carreño de Valdés headed an even larger and better-provisioned expedition from Pangasinan, but beset by native hostility, short supplies, difficult terrain, and adverse weather conditions, it had to be relieved by Captain Alonso Martín Quirante. The last expedition in 1624 comprised a force of 1,903 that included 893 Ilocanos and 855 Pangasinans.[80] The expeditions together cost a staggering 33,982 pesos and at the time were judged no less costly in Filipino labor and lives.[81] Despite their failure, the idea of developing the gold mines and pacifying the Igorots remained. One last effort occurred in the 1660s when, allied with a disaffected Igorot, Layuga, Admiral Pedro Durán de Monforte mounted an expedition from Candon made up of 100 Spaniards and 2,000 Filipinos.[82] It discovered seven gold mines, but they yielded little profit and after two to three years on the Cordillera, mounting native hostility forced the expedition to withdraw.

The Spanish maintained their interest in Ilocos due to its relatively dense native population and the trade in gold, but the climate proved unhealthy for Europeans. Nearly all the troops left by Salcedo at Vigan on his first exploratory expedition soon became ill and returned to Manila,[83] while Francisco Morante, a participant in the Goiti expedition, reported that many Spaniards had died in conflicts and from an unspecified illness.[84] Salcedo himself died of a fever in 1576.[85] In Luzon, malaria is generally found in the forested foothills above 800 feet, but in Ilocos the mountains come close to the coast, so expeditions would not have had to venture far inland before moving into a malarial zone. Although malarial resistance is not high in the Philippines, it is perhaps significant that G6PD deficiency associated with malaria resistance is highest in northwest Luzon, which suggests its greater prevalence in that region.[86] The forested foothills were places to be avoided and those involved in expeditions or cutting timber were vulnerable to infection.[87] As early as the 1580s Franciscans working in Ilocos judged that it was not a place where they could live because those assigned there shortly became "very ill looking, flabby and with colorless countenances" and others were afflicted with stomach ailments.[88] In the late sixteenth century the unhealthy climate was given as the main reason why so few Spaniards lived in Ilocos despite its being regarded as the richest province in the islands.[89] By 1591 Vigan possessed only five or six Spanish *vecinos*,[90] and in 1609 Antonio de Morga claimed that Spaniards no longer lived there.[91]

Another reason given for the decline of the province was its vulnerability to attack by Chinese and Japanese pirates. The Chinese and Japanese continued to frequent the west coast of Luzon in the sixteenth century, raiding or trading as the opportunity arose. While Manila was the main focus of trade, many Chinese merchants, by choice or due to adverse weather conditions, also traded on the Ilocos coast.[92] But not all contacts with the Chinese and Japanese were peaceful. In 1574 the notorious Chinese corsair Limahon appeared on the Ilocos coast, and there were many other smaller attacks by the Chinese, Japanese, and Borneans.[93] Such attacks not only destabilized the region, but also provided opportunities for the introduction of acute infections.

Missionary Expansion

While few Spaniards and secular officials resided in Ilocos and Pangasinan, the regular clergy were active there throughout the colonial period. Augustinians probably accompanied Salcedo's expedition to establish Vigan in 1574, but native hostility retarded missionary efforts, and it was not until 1578 that Franciscans based at Vigan and Tuley began the conversion of local peoples. By 1591 the Franciscans had left and their parishes had become secular benefices.[94] Meanwhile, in 1586 Augustinians established their first residences at Ilauag (Laoag), Batac, Tagudin, and Baratao (in Pangasinan),[95] and by 1612 they had thirty-one priests working in twelve parishes.[96] While the Augustinians soon became firmly established in Ilocos, missionary progress in Pangasinan was slow due to continuing unrest provoked by ill treatment and excessive exactions.[97] Initially the Franciscans and Augustinians both worked there for brief periods,[98] and it was not until 1587 that the Dominicans established a permanent presence at Binalatongan.[99] By 1596 they had founded five residences[100] and by 1613 had taken over the Augustinian parishes of Lingayen and Manaoag.[101] After that time, Pangasinan remained a predominantly Dominican province.

Ilocos and Pangasinan were part of the bishopric of Nueva Segovia that was established in 1595 with its seat in Nueva Segovia in Cagayan.[102] Despite official intentions, in 1604 the second bishop of Nueva Segovia, Diego de Soria, took up residence in Vigan, as did most of his successors.[103] The preference for Vigan probably reflected the declining importance of the province of Cagayan and the difficulties of administering the bishopric from so remote a location.[104] Despite the erection of the bishopric, there were few secular benefices in Ilocos, and the Augustinians administered most parishes. The Augustinians founded permanent missions in the lowlands, but their attempts to form settlements in the highlands were generally short-lived and any converts they made were transferred to the lowlands. The division between peaceable lowland populations and hostile highland groups noted on Salcedo's first expedition thus remained throughout the colonial period, though the distinction came to be couched in terms of converted and unconverted peoples.

To facilitate the conversion and administration of local populations, the Augustinians attempted to establish the *cabecera-visita* system, as outlined in chapter 3. In Ilocos this involved bringing communities together to form *cabeceras*, which they referred to as *ministerios*.[105] However, since lowland peoples needed to reside near their rice fields, only those who could afford to live away from their lands or had enough serfs to work them settled near the church, perhaps being attracted by Christian ritual and pageantry.[106] *Cabeceras* thus came to be dominated by economic and political elites.

The extent of Augustinian mission fields fluctuated during the seventeenth century, but overall progress was slow. Isabelo de los Reyes y Florentino has noted that in 1600 the Augustinians possessed eighteen *pueblos* in Ilocos and by the end of the seventeenth century only six or seven more had been founded.[107] The Augustinians expanded their missionary activities on three main fronts. The earliest attempts focused on the Igorots. The Augustinians were involved in the major expeditions aimed at discovering gold and these often resulted in the transfer of small numbers of converts to lowland missions. Hence, following the failure of Pedro Durán de Monforte's expedition in the 1660s, small numbers were settled at Bauang, Bangar, and Narvacan.[108] Throughout the colonial period the lowland missions were also boosted by small numbers of converts attracted from the highlands through the efforts of individual missionaries. In 1760 the Augustinians had charge of 146 converted Igorots and 148 *catecúmenos* in the aforementioned villages, Candon, Namacpacan, Agoo, and Aringay together.[109]

Another major arena of Augustinian activity was the Abra de Vigan. In 1598 fathers Esteban Marín and Agustín Miño, based at Bantay, penetrated the Abra Valley and established a settlement at Bangued to serve as a center for the conversion of Tinguians of the region.[110] In the early seventeenth century, Father Juan de Pareja baptized 3,000 souls and the *visitas* of Tayum, Sabangán, and Bukao (Dolores) were established.[111] However, these towns were in daily conflict with unconverted Tinguians in surrounding settlements. Missionary activity seems to have been intermittent during the latter part of the century. The region was considered unhealthy and the population hostile, so the Bangued mission was regarded as poor and was often vacant.[112] Despite intermittent missionary activity, in 1756 the bishop of Nueva Segovia reported that the Tinguians of Abra were peaceable but were reluctant to be baptized because they would have to pay tribute. He estimated they numbered 10,000 souls distributed in 100 villages or *rancherías* of one, two, or three families.[113] Spanish control of the region was not effective until the nineteenth century, when most modern-day towns were founded.[114] Meanwhile, some converted Tinguians moved away from the hostile frontier and settled between Narvacan and Candon.[115]

Further north, early mission centers were established at Laoag, Batac, and Bacarra,[116] and from there the interior highlands of northern Ilocos were approached from both the south and north. Following a revolt in Batac and Dingras in the late 1580s,[117] a *visita* was established at Dingras as a base for converting interior populations. In 1610 it possessed three priests in charge of 1,500 tributaries and 4,500 *almas de confesión*. Subsequent missionary progress was slow.[118] In the early eighteenth century Father Nicolás Fabro converted more than 1,000 Tinguian near Dingras and founded a settlement at San Juan, while concerted efforts from the 1740s led to the establishment of Banna, Santiago, and Parras.[119] In 1760 Banna and Santiago possessed 437 Tinguian converts and 250 *catecúmenos*, while small numbers were to be found at Batac and Magsingal.[120]

Meanwhile to the north, in 1607 a *visita* of Bacarra was established at Bangui at the instigation of its *encomendero*. Despite the early establishment of this *visita* and a ministry there in 1624,[121] a missionary push from Bangui did not occur until 1668, when Father Benito de Mena Salazar founded villages at Adan, Vera, and Bangbanglo (Nacpartian).[122] By 1714 this mission field had been abandoned, but Father José Herice resumed work there in 1720 and founded two new settlements at Adan and Vera.[123] In 1754 the Adan were said to comprise only one *pueblo* of sixty houses living under the protection of the Apayao, who were very numerous.[124]

The slow progress of the missions in Ilocos is evident in the relatively small numbers of converts who were baptized between 1754 and 1758. During this period only 463 baptisms were recorded; 41 of those were Adan, 11 Apayao, 63 Tinguian, and the remainder Igorot.[125] These numbers may be compared with estimates in

1788 of 10,000 for the Tinguian in Abra, of 10,000 converts from Vigan to Agoo, and of 10,000, probably of mixed ethnic origins, from Kavagan, Inbusi, Apayao, and Pangutgutan.[126] The lack of progress was blamed on the shortage of priests, the use of force on the expeditions, and the failure of converts to adapt to a new way of life.[127]

Missionary progress by the Dominicans in Pangasinan was equally slow. Although by the early seventeenth century 10,000 to 12,000 were reportedly paying tribute, they were described as only "half-pacified."[128] Cortes claims that the inhabitants gradually accepted Christianity after being impressed by miracles, acts of faith, and the seeming healing powers derived from the priests' knowledge of medicine.[129] However, the unrest caused by Spanish demands for tribute and labor, which were to increase during the Hispano-Dutch War, inevitably retarded the process of conversion. By 1621 the Dominicans had charge of ten parishes in Pangasinan and their sixteen priests were ministering to 25,000 souls.[130]

Toward the end of the seventeenth century, the Dominicans opened up active mission fields in the foothills to the northeast hoping to link up with Dominican missions in the Cagayan Valley. Missions were founded at San Bartolomé de Agno in 1687 and at Asingan in 1688.[131] At that time there were still said to be many heathens in the mountains, including many fugitives from Spanish administration, who found they could obtain everything they wanted by trade without being subject to tribute, *vandalas*, and *polos*. There were also many *rancherías* between the Agno and Tarlac rivers. Despite these settlements, the region was often referred to as the "despoblado," and in the late seventeenth century it was the focus of Dominican activity, with settlements being founded at Paniqui, Camiling, and Baruc (Gerona).[132] However, from about 1720 missionary efforts shifted from the conversion of highland groups to the consolidation of settlements on the plain and the creation of new *pueblos* within the jurisdiction of existing towns.[133] During the eighteenth century the number under Dominican control increased only marginally, from 11,039 tributaries, or a total population of about 45,000, in 1708 to 58,725 souls in 1800.[134] Even in the nineteenth century only a small proportion of the population lived in formal *pueblos*.[135]

Tribute, *Vandala*, and *Polo*

Only a few *encomiendas* were allocated in Pangasinan, but tribute payments constituted only one of the levies imposed on its inhabitants. The region was a major source of rice and timber for shipbuilding, both of which were in high demand during the Hispano-Dutch War. Nevertheless, the greater distance of the province from Manila and attacks by Zambals made overland communication hazardous, so it did not suffer from *vandalas* and *polos* on the same scale as neighboring Pampanga. Nevertheless, the burden was sufficient to promote political unrest and fugitivism.

Following the exactions made by early expeditions, the Crown attempted to regulate tribute payments. Initially, Filipinos were not supposed to pay tribute until they received Christian instruction. This should have applied to Pangasinans, but it is clear that from an early date some were paying tribute.[136] In any case, in 1591 all those who had received Christian instruction whether or not converted became liable for payment.[137] Among the goods demanded in Ilocos and Pangasinan was gold, which was never worked by the inhabitants but in pre-Spanish times had been obtained by trade. Even though gold became increasingly difficult to acquire as Spanish conquest disrupted trading relations,[138] in 1594 the tribute payable by the inhabitants of both regions was set at two *maes* of gold and one *gallina*, together with six reals payable in Pangasinan in either silver or rice and in Ilocos in *mantas* or rice.[139]

Despite attempts at regulating tribute payments, the amounts specified were often exceeded. In 1597 charges were brought against the tribute collector for Ilocos, Francisco Salgado, for having exceeded the official levy of three *tostones* or its equivalent and exacting large numbers of additional *gallinas*. He was also charged with forcing communities to pay for those who were absent or dead and imposing additional taxes (*derramas*) and *vandalas* in rice and honey for which those supplying them were not paid or received inadequate payments.[140] Excessive exactions precipitated revolts, such as that against the *encomenderos* of Dingras and Batac, which resulted in the death of six Spaniards in Vigan.[141] By the turn of the century the number of Ilocanos paying tribute had fallen from 12,000 to only 2,500.[142] While tribute income was falling throughout the islands, the decline in the province of Ilocos was regarded as particularly noteworthy.

Vandalas, or forced sales to the government, were also imposed in Pangasinan and they continued even after the Hispano-Dutch War had ended. In 1655 the levy amounted to 9,000 *cestos* or baskets of husked rice.[143] However, the *vandala* gradually declined in importance and came to be imposed mainly in times of emergency. It was levied for defense at Zamboanga in 1738[144] and during the English invasion of Manila in 1763, but not again until 1780.[145]

More oppressive, particularly in Pangasinan, was the demand for forced labor. In common with the inhabitants of southwest Luzon and Pampanga, Pangasinans were forced to extract timber and work in the local shipyards. While the main naval dockyard in the Philippines was at Cavite in Manila Bay, ships were also constructed locally, notably at Lingayen, where there was a good supply of timber and native labor.[146] Ships were generally built of hard molave wood that was found on the drier soils of the interior and transported to the coast by river.[147] The construction of individual ships required the mobilization of a substantial workforce. In 1689 the *alcalde mayor* of Pangasinan was drafting 2,000 workers to extract wood and 1,000 to collect bamboo and fuel, while others were forced to build his personal *champán*.[148] Labor in these activities was hard and workers were often ill-treated, so mortality rates were high. For these reasons, in 1604 the Dominicans burned the cut timber so that their charges would not have to be employed in the construction of galleons ordered by Governor Acu a.[149] The demand for ships was highest during the Hispano-Dutch War, but even in the eighteenth century galleons were being built in Pangasinan.[150]

While the distance of Ilocos from Manila and the shipyards at Cavite moderated the demands for labor, the region became the main source of sailcloth.[151] Communities there were forced to make sailcloth, for which they received only token payments and were often owed considerable sums.[152] Apart from these official levies, *alcaldes mayores* and priests often employed Ilocanos to spin and weave cloth illegally,[153] from which one *alcalde mayor* reportedly made 14,000 pesos in two years.[154]

Persistent levies and demands for labor fueled growing resentment that erupted into open revolts, costing many lives and resulting in towns being devastated and economic activities disrupted. Major revolts exploited kinship ties to muster troops, but the lack of a supra-*barangay* organization meant that movements lacked coordination and were eventually suppressed. This characterized the rebellion in 1660 that started in Pampanga and spread to Pangasinan, Ilocos, and Cagayan.[155] In Pangasinan, Andrés Malong was able to muster 8,000 rebels,[156] but he was eventually defeated and the town of Binalatongan destroyed. In Ilocos the rebellion was suppressed by 3,000 troops, who devastated the towns of Vigan, Bantay, and Santa Catalina, killing 100 people and capturing 1,500. Some 134 rebels were sentenced to death and others were condemned to ten years' servitude on galleys or in hospitals, schools, or the naval dockyard at Cavite.[157]

The secular authorities were aware of the scale of fraud and abuse and conducted two *visitas*. The first *visita* by *oidor* Alonso de Avella Fuertes in 1690 brought charges for excessive levies and issued orders regulating the exaction of tribute and labor; it also succeeded in adding 3,240.5 tributaries to Pangasinan's tribute rolls.[158] Nevertheless, several revolts occurred in the early eighteenth century, and abuses of the tribute system were still continuing in 1743 when Joseph Ignacio de Arzadún y Rebolledo conducted another *visita*.[159] Excessive levies continued to be a significant grievance that underlay the major insurrection led by Diego Silang. This revolt took advantage of the English occupation of Manila in 1762 and succeeded in temporarily driving Spanish officials from Vigan.[160] It took the heaviest toll of all since the Spanish exacted vengeance for the rebels' stubborn resistance. According to the Dominican Domingo Collantes, 10,000 to 12,000 rebels were killed and others fled.[161] Worst affected were the large towns of Binalatongan, Calasiao, and Mangaldan. There seems little doubt that these revolts contributed to Pangasinan's low growth rate of 0.02 percent a year in the second half of the eighteenth century.[162]

Demographic Trends in Ilocos and Pangasinan

Tracking demographic trends in Ilocos and Pangasinan during the colonial period is beset by a number of difficulties. Knowledge of populations of these regions was limited by the small number of Spanish residents and the fact that a significant proportion of the population remained outside effective Spanish administration even into the nineteenth century. Moreover, this proportion fluctuated with the intensity of missionary activity and with migration. Even though Ilocos and Pangasinan remained largely in the hands of the same missionary orders throughout the colonial period, the numbers they administered and who paid tribute fluctuated. In Pangasinan the Dominicans extended their mission field into the interior plain, but even in the eighteenth century the eastern and western fringes of the plain were still forested; only in the nineteenth century were these forests cleared and new towns founded, especially around Binalonan.[163] Similarly, in Ilocos, the Augustinians opened up mission fields on three fronts, but these were not always sustained because of the shortage of priests and native hostility. Therefore the accounts by observers, officials, and priests often referred to only part of the region, and the areas to which their figures referred were often ill-defined. The situation is complicated further by the fact that the boundaries between secular and ecclesiastical jurisdictions did not coincide precisely. The *alcaldía mayor* of Pangasinan extended as far north as Bacnotan,[164] thereby including not only those settlements administered by the Dominicans, but also four under Augustinian control. Until 1735 it also included Bolinao, which in 1607 passed from the Dominicans to Augustinian Recollects.[165]

It is generally assumed that in the early colonial period coastal peoples fled into the mountains to escape Spanish rule, while later missionary efforts reversed this process by transferring converts in the mountains to the lowlands. These movements are thought to have been particularly significant in Ilocos; Felix Keesing has suggested that rice terracing was introduced to the Kankanai, Lepanto, and Bontoc by coastal peoples fleeing from colonial rule.[166] While migration probably contributed to the apparent collapse of coastal populations in the sixteenth century and their marked increase in the eighteenth century, it is difficult to estimate the scale of these movements and their exact influence on demographic trends.

The first forty years of colonial rule were characterized by a dramatic decline that was prolonged through much of the seventeenth century by the demands of the Hispano-Dutch War. In the list of *encomiendas* drawn up in 1591, the province of Ilocos was recorded as having 17,230 tributaries and 68,520 souls.[167] In 1606 a similar list of *encomiendas* in the province of Ilocos reveals a marked decline to only 10,544.5 *tributos*,[168] though in 1610 the Augustinians were said to be ministering to 12,300 tributaries and a total of 36,900 people "de confesión."[169] Most likely the difference in the figures for 1606 and 1610 does not reflect demographic changes, but a difference between fiscal and church records. Assuming an estimate of 43,000 tributaries in 1570, these estimates suggest that by 1610 the tributary population of Ilocos had declined by about 70 percent.

It has been estimated that the population of Pangasinan in 1570 may have been about 40,000. By 1591 the number of tributaries in *encomiendas* appears to have declined to 5,900, or 22,600 persons. By this time the Dominicans had made little headway converting interior groups, so they would not have been included in these figures. In 1592 an expedition against the Zambals resulted in 3,500 being captured or killed. Although some were settled in already pacified communities, many remained in the forested interior.[170] To take account of those who had recently been brought under Spanish control as well as those who still remained outside, it is suggested that the total population in 1600 may have been about 30,000.

The decline of the native population in Ilocos and Pangasinan may have been more apparent than real. In Pangasinan it may be exaggerated because initially the population was overestimated. For example, it was anticipated that the *encomienda* of Bolinao would have 3,000 tributaries, but in 1582 only 400 had been pacified. In both regions part of the decline might also be attributed to fugitivism. There is evidence for fugitivism from Ilocos that was precipitated by Spanish expeditions and demands for tribute and labor, though observers also noted that the fugitives generally returned to their homes after a period.[171] Even though part of the decline in populations under Spanish control might be attributed to flight, it is doubtful that migration occurred on such a scale as to account for such a massive demographic collapse. Contemporary observers generally blamed other factors such as conquest itself, ill treatment, food shortages, epidemics, and raids by highland groups and by Chinese and Japanese pirates. In Pangasinan, Zambal attacks and native unrest resulted in further losses.

Outspoken critics of the Spanish expeditions to western Luzon were clear that forced exactions of gold had taken a heavy toll of the local population.[172] Expeditions not only resulted in many being killed in conflict, but they also stimulated fugitivism and disrupted subsistence activities and family life. Subsequent demands for tribute and labor prolonged this process. The seasonal climate and occasionally severe droughts and floods exacerbated food shortages.[173] A regional breakdown of decline in the tributary population of Ilocos between 1582 and 1610 (Table 11.3) suggests that it was greatest around Vigan, where Spanish demands were the highest and where flight was probably more easily effected. While the average level of decline in Ilocos during this period was 54.6 percent, in central Ilocos it was 67.6 percent.

Since even the combined populations of Ilocos and Pangasinan would have been too low to sustain acute infections in endemic form, outbreaks were dependent on re-introductions from outside the region. The first may have arrived with expe-

Table 11.3 Regional Decline in the Tributary Population of Ilocos in the Early Colonial Period

	1572	1582	1591	1610	Percent decline 1582–1610
South	4,168	8,300	5,300	4,900	-41.0
Central	4,417	6,800	5,530	2,200	-67.6
North	600*	12,000	6,400	5,200	-56.7
Total	-	27,100	17,230	12,300	-54.6

Sources: 1572 AGI PAT 24-21 fols. 1–12 Martín de Goiti 1570s. Refers to the number of houses.
1582 AGI PAT 23-9 and BR 5: 107–111 Miguel de Loarca [1582]. Refers to *hombres* or men.
1591 AGI PAT 25-38 fols. 6–9 and BR 8: 105 Relación punctual de las encomiendas 31 May 1591. Taken from the figures for individual towns. The summary figure is given incorrectly as 17,130.
1610 AGI AF 20-4-34 Memoria de los conventos y ministerios 1610. Excludes Agoo and Alingayen.
* Incomplete: The geographical divisions of the regions are indicated in Map 11.1.

ditions of conquest. The first smallpox epidemic to strike Luzon in colonial times occurred in 1574, when it was said to have spread throughout all the islands and caused the death of many natives.[174] It was in 1574 that Juan de Salcedo left Manila to establish Vigan, and the expedition probably carried the disease to the region. The epidemic could partially explain the sharp decline of the population between 1574 and 1582, though observers generally attributed it to the devastation caused by Spanish expeditions. Epidemics appear to have been less frequent in Pangasinan, though in 1612 many children were dying of smallpox when the Dominicans were undertaking the conversion of Filipinos at Binmaley.[175] The fact that children rather than adults were affected suggests that smallpox may have afflicted the region recently or that it was becoming endemic. Smallpox could have been introduced through regular contacts with Chinese and Japanese traders.[176]

The Seventeenth Century

Few population estimates exist for northwest Luzon in the seventeenth century, but available accounts suggest that population levels in Ilocos remained fairly stable; indeed in the mid-seventeenth century the region was still regarded as densely settled.[177] Ilocos was largely spared *vandalas* and *polos*, but there were intermittent demands for auxiliaries for expeditions into the Cordillera, and throughout the century a number of "natural" disasters including plagues of locusts, epidemics, and earthquakes affected individual communities and retarded population growth.

In Ilocos there were regular food shortages and famines with major shortfalls recorded in 1629, 1634, 1656, and 1686–1687.[178] In most cases the shortages were linked to particular events such as locust infestation, volcanic dust, or epidemics. Attention has already been drawn to the possible impact of climate change on agricultural production in the seventeenth century.[179] Tree-ring analyses of teak trees from east central Java suggest that the period from 1598 to 1679 was exceptionally dry, with only thirteen years reaching the average rainfall.[180] In areas with a marked seasonal climate, the impact of lower than average rainfall would be to extend the dry season, resulting in crop failure and famine. Ilocos certainly appears to have suffered from famines during the seventeenth century,[181] but with the exception of 1634 the dates do not coincide with the driest years indicated by the tree-ring data. Given differences in the climatic regimes within the Philippines, a perfect correlation is not expected, but other causes, such as external demands for labor, rather than the weather, were generally blamed for the food shortages.[182]

Epidemics also took a significant toll. Since new disease episodes generally depended on the re-introduction of infections from outside the Philippines, and given that acute infections have only short periods of communicability, generally less than two weeks, in colonial times most epidemics probably came from mainland Asia and Japan rather than the Americas. The greater proximity of Ilocos to these regions, and the fact that vessels trading at Manila often stopped on the Ilocos coast for provisions or to await more favorable weather, made it particularly exposed to re-infection, particularly prior to the 1630s. Contacts with China and Japan subsequently declined,[183] but there were nevertheless epidemics of smallpox in Ilocos in the 1650s and in 1685, and of "catarro," an upper respiratory infection, possibly a cold or influenza, in 1688.[184] In all these cases outbreaks were simultaneous in other parts of Luzon. The region is also unlikely to have escaped the general epidemic of "peste" in 1668 that resulted in 50,000 deaths in the Philippines as a whole or the epidemic of smallpox that afflicted Manila in 1705.[185] The apparent lack of coincidence in the timing and scale of epidemics and the intensity of foreign trade may be explained by the more extended intervals between disease outbreaks in the second half of the seventeenth century, which enabled non-immune populations to emerge. This meant that when diseases were introduced, they were associated with high mortality.

High mortality might also be associated with earthquakes and volcanic eruptions, which occurred in Ilocos in 1620, 1627, 1634, 1641, and 1645.[186] These events were probably not directly responsible for many deaths, but the dust they produced often destroyed crops and sometimes precipitated famines.

Unlike most other regions in Luzon, the population of Pangasinan appears to have increased throughout the seventeenth century, but this increase probably reflected, at least in part, the extension of Dominican activity and more effective registration. During the early seventeenth century the Pangasinans are unlikely to have been spared the epidemics that assaulted Ilocos, and they were hard-pressed by the demands for provisions and labor, particularly for shipbuilding and expeditions, which not only undermined agricultural production but in the latter case often took them through malarial foothills. Headhunting raids from the mountains also took a small but regular toll of lowland peoples. At particular risk was the village of Manaoag, where in 1633 a raid by 400 Zambals succeeded in killing sixty converts and capturing others.[187] In such circumstances, it is surprising that the population of Pangasinan continued to increase to 7,666.5 *tributos* in 1655.[188] More surprising still is the increase to 9,025.5 in 1689, since this was a period of considerable unrest that included the highly disruptive and destructive revolt of 1660. In fact, the tributary population increased by about 0.79 percent a year in the second half of the seventeenth century and was one of the highest growth rates in Luzon. The more than 10,916 tributaries in 1700 suggests that Pangasinan may have contained about 50,000 people and therefore exceeded its size before Spanish contact. In addition, a significant number would have been outside Spanish administration. The trends indicated by the quantitative data are difficult to reconcile with the qualitative evidence.

The Eighteenth Century

By the second half of the seventeenth century many factors that had contributed to demographic collapse in the late sixteenth and early seventeenth centuries had moderated, allowing the population to achieve a level of stability. As elsewhere in the Philippines the lack of population growth in Ilocos in the seventeenth century contrasted markedly with its rapid expansion in the eighteenth century. As indicated in Appendix D, the population of Ilocos more than quadrupled from conservative estimates of about 10,000 tributaries in 1700 to more than 40,000 in 1800. The tributary population grew by about 1.5 percent a year during the century as a whole, but growth was more marked in the second half of the century, when it was increasing by 1.8 percent per annum. By 1800 the population may have returned to pre-Spanish levels.

Population growth was less marked in Pangasinan. A census of the bishopric of Nueva Segovia in 1800 indicates that the region had a total population of 83,369,[189] to which might be added at least another 15,000 to account for those in Zambales,[190] giving an overall figure of about 100,000. This would give a growth rate of about 0.7 percent a year from 1700. Precise trends are difficult to determine since many accounts refer only to the numbers administered by the Dominicans, who were responsible for only about 70 percent of the population. However, it seems clear that growth was concentrated in the first half of the eighteenth century when the tributary population grew by 1.1 percent a year, after which the rate of increase slowed.

Population growth in the eighteenth century can be attributed in part to more active proselytizing, which resulted in more people being settled in lowland communities, though they were in the hundreds rather than thousands. As contacts with the interior increased, others may have drifted down to the coast voluntarily, perhaps encouraged by kinship ties and trading contacts that predated Spanish arrival.[191]

More effective administration probably accounted for much of the growth in the registered population. In 1794 it was noted that since the *visita* of Ilocos by *oidor* Arzadún y Rebolledo in 1743, tribute income had increased from 25,000 to 60,000 pesos despite a war and two or three outbreaks of smallpox and another unspecified epidemic.[192] These mortality crises took a considerable toll of the population. In 1756 "una peste tan cruel" struck, which caused a fever, headache, and cold and resulted in death within two or three days. In Ilocos it killed 8,344 people, including 885 in Vigan, most of whom were adults, and another 8,313 fell victim in Pangasinan.[193] The high adult mortality suggests that the disease had not afflicted the population for some time or that this was a particularly virulent strain. These figures represent a significant proportion of the total population, especially in Pangasinan, where losses accounted for about 15 percent of the population. Another epidemic, this time of smallpox, struck Pangasinan in 1789, killing 3,532 people, including 904 adults.[194] This smallpox epidemic appears to have been only one of two or three during the century, another possibly occurring in 1762–1763. There may also have been an outbreak of measles in Ilocos Norte in 1784.[195] Epidemics would have retarded population growth in the late eighteenth century, especially in Pangasinan, and this may explain some of the fluctuations that appear in the official statistics.

These epidemic crises occurred against a background of continuing demands for labor that disrupted agricultural production and family life, and they fomented unrest. During the Silang insurrection, the towns of Panglaguit and Telbang were totally destroyed by royal troops. Binalatongan not only lost about a quarter of its population of 2,000 *tributos*, but the city and surrounding lands were devastated, causing its inhabitants to flee.[196] Similar forms of disruption, though not this scale, occurred during other periods of unrest.

More effective Spanish enumeration may have augmented the registered population of Ilocos, but this cannot account for scale of the increase in the eighteenth century, particularly given the mortality crises that afflicted the region. Ken de Bevoise has suggested that birth rates regulated population growth to a greater extent in the early colonial period than they did in the nineteenth century.[197] However, this argument can only be taken so far because many factors that contributed to high mortality rates—food shortages, excessive labor, death in conflict, and epidemics—also suppressed birth rates through their impact on marriage patterns, stress, and nutrition. Nevertheless, Ilocano families reportedly did not practice infanticide,[198] and this may have contributed to the relatively dense population the Spanish initially encountered there and may have facilitated demographic recovery following mortality crises. Compared to other regions, recovery may also have been aided by the lower demands for provisions and labor and the relative absence of commercial agricultural estates that brought restructuring to native societies around Manila and in southwest Luzon. Ken De Bevoise suggests that population increase after the Hispano-Dutch War was due less to a decline in mortality and more to an increase in fertility due to greater economic and social stability.[199] Nevertheless, in Ilocos major epidemics, food shortages, and volcanic eruptions delayed recovery in the second half of the seventeenth century despite the high birth rate. Although mortality crises occurred in the eighteenth century, the balance of births and deaths was more favorable.

The rapid growth of the Ilocano population in the eighteenth century occurred against the background of increased agricultural commercialization that brought new conflicts over land. Land shortages appear to have been particularly acute around Laoag, where it was said there was scarcely enough land for 500 *tributantes* when there were 4,500.[200] Population pressure was relieved in part by migration into the Abra and Laoag valleys and the foothills, but the settlement of upland regions was effectively blocked by the presence of mountain groups.[201] Local opportunities exhausted, in the early nineteenth century Ilocanos sought lands further south, initially in La Union and later Pangasinan.[202] In 1802 the *alcalde mayor* of Zambales suggested that 10,000 *tributos* from Ilocos should be settled in that region to aid its agricultural development and defense.[203] Migration from Ilocos became an essential feature of demographic change in Pangasinan in the nineteenth century, but the increase in the eighteenth century suggests that the flow may have begun earlier.[204]

CHAPTER 12

Cagayan

In Spanish colonial times the Cagayan Valley formed the backbone of the Dominican province of Cagayan. It encompassed the present-day provinces of Cagayan and Isabela, as well as the northern cordilleran provinces of Apayao and Kalinga. When the Spanish arrived, the region was ridden by internal conflict and soon the "Cagayan nation" came to be regarded as the most warlike in the Philippines and as being "of much cost and no profit."[1] Nevertheless, the Spanish thought it essential to maintain a permanent presence there, and they considered developing a port because of the advantages of an open sea and the absence of navigational hazards such as islands or strong winds and currents. More important, it was seen as a stepping-stone to China and of strategic importance in countering a possible invasion by the Japanese.[2] Hence, in 1581 the city of Nueva Segovia was founded and in 1595 it became the seat of the bishopric of Nueva Segovia. In the seventeenth century, however, Spanish interest in Cagayan waned as commercial activities focused on Manila and as hopes of gaining entry to China and fear of Japanese attacks faded. During the seventeenth and eighteenth centuries, many groups in the Cagayan Valley remained resistant to colonial rule and their pacification by the Dominicans was protracted.

Juan de Salcedo first made contact with the inhabitants of Cagayan during his circumnavigation of the island of Luzon in 1572,[3] but he received a hostile reception and continued on his journey without establishing a settlement. He subsequently offered to undertake another expedition to Ilocos and Cagayan, but Governor Guido de Lavezaris entrusted the task to Field Marshal Martín de Goiti. However, this expedition only extended as far as Ilocos. Two later expeditions also failed to establish a Spanish presence in Cagayan. In 1574 a ship sent to the region by Governor Sande under Luis de Sahajosa was destroyed by the Chinese corsair Limahon,[4] and in 1580 another expedition dispatched to found the town of Valladolid was forced to return because its members fell ill.[5] It was not until 1581 that Captain Juan Pablos de Carrión succeeded in establishing a permanent Spanish settlement in Cagayan. Carrión's expedition encountered a Japanese fleet at the mouth of the Cagayan River but managed to establish a fort and withstand attacks from both the Japanese and hostile natives. Due to the region's proximity to Japan and China, Carrión was instructed not to return to Manila until he had pacified the region. He therefore established the town of Nueva Segovia at Lal-loc on the banks of the Cagayan River.[6]

Even though no permanent Spanish settlement was established in Cagayan until 1581, by then much of the region had already been allocated in *encomiendas*. When *encomiendas* were assigned in Ilocos in 1574, the region was still relatively unexplored, so it was stipulated that if there proved to be insufficient people to allocate, others would be assigned in Cagayan. In addition, between 1574 and 1575, in anticipation of the pacification of Cagayan, 9,500 "indios" in unspecified villages were allocated in seven fairly large *encomiendas* to captains who had been involved in the Ilocos expeditions.[7] The numbers allocated were clearly guesses because at that time Cagayan had not been explored. Unfortunately, it is not clear when the majority of *encomiendas* in the Cagayan Valley were distributed, but in 1588 Nueva Segovia had forty *vecinos encomenderos*.[8] The 1591 list of *encomiendas* indicates that many recipients were soldiers who had been involved in expeditions, including Carrión himself, who possessed one of the largest *encomiendas*, that of Sinavanga, with 1,000 *tributos*.[9]

Although *encomiendas* were allocated, it is clear that the population had not been pacified. Initially Carrión was ordered not to exact tribute for a year, but as late as 1588 Bishop Salazar reported that tribute was being collected from only 7,000 of the 26,000 men who had been pacified.[10] This suggests that only about a quarter of the population had been subjugated and was paying tribute. However, official exchequer accounts for the same year recorded that the inhabitants had not been assessed for tribute because they had not been fully pacified.[11] There seems little doubt that tribute was being exacted from at least some communities and that it contributed to the continuing unrest. In 1589 it was reported that the whole province of Cagayan was in rebellion and that many Spaniards had been killed. In response, Captain Pedro de Chaves was dispatched with four or five ships and fifty soldiers and 200 native conscripts. Meanwhile, the rebels burned their villages and fled to the hills, so all the expedition could do was destroy their crops and palm trees.[12] Other attempts at pacification also failed, and the citizens of Nueva Segovia, fearful of leaving their homes and dying of hunger, petitioned Governor Dasmariñas to be allowed to abandon the city.[13] But in response, Captain Fernando Becerra Montano was sent in 1590 with fifty to eighty soldiers to begin the pacification of the Cagayan Valley.

Becerra Montano's expedition spent a year trying to pacify groups throughout the Cagayan Valley. From the rivers and valleys that he purportedly pacified, the expedition appears to have extended as far south as the Magat Valley and also had contact with the Mandaya and Gaddang, among whom Alonso Sánchez, the *alguacil mayor* of Nueva Segovia, conducted a follow-up expedition.[14] Even though many groups were probably pacified on these expeditions, exchequer figures for 1594 record that only 6,256 were paying tribute.[15] It is worth noting that in 1591 the Cagayan Valley was also approached from the south by two expeditions intent on exploring the province of Tuy.[16] The first, headed by the governor's son Don Luis Pérez Dasmariñas, passed down the Magat Valley, while a second, led by Don Francisco de Mendoza, seized supplies at Furao and encountered some Spaniards at the garrison of San Pedro and San Pablo, but few details exist.[17]

The Cagayan Valley in 1570

In terms of its physical geography, Cagayan is perhaps the most easily defined region in northern Luzon. Unified by the north-flowing Cagayan River and its tributaries, this drainage basin is bounded on three sides by mountains that limit contact with neighboring regions.[18] The Cordillera Central and the Caraballo Mountains to the west and south respectively will be considered in chapter 13. To the east are the Sierra Madre Mountains, which rise to over 5,900 feet and fall precipitously to the coast. Here Juan Salcedo's expedition in 1572 found no village for one hundred leagues.[19] Much of the Cagayan Valley is covered with deep alluvial soils, mainly sandy loams, whose fertility is maintained by extensive annual flooding. The rainfall averages between 60 to 80 inches a year, though the encircling high mountains create a rain-shadow effect and there is a marked dry season between December and May.

When the Spanish arrived, the native inhabitants of the Cagayan Valley were linguistically and culturally diverse. However, this diversity was not generally recognized by Spanish officials and priests, who more often distinguished between Christian tribute payers, apostates known as *remontados*, and unconverted *infieles*.[20] In pre-Spanish times the Ibanag occupied the lower reaches of the Cagayan Valley, and the Itavi and Gaddang lived upvalley, while pockets of Negritos were to be found in the foothills on both sides of the valley.[21] Early observations indicate that the inhabitants of the Lower Cagayan harvested a lot of rice that was grown on naturally irrigated lands along the banks of rivers.[22] Taro and millet were probably also grown. In addition, palm trees were widely exploited and were so important to the economy that they were often strategically destroyed by expeditions of conquest. They also grew cotton, raised pigs and *gallinas*, and hunted deer and buffalo. The Cagayan River and its tributaries were exploited for fish, and on the coast fishing was the mainstay of the economy, so that here tribute payments were made in cash rather than crops.[23] Spanish observers also noted that the inhabitants of the Cagayan Valley possessed gold, which they obtained from the mountains and traded with the Chinese and Japanese either directly or through Ilocos.[24]

As will be shown below, early observers converged in their view that the Lower Cagayan Valley was densely populated despite the state of constant intervillage feuding. Leaders derived their status from success in warfare rather than noble descent and enhanced it by distributing booty they acquired and by providing for their followers in times of crisis. Warfare took the form of headhunting raids, in which few captives were taken. Their main weapons were spears, daggers, and long shields.[25] At the time the Spanish arrived, a native leader known as Guiab, with a select band of about 300 men, was attempting to extend his power over the province, killing and destroying the lands of those who failed to submit to his authority. Mindful of Spanish success against the Japanese, Guiab sought to enlist their help, but Guiab's enemies agreed to accept Spanish rule in return for their support. After hanging Guiab, the Spanish were surprised to find their allies then turned on them and rebelled.[26] This episode suggests the existence of warrior leadership and that leaders

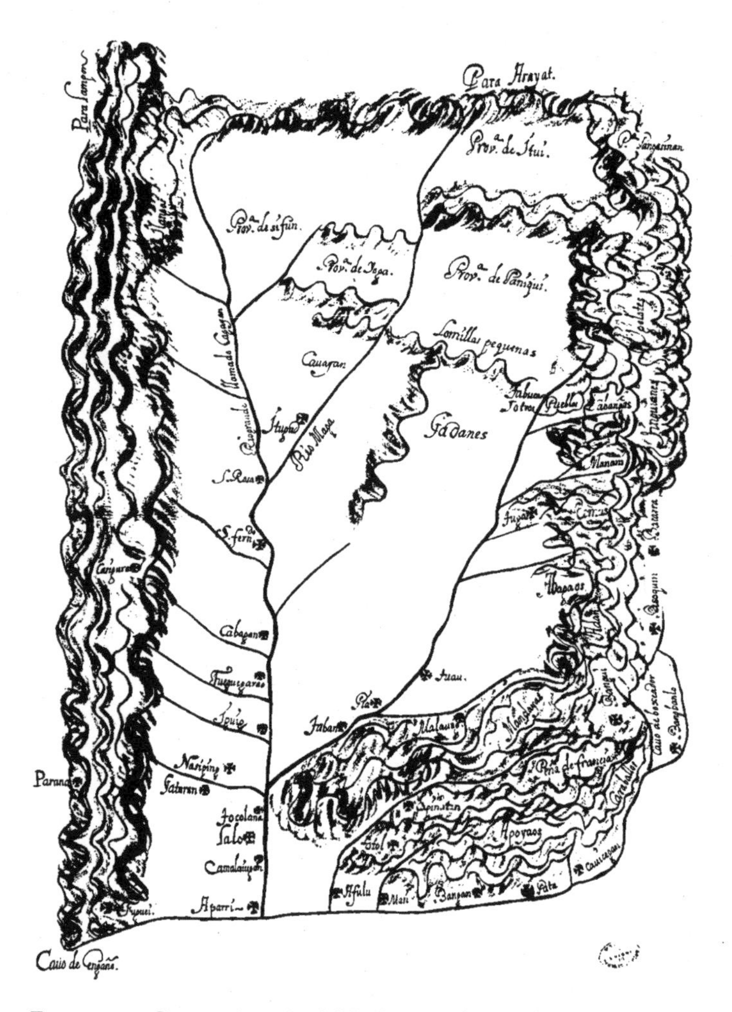

Figure 12.1. Cagayan in 1690. AGI Mapas y Planos Filipinas 140 Mapa de la vega del río Grande llamado Cagayan 1690.

were unable to exert power over a wide area. The Spanish were able to exploit these hostilities in conquering the region, but at a considerable cost of life.[27] In addition to losses sustained in intervillage feuding and unsuccessful attempts to pacify the region were losses from attacks by the Japanese, which were said to be more destructive in Cagayan than elsewhere.[28]

Slightly upriver on the flats to the west of the confluence of the Cagayan and Lower Chico were a group known as the Itavi, who spoke a different language related to Ibanag and Isneg.[29] There are only a few references to them in early colonial sources. The Dominican chronicler Diego de Aduarte recorded that in 1604 missionaries were working in "the estuary of Lobo and land of the Ytabes," where the inhabitants lived in many small settlements or *rancherías*.[30] The dispersed settlement pattern suggests that they were probably dry swidden cultivators.[31]

Further up the Cagayan Valley to the south of Tuguegarao was the district of Irraya, whose name derives from the Ibanag word meaning "upriver."[32] Some groups were known as Irraya, while others were called Gaddang or Gaddan. Still further upriver, and related to them, were the Yogad.[33] Their languages differed from Ibanag and Ifugao. Aduarte judged that the Gaddang were more difficult to subdue since they inhabited the hills and had little contact with either Spaniards or other groups.[34] In 1595 they had still not been assessed for tribute.[35] When the Spanish arrived, the Gaddang appear to have been dry-rice cultivators, for there are no references to wet-rice cultivation in the early colonial sources. The Yogad were probably also dry-rice farmers who adopted the plow about a century ago.[36] In the late twentieth century these groups were socially organized in nuclear family units that occasionally included a relative, thereby forming households of about four persons that were sometimes quite isolated.[37] In the eighteenth century, Father Antolín judged that the "Gadanes Yogades" from Tuao to Cauayan, including those inland, numbered 4,000. He claimed they occupied the best lands, forest, and rivers and therefore had access to good subsistence resources. They cultivated cotton in abundance, which they used for clothing, but they also painted their arms and hands, wore gold jewelry, and had gold teeth fillings. The flats of Diffun were described as so fertile that cotton, rice, maize, and sugar cane could be produced with little effort.[38] Father Antolín equated the Gaddang with the Paniqui, so that by the late eighteenth century some may have been living further south in the Magat Valley.

The Population of Cagayan in 1570

Estimating the population of the province of Cagayan in 1570 is particularly difficult since many groups had little contact with Spaniards and existing accounts refer to only limited parts of the valley, mainly to its lower reaches. Gaspar de San Agustín claimed that Juan de Salcedo in his circumnavigation of Luzon in 1572 was keen to proceed to Cagayan because he had heard rumors that it possessed "more than 40,000 men."[39] On receiving a hostile reception, he anchored on a small island at the mouth of the Cagayan opposite a village "where there were many people." Subsequently an "innumerable multitude" mustered with more than 300 boats, and, faced with "so many people," he decided not to engage them in battle but continue on his journey.[40] It is clear from this account that the lower reaches of the Cagayan were densely settled, but these observations cannot be extrapolated to the rest of the valley.

By the 1580s several expeditions had penetrated the Cagayan Valley, and Miguel de Loarca recorded that on the banks of the Cagayan River there were large settlements with 30,000 men.[41] What proportion of the valley this referred to is not clear. In 1590 it was claimed that Fernando Becerra Montano's expedition

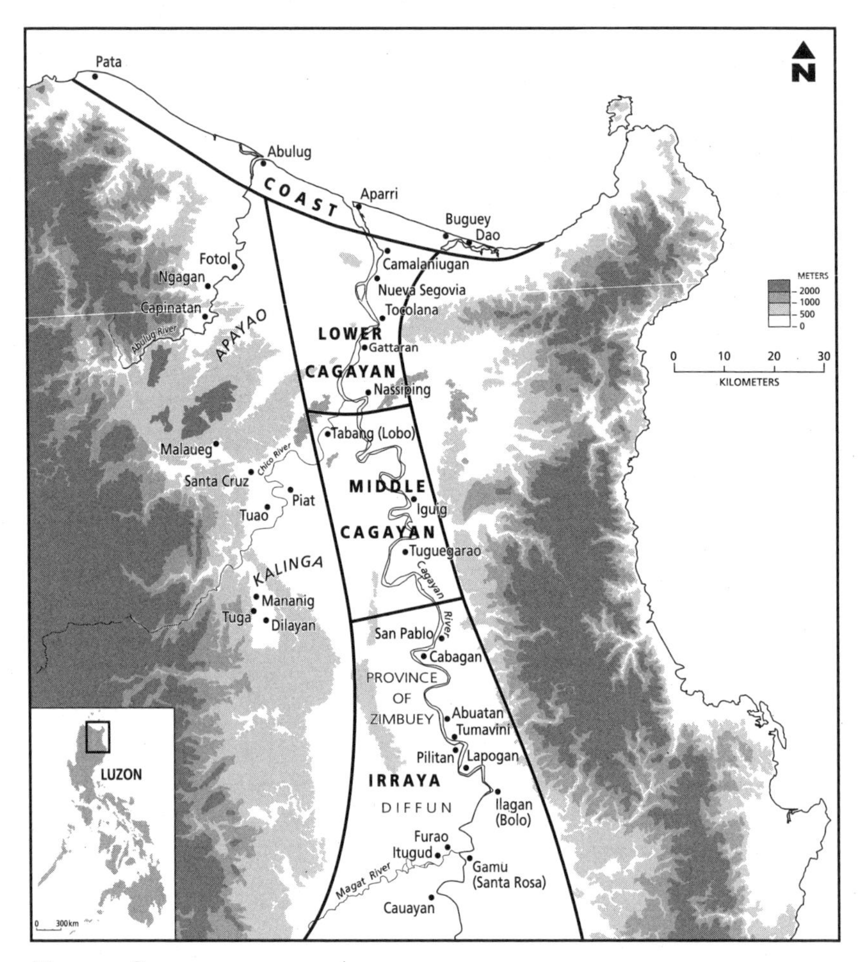

Map 12.1. Cagayan

had pacified 25,000 "hombres." In this case it is clear from the rivers and valleys it purportedly pacified that the expedition extended as far south as the Magat Valley but did not include groups on the coast or in the Lower Cagayan Valley, which were "at peace."[42] This expedition appears to have had at least some encounters with neighboring highland groups, for example, with the Mandaya at Fotol and probably with the Gaddang in the province of Zimbuey, located near Pilitan in Irraya, but it does not appear to have contacted those in the surrounding mountains. Hence, in 1593 it was said that Becerra Montano's expedition had found eight villages at the "estero de Zimbuey" that had rendered obedience, but it was rumored that there were many more settlements. The follow-up expedition led by Alonso Sánchez uncovered a further twenty villages containing more than 2,000 men.[43] This suggests that the 25,000 men reportedly pacified by Becerra Montano referred essentially to those living near the Cagayan River itself and that significant numbers remained outside Spanish control in the foothills. The list of *encomiendas* drawn up in 1591 probably did not contain information collected during these expeditions; indeed at that time only about 22 percent of the population living in Cagayan was described as being "at peace."[44] This was mainly on the coast and in the Lower Cagayan Valley; elsewhere the inhabitants were described as in rebellion or at war. Adding 22 percent to the figure of 25,000 men reputedly pacified by Becerra Montano would give a total of 30,500 for the valley. This is likely to be an underestimate since by then the population of the lower valley had already declined significantly. Also, as Alonso Sánchez's expedition indicates, large numbers were still outside Spanish control. Contact estimates of 40,000 men and a total population of about 160,000 are thus likely to be underestimates.

Progress in the Dominican Missions

Initially the Dominicans made few converts due to continuing native hostility that was aggravated by mistreatment by *encomenderos* and tribute collectors.[45] Don Rodrigo Ronquillo, the *encomendero* of Lobo, was singled out for particular condemnation and died in prison. By 1596 two missions had been established on the coast at Pata and Abulug (Tular), but in 1598 a four real increase in the tribute demanded sparked a revolt. This was suppressed by the *alcalde mayor*, Pedro de Chaves, and twelve of the leaders were executed.[46] The governor said he considered it prudent to punish a few leaders but admitted that *encomenderos* had given the natives cause to rebel, so once they had been pacified they were generally treated leniently.

The fragmented political organization of Cagayan communities initially helped facilitate in their subjugation, but later it became an obstacle to maintaining order and furthering conversions, particularly given the limited Spanish presence in the region. The province was insufficiently important economically or strategically to warrant a large military presence, for which more pressing needs existed elsewhere in the archipelago. Nevertheless, a garrison was maintained at Nueva Segovia[47] and small detachments of soldiers were located in a number of towns. While ostensibly there to protect Spanish officials and citizens, their activities often contributed to persistent hostile relations with local populations.

By 1610 the Dominicans possessed eleven ministries in Cagayan and had charge of 10,500 "indios,"[48] which included the two well-established missions at Pata and Abulug that together contained 1,900 "indios." Others had been established on the Lower Cagayan River near Nueva Segovia at Camalaniugan and slightly upriver at Tocolana. Still further upriver two more were founded at Nassiping at the junction of the Chico River and in the Lower Chico. Together these missions had charge of 4,400 "indios." The Dominicans had also begun to extend their activities up the Cagayan and into the western foothills. By 1610 they had established missions as far south as Malaueg, Tuguegarao, and Pilitan, where they had made 3,900 converts, and were beginning work among the *tingues* of Zimbuey. All the missions founded up to that date clustered in the Cagayan Valley or the coast; the only mission to be established in the foothills was at Fotol, where the Dominicans were ministering to 300 "indios" and were beginning to convert the Mandaya.

For the seventeenth century, information relating to the Cagayan Valley comes mainly from Dominican chronicles, particularly those of fathers Diego de Aduarte and Vicente de Salazar. These accounts, together with other Dominican sources, provide details of the newly opened mission fields, notably among the Mandaya and Kalinga, but say very little about the progress of Christian settlements along the banks of the Cagayan River, with the exception of the Irraya or Gaddang. Throughout the seventeenth century the province was described as in rebellion or only partially pacified. In the 1620s conflicts within the region were so serious that they were seen as constituting one of the four wars the Spanish were conducting in the Philippines, the others being in the island of Hermosa (Taiwan), Maluku, and Jolo.[49] In 1626 Governor Silva reported that an expedition had forced 1,000 rebels down from the mountains, and due to a general pardon more were coming down each day.[50] But the unrest continued and between 1627 and 1628 a particularly large punitive expedition composed of 2,000 "friendly Indians" destroyed eight villages and their lands.[51]

Missionaries working in the Middle Cagayan Valley faced difficulties in converting the Irraya and Gaddang, who were regarded as the most warlike inhabitants of the valley. When Nueva Segovia was founded, several forts were established because it was said that the province was on the frontier with the "fierce and barbarous" Irraya, who lived in the inaccessible mountains.[52] In 1608 three new missions were founded at Abuatan, Bolo, and Batavag, which with the previously established village of Pilitan together contained 2,000 houses.[53] However, in 1615 and 1621 revolts occurred in the first three missions, apparently inspired by some *aniteros* or shamans.[54] Father Pedro de Sancto Tomás attempted to draw them back from the mountains, but when he died in 1622 missionary efforts lapsed, though those settled at Maquila later moved south to found the mission of Cabagan in 1646.[55]

Not until 1673 were missionary efforts resumed in the Middle Cagayan Valley under Fathers Pedro Sánchez and Geronimo de Ulloa. At that time Cabagan marked the frontier between those who had been converted and heathen and apostate groups upriver. The banks of the Upper Cagayan were known to be densely populated and to harbor many apostates from Cabagan, Tuguegarao, and Iguig.[56] In 1678 it was resolved that Father Pedro Ximénez, based at Cabagan, should proceed with their conversion. He declined the offer of military support and settled some converts from Diffun at Santa Rosa.[57] Another 300 who lived further inland decided to settle at Cabagan, Santa Rosa, or the newly established settlement at Nuestra Señora de Victoria de Itugud. Finally another 100 formed the village of San Fernando at the site of the old mission at Bolo. When Father Ximénez was transferred to Apayao in 1684, two missionaries continued working in the area and by 1690 had baptized many in San Fernando (Ilagan), Santa Rosa, and Itugud. However, the converts were leaving because of excessive demands for services and ill treatment by soldiers in the garrison at Itugud.[58]

The missionaries' strategy, as elsewhere in the Philippines, was to work through existing leaders, so the Dominicans legitimized the status of native leaders, though this did not extend to shamans, whose position they attempted to undermine by destroying shrines and ritual objects. Neither did their tolerance extend to other native practices such as headhunting and slavery.[59] While native leaders may have been relatively easy to convert, in Cagayan it proved more difficult to bring its small, scattered communities together to form missions. The predominant form of agriculture practiced in the valley, particularly upriver and in the foothills, was dry-rice farming, where the characteristic settlement pattern was one of small hamlets or even single houses rather than large nucleated settlements.[60] Local populations saw few benefits from moving their homes away from their swiddens or adopting wet-rice cultivation using plows and *carabaos*, as the missionaries wished. On the coast, where this type of cultivation was already practiced and settlements were more nucleated, the missionaries' task was easier.

A major obstacle to missionary work was the oppressive exactions and trading activities of Spanish officials, *encomenderos*, and soldiers.[61] Abuses of the tribute system were apparent from its first introduction. The inhabitants of Cagayan were assessed for tribute in the late sixteenth century, but more than a century later the assessments had not been revised. According to native leaders, a fundamental problem was that part of the tribute had been assessed in cash that was impossible for them to obtain.[62] Also, the assessment in kind was undertaken at a time when the harvest was abundant and prices were low, so they claimed the tribute they were required to pay was normally worth about four times as much as they were assessed. Furthermore, it was exacted with "such cruelty" that families were forced to pay for those who were absent in the service of Spaniards or who had died. Abuses of the tribute system were particularly rife in times of shortage, when tribute was exacted in full even though it was said that families did not have a grain of rice left to support their children or to sow the following year, or even a single real with which to buy food or clothing.[63] Harassed by tribute collectors, many fled to other villages and provinces, often leaving their families, while others paid off their tribute debts through service.[64] As early as 1624 Father Ruiz claimed there were villages in Cagayan where one-third of the inhabitants were indebted and spent their whole lives as "half slaves."[65]

Excessive exactions were not limited to *encomenderos*, but were also made by Spanish officials and soldiers. Once formal communities had been established, they were often visited by *alcaldes mayores* and soldiers under the pretext of ensuring they had been pacified, but with the aim of indulging in trade and illegal exactions. Trade not only brought exploitation but also, it was alleged, hindered Christian conversion.[66] Many goods traded by the new converts such as iron, salt, cloth, tobacco, and wine were destined for groups living in the mountains, from whom they acquired gold and wax. Since those in the highlands obtained the goods they needed through this means, there was no incentive for them to settle in the missions. At the same time, the leaders of Christian communities who acted as intermediaries and benefited from this trade discouraged them from joining the missions, telling them they would be subject to tribute payments and forced labor.[67] In an attempt to encourage those living in the hills to settle in Christian villages, in 1642 the Crown banned all trade and communication with those in the highlands on pain of one hundred lashes and two years' service at Cavite, a ban that was reaffirmed in 1696.[68] The trade did not cease, however, for there were too many interested parties. While this problem was not unique in the Philippines, it was regarded as worse in Cagayan because of its remoteness.[69]

There is little doubt that the presence of soldiers greatly hindered missionary efforts. Due to the persistent threat of revolt, small numbers of soldiers were stationed throughout the region. In the 1680s, ten villages had small garrisons that generated considerable demands for goods and services. Particularly onerous was the transportation by river of soldiers and supplies to support them. At the end of the seventeenth century it was alleged that the villages of Nassiping, Gattaran, and Tocolana, located on the Cagayan, together with those of Capinatan, Fotol, and Abulug on the coast had been "destroyed" by such demands and that many had fled to the mountains or to other provinces. It was claimed that villages that fifty years earlier had contained 600 or 700 *tributos* had been reduced to 100. Demands were equally onerous in communities where garrisons were established. Here the inhabitants were required to build houses for the soldiers, clear their lands, and carry out many other services; they were in effect slaves of the commander of the garrison.[70] The Dominicans and native leaders were thus united in their opposition to the military presence. The former maintained they could achieve more without the presence of soldiers, citing one priest who went to Capinatan without an escort and in eight months had converted 1,300 Mandaya.[71]

Even where converts had formed Christian communities, excessive exactions, epidemics, or famines might cause them to flee or rebel. In response, punitive expeditions often destroyed their fields and palm trees in an attempt to force them to return,[72] but this did little more than alienate them further. Thus the missionaries came to distinguish those who had been converted but had rejected Christianity and deserted their settlements—the *remontados*—from pagan groups.[73] In 1678 there were said to be 4,000 apostates living among pagans in the mountains,[74] and a decade later the Dominican provincial recorded that fifty leagues upriver there were three or four very numerous "nations" to which many apostates had fled, of which the most important were the "Gadanes, Sifun, Yoga[d] and Paniqui."[75] Later in the eighteenth century, 600 Gaddang and Yogad were living in missions in the province of Paniqui.[76]

In the early eighteenth century, progress continued to be slow, but the opening up of the road from Pangasinan to Cagayan in 1739 enabled the extension of missionary efforts into the Upper Cagayan Valley.[77] Although details are lacking, it seems that the Dominicans continued working in the Upper Cagayan in the early eighteenth century. In 1711 Father Juan Martínez reported that in the province of Irraya they had formed six villages, three quite large and three medium-sized.[78] The two missions that are consistently mentioned in Dominican sources are Santa Rosa and Tumavini. In 1741 the mission of Santa Rosa, which housed 170 souls, had been joined to that of Itugud at Gamu, while the previous year a smallpox epidemic had caused one-third of the population of Tumavini to flee.[79] Meanwhile, in 1740 the mission of San Martín de Furao was founded as a *visita* of Gamu and a few years later San Juan Bautista de Lapogan became a *visita* of Tumavini.[80]

Demographic Trends in the Cagayan Valley

Although the inhabitants of the Cagayan Valley were spared the enormous burden of *polos* and *vandalas* and there was only a limited Spanish presence in the region, conquest was protracted and subsequently demographic recovery was slow. While epidemics periodically took a heavy toll, the impression is that losses were sustained at a lower level over a longer period, with malaria probably taking a regular toll of the infant population, and expeditions and missionization intermittently undermining subsistence activities and disrupting social relations. Tracking demographic trends is particularly difficult since significant numbers took refuge further up the Cagayan Valley and in the surrounding mountains. While this may have led to a shift in the concentration of population, it may not have altered its overall size. Demographic trends are difficult to determine since Dominican records and tributary counts generally refer only to those living in Christian villages or missions. Populations in these communities fluctuated considerably, in large part with the intensity of missionary activity.

Among the most common causes cited for the failure of the population in the Cagayan Valley to expand were excessive demands for tribute, goods, and services by *encomenderos*, Spanish officials, soldiers, and priests. While ill treatment might have contributed to the decline, greater demographic effects derived from the destabilizing effect they had on local communities. Demands for services drew labor from subsistence and resulted in the extended separation of spouses, which reduced fertility.[81] Unable to meet tribute demands, many sought work with Spaniards or *principales* to pay off their debts, while others opted to flee into the interior. Despite the relative fertility of the Cagayan Valley, there are many references to food shortages in the region. Julián Malumbres notes there were droughts in 1624, 1651, and 1659, plagues of locusts in 1599, 1631, and 1645, and a major famine occurring in 1659 when corpses were to be found in "twos and threes."[82] Bad weather or locusts were responsible for some of these, but in some cases they were aggravated, if not caused, by the burdens placed on the inhabitants to provide goods and services and by the disruption caused by military expeditions and forced relocations associated with missionary activity. Although missionization was often accompanied by attempts to improve agricultural production, mainly through the introduction of plows, *carabaos*, and sometimes irrigation, mission communities were often unstable due to attacks by hostile neighbors and the propensity of their inhabitants to flee in the face of crises, ill treatment, demands for labor and tribute, or encouragement by outsiders. For these reasons, missionization probably did little to improve food security in the valley.

Apart from the disruptive impact of conquest and missionization, inhabitants of the Cagayan Valley were periodically hit by major epidemics and suffered from a number of chronic infections. Acute infections appear to have contributed significantly to mortality in the Cagayan Valley in colonial times, since limited contacts in pre-Spanish times would have limited the introduction of infections and thus the ability of local inhabitants to develop some immunity. Therefore when epidemics, notably smallpox, struck, they were associated with high mortality among both adults and children. Outbreaks were highly correlated with new movements into the region by Spanish officials, soldiers, and missionaries. When the Dominicans began working in Apayao in 1684 after a lapse of some forty years, their reappearance was accompanied by an outbreak of smallpox in which many adults as well as children died.[83] Until the early eighteenth century, Spanish contact focused on the Lower Cagayan Valley, through which most acute infections probably entered. However, the opening of the road from Pangasinan to the Cagayan Valley in 1739 vastly increased movements through the Upper Cagayan Valley, and within two years a major epidemic of smallpox had assaulted the missions of Ituy and Paniqui and spread to Tumavini.[84]

The precise impact of epidemics varied locally according to the length of time that had elapsed since the last outbreak. About 1590 there was reportedly a "contagious epidemic" in Cagayan and in 1595 a "great epidemic of smallpox" that resulted in the death of a large number of infants who were among the first to be buried in the cathedral of Nueva Segovia.[85] The latter epidemic was almost certainly related to the major outbreak in Manila in the same year.[86] The observation that mortality was particularly high among children suggests that the region had been recently affected, possibly by the unspecified epidemic of 1590. High mortality might also be associated with particularly virulent strains, even in areas where there were frequent contacts. In 1757 Aparri was struck by a particularly deadly disease that in three months claimed the lives of 386 people, of whom more than 200 were tributaries. In fact it was suspected that 1,000 had died.[87] The impact of epidemics was often amplified by the propensity of the inhabitants to flee and spread the contagion, as well as the need to avenge the deaths, which were often attributed to sorcery, which promoted intervillage conflict.[88]

These epidemics occurred against a background of chronic infections and malaria. In the twentieth century the inhabitants of the Upper Cagayan Valley suffered from tuberculosis, leprosy, many internal parasites, skin diseases, and malaria.[89] This repertoire of infections may not have differed significantly from that in early colonial times, except that they probably increased in frequency in the nineteenth century as the commercialization of the economy brought changes to rural environments and living conditions. Malaria is endemic throughout Luzon between 800 and 2,000 feet. While the Lower Cagayan Valley and the valley bottom lay outside this zone, malaria was probably prevalent in the surrounding foothills and further upriver.[90]

Missionaries moving into these areas commonly fell ill, which sometimes resulted in the suspension of missionary activity. From the Spanish perspective, Cagayan had "an extremely unhealthy disposition and bad climate."[91] However, Spaniards were not the only victims of malaria; lowlanders who fled to the interior hills to escape Spanish exactions may also have been afflicted, since unlike their highland neighbors they would not have had immunity to the disease. This was the experience of colonists involved in extracting timber and cash crop development in the nineteenth century, though these activities also brought social and environmental changes that encouraged malaria's spread.[92] Malaria would have shortened life expectancy and held back population growth by taking a regular toll of infants. Medical care, as elsewhere in the islands, was limited. The province possessed two hospitals: one established by *real cédula* for Spaniards and priests in Nueva Segovia and the other maintained by the Dominicans for the native inhabitants at Tocolana.[93]

Unfortunately there is little evidence for fertility in Cagayan in the early colonial period. Among the Ibanag, divorce was relatively easy and someone who was married only once was the exception rather than the rule.[94] These customs would have facilitated the formation of new unions where relations between spouses were disrupted by prolonged absences perhaps associated with labor demands. However, divorce was incompatible with Catholicism and would have been discouraged by priests and missionaries. Although information exists on the size of Christian villages and missions, particularly in the eighteenth century, it is often difficult to assess whether the changes reflect differences in vital rates or increased missionary activity. Dominican sources generally provide details on the numbers of tributaries and souls, but not other population categories. However, one account in 1758 gives a more detailed breakdown for the whole valley that enables adult-to-child ratios to be calculated.[95] The figures generally show that the population was only replacing itself, though there are wide variations between individual settlements. Adult-to-child ratios on the coast and in the Lower Cagayan were 1:0.96 and 1:0.97 respectively, whereas upvalley they exceeded 1:1.[96] The lower ratios on the coast and Lower Cagayan may reflect more difficult conditions of life due to labor demands and other levies that might have resulted in, among other things, a higher age at marriage.

Demographic trends in Cagayan are characterized by a marked decline in the early colonial period followed by a slow recovery through the eighteenth century. Cagayan does not appear to have participated in the major demographic expansion that occurred in most regions of Luzon in the eighteenth century. The decline in the sixteenth century was associated with epidemics and attempts to pacify the region, and it continued into the seventeenth century, when the number of tributaries, excluding the Babuyanes, fell by about half from 22,050 in 1591 to 10,500 in 1610 (Table 12.1).[97] Broken down by region, losses were significantly higher in the Lower and Middle Cagayan, where Spanish activities were concentrated, than on the coast. How far this decline was apparent rather than real is difficult to gauge. Part of the decline might be explained by differences in the purposes for

Table 12.1 Estimates of the Tributary Population in the Cagayan Valley by Region in the Early Colonial Period

	1591 *tributos*	**1606** *tributos*	**1610** *indios*	**1591–1610 percent decline**
Coast	3,800	2,202	1,900	50.0
Lower Cagayan	3,950	833	1,700	54.7
Middle Cagayan	7,550	4,311	3,000	61.3
Irraya	2,750	1,605	1,600	41.8
Apayao and Kalinga	4,000	2,623	2,300	42.5
TOTAL	22,050	11,574	10,500	52.4

Sources: 1591 AGI PAT 25-38 fols. 9–14 Relación punctual de las encomiendas 31 May 1591. These figures exclude 1,400 in the Babuyan islands.
1606 AGI AF 29-87 Memorial y lista de las encomiendas 1606.
1610 AGI AF 20 and BR 17: 211 Baltasar Fort 1610.

Note: For boundaries of the regions see Map 12.1.

which various accounts were drawn up. Whereas accounts of *encomiendas* in 1591 and 1606 attempted to be comprehensive, even though the precise figures were often unknown, those reported by the Dominicans in 1610 related only to those they had converted. Hence, the apparently lower level of decline on the coast might be explained by the fact that ministries were well-established there, whereas farther up the Cagayan Valley they were still in the process of formation. Also, the figures for 1591 are significantly more generalized than those for 1606 and may have been based on estimates rather than counts, since at that time much of the valley had still not been pacified. Hence, the figures for 1591 might overestimate the numbers present and thereby the extent of decline between 1591 and 1610. It is difficult to estimate what proportion of the difference may be accounted for by high mortality as opposed to desertion or different methods of recording. Nevertheless, the figures do indicate a significant decline.

The population continued to decline slowly through the seventeenth century, perhaps reaching its nadir toward the end of the century. The more rapid decline in the first part of the century is likely to have been related to continued unrest and Spanish attempts to pacify the region. However, desertions encouraged by excessive exactions and ill treatment probably accounted for higher losses.[98] It has already been noted that in 1678, 4,000 neophytes were reputedly living among pagans in the mountains.[99] At times these losses were countered by Dominican success in settling new converts in the missions, but between 1622 and 1673 their attempts to extend the mission field in the Cagayan Valley were suspended, though intermittent contacts continued with the Apayao. By 1700 there were about 6,000 *tributos* living in settled communities, which represents a loss of about 0.29 percent a year after 1655. However, Juan de Varona y Velásquez's observation in 1746 that in the mountains of

Cagayan there were "very many more pagans than those registered and baptized"[100] was probably equally true in 1700; indeed the proportion is likely to have been greater since the Dominicans achieved some success in drawing converts from the hills in the early eighteenth century. At a guess there may have been 15,000 *tributos* or families in the whole valley in 1700. This would not include any who resided outside the valley in the Cordillera, whose numbers for the purposes of this study have been included in estimates for the latter region.

During the eighteenth century the population under Spanish administration was growing at the slowest rate in the island of Luzon, averaging only 0.4 percent a year. It grew more rapidly in the early part of the century when the Dominicans made more concerted efforts to settle pagan groups in formal settlements, particularly after the opening of the road from Pangasinan to Cagayan. However, mission growth was often retarded by epidemics. Nevertheless, by midcentury the number of *tributos* had increased by about 47 percent to 8,660.[101] Part of the increase can be attributed to the transfer of inhabitants from the Babuyan and Batan Islands to the coast of Cagayan to enable their more effective administration. In 1741 it was reported that 896 persons from the island of Calayan had been resettled at Babaitan between Aparri and Camalaniugan, and another 108 had been settled at Tagga between Fotol and Abulug.[102] By 1746, 993 *almas* had been aggregated to the mission of Buguey and a further 349 established at Tagga, in addition to which small numbers were found in towns in the Lower Cagayan. Many had been reluctant to move; indeed many fled and others deserted back to the Babuyanes after settlement on the coast, and the numbers on the Cagayan coast declined. By the 1770s the number of souls at Buguey and Dao (Babuyanes) had fallen to about 400.[103]

According to fiscal records (see Appendix E), during the second half of the eighteenth century Cagayan was the only province in Luzon where the tributary population did not change significantly. For this period there is relatively abundant evidence for the population in Dominican accounts and in *visitas* of the region by royal officials, such as those by Juan de Varona y Velásquez in 1746 and Joseph de Figueroa in 1787.[104] Almost continuous records in the form of *estados de almas* for individual villages in Cagayan exist in the Dominican archives from the 1760s. Although there are sometimes inexplicable differences in the populations given for specific villages, overall trends suggest that the population increased from 6,734.5 *tributos* in 1758 to 8,894.5 *tributos* in 1800, a rate of 0.66 percent a year (see Table 12.2).[105]

These figures include those Apayao and Kalinga living in settled communities on the fringes of the highlands, but not those in highland missions, who will be discussed in chapter 13. Also, they do not include those who may have fled to interior regions outside the Cagayan Valley, such as Ituy and Paniqui. Meanwhile, fiscal accounts reveal that the numbers of people actually paying tribute between 1750 and 1792 declined by about 0.03 percent a year. Even though the population as a whole may have expanded, Cagayan registered the lowest population growth during this period.

TABLE 12.2 Estimates of the Tributary Population of the Cagayan Valley by Region

	1591	1606	1708	1746	1758	1767	1775	1787	1800
Coast	3,800	2,202	1,520	1,343	1,356	1,183	1,271.5	1,421.5	1,566.5
Lower Cagayan	3,950	833	1,341.25	1,378.5	926.5	1,245.5	1,102	1,391.5	1,056
Middle Cagayan	7,550	4,311	1,076.5	2,063.5	1,861.5	1,841.5	1,845.5	2,101	2,112
Irraya	2,750	1,605	800.75	1,633	1,679	2,195	2,556.5	2,654	2,450.5
Apayao and Kalinga	4,000	2,623	1,299.25	1,560	911.5	1,738.5	1,814.5	1,952	1,709.5
TOTAL	22,050	11,574	6,037.75	7,978	6,734.5	8,203.5	8,590	9,520	8,894.5

Sources: 1591 AGI PAT 25-38 fols. 9–14 Relación punctual de las encomiendas 31 May 1591.
1606 AGI AF 29-87 Memorial y lista de las encomiendas 1606.
1610 AGI AF 20 and BR 17: 211 Baltasar Fort 1610.
1708 AGI AF 296 Certificación jurídica de los oficiales reales 21 June 1708.
1746 Malumbres, *Cagayan*, 298–315, Juan de Varona y Velásquez 3 Mar. 1746.
1758 APSR Cagayan 18 doc. 1 Mapa de los pueblos y almas . . . 1758.
1767 APSR Cagayan 18 doc. 3 Estadísticas o estados de almas 1758–1805 and Cagayan 26 doc. 7 Estadísticas o estados de almas 1758–1800.
1775 APSR Cagayan 18 doc. 3 Estadísticas o estados de almas 1758–1805 and Cagayan 26 doc. 7 Estadísticas o estados de almas 1758–1800.
1787 PNA Erección de pueblos Cagayan 1749–1926 Joseph de Figueroa 30 Sep. 1787.
1800 APSR Cagayan 18 Número de almas del obispado de Nueva Segovia 1800.

Note: Where *tributantes* are given in the document the number has been divided by two to make the data comparable. Figures exclude the Babuyan Islands. For the boundaries of the regions see Map 12.1.

Part of the failure of the population to expand significantly might be attributed to two main causes: the imposition of the tobacco monopoly and environmental disasters. The ban on tobacco cultivation in Cagayan in 1785 precipitated economic hardship, rendered many unable to pay tribute, and encouraged emigration. Against this background of harsh economic conditions, in 1788 and 1789 the province was afflicted by typhoons, floods, and plagues of rats and locusts, which created such severe food shortages that provisions had to be imported from Pangasinan and Ilocos. Writing in 1791, the *alcalde mayor*, Manuel Garay, claimed that 4,000 to 5,000 people had died or left the province.[106] While some blamed the crisis on the tobacco monopoly, others held natural disasters responsible. Yet others asserted that emigration was occurring before the monopoly was imposed and was in response to demands for tribute and service.

During the colonial period the balance of population in the Cagayan Valley seems to have shifted upvalley. Table 12.2 indicates the tributary population for different sections of the valley. Between 1591 and 1800 the proportion living on the coast remained fairly constant at about 20 percent. However, the percentage in the Lower and Middle Cagayan together declined from 64 to 44 percent, while in the province of Irraya it increased from 15 to 34 percent. Part of the shift was almost certainly due to migrants from the Lower and Middle Cagayan moving upriver to escape Spanish control. However, part of the decline in the Lower and Middle Cagayan derived from the more disruptive impact of Spanish activities that contributed to high mortality and destabilized native societies. Hence the shifting balance between the regions may have derived more from population decline in the Lower and Middle Cagayan than to an increase in the province of Irraya, where population levels between 1591 and 1800 remained fairly constant. This does not mean that migration was not a factor contributing to the *relative* demographic importance of Irraya, for it could have buoyed up an otherwise declining population. In the late sixteenth century the population of Irraya may have been greater than what was recorded at the time, since the region had not been pacified and was not well-known. This might mean that the underlying demographic trend in the region was more negative than the figures suggest. Furthermore, there is evidence from the seventeenth century that the province of Irraya was losing population to regions even further upriver, such as Paniqui. Migration from the Lower and Middle Cagayan may have been able to sustain populations in the province of Irraya.

CHAPTER 13
Interior Luzon

The mountain region that forms the backbone of northern Luzon constitutes a formidable landscape of rugged, forested terrain dissected by deep canyons and fast-flowing rivers. Composed of three mountain ranges, the Cordillera reaches between 8,000 and 9,000 feet in the south and descends to about 3,000 feet in the north.[1] It receives high rainfall, between 70 and 120 inches a year, which feeds the tributaries of some of Luzon's major rivers, such as the Magat, Chico, Agno, and Abra. In colonial times these river valleys constituted the main routes of access to the Cordillera.

Colonial sources contain numerous references to native groups living in the Cordillera, many of which are difficult to identify with cultural-linguistic groups that are distinguished today. Mountain dwellers were often referred to collectively as Igorot or Tinguian. The former term was derived from the Manila Tagalog word for "mountaineer" and was more commonly applied to groups in the central and southern Cordillera,[2] while those in the north were often referred to as Tinguian, a term derived from the Malay word *tingii*, meaning "high" or "elevated."[3] These collective names embraced the cultural-linguistic groups known today as the Isneg (Apayao), Kalinga, Bontoc, Ifugao, Gaddang, Kankanai, Ibaloi, and Isinai (Ituy). At present there are significant differences in the types of agriculture practiced by these groups. The northern Kankanai, Ifugao, Bontoc, and southern Kalinga practice wet-rice cultivation, whereas in Benguet and adjacent parts of Ifugao and Bontoc swidden cultivation based on root crops predominates. The northern Kalinga and Apayao are dry-rice cultivators, while the southern Kalinga and northern Bontoc practice both types of cultivation.[4]

A major issue in ethnohistorical research in northern Luzon is the antiquity of wet-rice cultivation and the construction of rice terraces, particularly in regions occupied by the Ifugao and Bontoc.[5] Early research, notably by Otley Beyer, argued that the ancestors of the Ifugao and Bontoc introduced wet-rice cultivation from south China about 1500 BC.[6] This was accepted wisdom until the 1960s, when Felix Keesing used ethnohistorical evidence to argue for the local development of terracing techniques introduced by refugees from Spanish control in the lowlands.[7] Francis Lambrecht, citing evidence from Ifugao epic tales, has also suggested that terracing may date back only to the early seventeenth century.[8] More recent ethnographic, ethnohistorical, and archaeological research has favored a more local origin for the development of irrigated rice terraces. Although there is evidence for the construction of terraces in pre-Spanish times, there is as yet no evidence that they were irrigated.[9] The debate is relevant to this study because the existence of particular subsistence patterns may imply certain settlement patterns and population densities.

During the early colonial period the Spaniards did not establish a permanent presence on the Cordillera. The existence of gold at times prompted military expeditions through the region, while the missionary orders, especially the Dominicans, established missions on its fringes, from which they often conducted exploratory expeditions further inland. The documentary evidence available is therefore patchy and for some regions, such as those inhabited by the Kalinga, Bontoc, and Ifugao, virtually non-existent. Population movements also complicate efforts to trace the history of individual groups. Highland populations were augmented by groups fleeing from lowlands, while within the Cordillera itself the presence of Spaniards or hostile neighbors caused some to retreat further inland or to settle in lowland missions.

Given the fragmentary nature of the documentary record and the difficulty of tracing the history of the major cultural-linguistic groups, the following discussion focuses on the geographical regions that were commonly referred to in documentary sources and for which it is possible to trace broad developments through the colonial period. This focus on geographical rather than cultural areas is not such a drawback as it might seem, for in pre-Spanish times groups in the interior mountains shared a more uniform culture. This later became differentiated according to different ecological conditions and, in the nineteenth century, as the population increased and ethnic consciousness was raised through the creation of subprovinces with ethnic designations.[10]

A broad division will be made between the northern and southern Cordilleras, since contacts and attempts to occupy these two areas were conducted from different bases. For the most part the Apayao and Kalinga in the northern Cordillera came into contact with Spaniards moving up the Cagayan Valley. Groups in the southern Cordillera, on the other hand, were approached mainly from the south and west.[11] Here two regions are distinguished. The first comprises the Isinai and Yogad in the Magat Valley, in the region that became known as Ituy and Paniqui, and includes neighboring groups such as the Italon, Abaca, and Ilongot to the east and in the Caraballo Mountains. The second is the territory inhabited by the Igorot that in turn is divided into three sections that relate to the direction, nature, and intensity of Spanish contacts and to some degree to different cultural-linguistic groups. Spaniards who approached the region around Kayan from the Abra Valley (Map 13.1) encountered the Kankanai or Lepanto, who unlike their neighbors to the south were wet-rice cultivators. The more southern Benguet region, where gold mines were located, was approached from the Agno Valley or from missionary bases in the Magat Valley. Today the inhabitants of this region are known as Ibaloi, but in colonial sources they were generally referred to as "Igolotes" or "Igorotes." To the

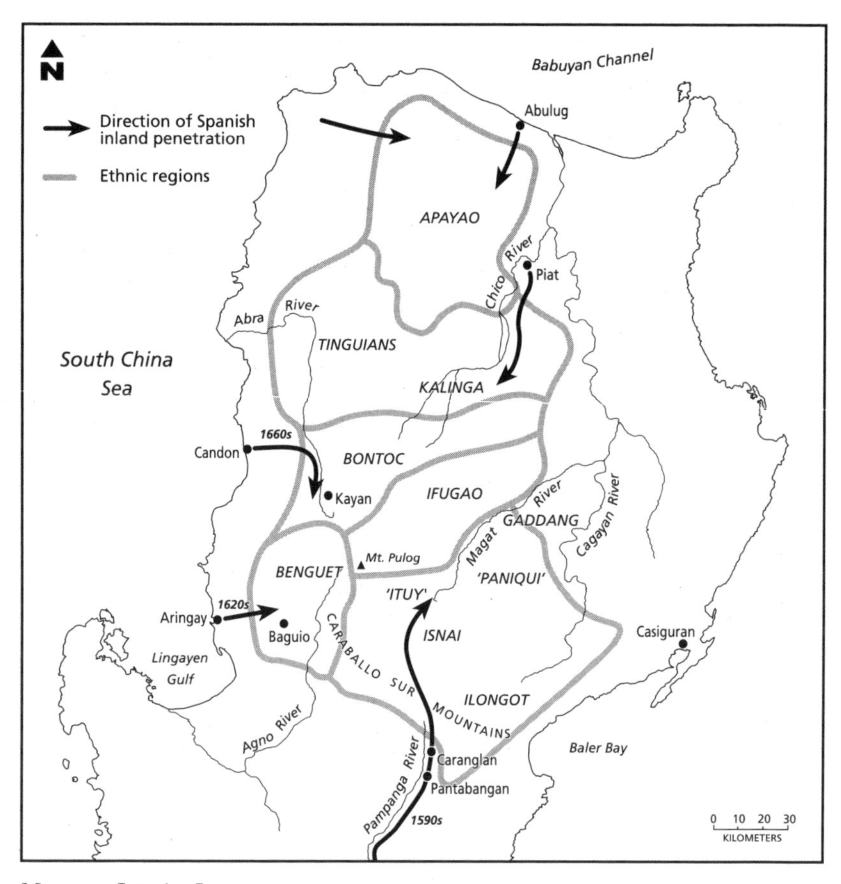

Map 13.1. Interior Luzon

north and east were the Ifugao, who were contacted by Spaniards approaching the Magat Valley only toward the end of the eighteenth century.

The Southern and Central Cordillera

The discussion of the demographic history of groups within the southern and central Cordillera is structured around the incidence and timing of Spanish contacts in the region, so it is useful to review them briefly. First contacts with groups living in the southern and central Cordillera may have been with expeditions penetrating the Upper Cagayan Valley via the Cagayan and Magat rivers. In any case, by 1591 six *encomiendas* had been distributed south of the confluence of the Cagayan and Magat rivers and were said to contain 4,550 *tributos* or 18,200 *almas*.[12] However, these numbers clearly represented only a proportion of those living in the region and there is some doubt over their accuracy since no permanent Spanish presence had been established there and the region was described as "in rebellion." Other early expeditions from the south in search of gold and a route to Cagayan achieved little.[13]

Subsequently, from the late sixteenth century, three periods of expeditionary activity focused on different parts of the southern Cordillera. The first, in the 1590s, concentrated on the region that became known as Ituy and Paniqui. This was reached by traveling up the Pampanga River and over the Caraballo Sur Mountains through the Balete Pass.[14] After these military expeditions failed to secure a permanent Spanish foothold, intermittent contacts occurred with Franciscans working out of Casiguran and with Dominicans in Pangasinan. Later, in the 1620s, military expeditions from Aringay and Duplas encountered Igorot in Benguet. Finally, in the 1660s an expedition from Candon in Ilocos crossed the Malaya range and, approaching from the north, made contact with Igorot communities at Kayan and Lubon.

More intense missionary activity in the early eighteenth century established permanent missions in the Magat Valley, and in 1739 a road was opened between Pangasinan and Cagayan. Forts were established in the Magat Valley for the protection of the missions and travelers, from which soldiers carried out punitive raids to the west and north and first came into contact with the Ifugao. However, by the end of the eighteenth century Ifugao and Bontoc territory was still virtually unknown.

Ituy and Paniqui

Groups known today as the Isinai, Gaddang, and Yogad occupied the region of Ituy and Paniqui. In the mid-eighteenth century the inhabitants of Ituy were referred to as Isinai and those of Paniqui as Yogad or Gaddang.[15] The inhabitants of Ituy and Paniqui had contacts with a number of groups nearby. On the slopes of the Cordillera Central west of Paniqui were the Ifugao, and to the south and the east were an Igorot group, the Igolot, who cultivated root crops and traded gold with the Isinai.[16] To the east of the Magat Valley were the Ilongot, who were neighbors of the Italon and Abaca and were cultivators of dry rice and roots. Some Igolot and Ilongot joined the Ituy missions in the eighteenth century, but they generally resisted conversion.[17]

The region of Ituy and Paniqui was located above the Magat gorge around present-day Aritao, Dupax, and Bayombong, where Magat Valley opens out to form flatlands. Spaniards explored it at an early date during their attempts to find gold. In 1591 Governor Dasmariñas commissioned three expeditions led by his son, Luis Pérez Dasmariñas, Francisco de Mendoza, and Pedro Sid. Accounts of these expeditions and the two subsequent ones by Toribio de Miranda and Captain Clavijo between 1594 and 1595 provide some insight into the culture and population of the region.[18]

Expeditions approached Ituy and Paniqui from the south and entered the Upper Magat Valley near present-day Aritao.[19] Its inhabitants were said to comprise two provinces, "Dangla" and "Guamangui."[20] The Dasmariñas expedition recorded the presence of 590 well-built houses in the communities of Tuy, Burat, Baguay (Buhay), and Bantal in the province of "Dumaqui," the last two together comprising

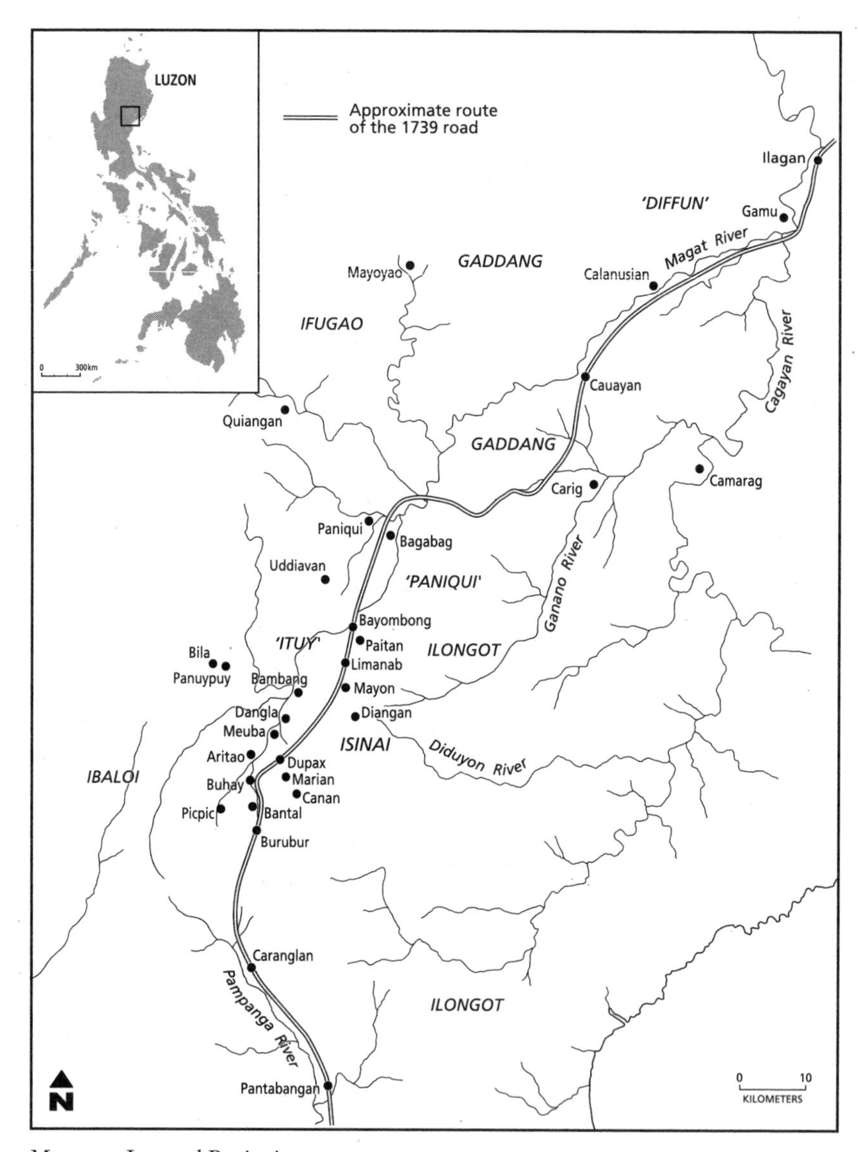

Map 13.2. Ituy and Paniqui

500 houses and the other two 60 and 30 respectively.[21] Toribio de Miranda's subsequent expedition revealed several other settlements in the same area: Guilaylay and Anit, which had 40 and 70 houses respectively, and another two—Sicat and Marangui—whose populations were not recorded. Taking the number of houses reported on these two expeditions and assuming a household size of four suggests a minimum population of 2,800, to which an additional 440 might be added for

the two settlements whose populations were not recorded.[22] It is not clear whether these communities formed nucleated settlements or were more dispersed. The settlements of Ituy and Paniqui were generally referred to as "pueblos" rather than "rancherías," but in the early seventeenth century the Franciscans noted that the inhabitants "were scattered in rancherías, without villages or government."[23] Such contradictions in the accounts might be explained by differences in the groups encountered, with well-formed villages found on the flats and more dispersed settlements in the surrounding hills. A similar range of settlement sizes was found among the thirteen Isinai settlements named by Alejandro Cacho in 1717, but by then the largest possessed only 200 houses,[24] less than half the size of the largest found in the late sixteenth century.[25]

Settlements seem to have been smaller in the Dangla Valley. Here in 1594 Toribio de Miranda recorded that the settlements of Agulan and Palan each had 80 houses and Irao 60, and he listed another thirteen settlements with an unspecified number of houses.[26] His account refers to small villages and "ranchos," and the impression is that the settlement pattern was more dispersed than in Ituy. In 1739 the Franciscan missionary Manuel del Río y Flores described the settlement pattern of Paniqui as follows: "the villages, although they are not large are many, for along the banks of the River Magat alone . . . there are eighteen villages, large and small."[27] Using a conservative estimate of 50 houses per settlement for those communities for which Miranda does not provide figures suggests a total of 870 houses with about 3,480 inhabitants in the Dangla Valley in 1594. Miranda's expedition also ventured over a mountain named St. Cecilia's Peaks to what was probably the Ganano Valley. Here it visited two deserted villages and six others with a total of 514 houses, including three with more than 100 houses, and an estimated total population of 2,570. The Ganano Valley was probably inhabited by the Gaddang, discussed in chapter 12.

Excluding the Ganano Valley, the estimated population of 6,720 for the province of Ituy and Paniqui in the 1590s falls short of the number of inhabitants contained in reports summarizing the achievements of the expeditions. Following the first three expeditions, Governor Dasmariñas reported to the Crown that in the province of Tuy, which clearly included the Dangla Valley, 15,000 "tributantes" had rendered obedience to the Crown.[28] However, summarizing the achievements of all the expeditions up to 1609, Juan Manuel de la Vega commented that even if the province of Tuy proved to have no other riches, at least 100,000 souls had been pacified.[29] That such a large population had been pacified seems unlikely, but the figure might be credible as an estimate for the total number living in the region. The existence of large populations is also implied by the fact that the Augustinians who accompanied the Dasmariñas expedition estimated that to effect the conversion of the inhabitants of Tuy, forty missionaries would be required.[30] Calculated at the contemporary norm of one priest for every 500 *tributos* or 2,000 souls, this suggests a population of about 80,000 souls. The precise region to which the figure refers is unclear and the estimates may appear high, but in the early colonial period the province of Tuy was consistently described as densely settled.[31]

Support for the existence of dense populations in Ituy and Paniqui in the early colonial period is found in the memorial written by Father Francisco Antolín in 1787 entitled *Discurso sobre el gentió y población de esta misión de Ituy y Paniqui*.[32] With a lifetime's experience as a missionary in the region, he posed the question as to why the population of the mountain provinces had declined. Without giving his source, he noted that estimates had suggested that these provinces had once possessed 400,000 *almas*, which he thought was an exaggeration. At the time of writing he estimated that there were only 82,900 *almas*, a figure he regarded as "prudent." He attributed the high level of depopulation to the spread of disease that accompanied the opening of communications between the highlands and lowlands in the eighteenth century. Of the total of 82,900 *almas*, he estimated that the Ituy or Isinai accounted for 3,900 *almas*, the Gaddang or Paniqui 10,000 *almas* and the Italon, Ibaloi, and Ilongot 4,000 *almas*, or together 22 percent of the total.[33] It seems unlikely that Ituy and Paniqui accounted for exactly the same proportion of the population of the mountain provinces as they had in the sixteenth century, for the Gaddang probably moved into the province of Paniqui during the colonial period. The proportion might therefore be considered high when applied to the sixteenth century, and a figure of 20 percent or less might be more appropriate. Using the figure of 400,000 *almas* for the mountain provinces as a whole would suggest a population for Ituy and Paniqui in the sixteenth century of about 80,000 *almas*, a figure that is consistent with the observations of the participants of early expeditions. Even taking a lower estimate of 300,000 *almas* would suggest a population of 60,000 *almas*. These estimates are very crude since they assume that demographic change during the early colonial period was uniform throughout the mountain provinces, which is unlikely. Furthermore the regions are not precisely delineated and thus may not be strictly comparable. Nevertheless, they do suggest that a sizeable population existed in Ituy and Paniqui in the sixteenth century. For the purposes of calculating a total population of the interior highlands in pre-Spanish times, a conservative estimate of 60,000 *almas* will be assumed.

Evidence for dense populations in the province of Ituy and Paniqui is supported by the accounts of early expeditionaries who described it as temperate, fertile, and densely settled.[34] The Isinai in particular were regarded as excellent farmers.[35] Rice was the dominant staple and described as "the best that is harvested in the Indies."[36] Most accounts refer to the cultivation of dry rice,[37] but some rice may have been irrigated.[38] This is also suggested by an account of the establishment of permanent missions on the valley flats in the eighteenth century that describes how the inhabitants had to be instructed in how to use plows to prepare the land for irrigation, since previously they had only used dibbles.[39] In addition to dry rice, root crops may also have been cultivated on the hillsides. In fact, in the early seventeenth century the inhabitants of Burubur in Ituy were described as cultivators of gabi and sweet potatoes and obtained their rice through trade with lowland villages.[40]

Relatively little information exists on the population of Ituy and Paniqui during the seventeenth century, since missionaries only worked there for short periods and were hampered in their efforts by the rugged terrain, dispersed population, native hostility, and disease.[41] In the late seventeenth century, Dominicans working in the Upper Cagayan moved upvalley to Diffun, Yogad, and Paniqui and founded three missions near the confluence of the Cagayan and Magat. Partly spurred by this success, the Dominican provincial, Cristóbal Pedroche, urged the authorities to construct a road from Pampanga to Cagayan so that many *infieles*, including many apostates, could be converted. Although the project received official support in 1696, it was abandoned due to sickness and native hostility.[42] A few years later the Dominican provincial, Father Francisco Ximénez, estimated that from Ituy to Cagayan alone there were 100,000 families and more than 400,000 souls in need of conversion.[43] It was not until 1739 that Dominicans, who had begun work in Paniqui in 1736,[44] linked up with Augustinians based in Ituy.[45] Meanwhile, between 1715 and 1723, Augustinians headed by Father Alejandro Cacho had extended their efforts to the Magat Valley from bases at Pantabangan and Caranglan, baptizing 695 people and founding four new missions among the Isinai at Buhay, Picpic, Marian, and Canan.[46] By 1740 they had reduced eighteen native settlements to nine and baptized 2,755 neophytes.[47] The Augustinians wished to focus their attention elsewhere and, seeing that the Dominicans were committed to the region and had built a road from Asingan to Buhay, they formally ceded control of the missions to the Dominicans in 1742.[48]

When the Dominicans assumed control of the province of Ituy, they were ministering to about 2,500 Christians and 1,000 neophytes,[49] but further progress was slow. Apart from an epidemic of *viruelas* that afflicted Puncan (in Italones), Cadayan, and the Igorot in 1741, the missions were destabilized by headhunting raids by the Panuypuy and by surrounding heathen groups who encouraged the converts to flee or rebel.[50] In 1745 the Dominicans, who were to the point of abandoning the mission field, received military support that destroyed the Panuypuy stronghold at Ajanas, Bila, and five other villages, killing 276 Panuypuy and 130 others.[51] The survivors retreated north, where they remained hostile to Spanish rule, occasionally attacking the missions and supporting fleeing apostates.[52] Nevertheless, the decisive defeat of the Panuypuy created relatively peaceful conditions that enabled 200 Igorot to be baptized and 700 heathens to settle in the missions.[53]

Seven years after they had assumed control of Ituy, the Dominicans had reduced the number of missions to five and were ministering to 2,719 converts and *infieles*, the majority of them Isinai and Igorot. They had also begun to convert and baptize the Ilongot. The only groups that remained hostile to missionization were the Ipituy and Panuypuy, who continued to harass the missions.[54] Despite these raids and being visited by epidemics in 1758 and 1786, accounts of the Ituy missions in the second half of the eighteenth century reveal a steady growth in their populations,[55] rising from 3,239 souls in 1751 to 5,621 in 1800 (Table 13.1). The movement of the garrison at Aritao to Carig in 1772 reflected the greater stability of the Ituy missions and their declining need for defense.[56]

When Father Antonio Campo made the first journey along the newly opened road linking Pangasinan and Paniqui in 1739, he compiled a detailed list of the

Table 13.1 Total Populations in the Missions of Ituy and Paniqui, 1747 to 1800

Missions of Ituy	**1747**	**1751**	**1785**	**1787**	**1790**	**1796**	**1799**	**1800**
Buhay (Aritao)	624	486	758	793	1,013	1,218	1,248	1,330
Dupax and Meuba	1,268	1,290	1,304	1,398	1,644	1,829	1,745	1,856
Rosario	188	288						
Santa María (includes Batu, Paetan)	229	315						
Bambang (includes Ylamanap, Diangan, Mayon)	410	860	1,393	1,597	1,704	1,888	2,248	2,435
Balsain				161				
TOTAL	2,719	3,239	3,455	3,949	4,361	4,935	5,241	5,621
Missions of Paniqui								
Bayombong	470	312	1,740	1,728	1,896	2,755	1,506	1,745
Daruyag (later includes Angadanan and Gapat)	309	134	833	1,136	915	889	893	831
Gapat (Santa Cruz)	123	140						
Bagabag	213	450	834	1,562	1,199	1,517	1,608	1,602
Dagay	28	200						

Lacab		200						
Carig	200	150	1,273	1,109	1,056	1,047	1,220	1,003
Lappau	204	339						
Camarag			1,617	1,708	1,326	1,234	1,201	1,033
Cauayan	265	556	654	1,175	1,167			
Calanusian		218		668	589	2,088	2,098	2,144
Lumabang				831	876			663
TOTAL	1,812	2,699	6,951	9,917	9,024	9,530	8,526	9,021
GRAND TOTAL	4,531	5,938	10,406	13,866	13,385	14,465	13,767	14,642

Sources: 1747 APSR Cagayan 29 no doc. number Vicente Salazar 8 July 1747 and APSR Cagayan 30 Compendio cronológico, Francisco Antolín, 1787.
1751 APSR Cagayan 28 doc. 15 Joseph Herrera 16 Dec. 1753.
1785 PNA Patronato Unclassified Nicolás de Cora 20 Sept. 1785.
1787 APSR Cagayan 30 Compendio cronológico, Francisco Antolín, 1787.
1790 APSR Cagayan 1 doc. 7 Pedro Mártir Fernández 6 Mar. 1790 also in APSR Cagayan 28 doc. 31 Francisco Antolín, no date [1789].
1796 PNA Patronato 1720–1799 Certificación de las almas y tributos que administran los religiosos de la provincia del Santísimo Rosario . . . 1796.
1799 Malumbres, *Isabela*, 99–100, Dominican Provincial, Pedro Galán 1799.
1800 APSR Cagayan 18 Número de almas del obispado de Nueva Segovia 13 Mar. 1801.

communities he encountered on the stretch between Bayombong and Cauayan and in the nearby hills and valleys.[57] He listed 127 settlements with 2,283 houses, which might suggest a population of about 11,500. The settlements averaged about eighteen houses each, though nearly half had fewer than ten and only about 10 percent had more than thirty. Settlements were slightly larger on the flats than in the hills. In 1739 Father Manuel del Río y Flores also described the region of Paniqui as possessing many, though not very large, settlements, including eighteen on the banks of the river,[58] and elsewhere gave an account of eighty-five unconverted communities on the flats of Ituy and Paniqui.[59]

Compared to the natives of Ituy, the inhabitants of Paniqui were resistant to conversion, though the Augustinians managed to establish a mission at Bayombong.[60] In 1741 there were 400 Christians at Bayombong, Gapat, and Bagabag, and two more missions had been established at Carig and Lapao with 400 *infieles* and forty-three families.[61] These missions possessed only a fraction of the population that lived in the surrounding *rancherías*. Around Bagabag alone there were said to be twenty *rancherías* with twenty, thirty, fifty, and sixty families, though the town itself possessed only 180 *almas*.[62] In 1747 the Paniqui missions had only 1,812 converts and *infieles*.[63] Progress with conversions was slow because of the shortage of missionaries and because it was said that those who settled in the missions joined not to be converted but for other reasons, such as to escape the threat of their more powerful neighbors, to seek social advancement, or to evade punishment for debts or crimes.[64] Some who escaped the missions encouraged those in the mountains to remain hostile.[65] Conditions of open hostility between those living in the hills and those in the missions resulted in raids and counterraids that caused significant mortality and destabilized the missions. In 1752 a fort was established at Bagabag, and in the early 1770s military expeditions aimed at punishing the hostile Igorot resulted in 1,000 being settled in lowland missions. Here they were taught how to cultivate rice and were provided with houses, pigs, and chickens, as well as plots for cultivating maize and sweet potatoes.[66] By 1774 the bishop of Nueva Segovia was able to report that missionaries in Paniqui were working among 3,000 Christians and heathens. However, a considerable proportion of the mission population was living outside the missions. For example, in 1775 the mission of Camarag had a population of 2,066, of which 1,200 had returned to the mountains.[67] The *alcalde mayor* of Cagayan, Joseph de Figueroa, considered that only those born in the missions remained there.[68]

Despite the difficulties of settling and retaining people in the missions, during the second half of the eighteenth century, the recorded total population of Ituy and Paniqui more than trebled from 4,531 in 1747 to 14,465 in 1796. The growth was particularly marked in the Paniqui missions, whose population quintupled, though this was due in part to migration up the Cagayan Valley by groups, such as the Gaddang, who sought refuge in the missions from attacks by the Ifugao. Although mission populations increased, they were unstable and often represented only a proportion of those living in the wider region. In 1788 Father Antolín reported that the mission of Ituy and Paniqui comprised twelve *pueblos* with 14,000 *almas*, of whom about 1,000 were "infieles catecumenos." At the same time he suggested that the number of *infieles* living outside the missions was "considerable" and included the Igorot, who were "quite numerous."[69] Therefore the population of Ituy and Paniqui at the end of the eighteenth century may have been between 18,000 and 20,000, and on this basis had declined by about two-thirds since the Spanish had first arrived in Luzon.

The Italon and Abaca

To the east of Ituy and Paniqui in the Caraballo Mountains were the Italon and Abaca. The Augustinians began working among them in 1695, approaching them via the Pampanga River and establishing bases at Bongabón, Pantabangan, and Caranglan.[70] In 1702, Father Antolín de Alzaga reported that the Italon had fifty-six well-kept villages on the banks of two fast-flowing rivers that drained north. They had tall houses and took great care of their crops, storing the seeds in granaries to avoid shortages. Others noted they had "fields of rice, sugar and garden vegetables" and had more food than they needed.[71] According to Father Alzaga the Italon were monogamous and did not permit divorce or concubinage. Meanwhile the Abaca formed two jurisdictions, Pantabangan and Caranglan, with six and four villages respectively. The settlements of both the Italon and Abaca comprised about 100 to 150 families.[72] Although the Italon and Abaca were said to be very similar, some Abaca had several wives. Due to similarities in the language and settlements of the Abaca and Negritos, Father Cacho believed the Abaca were a mixed racial group descended from the Italon and Baluga (Negritos). The Baluga were nomadic hunters and described as "wild and unruly."[73]

By 1704 the Augustinians had established five villages the mountains of Caranglan and Pantabangan at Santo Tomás de Villanueva, Santo Cristo de Burgos, San Agustín, San Pablo, and San José. These villages comprised 540 families, of whom 469 adults had been baptized and more than 800 were under Christian instruction, but there were many others in the mountains.[74] By 1707 six other settlements had been established, one among the Abaca at San Miguel and the other five possessing several hundred Baluga.[75] A secular *visita* of the Italon and Isinai in 1723 reported that since 1702 at least 3,413 people had been baptized. By then the Augustinians had five missions, each with several *visitas* and containing mixed populations of Italon, Abaca, Isinai, Baluga, Aeta, Zambal, and Igorot. The Augustinians apparently taught them how to cultivate rice, coconuts, and other vegetables, which they claimed meant the population now had sufficient food whereas before they lived on wild roots and game.[76] By the time the Augustinians relinquished the Ituy missions in 1739, they had reduced the number of settlements among the Italon from eighteen to fifteen.[77] Subsequently in 1753 they were transferred to Franciscan administration. In 1818 Pantabangan and Caranglan had a combined population of only 1,254.[78]

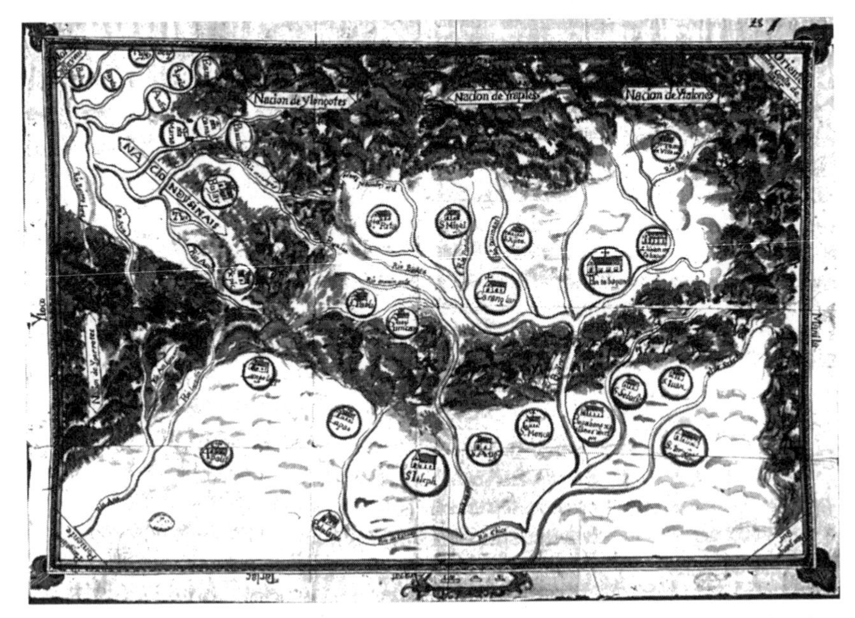

Figure 13.1. Native groups in the mountains of Pantabangan and Caranglan under the Augustinians in 1723. AGI Mapas y Planos Filipinas 148 Mapa de los pueblos existentes en los montes de Pantabangan y Caranglan . . . pertenecientes a las misiones de los religiosos de San Agustín 1723.

Igorot Territory

The term "Igorot" or "Igolot" was a collective name for mountain groups mainly in the southern and central Cordillera. As noted above, due to differences in direction, nature, and intensity of Spanish contacts and to some extent the culture and language of these groups, their demographic history will be considered in three parts. The first examines the wider region of Benguet, the second considers the northern Kankanai and Bontoc, and the third discusses the more remote Ifugao. While evidence for the size of Igorot groups will be considered in passing, due to the fragmentary nature of the documentary record and lack of clarity concerning the precise groups or regions to which the estimates refer, the Igorot population as a whole will be discussed at the end of this section.

The Wider Benguet Region

Reports from early military and missionary expeditions provide glimpses of Igorot culture in the Benguet region, but the most detailed accounts date from the eighteenth century. Although Father Francisco Antolín spent much of his life in the mission at Dupax in the province of Ituy and Paniqui, he became fascinated with the neighboring Igorot, about whom he compiled a number of book-length reports.[79] The Augustinian fathers Pedro de Vivar and Manuel Carrillo also wrote valuable accounts in the 1750s, as did Father Benito Herosa, who was based on the lower Agno River in the 1780s.[80]

The basic subsistence pattern of the Benguet Igorot does not appear to have changed significantly until the early nineteenth century. Prior to that time their main crops were root crops—sweet potatoes, gabi, and ube—which were grown in swiddens that could only be cultivated for three years before they became overgrown and had to be abandoned.[81] The region's climate was generally too wet to permit the cultivation of maize. Fruit was not abundant, but some sugar cane and tobacco were grown. During the colonial period, rice was only grown in small quantities "in the hills"[82] or else obtained by trade from groups at lower elevations. They also consumed large quantities of meat, particularly pork, which they likewise obtained by trade.[83] In the early nineteenth century, root crops were still the main staples. Commander Guillermo Galvey's expedition to Benguet in 1829 reported that the land was irrigated, but he specifically noted that no paddy rice was grown.[84] However, further north in Kapangan the land was described as "well cultivated with rice, camote and gabi." Similarly, around Kabayan in the Upper Agno Valley there were "many fields of rice."[85] Fifty years previously, observers had found little rice and no granaries here, which suggest that wet-rice cultivation had only recently spread to the region, perhaps from the Ifugao.[86] The increased size of settlements, to be described below, also supports this change in subsistence.

Swidden cultivation was associated with the frequent movement of both houses and plots, though judging by early twentieth-century accounts seldom more than a few miles.[87] In the seventeenth century, it was said that they moved for the smallest reason, easily building new houses and pulling up their root crops and transplanting them elsewhere.[88] Their seminomadic existence made it difficult for observers to estimate populations or to identify communities over extended periods. Hence in 1789 Father Antolín noted that many villages listed by Father Campo in 1739 no longer existed.[89]

The settlement pattern of Benguet consisted of small, dispersed *rancherías*, and it did not change significantly during the colonial period. In the early seventeenth century, settlements averaged ten to twelve houses and were located on defensive sites,[90] while in the 1750s the figures provided by Fathers Carrillo and Vivar suggest they averaged between seventeen and nineteen houses.[91] Some settlements were slightly larger, but they did not generally exceed thirty to forty houses[92]; indeed in 1756 Father Vivar commented that Tonglo with 64 *tributos* and 220 souls was the largest he had seen.[93] In the nineteenth century, however, Benguet itself possessed 500 houses and Capangan 300, though they did not form compact settlements but consisted of small groups of houses "here and there."[94] Each *ranchería* comprised a separate kin group presided over by elders, whose authority was based on the ownership of stores of rice or other foods, which signified that they had more alliances or slaves to cultivate their lands.[95] In 1780 Father Herosa suggested that two or three married couples inhabited each house, but he was probably referring to the houses of leaders. The Benguet Igorot were not polygamous nor did they practice adultery, but divorce was easy and a man would leave his wife if she was unable to bear children or proved unsuitable.[96]

Infanticide appears to have been widely practiced for a variety of reasons. It was the custom for children who experienced an unusual delivery, such as being born with the feet first or with their umbilical cords around their necks, or born blind or with other congenital defects. Such infants were thought to have tried to kill their mothers or would live miserable lives. Infanticide was also practiced to achieve child spacing and thereby allow women to continue with their daily activities.[97] Few families had more than six children. It was suggested that hard domestic and agricultural labor contributed to their lack of fecundity, while the absence of men on trading expeditions may also have had an impact on fertility.[98] In the early twentieth century, the marked gender division of labor was attributed to the needs of defense; while men guarded against attack, women had to work in the fields.[99] These observations are consistent with Anthony Reid's argument presented in chapter 5 that correlates the hard labor and insecurity associated with swidden cultivation with smaller families.[100]

The Igorot attracted Spanish interest because they occupied of one of the main gold-producing areas of the Philippines. During the early colonial period expeditions in search of gold deposits brought back information on the territory occupied by the Igorots. In 1609 Juan Manuel de la Vega drew up an account of what was known of the region at that time. The "Ygolotes" were judged to number 18,000 to 20,000 "indios." They were said to be headhunters and at war with their neighbors, but were generally well-disposed. They were described as not being cultivators, partly because of the shortage of land in their rugged, pine-clad territory, but also because they could obtain their food—rice, pigs, and *carabaos*—in exchange for gold, which they only extracted when they needed to trade.[101] In the 1620s a further three expeditions were conducted by Captain García de Aldana y Cabrera,[102] Sergeant Major Antonio Carreño de Valdés, and Captain Alonso Martín Quirante,[103] which penetrated from the west rather than through Ituy. Based on the number of villages he encountered, Captain Aldana reasoned that the Benguet region possessed 15,000 souls, though elsewhere he alluded to the Igorot's being able to muster 7,000 people who could bear arms.[104] Captain Quirante estimated that the Igorot numbered only 1,000 men, though he was probably referring only to those living around the mines near Baguio, since he noted other Igorot elsewhere.[105]

There was one last protracted effort to pacify the Igorot and open up gold mines in the late 1660s, but the expedition approached Igorot territory via the Abra Valley and focused on the Kankanai region, to be discussed below. Meanwhile, in the Benguet region the Igorot resisted Spanish attempts to establish a permanent presence on the Cordillera, though in 1688 the Dominicans established the mission of San Bartolomé de Agno for those panning gold in the River Agno[106] and for Alaguet and Igorot converts.[107] This mission lasted more than twenty years until a dispute with the Igorot resulted in its being burned to the ground in 1709 or 1710.[108] The Dominicans had no illusions about attracting large numbers down from the highlands, since the mountain dwellers obtained everything they wanted from trade with Christian villages, even though this trade was banned in 1642 and 1695.[109] They feared that if they settled in the lowlands they would be subject to tribute payments, *polos*, and *vandalas*.[110] Even so, in the early eighteenth century there was a continuous trickle of Igorot to the lowlands, where they settled in the Christian villages of Agoo, Bauang, and Bacnotan in Ilocos[111] and in the missions of Ituy.[112] In 1732 a new mission, San Joseph, was also established for the Igorot near Malionglióng at the site of the previous mission of San Bartolomé,[113] but direct contact between Spaniards and Igorot on the Cordillera did not occur until the road from Pangasinan to Cagayan was constructed in 1739.

As noted in the discussion of the missions of Ituy and Paniqui, when this overland link was opened up, the Dominicans aimed to establish a short road that passed through Igorot territory from Asingan to Buhay.[114] Father Antonio Campo made the first journey along this trail in 1739 when he compiled a list of 108 Igorot settlements along the route. These included nineteen *rancherías* of Apsay Igorot at the junction of the Rivers Agno and Ambayaban and overlooking the Valley of Ituy, thirty settlements of Yumanguies, and twenty Awa settlements. He also included eighteen others located along the planned road from Bayombong to Bangar in Ilocos.[115] As will be shown below, in the 1750s settlements in this region averaged about seventy people, which would suggest a total population in 1739 of about 7,560. However, this number probably represented only a proportion of Igorot settlements, since in 1755 Father Antonio Lobato reported more than twice the number of Awa settlements that had been noted by Father Campo.[116]

The Dominicans undertook most missionary work among the Igorot, but from 1747 Augustinians began working out of Ilocos and soon established a residence at Tonglo near present-day Baguio.[117] According to the Augustinian provincial, Manuel Carrillo, by 1755 they had managed to convert 1,772 persons in twenty-six named settlements. It is difficult to identify many of these settlements today, but they appear to have been located on the western fringes of the western Cordillera near the present-day towns of Tubao, Pugo, Tuba, and Sablan.[118] Father Carrillo also noted that many other small, unnamed communities had rendered obedience.[119] Enthusiastic about their conversion, Provincial Carrillo encouraged Father Pedro de Vivar to extend missionary efforts deeper into the Cordillera. This he did, and in 1756 he compiled a list of thirty settlements that included sixteen new settlements, which together had 2,034 souls. It included settlements around Baguio not included in Father Carrillo's list, and it noted that there were another twenty-nine settlements three days further east. Together the two lists indicate the presence of seventy-one settlements, forty-two named and twenty-nine unnamed, and his figures suggest an average of about seventy souls per settlement, giving an estimated total population for the region of about 4,970.[120] Figures given by Francisco de Córdoba, an Augustinian who did the initial reconnaissance, differ only slightly.[121] The difference in the figures provided by Fathers Campo and Vivar suggests the population declined between 1739 and 1756. This is feasible given that in 1754 Ilocos was hit by a major epidemic that may well have spread into Igorot territory,[122] but it could also reflect differences in the precise groups they encountered. In fact, missionary advance was slow due to the shortage of missionaries, the lack of gifts to offer potential converts, and the dispersed population.[123] The Dominican response to Augustinian activity was to re-open the old trail. In 1755, Fathers Cristóbal Rodríguez and Antonio Lobato, based in Dupax, attempted to open a direct road to Pangasinan, but rather than following the old route, they moved into the headwaters of the Kayapa, where they claimed there were forty-eight Awa settlements.[124]

Missionary efforts, by now headed by the Dominicans, were brought to an abrupt end in 1759, when, faced with continual attacks on travelers and settlements, the *alcalde mayor* of Pangasinan, Don Manuel Arza y Urrutia, led a major expedition of more than 1,000 conscripts from Bauang to force the Igorot to settle in permanent settlements. The venture destroyed many Igorot settlements and fields and, after finding the mission of Tonglo deserted, continued to devastate thirty-five surrounding villages.[125] Stiff native resistance prevented deeper penetration toward the Acupan mines, and the expedition withdrew. During the late eighteenth century, no further attempts were made to subdue the Igorot from the Ilocos coast, though some drifted down to the lowland missions there.[126]

The Northern Kankanai and Bontoc Region

Spaniards approached the northern Kankanai and Bontoc from the north and west. Contact with Augustinian missionaries dated from the late sixteenth century, when Esteban Marín, based in Tagudin, was said to have baptized more than "2,000 Igorots."[127] Some Augustinians continued working in the adjacent Abra Valley, but the most sustained contact followed an expedition by Admiral Pedro Durán de Monforte in 1667. This force of some 100 Spaniards, three Augustinian missionaries, and 2,000 Filipinos penetrated Igorot territory through the Abra Valley and found seventy-seven Igorot settlements and seven gold mines.[128] The Augustinians established their first church on the Cordillera at Kayan, which, according to the Augustinian chronicler Casimiro Díaz, possessed 150 houses, and Lubon a few less.[129] During two to three years' sojourn in the region, the expedition explored 150 villages "from the heights of Kayan to the mountains of Cagayan." Díaz names thirty-eight villages that submitted to Spanish rule and notes there were nine others in the Loo Valley. He names a further fifteen villages that rendered some form of obedience and says there were more than a hundred other villages of lesser importance. Assuming that the named villages, including those in the Loo Valley, averaged about fifty houses and the unnamed ones only twenty houses, and that the average household size was four, the total population may have been just over 20,000. This is likely to have been an underestimate, for, as will be shown below, in the early nineteenth century settlements around Kayan averaged seventy-five houses. There is no indication as to how the expedition obtained its supplies, but Felix Keesing argues that some wet-rice cultivation must have been practiced for an expedition of this size to survive.[130] The expedition was eventually forced to withdraw, taking with it some converts who were settled in Bauang (Baratao), Bangar, and Narvacan.[131]

The spectacular failure of the Monforte expedition discouraged major expeditions into Kankanai territory for nearly a century. However, the Augustinians continued to work on the western fringes of the region and encouraged small numbers to settle in the lowland settlements of Tagudin, Bangar, and Namacpan.[132] In Tagudin, forty to fifty persons from the Kayan-Bila area were being baptized annually.[133] Further observations on the Kankanai and Bontoc are not available until the nineteenth century. In 1811 Soliman, an Igorot leader from Kayan, sought to extend his authority by allying with the Spanish, but this precipitated a revolt in which only nine settlements, mainly around Kayan, supported him, while seventeen, including the prominent communities of Besao, Batuko, and Sabangan, were opposed.[134] At that time Kayan was the largest settlement with 150 houses, while the average size was 75.

More informative are the accounts of Commander Guillermo Galvey, who between 1829 and 1839 conducted no fewer than forty-five punitive and exploratory expeditions into the Cordillera with the aim of suppressing the contraband trade in tobacco. One expedition in 1833 focused on the Upper Agno, Suyoc, and Kayan areas. At that time Kayan had 250 houses and excellent "fields of rice," which were harvested two or three times a year, and there were other large settlements such as Magecimuy, with 280 houses.[135] Later ethnographic notes on the Igorot published by Sinibaldo de Mas made a distinction between the Burik and the Besao. The former, who lived around the gold mines of Suyoc and the copper mines of Mankayn, had many irrigated rice fields and cattle, while to the north the Besao were described as having large towns and many well-irrigated rice fields.[136] By then it seems wet-rice cultivation was well-established and that settlements there were larger than among the Igorot of Benguet.

The Ifugao

Only limited documentary evidence exists for the Ifugao before the early nineteenth century. The first recorded direct contact between the Ifugao and Spaniards occurred in 1736, when the Augustinian Father Diego de la Torre set out from Ilagan to establish a road to Cagayan.[137] It was not until the mid-eighteenth century, however, that growing hostility between the Ifugao and those settled in the Magat Valley prompted several military expeditions. At the time it was thought that Ifugao hostility stemmed from their displacement from the Magat Valley by groups such as the Gaddang and Yogad moving up the Cagayan Valley.[138] Their response was to try and exact tribute from the newcomers as well as conduct headhunting raids on them and rustle their cattle. In 1752 a fort was built at Bagabag for the protection of the missions and travelers, and from there troops made regular sorties against the Igorot, destroying their homes and fields and settling some in the missions.[139] In 1778 an expedition into the mountains of Buag resulted in 420 adults and children from six settlements being settled in the mission of Uddiavan in the Magat Valley.[140]

Even though some Ifugao settled in the missions and on occasions continued to trade in the Magat Valley, their raids and Spanish military retaliations resulted in a hardening of attitudes and reduced contact between those living in the missions and those outside. Because of this, knowledge about the Ifugao remained limited. Undaunted by the hostile environment, the Dominicans continued to be optimistic about the conversion of the Ifugao, often accompanying military expeditions and in peaceful interludes reconnoitering Ifugao territory for themselves. One such Dominican was Father Juan Molano, who visited the Quiangan region in 1801.[141] There he observed large expanses of irrigated rice fields and well-constructed houses and granaries. The inhabitants also grew sweet potatoes, gabi, ubi, onions, and many mongos, but not bananas or palms. The town of Quiangan itself had 186 houses, while the four adjoining villages had between ten and forty houses. Altogether, he named twenty villages, which, excluding three whose population was not known but two of which were described as large, together contained about 1,070 houses. He noted that there were many children and enough work for four or five missionaries. The large expanses of irrigated rice terraces similarly impressed Commander Guillermo Galvey, whose expedition to Quiangan in 1832 reported that they were so extensive that they could support 30,000 people.[142] He went on to list twenty-seven settlements belonging to the Ifugao. On a later expedition to Quiangan and Mayayao in 1836, Galvey reported that around Mayayao the whole hillside was covered with irrigated rice terraces and could support 20,000 souls.[143]

The Igorot Population

Describing demographic trends among Igorot groups during the early Spanish period is difficult due to the fragmentary documentary record and later changes to Igorot subsistence and settlement patterns as a result of migration, contact, or local innovation. Superimposed on these processes were periodic mortality crises associated with military expeditions and epidemics that affected both mortality and fertility. Given these limitations, the discussion will take a retrospective view starting with population estimates made by Father Francisco Antolín in the late eighteenth century (see Table 13.2). His estimates of the Igorot population are the most detailed and probably the best informed.[144] Despite his considerable knowledge and experience, his figures appear low and are not wholly consistent with other observations he makes. He conceded that Igorot territory was once more extensive and that contact with Spaniards had forced them to retreat inland. However, he maintained that estimates suggesting they numbered 400,000 *almas* were exaggerated and said they had been made without exploring the region sufficiently, which was like "trying to tell the number of trees in a thick forest at a single glance." Nevertheless, he judged the Igorot nation to be "very populous" and their houses and *rancherías* "many," and elsewhere he described Igorot territory as being "moderately well populated."

Father Antolín provided estimates for thirteen groups, four of which relate to the territory of the Igorot discussed here. Two estimates probably drew on the

Table 13.2 Total Populations of Interior Luzon According to the Dominican Father Francisco Antolín, 1789

Ethnic groups and geographical regions	**Estimate in *almas***	**Discussed under**
Ituy or Isinay	3,900	Ituy and Paniqui
Gaddang or Paniqui	10,000	Ituy and Paniqui
Italones, Ibilaos, and Ilongotes	4,000	Ituy and Paniqui
Baler, Casiguiran, Palanan	4,000	Ituy and Paniqui
Gamu, Furao, Ilagan,	6,000	Northern sierra
Tumavini, Catalangan		(Gaddang and Kalinga)
Gadanes Yogades from Tuao to Cauayan including those living in the interior	4,000	Northern sierra (Gaddang and Kalinga)
Igorrotes of Quiangan and other villages opposite Bagabag	6,000	Igorots (Ifugao)
Yumanguies, Ava, Leaban, and other interior pagans	5,000	Igorots (Benguet)
Tino[k] and other pagans opposite the Matuno River	5,000	Igorots (Benguet)
From Vigan to Agoo there are *rancherías* of pagan Igorots and others	10,000	Igorots (Ilocos, Kankanai, Benguet)
Tinguianes who live in the Abra of Vigan according to the decree of Señor Fuentes	10,000	Tinguians of Abra (Ilocos)
Opposite San Jacinto y Asingan there are various pagans	5,000	Pangasinan
Mining regions of Cauayan, Imbussi, Apaiao, Pagutentan	10,000	Within Igorot territory but assumed to be of varied ethnic origins.

Source: AUST Libro de Becerro 37 fols. 250r and v Discurso sobre el gentio . . . Francisco Antolín 1789.

Note: The names of ethnic groups are as they appear in the source.

recent exploratory expeditions. The "Yumanguies, Ava, Leaban and other pagans in the interior" were estimated at 5,000 souls and another 5,000 were to be found in the region of Tino[k], including other pagans "opposite the River Matuno."[145] Even further north, the Igorot of Quiangan (Ifugao) were estimated at 6,000, while to the west in the foothills of Ilocos between Vigan and Agoo there were another 10,000. In addition to these 26,000 souls, another 10,000 of varied ethnic origins were living in the mining regions. Elsewhere, Father Antolín suggests, the Igorot were at least five times more numerous than the Tinguian of Ilocos, who Bishop Fuentes had recently reported numbered 10,000. This would suggest a population of 50,000. From his map of Igorot territory, it appears that Father Antolín was using the term Igorot to apply only to those groups discussed above. In 1898 the total population of the *comandancías* of Benguet, Bontoc, Quinagan, Lepanto, and Amburayan was 121,888.[146] This would represent an increase of about 0.8 percent a year over the previous century, which seems high given the relatively low fertility among these groups and the disruptive effects of military campaigns in the early nineteenth century.[147] Most likely, Father Antolín's figure of 50,000 was an underestimate. At the time he was writing, little contact had been made with the Ifugao, who, as noted above, in the nineteenth century were revealed to be very numerous, perhaps numbering 20,000 to 30,000. It is not unreasonable therefore to add about 20,000 to the figure of 50,000, to give a conservative estimate for the Igorot of 70,000 in the late eighteenth century.

It is even more difficult to trace demographic trends during the early colonial period because estimates were often derived from fleeting observations made during expeditions and often did not specify the boundaries of the region they referred to or the groups they encompassed. The earliest estimates relate to expeditions that explored the Upper Magat Valley in the late sixteenth century. These estimated that the gold-mining region occupied by the Igorot possessed between 18,000 and 20,000 "indios."[148] Assuming this to be the Benguet region, the figure might be compared with the 10,000 souls estimated by Father Antolín for the end of the eighteenth century, though it is doubtful that the expeditions had acquired information on groups as far north as those referred to by Father Antolín. Other important estimates relate to Captain Aldana's expedition in 1620 that explored the southwest corner of Benguet around Boa and the Antamoc mines. Aldana's account provides two contradictory estimates. He claimed that there were more than 7,000 "Igolotes" "who bore arms," which suggests they were adult males, but then he goes on to say that on the basis of the number of villages in the region, which he says were very many, there were more than "15,000 almas con la chusma."[149]

There are no estimates of the Igorot population in the late seventeenth century, and even the early and mid-eighteenth-century accounts such as those written by Fathers Carrillo and Vivar cover only part of the region. However, the list of settlements drawn up by Father Campo in 1740 gives the names of 108 *rancherías* for a wider area that encompassed the greater part of Benguet, which as has been estimated above may have possessed 7,560 *almas*, though this is likely an underestimate.[150] Nevertheless, by comparison with figures reported by expeditions in the early seventeenth century it suggests that the population had declined.

Father Antolín, looking back at demographic trends in early colonial times, was also certain that the population had declined. Nevertheless, he suggested that the Igorot had a moderate population because they had sufficient food and had escaped smallpox and other diseases by isolating themselves. They had also been spared from hard labor in extracting timber, rowing boats, and acting as porters, and they did not have prolonged wars. On the other hand, he noted that certain factors discouraged population increase. These included infanticide and the fact that women were treated like slaves and subject to hard labor so that they miscarried or became infertile.[151] He argued that the cessation of these practices would encourage population growth, as it had done among converts in Ilocos and Pangasinan. He therefore attributed population decline more to low fertility than to high mortality. Nevertheless, his comments are contradictory, for elsewhere he noted epidemics had had a devastating impact.

If the Igorot population did decline, what were the factors responsible? Expeditions and missionary efforts often resulted in the transfer of small numbers of Igorot to the lowlands, while others settled there voluntarily. While this may have contributed to population decline in the highlands, some lowland inhabitants fleeing from tribute payments and forced labor would have countered it. It is difficult to ascertain what the balance of these movements might have been, though it is noteworthy that neither movement attracts significant attention in the documentary sources.

Father Antolín considered that until the opening up of communications, the Igorot had been spared the scourge of epidemics due to their remoteness and their practice of closing off roads to prevent diseases from spreading.[152] He also noted that missionization facilitated the spread of smallpox, measles, *bubas*, and other diseases, from which their previous isolation had protected them.[153] Hence, the opening of the road to Cagayan in 1739 was immediately followed by an outbreak of smallpox in 1740–1741 that afflicted large numbers of Ilongot, Panuypuy, and others.[154] Although this may have been the first smallpox epidemic to hit the area within living memory, it may not have been the first to strike the Igorot, for in 1656 a major epidemic was said to have struck the interior mountains, leaving them deserted.[155] Nevertheless, following the construction of the road in the eighteenth century, the frequency of disease outbreaks increased. In 1758 Dupax was afflicted by "peste," and a few years later 700 died of smallpox. This was apparently the first time the disease had struck the population and there was one day when 60 people died. Then another 500 died in a second "peste" and subsequently there were another two outbreaks of smallpox, though the impact was not as great as in the first, when many adults died. Another significant epidemic occurred in 1786 when a "peste" spread from Manila to Bagabag and its surrounding region and killed more than 1,000 people, while another 200 died in the revolt it provoked.[156]

Among mountain peoples the impact of epidemics was heightened by the practice of abandoning the sick without shelter or sustenance.[157] This practice was still common among the Igorot in the early nineteenth century and was regarded as one of the main causes of high mortality associated with smallpox.[158] Fertility was also affected by epidemics and disease. Father Antolín noted that following the 1786 epidemic of "peste" there had been a fall in baptisms due to the lack of conceptions.[159] "Mal gálico" or syphilis, which had formerly been unknown, also became common among men and women following the opening of the road to Cagayan in 1739.

Military expeditions adversely affected populations by both inflicting casualties and causing major disruption to subsistence activities and marital life. Father Antolín himself reflected on what had happened to the hundred families of Panuypuy who had been such a threat to the missions in the early part of the eighteenth century. He noted that some survivors had retreated inland, two or three families were living in Aritao, and six or seven each in Dupax and near Ileaban.[160] The experience of the Panuypuy was perhaps exceptional, but other groups who were the object of punitive raids were also likely to have been similarly dispersed, forcing them to adapt to new social and environmental conditions. Many preferred to throw in their lot with Christian villages, so that during the late eighteenth century the populations of nearby missions expanded considerably, in part due to fear of military expeditions.[161]

The Igorot population appears to have suffered a significant decline in the second half of the eighteenth century. If, as estimated above, the population in the 1780s was about 70,000, then it may have been about 100,000 in 1700. This is little more than an educated guess, and the suggested level of decline may be too high. However, it takes account of the indirect and well as direct impact of epidemics. Although not all communities would have been affected to equal degrees, the fact that losses in this region were being sustained among the adult population meant that epidemics might result in an immediate loss of reproductive capacity, reduce agricultural labor inputs, and cause family breakdown.[162] Moreover, such crises occurred in the context of social practices that promoted low fertility and retarded demographic recovery.

Earlier demographic trends are almost impossible to track. In the sixteenth and seventeenth centuries, some losses occurred as a result of epidemics and expeditions, especially on the fringes of the region, but the population may have been boosted by people moving from the lowlands. Therefore, in the absence of other evidence it will be assumed that the Igorot population was broadly the same in 1570 as it was in 1700. However, at the local scale there would have been significant spatial and temporal differences in demographic trends. Descriptions of agricultural practices and settlement patterns suggest that the Benguet Igorot were less populous than those in Bontoc and the Ifugao; they are also likely to have declined more markedly during the colonial period due to more regular outside contacts and possibly more frequent epidemics. The spatial balance of population would thus have been rather different at the end of the eighteenth century than it had been in 1570.

The Northern Cordillera

Missionaries approached the Apayao and Kalinga in the northern Cordillera primarily from the Cagayan Valley, hence they are considered separately from other inhabitants of the mountain provinces. Little information exists on this region prior to the arrival of Dominicans in the early seventeenth century. The northwest coast of Cagayan that bordered on the Apayao was pacified at an early date and its inhabitants distributed in *encomiendas*. However, the Spanish only penetrated inland to the Lower Chico Valley. In 1591 only one *encomienda* existed at the "estuary of Lobo," where 4,000 tributaries and 16,000 souls existed.[163] Subsequently the Apayao and Kalinga regions became the focus of distinct Dominican missionary efforts.

The Apayao

The inhabitants of Apayao province are known today as the Isneg, but in early colonial times were referred to either as the Apayao, after the river of that name, or more commonly as the Mandaya, meaning "upstream" in Isneg. The term Isneg appears to have derived from the Ilocano word *tineg*, meaning "enemy," which was applied to both the Kalinga and Isneg. The name lost the connotation of enemy and was eventually adopted by the Isneg themselves.[164]

The Mandaya were predominantly dry-rice farmers who also grew gabi and sweet potatoes and who hunted and fished. They lived in small hamlets along rivers and streams.[165] In the late twentieth century, they lived in individual extended family households.[166] This pattern of residence is unusual in interior Luzon, and historical accounts throw little light on its origins. What is evident, however, is that there was no political organization that extended beyond communities that were composed of clusters of extended families. The Mandaya were renowned headhunters who conducted raids for prestige, as a qualification for marriage, and for revenge and ritual.

Dominican missionaries worked among the Mandaya more or less continuously until the eighteenth century, but progress was slow and the mission was eventually abandoned in 1769. In 1608 the Dominicans established a mission at Fotol and within a few years had converted 300 Mandaya (Map 12.1). By 1619 they had established another mission further up the Abulug River at Capinatan, and a third, called Santa Cecilia, may also have been initiated.[167] However, progress came to an abrupt halt in 1625 when a revolt in Capinatan fomented by some unconverted Mandaya left two missionaries dead and Fotol in ruins.[168] The following year a Spanish punitive expedition tried to force the rebels down from the hills by destroying their crops and palm trees, but to little effect.[169]

In 1631 Father Jerónimo de Zamora arrived in Fotol and the following year he and Father Luis Oñate undertook the first of several expeditions up the Abulug River. Within a year 800 Mandaya had been baptized. Apparently many more wanted to be converted, but the Dominicans lacked the personnel to continue the mission, and they returned to the lowlands, where they were ministering to 8,000 *almas de confesión*.[170] Some were skeptical of the ease and speed with which the Mandaya had been converted, believing them to be fickle and of little capability.

Whether or not their skepticism was justified, other factors were instrumental in a revolt among the Mandaya in 1639. This revolt was provoked by mistreatment by soldiers stationed at a local garrison, possibly at Capinatan.[171] From then missionary activity appears to have lapsed until 1684, when Father Pedro Ximénez was transferred there from the Irraya mission in the Upper Cagayan. At Fotol he found the inhabitants dying of hunger because they had been unable to farm due to threats from unconverted Mandaya around Capinatan.[172] The following year this region was afflicted by an epidemic of smallpox, which resulted in many coming down from their *rancherías* in search of baptism, including many adults who subsequently died.[173] By 1686, 1,300 *almas* had reportedly been baptized, a not insignificant number given the dispersed settlement pattern, and by 1689 two new missions had been established at Nuestra Señora del la Peña de Francia and at Ngagan between Fotol and Capinatan. According to Julián Malumbres, the first mission had 2,000 *infieles*.[174] Like their predecessors, these new missions were short-lived, for in the absence of missionaries they were attacked by neighbors who opposed their conversion. As a result most fled to the mountains, leaving only 134 converts who were moved to Camalaniugan.[175]

The Dominican historian Vicente de Salazar recorded that after 1689 the Apayao mission ended. Nevertheless, small numbers of converts remained in Fotol and Capinatan, which in the early eighteenth century together possessed about 140 *tributos*.[176] Also, some missionary activity was still taking place in more remote regions when Father José Tomás Marín made two journeys across the province of Apayao in 1740 and 1741. At that time Fotol had 250 *almas de confesión*, and Capinatan, which had been moved to a new site to facilitate its administration, had 81. In addition, there were twenty new converts and seven apostates in the new mission of San Antonio de Ngagan, where 104 *catecumenos* from nine surrounding villages were building their homes.[177] The mission at Ngagan was short-lived, for in 1769 it, Fotol, and Capinatan had been aggregated and moved to a new site for their protection against their hostile neighbors.[178] Fotol continued to appear in censuses and tribute lists, but new attempts to convert those in the interior had to wait for another century.

Further south, bordering on Kalinga territory, in 1778 Father Antonio Feijas compiled a list of settlements in the hinterland of the missions of Malaueg, Mavanan, and Santa Cruz. While most of these were found among the northern Kalinga, those on the Matalag, Nabbuagan, and Tumuttut rivers, as well as twenty-seven *ranchos* located further north, were in Apayao territory. Settlements in the three valleys included 420 houses, with communities averaging between fifteen and thirty houses.[179] Using the contemporary multiplication factor of four suggests a total population for these settlements of 1,680. However, this multiplier may not be appropriate for the Mandaya, who in the late twentieth century resided in extended family units with an average size of household of about 9.5.[180] The total population may therefore have been at least twice this size.

Most contact with the Mandaya was from the east, but from the mid-seventeenth century Augustinians working out of Ilocos had intermittent contact with them. Felix Keesing argues that the absence of early records of people living in this area suggests they may have arrived there as refugees from Spanish control in the lowlands or from the Upper Apayao region, where concerted missionary efforts began in 1668.[181]

Writing in 1763, the Augustinian historian Antonio Mozo described Apayao (Mandaya) territory as extending for about thirty leagues and comprising "many thousands of souls."[182] This excluded the neighboring Adan, whom he described as another nation that was less powerful and was "of fewer people." Very little is known of the Apayao in the nineteenth century. In 1890 an anonymous account calculated that the Apayao numbered 6,872,[183] while in 1898 the population of the whole *comandancia* of Apayao, which included some non-Apayao groups, was estimated at 12,000.[184] Given the extensive area inhabited by the Apayao, this would have been a very low population density. In the 1930s Morice Vanoverbergh estimated that they numbered 9,000 and suggested they had declined due to the unhealthy climate, high infant mortality, the lack of medical care, and easy divorce.[185] Such factors may also have contributed to low population levels in the colonial period. However, compared to other regions, the Apayao were relatively isolated and during the colonial period may not have suffered a significant decline, though they may have been struck by an occasional epidemic from which low fertility would have slowed recovery. If the population was about 12,000 in 1800, a decline of 10 or 20 percent during the colonial period suggests a population in 1570 of between 13,300 and 15,000.

The Kalinga of the Chico River and Their Neighbors

The Kalinga occupy a significant proportion of the Chico Valley region. In recent times a distinction has been made between the southern and northern Kalinga. The former inhabit large villages and are essentially wet-rice cultivators, but also grow dry rice and, unlike the Ifugao, Bontoc, and Kankanai, cultivate few roots.[186] Among the northern Kalinga, on the other hand, dry-rice cultivation predominates. Here populations are lower and hamlet-sized settlements of between six and thirty houses are more characteristic. The northern Kalinga are thus more akin to their northern neighbors, the Apayao. It is thought that wet-rice cultivation spread to the southern Kalinga only a few centuries ago, prior to which swidden cultivation based on root crops predominated.[187] The chronicler Diego de Aduarte describes how in the lower Chico Valley in the early seventeenth century the Dominicans congregated the dispersed population into large villages and established fields around them, suggesting that there was a change from shifting to permanent cultivation, probably of wet rice.[188]

Among the Kalinga the predominant residence unit was the nuclear family. Ethnographic studies of the southern Kalinga at Lubuagan and the northern Kalinga at Mabaca in the late 1950s recorded household sizes of about 4.8 persons and 5.5

persons respectively. At that time fertility was high, with women averaging seven children, with some having as many as fifteen. However, only three or four normally survived beyond puberty, with diarrhea being the main cause of infant and child mortality.[189] Headhunting and warfare also contributed to low population levels. Headhunting involved fewer individuals and often focused on vulnerable persons such as old men, the infirm, or unprotected women and children.[190] With the availability of modern weapons, headhunting has been preferred to warfare since it results in less bloodshed, but the balance may have been different in the past.

The first missions to be founded among the Kalinga were established at Piat and Lobo (Tabang) in 1604 and another further upriver at Tuao in 1612 (Map 12.1).[191] Tabang was established with 500 tributaries and the other two with more than 1,000 each. By 1617 another mission had been established at Malaueg. Little is known of these missions until 1688, when Father Juan Yñiguez was entrusted with the conversion of the inhabitants of Mananig and groups living in the mountains near Tuao, who were regarded as the most warlike in the province.[192] Six leagues south of Tuao, Father Yñiguez established the mission of San José at Tuga, but it was later moved closer to Tuao, of which it became a *visita* in 1710. Many neophytes opted to flee and its remaining inhabitants were transferred to Tuao.[193] Slightly before Tuga was founded, Father Joseph Galfaroso extended missionary activity west from Malaueg up the Matalag River, where the mission of Santa Cruz de Gumpat was founded about 1693.[194] The mission also made little progress and the general revolt in Cagayan in 1718 encouraged many to flee. At that time, Tuao had only thirty *almas* and the mission at Santa Cruz possessed only "apostates and heathens."[195]

Even though missionary efforts had little success, they were later resumed both to the south of Tuao and to the west of Malaueg. The Dominicans tried to establish a mission upriver from Tuao in the Alioc region, but in 1723 its inhabitants fled, and sometime between 1729 and 1731 the remaining converts were moved downriver to a new site at Orag.[196] The mission was destabilized by conflicts between different factions of Kalinga who had been settled there, but following an attack on the mission in 1741 military *entradas* managed to settle 132 fugitives at Orag or between Piat and Nassiping.[197] By the time Father Tomás Marín visited the mission in 1743, six expeditions had been undertaken into the mountains of Mananig, Calavan, Dilayan, Tubog, Concalan, and Calayug, and the population of the mission of Orag had increased to 349 *almas*.[198] Meanwhile Piat had 1,019 *comuniones* and Tabang 331.[199]

During the second half of the eighteenth century, the population of the Orag mission seems to have fluctuated around 300 *almas*,[200] but in 1757 it was hit by a smallpox epidemic that struck the Cagayan region. It not only caused high mortality, but exacerbated fugitive tendencies. Between 1757 and 1764, sixty-four died and in 1758 sixty-seven were registered as tributaries in other towns and provinces.[201] By 1773, the mission of Orag comprised three settlements, the other two being at Santa Catalina de Sena and Bubug.[202] Together they contained 755 *almas*, of whom 219 had been born outside the missions. Father Tomás de Anibarra reported that there were 18,000 potential converts in the hills around Tuao, among whom were many apostates who were considered more difficult to settle in the missions than those who had never been converted.

Dominican records provide continuous information on mission populations from the late 1750s to the nineteenth century (Table 13.3).[203] Overall, they give the impression that there were only minor fluctuations in population, but underlying them there was probably a considerable population turnover. The proportions living in the three areas of Tuao, Malaueg, and Piat did not change substantially.[204] The populations of the Tuao and Orag missions reached a peak in the late 1770s and 1780s when they contained about 3,700 *almas*, after which they declined slightly. Comparing the figures for these missions with that of 755 *almas* given by Father Anibarra in 1773 suggests that only about 20 percent were living in the missions.

To the northwest, the mission of Santa Cruz was re-established in 1722, and in 1725 Mavanan was founded. When the inhabitants of Orag revolted in 1741, missionaries dissuaded those at Santa Cruz and Mavanan from so doing, and by 1743 Santa Cruz had 226 *almas* and was drawing converts from settlements two to three days' walk away at Nabuagan, Tumutud, Tabaran, and Nabbayugan.[205] Mavanan partially drew on the same catchment area as Santa Cruz and in 1743 had 144 *almas*.[206] The mission averaged 200 to 300 souls until the 1770s, when some were killed by converts from Tuao and they became hostile. Others died in "pestes y viruelas" and some who fled to escape the epidemics did not return.[207] These processes are reflected in the populations of the missions of Santa Cruz, Malaueg, and Mavanan, which show an increase to the 1770s, but thereafter show greater fluctuations than Tuao and Orag.

During the second half of the eighteenth century, the total population of the northern Kalinga missions fluctuated between about 6,000 and 7,000 *almas*. Given his firsthand knowledge of the region, Father Anibarra's figure of 18,000 potential converts in the mountains around Tuao was probably reasonably accurate.[208] Therefore, the total population of the region in 1800 may have been around 25,000. At that time, the northern Kalinga were more populous than their northern neighbors, the Apayao, and they were probably also more populous in 1570. Dominican accounts at the beginning of the seventeenth century make it clear that even before the establishment of wet-rice cultivation, the region was more densely settled than that of the Apayao. Nevertheless, the population would have expanded with the extension of wet-rice cultivation. However, any growth would have been countered by high mortality associated with epidemics, from which demographic recovery would have been retarded by low fertility and intertribal conflict. The population of the region in 1570 therefore may not have been significantly different from that in 1800.

Demographic Trends in the Cordillera

It has been estimated here that the population of the mountain provinces as a whole in 1800 may have been about 127,000 (Table 13.4). If anything this figure is probably an underestimate since large parts of the Cordillera were still unknown or had been

Table 13.3 Total Populations of Missions in the Chico Valley, 1758 to 1805

	1758	1764–1765	1766–1767	1770	1773	1774	1774–1775	1775–1776	1776–1777	1779–1780
Tuao	2,712	2,770	2,750	2,596	2,676	3,020	2,849	2,882	3,007	3,713
Orag		55	700	571	705	841	831	688	836	
TOTAL	2,712	2,825	3,450	3,167	3,381	3,861	3,680	3,570	3,843	3,713
Malaueg	1,122	1,030	1,098	952	1,050	1,117	1,053	1,233	1,201	1,116
Mavanan		264	255	232	300	299	262	277	305	212
Santa Cruz	355	431	302	342	364	359	395	446	337	227
TOTAL	1,122	1,649	1,784	1,486	1,692	1,780	1,674	1,905	1,952	1,665
Piat	1,590	1,751	1,515	1,508	1,526	1,639	1,592	1,668	1,742	1,595
Tabang	455	484	503	364	424	366	416	431	419	407
TOTAL	2,045	2,235	2,018	1,872	1,950	2,005	2,008	2,099	2,161	2,002
GRAND TOTAL	5,879	6,709	7,252	6,525	7,023	7,646	7,362	7,574	7,956	7,380

Sources:

1758 APSR Cagayan 18 doc. 1 Mapa de los pueblos y almas . . . 1758.

1764–1765, 1766–1767, 1770, 1773, 1774–1775, 1775–1776 1776–1777, 1779–1780, 1783–1784, 1786–1787, 1789–90 APSR Cagayan 18 doc. 3 Estadísticas ó estados de almas 1758–1805 and Cagayan 26 doc. 7 Estadísticas ó estados de almas 1758–1800.

1788 APSR Cagayan 18 doc. 1 Estadísticas ó estados de almas 1758–1805.

1794–1797 APSR Cagayan 18 doc. 3 Estadísticas ó estados de almas 1758–1805 and Cagayan 26 doc. 7 Estadísticas ó estados de almas 1758–1800.

1800 APSR Cagayan 18 Número de almas del obispado de Nueva Segovia 1800.

1803 APSR Cagayan l 1 doc. 11 Número de almas de la provincia de Cagayan 29 Nov. 1803.

1805 APSR Cagayan 18 doc. 3 Estadísticas ó estados de almas 1758–1805 and Cagayan 26 doc. 7 Estadísticas ó estados de almas 1758–1800.

1783–1784	1786–1787	1788	1789–1790	1794	1795	1796	1797	1800	1803	1805
3,535	3,733	3,744	3,783	3,416	3,383	3,144	3,278	3,040	2,995	3,060
3,535	3,733	3,744	3,783	3,416	3,383	3,144	3,278	3,040	2,995	3,060
1,298	1,311	1,254	863	1,754	1,464	1,555	1,812	1,589	1,918	1,687
228	200	179	184			253				254
223	217	202								
1,753	1,734	1,650	1,249	1,754	1,464	1,808	1,812	1,589	1,918	1,941
1,720	2,063	1,706	1,971	1,713	1,661	1,762		1,280	1,618	1,885
455	440	447	457	403	477	466		400	422	431
2,175	2,503	2,153	2,428	2,116	2,138	2,228		1,680	2,040	2,316
7,463	7,970	7,547	7,460	7,286	6,985	7,180	5,090	6,309	6,953	7,317

TABLE 13.4 Estimates of the Total Population of Interior Luzon, 1570 to 1800

Region	**Estimated total population 1570**	**Estimated total population 1800**	**Percentage change**
Ituy and Paniqui	60,000	20,000	66.7
Igorot territory	100,000	70,000	30.0
Kalinga of the Chico Valley	25,000	25,000	0.0
Apayao	14,150	12,000	15.2
TOTAL	199,150	127,000	36.2

Note: See the text for a discussion of these estimates.

explored only superficially. At that time, the population was concentrated in the areas inhabited by the Bontoc, Ifugao, and southern Kalinga. These societies possessed more intensive forms of agricultural production and had come into less sustained contact with outsiders. They may also have experienced some immigration.

The population of interior Luzon in 1570 has been estimated at a conservative 199,150, which represents an overall decline of nearly 36 percent. However, not all groups in the Cordillera experienced the same level of decline, partly because the population distribution in 1570 differed from that in 1800. In 1570 wet-rice cultivation was not widespread or well-established among the Isinai, southern Kankanai, and southern Kalinga, whose populations grew during the colonial period. On the other hand, levels of decline varied across the region, with losses being greatest where expeditions often destroyed communities and crops and sometimes brought epidemic disease, social change, and resettlement. These processes appear to have had their greatest impact in Ituy and Paniqui, where the population may have fallen by about half between 1570 and 1800, from about 40,000 to 20,000. Losses would also have been high on the western fringes of Benguet, which were easily accessible from Ilocos. On the other hand, regions remote from outside contact were not only spared these ravages, but to varying degrees became zones of refuge for those wishing to escape Spanish control. Population levels in much of Igorot territory were therefore maintained to a greater degree during the colonial period, though even there epidemics probably took a toll. While the documentary evidence provides support for these observations, the figures themselves are little more than reasoned guesses. Archival research on the mountain provinces in the nineteenth century might throw considerable light on demographic trends in earlier periods, but is beyond the scope of this book. I fully expect the estimates here to be modified in the light of future research.

PART V

Conclusion

CHAPTER 14
Demographic Change in the Early Spanish Philippines

In general terms, demographic trends following European contact in both Southeast Asia and the Americas followed a similar trajectory, with indigenous peoples in both regions experiencing a significant decline followed by a slow recovery. In Southeast Asia the decline does not appear to have been as great, but it extended through the seventeenth century, whereas by then native populations in some parts of the Americas had begun to recover.[1] In Spanish America, however, population increase was slow and growth did not reach the spectacular rates that characterized demographic recovery in Southeast Asia from the eighteenth century.[2] Hence, despite the Philippines' being subject to the same colonial power as Spanish America, broad demographic trends in the Philippines showed greater similarities to those in Southeast Asia than to those in the Americas. The initial impact of conquest and the types of transformations the Spanish sought to bring to native societies in both regions were similar, but what made the Philippines different from Spanish America was the geographical location of the islands, their physical configuration, and the character of the natural resources and societies to be found there. These factors were also significant in explaining why, although the Philippines may have followed a similar demographic trajectory to other Southeast Asian societies, there were differences in the relative importance of factors underlying population trends in these two regions.

Low Population Densities in Pre-Spanish Times

One necessary aim of this study was to refine estimates for the population of the Philippines at the time of Spanish arrival. Through an examination of the evidence for each region in the Visayas and Luzon, it has been suggested that in 1565 the population of these islands together was about 1.43 million, with nearly 73 percent being in Luzon. To this number might be added a further 5 to 10 percent to take account of the inhabitants of smaller islands and others who escaped official attention. These figures do not include Mindanao and other islands in the southern archipelago. This would suggest a maximum population of about 1.57 million at the time the Spanish arrived. While this estimate may appear precise, given the fragmentary nature of the evidence on which it is based and the need to make many assumptions about the influence of epidemics and political, economic, and social changes that were associated with colonial rule, it must be regarded as having a margin of error. While the estimate of 1.57 million is higher than suggested in other studies, it confirms earlier findings that the population density of the Philippines was low.[3] Densities appear to have been slightly higher in Luzon than in the Visayas, but they still averaged less than ten persons per square kilometer; only around Manila and in Ilocos did densities exceed twenty persons per square kilometer.[4]

Anthony Reid had argued that the most significant factor holding back population growth in Southeast Asia through the eighteenth century was interpolity warfare. It is recognized that its demographic impact derived not so much from the numbers killed in conflict, since the aim was to capture sources of labor, but from the disruption it caused to subsistence activities and its impact on fertility through the prolonged or permanent separation of spouses, encouraging birth control, and inducing unconscious stressed-related amenorrhea.[5] Certainly interpolity conflict was common throughout much of the Visayas and Luzon in pre-Spanish times. Ilocos appears to have been the exception, and its absence could have contributed to higher population densities there.

Research in other regions of Southeast Asia suggests other factors that may have been more significant in explaining low population densities. Peter Boomgaard has stressed the importance of marriage practices and birth control in explaining low fertility in the Indonesian archipelago,[6] while David Henley has collected evidence from Sulawesi and elsewhere to suggest that lower birth rates prevailed in slave-owning societies.[7] The research here supports the view that fertility was a significant factor in maintaining low population densities in the Philippines, particularly in the Visayas, where small families were preferred and abortion and infanticide were widely practiced. Here marriages were also delayed by high bridewealth, and the widespread use of penis inserts may have affected fecundity. Similar practices were found among groups that inhabited the interior highlands of Luzon, but they were not common in Tagalog society, where large families were favored. Similarly, slavery and debt bondage seem to have been more prevalent in the Visayas, perhaps because of the Visayans' more precarious form of subsistence or the need to acquire slaves for bridewealth. These social practices would not only have functioned to limit population growth and promote low fertility, but they would also have made it difficult for communities to recover from major demographic crises associated with famines or epidemics.

Another factor that may have contributed to low population densities in precolonial Southeast Asia that has received scant attention from demographic historians is disease. There is some recognition that the warm, humid climate of the tropical lowlands favored the spread of infections,[8] but the disease environment has not generally been considered in detail, possibly because early descriptions suggested that Southeast Asians were very healthy and/or that they had acquired some immunity to acute infections in pre-Spanish times.[9] However, this study has suggested that enteric diseases, malaria, dengue, leprosy, yaws, and possibly schistosomiasis and tuberculosis were probably endemic in at least some islands in pre-Spanish times, some of which would have enhanced infant and child mortality in particular. The Visayas were generally regarded as healthier than Luzon, perhaps because environmental conditions there were less favorable for the spread of certain diseases, such as malaria, or also because of the lower population densities. Mathematically it can be shown that chronic infections that kill a significant proportion of children within ten years of birth have a more significant effect on the general level of mortality and rate of population growth than high death rates from infrequent epidemics.[10] But the Philippines suffered from both. Superimposed on the regular toll that chronic infections may have taken were periodic epidemics that continued to cause high mortality because populations failed to reach thresholds necessary for acute infections to become endemic and for local populations to acquire immunity to them. However, while single epidemics would have caused high mortality, due to the dispersed settlement pattern and difficulties of communication between and within the islands, each is likely to have affected only a small number of islands and communities before it died out.

Other possible influences on population densities were periodic famines and environmental hazards, such as typhoons, floods, and volcanic eruptions, which were frequently recorded in both the Philippines and the rest of Southeast Asia in colonial times.[11] While colonial rule often amplified their effects, their role in maintaining low population densities in precolonial times has probably been underestimated. David Henley has also drawn attention to limitations on agricultural production in precolonial Southeast Asia, which he argues reflected edaphic and climatic conditions and restricted the external demand for commodities.[12] While the more environmentally deterministic features of his argument cannot be accepted, there is some support for his proposition from the Philippines, where fertile, cultivable land was often limited and intensive forms of agricultural production, particularly those based on artificial irrigation that can support high population densities, were generally absent until the late eighteenth and nineteenth centuries. Low agricultural productivity, periodically exacerbated by natural hazards, would have adversely affected nutrition, maintained high levels of infant and child mortality, and retarded population growth. In pre-Spanish times, therefore, a number of interrelated factors functioned to maintain low population densities.

Temporal and Regional Population Trends in the Early Spanish Philippines

The colonial period saw major economic, social, and political changes that affected the nature of warfare, birth and marriages practices, and patterns of subsistence, while epidemics and environmental disasters continued to afflict the region. Many of these changes had adverse effects on demographic change, but others indirectly encouraged population growth. As elsewhere in Southeast Asia, the balance of these factors shifted over time, with the Filipino population experiencing a significant decline in the seventeenth century followed by a substantial expansion in the eighteenth century. While this pattern characterized the Philippines as a whole, there were considerable regional differences in the level and timing of demographic decline and recovery. These diverse trends are worth summarizing here since they can contribute to the general debate over the causes of demographic change in the wider Southeast Asian archipelago.

The Initial Impact of Conquest

The decline of the Filipino population in the early colonial period has generally been attributed to the demands for provisions and labor generated by the Hispano-Dutch War, which has often obscured the prior impact of Spanish conquest. Yet this study has shown that by 1600 the overall population of the islands may have already declined by about 36 percent, though this figure masks important regional differences (Table 14.1). While average population losses were higher in the Visayas at about 42 percent, the decline was highest in those islands that experienced the most sustained contacts with Spaniards or, in the case of Bohol, were subject to Portuguese and Moro raids. Although Cebu was the initial focus of Spanish settlement in the Visayas, here the level of decline was moderated by the early Spanish move to Luzon. On the other hand, losses were highest in Panay, which continued to be an important source of provisions and labor, first for the occupation of Luzon and later for garrisons and to support the Hispano-Dutch War. In Luzon the decline was greatest in Ilocos, Cagayan, Bikol, and Pampanga, which all lost more than 40 percent of their populations. Prior to 1600 there was little Spanish permanent settlement in the first three regions, where elevated losses were associated with their particularly brutal or protracted conquest, which either resulted in high mortality or encouraged fugitivism. In the case of Pampanga, however, excessive demands for provisions and labor, due to its proximity to Manila, contributed to higher losses than in Manila Bay itself, where population losses were compensated for in part by immigration. Meanwhile, in the interior highlands the decline was probably minimal due to limited contact.

Losses of the order of 36 percent are significant in the context of arguments that the conquest of the Philippines occurred with little bloodshed. It is clear that the Ordinances of 1573, aimed at bringing about the peaceful subjugation of newly discovered territories, had little impact on the course of conquest in the Philippines. Initial Spanish-Filipino contacts resulted in heavy loss of life, with ecclesiastics condemning the activities of the conquistadors and soldiers. The chronicle of conquest differed little from that in many parts of Spanish America. The high level of conflict and bloodshed may be explained in part by the difficulties the Spanish experienced in securing supplies from societies that did not produce large surpluses and in achieving political control of regions where the authority of leaders was not extensive. In such cases subjugation had to be undertaken piecemeal and often required the use of military force, a process most clearly exemplified in the conquest of the Cagayan Valley. As in Spanish America, the conversion and "civilization" of such societies was eventually left to the missionary orders, but not before military subjugation had exacted its toll.

In Spanish America the exceptionally high mortality that characterized the early conquest period has been associated with the introduction of Old World diseases. The Philippines continued to be afflicted by epidemics that in the early colonial period took a heavy toll, with mortality rates in particular places reaching levels as high as in early Spanish America. However, their overall impact was moderated because the dispersed settlement pattern and slow transport through the islands meant that their impact was localized. Indeed, Ken De Bevoise argues that the impact of acute infections in the Philippines was felt most profoundly not in the early colonial period, but in the nineteenth century, when population growth and improved communications greatly facilitated their spread.[13] Although there is some debate over the relative contribution of Old World diseases and conquest to demographic collapse in the Americas, the former is generally considered to have been more significant. In the Philippines, however, the reverse would seem to be the case.

The Demographic Crisis of the Seventeenth Century

The evidence for demographic trends in the Philippines during the seventeenth century is very fragmentary, and undue reliance has to be placed on fiscal records, which often reflect the level of administrative efficiency or fugitivism and are therefore an imperfect guide to changes in vital rates. Nevertheless, excluding the interior of the island, they suggest that the tributary population of Luzon fell by about 46 percent in the early seventeenth century.[14] Levels of decline were particularly high in those provinces subject to the *polo* and *vandala*, such as Pampanga and southwest Luzon, and were somewhat lower in Ilocos and Pangasinan, which were largely spared these levies. Meanwhile, falling numbers of tributaries in Cagayan almost certainly reflects weakening administrative control, while in Bikol, Moro raids caused high mortality, disrupted agricultural production and family life, and promoted fugitive tendencies.

In contrast to Luzon, the tributary population of the Visayas in the early seventeenth century remained almost constant. However, this trend masked considerable variation between the islands. The population of Cebu seems to have recovered once the Spanish effectively abandoned the island for Luzon, while the impact of the Hispano-Dutch War, through the demands it generated for provisions and troops, prolonged the decline in Panay. The tributary population of Leyte and Samar together also declined by 37 percent, due in part to Moro raids.

In the second half of the seventeenth century, demographic decline in Luzon began to be reversed, although growth was slow. Regions that had been subject to the *polo*, such as Pampanga and southwest Luzon, generally showed a slight increase in the tributary populations, whereas outlying regions continued to register slight declines, as did the Visayas as a whole. It is suggested here that the more sluggish recovery of the Visayan population might be attributed to lower fertility resulting from a degree of persistence, despite missionary efforts to suppress them,

TABLE 14.1 Demographic Trends in Luzon and the Visayas, 1565 to 1800

	1565/1570	1565/1570	1600	1600
	TRIBUTARY POPULATION	TOTAL POPULATION	TRIBUTARY POPULATION	TOTAL POPULATION
Manila	10,750	43,000	6,700[1]	36,000[2]
Southwest Luzon	30,000	120,000	22,600	90,200
Pampanga and Bulacan	30,000	120,000	15,000[2]	60,000[2]
Pangasinan	10,000	40,000	5,900	30,000[2]
Ilocos	43,000	172,000	17,230	68,520
Cagayan	40,000	160,000	22,050	88,200
Bikol	37,500	150,000	22,160	88,840
Mindoro	10,000	40,000	2,034[1]	32,000
Interior		199,150		190,000[2]
TOTAL LUZON	211,250	1,044,150	113,674	683,760
Cebu	7,000	28,000	5,730	23,000
Panay	50,000	200,000	25,000	100,000
Negros	7,500	30,000	6,250	25,000
Bohol	6,250	25,000	2,375	9,500
Leyte	15,000	60,000	8,750	35,000
Samar	10,000	40,000	7,500	30,000
TOTAL VISAYAS	95,750	383,000	55,425	221,700
GRAND TOTAL	307,000	1,427,150	169,099	905,460

Sources: 1565/1570 See Table 5.1 for the Visayas and the text for figures for Luzon.

1600 Tributary and total populations for Luzon are taken from 1591 except where other figures available from Appendixes (1) or estimated in the text (2). For figures for the Visayas see Table 5.2.

1700 Tributary figures for Luzon taken from AGI Contaduría 1253 fols. 111–120 Oficiales reales 1700, except where estimated in the text (2), and total populations are broadly estimated from tributary populations. For

Percent change 1565/1600 TOTAL POPULATION	**1700** TRIBUTARY POPULATION	**1700** TOTAL POPULATION	**1800** TRIBUTARY POPULATION	**1800** TOTAL POPULATION	**Population nadir**
16.3	7,224	32,000	14,949	70,000	Early 18th century
24.8	12,425	65,000	40,642	195,000	Early 17th century
50	12,305	52,000	36,440	155,500	Mid-17th century
25	10,916	50,000	21,696	100,000	Early 17th century
60.2	10,166	42,000	44,000	211,786	Late 17th century
44.9	15,000[2]	60,000	10,345	40757	Early 18th century
40.8	6,983	30,000	33,250	165,000	Early 17th century
20	1,878	26,000	3,244	20,000	Mid-17th century
4.6	170,000		127,000		18th century
34.5	76,897	527,000	204,566	1,085,043	
17.9	5,000	20,000	21,441	60,000	Early 18th century
50.0	25,000	100,000	43,971	235,000	Mid- to late 17th century
16.7	3,200	12,800	5,492	30,000	Late 17th/early 18th century
62.0	3,750	15,000	13,357	55,000	Late 17th century
41.7	6,250	25,000	8,657	40,000	Late 17th century
25.0	8,750	35,000	10,674	50,000	Late 17th century
42.1	51,950	207,800	103,591	470,000	
36.6	128,847	734,800	308,157	1,555,043	

the Visayas tributary populations are estimated by dividing by four the total populations in Table 6.5. For Interior Luzon see the text.

1800 Tributary populations are calculated from *tributos* for 1792 using the estimated growth rate per annum for 1792–1812 (AUST Libro 229 no. 1 Estatística [*sic*] de las Yslas 1815. For Bohol the tributary population is interpolated from figures for *tributos* in 1785 and 1815 in Appendix D. For Interior Luzon see the text.

of pre-Spanish marriage and birth practices that functioned to limit family size. In contrast, further north, the Tagalogs, Pampangans, and Ilocanos favored large families and did not normally practice infanticide.

Two other factors that possibly had different impacts in Luzon and the Visayas were epidemics and food shortages. During the first half of the seventeenth century, the inhabitants of some regions, notably surrounding Manila Bay, may have begun to acquire some immunity to acute infections as the opportunities for the introduction of disease expanded with increased contacts with China and Japan.[15] Over time the constant re-introduction of infections may have enabled a more immune population to emerge, as those who were less resistant died in epidemics and those who were more resistant survived to reproduce. Although fewer foreign traders visited the Visayas, diseases might spread to the islands from other regions, for example, with missionaries, troops, ships, or Moro raids. The Visayas were indeed visited periodically by epidemics, but their impact does not appear to have been as great. Although in the second half of the seventeenth century the frequency of epidemics in Luzon appears to have declined due to reduced external contacts, the higher population density would have facilitated the spread of those that were introduced. This, coupled with the more extended intervals between outbreaks, meant that when epidemics did strike they were often associated with high adult mortality. Even in the nineteenth century, despite the introduction of vaccination, which was not very effective, smallpox epidemics continued to cause high mortality and were considered to be a major factor holding back population growth.[16]

Comparing the initial impact of Spanish conquest on native peoples in the Philippines and in Spanish America, it is clear that although the losses sustained in the Philippines during the first 150 years of Spanish rule were substantial, they were generally lower than in the Americas. Between 1565 and 1655 the tributary population of Luzon and the Visayas declined from about 307,000 to 103,669, which represents a depopulation ratio of about 3:1.[17] This is significantly lower than the level of decline experienced in most regions of the Americas. Henry Dobyns has estimated that between first contact and the lowest recorded population for different regions, which for many areas was in the mid-seventeenth century, American populations generally declined by a ratio of 25:1 or 20:1.[18] Subsequent research has indicated that depopulation ratios varied widely, with losses being higher in the tropical lowlands and in Amazonia, and lower in the highlands.[19] It might be expected that the level of decline in the Philippines might have approached that of the tropical lowlands of Spanish America given similarities not only in environmental conditions, but also in the nature of indigenous societies found there and the mechanisms the Spanish used to bring about their subjugation and integration into colonial society.[20] However, the depopulation ratio for the Philippines is even lower than the lowest ratios in the Americas, which have been calculated for the highlands of Middle America and the Andes at about 4:1 to 5:1.[21]

In accounting for this lower level of decline, it would seem that the initial conquest of the Philippines was little different from that in many parts of Spanish

America. New colonial legislation promoting the peaceful acquisition of new territories was largely a dead letter in the Philippines. However, the impact of Spanish colonial rule was moderated by the islands' remote geographical location and the limited opportunities it offered for wealth creation, which discouraged Spanish immigration. Geography also played a role in moderating the impact of Old World diseases. While many studies have suggested that the main factor accounting for the relatively low level of population decline in the Philippines was the immunity Filipinos had acquired to Old World diseases in pre-Spanish times, this study has shown that this proposition has little foundation. The impact of epidemics was moderated not by any immunity Filipinos had acquired, but by the low population density and dispersed settlement pattern that limited the spread of disease.

Demographic Recovery in the Eighteenth Century

This study has focused primarily on the sixteenth and seventeenth centuries, while using sources from the eighteenth century and beyond for regions where evidence is scant for the early contact period. It has also used census and fiscal data to gain an overview of demographic trends during the eighteenth century. The most marked feature of the eighteenth century is that all regions experienced an increase in their tributary populations, with most regions exceeding 1 percent growth a year (see Appendix E). The only regions in Luzon where the population did not expand significantly were Cagayan and the interior highlands, where the opening of the road from the Central Plain of Luzon to Cagayan led to more sustained contact and introduced epidemic disease. While the populations of all regions increased during the eighteenth century, growth was more marked in the first half of the century. Between 1700 and 1750 the tributary population of Luzon and the Visayas grew by an average of 1.4 percent a year, but slowed to 0.6 percent in the second half of the eighteenth century. Growth was particularly slow in the Visayas, and especially Leyte and Samar, which suffered badly from Moro raids. A full analysis of the factors that might account for this marked increase and for differences in the rate of growth between regions would require further research into the economic, social, and political processes occurring at the time and is beyond the scope of this book. A vast amount of documentation for the eighteenth-century Philippines exists in the Archivo General de Indias in Seville, but it has scarcely been used by researchers. Nevertheless, the pattern of change in the eighteenth century can be discerned to a sufficient degree to enable a preliminary discussion of demographic trends in the Philippines in the wider Southeast Asian context.

The Philippines in the Context of the Demographic Trends in Southeast Asia

The Philippines appear to have followed the same demographic trend as other parts of the Southeast Asian archipelago, that is, suffering a significant decline through the seventeenth century followed by an increase in the eighteenth or nineteenth centuries, the timing and scale of which varied regionally. While these broad population movements might be similar, the factors underlying them appear to have been different.

Anthony Reid has argued that the seventeenth century was one of economic and demographic crisis in Southeast Asia as a whole due to an increase in military conflict and harsh conditions imposed by colonial rule in certain export-producing regions.[22] Reid argues that warfare increased in intensity as European weapons became available and as rivalry over trade increased between emerging city ports and with Europeans who sought to wrest the control of trade from native leaders and eliminate their competitors. Second, he suggests that mortality was high in Dutch VOC–controlled areas, particularly in the spice-producing islands of Maluku and parts of Java, due to harsh conditions associated with the extraction of export commodities. Maluku also suffered heavy losses during the Hispano-Dutch War. Elsewhere the impact of colonial rule in Southeast Asia up to the nineteenth century was largely indirect.

Though the Hispano-Dutch War did have a significant demographic impact in the Philippines, from the above observations, it appears that factors influencing population trends were somewhat different. This study has shown that the conquest of the islands was a bloody affair but that interpolity conflict within the Philippines diminished rather than increased during the early colonial period. Spain's weak financial position and tenuous foothold in Asia meant that it was generally forced to adopt a defensive rather than aggressive stand in Southeast Asia. External threats by Moros and the Dutch, while they inflicted periodic losses, seem to have unified Filipinos rather than exacerbated internal conflicts. Therefore, once the Hispano-Dutch War had ended, warfare was probably not a significant constraint on population growth, except perhaps in some limited interior regions.

The colonial economy of the Philippines also differed from much of the Southeast Asian archipelago. The commercial economy of the Philippines revolved around its role as an entrepôt rather than as a producer of export commodities. With the exception of regions in the hinterland of Manila, the degree of restructuring of native economies therefore was considerably less than in some other islands in the Southeast Asian archipelago, notably those that depended on the commercial production of spices (cloves, mace, nutmeg, and later pepper). The limited evidence that exists for demographic trends in regions such as Maluku, Sulawesi, and parts of Java, which came under formal Dutch control, suggests that the impact of colonial rule varied.[23] While the brutal conquest of the Banda islands resulted in the virtual extinction of its indigenous population,[24] the population in Ambon and the Lease Islands in Central Maluku between 1634 and 1674 declined by about 14 percent, after which it began to recover.[25] Why, if commercial activities were more limited in the Philippines, were levels of demographic decline generally higher than in Central Maluku?

This study suggests that the greater decline may be partially explained by the more pervasive nature of Spanish colonial rule. The dependence of the colony on tribute payments for its survival coupled with the imperative to "civilize" and convert Filipinos to Catholicism required the effective integration of communities into colonial society. These processes brought significant restructuring to Filipino societies, involving changes to subsistence practices, land tenure, settlement patterns, family structures, beliefs, and social customs that had implications for demographic trends. These changes occurred not only in and around the centers of Spanish settlement, but also to different degrees in remote regions and islands. Through adopting a regional approach, this study has been able to highlight the nature and intensity of colonial contact and the ease with which native Filipino communities could be incorporated into colonial society and their importance in understanding geographical and temporal variations in demographic trends.

Reid has also suggested that climatic change, specifically a decline in rainfall, perhaps linked to the Little Ice Age in the northern hemisphere, might have affected agricultural production and contributed to population decline in Southeast Asia in the seventeenth century. Evidence has been presented here for drought-induced food shortages in Cebu and Ilocos in the seventeenth century. These are both regions of relatively low rainfall and porous soils where there were periodic shortages of food in pre-Spanish times. Here agriculture would have been particularly vulnerable to climatic changes, but whether these food shortages were symptomatic of normal variations in production that might be expected from year to year or whether they reflected broader climatic changes is not clear. Other areas also suffered from periodic shortages, but these were generally related to human factors, such as Moro raids or labor being withdrawn from subsistence activities.

For the Philippines, therefore, demographic decline in the seventeenth century was the outcome of a complex interaction of factors that included the Hispano-Dutch War, the restructuring of Filipino communities, and periodic famines, epidemics, and Moro raids. Like others factors that contributed to elevated mortality, they varied geographically in part because of the nature of the societies affected. But not all structural changes had a negative impact. Some had a positive impact on fertility, which both moderated the level of decline and encouraged population growth. Although the evidence from much of the Southeast Asian archipelago is scant, it would seem that the Philippines were the first to emerge from the demographic crisis of the seventeenth century.[26]

At the same time as scholars have speculated on the causes of demographic decline in Southeast Asia in seventeenth century, they have also reflected on the causes of its dramatic recovery, mainly from the mid-eighteenth century. At that time growth rates exceeded 1 percent a year, a figure that was extremely high by world standards at the time.[27] A wide variety of explanations have been proposed, but discussions have tended to focus on whether the main driver of population growth was reduced mortality or increased fertility.

Just as Reid has argued that warfare was the main cause of population decline in the seventeenth century, so he has suggested that the suppression of warfare or the peace imposed by colonial rule, or the *pax imperica*, was a major factor behind declining death rates and increased birth rates. He argues that where internal conflict was not suppressed, growth was much slower.[28] The evidence from the Philippines provides some support for the role played by warfare. Compared to other Southeast Asian regions, internal conflicts, except between Spaniards and Filipinos in the initial conquest of the islands, do not appear to have been as common in the early colonial period as they were elsewhere in Southeast Asia, and their absence in the Philippines may partially explain the relatively precocious recovery of its population. However, external conflicts with Moro groups from the second half of the eighteenth century raised mortality and probably contributed to a slowing of the rate of growth, to the extent that the populations of Leyte and Samar, which were worst hit by Moro raids, actually declined.[29] Demographic trends were therefore influenced to some extent by warfare, but by external rather than internal conflicts.

Other influences on mortality do not appear to have changed significantly during the eighteenth century. It has been suggested that the spread of American crops such as maize, cassava, and sweet potatoes may have improved nutrition in some regions, but estimating their significance is not easy.[30] The islands also continued to be afflicted by natural disasters, famines, and epidemics, and like other regions in the Southeast Asian archipelago, the impact of acute infections was not moderated until the nineteenth century, when population increase and quicker communications enabled such diseases to become endemic. Smallpox vaccination was ineffective and malaria control and public works to improve sanitation and hygiene had to wait until the twentieth century.[31] Mortality is unlikely to have declined significantly in the eighteenth century.

Other explanations for the rapid expansion of the population in the eighteenth and nineteenth centuries have placed greater emphasis on increased fertility occasioned by changes in subsistence patterns or social practices.[32] It has been suggested that population growth in Southeast Asia was encouraged by the creation of more stable communities, often formed as a result of a shift from swidden to permanent wet-rice cultivation.[33] This may have affected fertility in several ways. First, it could have raised agricultural productivity and led to an improvement in nutrition, which may have reduced infant and child mortality, though there would have been few benefits where people lost access to land, worked as wage laborers, or were subject to heavy tribute levies. Whether or not nutrition improved, Boomgaard suggests that by creating a larger demand for labor, wet-rice cultivation also provided an incentive for women to have more children. Related to this, and perhaps more significant in the Philippine context, is the general argument that sedentism encouraged population growth through reducing miscarriages and removing the necessity for child spacing. This process may have had some influence on fertility among some nomadic or seminomadic groups.

Probably more significant were changes to birth and marriage practices. Most likely the suppression of infanticide, abortion, penis inserts, and slavery and the reduction in bridewealth would have all facilitated population growth and enabled communities to recover more easily from epidemic and environmental crises. Their suppression, while by no means complete, might have made a greater contribution to population growth in the Philippines than elsewhere in Southeast Asia due to the more pervasive influence of the Catholic Church. This may have been especially true in the Visayas, where these social practices were more prevalent in pre-Spanish times. For nineteenth-century Sulawesi, David Henley has argued that such changes to birth and marriages practices were associated with the rapid commercialization of the economy,[34] but this study suggests that broader cultural changes including those to religious beliefs, though often only partial, might also have had similar effects.

Demographic change reflects the complex interplay of economic, social, political, and environmental processes. While demographic trends were broadly similar in the Philippines and the Southeast Asian archipelago, the geographical location of the islands and their economic isolation imposed by Spain's mercantilist policies meant that to some extent the islands were less integrated into the Southeast Asian economy than many other islands. Hence, while demographic trends were similar in both regions, differences in the nature of colonial rule and in the native societies it affected, as well as the environments they inhabited, meant that the importance of different factors varied not only between the Philippines and the rest of Southeast Asia, but also between different islands and regions within the Philippine archipelago.

Appendixes

Appendix A: Epidemics in Luzon and the Visayas 1565 to 1800

Date	Luzon or Visayas	General (G) or Local (L)	Region	Sources
1572	V	?	Panay	In Panay "habido gran hambre entre los naturales desta isla y pestilencia que han muerto más de la mitad" (AGI PAT 24-25-2 and BR 3: 170 Relación del descubrimiento y conquista de la isla de Luzon 20 Apr. 1572)
1574	V/L	G		"gran enfermedad de viruela" in all the islands resulting in many deaths (AGI AF 6 Guido de Lavezaris 16 July 1574) "enfermedad general de viruelas que no ha perdonado ni niño ni moço ni viejo . . . ha muerto muchas gente de ellas" (AGI AF 84-4 and Rodríguez, *Historia*,185, Martín de Rada 30 June 1574).
1590	L	G	Cagayan	"epidemia contagiosa" in Cagayan (Malumbres, *Cagayan*, 32)
1591	L	G	Manila	In Manila "enfermedad peligrosa de calenturas malignas y contagiosas" (Colin, *Labor evangélica*, 1: 561–562)
1592	L	L	Manila	In Manila "muertes enfermedades communes a indios y españoles (AGI AF 18B and BR 8: 237 Gómez Pérez Dasmariñas 31 May 1592, AGI 18B Vecinos de la ciudad de Manila 31 May 1592).
1590s	L	G	Balayan	"peste de viruela" that the natives called *bolotong*. Killed adults as well as children and old people in Balayan (Chirino, *Relación*, 21, 254).
1595	L	G		"habido gran mortandad entre los naturales que han muerto gran suma de indios . . . que se han de acabar como en Santo Domingo (AGI AF 35 Juan Núñez 24 June 1595). In Cagayan "un gran peste de viruelas que lleva a la tumba gran cosecha de párvulos" (Malumbres, *Cagayan*, 33).
1596	L	G	Manila (Antipolo)	Last year there was a "pestilencia" in Antipolo (ARSI Phil 9 fol. 313 Francisco Almerique 23 June 1597). Many died of "pestes y enfermedades" (ARSI Phil 10 fols. 5–12 Diego Garcia 8 June 1600).
1596 –1597	V	G	Bohol, Samar	"Murieron de ella tantos que quedaron yermas algunas comarcas" (Colin, *Labor evangélica*, 2: 134–136, 156). In Bohol it was described as "una pestilencia que con dolor de estomago y cabeza los acababa, de que se despoblaron en esta isla pueblos

				enteros" (Chirino, *Relación*, 93, 333). When the Jesuits arrived in Samar there was an "enfermedad" from which many died (ARSI Phil 5 fols. 1–33 Diego Sánchez 27 June 1597). It was said to be worse among children, although some adults and old persons also died (Colin, *Labor evangélica*, 2: 143n).
1599	L	L	Manila (Antipolo, San Juan del Monte)	Unspecified epidemic broke out in Manila and spread throughout the province as far as Antipolo and San Juan del Monte (Chirino, *Relación*, 128–132, 373–375).
1612	L	L	Pangasinan (Binmaley)	When the Dominicans were converting Filipinos at Binmaley in about 1612, many children were dying of smallpox (Aduarte, *Historia*, 1: 390, also BR 32: 20).
1626	V	L	Samar (Catbalogan)	Catbalogan in Samar suffering from "viruelas genero de peste" (NL Ayer 1300 VA I: 523–545 Relación del estado . . . 1626)
1628	L	L	Manila	Unspecified "peste" or "epidemia" in Manila of which many people died. Afflicts Spaniards in particular. It was suggested that it was introduced by Kafirs or blacks brought from India by the Portuguese, due to fish poisoning or as a punishment for stealing the holy sacrament from the cathedral (Murillo Velarde, *Historia*, 38; Díaz, *Conquistas*, 255).
1630	L	L	Manila	Nun in the convent of Santa Clara in Manila dies of "sarampión" (AGI AF 8-12 Juan Niño de Tavora 27 Nov. 1630).
1630	L	L	Cavite (Silang)	Unspecified "epidemia" in Silang from which many died (Murillo Velarde, *Historia*, 71).
1652	L	L	Manila	"peste general de viruelas" in Taytay (AGI AF 15-37 Provincial of Augustinians, Thomás de San Gerónimo 1686).
1652	V	G	Cebu	In Cebu a "peste de viruelas" from which many died (Díaz, *Conquistas*, 271).
1652 –1653	L	L	Contracosta (Casiguran, Palanan)	In Casiguran and Palanan (*contracosta*) "mortandad general de viruelas" (PNA Cedulario (1636–1656), pp. 296–303 Real cédula 26 Mar. 1654).
1653?	L	?	Laguna (Tayabas)	PNA Cédulario 16 (Bound vol. 1636–1656) pp. 121–127 Commission to the *alcalde mayor* of Tayabas 27 June 1673.
1656	L/V	G		Epidemic of "viruelas" in which many died (Díaz, *Conquistas*, 255; Murillo Velarde, *Historia*, 252). For Ilocos, see Reyes y Florentino, *Historia de Ilocos*, 2: 96.

Appendix A *(continued)*

Date	Luzon or Visayas	General (G) or Local (L)	Region	Sources
1668	L/V	G		More than 50,000 people died, including some Spaniards, in a "peste general" (AGI AF 9-51 Diego de Salcedo 25 June 1668; AF 23-32 Audiencia June 1668).
1685	L	L	Cagayan and Ilocos	"peste de viruelas" in Cagayan after the Dominicans enter and in which adults also died (AGI AF 83-203 Dominican provincial, February 1695). Among the Apayao, adults as well as children died (AGI AF 83-82 Bartolomé Marrón 8 Feb. 1690, AF 83-203 Dominican provincial February 1695; Salazar, *Historia*, 395). In Ilocos it killed adults and children (Reyes y Florentino, *Historia de Ilocos*, 2: 141).
1687 -1688	L	L	Cagayan	In Cagayan "pestilencial epidemia de catarros" from which many died, especially children and old people (Díaz, *Conquistas*, 794–795). In Ilocos many children and old people died (Reyes y Florentino, *Historia de Ilocos*, 2: 141).
1692	V	L	Leyte (Dagami)	In Dagami in Leyte "una epidemia maligna de frios y calenturas acompañadas de cámaras de sangre" (ARSI Phil 8 fols. 26–47 Magino Sola 11 June 1696).
1705 -1706	L	G	Manila and interior	Devastation by "viruelas" that began in Manila and spread to mountains where it was unknown (ARSI Phil 8 fols. 74–133 Antonio Succio 25 Jan. 1707)
1716	L	L	Ilocos - Batac	Smallpox epidemic in Ilocos Norte (Historical Data Papers Ilocos Norte–Batac, p. 287).
1718	?	?		"epidemia de viruelas" (Díaz, *Conquistas*, 556).
1723	L	L	Interior Luzon (Ituy and Italones)	"epidemias de calenturas y unciones a la garganta" among the Isinai and Italon (AGI AF 140 Márquez de Torrecampo 30 June 1725).
1740	L	L	Interior Luzon (Ituy)	Indians in Buhay (Ituy) are "atemorizados por las viruelas" (AUST Libro 79 fols 50–51 Juan Ormaza 7 Dec. 1740).

1741	L	L	Interior Luzon (Italones and Igorots)	"viruelas" in Puncan (Italones), Cadayan, and among the Igorot (APSR Cagayan 29 no doc. no. Juan Ormaza 19 Mar. 1741, Antonio Campo 26 Feb. 1741).
1741	L	L	Pangasinan	Indians from Pantabangan (Pangasinan) fleeing from "viruelas" (APSR Pangasinan 1 doc. 19 Alejandro Cacho 22 Dec. 1741).
1741	L	L	Interior Luzon (Ituy and Paniqui)	Epidemic of smallpox in Ituy and Paniqui spreads to Tumavini (APSR Cagayan 1 doc. 2 No author, 13 July 1741).
1754	L	G		14,000 died of "una pestilencial epidemia tan cruel" in villages administered by Augustinians (Pérez, *Relaciones agustinianas*, 122 Manuel Carrillo 20 Mar. 1758).
1754	L	L	Ilocos (Batac)	Cholera epidemic in October and November kills 700 (Historical Data Papers Ilocos Norte–Batac p. 287)
1756	L	L?	Pangasinan and Ilocos	A "peste tan cruel de calenturas dolor de cabeza y resfriado" kills 16,657 people in Pangasinan and Ilocos (AGI AF 293 Bishop of Nueva Segovia 20 June 1756).
1754 -1756	L	L	Laguna	Unidentified "peste" results in the death of 7,124 persons in Laguna (PNA Erección de pueblos Laguna 1755–1886 Governor Arandía Santisteban 24 Mar. 1756, Alcalde Mayor Fernández de Guevara 27 July 1756, 24 Mar. 1756). The sources provide details of the numbers dying in each village, but numbers include the victims of Moro raids and the eruption of Taal volcano.
1757	L	L	Cagayan	Unidentified "peste" causing high mortality at Aparri and in the Chico Valley (APSR Cagayan 16 no. 12 Vélez 15 Mar. 1757, APSR Cagayan 18 doc. 3 No author December 1764).
1758	L	L	Interior Luzon (Ituy–Dupax)	"mortandad de viruelas" at Dupax (AUST Libro de Becerro 37 fol. 252 Discurso sobre el gentio . . . Antolín 1789).
1762 -1763	L	L	Ilocos (Batac)	Smallpox epidemic in Ilocos Norte (Historical Data Papers Ilocos Norte–Batac, p. 287)
1768	L	L	Ilocos (Batac)	Cholera epidemic in December 1768 to February 1769 kills 800 (Historical Data Papers Ilocos Norte–Batac, p. 288)

Appendix A *(continued)*

Date	Luzon or Visayas	General (G) or Local (L)	Region	Sources
1784	L	L	Ilocos (Batac)	Measles epidemic in Ilocos Norte (Historical Data Papers Ilocos Norte–Batac, p. 289)
1784	L	L	Batanes	A "peste" kills 30,000 in Batanes (PNA Erección de pueblos Batanes 1784–1898 Josef de Huleva y Malgarejos 5 Mar. 1784).
1786	L	L	Manila	Two epidemics of "calenturas con vómitos y tos fuerte, then sarampión" which was particularly devastating among children, asthmatics, and the weak (Lilly Philippine Ms II García Herreros 7 June 1786).
1786	L	L	Manila, Interior Luzon (Ituy–Bagabag)	A "peste" spread from Manila inland to Bagabag (AUST Libro de Becerro 37 fol. 253 Discurso sobre el gentio . . . Francisco Antolín 1789).
1789	L	L	Pangasinan	Epidemic of smallpox kills 3,532 people (AUST Libro 17 fol. 2 and APSR Pangasinan 12 Mapa de los que han muerto . . . 1789).

Appendix B: Large-Scale Moro Raids on the Visayas and Bikol

Date	Number captured or killed	From	Islands	Source
1595	1,500	Mindanao and Ternate	Visayas, including Cebu	AGI AF 18B Luis Gómez Dasmariñas 6 Dec. 1595, 30 June 1597; AF 6 Francisco Tello 12 July 1599.
1599	800	3,000 Magindanao in 50 boats under Sirongan and Sali	Cebu, Negros, Panay	*Joseph Calvo*, 4; Torrubia, *Dissertación*, 13; Montero y Vidal, *Piratería*, 1: 146; Costa, *Jesuits*, 282. Costa refers to 300 rather than 3,000 men.
1600	800–1,400. *Cabildo* of Manila says 800 captured in Bantayan and 600 in Panay.	800 Magindanao in 60 *navios pequeños*. García refers to 40 boats. Others refer to the boats as *caracoas*.	Destroy Bantayan, attack Arévalo on Panay and Baclayon on Bohol	ARSI Phil 5 fols. 75–92 Juan de Ribera 1 June 1601; ARSI Phil 10 fols. 65–68 Diego García 25 June 1601; AGI AF 35-70 Cabildo of Manila 20 July 1601; Chirino, *Relación*, 184, 435; *Joseph Calvo*, 5; Torrubia, *Dissertación*, 16; Redondo y Sendino, *Breve reseña*, 32–33; Montero y Vidal, *Piratería*, 1: 146–147. Montero y Vidal says 8,000 in 70 boats; Calvo, Torrubia, and Redondo y Sendino say 4,000 in 70 boats.
1602	700 in Calamianes only	145 *navios* (60 from Magindanao, 50 from Ternate, Sangil and Tagolanda, and 35 from Basilan)	Calamianes, Mindoro and southern Luzon	AGI AF 19 Pedro de Acuña 26 Sept. 1602; Majul, *Muslims*, 117.
1603	700 (Gregorio López gives 800).	1,000 Magindanao in 50 *caracoas* under Bwisan	Leyte (Dulag, Palo, Lingayon).	AGI AF 84-154 Gregorio López 10 Dec. 1603; ARSI Phil 10 fols. 159–176 Melchor Hurtado 6 Oct. 1604, Colin, *Labor evangélica*, 1: 207n, 2: 370–379, 387, 88; Murillo Velarde, *Historia*, 65; Costa, *Jesuits*, 292–296.
1604	?	Camucones	Calamianes	Colin, *Labor evangélica*, 1: 207n, 2: 370–371n; Majul, *Muslims*, 118; Costa, *Jesuits*, 301.

Date	Number captured or killed	From	Islands	Source
1604	160 and many others killed	Caragas in 18 *caracoas*	Western Leyte (Baybay and Poro).	Colin, *Labor evangélica*, 2: 388–390; Costa, *Jesuits*, 301.
1607	?	Sanguiles and Caragas	Leyte (Baybay, Ogmuc and Carigara).	Colin, *Labor evangélica*, 1: 212.
1608	?	Magindanao in 67 *caracoas*	Leyte, Samar, and Negros	ARSI Phil 14 fol. 41 Cristóbal Jiménez 8 Mar. 1608, Phil 10 fols. 235r–235v Fabrizio Sarsali 20 Mar. 1608; AGI AF 20 Audiencia 8 July 1608, AF 60-10 Relación de la armada 1608; Colin, *Labor evangélica*, 3: 167, 180; Costa, *Jesuits*, 308.
1613	1,000 plus	Magindanaos and Caragas in 3 squadrons	Leyte and Samar 400 taken from Dulag, 600 from Samar towns also attack Palo	Colin, *Labor evangélica*, 3: 336–339; Calvo, *Joseph Calvo*, 6; Costa, *Jesuits*, 311.
1616	400 captured 200 killed	Sulus in 60 *caracoas*	Pantao in Camarines	BR 27: 195 Juan Grau y Monfalcón 1637; AGI AF 38-1 and BR 18: 185 Sebastián de Pineda 26 May 1619; Colin, *Labor evangélica*, 3: 532; Montero y Vidal, *Piratería*, 1: 153–154; Saleeby, *History of Sulu*, 175; Majul, *Muslims*, 123; Mallari, "Muslim Raids," 262. The number of *caracoas* varies in the accounts.

1625	40 captured in Catbalogan and 20 old persons, women and children killed. Díaz says 50 captured.	Camucones in 24 *joangas*	Sack Catbalogan in Samar	NL Ayer 1300 VA I: 523–545 Relación del estado . . . 1626; Díaz, *Conquistas*, 242; Montero y Vidal, *Piratería*, 1: 155; Murillo Velarde, *Historia*, 29–30; Saleeby, *History of Sulu*, 175.
1627	300 captured in Pantao, 300 in Ogmuc, and 150 captured and killed in Bantayan.	2,000 Sulus in 30 *caracoas* under Raja Bongsu	Bantayan and Ogmoc in Leyte on way home from sacking Pantao.	NL Ayer 1300 VA I: 551–607 Relación de lo sucedido . . . 1628; AGI AF 30 Juan Niño de Tavora 4 Aug. 1628; Medina, *Historia de los sucesos*, 137; Costa, *Jesuits*, 323.
1627	?	Camucones	Came to Otón	NL Ayer 1300 VA I: 551–607 Relación de lo sucedido . . . 1628
1629	?	Joloanos and Camucones in 36 *caracoas* under Datu Ache	Visayas—especially Capul, Palapag, Paranas (Samar), Dagami (Leyte), and Baclayon (Bohol).	Murillo Velarde, *Historia*, 44–45; Montero y Vidal, *Piratería*, 1: 156; Saleeby, *History of Sulu*, 176; Costa, *Jesuits*, 323.
1632	?	Joloes, Sangiles, and Caragas	Leyte (Cabalian, Sogor, Hinunangan).	ARSI Phil 7 fols. 1–80 Juan de Bueras 21 June 1632; Murillo Velarde, *Historia*, 64; Costa, *Jesuits*, 323–324.
1634	Says worst in Ogmuc where 200 captured	1,500 Magindanaos and Sulus in 18 *caracoas*	Dapitan, Bohol (Maribohoc and Inabangan), Leyte (Cabalian, Sogor, Canamucan), Baybay, and Ogmuc)	AGI AF 8-104 Relation of the glorious victories . . . 1638; Colin, *Labor evangélica*, 3: 792; Murillo Velarde, *Historia*, 70–71; Torrubia *Dissertación*, 32; Montero y Vidal, *Piratería*, 1: 159–160; Díaz, *Conquistas*, 322; Costa, *Jesuits*, 324.

APPENDIX B *(continued)*

Date	Number captured or killed	From	Islands	Source
1634	?	Camucones	Batan, Domayan, Mahanlar, Aklan, and Bahay (Batan)	Corpuz, *Roots*, 1: 146.
1636	650	Magindanaos in 4 *caracoas* and 3 smaller boats under Datu Tagal	Calamianes, Cuyo, and Mindoro	BR 27: 215–226 No author, no date [1637]; Majul, *Muslims*, 133.
1636	100 captured in Ibabao	Camucones—a flotilla.	Samar and Albay.	Jesús, *Historia general*, 285; Montero y Vidal, *Piratería*, 1: 163; Costa, *Jesuits*, 383. Encountered by Magindanaos on the journey back from Calamianes, Cuyo, and Mindoro.
1640		3 *joangas* of Borneyes and Camucones	Near Mindoro and Lubang, Marinduque	Murillo Velarde, *Historia*, 123.
1648	?	Camucones and Mindanaos allied with the Dutch	Sacked towns of Capalongan, Paracale, Bacón, Albay, and Tabaco in Camarines	Retana, *Archivo bibliófilo Filipino*, 1: 1–13, Entrada de la seráphica religion 1649.
1657	1,000 captured	Mindanaos under Datu Salicala	Unspecified but reached Bay of Manila	Montero y Vidal, *Piratería*, 1: 239; Murillo Velarde, *Historia*, 253.
1655	80 captured	Sulus under Linao, Libot, and Sacahati from Tawi-Tawi in 13 boats	Costa de Bohol, Leyte, and Masbate	Montero y Vidal, *Piratería*, 1: 244; Majul, *Muslims*, 162; Mallari, "Muslim Raids," 267.

1663	Many captured and killed	Joloes in 60 *joangas*	Burn Poro, Baybay, Sogor, Cabalian, Basey, Bangajon, Guinobatan, and Capul	Murillo Velarde, *Historia*, 275; Montero y Vidal, *Piratería*, 1: 245–246; Torrubia, *Dissertación*, 63.
1722 -1723	?	Moros	Negros	Costa, *Jesuits*, 543; Martínez Cuesta, *History of Negros*, 124.
1730	?	Sulus from Tawi-Tawi in 20 large boats and other smaller ones with 3,000 men.	Rob and capture natives on Paragua and isla de Dumaran, then to Taytay	Montero y Vidal, *Piratería*, 1: 261–262; Saleeby, *History of Sulu*, 179; Costa, *Jesuits*, 543.
1740	26 killed and 28 women and children captured		Sorsogón	Mallari, "Muslim Raids," 269.
1746	?	Tirones	Gate in Sorsogón	Mallari, "Muslim Raids," 269.
1753 -1754	Large numbers taken in many locations		Visayas, Mindoro, Camarines, and Batangas	NL Ayer 1328 Pedro Manuel de Arandía 1755; Montero y Vidal, *Piratería*, 1: 309–311, and *Historia general*, 1: 515–518; Saleeby, *History of Sulu*, 185; Costa, *Jesuits*, 549.
1756	70 killed and 200 captured	Moros	Tucgaguan in Negros	Martinez Cuesta, *History of Negros*, 125.
1757	8,000 captured and killed	Moros	Camarines and Visayas including Panay	AGI AF 293 Bishop of Nueva Caceres 29 June 1758; Montero y Vidal, *Piratería*, 1: 328.
1770	100 captured	Moros	Bangajon (Samar)	Cruikshank, *Samar*, 239.
1771	Many killed	Moros	Paranas (Samar)	Cruikshank, *Samar*, 239.
1774 or 1775	500 captured and some killed	Moros	Catubig (Samar)	Cruikshank, *Samar*, 255; Huerta, *Estado*, 297.

Date	Number captured or killed	From	Islands	Source
1785	130 captured	43 *pancos* with 200 Moros	Talaban, Himamaylan, and Binalbagan (Negros)	Barrantes, *Guerras piráticas*, 134; Montero y Vidal, *Piratería*, 1: 355; Martínez Cuesta, *History of Negros*, 124.
1789	Over 400 captured	Moros	Ajuy and Barotac near Iloilo	Montero y Vidal, *Piratería*, 1: 355–356; Barrantes, *Guerras piráticas*, 136.
1793	120 captured	Moros	A village in Leyte	Montero y Vidal, *Piratería*, 1: 356; Barrantes, *Guerras piráticas*, 140.

Appendix C: Tributary Populations for the Visayas Given in Documentary Sources 1571 to 1626

	1571	**1582**	**1591**	**1606**	**1626**
Cebu	6,000	5,100	3,170	3,518	3,900
Panay	28,000	23,340	22,990	18,125	12,700
Negros	32,000	7,000	3,037	2,184	3,000
Bohol	not given	2,000	not given	1,050	1,500
Leyte	23,000	15,260	6,597	4,970	6,500
Samar	19,000	6,150	2,636	5,486	4,800
TOTAL	108,000	58,850	38,430	35,333	32,400

Sources: 1571 AGI PAT 24-19 Hernando Riquel 2 June 1576.

1582 BR 5: 43–59 Miguel de Loarca [1582]. The figure for Leyte is 14,260–15,260 (includes the islands of Panaon, Maripipi, and Macagua) and for Negros 6–7,000.

1591 AGI PAT 25-38 Relación punctual de las encomiendas 31 May 1591. Figures for Cebu are inflated and figures for Samar and Leyte are deflated because *encomiendas* that were held jointly are all included under Cebu. The figure for Bohol is not listed separately, but probably included in Bantayan. The figure for Panay includes Cuyo.

1606 AGI AF 6 Memoria y lista de las encomiendas [1606]. The figures for Masbate and Mindanao, which came under the jurisdiction of the *alcalde mayor* of Cebu, have not been included. The figures for the islands of Bantayan and Bohol have been divided equally between the jurisdictions of Cebu and Bohol. Panay includes the islands of Tablas, Romblon, Cuyo, and other adjacent islands.

1626 Rodriguez, *Historia*, 2: 72–74, Pedro de Arce 1626. The figure excludes 1,400 in Calamianes and 1,000 in Balayan.

Note: These figures often differ from the summaries for broad jurisdictions contained in the accounts above because they are based on the populations of individual towns in each island.

Appendix D: Regional Population Estimates

BALAYAN (BATANGAS)

Date	Tributary population	Total population	Source
Pre-1582	20,000 *indios*		AGI PAT 23-8 and BR 5:202–204 Report on saleable offices, no date. Covers Bonbon, Balayan, and Mindoro.
[1582]	5,000 men		AGI PAT 23-9 and BR 5: 87–89 Miguel de Loarca [1582]. In Bonbón, Balayan, and Batangas.
1588	9,000 *tributarios*		AGI AF 74 and Rodríguez, *Historia*, 15: 355–356, Domingo de Salazar 25 June 1588. In Balayan and Calilaya together.
1591	6,600 *tributos*	26,400 *almas*	AGI PAT 25-28 fols. 14–15 Relación punctual de las encomiendas 31 May 1591.
1606	4,478 *tributos*		AGI AF 29-87 Memoria y lista de las encomiendas [1606].
1655	2,162.5 *tributos*		AGI AF 22-7-20 fol. 11 Jueces oficiales de la real hacienda 16 June 1655.
1656	2,500 *tributarios*		Colin, *Labor evangélica*, 1: 21.
1700	2,654.5 *tributos*		AGI CO 1253 Oficiales reales 1700.
1735	3,151 *tributos*	17,128 *almas*	San Antonio, *Philippine Chronicles*, 80, 197, 218. Includes 2,500 *almas* in the *contracosta*.
1735	3,208 *tributos*		AGI CO 1266 Oficiales reales 1735.
1745	6,671 *tributos de naturales*		AGI AF 182 Calderón Enriques 8 July 1747.
1750	5,823 *tributos*		AGI CO 1276B Oficiales reales 1750.
1778	10,061.5 *tributos enteros*	42,613 *indios*	AGI IG Demonstración de clases de naciones habitantes . . . que comprehende este arzobispado 9 Dec. 1778.
1785		49,689 *indios*	AGI IG 1527 Extracto del número de habitantes que comprehende el arzobispado de Manila 1785.
1792	12,690 *tributos de naturales*	64,680 *almas*	AUST Libro 229 no. 1 Estatística [*sic*] de las Yslas Filipinas 1815. Plus 246 tributary *mestizos*. *Almas* include *mestizos*.
1805	16,261 *tributos*	81,035 *almas*	AUST Libro 229 no. 1 Estatística [*sic*] de las Yslas Filipinas 1815. *Tributos* and *almas* include *mestizos*.

Appendix D *(continued)*

BALAYAN (BATANGAS) *(continued)*

Date	Tributary population	Total population	Source
1809	19,680 *tributos*	127,920 *almas*	Comyn, *Estado*, App. 1.
1812	17,902 *tributos de naturales*	91,902 *almas*	AUST Libro 229 no. 1 Estatística [*sic*] de las Yslas Filipinas 1815. Plus 478.5 tributary *mestizos*. *Almas* include *mestizos*.
1815	19,889 *tributos de naturales*	128,585 *almas*	AUST Libro 229 no. 1 Estatística [*sic*] de las Yslas Filipinas 1815. Plus 509.5 tributary *mestizos*. *Almas* include *mestizos*.
1818	21,771 *tributos*	112,120 *almas*	Aragón, *Estados de la población*, B 1: 367. 1818.

BIKOL

Date	Tributary population	Total population	Source
At contact	100,000 *hombres de armas*		San Agustin, *Conquistas*, lib. 2 cap. 7: 355.
1574	20,000 *hombres* pacified		AGI AF 6 Guido de Lavezaris 17 July 1574. In the Bikol Valley and Camarines alone.
[1582]	22,700 men		AGI PAT 23-9 and BR 5: 52–53, 93–101 Miguel de Loarca [1582]. Excludes 4,500 in Masbate and Catanduanes and 1,300 in the *contracosta*.
1588	23,000 *tributantes*		AGI AF 74 and Rodríguez, *Historia*, 15: 357, Domingo de Salazar 25 June 1588. 20,000 in Camarines and 3,000 in Catanduanes.
1591	21,360 *tributos*	88,840 *almas*	AGI PAT 25-38 Relación punctual de las encomiendas 31 May 1591. In addition there were 800 *tributos* and 3,200 *almas* in Masbate and Burias together. There is an arithmetic error in the document, which gives summaries for Camarines and Bikol as 21,660 and 86,640 respectively.
1594	21,767.5 *tributos*		AGI CO 1202 fols. 179r–186v Cargo de tributos 1594. Excludes Masbate and Burias.
ca. 1594	12,450 *tributos*	31,000 *almas*	AGI AF 79 and BR 9: 98–101 Francisco de Ortega, no date [ca. 1594]. Includes 550 *tributos* for Masbate and 4,000 for Catanduanes.

Appendix D *(continued)*

BIKOL

Date	Tributary population	Total population	Source
1590s	10,920 *tributos*		Alcalá, *Chrónica*, 71. Under the Franciscans. No figure is given for Tabuco or Naga.
1601	12,597.5 *tributos*		AGI CO 1205 Cargo del situado 1601. In 27 *encomiendas*.
No date [1599]	16,559 *tributos*		AGI PAT 25-54 Memoria de las personas beneméritas, n.d. Includes 12,700 under 17 private *encomenderos* and 3,859 under the Crown.
1606	7,725 *tributos*		AGI AF 29-87 Memoria y lista de las encomiendas 1606. Excludes Catanduanes and Masbate. 5,896 under 16 *encomenderos* and 1,829 under the Crown.
1618		150,000 *almas*	BR 18: 95 Pedro de Bivero 1618. Including Negritos.
1622		59,200 *cristianos*	Abad, "Los franciscanos," 418–419, Alonso de Montemayor 16 July 1622. In Albay and Camarines. The islands do not appear to have been included.
1622		56,800 *cristianos*	AGI AF 74 and BR 20: 235 Miguel García Serrano 31 July 1622, AF 74 Serrano 25 July 1626.
1649	8,890 *tributos*	35,410 *personas*	Retana, *Archivo del bibliófilo Filipino*, 1: 1–13, Entrada de la seráfica religión 1649. Includes Paracale and Capalongan listed under the province of Tagalos.
1655	10,165 *tributos*		AGI AF 222-7-20 fol. 11 Jueces oficiales de la real hacienda 16 June 1655. 6,212 in Camarines and 3,953 in Ibalon and Catanduanes.
1700	6,982.5 *tributos*		AGI CO 1253 Oficiales reales 1700. 5,194.5 in Camarines and 1,788 in Ibalon and Catanduanes.
1709	7,006.5 *tributos*	24,340 *almas*	AGI AF 296 Razón de la gente adminstrada en esta provincia de San Gregorio 1709. Camarines only. Document gives 14,013 *tributantes*.
1735	12,430.5 *tributos*		AGI CO 1266 Oficiales reales 1735. 8,600 in Camarines and 3,830.5 in Ibalon and Catanduanes..

Appendix D *(continued)*

BIKOL *(continued)*

Date	Tributary population	Total population	Source
1735		95,736 *almas*	San Antonio, *Philippine Chronicles*, 219–220. 36,981 under secular clergy and 56,555 under religious orders, in addition to 2,100 in new missions in Camarines, Albay and Catanduanes, Masbate, and other islands.
1735	13,173 *tributos*		San Antonio, *Philippine Chronicles*, 62–65. In Camarines and Albay.
1750	19,041 *tributos*		AGI CO 1276B Oficiales reales 1750. 12,080.5 in Camarines and 6,960.5 in Albay, including Ibalon and Catanduanes.
1751	11,110.5 *tributos*	56,119 *almas*	Sánchez Fuertes, "Estado de las misiones," 146–151. The original is in AGI AF 323 Tabla y noticia, 1 May 1751. Only those in Camarines under the Franciscans.
1780	54,883 *tributantes naturales*	126,109 *almas*	las almas . . . Obispo de Caceres AGI IG 1527 Plan general de todas 1780. Plus 144 Negritos.
1792	28,949.5 *tributos de naturales*	145,264 *almas*	AUST Libro 229 no. 1 Estatística [*sic*] de las Yslas Filipinas 1815. Plus 307.5 tributary *mestizos*. *Almas* include *mestizos*.
1798	31,836 *tributantes*	73,917 *almas*	PNA Patronatos 1720–1799 Re sumen del estado . . . Sebastián Recuenco 4 July 1798. Numbers under Franciscan Observants.
1805	35,575 *tributos*	177,874 *almas*	AUST Libro 229 no. 1 Estatistica [*sic*] de las Yslas Filipinas 1815. *Tributos* and *almas* include *mestizos*.
1809	40,590 *tributos*	263,835 *almas*	Comyn, *Estado*, App. 1.
1812	41,051.5 *tributos de naturales*	122,775 *almas*	AUST Libro 229 no. 1 Estatística [*sic*] de las Yslas Filipinas 1815. Plus 652 tributary *mestizos*. *Almas* include *mestizos*.
1815	36,254 *tributos de naturales*	214,070 *almas*	AUST Libro 229 Estatística [*sic*] de las Yslas Filipinas 1815. Plus 372.5 tributary *mestizos*. *Almas* include *mestizos*.

Appendix D *(continued)*

BOHOL

Date	Tributary population	Total population	Source
Antigua-mente	Over 10,000 *moradores* or *familias*		Colin, *Labor evangélica*, 1: 35 and 2: 152n.
[1582]	2,000 *indios*		AGI PAT 23-9 and BR 5: 45–46 Miguel de Loarca [1582].
1588	600 *tributantes*		AGI AF 74 and Rodríguez, *Historia*, 15: 364, Domingo de Salazar 25 June 1588.
ca. 1594	1,000 *tributantes*	Which are 4,000 *almas*	AGI AF 79 and BR 9: 98 Francisco de Ortega, no date [ca. 1594].
1599		4,000 *almas*	ARSI Phil 9 fols. 372–375 Diego García 10 July 1599.
1600		9,500 *personas*, of whom 700 were converted	ARSI Phil 10 fols. 26–27 Diego García 7 July 1600.
1601		3,000 *almas cristianos*	ARSI Phil 5 fols. 171–194 Juan de Ribera 1 June 1601.
1605		8,500 *almas* of whom 7,000 were converted	ARSI Phil 5 fols. 171–194 Gregorio López 5 June 1605. Includes the islands of Fuegos and Baslao.
1606	2,000 *tributos*	4,000 *almas*	ARSI Phil 14 fols. 28–29 Diego Laurencio 4 Apr. 1606.
1606	1,050 *tributos*		AGI AF 6 Memoria y lista de las encomiendas [1606].
1610	2,190 *tributos*		AGI AF 20 Gregorio López 1610. Includes Siquior. An error gives the summary as 2,200.
1620	2,000 *tributa*		ARSI Phil 11 fols. 115–118 Historiae Provinciae Philippinarum 15 July 1620.
1626	1,500 *tributos*		Rodriguez, *Historia*, 2: 74, Pedro de Arce July 1626.
1656	1,200 *tributarios*		Colin, *Labor evangélica*, 3: 791. Razón del número de religiosos . . . 1656.
1659	1,100 married persons (*uxorati*)	4,124 *almas*	ARSI Phil 2 II fols. 314–317 Catologus christianorum 1659. Includes 396 slaves.
1675	2,160 married persons (*uxorati*)	7,420 *almas*	ARSI Phil 2 I fols. 412–415 Catologus christianorum 1675.

Appendix D *(continued)*

BOHOL *(continued)*

Date	Tributary population	Total population	Source
1690	1,200 *tributos*		ARSI Phil 12 fols. 138–148 Alejo López 1690.
1696	4,209 married persons (*uxorati*)	11,091 *almas*	ARSI Phil 14 fols. 106–109 Catologus christianorum 1696. Includes 237 slaves.
1697	1,200 *tributos*		Gemelli Careri, *Voyage Around the World*, 441.
1735	8,114 *tributos de indios*		Martínez de Zúñiga, *Estadismo*, 2: 62.
1737	11,256 married persons (*uxorati*)	29,898 *almas*	ARSI Phil 14 fols. 110–113 Catologus christianorum 1737. Includes 35 slaves.
1743	10,446 married persons (*uxorati*)	28,144 *almas*	ARSI Phil 14 fols. 114–117 Catologus christianorum 1743.
ca. 1749		37,022 *almas*	Murillo Velarde, *Historia*, Appendix 9.
1755	14,046 married persons (*uxorati*)	41,239 *almas*	ARSI Phil 14 fols. 118–121 Catologus christianorum 1755. Includes 11 slaves.
1768	5,810 *tributos enteros*		PNA Patronatos (Unclassified) Provincial Aquino 19 Oct. 1785. When the regulars left.
1778	16,974 *tributantes*	41,940 *almas*	Redondo y Sendino, *Breve reseña*, 143.
1785	8,546 *tributos enteros* plus 4,000 *tributos alzados*	43,053 *almas*	PNA Patronatos (Unclassified) Provincial Aquino 19 Oct. 1785.
1815	14,219.5 *tributos de naturales*		AUST Libro 171 and 229 Censo del archipelago 1815.
1818	30,015 *tributos naturales y mestizos*	88,671 *almas*	Aragón , *Estados de la población* 1818.

Appendix D *(continued)*

CAGAYAN

Date	**Tributary population**	**Total population**	**Source**
At contact	more than 40,000 men		San Agustín, *Conquistas*, lib. 2 cap 13: 386.
[1582]	more than 30,000 men		AGI PAT 23-9 and BR 8: 99–101 Miguel de Loarca [1582].
1588	30,000 *hombres*		AGI AF 74 and Rodríguez, *Historia*, 15: 352–353, Domingo de Salazar 25 June 1588 Includes 4,000 in Babuyanes. Tribute only being collected from 7,000.
1591	22,050 *tributos*	88,200 *personas*	AGI PAT 25-38 fols. 9–14 Relación punctual de las encomiendas 31 May 1591 Excludes 1,400 *tributantes* and 5,600 *personas* in the Babuyanes.
1593	25,000 *hombres* had been pacified		AGI PAT 25-44 Interrogatorio . . . Gabriel de Mercado 5 Feb. 1593.
ca. 1594	10,400 *tributos*	More than 40,000 *almas*	AGI AF 79 and BR 9: 101 Francisco de Ortega, no date [ca. 1594] Contained in 12 *encomiendas*.
1606	11,574 *tributos*		AGI AF 29-87 Memorial y lista de las encomiendas [1606].
1610	10,500 *indios*		AGI AF 20 and BR 17: 211 Baltasar Fort 1610. Excludes new conversions.
1618	12,000–13,000 *tributos*		BR 18: 101 Pedro de Bivero 1618. Of whom 1,500 pay tribute to the Crown.
1655	6,748.5 *tributos*		AGI AF 22-7-20 fols. 10–12 Jueces oficiales reales 16 June 1655. 3,810.5 under the Crown and 2,938 private.
1700	5,911.5 *tributos*		AGI CO 1253 fols. 111–120 Oficiales de la real hacienda . . . 1700.
1708	6,037.75 *tributos*		AGI AF 296 Certificación jurídica de los oficiales reales 21 June 1708.
1735	6,678.5 *tributos*		AGI CO 1266 fols. 130–146 Oficiales de la real hacienda . . . 1735.
1735	7,036 *tributos*	25,752 *almas*	San Antonio, *Philippine Chronicles*, 70, 224. Excludes a large number outside administration and infants.
1746	7,978 *tributos*	33,778 *almas*	Malumbres, *Cagayan*, 298–315, Juan de Varona y Velásquez 3 Mar. 1746. Excludes 2,821 *almas* in active missions.
1750	8,660.5 *tributos*		AGI CO 1276B fols. 185–199 Oficiales de la real hacienda . . . 1750.

APPENDIX D *(continued)*

CAGAYAN *(continued)*

Date	Tributary population	Total population	Source
1758	13,469 *tributantes*	35,632 *almas*	APSR Cagayan 18 doc. 1 Mapa de los pueblos y almas . . . 1758.
1767	8,203.5 *tributos*	37,526 *almas*	APSR Cagayan 18 doc. 3 Estadísticas ó estados de almas 1758–1805 and Cagayan 26 doc. 7 Estadísticas ó estados de almas 1758–1800.
1775	8,590 *tributos*	38,931 *almas*	APSR Cagayan 18 doc. 3 Estadísticas ó estados de almas 1758–1805 and Cagayan 26 doc. 7. Estadísticas ó estados de almas 1758–1800.
1780	9,393 *tributos enteros*	41,388 *almas*	AGI IG 1527 fol. 885. Plan demonstrativo de los pueblos . . . Cagayan 1780.
1787	18,079 *tributantes*	42,481 *almas*	AGI IG 1527. Mapa de los pueblos tributantes y almas . . . Cagayan 1787. Bishop of Nueva Segovia. *Almas* include children and *catecúmenos*, but exclude those in interior missions and Negroes.
1787	9,520 *tributos*		PNA EP Cagayan 1749–1926 Figueroa 30 Sept. 1787.
1792	8,539 *tributos de naturales*	42,695 *almas*	AUST Libro 229 no. 1 Estatística [*sic*] de las Yslas Filipinas 1815.
1800	8,894.5 *tributos*	40,757 *almas*	APSR Cagayan 18 Número de almas del obispado de Nueva Segova 1800.
1805	12,837.5 *tributos*	64,187 *almas*	AUST Libro 229 no. 1 Estatística [*sic*] de las Yslas Filipinas 1815. *Tributos* and *almas* include *mestizos.*
1809	11,808 *tributos*	76,752 *almas*	Comyn, *Estado*, App. 1.
1812	13,875 *tributos*	69,452 *almas*	AUST Libro 229 no. 1 Estatística [*sic*] de las Yslas Filipinas 1815. Plus 15.5 tributary *mestizos. Almas* include *mestizos.*
1815	13,564 *tributos de naturales*	82,385 *almas*	AUST Libro 229 no. 1 Estatística [*sic*] de las Yslas Filipinas 1815. Plus 14.5 tributary *mestizos. Almas* include *mestizos.*
1818	13,363 *tributo* or *familias*	61,322 *almas*	Aragón, *Estados de la población* B1 Appendix, 1818. Includes Ituy and Paniqui.

Appendix D *(continued)*

CEBU

Date	**Tributary population**	**Total population**	**Source**
1571	6,000 *indios*		AGI PAT 24-19 Hernando Riquel 2 June 1576. In three *encomiendas* given by Legazpi. In addition an unspecified number were allocated to the Crown.
[1582]	5,100 *indios*		AGI PAT 23-9 and BR 5: 43–59 Miguel de Loarca [1582]. Includes 300 in Mactan, 300 Camotes, 1,000 in Bantayan.
1591	3,170 *tributos*	12,680 *almas*	AGI PAT 25-38 fols. 23–27 Relación punctual de las encomiendas 31 May 1591.
ca. 1594	4,000 *tributos*		AGI AF 79 and BR 9: 97 Francisco de Ortega, no date [ca. 1594]. Under eight *encomenderos*, but the south was not well known.
1606	3,518 *tributos*		AGI AF 6 Memoria y lista de las encomiendas [1606].
1626	3,900 *tributos*		Rodriguez, *Historia*, 2: 72–74, Pedro de Arce July 1626. Of which 150 were on the island of Maripipi.
1655	8565.5 *tributos*		AGI AF 22-7-20 fols. 10–12 Oficiales reales 16 Mar. 1655. Includes the whole province of Cebu. 1,641.5 in Crown encomiendas, 6,924 private.
1660	5,000 *tributarios*, plus 300 in Bantayan and other small islands.		Colin, *Labor evangélica*, 1: 39.
1667	5,000 *tributos* or *familias*		AGI AF 82-57 Bishop of Cebu 25 Feb. 1667.
1712	3,600 *familias* under Augustinians on island of Cebu	10,000 *personas*	Lopez Memorial Museum. Book of cédulas and autos 1707–1713 Joseph López 24 June 1712.
1738	4,411.5 *tributos*		NL Ayer 1300 and VA IV: 335–408 no author 1738. Based on the last *cuenta general.*
1770s		41,480 total population	Cullinane and Xenos, "Population Growth in Cebu," 94.
1778	7,754 *tributantes*	21,612 *almas*	Redondo y Sendino, *Breve reseña*, 138. Under the Augustinians only.
1792	17,798.5 *tributos de naturales*	91,740 *almas*	AUST 229 no. 1 Estatística [*sic*] de las Yslas Filipinas 1815. Plus 549.5 tributary *mestizos*. *Almas* include *mestizos*.

Appendix D *(continued)*

CEBU *(continued)*

Date	Tributary population	Total population	Source
1805	23,075.5 *tributos*	115,377 *almas*	AUST 229 no. 1 Estatística [*sic*] de las Yslas Filipinas 1815. *Tributos* and *almas* include *mestizos*.
1809	23,370 *tributos*	151,905 *almas*	Comyn, *Estado*, Appendix 1.
1812	28,348.5 *tributos de naturales*	146,565 *almas*	AUST 229 no. 1 Estatística [*sic*] de las Yslas Filipinas 1815. Plus 971.5 tributary *mestizos*. *Almas* include *mestizos*.
1815	12,808.5 *tributos de naturales*		AUST Libro 171 ands 229 Censo del archipelago 1815. Includes Siquior with 1,100 and Poro (Camotes) with 160. Plus 755 *tributos de mestizos*.
1815	27,029.5 *tributos de naturales*	168,910 *almas*	AUST 229 no. 1 Estatística [*sic*] de las Yslas Filipinas 1815. Plus 924.5 tributary *mestizos*. *Almas* include *mestizos*.
1818	14,991 *tributos naturales y mestizos*	79,755 *almas*	Aragón, *Estados de la población* 1818.

ILOCOS

Date	Tributary population	Total population	Source
At contact	400,000 *indios*		AGI PAT 24-27 fol. 4 and BR 34: 262 Francisco de Ortega 6 June 1573. In the province of Ilocos and three others in the *contracosta*.
1573	40,000 *indios*		AGI PAT 24-27 fol. 4 and BR 34: 262 Francisco de Ortega 6 June 1573. In the province of Ilocos and three others in the *contracosta*.
1574	45,600 *indios*		AGI PAT 24-19 fols. 48, 50–54 Hernando Riquel 2 June 1574. See the text for the calculation.
1570s	9,185 houses		AGI PAT 24-21 fols. 1–12 Martín de Goiti 1570s.
[1582]	26,100 men		AGI PAT 23-9 and BR 5: 107–111 Miguel de Loarca [1582].
1588	27,000 *tributarios*		AGI AF 74 and Rodríguez, *Historia*, 15: 351, Domingo de Salazar 25 June 1588.

Appendix D *(continued)*

ILOCOS *(continued)*

Date	Tributary population	Total population	Source
1591	17,130 *tributos*	68,520 *almas*	AGI PAT 25-38 fols. 6–9 Relación punctual de las encomiendas 31 May 1591. The actual figures sum to 17,230.
1606	10.544.5 *tributos*		AGI AF 29-87 Memoria y lista de las encomiendas [1606].
1610	12,300 *tributos*	36,900 *indios de confesión*	AGI AF 20-4-34 Memoria de los conventos y ministerios 1610. Excludes Alingayen and Agoo, which together had 2,300 *tributos* and 5,900 *indios de confesión*.
1618	14–15,000 *tributos*		BR 18: 100 Pedro de Bivero 1618.
1655	10,493 *tributos*		AGI AF 22-7-20 fol. 11 Jueces oficiales de la real hacienda 16 June 1655.
1656	9,000 *tributarios*		Colin, *Labor evangélica*, 1: 24.
1700	10,166 *tributos*		AGI CO 1253 Oficiales de la real hacienda . . . 1700.
1712	10,480 families	40,000 *almas de confesión*	Lopez Memorial Museum. Cédulas y autos 1707–1712. Augustinian Joseph López 24 June 1712.
1735	10,041 *tributos enteros*	51,453 souls	San Antonio, *Philippine Chronicles*, 71, 223. Souls under the Augustinians.
1735	10,165.75 *tributos*		AGI CO 1266 Oficiales reales 1735.
1738	8,665.75 *tributos*		NL Ayer 1300 Informe dado por D. José Niño Villaviciencio 4 Feb. 1738. From whom rice was levied.
1743	22,773 *tributos*		PNA Cedulario 1738-44: 120–130 Oficiales reales 21 Sept. 1743. 2,700 were *infieles*.
1744	22,681 *tributos*		PNA Cedulario 1738-44: 120–130 Oficiales reales 6 July 1744. 1,449 were *infieles tinguianes*.
1750	19,166.5 *tributos*		AGI CO 1276B Oficiales reales 1750.
1760	17,283 *tributos*	74,541 *almas*	NL Ayer Ms 1449 (Box) and BR 48: 53–57 Razón de los pueblos, Pedro Velasco 16 Apr. 1760. Under Augustinians. Figures exclude newly converted Tinguians and Igorots. Plus 3,064 *tributantes* and 12,806 *almas* in La Union.
1764	21,280 *tributos*		Pedro Vivar cited in Routledge, *Diego Silang*, 5. Under the Augustinians.

Appendix D *(continued)*

ILOCOS *(continued)*

Date	Tributary population	Total population	Source
1774	23,058 *tributos* plus 4,558 in La Union		PNA EP Cagayan 1749–1926 Miguel García San Esteban 20 Sept. 1774. Also in *Philippiniana Sacra*, 6: 76–81. Includes those under the secular clergy as well as Augustinians. About two-thirds were under the Augustinians.
1778	51,439.5 *tributos enteros*	236,888 *almas*	AGI IG 1527 Estado general 31 Aug. 1788. The figure for *almas* is for *naturales* only and it includes 2,098 Tinguians.
1780	31,672.5 *tributos enteros*	149,482 *almas*	AGI IG 1527 fol. 884 Plan demonstrativo de los pueblos 26 Apr. 1780. *Almas* include 1,285.5 *infieles* who pay tribute.
1787		110,956 *almas*	*Mapa general de las almas* 1820. Plus 18,392 *almas* in La Union.
1787	71,150 *tributantes*	152,706 almas	AGI IG 1527 Mapa de los pueblos tributantes y almas . . . Bishop of Nueva Segovia 1787.
1792	40,626 *tributos de naturales*	205,590 *almas*	AUST Libro 229 no. 1 Estatística [*sic*] de las Yslas Filipinas 1815. Plus 492 tributary *mestizos*. *Almas* include *mestizos*.
1793	41,260 *tributos*	Over 170,000 *almas*	NL Ayer 1333 (shelf) Descripción de la provincia de Ilocos ca. 1794.
1796	43,572 *tributos*	184,704 *almas*	PNA EP Ilocos Sur y Norte 1807–1897 Juan de Cuellar 16 July 1798. These totals are incorrectly calculated in the manuscript. Includes La Union.
1797		151,037 almas	*Mapa general de las almas* 1820. Plus 21,147 in La Union.
1800	44,531 *tributos de naturales*	212,486 almas	APSR Cagayan 18 Numero de almas del Obispado de Nueva Segovia 1800. Also in Fernández, "Dominican Apostolate," opposite p. 178. *Almas* include about 700 Spaniards and *mestizos*. Excludes La Union.
1805	45,746.5 *tributos*	228,732 *almas*	AUST Libro 229 no. 1 Estatística [*sic*] de las Yslas Filipinas 1815. *Tributos* and *almas* include *mestizos*.
1807	56,236 *tributos*		PNA EP Ilocos Sur y Norte 1807–1897 Sumario general de los tributos 1807.

Appendix D *(continued)*

ILOCOS *(continued)*

Date	Tributary population	Total population	Source
1807		173,618 *almas*	*Mapa general de las almas* 1820. Plus 28,178 *almas* in La Union.
1809	55,580 *tributos*	361,270 *almas*	Comyn, *Estado*, App. 1.
1812	49,643 *tributos*	251,280 *almas*	AUST Libro 229 no. 1 Estatística [*sic*] de las Yslas Filipinas 1815. Plus 613 tributary *mestizos*. *Almas* include *mestizos*.
1815	55,423 *tributos de naturales*	361,840 *almas*	AUST Libro 229 no. 1 Estatística [*sic*] de las Yslas Filipinas 1815. Plus 665 tributary *mestizos*. *Almas* include *mestizos*.
1817	83,976 *tributantes*	175,586 *almas*	*Mapa general de las almas* 1820. Plus 11,958 *tributantes* and 24,447 *almas* in La Union.
1818	58,484 *tributos* or *familias*	282,843 *almas*	Aragón, *Estados de la población* B2: 90, App. 1. 1818.

LAGUNA DE BAY

Date	Tributary population	Total population	Source
Pre 1582	30,000 *indios*		AGI PAT 23-8 and BR 5: 202–504 Report on saleable offices, no date.
[1582]	9,300 men		AGI PAT 23-9 and BR 5: 87–89 Miguel de Loarca [1582].
1588	11,000 *indios tributarios*		AGI AF 74 and Rodríguez, *Historia*, 15: 354, Domingo de Salazar 25 June 1588.
1591	9,600 *tributos*	39,200 *almas*	AGI PAT 25-28 fols. 14–15 and Relación punctual de las encomiendas 31 May 1591. This figure excludes Tayabas, Lucban, and Taytay listed under the jurisdiction of Laguna.
1590s	7,620 *tributos*	22,093 *cristianos*	Alcalá, *Chrónica*, 68–72. Under Franciscans. In 1610 there were an additional 3,000 *tributos* and 9,000 *indios* in Laguna under Augustinians (AGI AF 20-4-34 Memoria de los conventos 1610).
1606	8,724 *tributos*		AGI AF 29-87 Memoria y lista de las encomiendas [1606].
1622		34,900 *cristianos*	Abad, “Los franciscanos,” 418–419, Alonso de Montemayor 16 July 1622. Under Franciscans.

Appendix D *(continued)*

LAGUNA DE BAY *(continued)*

Date	Tributary population	Total population	Source
1649	4,930 *tributos*	19,040 *personas*	Retana, *Archivo del bibliófilo filipino*, 1: 1–13, Entrada de la seráfica religión 1649. Under Franciscans.
1655	5,931.5 *tributos*		AGI AF 22-7-20 fol. 11 Jueces oficiales de la real hacienda 16 June 1655.
1656	6,000 *tributantes*		Colin, *Labor evangélica*, 1: 24.
1700	6,722.5 *tributos*		AGI CO 1253 Oficiales reales 1700.
1709	6,601 *tributos*	21,293 *almas*	AGI AF 296 Razón de la gente adminstrada en esta provincia de San Gregorio 1709. Document gives 13,202 *tributantes*. Under Franciscans
1735	8,122 *tributos*	40,534 *almas* under Franciscans; 2,600 under Augustinians	San Antonio, *Philippine Chronicles*, 79, 197, 205. In addition there were 400 converted souls in the mountains of Daraetan.
1735	7,790 *tributos*		AGI CO 1266 Oficiales reales 1735.
1750	10,034.5 *tributos*		AGI CO 1276B Oficiales reales 1750.
1751	8,224 *tributos enteros*	36,560 *almas*	Sánchez Fuertes, "Estado de las misiones," 155–159. Copy of document in AGI AF 323 Tabla y noticia 1 May 1751. Under Franciscans.
1756	18,518 *tributarios*	39,137 *personas*	PNA EP Laguna 1755–1886. Fernández de Guevara 27 July 1756.
1778	10,978 *tributos enteros*	49,597 *indios*	AGI IG Demonstración de clases de naciones habitantes . . . que comprehende este arzobispado 9 Dec. 1778.
1784	18,698 *tributantes*	44,618 *almas*	AAM Padrones 1760–1796 Plan de tributos y almas 1784. Under Franciscans, excluding haciendas.
1785		53,961 *indios*	AGI IG 1527 Extracto del número de habitantes que comprehende el arzobispado de Manila 1785.
1792	11,076.5 *tributos de naturales*	63,475 *almas*	AUST Libro 229 no. 1 Estatística [*sic*] de las Yslas Filipinas 1815. Plus 1,618.5 tributary *mestizos*. *Almas* include *mestizos*.
1798	12,630.5 *tributos enteros*	56,369 *almas*	PNA Patronatos 1720–1799 Resumen del estado . . . Sebastián Recuenco 4 July 1798. Under Franciscans. Given as 25,261 *tributantes* in document.

Appendix D *(continued)*

LAGUNA DE BAY *(continued)*

Date	Tributary population	Total population	Source
1802	15,745.5 *tributos enteros*		PNA Tributos Laguna 1802–1807. Excludes *mestizo* tributaries and *reservados*.
1803	16,074 *tributos enteros*		PNA Tributos Laguna 1802–1807. Excludes *mestizo* tributaries and *reservados*.
1804	16,503 *tributos enteros*		PNA Tributos Laguna 1802–1807. Excludes *mestizo* tributaries and *reservados*.
1805	13,311.5 *tributos*	66, 557 *almas*	AUST Libro 229 no. 1 Estatística [*sic*] de las Yslas Filipinas 1815. *Tributos* and *almas* include *mestizos*.
1805	16,869 *tributos enteros*		PNA Tributos Laguna 1802–1807. Excludes *mestizo* tributaries and *reservados*.
1806	17,072.5 *tributos enteros*		PNA Tributos Laguna 1802–1807. Excludes *mestizo* tributaries and *reservados*.
1807	17,234.5 *tributos enteros*		PNA Tributos Laguna 1802–1807. Excludes *mestizo* tributaries and *reservados*.
1807		54,273 *almas*	AAM Visitas de las iglesias 9a (1751–1817) Visita of Laguna, Juan Antonio Zulaybar, 1806, 1807. Excludes haciendas and 4,989 in Santa Rosa.
1809	14,760 *tributos*	95,940 *almas*	Comyn, *Estado*, Appendix 1.
1812	16,339 *tributos de naturales*	83,895 *almas*	AUST Libro 229 no. 1 Estatística [*sic*] de las Yslas Filipinas 1815. Plus 439.5 tributary *mestizos*. *Almas* include *mestizos*.
1815	19,255 *tributos*	107,963 *almas*	AUST Libro 229 no. 1 Estatística [*sic*] de las Yslas Filipinas 1815. Plus 382 tributary *mestizos*. *Almas* include *mestizos*.
1818	20,144 *tributos* or *familias*	86,680 *almas*	Aragón, *Estados de la población* B2: App. 3. 1818.

Appendix D *(continued)*

LEYTE

Date	Tributary population	Total population	Source
1571	23,000 *indios*		AGI PAT 24-19 Hernando Riquel 2 June 1576.
[1582]	14,000–15,000 *indios*		AGI PAT 23-9 and BR 5: 43–59 Miguel de Loarca [1582]. Plus 260 in the islands of Panaon, Maripipi, and Maçagua.
1588	15,000–16,000 *tributantes*		AGI AF 74 and Rodríguez, *Historia*, 15: 364, Domingo de Salazar 25 June 1588.
1591	6,597 *tributos*	25,432 *almas*	AGI PAT 25-38 fols. 23–27 Relación punctual de las encomiendas 31 May 1591.
ca. 1594	ca. 5,000 *tributantes*	10,000 *almas*	AGI AF 79 and BR 9: 96 Francisco de Ortega, no date [ca. 1594]
1594		70,000 *almas*	ARSI Phil 9 fols. 293–294 Antonio Sedeño 19 June 1594.
1600		24,500 *almas* plus 11,000—12,000 who had not been ministered to	ARSI Phil 10 fols. 26–27 Diego García 7 July 1600. Only 4,946 had been baptized.
1600		30,000 *almas*	ARSI Phil 10 fol. 17 Juan de Ribera 21 June 1600.
1600	7,380 *tributos*	29,520 *personas*	ARSI Phil 5 ff.75–92 Juan de Ribera 1 June 1601. Colin, *Labor evangélica*, 2: 122, rounds this to "más de 30,000 ánimas."
1606	4,970 *tributos*		AGI AF 6 Memoria y lista de las encomiendas [1606]
1610	6,523 *tributos*		AGI AF 20 Gregorio López 1610. 2,420 in Carigara and 4,103 in Dulac.
1620	6,800 *tributa*		ARSI Phil 11 fols. 115–118 Historiae Provinciae Philippinarum 15 July 1620. 3,000 in Leyte and 3,800 in Dulac.
1626	6,500 *tributos*		Rodriguez, *Historia*, 2: 72–74, Pedro de Arce July 1626. 3,000 in Carigara and 3,500 in Dagami.
1656	4,000 *tributarios*		Colin, *Labor evangélica*, 3: 793. Razón del número de religiosos . . . 1656. 2000 in Carigara and 2,000 in Dagami.
1659	4,441 married persons (*uxorati*)	12,092 *almas*	ARSI Phil 2 II fols. 314–317 Catologus christianorum 1659. Includes 161 slaves.

Appendix D *(continued)*

LEYTE *(continued)*

Date	Tributary population	Total population	Source
1675	7,615 married persons (*uxorati*)	15,121 *almas*	ARSI Phil 2 I fols. 412–415 Catologus christianorum 1675.
1690	4,000 *tributos*		ARSI Phil 12 fols. 138–148 Alejo López 1690. 2,000 each in Dagami and Carigara.
1696	9,162 married persons (*uxorati*)	21,467 *almas*	ARSI Phil 14 fols. 106–109 Catologus christianorum 1696. Includes 235 slaves.
1697	9,000 tributaries		Gemelli Careri, *Voyage around the World*, 441.
1714		15,000—16,000 *almas*	ARSI Phil 8 fols. 142–149 Letras anuas . . . de los años 1713 y 1714.
1735	7,678 *tributos de indios*		Martínez de Zúñiga, *Estadismo*, 2: 69.
1735	11,331 *tributos*		San Antonio, *Philippine Chronicles*, 86. 8,568 under the Crown, 2,762 in private *encomiendas*.
1737	15,324 married persons (*uxorati*)	39,815 *almas*	ARSI Phil 14 fols. 110–113 Catologus christianorum 1737.
1743	15,955 married persons (*uxorati*)	41,405 *almas*	ARSI Phil 14 fols. 114–117 Catologus christianorum 1743.
ca. 1749		47,064 *almas*	Murillo Velarde, *Historia*, App. 9.
1755	16,381 married persons (*uxorati*)	47,462 *almas*	ARSI Phil 14 fols. 118–121 Catologus christianorum 1755. Includes 7 slaves.
1778	12,865 *tributantes*	34,074 *almas*	Redondo y Sendino, *Breve reseña*, 141–142.
1792	7,675 *tributos*	38,532 *almas*	AUST 229 no. 1 Estatística [*sic*] de las Yslas Filipinas 1815. Plus 30 tributary *mestizos*. *Almas* include *mestizos*.
1805	17,190 *tributos*	85,950 *almas*	AUST 229 no. 1 Estatística [*sic*] de las Yslas Filipinas.1815. *Tributos* and *almas* include *mestizos*.
1809	10,455 *tributos*	68,007 *almas*	Comyn, *Estado*, App. 1.
1812	10,370 *tributos de naturales*	52,390 *almas*	AUST 229 no. 1 Estatística [*sic*] de las Yslas Filipinas 1815. Plus 108 tributary *mestizos*. *Almas* include *mestizos*.
1815	10,196 *tributos de naturales*	62,295 *almas* (51,492 *almas* for families of *tributos* and 10,804 for *reservados*)	AUST 229 no. 1 Estatística [*sic*] de las Yslas Filipinas 1815. Plus 102.5 tributary *mestizos*. *Almas* include *mestizos*.
1818	8,124 *tributos* or *familias*	40,623 *almas*	Aragón, *Estados de la población* 1818.

Appendix D *(continued)*

MINDORO

Date	Tributary population	Total population	Source
1572	Over 15,000 *hombres*		AGI PAT 24-25 and Rodríguez, *Historia*, 14: 97, Relación del descubrimiento 20 Apr. 1572.
[1582]	1,300 *indios*		AGI PAT 23-9 and BR 5: 111–113 Miguel de Loarca [1582]. In Mindoro, Lucban (Lubang), Elin, and another island.
1588	5,000 *casas* of which 2,000 pay tribute		AGI AF 74 and Rodríguez, *Historia*, 1: 368, Domingo de Salazar 25 June 1588. There were an additional 500 *tributantes* in Lubang.
1588	1,733.5 *tributos*		AGI CO 1200 fols. 118v–119v Cargo de dinero de tributos 1588.
1591	700 *tributos*	2,800 *personas*	AGI PAT 25-38 fol. 31 Relación punctual de las encomiendas 31 May 1591. In addition here were 500 *tributos* in Lucban and 700 *tributos* in Marinduque.
ca. 1594	2,000 *indios tributantes*		AGI AF 79 and BR 98 Francisco de Ortega, no date [ca. 1594].
No date [1599]	2,034 *tributos*		AGI PAT 25-54 Memoria de las personas beneméritas, n.d.
1606	1,870 *tributos*		AGI AF 6 Memoria y lista de las encomiendas [1606]. Plus 760 in Marinduque.
1608	2,091 *tributos*		AGI AF 7 Relación de las rentas . . . que SM tiene 18 Aug. 1608.
1624	1,623.5 *tributos*		AGI AF 30-109 Contador de cuentas 18 Aug. 1624. In Mindoro and Lubang under the Crown.
1630	1,612 *tributos*		Grau y Monfalcón, *Memorial informativo*, 4v, also in BR 27: 82 1637.
1655	1,511.5 *tributos*		AGI AF 22 R7 N12 Oficiales reales 16 June 1655.
1656	1,700 *tributarios*		Colin, *Labor evangélica*, 1: 28.
1697	1,700 inhabitants		Gemelli Careri, *Voyage around the World*, 437.
1700	1,878.5 *tributos*		AGI CO 1253 Oficiales reales 1700.
1735	2,013.5 *tributos*		AGI CO 1266 Oficiales reales 1735.
1735	2,034 *tributos enteros*	7,552 souls	San Antonio, *Philippine Chronicles*, 105, 203; Martínez de Zúñiga, *Estadismo*, 2: 69.

Appendix D *(continued)*

MINDORO *(continued)*

Date	Tributary population	Total population	Source
1750	2,864 *tributos*		AGI CO 1276B Oficiales reales 1750.
1792	2,993 *tributos de naturales*	14,965 *almas*	AUST 229 no. 1 Estatística [*sic*] de las Yslas Filipinas 1815.
1805	3,141.5 *tributos*	15,707 *almas*	AUST 229 no. 1 Estatística [*sic*] de las Yslas Filipinas 1815. *Tributos* and *almas* include *mestizos.*
1809	2,026 *tributos*	13,169 *almas*	Comyn, *Estado*, App. 1.
1812	3,665.5 *tributos de naturales*	18,405 *almas*	AUST 229 no. 1 Estatística [*sic*] de las Yslas Filipinas 1815. Plus 15.5 tributary *mestizos. Almas* include *mestizos.*
1815	4,145.5 *tributos de naturales*	24,650 *almas*	AUST 229 no. 1 Estatística [*sic*] de las Yslas Filipinas 1815.
1818	3,717 *tributos* or *familias*	18,796 *almas*	Aragón, *Estados de la población* 1818.

NEGROS

Date	Tributary population	Total population	Source
1571	32,000 *indios*		AGI PAT 24-19 Hernando Riquel 2 June 1576.
1572	20,000 *hombres*		AGI PAT 24-25 Relación del descubrimiento 20 Apr. 1572.
[1582]	6,000 or 7,000 *indios*		BR 5: 46–49 Miguel de Loarca [1582]. Excluding Negritos.
1591	3,037 *tributos*	12,120 *almas*	AGI PAT 25-38 fols. 27–31 Relación punctual de las encomiendas 31 May 1591.
ca. 1594	4,500 "pagan tributo."	20,000 *almas* more or less	AGI AF 79 and BR 9: 96–97 Francisco de Ortega, no date [ca. 1594]
1600		8,000 *almas* in the jurisdiction of Tanay	ARSI Phil 10 fols. 26–27 Diego García 7 July 1600.
1606	2,184 *tributos*		AGI AF29 Memoria y lista de las encomiendas [1606].
1626	3,000 *tributos*		Rodriguez, *Historia*, 2: 72–74, Pedro de Arce July 1626.
1660	2,166 *tributos*	12,635 *almas*	Martínez Cuesta, *History of Negros*, 44, refers to AGI AF 352 Relación de las encomiendas 1660.

Appendix D *(continued)*

NEGROS *(continued)*

Date	Tributary population	Total population	Source
1697	3,000 pay tribute		Gemelli Careri, *Voyage Around the World*, 443.
1701	1,647 *tributos*	9,607 *almas*	Martínez Cuesta, *History of Negros*, 108.
1713	1,367 *tributos*	7,974 *almas*	Martínez Cuesta, *History of Negros*, 108. The same figures are given for 1740.
1718	1,600 *familias*		Díaz, *Conquistas*, 34.
1734	5,741 *tributos de indios*		Martínez de Zúñiga, *Estadismo*, 2: 88.
1745	4,732 *tributos*	27,603 *almas*	Martínez Cuesta, *History of Negros*, 108.
1751	4,479 *tributos*	26,127 *almas*	Martínez Cuesta, *History of Negros*, 109.
1755	4,846 *tributos*	28,268 *almas*	Martínez Cuesta, *History of Negros*, 109.
1761	4,842 *tributos*	26,245 *almas*	Martínez Cuesta, *History of Negros*, 109.
1776	4,306 *tributos*	25,128 *almas*	Martínez Cuesta, *History of Negros*, 109.
1779	5,319 *tributos*	31,027 *almas*	Martínez Cuesta, *History of Negros*, 109.
1781	4,191 *tributos*	24,550 *almas*	Martínez Cuesta, *History of Negros*, 109.
1785	4,048 *tributos*	23,613 *almas*	Martínez Cuesta, *History of Negros*, 109.
1790	4,615 *tributos*	26,915 *almas*	Martínez Cuesta, *History of Negros*, 109.
1792	5,341 *tributos de naturales*	26,705 *almas*	AUST Libro 171 and 229 Estatística [*sic*] de las Yslas Filipinas 1815.
1794	4,438 *tributos*	25,879 *almas*	Martínez Cuesta, *History of Negros*, 109.
1805	6,057 *tributos de naturales y mestizos*	26,705 *almas*	AUST Libro 229 Estatística [*sic*] de las Yslas Filipinas 1815. *Tributos* and *almas* include *mestizos*.
1809	6,396 *tributos*	41,574 *almas*	Comyn, *Estado*, App. 1.
1812	5,727 *tributos de naturales*	28,967 *almas*	AUST Libro 229 Estatística [*sic*] de las Yslas Filipinas 1815. Plus 66.5 tributary *mestizos*. *Almas* include *mestizos*.
1815	7,266.5 *tributos de naturales*	43,275 *almas*	AUST Libros 171 and 229 Censo del archipelago 1815 and AUST Libro 229 Estatística [*sic*] de las Yslas Filipinas 1815. Plus 90 tributary *mestizos*. *Almas* include *mestizos*.
1818	7,356 *tributos* or *familias*	35,445 *almas*	Aragón, *Estados de la población* 1818.

Appendix D *(continued)*

PAMPANGA AND BULACAN

Date	Tributary population	Total population	Source
pre-1582	30,000 *indios*		AGI PAT 23-8 and BR 5: 202–204 Report on saleable offices, no date. Under the *alcalde mayor* of Pampanga prior to the creation of the *alcaldía mayor* of Bulacan.
[1582]	18,770 men		AGI PAT 23-9 and BR 5: 84–85 Miguel de Loarca [1582].
1588	22,000 *tributarios*		AGI AF 74, Colin, *Labor evangélica*, 2: 677, and Rodríguez, *Historia*, 15: 350, Domingo de Salazar 25 June 1588.
1591	18,680 *tributos*	74,720 *almas*	AGI PAT 25-38 fols. 6–9 and BR 8: 105 Relación punctual de las encomiendas 31 May 1591.
[1594]	23,500 *tributantes*	90,000 *almas*	AGI AF 74 and BR 9: 103 Francisco de Ortega, n.d. [1594]
1606	13,600 *tributos*		AGI AF 29-87 Memoria y lista de las encomiendas [1606]. Includes Bulacan.
1610	14,800 *tributos*	44,100 *indios de confesión*	AGI AF 20-4-34 Memoria de los conventos y ministerios 1610. Under Augustinians.
1655	11,004 *tributos*		AGI AF 22-7-20 fol. 11 Jueces oficiales de la real hacienda 16 June 1655. 3,539 in Bulacan, 7,139.5 in Pampanga and 325.5 in Mariveles.
ca. 1656	8,000 *tributarios*		Colin, *Labor evangélica*, 1: 24.
1700	12,304.75 *tributos*		AGI CO 1253 Oficiales de la real hacienda . . . 1700. 7,363.25 in Pampanga, 4,393.5 in Bulacan, and 548 in Mariveles.
1712	8,100 families	26,000 *almas* de confesión	Lopez Memorial Museum. Cédulas y autos 1707–1713. Augustinian Provincial Joseph López 24 June 1712. Plus about 800 families in new reductions. Pampanga only.
1735	15,390.5 *tributos*		AGI CO 1266 Oficiales reales 1735. 9,662.25 in Pampanga, 5,194.5 in Bulacan, and 533.5 in Mariveles.
1735	15,395 *tributos*	83,318 *almas*	San Antonio, *Philippine Chronicles*, 75–76, 197–198. 10,145 *tributos* in Pampanga and 5,250 in Bulacan. Includes 870 Sangleys. *Almas* under Augustinians are: 23,305 in Bulacan and 38,513 in Pampanga, plus 4,500 converted *almas* in missions. In addition the Dominicans had charge of 16,000 in several towns and missions (p. 202).

Appendix D *(continued)*

PAMPANGA AND BULACAN *(continued)*

Date	Tributary population	Total population	Source
1738	13,030.5 *tributos*		NL Ayer 1300 VA IV: 335–408 Informe dado por . . . D. José Niño Villaviciencio 4 Feb. 1738. 4,963.5 in Bulacan and 8,067 in Pampanga.
1750	20,148.25 *tributos*		AGI CO 1276B Oficiales reales 1750. 11,488.25 in Pampanga, 7,395.5 in Bulacan, and 1,264.5 in Mariveles.
1760	17,723 *tributos*	93,672 (Pampanga only 57,761)	NL Ayer Ms 1449 (Box) and BR 48: 53–57 Razón de los pueblos, Pedro Velasco 16 Apr. 1760. In Bulacan and Pampanga. In addition there were 662 Zambales, Igorots, and Balugas in missions.
1779	25,219.5 *tributos enteros*	117,075 *almas naturales*	AGI IG 1527 Demonstración de clases de naciones . . . 9 Dec. 1778. 10,991 in Pampanga and 11,081 in Bulacan. Includes 259 in missions and 2,888.5 in Batan.
1785		127,169 *indios*	AGI IG 1527 Extracto del número de habitantes 1785. Includes Pampanga, Bulacan, Batan, and missions.
1792	31,783.5 *tributos*	152,762 *almas*	AUST Libro 229 no. 1 Estatística [*sic*] de las Yslas Filipinas 1815. Plus 4,769 tributary *mestizos*. *Almas* include *mestizos*.
1805	44,923 *tributos*	184,204 *almas*	AUST Libro 229 no. 1 Estatística [*sic*] de las Yslas Filipinas 1815. *Tributos* and *almas* include *mestizos*.
1806/1809		74,210 *almas* in Pampanga and 93,698 in Bulacan	AAM Santa visita de las iglesias 9A Testimonio de la visita de Fray Juan Antonio Zulaybar, Pampanga 1806, Bulacan 1809. No information for Santa Rita and Minalin in Pampanga.
1809	41,820 *tributos*	271,810 *almas*	Comyn, *Estado*, App. 1.
1812	41,720.5 *tributos de naturales*	215,314 *almas*	AUST Libro 229 no. 1 Estatística [*sic*] de las Yslas Filipinas 1815. Plus 5,972.5 tributary *mestizos*. *Almas* include *mestizos*.
1815	43,337.5 *tributos de naturales*	295,537 *almas*	AUST Libro 229 no. 1 Estatística [*sic*] de las Yslas Filipinas 1815. Plus 5,976 tributary *mestizos*. *Almas* include *mestizos*.
1818	54,308 *tributos* or *familias*	254,795 *almas*	Aragón, *Estados de la población* 1818. In Pampanga, Bulacan, and Batan. There is an arithmetic error in the document in the calculation of *almas*.

Appendix D *(continued)*

PANAY

Date	Tributary population	Total population	Source
At contact	more than 70,000 *familias*		Lilly Library Lot 512 fols. 1–54 Francisco Combés, no date.
1566	50,000 *familias*		Colin, *Labor evangélica*, 1: 31; San Agustín, *Conquistas*, lib. 2 cap. 11: 377.
1571	28,000 *indios*		AGI PAT 24-19 Hernando Riquel 2 June 1576.
[1582]	20,000 *indios* plus 3,340 in neighboring islands		AGI PAT 23-9 and BR 5: 68–79 Miguel de Loarca [1582].
1582	15,000 *tributantes*		AGI AF 52-7 Interrogatorio . . . Enríquez de Guzmán 19 Mar. 1582.
1588	22,000 *tributarios*, of which 3,000 under the Crown		AGI AF 74 and Rodríguez, *Historia*, 15: 359, Domingo de Salazar 25 June 1588.
1591	22,990 *tributos enteros*	90,220 *almas*	AGI PAT 25-38 Relación punctual de las encomiendas 31 May 1591. Includes 1,000 tributary Indians for the island of Cuyo.
ca. 1594	About 25,000 *tributantes*	100,000 *almas*	AGI AF 79 and BR 9: 97 Francisco de Ortega, no date [ca. 1594].
1606	18,125 *tributos*		AGI AF 6 Memoria y lista de las encomiendas [1606].
1610	15,500 *tributos*	49,500 *indios*	AGI AF 20 Memoria delos conventos y ministerios [1610].
1618	30,000 *tributos*, but includes western Negros		BR 18: 102, Pedro de Bivero 1618.
1626	12,700 *tributos*		Rodriguez, *Historia*, 2: 72–74, Pedro de Arce July 1626. Excludes 1400 in Calamianes. 10,300 under the Augustinians and 2,400 under the secular clergy.
1660	16,361 *tributarios*		Colin, *Labor evangélica*, 1: 31. These are the same figures given by Gemelli Careri, *Voyage*, 438, in 1697. 9,400 under the Crown and 6,900 under private individuals.
1660s	16,000 *familias*		Lilly Library Lot 512 fols. 1–54 Francisco Combés, no date.
1698	14,000 *tributarios*, of which 6,000 under the Crown		San Agustín, *Conquistas*, lib. 2 cap. 11: 377.

Appendix D *(continued)*

PANAY *(continued)*

Date	Tributary population	Total population	Source
1714	13,635.5 *tributos* in Augustinian parishes		Rodríguez, *Historia*, 2: 391, Sebastián Foronda 1714.
1718	20,000 *tributos* "sin otras muchas . . . por los montes"		Díaz, *Conquistas*, 35.
1735	20,962 *tributos*		San Antonio, *Philippine Chronicles*, 101. 2,655 in private *encomiendas*; the rest under the Crown. 11,965 in Otón and 9,267 in Panay.
1735	25,962 *tributarios*		Redondo y Sendino, *Breve reseña*, 138; Martínez de Zúñiga, *Estadismo*, 2: 93, 96. 16,695 in Otón and 9,267 in northern Panay with Romblon, Tablas, and other islands. 18,307 under the Crown; 7,655 in private *encomiendas*. Excludes Calamianes with another 1,384 *tributantes* all under the Crown.
1760	24,498 *tributos de hombres y mujeres* under Augustinians	88,993 calculated from other population categories	NL Ayer 1449 (Box) Razón de los pueblos . . . Pedro Velasco 1760.
1765	24,832 *tributantes enteros*	106,319 calculated from other population categories	BL Additional Mss. 13,976 Lista de los conventos y ministerios que tiene esta provincia del santísimo nombre de jesús destas islas . . . Valladolid 1765. Of which 20,179 *casados tributantes enteros* and 9,306 *solteros y solteros tributantes medios* under Augustinians.
1778	23,685 *tributos* (47,370 *tributantes* under Augustinians)	101,707 *almas*	Redondo y Sendino, *Breve reseña*, 139–141.
1792	38,992 *tributos de naturales*	195,991 *almas*	AUST 229 no. 1 Estatística [*sic*] de las Yslas Filipinas 1815. Plus 206 tributary *mestizos*. *Almas* include *mestizos*.
ca. 1800	50,470 *tributos*		Martínez de Zúñiga, *Estadismo*, 2: 113.
1805	45,610 *tributos*	228,049 *almas*	AUST 229 no. 1 Estatística [*sic*] de las Yslas Filipinas 1815. *Tributos* and *almas* include *mestizos*.
1809	45,287 *tributos*	294,365 *almas*	Comyn, *Estado*, App. 1.

Appendix D *(continued)*

PANAY *(continued)*

Date	Tributary population	Total population	Source
1812	52,656 *tributos de naturales*	264,522 *almas*	AUST 229 no. 1 Estatística [*sic*] de las Yslas Filipinas 1815. Plus 248.5 tributary *mestizos*. *Almas* include *mestizos*.
1815	25,954.5 *tributos* under Augustinians of a total of 46,021		AUST Libro 229 Censo del archipelago 1815.
1815	45,021.5 *tributos de naturales*	264,950 *almas*	AUST 229 no. 1 Estatística de las Yslas Filipinas 1815. Plus 167.5 tributary *mestizos*. *Almas* include *mestizos*.
1818	38,870 *familias tributarios* under Augustinians of a total of 61,604	194,364 under Augustinians of a total of 292,760 *almas*	Buzeta and Bravo, *Diccionario geográfico*, vol. 1: 301 for Antique, vol. 1 pull out for Capiz, vol. 2, cuadro 2 for Iloilo.

PANGASINAN

Date	Tributary population	Total population	Source
1573	2,835 houses		AGI PAT 24-21 Martín de Goiti 1573. 2,800 in Pangasinan and 30 in Burinao (Bolinao).
1574	10,000 *indios*		AGI PAT 24-19 fols. 51–54 Hernando Riquel 2 June 1576. 5,000 in private *encomiendas*, 1,000 under the Crown. In addition 3,000 in the river Bolinao and isleta Lunboy and 1,000 on the coast of Zambales and in the river of Tugui and Dingue.
[1582]	5,400 *hombres de paz*		AGI PAT 23-9 and BR 5: 102–105 Miguel de Loarca [1582]. 4,000 in Pangasinan, 400 at Bolinao and an additional 1,000 in Zambales.
1588	5,000 *tributos pacíficos*		AGI AF 74 and Rodríguez, *Historia*, 15: 351, Domingo de Salazar 25 June 1588. Of these 1,500 were under the Crown.
1591	5,900 *tributos enteros* [6,000]	22,600 *personas* [24,000]	AGI PAT 25-38 fol. 6 Relación punctual de las encomiendas 31 May 1591. The summary says that Pangasinan has about 6,000 *tributos enteros* who are 24,000 *personas*.

Appendix D *(continued)*

PANGASINAN *(continued)*

Date	Tributary population	Total population	Source
1593	5,000 *indios*		APSR Pangasinan 1 doc. 1 Alonso Jiménez 11 Aug. 1593 or 12 Aug. 1593.
1606	5,303.5 *tributos*		AGI AF 29-87 Memoria y lista de las encomiendas [1606]. Includes 374.5 at Agoo paying tribute to the Crown.
1610	3,900 *indios*		AGI AF 20 Baltasar Fort 1610. In Dominican doctrinas.
1618	10,000 to 12,000 half-pacified tributes		BR 18: 97 Description of the Philippine Islands, Pedro de Bivero 1618. 2,000 of whom paid tribute to the Crown.
1622		25,000 *almas*	AGI AF 74 and BR 20: 230 Miguel García Serrano 31 July 1622. Administered by the Dominicans.
1655	7,666.5 *tributos*		AGI AF 9-3-45 and AF 22-7-20 Oficiales reales 16 June 1655. Of these 2,454 paid tribute to the Crown.
1689	9,025.5 *tributos*		AGI AF 83-133 and APSR Pangasinan 1 doc. 3 Autos sobre los informes de los alcaldes 4 Mar. 1689. 7,648.5 under Dominicans and 1,377 under Augustinians.
1700	10,916 *tributos*		AGI CO 1253 Oficiales de la real hacienda . . . 1700.
1708	11,039 *tributos*		AGI AF 296 Certificación jurídica de los oficiales reales 21 June 1708. Includes 340 *mestizos*.
1735	14,124.5 *tributos*		AGI CO 1266 Oficiales reales 1735.
1735	14,661 *tributos*	56,875 *almas*	San Antonio, *Philippine Chronicles*, 73, 223. Of the *almas* 8,875 were under Augustinians and about 48,000 under the Dominicans.
1743	18,790.5 *tributos*		PNA Cedulario 1748–1764: 259–260 Real cédula 18 June 1752. Includes Sangleyes and those recently converted.
1750	18,586.25 *tributos*		AGI CO 1276B Oficiales reales 1750.
1751		50,694 *almas* excluding infants	Collantes, *Historia de la provincia*, 587.
1758	24,765 *tributantes*	55,386 *almas*	APSR Pangasinan 11 Mapa de los pueblos y las almas . . . de Pangasinan 1758.
1770	17,645 *tributantes*	33,450 *almas*	APSR Pangasinan 11 Mapa de los pueblos y las almas . . . de Pangasinan 1770.

Appendix D *(continued)*

PANGASINAN *(continued)*

Date	Tributary population	Total population	Source
1774	10,600 *tributos*		PNA Erección de pueblos Cagayan 1749–1926 Miguel García San Esteban 20 Sept. 1774. Also in *Philippiniana Sacra*, 6: 75–76.
1775	20,303 *tributantes naturales*	41,015 *almas naturales*	APSR Pangasinan 11 Mapa de los pueblos y las almas . . . de Pangasinan 1775.
1776	20,645 *tributantes naturales*	39,545 *almas naturales*	APSR Pangasinan vol. 11 Mapa de los pueblos y las almas . . . de Pangasinan 1776.
1779	29,388 *tributantes*	63,303 includes 1,964 *mestizos*	AGI IG 1527 Padrón general de personas . . . Pangasinan, Antonio Vilella, *alcalde mayor* 1779.
1787	31,542 *tributantes naturales*	72,649 *almas naturales*	AGI IG 1527 Mapa de los pueblos tributantes y almas . . . 1787 Bishop of Nueva Segovia.
1792	19,010.5 *tributos*	98,184 *almas*	AUST Libro 229 no. 1 Estatística [*sic*] de las Yslas 1815. Includes Zambales. Plus 626.5 tributary *mestizos*. *Almas* include *mestizos*.
1795	28,005 *tributantes*	60,743 *almas naturales*	APSR Pangasinan 12 Mapa en que se declara el número de individuos . . . 12 Aug. 1795. Does not include Zambales.
1800	30,732 *tributantes*	83,369 *almas*	APSR Cagayan 18 Número de almas . . . 1800. Also in Fernández, "Dominican Apostolate," opposite p. 178.
1805	25,469 *tributos*	127,345 *almas*	AUST Libro 229 no. 1 Estatística [*sic*] de las Yslas Filipinas 1815. Includes Zambales. *Tributos* and *almas* include *mestizos*.
1809	28,290 *tributos*	183,885 *almas*	Comyn, *Estado*, App. 1. Includes 3,690 *tributos* and 23,985 *almas* in Zambales.
1812	26,525 *tributos de naturales*	135,297 *almas*	AUST Libro 229 no. 1 Estatística [*sic*] de las Yslas Filipinas 1815. Includes Zambales. Plus 534.5 tributary *mestizos*. *Almas* include *mestizos*.
1815	27,224 *tributos de naturales*	158,024 *almas*	AUST Libro 229 no. 1 Estatística [*sic*] de las Yslas Filipinas 1815. Includes Zambales. Plus 555 tributary *mestizos*. *Almas* include *mestizos*.
1818	30,440 *tributos* or *familias*	138,163 *almas*	Aragón, *Estados de la población* 1818.

Appendix D *(continued)*

SAMAR

Date	**Tributary population**	**Total population**	**Source**
1571	19,000 *indios*		AGI PAT 24-19 Hernando Riquel 2 June 1576.
[1582]	6,150 *indios*		AGI PAT 23-9 and BR 5: 43–59 Miguel de Loarca [1582].
1588	3,000 *tributantes*		AGI AF 74 and Rodríguez, *Historia*, 15: 366, Domingo de Salazar 25 June 1588.
1591	2,636 *tributos*	10,544 *almas*	AGI PAT 25-38 ff. 23–27 Relación punctual de las encomiendas 31 May 1591. Excludes *encomiendas* that included other islands.
ca. 1594	3,000 *tributantes* in Samar and 800 in Ibabao	more than 10,000 *almas* in Samar alone	AGI AF 79 and BR 9: 98 Francisco de Ortega, no date [ca. 1594].
1600		8,430 *personas* in mission of Tinagon and 14,000–15,000 *almas* in Ibabao	ARSI Phil 10 fols. 26–27 Diego García 7 July 1600.
1606	5,186 *tributos*		AGI AF 6 Memoria y lista de las encomiendas [1606].
1610	5,773 *tributos* (2,823 Tinagon, 2,950 Palapag)		AGI AF 20 Gregorio López 1610.
1620	5,500 *tributa*		ARSI Phil 11 fols. 115–118 Historiae Provinciae Philippinarum 15 July 1620. 2,500 in Tinagon and 3,000 in Palapag.
1626	4,800 *tributos*		Rodriguez, *Historia*, 2: 72–74, Pedro de Arce July 1626. Excludes 1,400 in Calamianes and 1,000 in Balayan. 2,200 in Catbalogan and 2,600 in Ibabao.
1656	3,000 *tributarios*		Colin, *Labor evangélica*, 3: 793–795. Razón del número de religiosos . . . 1656. 1,400 in Catbalogan and 1,600 in Palapag.
1659	3,661 married persons (*uxorati*)	11,952 *almas*	ARSI Phil 2 II fols. 314–317 Catologus christianorum 1659. Includes 450 slaves.
1675	9,268 married persons (*uxorati*)	22,656 *almas*	ARSI Phil 2 I fols. 412–415 Catologus christianorum 1675.

Appendix D *(continued)*

SAMAR *(continued)*

Date	Tributary population	Total population	Source
1690	3,400 *tributos* (1,700 each in Catbalogan and Palapag)		ARSI Phil 12 fols. 138–148 Alejo López 1690.
1696	10,410 married persons (*uxorati*)	31,995 *almas*	ARSI Phil 14 fols. 106–109 Catologus christianorum 1696. Includes 1,718 slaves.
1735	3,042 *tributos de indios*		Martínez de Zúñiga, *Estadismo*, 2: 67.
1737	18,470 married persons (*uxorati*)	47,479 *almas*	ARSI Phil 14 fols. 110–113 Catologus christianorum 1737. Includes 29 slaves.
1743	15,889 married persons (*uxorati*)	44,338 *almas*	ARSI Phil 14 fols. 114–117 Catologus christianorum 1743. Includes 20 slaves.
ca. 1749		57,414 *almas*	Murillo Velarde, *Historia*, App. 9.
1755	19,819 married persons (*uxorati*)	57,603 *almas*	ARSI Phil 14 fols. 118–121 Catologus christianorum 1755.
1766		46,500 total population	Cruikshank, "Moro Impact," 163.
1768	10, 641 *tributantes*	22,900 *almas*	PNA Patronatos Unclassified Plan de tributos y almas . . . de 68 hasta el presente de 85 12 Sept. 1785. Only those transferred to the Franciscans.
1770		33,350 total population	Cruikshank, "Moro Impact," 163.
1779	17,671 *tributantes*	41,358 *almas*	Redondo y Sendino, *Breve reseña*, 142–143. 12,511 under the Franciscans and 5,160 under the Augustinians.
1784	15,723.5 *tributos*	46,696 *almas*, includes 70 Negritos or cimarrones	PNA Patronatos Unclassified (Bound volume) Plan de tributos y almas . . . 1785. Includes *mestizos*.
1792	9,557 *tributos de naturale*	48,242 *almas*	AUST 229 no. 1 Estatística [*sic*] de las Yslas Filipinas 1815. Plus 90.5 tributary *mestizos*. *Almas* include *mestizos*.
1800		42,000 total population	Cruikshank, "Moro Impact," 163.
1805	10,749.5 *tributos*	53,747 *almas*	AUST 229 no. 1 Estatística [*sic*] de las Yslas Filipinas 1815. *Tributos* and *almas* include *mestizos*.
1809	13,630 *tributos*	88,595 *almas*	Comyn, *Estado*, App. 1.
1812	12,598 *tributos de naturales*	63,737 *almas*	AUST 229 no. 1 Estatística [*sic*] de las Yslas Filipinas 1815. Plus 147 tributary *mestizos*. *Almas* include *mestizos*.

Appendix D *(continued)*

SAMAR *(continued)*

Date	Tributary population	Total population	Source
1815	12,879 *tributos de naturales*	75,374 *almas*	AUST 229 no. 1 Estatística [*sic*] de las Yslas Filipinas 1815. Plus 139.5 tributary *mestizos*. *Almas* include *mestizos*.
1818	12,541 *tributos* or *familias*	57,922 *almas* (includes 97 soldiers)	Aragón, *Estados de la población* 1818.

TAYABAS

Date	Tributary population	Total population	Source
Pre-1582	20,000 *indios*		AGI PAT 23-8 and BR 5: 202–204 Report on saleable offices, no date, covers Bonbon, Balayan, and Mindoro.
[1582]	3,600 men		AGI PAT 23-9 and BR 5: 90–93 Miguel de Loarca [1582].
1588	9,000 men		AGI AF 74 and Rodríguez, *Historia*, 15: 356, Domingo de Salazar 25 June 1588. In Balayan and Calilaya together.
1591	6,200 *tributos enteros*	24,600 *almas*	AGI PAT 25-28 ff. 14–15 Relación punctual de las encomiendas 31 May 1591. Includes Tayabas and Lucban entered under Laguna.
1606	5,493.5 *tributos*		AGI AF 29-87 Memoria y lista de las encomiendas [1606].
1622		15,100 *cristianos*	Abad, "Los franciscanos," 417–418 Alonso de Montemayor 16 July 1622.
1649	2,390 *tributos*	9,380 *personas*	Retana, *Archivo del bibliófilo filipino*, 1: 1–13, Entrada de la seráfica religión 1649.
1655	2,905.5 *tributos*		AGI AF 22-7-20 fol. 11 Jueces oficiales de la real hacienda 16 June 1655.
1656	Over 2,500 *tributarios*		Colin, *Labor evangélica*, 1: 21. Plus another 2,500 in Balayan.
1700	1,631.5 *tributos*		AGI CO 1253 Oficiales reales 1700.
1709	2,756 *tributos enteros*	9,698 *almas*	AGI AF 296 Razón de la gente adminstrada en esta provincia de San Gregorio 1709. Given as 5,512 *tributantes*.
1735	2,004 *tributos*	19,748 *almas*	San Antonio, *Philippine Chronicles*, 69, 217–218.

Appendix D *(continued)*

TAYABAS *(continued)*

Date	Tributary population	Total population	Source
1735	1,817.5 *tributos*		AGI CO 1266 Oficiales reales 1735.
1750	4,386 *tributos*		AGI CO 1276B Oficiales reales 1750.
1751	4,391 *tributos enteros*	23,096 *almas*	Sánchez Fuertes, "Estado de las misiones," 152–155. Copy of a document in AGI AF 323 Tabla y noticia, 1 May 1751. Under Franciscans. Calculated from individual villages since the summaries contain errors. Includes 1,218 in the missions including some Negritos.
1768	5,172 *tributos enteros*		PNA Erección de pueblos Tayabas 1755–1896 Cuenta de los reales tributos 13 Dec. 1771.
1792	6,732.5 *tributos de naturales*	33,747 *almas*	AUST Libro 229 no. 1 Estatística [*sic*] de las Filipinas Yslas 1815. Plus 17 tributary *mestizos*. *Almas* include *mestizos*.
1805	8,516.5 *tributos*	42,582 *almas*	AUST Libro 229 no. 1 Estatística [*sic*] de las Filipinas Yslas 1815. *Tributos* and *almas* include *mestizos*.
1809	11,070 *tributos*	71,9155 *almas*	Comyn, *Estado*, Appendix 1.
1812	8,702 *tributos de naturales*	43,667 *almas*	AUST Libro 229 no. 1 Estatística [*sic*] de las Yslas Filipinas 1815 Plus 31.5 tributary *mestizos*. *Almas* include *mestizos*.
1815	10,116.5 *tributos de naturales*	62,861 *almas*	AUST Libro 229 no. 1 Estatística [*sic*] de las Yslas Filipinas 1815. Plus 33.5 tributary *mestizos*. *Almas* include *mestizos*.
1818	11,089 *tributos* or *familias*		Aragón, *Estados de la población* 1818.

TONDO

Date	Tributary population	Total population	Source
[1582]	4,860 men or *indios*		AGI PAT 23-9 and BR 5: 86–87 Miguel de Loarca [1582]. Incomplete. No figures given for Quiapo and Santa María.
1588	7,500 *indios* of whom 4,000 paid tribute to the Crown		AGI AF 74, Rodríguez, *Historia*, 15: 346 and BR 8: 32 Domingo de Salazar 25 June 1588.

Appendix D *(continued)*

TONDO *(continued)*

Date	Tributary population	Total population	Source
1591	8,900 *tributos enteros*	35,600 *almas*	AGI PAT 25-38 Relación punctual de las encomiendas 31 May 1591. Excludes 40 *Chinos* and Cavite and Maragandon.
1598	6,693 *tributos enteros*	26,772 *almas*	Cushner, *Landed Estates*, 99, cites AGI CO 1253.
1606	5,382 *tributos*		AGI AF 6 Memoria y lista de la encomiendas [1606].
1608	3,992 *tributos*		AGI AF 7-42 and BR 14: 243–244 Relación de las rentas y aprovechaminetos 18 Aug. 1608 (Crown *encomiendas* only). Plus 100 tributary *vagamundos*.
1630	5,031 *tributos*		BR 27: 82 Grau y Monfalcón 1637.
1655	7,112.5 *tributos*		AGI AF 9 R3 N45 Jueces oficiales 16 June 1655. 6,130.5 *tributos* paying to Crown and 982 to private individuals.
1700	7,224.5 *tributos*		AGI CO 1253 Oficiales de la real hacienda 1700.
1735	6,293.5 *tributos*		AGI CO 1266 Oficiales reales 1735.
1735	6,361 *tributos enteros*	Incomplete	San Antonio, *Philippine Chronicles*, 77, 197. The Augustinians have 21,959 *almas* and there were another 7,900 in suffragant administrations (p. 204).
1750	13,194 *tributos*		AGI CO 1276B Oficiales reales 1750.
1778	22,816 *tributantes*		AGI IG 1527 fol. 793 Indice y mapa general del número de los tributantes 1778. According to the *corregidor*.
1778	11,580.5 *tributos enteros*	81,133 *almas*	AGI IG 1527 Demonstración de clases de naciones habitantes . . . 1778. *Almas* include people of all races.
1785		66,913 *indios*	AGI IG 1527 Extracto del número de habitantes 1785.
1792	13,231 *tributos de naturales*	66,155 *almas*	AUST Libro 229 no. 1 Estatística [*sic*] de las Yslas Filipinas 1815. Plus 3,184 tributary *mestizos*. *Almas* include *mestizos*.
1805	21,489.5 *tributos*	107,447 *almas*	AUST Libro 229 no. 1 Estatística [*sic*] de las Yslas Filipinas 1815. *Tributos* and *almas* include *mestizos*.
1809	22,140 *tributos*	145,910 *almas*	Comyn, *Estado*, App. 1.

Appendix D *(continued)*

TONDO *(continued)*

Date	Tributary population	Total population	Source
1812	17,995.5 *tributos de naturales*	89,977.5 *almas*	AUST Libro 229 no. 1 Estatística [*sic*] de las Yslas Filipinas 1815. Plus 4,445.5 tributary *mestizos. Almas* include *mestizos.*
1815	18,215 *tributos de naturales*	154,350 *almas*	AUST Libro 229 no. 1 Estatística [*sic*] de las islas Filipinas 1815. Plus 4,283.5 tributary *mestizos. Almas* include *mestizos.*
1818	25,715 *tributos* or *familias*	149,695 *almas*	Aragón, *Estados de la población* 1818.

Appendix E: Growth in the Number of Tribute Payers According to Fiscal Accounts, 1591 to 1792

Jurisdiction	Tributaries 1591	Tributaries 1655	Tributaries 1700	Tributaries 1735	Tributaries 1750	Tributaries 1792	Growth rate 1591–1655	Growth rate 1655–1700	Growth rate 1700–1750	Growth rate 1750–1792	Growth rate 1700–1792
Manila and Tondo	8,900	7,112.5	7,224.5	6,293.5	13,194	13,231	-0.4	0.0	1.2	0.0	0.7
Laguna	9,600	5,931.5	6,722.5	7,790	10,034.5	11,076.50	-0.8	0.3	0.8	0.2	0.5
Balayan	6,600	2,162.5	2,654.5	3,208	5,823	12,690	-1.7	0.5	1.6	1.9	1.7
Tayabas	6,200	2,905.5	1,631.5	1,817.5	4,386	6,733	-1.2	-1.3	2.0	1.0	1.5
Puerto de Cavite	570	0	1,416.5	1,198.5	4,421.75	5,426	0.0	16.1	2.3	0.5	1.5
Pampanga and Bulacan	18,680	10,678.5	11,756.75	14,856.75	18,883.75	31,783.5	-0.9	0.2	0.9	1.2	1.1
Pangasinan	5,900	7,666.5	10,916	14,124.75	18,586.25	19,010.5	0.4	0.8	1.1	0.0	0.6
Ilocos	17,230	10,493	10,165.75	10,904.25	19,166.5	40,626	-0.8	-0.1	1.3	1.8	1.5
Cagayan	23,450	6,748.5	5,911.5	6,678.5	8,660.5	8,539	-1.9	-0.3	0.8	0.0	0.4
Bikol and Masbate	22,160	10,165	6,982.5	12,430.5	19,041	28,949.5	-1.2	-0.8	1.2	2.0	1.5
Mindoro	1,900	1,511.5	1,878.5	2,013.5	2,864	2,993	-0.4	0.5	0.8	0.1	0.5

Appendix E *(continued)*:

Jurisdiction	**Tributaries 1591**	**Tributaries 1655**	**Tributaries 1700**	**Tributaries 1735**	**Tributaries 1750**	**Tributaries 1792**	**Growth rate 1591–1655**	**Growth rate 1655–1700**	**Growth rate 1700–1750**	**Growth rate 1750–1792**	**Growth rate 1700–1792**
LUZON	121,190	65,375	67,260.5	81,315.75	125,061	181,058	-1.0	0.1	1.2	0.9	1.1
Leyte and Samar	9,233	5,734.5	7,351.5	11,765.5	18,895.5	17,232	-0.7	0.6	1.9	-0.2	0.9
Panay and Negros	26,027	23,994	13,190.5	19,736.5	29,128.5	44,333	-0.1	-1.3	1.6	1.0	1.3
Cebu	3,170	8,565.5	6,150	7,790.25	13,656.25	17,798.5	0.0	1.5	1.6	0.6	1.2
VISAYAS	38,430	38,294	26,692	39,292.25	61,680.25	79,363.5	0.0	-0.8	1.7	0.6	1.2
CALAMIANES, MINDANAO, AND MARIVELES	5,820	4,605.5	3,848	4,325	6,866	6,618.5	-0.4	-0.4	1.2	-0.1	0.6
TOTAL	165,440	108,274.5	97,800.5	124,933.05	193,607.25	267,040	-0.7	-0.2	1.4	0.8	1.1

Sources: 1591 AGI PAT 25-38 Relación punctual de las encomiendas 31 May 1591.
1655 AGI AF 22-7-20 Oficiales reales 16 June 1655.
1700 AGI Contaduría 1253 fols. 111–120 Oficales reales 1700.
1735 AGI Contaduría 1266 fols. 130–146 Oficiales reales 1735.
1750 AGI Contaduría 1276B fols. 185–199 Oficiales reales 1750.
1792 AUST Libro 229 no. 1 Estatística [*sic*] de las Yslas 1815.

Abbreviations

AAM Archdiocesan Archives of Manila

AGI Archivo General de Indias, Seville
- AF Audiencia de Filipinas
- CO Contaduría
- IG Indiferente General
- MP Mapas y Planos
- PAT Patronato

APSR Archivo de la Provincia del Santo Rosario, University of Santo Tomas, Manila

ARSI Archivum Romanum Societatis Iesu, Rome
- Phil Provincia Philippinarum

AUST Archive of the University of Santo Tomas, Manila

BR Blair, Emma H., and James A. Robertson. *The Philippine Islands, 1493–1803.* 55 vols. Cleveland: A. H. Clark, 1903–1909.

CDI *Colección de documentos inéditos relativos al descubrimiento, conquista y organización de las antiguas posesiones españoles de América y Oceanía.* 42 vols. Madrid, 1864–1884.

CDIU *Colección de documentos inéditos relativos al descubrimiento, conquista y organización de las antiguas posesiones españoles de ultramar.* 25 vols. 2nd Series. Madrid: Real Academia de la Historia, 1885–1932.

NL Newberry Library, Chicago

VA Ventura de Arco transcripts

PNA Philippine National Archive, Manila
- EP Erección de pueblos

Notes

Chapter 1: A World Apart?

1. Cushner, *Spain in the Philippines*; Hidalgo Nuchera, *Encomienda*; Noone, *Discovery and Conquest*; Phelan, *Hispanization*.

2. Costa, *Jesuits*; Fernández, *History of the Church*; Rafael, *Contracting Colonialism*.

3. Denevan, *Native Population*, xxix; Dobyns, "Estimating Aboriginal American Population," 415. Estimates for the native population of the Americas in 1492 range from as low as Alfred Kroeber's 8.4 million (Kroeber, *Cultural and Natural Areas*, 166) to Henry Dobyns's 90 to 112.5 million (Dobyns, "Estimating Aboriginal American Population," 415). Denevan's estimate of about 54 million in 1492 is preferred since it is based on a review of recent research on each major region of the Americas.

4. Phelan, "Free Versus Compulsory Labor," 192.

5. Phelan, *Hispanization*, 100–102, and "Free Versus Compulsory Labor," 192–194.

6. Corpuz, *Roots*, 1: 54, 529, suggests between 1 million to 1.25 million, and De Bevoise, *Agents*, 18, no more than 1.2 million. Other authors suggest lower estimates. Believing the early accounts to be exaggerated, David Barrows ("History of Population," 411, 442–443) suggests there were only 500,000 to 750,000, while Anthony Reid ("Low Population Growth," 36) estimates that the population of Luzon and the Visayas in 1600 was 800,000. These estimates are nearly all based on the list of *encomiendas* drawn up in 1591 (AGI PAT 25-38 fols. 6–9 and BR 8: 105 Relación punctual de las encomiendas 31 May 1591), which includes only 100 tributaries in Mindanao.

7. VanderMeer, "Population Patterns," 315–337; Cullinane and Xenos, "Growth of Population in Cebu," 80–105; Martínez Cuesta, *History of Negros*, 42–51, 105–110.

8. Reid, "Low Population Growth."

9. N. David Cook (*Demographic Collapse*, 70) has shown how six major epidemics in the sixteenth century might have reduced the population of Peru by between 79 and 92 percent. For a discussion of the impact of Old World diseases in the Americas, see Crosby, "Virgin Soil Epidemics"; Dobyns, "Estimating Aboriginal American Population," 410–414; Cook, *Born to Die*; Cook and Lovell, *'Secret Judgments of God'*. The scale and timing of their impact remain issues of debate (Roberts, "Disease and Death," 1245–1247; Henige, *Numbers from Nowhere*, 167–183).

10. Doeppers, "Hispanic Influences," 61; Larkin, *Pampangans*, 16; Owen, *Death and Disease*, 9; Phelan, *Hispanization*, 106, 156; Reid, *Southeast Asia*, 1: 57–58.

11. Fernández Arias, *Paralelo*, 21–28.

12. Phelan, "Free Versus Compulsory Labor," 190, 192.

13. Bauzon, *Deficit Government*.

14. Phelan, *Hispanization*, 13. See also Fernández Arias, *Paralelo*, 31, and Spate, *Spanish Lake*, 157.

15. AGI AF 74 and BR 7: 29–51 passim Domingo de Salazar 25 June 1588.

16. For succinct accounts of these voyages, see Cushner, *Spain in the Philippines*, 21–45, and *Isles of the West*, 29–56; Noone, *Discovery and Conquest*, 261–399 passim.

17. For Legazpi's instructions see *CDIU* 2: 145–200 Instructions to Legazpi 1 Sept. 1564, which are summarized in BR 2: 89–100. The Augustinian friar Andrés de Urdaneta questioned whether the Philippines fell in Portuguese jurisdiction, but the Crown did not seem to be unduly bothered by this potential area of dispute (Cushner, *Spain in the Philippines*, 41).

18. Hanke, *Spanish Struggle*, 31–36.

19. Seed, *Ceremonies*, 71–97.

20. Hanke, *Aristotle*, 28–73, and *Spanish Struggle*, 111–132.

21. *CDI* 16: 152 Ordenanzas de Su Magestad 13 July 1573; *Recopilación* 2 lib. 4 tit. 1 ley 6: 2 11 June 1621.

22. *CDIU* 3: 325–329 Petición . . . Miguel de Legazpi [1567]; Hidalgo Nuchera, *Encomienda*, 30–31.

23. AGI AF 339 lib.1 fols. 1r–2v and BR 34: 236 Carta real 16 Nov. 1568.

24. AGI AF 339 lib. 1 fols. 175r–176r Real cédula 1 Apr. 1580.

25. Hanke, *Spanish Struggle*, 152, 158; Costa, "Church and State," 319, 334.

26. Phelan, "Some Ideological Aspects"; Costa, "Church and State"; Hanke, *Spanish Struggle*, 139–146, and *Cuerpo de documentos*, xxxix–li.

27. AGI AF 339 lib. 1 fols. 57v–58r Real cédula 7 Nov. 1574, AF 339 lib. 1 fols. 181–184v Real cédula 24 Apr. 1580, AF 339 lib. 1 fol. 193v Real cédula 9 Aug. 1589; Gayo Aragón, "Ideas jurídico-teológicos," 201, 205.

28. The ban was issued in 1679 (AGI AF 24-28 Real Cédula 12 June 1679) but only became fully effective in 1692 (Cortes, *Pangasinan*, 88; Scott, *Slavery*, 36–38, 61).

29. BR 19: 235–246 Hernando Ríos Coronel 1621; Headley, "Spain's Asian Presence," 635.

30. AGI PAT 24-25 Juan Pacheco Maldonado 20 Apr. 1572, PAT 24-38 and BR 3: 57 Miguel de Legazpi no date, PAT 24-4-7 Juan de la Isla no date, PAT 24-25 and BR 3: 168 Relación del descubrimiento 20 Apr. 1572.

31. AGI PAT 24-21 Martín de Goiti 9 Dec. 1572.

32. Tegengren, "Gold," 564–566; Schurz, *Manila Galleon*, 46–47.

33. Morga, *Sucesos*, 304–309; Spate, *Spanish Lake*, 222; Villiers, "Manila and Maluku," 145–149.

34. Headley, "Spain's Asian Presence," 636–637.

35. AGI AF 6 and BR 4: 50, 58–73, 93 Francisco de Sande 7 June 1576. See also BR 6: 197–233 Memorial to the Council of the Indies 19 Apr. 1586.

36. Boxer, "Spanish and Portuguese Projects," 132; Costa, *Jesuits*, 50–52, 85–88.

37. Parker, *Grand Strategy*, 286. Nevertheless, there were two expeditions to Cambodia in 1596 and 1598 (Boxer, "Spanish and Portuguese Projects," 130–131).

38. In fact it was not wholly a subsidy because part of the cash remitted from Mexico came from duties on goods from the Philippines levied in Acapulco (Bauzon, *Deficit Government*, 50–76; Fradera, *Colonia más peculiar*, 54–69).

39. TePaske, "New World Silver," 434–435; Chaunu, *Les Philippines*, 114–116; Villiers, "Manila and Maluku," 154–155. The Spanish retained control of Maluku between 1606 and 1662.

40. Borah, *Early Colonial Trade*, 118–127.

41. Boxer, "Plata es Sangre," 464. After 1620 trade may have declined as the Dutch began to divert Asian trade away from Manila and as internal problems in China reduced the flow of silk and spices to the Philippines, but contraband trade continued (TePaske, "New World Silver," 437).

42. Schurz, *Manila Galleon*, 44.

43. Spate, *Spanish Lake*, 221.

44. Reid, "Low Population Growth," 37–43, and *Southeast Asia*, 1:15–18; Boomgaard, *South East Asia*, 111–139, and "Bridewealth and Birth Control"; Henley, "Population and Means of Subsistence."

45. Reid, "Seventeenth-Century Crisis," 49–50, and "South-East Asian Population History," 46–49.

Chapter 2: The Role of Disease

1. McNeill, *Plagues and Peoples*, 109–110.

2. Reid, "Low Population Growth." It is briefly acknowledged by Boomgaard, *Southeast Asia*, 119.

3. For a succinct account of these issues see Ramenofksy, *Vectors of Death*, 138–141.

4. Black, "Infectious Diseases," 515–518, and "Modern Isolated Pre-Agricultural Populations," 45–49; Cockburn, "Infectious Diseases," 50; Fenner, "Effects of Changing Social Organisation," 48–68; Garruto, "Disease Patterns," 560–564; McKeown, *Origins of Human Disease*, 38, 49.

5. Bartlett, "Measles Periodicity," 48–70.

6. Black, "Measles Endemicity," 210.

7. Black, "Infectious Diseases," 515–518.

8. Fenner et al., *Smallpox*, 118.

9. Cliff and Haggett, *Atlas*, 245–257; Neel, "Health and Disease," 155–168.

10. Anderson and May, "Population Biology," 515–518; Thornton et al., "American Indian Population Recovery," 30–39.

11. Cliff and Haggett, *Atlas*, 245–257.

12. Jannetta, *Epidemics and Mortality*, 19–21; Lilienfeld and Lilienfeld, *Foundations of Epidemiology*, 61–62.

13. Ramenofsky, *Vectors of Death*, 146.

14. McNeill, *Plagues and Peoples*, 60–61.

15 Junker, *Raiding*, 239–246.

16. Hutterer, "Evolution of Philippine Lowland Societies," 295–298, and "Prehistoric Trade," 178–181; Junker, *Raiding*, 378.

17. Goodman and Martin, "Reconstructing Health Profiles," 32.

18. For this study the following Tagalog dictionaries were used: Ruiz, *Bocabulario Tagalo* [comp. 1580?] Marsden Collection M2/17, King's College London; San Buenaventura, *Vocabulario de lengua Tagala* (Pila, 1613); Santos, *Vocabulario de la lengua Tagala* (Manila, 1703). Visayan dictionaries consulted were Sánchez, *Vocabulario de la lengua Bisaya* [comp. 1617] (Manila, 1711) and Mentrida, *Diccionario de la lengua Bisaya, Hiligueina y Haraya de la isla de Panay* [comp. 1637] (Manila, 1841). Other dictionaries include Lisboa, *Vocabulario de la lengua Bikol* [comp. 1628] (Manila, 1865) for Bikol, and López, *Vocabulario de la lengua Iloca* [comp. ca. 1627] Marsden Collection M2, King's College London for Iloko. A detailed discussion of the dictionaries is the subject of a separate paper: Newson, "Disease and Immunity," 1833–1850.

19. McNeill, *Plagues and Peoples*, 110.

20. Gwei-Djen and Needham, "Disease of Antiquity in China," 348; Jannetta, "Diseases of the Premodern Period in Japan," 380; Bamber, "Premodern Period in Southeast Asia," 429.

21. For details of the terms see Newson, "Disease and Immunity," 1836–1845.

22. Chirino, *Relación*, 259; Morga, *Sucesos*, 249; Reid, *Southeast Asia*, 1:51.

23. McNeill, *Plagues and Peoples*, 89, 110.

24. Russell, *Malaria*, 50; Salazar et al., "Malaria Situation," 709–711; De Bevoise, *Agents*, 142–149.

25. Boomgaard, "Morbidity and Mortality in Java," 56–57.

26. Snow et al., "Evidence for Early Rice Cultivation," 3–11.

27. Wheatley, *Nagara*, 82–89; Hall, "Economic History," 188; Glover and Higham, "New Evidence for Early Rice Cultivation," 426, 433.

28. Keesing, *Ethnohistory*, 305–307; Scott, *Barangay*, 36, 180–181, 199–200, 266–267.

29. Motulsky et al., "Glucose-6-phosphate dehydrogenase," 102, 106; Livingstone, *Frequencies of Hemoglobin Variants*, 37–39. In many parts of Southeast Asia malarial resistance takes the form of high frequencies of abnormal hemoglobin E. In areas where malaria is endemic it has replaced GP6D deficiency as the most prevalent form of red cell defect that confers some resistance to malaria. In the Philippines, however, this replacement has not yet occurred.

30. For example, AGI AF 34 Juan Maldonado et al. 1577, AF 29-31 Andrés Cabchuela et al. 20 May 1582; San Agustín, *Conquistas*, lib. 2 cap. 6: 346–347, cap. 7: 353–355.

31. Ruiz, *Bocabulario Tagalo.*

32. Hayes et al., "Dengue," 43–44; Siler et al., *Dengue*, 9, 21, 128, 157, 225.

33. Farley, *Bilharzia*, 159, 163; Tabangui and Pasco, "Control of *Schistosomiasis japonica*," 302.

34. Farris, "Diseases of the Premodern Period in Japan," 380; Gwei-Djen and Needham, "Diseases of Antiquity in China," 347; Magner, "Diseases of the Premodern Period in Korea," 398.

35. Abad, "Los franciscanos," 429–430; Guerra, *El hospital*, 540, 546.

36. Garruto, "Disease Patterns," 561; McNeill, *Plagues and Peoples*, 166.

37. Leung, "Diseases of the Premodern Period in China," 356; Jannetta, "Diseases of the Premodern Period in Japan," 388; Magner, "Diseases of the Premodern Period in Korea," 395.

38. AGI PAT 23-9 and BR 5: 66–67 Miguel de Loarca [1582].

39. AGI AF 74 Expediente sobre la cobranza de tributos [ca. 1591].

40. Santos, *Vocabulario de la lengua Tagala.*

41. Ruiz, *Bocabulario Tagalo.*

42. Boomgaard, "Morbidity and Mortality," 51.

43. Yepes, *Etnografía*, lib. 3 cap. 23: 145.

44. Johnston, "Tuberculosis," 1062.

45. Yepes, *Etnografía*, lib. 3 cap. 24: 149.

46. Brewer, "Tuberculosis," 331–333; De Bevoise, *Agents*, 94–96.

47. For high mortality among Spaniards see AGI PAT 25-36 Santiago de Vera 26 June 1587, AF 59-31 Información del hospital de Manila 16 Feb. 1594, AF 59-23 Francisco Morante 8 June 1595; ARSI Phil 12 fols. 1–12 Ignacio Alcina 24 June 1660.

48. Alcina, *Historia*, lib. 1 cap. 5: 17.

49. De Bevoise, *Agents*, 148–149.

50. Bellwood and Omar, "Trade Patterns," 158–159; Lim, *Evidence of Ceramics*, 39–40.

51. Hopkins, *Princes and Peasants*, 112–113; Fenner et al., *Smallpox*, 228.

52. Fenner et al., *Smallpox*, 217, 225; Jannetta, *Epidemics and Mortality*, 29–30; Leung, "Diseases of the Premodern Period in China," 357.

53. De Bevoise, *Agents*, 18.

54. Dunstan, "Late Ming Epidemics," 1–59; Farris, *Population*, 156–161; Jannetta, *Epidemics and Mortality*, 48–49; McNeill, *Plagues and Peoples*, 269–276; Twitchett, "Population and Pestilence," 43.

55. McNeill, *Plagues and Peoples*, 111.

56. Farris, *Population*, 71; Magner, "Diseases of the Premodern Period in Korea," 377; Twitchett, "Population and Pestilence," 46.

57. Leung, "Diseases of the Premodern Period in China," 355.

58. Hopkins, *Princes and Peasants*, 104–106; Farris, *Population*, 72–73; Jannetta, *Epidemics and Mortality*, 43–44, 68–69, 188; Fenner et al., *Smallpox*, 216–217.

59. McNeill, *Plagues and Peoples*, 128.

60. Jannetta, *Epidemics and Mortality*, 49–50.

61. Farris, "Diseases of the Premodern Period in Japan," 377, 379, 382–383; Magner, "Diseases of the Premodern Period in Korea," 393.

62. Leung, "Diseases of the Premodern Period in China," 354, 356.

63. McNeill, *Plagues and Peoples*, 128; Twitchett, "Population and Pestilence," 42–45, 62n27, 65n76.

64. Farris, "Diseases of the Premodern Period in Japan," 383; Jannetta, *Epidemics and Mortality*, 193.

65. McNeill, *Plagues and Peoples*, 153–154.

66. For example, AGI PAT 24-17 and BR 3: 72–104 Relación de lo sucedió . . . 8 May 1570, PAT 24-9 Juan de Alva 20 July 1570, PAT 24-25 Juan Pacheco Maldonado 20 Apr. 1572, PAT 24-23 Miguel de Legazpi 11 Aug. 1572.

67. AGI PAT 24-9-7 Juan de Alva 20 July 1570; Scott, *Cracks*, 88, and *Barangay*, 72.

68. ARSI Phil 10 fols. 104–107 Mateo Sánchez 12 Apr. 1603; Alcina, *Historia*, lib. 2 cap. 5: 148.

69. Rabor, *Philippine Flora and Fauna*, 11: 146–167.

70. Harden, "Typhus," 1080–1084.

71. Wheatley, *Golden Khersonese*, 283; Samuels, *Contest for the South China Sea*, 11.

72. Fenner, "Smallpox in Southeast Asia," 235–236; Fenner et al., *Smallpox*, 228.

73. Wolters, *Early Indonesian Commerce*, 63.

74. Wolters, *Early Indonesian Commerce*, 78, 95–117.

75. Lim, *Evidence of Ceramics*, 40–41.

76. Chang, *Sino-Portuguese Trade*, 19–20; Scott, *Prehispanic Source Materials*, 62–66, and *Filipinos in China*, 2–7.

77. Clark, *Community, Trade and Networks*, 117.

78. Chang, *Sino-Portuguese Trade*, 26–28; Wheatley, *Golden Khersonese*, 75–77.

79. Andaya and Ishii, "Religious Developments," 513–519.

80. Fox, "Archaeological Record," 57–60; Hutterer, "Prehistoric Trade," 179; Junker, *Raiding*, 198.

81. BR 34: 377 Relation of the Philippine islands, no author, ca. 1586; Cortesão, *Suma Oriental*, 1: 121; Scott, *Prehispanic Source Materials*, 83–84.

82. De Bevoise, *Agents*, 18.

83. Manguin, "Southeast Asian Ship," 276; Needham, *Science and Civilization*, 460–477.

84. BR 3: 242 Hernando Riquel 1573; AGI AF 6 and BR 4: 54 Francisco de Sande 8 June 1576; Cortesão, *Suma Oriental*, 1: 133–134.

85. Needham, *Science and Civilization*, 469–470. There is some controversy over whether Marco Polo ever visited China, but if he did not the information would have been acquired second-hand. See Wood, *Did Marco Polo Go to China?*

86. AGI PAT 24-25 Juan Pacheco Maldonado 20 Apr. 1572.

87. AGI PAT 24-25 Juan Pacheco Maldonado 20 Apr. 1572, PAT 23-9 and BR 5: 105–107 Miguel de Loarca 1582, PAT 25-2 Santiago de Vera 20 June 1585; Boxer, *South China*, xxiv–xxv.

88. AGI AF 6 and BR 2: 238 Miguel de Legazpi 23 July 1567, PAT 24-38 and BR 3: 57 Miguel de Legazpi, no date, AF 29-3bis Guido de Lavezaris et al. 26 July 1567, PAT 24-23 Miguel de Legazpi 11 Aug. 1572, PAT 24-25 Juan Pacheco Maldonado 20 Apr. 1572, PAT 24-12 Andrés de Mirandaola 8 Jan. 1574.

89. Chau Ju-Kua, "Description of the Philippines," 71–72; Wheatley, "Geographical Notes," 50, 64, 67, 80, 83, 90, 125; Scott, *Prehispanic Source Materials*, 74.

90. BR 18: 99 Pedro de Bivero 1618; Morga, *Sucesos*, 308.

91. Lim, *Evidence of Ceramics*, 52–54.

92. Hutterer, "Evolution of Philippine Lowland Societies," 295–298, and "Prehistoric Trade," 178–181.

93. AGI PAT 23-6 Antonio Andrada, n.d; Doeppers, "Hispanic Influences," 33; Morga, *Sucesos*, 252–253.

94. Noone, *Discovery and Conquest*, 405.

95. Haggett, "Prediction and Predictability," 9–14, 17.

96. Smallpox is called *bolotong* (Tagalog), *buti* (Visayan), *burtong* (Iloko), and *poco* (Bikol); measles *tiplas, tipdas* (Tagalog, Visayan, Bikol) and *darap* (Visayan). Mumps was known in Tagalog as *bayiqui or bicqui*. For the dictionaries see note 18.

97. Hart, *Bisayan Filipino and Malayan Humoral Pathologies*, 64.

98. AGI PAT 24-25 no author 20 Apr. 1572, AF 84-2 no author, no date.

99. AGI AF 6 Guido de Lavezaris 16 July 1574.

100. AGI AF 84-4 and Rodríguez, *Historia*, 14: 185 Martín de Rada 30 June 1574.

101. Colin, *Labor evangélica*, 1: 561–563.

102. ARSI Phil 9 fol. 276 Antonio Sedeño 7 July 1592, cited in Costa, *Jesuits*, 143.

103. Chirino, *Relación*, 21, 254.

104. In an earlier paper I suggested they might have been the same disease ("Old World Diseases," 28).

105. AGI AF 35 Juan Núñez 24 June 1595.

106. ARSI Phil 9 fol. 313 Francisco Almerique 23 June 1597; see also ARSI Phil 10 fols. 5–12 Diego García 8 June 1600.

107. Malumbres, *Cagayan*, 33.

108. De Bevoise, *Agents*, 98. See also Boomgaard ("Crisis Mortality," 200) on the incidence of smallpox in Indonesia, in which he claims that it probably did not become endemic until the nineteenth century.

109. Reid, *Southeast Asia*, 2: 10.

110. Newson, "Disease and Immunity," 1843.

111. Díaz, *Conquistas*, 555.

112. Boomgaard, "Crisis Mortality," 199–200. For the periodicity of smallpox see Fenner et al., *Smallpox*, 178; and Hopkins, *Princes and Peasants*, 117, 122.

113. De Bevoise, *Agents*, 102–113.

114. Grau y Figueras, *Memoria sobre la población*, 9; Mas y Sans, *Informe*, 1: 20.

Chapter 3: Colonial Realities and Population Decline

1. Fradera, *Colonia más peculiar*, 21–23, 74–75; Hidalgo Nuchera, *Recta administración*, 22.

2. Fradera, *Colonia más peculiar*, 49.

3. Reid, *Southeast Asia*, 2: 32–36, 62–67, 208–214; Andaya and Ishii, "Religious Developments," 528–529.

4. Phelan, "Some Ideological Aspects," 210.

5. Barrows, "Governor-General," 240–242; Cunningham, *Audiencia*, 76.

6. Morga, *Sucesos*, 311; AGI AF 8-3 and BR 22: 226–242 Juan Niño de Tavora 2 Aug. 1628; Cunningham, *Audiencia*, 30.

7. AGI PAT 25-11 and BR 5: 274–318 Real cédula 5 May 1583; Cunningham, *Audiencia*, 48–54.

8. AGI AF 74 Domingo de Salazar 25 June 1588.

9. Corpuz, *Bureaucracy*, 32.

10. AGI AF 18B and BR 10: 81 Antonio de Morga 8 June 1598.

11. Haring, *Spanish Empire*, 129, says these two officials performed essentially the same functions. See also Cunningham, *Audiencia*, 27; Phelan, *Hispanization*, 128; Corpuz, *Bureaucracy*, 92–107.

12. Prior to the arrival of Governor Gonzalo Ronquillo in 1580, there had been only three or four, but within three years they had multiplied to ten or sixteen (AGI AF 59-7 Información que hizo el obispo 19 Mar. 1582, AF 6 and Retana 3: 6 Bishop Domingo de Salazar [1583]).

13. AGI AF 18B and BR 11: 87–92 Fiscal Salazar y Salcedo 21 July 1599, AF 7-42 and BR 14: 243–269 Relación de las rentas 18 Aug. 1608 and NL Ayer 1300 VA I: 431–441 Pedro de Bivero 1618.

14. AGI AF 27 and BR 18: 315 Hernando Ríos Coronel [1619].

15. AGI AF 34 and BR 10: 110–113 Antonio de Morga, no date [late 1590s], AF 7-42 and BR 14: 243–269 Relación de las rentas 18 Aug. 1608.

16. The criticisms of the conduct of *alcaldes mayores* are too numerous to list. For examples of their abuses see AGI AF 74 and BR 5: 188–189 Bishop Salazar 20 June 1582, PAT 24-29 and BR 3: 253–259 Martín de Rada 21 June 1574, AF 6 Domingo de Salazar [1583], AF 18B and BR 10: 75–102 Antonio de Morga 6 June 1598, AF 27 and BR 18: 315–317 Hernando Ríos Coronel 1619–1620, AF 84-211 Relación de las muchas mieses . . . Fathers Jesús and San Joseph, no date.

17. AGI PAT 23-8 and BR 5: 202–204 Report on saleable offices, no date.

18. AGI AF 18B and BR 11: 33–35 Autos para el buen gobierno 7 Jan. 1598.

19. Corpuz, *Bureaucracy*, 109–113; Phelan, *Hispanization*, 124–125.

20. Phelan, *Hispanization*, 126–127; Owen, "Principalia," 303–304.

21. Hidalgo Nuchera, *Recta administración*, 83–84.

22. Spalding, "Social Climbers," 645–664.

23. Owen, "Principalia," 309–310.

24. Corpuz, *Bureaucracy*, 115, takes a rather different view, arguing that the Spanish placed excessive burdens on native officials, treating them with contempt and causing them to lose respect.

25. Spate, *Spanish Lake*, 221. See also Rafael, *Contracting Colonialism*, 18–21.

26. AGI AF 19 and BR 14: 167 Rodrigo Díaz Guiral 30 June 1606.

27. Cushner, *Spain in the Philippines*, 98–99.

28. AGI AF 74 and BR 20: 231–232 Miguel García Serrano 31 July 1622; Phelan, *Hispanization*, 47–48.

29. Phelan, *Hispanization*, 48; Foronda and Foronda, *Samtoy*, 7.

30. Keesing, *Ethnohistory*, 27–28.

31. AGI AF 297-39 La ciudad de Manila 13 July 1714.

32. Medina, *Historia*, 149.

33. A *mae* was generally valued at 2.5 reals.

34. AGI PAT 24-29 and BR 3: 265–270 Guido de Lavezaris, no date, AF 34-15 Guido de Lavezaris 17 July 1574.

35. AGI PAT 24-29 and BR 3: 255–257 Martín de Rada 21 July 1574.

36. BR 6: 161 Memorial to the Council of the Indies 19 Apr. 1586; AGI AF 18A Audiencia 26 June 1586, AF 339 lib. 1 fol. 171v Real cédula 9 Aug. 1589; Phelan, "Some Ideological Aspects," 233.

37. Hidalgo Nuchera, *Encomienda*, 135–200.

38. AGI AF 19-7 Testimonio sobre la tasación . . . 28 Sept. 1604.

39. Phelan, *Hispanization*, 100, and "Free Versus Compulsory Labor," 193–196.

40. AGI AF 20 Bernardo de Santa Catalina, Dominican Provincial 9 July 1616, Vicente de Sepúlveda, Augustinian Provincial 13 Aug. 1616; Phelan, "Free Versus Compulsory Labor," 193.

41. BR 50: 204 Ordinances of good government 1696.

42. AGI AF 34-52 Diego de Zarate 10 June 1581.

43. NL Ayer 1301 Visita de Joseph Ignacio de Arzadún y Rebolledo 28 Mar. 1743; Phelan, "Free Versus Compulsory Labor," 191–192. Those exempt were *cabezas de barangay*, their eldest sons and successors, church singers and sacristans, porters and cooks working for convents and churches, all officers of justice, Pampangans who served as soldiers and in other capacities in Manila, Cavite and other *presidios*, and their wives during their tours of duty (BR 50: 203–204 Ordinances of good government 1696; Moreno y Díaz, *Manual*, 47–48).

44. AGI AF 329 lib. 2 fols. 83r–85r Real cédula 26 May 1609.

45. AGI AF 340 lib. 3 fols. 26r–26v Real cédula 6 Mar. 1608, AF 27 and BR 18: 316 Hernando Ríos Coronel 1619–1620, AF 9-6 Diego Fajardo 31 July 1649.

46. AGI AF 340 lib. 3 fols. 414–441v Real cédula 1 May 1608, AF 20 Juan de Espinosa 18 Aug. 1617, AF 7-53 Alonso Fajardo 10 Aug. 1618, AF 38-1 Sebastián de Pineda 26 May 1619, AF 329 lib. 2 fols. 301v– 313v Real cédula 10 Aug. 1619, AF 27 and BR 18: 327 Hernando de los Ríos Coronel 1619–1620, AF 80 and BR 19: 72–77 Pedro de San Pablo 7 Aug. 1620, AG 340 lib. 4 fols. 181v–182v Real cédula 8 Dec. 1628, AF 9-6 Diego Fajardo 13 July 1649.

47. *Recopilación* 2 lib. 4 tit. 12 ley 14: 42 Real cédula 20 Nov. 1578; Ots Capedqui, *España en América*, 29–32, 82.

48. AGI PAT 25-60 fols. 41–42 Juan de Plasencia 4 Oct. 1589; Cushner, *Landed Estates*, 8–10; Scott, *Barangay*, 229–230.

49. Cushner, *Landed Estates*, 18–19, 27–30, 66; Cushner, "Meysapan," 31.

50. Roth, *Friar Estates*, 45–49; Borromeo, "Cadiz Filipino," 73–77.

51. Cushner, *Landed Estates*, 23–36, and "Meysapan," 32–39, describes the piecemeal growth of several religious haciendas in the Tondo region.

52. Cushner, "Meysapan," 33.

53. Roth, "Casas de Reservas," 118–119.

54. Other small numbers of *casas de reservas* were given to Spaniards and native Filipinos as rewards for services (Camara Dery, *Pestilence*, 31–36).

55. The right of the *gobernadorcillo* to designate *casas de reservas* was banned in 1691, but the order was ineffective (Cushner, *Landed Estates*, 52–53).

56. Roth, "Casas de Reservas," 117, 120–121; Cushner, *Landed Estates*, 51.

57. Roth, "Church Lands," 138–142.

58. Majul, *Muslims*, 36–46; Reid, *Southeast Asia*, 2: 132–135, for a useful map of the spread of Islam.

59. Saleeby, *History of Sulu*, 158–164; Majul, *Muslims*, 51–64, and "Islamic and Arab Cultural Influences," 64–68.

60. Ileto, *Magindanao*, 3–6; Scott, *Barangay*, 173–176.

61. Scott, *Barangay*, 175; Costa, *Jesuits*, 299.

62. Nicholl, "Brunei Rediscovered," 45; Bellwood and Omar, "Trade Patterns," 158–160.

63. Saleeby, *History of Sulu*, 171.

64. Scott, *Cracks*, 48.

65. *CDIU* 2: 184, 188–189 Instrucción . . . a Miguel de Legazpi 1 Sept. 1564.

66. AGI AF 339 lib. 1 fols. 1r–2v and BR 34: 237 Real cédula 16 Jan. 1568.

67. *Recopilación* 2 lib. 2 tit. 2 ley 12: 204 Reales cédulas 4 July 1570 and 29 May 1620; Hanke, *Spanish Struggle*, 145; Cunningham, *Audiencia*, 57n26.

68. Majul, *Muslims*, 81–83.

69. AGI AF 18B Antonio de Morga 6 July 1596. These expeditions also aimed to gain control of the trade with China and within the archipelago (Scott, *Cracks*, 47).

70. AGI AF 6 Francisco Tello 12 July 1599.

71. Junker, "Trade Competition," 248–255, and *Raiding*, 339–343.

72. Majul, *Muslims*, 125, 167.

73. Tarling, *Piracy*, 6–8, 146. Tarling (*Sulu and Sabah*, 4) later speaks of frustration rather than decline.

74. Torrubia, *Dissertación*, 32; Calvo, *Joseph Calvo*, 17; Majul, *Muslims*, 125; Reid, *Southeast Asia*, 2: 22–23, 32.

75. Reid, *Southeast Asia*, 1: 133.

76. Warren, *Sulu Zone, 1768–1898*, xvi, 198–200, and *World Capitalist Economy*, 46.

77. BR 17: 64 1610 from Annuae Litterae Societatis Jesu (Dilingae, 1610).

78. Montero y Vidal, *Piratería*, 2: 153; Costa, *Jesuits*, 311.

79. NL Ayer 1300 VA I: 523–545 Relación del estado 1626; Costa, *Jesuits*, 319, 321.

80. Tarling, *Sulu and Sabah*, 7–8; BR 29: 98 Relation of the glorious victories, 1638; BR 27: 358 Sebastián Hurtado de Corcuera 20 Aug. 1637; Mallari, "Muslim Raids," 268n42; Casino, "Two Kingdoms," 740–741.

81. Majul, *Muslims*, 123.
82. NL Ayer 1300 VA I: 523–545 Relación del estado 1626, VA I: 551–607 Relación desde el mes de Julio 1628; Costa, *Jesuits*, 321.
83. ARSI Phil 12 fols. 1–12 Ignacio Alcina 24 June 1660.
84. Prieto Lucena, *Manrique de Lara*, 121–137.
85. Costa, *Jesuits*, 540–543.
86. Tarling, *Sulu and Sabah*, 10–13.
87. Saleeby, *History of Sulu*, 185.
88. Montero y Vidal (*Piratería*, 1: 334–336) provides three pages of raids that occurred during the 1760s.
89. Nort, *Description*, 38–47; San Agustín, *Conquistas*, lib. 3 cap 5: 605–606; Morga, *Sucesos*, 177–184.
90. Boxer, *Dutch Seaborne Empire*, 24–25.
91. San Agustín, *Conquistas*, lib. 3 cap. 28: 736; Colin, *Labor evangélica*, 1: 214–215, 3: 221, 232–242; Blumentritt, *Ataques*, 18–21; Schurz, *Manila Galleon*, 346; Morales Maza, *Augustinians*, 144.
92. Colin, *Labor evangélica*, 3: 328–329.
93. San Agustín, *Conquistas*, lib. 3 cap. 30: 748; Blumentritt, *Ataques*, 31; Costa, *Jesuits*, 336; Colin, *Labor evangélica*, 1: 631–632; Morales Maza, *Augustinians*, 144. Unfortunately Speilbergen provides no details of this encounter in the account of his circumnavigation (*East and West Indian Mirror*).
94. Schurz, *Manila Galleon*, 348–350.
95. Morales Maza, *Augustinians*, 148.
96. Blumentritt, *Ataques*, 52–59.
97. Morga, *Sucesos*, 232; San Agustín, *Conquistas*, lib. 3 cap. 25: 719.
98. Phelan, *Hispanization*, 100–102.
99. Reid, *Southeast Asia*, 2: 294–295.
100. Reid, *Southeast Asia*, 2: 291–296.
101. Boomgaard, "Crisis Mortality," 193–197, and *Southeast Asia*, 91–105, 122–127.

Chapter 4: Interpreting the Evidence

1. Scott, *Prehispanic Source Materials*, 63–90.
2. For overviews of Spanish colonial sources and the difficulties of interpretation, see Borah, "Historical Demography of Latin America," 175–205; Borah, "Historical Demography of Aboriginal and Colonial America," 13–34; Owen, "Philippine Historical Demography."
3. *CDIU* 3: 459 Miguel de Legazpi, no date.
4. AGI AF 74 and BR 7: 269–274 Expediente sobre la cobranza 1591; Costa , *Jesuits*, 58–59.
5. Borah, "Historical Demography of Aboriginal and Colonial America," 20–21, 24–26; Dobyns, "Estimating Aboriginal American Population," 398. For an unconstructive review of methods used to estimate aboriginal populations, see Henige, *Numbers from Nowhere*.
6. Cook and Simpson, *Population of Central Mexico*, 18–30, urge caution in dismissing early missionary and military estimates on the basis of ulterior motives without due evaluation of the context and other evidence available.

7. Borah, "Historical Demography of Latin America," 182.

8. Ricard, *Spiritual Conquest of Mexico*, 83–95.

9. Although referring primarily to nineteenth-century sources, Michael Cullinane provides an excellent account of the relationship between civil and ecclesiastical records in "Accounting for Souls."

10. Few authors have examined in detail the reliability of the figures presented in such accounts. Notable exceptions are Onofre Corpuz and Norman Owen, though their comments relate largely to figures for the late colonial period and for the Philippines as a whole. See Corpuz, *Roots*, 515–569, and Owen, "Philippine Historical Demography."

11. AGI PAT 25-38 and BR 8: 96–141 Relación punctual de las encomiendas 31 May 1591.

12. AGI PAT 24-19 Hernando Riquel 2 June 1576. The whole of this document has not been published. Some details are contained in Colin, *Labor evangélica*, 1: 135, 157–158, though the transcription contains many errors and fails to include the names of all communities.

13. Hidalgo Nuchera, *Encomienda*, 40–49.

14. AGI PAT 23-9 and BR 5: 34–187 Relación de las Yslas Filipinas, Miguel de Loarca [1582]; Cullinane and Xenos, "Growth of Population," 83–84.

15. AGI AF 74 and Rodríguez, *Historia*, 1: 343–370, quotation on p. 369 Domingo de Salazar 25 June 1588.

16. AGI AF 29-87 Memorial y lista de las encomiendas 1606.

17. Hidalgo Nuchera, *Encomienda*, 249–333, gives figures for these *encomiendas* by civil district.

18. Corpuz, *Roots*, 532–535.

19. BR 18: 93–106 Pedro de Bivero 1618; AGI AF 9 R3 N45 and AF 22-7-20 Oficiales reales 16 June 1655.

20. Corpuz, *Roots*, 537–539.

21. San Antonio figures for Luzon add up to 83,144 *tributos* and the treasury accounts to 81,315.75 *tributos* (see Appendix E).

22. San Antonio, *Philippine Chronicles*, 225.

23. Browning, "Preliminary Comments on the 1776 Population Census," 5–13.

24. These are to be found in AGI IG 1527 and AF 495 to 500.

25. Hidalgo Nuchera, *Encomienda*, 201–208. In the nineteenth century, single men were liable at age eighteen and women at age twenty (Moreno y Díaz, *Manual*, 33).

26. Corpuz, *Roots*, 536–557.

27. González and Mellafe, "Función de la familia," 69, have calculated that family size in Huánuco, Peru, fell from about 6.0 in pre-Conquest times to 2.5 in 1560.

28. See Corpuz, *Roots*, 521–526.

29. In 1563 the Council of Trent made the registration of births and marriages compulsory and in 1614 the *Rituale Romanum* made the registration of confirmations and deaths compulsory. However, the compulsory registration of baptisms and marriages appears to have been introduced in Mexico in 1555 (Borah, "Historical Demography of Latin America," 27).

30. The catalogue of the Church of Jesus Christ of Latter-day Saints in Salt Lake City, Utah, constitutes a partial guide to the parish records that exist. See http://www.familysearch.org/Eng/Library/FHLC/frameset_fhlc.asp (accessed 25 August 2008). Analyses of nineteenth-century parish registers, such as those by Cullinane and Smith

for Cebu, by Owen for Bikol, and by Ng for Nagcarlan, demonstrate the value and limitations of using of these sources (Owen, "Philippine Historical Demography," 15–23).

31. Corpuz, *Roots*, 326–337.

32. Owen, "Life, Death and the Sacraments," 242–245.

33. AGI AF 74 and BR 20: 226–248 García Serrano 31 July 1622.

34. APSR Cagayan 18 Número de almas del obispado de Nueva Segovia; AAM Planes de almas 1812–1840 Plan general del arzobispado de Manila 1812. An earlier but incomplete account exists for the bishopric of Cebu in 1778 (Plan de almas de la diócesis de Cebu del año 1778 in Redondo y Sedino, *Breve reseña*, 139–146).

35. Plasencia, "Relación del culto."

36. Alcina, *Historia*; Scott, *Barangay*, 2.

37. Antolín, *Notices*, xii.

38. AUST Becerro 37 Discurso sobre el gentio, Francisco Antolín, 1787.

39. Scott, *Barangay*.

40. Morga, *Sucesos*, 245–323.

41. Quirino and García, "Manners," 330–342.

42. See Junker, *Raiding*, 40–53, 144, 151. See also the commentary by Scott, *Prehispanic Source Materials*, 1–32.

43. Spencer, "Rise of Maize," 9–15; VanderMeer, "Populations Patterns," 328; Cullinane and Xenos, "Growth of Population," 98–99.

44. Goodman and Martin, "Reconstructing Health Profiles," 11–60.

45. Cullinane and Xenos, "Growth of Population," 94–105; Owen, *Prosperity*, 116; Corpuz, *Roots*, 166.

46. Fradera, *Colonia más peculiar*, 75–77.

47. Corpuz, *Roots*, 167–177; Cullinane and Xenos, "Growth of Population," 88–89.

48. Mörner, *Race Mixture*, 45–48.

49. AUST Libro 229 no.1 Estatística de las islas Filipinas 1815. See Corpuz, *Roots*, 253–268, for a succinct account of the numbers of Chinese and Chinese *mestizos* during the early colonial period.

50. Moreno y Díaz, *Manual*, 30–31.

51. Doeppers, "Evidence from the Grave," 269; Cullinane, "Changing Nature," 257–262.

52. See Corpuz, *Roots*, 515–614, for a review of these sources.

53. VanderMeer, "Population Patterns," 315–337; Cullinane and Xenos, "Growth of Population," 80–105; Martínez Cuesta, *History of Negros*, 42–51, 105–110.

Chapter 5: Conquest and Depopulation before 1600

1. For detailed accounts of Legazpi's route through the Visayas, see Cushner, *Spain the Philippines*, 45–54, and *Isles of the West*, 57–100; Noone, *Discovery and Conquest*, 261–399 passim; *CDIU* 2: 394–427 Esteban Rodríguez [1565]; BR 2: 196–216 Miguel de Legazpi 1565.

2. BR 2: 213 Miguel de Legazpi 1565.

3. Wernstedt and Spencer, *Philippine Island World*, 445–446.

4. AGI PAT 23-9 and BR 5: 114–117 Miguel de Loarca [1582]; Quirino and García, "Manners," 397 and plate 7; Zorc, *Bisayan Dialects*, 11, 17, 32. The predominant dialect is Cebuano, which is spoken in the central Visayas as well as eastern Negros and western

Leyte, but other significant dialects are Hiligaynon, which is found in most of Panay and western Negros, Waray in Samar and western Leyte, and Aklanon in northwest Panay.

5. Chirino, *Relación de las islas Filipinas* [1604]. For Alcina's books 1 and 2 see *Historia* and for books 3 and 4 see Yepes, *Etnografía*. For more information on these sources see chapter 4.

6. ARSI Phil 5 fols. 1–33 Diego Sánchez 27 June 1597.

7. AGI PAT 23-9 and BR 5: 34–187 Relación de las Yslas Filipinas, Miguel de Loarca [1582]; Quirino and García, "Manners," 347–366. A photocopy exists at the Newberry Library at NL Ayer Ms 1409a (shelf).

8. Pigafetta, *First Voyage*, 31–70.

9. Scott, *Barangay*, 17–157.

10. Bellwood, "Southeast Asia before History," 112–113, 115.

11. Pigafetta, *First Voyage*, 67. There are some inconsistencies in accounts of the expedition. Pigafetta refers to Negritos in the island of Panglao south of Bohol, but Francisco Alvo refers to an island called Panilongo west of Cebu, which is taken to be Negros (Martínez Cuesta, *History of Negros*, 7).

12. *CDIU* 2: 410–418 Esteban Rodríguez [1565].

13. AGI PAT 23-9 and BR 5: 46–47 Miguel de Loarca [1582].

14. Gemelli Careri, *Voyage around the World*, 442–443.

15. Blumentritt, *An Attempt at Writing a Philippine Ethnography*, 22. Martínez Cuesta, *History of Negros*, 20n12, notes that this figure was drawn from another source, which did not distinguish among the pagans found in Negros. See also Díaz Arenas, *Memorias históricas*, cuaderno 5.

16. Rahmann and Maceda, "Notes on the Negritos," 815.

17. Mozo, *Noticia*, 142.

18. Díaz Arenas, *Memorias históricas*, cuaderno 5; Rahmann and Maceda, "Negritos of Iloilo," 865.

19. Cadeliña, "Adaptive Strategies," 96.

20. Martínez Cuesta, *History of Negros*, 9. On the Negritos, see Cadeliña, "Adaptive Strategies"; Oración, "Notes on the Culture of Negritos"; and Rahmann and Maceda, "Notes on the Negritos."

21. San Agustín, *Conquistas*, lib. 2 cap. 11: 376–377. The Spanish reads "sin rey, ni señor, ni población."

22. For crops grown, see Alcina, *Historia*, lib. 1 caps. 7–13: 21–70; Pigafetta, *First Voyage*, 64.

23. *CDIU* 2: 419 Esteban Rodríguez [1565]; *CDIU* 3: 125, 130 Relación muy circunstaciada 1567; *CDIU* 3: 326 Relación de las islas del Poniente [1565]; AGI PAT 23-9 and BR 5: 42–43, 54–55 Miguel de Loarca [1582]; VanderMeer, "Population of Cebu," 319, 321–322.

24. AGI PAT 23-9 and BR 5: 168–169 Miguel de Loarca [1582]; Pigafetta, *First Voyage*, 32–33.

25. AGI PAT 23-9 and BR 5: 44–45 Miguel de Loarca [1582]; Quirino and García, "Manners," 416.

26. *CDIU* 2: 408 Esteban Rodríguez [1565]; AGI PAT 23-9 and BR 5: 44–47, 54–55 Miguel de Loarca [1582]; PNA Patronatos (Unclassified) Thomás de Aquino 19 Oct. 1785.

27. ARSI Phil 5 fols. 1–33 Diego Sánchez 27 June 1597.

28. Junker, *Raiding*, 327–329.

29. Pigafetta, *First Voyage*, 47, 50, 56–57; Junker, *Raiding*, 320–321, 330.

30. Alcina, *Historia*, lib. 1 cap. 28: 246, lib. 2 cap. 5: 148; ARSI Phil 10 fols. 104–107 Mateo Sánchez 12 Apr. 1603; ARSI Phil 12 fols. 138–148 Alejo López 1690. Alcina, *Historia*, lib. 1 cap. 28: 246.

31. Colin, *Labor evangélica*, 3: 256.

32. ARSI Phil 5 fols. 1–33 Diego Sánchez 27 June 1597; Pigafetta, *First Voyage*, 41; Scott, *Cracks*, 88.

33. For example, AGI PAT 24-9 Juan de Alva 20 July 1570; AGI PAT 24-25 and BR 3: 170 Relación del descubrimiento 20 Apr. 1572; AF 6 and BR 5: 26 Gonzalo Ronquillo de Peñalosa 16 June 1582; PAT 23-9 and BR 5: 66–67 Miguel de Loarca [1582].

34. *CDIU* 2: 264, 303–304 Relación circunstaciada [1565].

35. For example, AGI PAT 24-25 and BR 3: 170 Relación del descubrimiento 20 Apr. 1572.

36. Yepes, *Etnografía*, lib. 4 cap. 8: 207.

37. For example, AGI PAT 23-9 and BR 5: 146–147 Miguel de Loarca [1582]; Quirino and García, "Manners," 414–415.

38. Yepes, *Etnografía*, lib. 3 cap. 5: 31–36.

39. ARSI Phil 12 fols. 138–148 Alejo López 1690.

40. Henley, "Population and the Means of Subsistence."

41. Boserup, *Conditions of Agricultural Growth*.

42. Junker, *Raiding*, 235.

43. Hutterer, "Evolution of Philippine Lowland Societies," 294; Junker, *Raiding*, 22–23, 243, 246–260.

44. AGI PAT 23-9 and BR 5: 120–121 Miguel de Loarca [1582].

45. For foreign trade see AGI AF 6 and BR 2: 238 Miguel de Legazpi 23 July 1567, PAT 23-7 and BR 3: 202 Diego de Artieda, no date, PAT 24-23 Miguel de Legazpi 11 Aug. 1572; Morga, *Sucesos*, 308; Chau Ju-Kua, "Description of the Philippines," 71–72; Wheatley, "Geographical Notes," 50, 64, 67, 80, 83, 90, 125; Scott, *Barangay*, 76.

46. *CDIU* 3: 463 Miguel de Legazpi, no date; AGI AF 84-2, PAT 23-9 and BR 5: 94–95, 98–99 Diego de Herrera, no date [1573]; see also AGI PAT 23-10, BR 2: 72 and *CDI* 5: 141 García Descalante Alvarado 1 Aug. 1548; *CDIU* 3: 213 Relación muy circunstanciada 1567; AGI PAT 24-12 and BR 3: 223–224 Andrés de Mirandaola 8 Jan. 1574; Colin, *Labor evangélica*, 1: 52; Tegengren, "Gold," 593–594.

47. Pigafetta, *First Voyage*, 68; Morga, *Sucesos*, 261; ARSI Phil 5 fols. 1–33 Diego Sánchez 27 June 1597.

48. Reid, *Southeast Asia*, 1: 96–100; Junker, *Raiding*, 270.

49. BR 2: 223 Anon. 1566.

50. Hutterer, *An Archaeological Picture*, 37, 56; Nishimura, "Long Distance Trade," 141–142, 145.

51. *CDIU* 3: 467 Miguel de Legazpi, no date; BR 2: 86 Andrés de Urdaneta 1561; BR 4: 74 Francisco de Sande 7 June 1576; Yepes, *Etnografía*, lib. 3 cap 6: 40; Junker, *Raiding*, 271–272; Reid, *Southeast Asia*, 1: 109; Scott, *Barangay*, 55.

52. Yepes, *Etnografía*, lib. 3 cap 6: 40, 42.

53. Chirino, *Relación*, 8, 240; Morga, *Sucesos*, 263.

54. Quirino and García, "Manners," 397–398, 412 plates 7–9, 11; Yepes, *Etnografía*, lib. 3 cap. 6: 37–39, cap. 7: 43–45.

55. Echevarría, *Rediscovery in Southern Cebu*, 20–77; Fenner, *Cebu*, 18–19; Junker, *Raiding*, 269.

56. AGI PAT 23-7 and BR 3: 203 Diego de Artieda, no date; McCoy, "The Queen Dies Slowly," 301.

57. Hutterer, "Evolution of Philippine Lowland Societies," 295–296; Junker, *Raiding*, 22–23, 222–231. For a colonial account of this pattern, see Yepes, *Etnografía*, lib. 4 cap. 1: 158. For the Bais-Tanjay region see Junker, *Raiding*, 113–118.

58. Scott, *Cracks*, 88.

59. AGI PAT 23-9 and BR 5: 67–71 Miguel de Loarca [1582].

60. Yepes, *Etnografía*, lib. 4 cap. 1: 160.

61. AGI PAT 23-9 and BR 5: 49 Miguel de Loarca [1582]; Yepes, *Etnografía*, lib. 4 cap. 1: 158–162.

62. *CDIU* 3: 459 Miguel de Legazpi, no date. "de dos en dos en 6 en 10."

63. Yepes, *Etnografía*, lib. 4 cap. 3; Quirino and García, "Manners," 409; Pigafetta, *First Voyage*, 50. See also Junker, *Raiding*, 145–164, and Scott, *Barangay*, 57–62.

64. Pagès, *Travels*, 1: 187.

65. Quirino and García, "Manners," 410.

66. Scott, *Barangay*, 129. For contemporary accounts, see Morga, *Sucesos*, 271–272; Quirino and García, "Manners," 407; Yepes, *Etnografía*, lib. 4 cap. 8: 207.

67. AGI PAT 23-9 and BR 5: 147–149 Miguel de Loarca [1582].

68. Scott, "Oripun," 140–141.

69. AGI PAT 23-9 and BR 5: 143–147 Miguel de Loarca [1582]; Quirino and García, "Manners," 414–415; Chirino, *Relación*, 363–364. See Scott, "Oripun," 142–145, and *Barangay*, 133–135, and Aguilar, *Clash of Spirits*, 68–69, for recent discussions of the nature of slavery in the Visayas.

70. BR 3:55 Miguel de Legazpi, no date [1567]; AGI PAT 23-7 and BR 3: 197–198 Diego de Artieda, no date; BR 3: 287 Guido de Lavezaris [1575]; AGI AF 84-4 and Rodríguez, *Historia*, 14: 185–186 Martín de Herrada 21 June 1574; Rodríguez, *Historia*, 14: 477–479 Rada 16 July 1577; AGI PAT 23-9 and BR 5: 116–117 Miguel de Loarca [1582]; Quirino and García, "Manners," 407; Chirino, *Relación*, 120–121, 363–364; Yepes, *Etnografía*, lib. 4 cap. 5: 186–190, caps. 10–11: 218–230; Morga, *Sucesos*, 272; Scott, *Barangay*, 153; Junker, *Raiding*, 344, 384–385.

71. AGI AF 84-4 and Rodríguez, *Historia*, 14: 185 Martín de Herrada 21 June 1574; Rodríguez, *Historia*, 14: 479 Rada 16 July 1577.

72. AGI PAT 23-9 and BR 5: 134–135 Miguel de Loarca [1582]; Quirino and García, "Manners," 404, 415–416.

73. AGI PAT 25-45 Breve sumario 1593; Yepes, *Etnografía*, lib. 4 cap. 5: 184–185 cap. 8: 207.

74. Chirino, *Relación*, 121, 364.

75. Reid, *Southeast Asia*, 1: 160.

76. Alcina, *Historia*, lib. 4 cap. 13: 205.

77. Jocano, *The Philippines*, 31.

78. Boomgaard, *Children of the Colonial State*, 143–145.

79. AGI PAT 23-9 and BR 5: 158–161 Miguel de Loarca [1582]; Scott, *Barangay*, 140.

80. Chirino, *Relación*, 319–322; Yepes, *Etnografía*, lib. 4 cap. 12: 231–236.

81. AGI PAT 23-9 and BR 5: 144–145, 154–155 Miguel de Loarca [1582].

82. Ibabao was the eastern part of the island of Samar.

83. Yepes, *Etnografía*, lib. 4 cap. 12: 242.

84. AGI PAT 23-9 and BR 5: 157–159 Miguel de Loarca [1582]; Quirino and García, "Manners," 410–411; Morga, *Sucesos*, 275; Phelan, *Hispanization*, 19; Scott, *Barangay*, 141.

85. Chirino, *Relación*, 82, 321; Morga, *Sucesos*, 275; Yepes, *Etnografía*, lib. 4 cap. 14: 252; Colin, *Labor evangélica*, 2: 126.

86. AGI PAT 23-9 and BR 5: 118–119 Miguel de Loarca [1582]; Pigafetta, *First Voyage*, 58; Yepes, *Etnografía*, lib. 4 cap. 14: 253.

87. Chirino, *Relación*, 81, 219, 326.

88. Jocano, *The Philippines*, 31.

89. *CDIU* 3: 461 Miguel de Legazpi, no date; AGI PAT 23-9 and BR 5: 116–119 Miguel de Loarca [1582]; Pigafetta, *First Voyage*, 58; Morga, *Sucesos*, 278; Quirino and García, "Manners," 417–418; Cavendish, "Admirable and Prosperous Voyage," 42; Alcina, *Historia*, lib. 1 cap. 4: 13.

90. Brown et al., *Penis Inserts*, 11–12, 20.

91. Yepes, *Etnografía*, lib. 3 cap. 23: 144.

92. Morga, *Sucesos*, 278.

93. Alcina, *Historia*, lib. 1 cap. 4: 13.

94. Carletti, *Voyage around the World*, 83–84.

95. Appell, "Penis Pin," 205.

96. For a brief review of these practices in the Philippines, see Pedrosa, "Abortion and Infanticide."

97. AGI PAT 23-9 and BR 5: 118–119 Miguel de Loarca [1582].

98. Quirino and García, "Manners," 413; Rodríguez, *Historia*, 14: 481 Martín de Rada 16 July 1577.

99. Rodríguez, *Historia*, 14: 481 Martín de Rada 16 July 1577; Colin, *Labor evangélica*, 2: 149.

100. Yepes, *Etnografía*, lib. 3 cap. 23: 143–144.

101. Quirino and García, "Manners," 427.

102. Reid, "Low Population Growth," 39–41, and *Southeast Asia*, 1: 161–162.

103. Quirino and García, "Manners," 413.

104. Yepes, *Etnografía*, lib. 3 cap. 17: 110.

105. Reid, "Low Population Growth," 38.

106. Legazpi had license to take between 300 and 350 soldiers and sailors (*CDIU* 2: 146 Instructions to Miguel de Legazpi 1 Sept. 1564; *CDIU* 2: 374–375 Relación muy circunstanciada . . . Esteban Rodríguez [1565]).

107. The 1567 expedition brought 200 soldiers to reinforce the garrison.

108. Morales Maza, *Augustinians*, 47.

109. Morales Maza, *Augustinians*, 79–82.

110. AGI PAT 24-9 Juan de Alva 28 July 1570.

111. AGI PAT 24-9 and Rodríguez, *Historia*, 14: 41–42 Martin de Rada 21 July 1570.

112. AGI PAT 24-23 and Rodríguez, *Historia*, 14: 118 Miguel de Legazpi 11 Aug. 1572. For the authority to distribute *encomiendas*, see AGI AF 339 lib. 1 fols. 1v–2v and BR 34: 235–255 Real cédula 16 Nov. 1568.

113. AGI PAT 24-19 Hernando Riquel 2 June 1576.

114. BR 5: 40–43, 67–68 Miguel de Loarca 1582; AGI AF 74 and BR 7: 42–43 Domingo de Salazar 25 June 1588.

115. ARSI Phil 10 fols. 104–107 Mateo Sánchez 12 Apr. 1603.

116. Hidalgo Nuchera, *Encomienda*, 212–224.

117. AGI PAT 23-21, and Rodríguez, *Historia*, 14: 228 No author 17 Sept. 1574; San Agustín, *Conquistas*, lib. 2 cap. 8: 358, lib. 3 cap. 5: 604; Colin, *Labor evangélica*, 1: 176; Tantuico, *Leyte*, 116; Regalado and Franco, *History of Panay*, 122.

118. Costa, *Jesuits*, 145; Colin, *Labor evangélica*, 2: 152.

119. AGI AF 18B and BR 11: 33–35 Autos para el buen gobierno 7 Jan. 1598.

120. ARSI Phil 10 fols. 104–107 Mateo Sánchez 12 Apr. 1603.

121. San Agustín, *Conquistas*, lib. 1 cap. 27: 191–193, lib. 2 cap. 9: 363, lib. 2 cap. 22: 439. In 1580 another convent was established at Tanjay to cover the east coast (San Agustín, *Conquistas*, lib. 2 cap. 36: 363). See also Martíñez Cuesta, *History of Negros*, 34–35.

122. AGI AF 74, Rodríguez, *Historia*, 15: 364, 366 and BR 7: 47–48 Domingo de Salazar 25 June 1588. In fact the Augustinians undertook some work in Leyte in the early 1580s (San Agustín, *Conquistas*, lib. 2 cap. 36: 533; Rodríguez, *Historia*, 15: 364n 1705; Tantuico, *Leyte*, 117).

123. Rodríguez, *Historia*, 1: 168.

124. Rodríguez, *Historia*, 1: 300. The others were in Mindoro (2) and Bantayan (1).

125. AGI PAT 25-38 Relación punctual de las encomiendas 31 May 1591.

126. AGI AF 79, BR 9: 95–115 and Rodríguez, *Historia*, 1: 339–342 Francisco de Ortega, no date [ca. 1594].

127. AGI AF 339 lib. 2 fol. 49r and BR 9: 120–121 Real cédula 27 Apr. 1594.

128. ARSI Phil 9 fols. 293–294 Antonio Sedeño 19 June 1594.

129. NL Ayer 1342 Extracto y noticia, no date [1596].

130. Pigafetta, *First Voyage*, 35–43.

131. *CDI* 14: 158–160 Gerónimo de Santisteban 22 Jan. 1547.

132. *CDIU* 2: 264 and Rodríguez, *Historia*, 14: 445 Relación circunstanciada [1565]; *CDIU* 2: 403 Esteban Rodríguez [1565].

133. *CDIU* 3: 160–162, 165–166, 212 Relación muy circunstanciada [1567].

134. AGI PAT 24-19 Hernando Riquel 2 June 1576. Tantuico (*Leyte*, 115) suggests the following communities were assigned: Marakaya, Ormok, Kalbakan, Suod, Kanamokan, Hilongos, and the region at the mouth of the rivers of Belugu, Palu, Vito, Makay, Vinkay, Hinunangan, Hinundayan, Kabalain, and Minaya.

135. AGI PAT 23-9 and BR 5: 49–51 Miguel de Loarca [1582].

136. AGI AF 74, BR 7: 47 and Rodríguez, *Historia*, 15: 364 Domingo de Salazar 25 June 1588.

137. AGI PAT 25-38 Relación punctual de las encomiendas 31 May 1591. These figures include the islands of Panaon, Maripipi, and Maçagua.

138. AGI AF 79 and BR 9: 96 Francisco de Ortega, no date [ca. 1594].

139. ARSI Phil 9 fols. 293–294 Antonio Sedeño 19 June 1594.

140. ARSI Phil 5 fols. 1–33 Diego Sánchez 27 June 1597. See also Chirino, *Relación*, 309.

141. ARSI Phil 10 fol. 17 Juan de Ribera 21 June 1600; ARSI Phil 5 fols. 75–92 Juan de Ribera 1 June 1601. Colin, *Labor evangélica*, 2: 122, rounds this to “más de 30,000 ánimas.”

142. ARSI Phil 10 fols. 26–27 Diego García 7 July 1600. Of this number only 4,946 had been baptized.

143. Colin, *Labor evangélica*, 2: 135–136.

144. AGI PAT 24-19 Hernando Riquel 2 June 1576. Paita was later recorded as being in Ibabao (AGI PAT 25-38 N27 Relación punctual de las encomiendas 31 May 1591).

145. AGI PAT 23-9 and BR 5: 54–59 Miguel de Loarca [1582].

146. AGI AF 74, BR 7: 48 and Rodríguez, *Historia*, 15: 366 Domingo de Salazar 25 June 1588.

147. AGI AF 29 Memoria y lista de encomiendas [1606]. Bishop Ortega suggested lower figures of 3,000 and 800 *tributantes* for Samar and Ibabao respectively in 1594 (AGI AF 79 and BR 9: 98 Francisco de Ortega, no date).

148. ARSI Phil 10 fols. 26–27 Diego García 7 July 1600.

149. Chirino, *Relación*, 83–83, 322–323; Colin, *Labor evangélica*, 2: 143n.

150. Díaz Arenas, *Memorias históricas*, cuaderno 5. In 1849, 25,964 people, or 25 percent of the island's population, was living in the "montes."

151. Pigafetta, *First Voyage*, 67.

152. *CDIU* 2: 408 Esteban Rodríguez [1565].

153. The numbers contained in different reports vary slightly (AGI PAT 23-24, AF 29-1 and BR 2: 184 Oficiales reales 28 May 1565, PAT 23-17 15 Apr. 1565 Información en la isla de Bohol 25 Mar. 1565; BR 2: 208 Miguel de Legazpi [1565]; AGI AF 34 Andrés de Mirandaola 28 May 1565, PAT 26-13 and *CDIU* 2: 293–295 Relación circunstanciada [1565]; San Agustín, *Conquistas*, lib.1 cap. 2: 157.

154. Yepes, *Etnografía*, lib. 4 cap. 1: 160.

155. ARSI Phil 5 fols. 75–92 Juan de Ribera 1 June 1601; ARSI Phil 14 fols. 23–24 Valerio Ledesma 28 Apr. 1601.

156. AGI PAT 24-19 Hernando Riquel 2 June 1576.

157. AGI PAT 23-9 and BR 5: 45–46 Miguel de Loarca [1582]

158. Chirino, *Relación*, 94. See also ARSI Phil 5 fols. 1–33 Diego Sánchez 27 June 1597.

159. ARSI Phil 10 fols. 26–27 Diego García 7 July 1600. In an earlier letter he suggests there were more than 8,000 *almas* (ARSI Phil 10 fols. 5–12 Diego García 8 June 1600).

160. ARSI Phil 5 fols. 171–194 Gregorio López 5 June 1605.

161. Chirino, *Relación*, 93, 333.

162. Colin, *Labor evangélica*, 1: 35, 2: 152.

163. Pigafetta, *First Voyage*, 43, 52–53.

164. *CDIU* 2: 323 Relación circunstanciada . . . [1565].

165. *CDIU* 2: 418 Esteban Rodríguez [1565].

166. *CDIU* 3: 159 Relación muy circunstaciada [1567].

167. AGI PAT 23-16 no author, no date; *CDIU* 2: 322 Relación circunstanciada . . . [1565].

168. AGI PAT 24-19 Hernando Riquel 2 June 1576.

169. AGI PAT 24-23 Miguel de Legazpi 11 Aug. 1572.

170. AGI PAT 24-25 Relación del descubrimiento 20 Apr. 1572. The term used was "mal poblada."

171. AGI AF 84-2 no author, no date [1572].

172. AGI PAT 23-9 and BR 5: 38–49 Miguel de Loarca [1582].

173. VanderMeer, "Population Patterns," 320.

174. VanderMeer, "Population Patterns," 319–320.

175. See VanderMeer, "Population Patterns," 322. AGI AF 6 and BR 4: 70 Francisco de Sande 7 June 1576, refers to land as "pobre," BR 18: 103 Pedro de Bivero 1618 comments it was "rugged and mountainous," and Alcina, *Historia*, lib. 1 cap. 5: 14, just refers to Cebu being less fertile than Panay.

176. AGI AF 6 and BR 2: 241 Miguel de Legazpi 26 June 1568.

177. Cullinane and Xenos, "Growth of Population," 85–87.

178. AGI PAT 23-9 and BR 5: 38–49 Miguel de Loarca [1582].

179. AGI AF 79 and BR 9: 97 Francisco de Ortega, no date [ca. 1594]. This figure omits Bantayan.

180. AGI AF 79 and BR 9: 95–119 Francisco de Ortega, no date [ca. 1594].

181. AGI PAT 23-21 and Rodríguez, *Historia*, 14: 222 Relación de la orden [17 Sept. 1574]. See also *CDIU* 2: 334 Relación circunstanciada . . . [1565]; AGI PAT 24-16 and Rodríguez, *Historia*, 14: 38 Diego de Herrera 16 Jan. 1570.

182. Cullinane and Xenos, "Growth of Population," 94, 105.

183. VanderMeer, "Population Patterns," 325.

184. See Appendix D.

185. San Agustín, *Conquistas*, lib. 2 cap. 11: 377.

186. See, for example, *CDIU* 3: 153, 188 Relación muy circunstaciada [1567].

187. AGI PAT 24-9 and Rodríguez, *Historia*, 14: 41–42 Martín de Rada 21 July 1570. The Bay of Ibalon is Sorsogón in Bikol.

188. AGI PAT 23-21 and Rodríguez, *Historia*, 14: 222–224 No author 17 Sept. 1574. A slave was only worth 0.5 *fanega* or less of rice.

189. AGI PAT 24-25 and BR 3: 170 Relación del descubrimiento 20 Apr. 1572.

190. AGI PAT 23-21 and Rodríguez, *Historia*, 14: 223–224 No author 17 Sept. 1574.

191. Abuses resulted in three *encomenderos* being murdered prior to 1576 and in two revolts in Antique in the 1580s (AGI PAT 24-19 Hernando Riquel 2 June 1576; Regalado and Franco, *History of Panay*, 122).

192. Of the total of 22,990 in Panay, 2,850 were under the Crown and 8,700 were in *encomiendas* for which a figure was given in 1571 (AGI PAT 25-38 Relación punctual de las encomiendas 31 May 1591).

193. AGI AF 84-2 No author, no date [1572]. However, he also noted there had been reports of 50,000 in other rivers and estuaries, and on the coast of Otón there were 50,000 "indios."

194. AGI PAT 23-9 and BR 5: 68–79 Miguel de Loarca [1582].

195. AGI AF 79 and BR 9: 97 Francisco de Ortega [ca. 1594].

196. *CDIU* 2: 411 Esteban Rodríguez [1565]. Possibly present-day Zamboanguita (Martínez Cuesta, *History of Negros*, 28).

197. *CDIU* 3: 129–135, 222 Relación muy circunstanciada [1567].

198. AGI PAT 24-19 Hernando Riquel 2 June 1576. Colin, *Labor evangélica*, 1: 157–158, omits an *encomienda* to Francisco Téllez of 2,000 Indians. Martínez Cuesta, *History of Negros*, 31, incorrectly gives the figures as eleven *encomiendas* of 2,000.

199. AGI PAT 23-9 and BR 5: 47–48 Miguel de Loarca [1582]; San Agustín, *Conquistas*, lib. 2 cap. 36: 533.

200. AGI PAT 24-25 Relación del descubrimiento 20 Apr. 1572.
201. AGI PAT 23-9 and BR 5: 46–48 Miguel de Loarca [1582].
202. AGI AF 74 and Rodríguez, *Historia*, 15: 363 Domingo de Salazar 25 June 1588; Rodríguez, *Historia*, 1: 300.
203. AGI AF 74 and Rodríguez, *Historia*, 15: 363 Domingo de Salazar 25 June 1588.
204. AGI AF 79 and BR 9: 96–97 Francisco de Ortega, no date [ca. 1594]
205. Martínez Cuesta, *History of Negros*, 38.
206. AGI PAT 25-38 Relación punctual de las encomiendas 31 May 1591.
207. ARSI Phil 10 fols. 26–27 Diego García 7 July 1600; Colin, *Labor evangélica*, 1: 402, 2: 289; Costa, *Jesuits*, 186–187.
208. Martínez Cuesta, *History of Negros*, 7.
209. Reid, "Low Population Growth," 36, and *Southeast Asia*, 1: 14.
210. Reid, "Low Population Growth," 37–43, and *Southeast Asia*, 1: 15–18.
211. AGI 6 and BR 2: 241 Miguel de Legazpi 26 June 1568, PAT 24-16 Diego de Herrera 16 Jan. 1570, AF6 and BR 4: 70 Francisco de Sande 7 June 1576, PAT 23-9 and BR 5: 116–117 Miguel de Loarca [1582], AF 84-4 and BR 34: 391 Relation of the Philippine Islands [1586].
212. Chirino, *Relación*, 258; Morga, *Sucesos*, 249.
213. Tabangui and Pasco, "Control of *Schistosomiasis japonica*," 302–308.
214. Newson, "Disease and Immunity," 1839.
215. Russell, *Malaria*, 9; Salazar et al., "Malaria Situation in the Philippines," 709.
216. VanderMeer, "Population Patterns," 333–334.
217. See chapter 2.
218. Yepes, *Etnografía*, lib. 3 cap. 24: 149.
219. ARSI Phil 5 fols. 1–33 Diego Sánchez 27 June 1597.
220. Reid, *Southeast Asia*, 1: 50.
221. Marcy, "Factors Affecting the Fecundity," 309.
222. *Recopilación* 2 lib. 6 tit. 1 ley 3: 190 Real cédula 17 Apr. 1581.
223. Henley, *Food, Fertility and Fever*, 370–373; Henley, "Population and the Means of Subsistence," 365–368. See also Boomgaard, "Human Capital, Slavery and Low Rates of Economic and Population Growth," 92.

Chapter 6: Wars and Missionaries in the Seventeenth-Century Visayas

1. Morales Maza, *Augustinians*, 233–234.
2. NL Ayer 1449 (Box) Razón de los pueblos . . . Pedro Velasco 16 Apr. 1760.
3. BR 9: 150–153 Papal bull 17 June 1595.
4. Gemelli Careri, *Voyage around the World*, 442; Le Gentil, *Voyage*, 138; Fenner, *Cebu*, 36–38.
5. Cullinane, "The Changing Nature of the Cebu Urban Elite," 255.
6. PNA Patronatos Unclassified (Bound vol.) Pedro Martínez 18 Oct. 1785; PNA Patronatos Unclassified (Bound vol.) Franciscan Provincial 19 Sept. 1785.
7. Cavada y Méndez de Vigo, *Historia geográfica*, 2: 325.
8. PNA Patronatos Unclassified (Bound vol.) Thomás de Aquino 19 Oct. 1785.
9. AGI AF 6 and BR 5: 24 Gonzalo Ronquillo de Peñalosa 16 June 1582, AF 74 and Rodríguez, *Historia*, 15: 358–359 Domingo de Salazar 25 June 1588; San Agustín, *Conquistas*, lib. 2 cap. 11: 376.

10. San Agustín, *Conquistas*, lib. 2 cap 37: 545.

11. Prieto Lucena, *Manrique de Lara*, 137–138.

12. BR 27: 126–134 Juan Grau y Monfalcón 1637; see also Prieto Lucena, *Manrique de Lara* 102–103, 134.

13. Prieto Lucena, *Manrique de Lara*, 102, 134. Even in 1739 there were 200 Spanish soldiers and 100 Pampangans, and a coastguard of 96 *forzados* (BR 47: 86–160 Fernando Valdés Tamón 1739).

14. San Agustín, *Conquistas*, lib. 3 cap. 25: 719.

15. AGI AF 30 Oficiales reales 7 Sept. 1627

16. NL Ayer 1300 VA IV: 335–408 Jose Antonio Niño de Villavicencio 4 Feb. 1738.

17. Schurz, *Manila Galleon*, 195–196. Others were built at Masbate, Marinduque, Mindoro, and in Pangasinan.

18. Tantuico, *Leyte*, 154. See also Costa, *Jesuits*, 290, 343; Chirino, *Relación*, 206, 459.

19. AGI AF 76 and BR 4: 7 Francisco de Sande 7 June 1576, PAT 23-9 and BR 5: 70–77 Miguel de Loarca [1582]; Morga, *Sucesos*, 268.

20. San Antonio, *Philippine Chronicles*, 87; Martínez de Zúñiga, *Estadismo* 2: 88.

21. San Agustín, *Conquistas*, lib. 2 cap. 11: 375; Medina, *Historia*, 85.

22. AGI AF 329 lib. 2 fols. 83r–85r and BR 17: 81 Real cédula 26 May 1609, AF 340 lib 3 fols. 63v–64r Real cédula 29 May 1620.

23. AGI AF 27 and BR 18: 297 Fernando de los Ríos Coronel 1619–1620; Lilly Philippine Ms II Informe sobre varios abusos, no date; Colin, *Labor evangélica*, 2: 390; Calvo, *Joseph Calvo*, 45.

24. AGI PAT 23-9 and BR 5: 66–67 Miguel de Loarca [1582].

25. BR 18: 102 Pedro de Bivero 1618.

26. Colin, *Labor evangélica*, 1: 39; San Antonio, *Philippine Chronicles*, 87, 89; Martínez de Zúñiga, *Estadismo*, 2: 88; Martínez Cuesta, *History of Negros*, 130; Reyes y Florentino, *Islas Visayas*, 10.

27. AGI AF 9-13 Información hecha . . . de los tratos 1650; Martínez Zúñiga, *Estadismo*, 2: 96; San Antonio, *Philippine Chronicles*, 101.

28. Spencer, "Rise of Maize," 9–15; VanderMeer, "Populations Patterns," 328; Cullinane and Xenos, "Growth of Population," 98–99.

29. Díaz, *Conquistas*, 270–271.

30. Some observers doubted the veracity of this account (San Agustín, *Conquistas*, lib. 2 cap. 11: 376n1).

31. Costa, *Jesuits*, 275–276.

32. Martínez Zúñiga, *Estadismo*, 2: 90.

33. Medina, *Historia*, 36 [1630].

34. Cullinane, "The Changing Nature of the Cebu Urban Elite," 254.

35. Fenner, *Cebu*, 42–43.

36. At the beginning of the nineteenth century the Augustinians possessed two estates consisting of 22,000 acres (Cullinane, "The Changing Nature of the Cebu Urban Elite," 254).

37. Cushner and Larkin, "Royal Land Grants," 105.

38. Aguilar, *Clash of Spirits*, 75. This practice was noted elsewhere in the Philippines, but not specifically in the Visayas.

39. AGI AF 19-7 Testimonio sobre la tasación 28 Sept. 1604, AF 8-5 and BR 22: 255–268 Juan Niño de Tavora 4 Aug. 1628.

40. For later *tasaciones* see AGI AF 296 Certificación de los oficiales reales 13 July 1709.

41. AGI PAT 24-29 and BR 3: 268 Martín de Rada 21 June 1574; Rodríguez, *Historia*, 14: 493 Martín de Rada 16 July 1577. This was also implicit in Guido de Lavezaris's original *tasación*.

42. AGI AF 8-5 and BR 22: 255–268 Juan Niño de Tavora 4 Aug. 1628.

43. AGI AF 27 and BR 18: 316 Hernando de los Ríos Coronel 1619–1620.

44. AGI AF PAT 25-16 Vargas 15 June 1584 only partially transcribed in BR 6: 47–53; AGI AF 6 and Retana, *Archivo del bibliófilo filipino*, 3: 4–8 Domingo de Salazar 1583.

45. AGI AF 7-53 and BR 18: 130 Alonso Fajardo de Tença 10 Aug. 1618, AF 27 and BR 18: 316 Hernando de los Ríos Coronel 1619–1620.

46. Yepes, *Etnografía*, lib. 3 cap. 20: 125.

47. Díaz, *Conquistas*, 133; Murillo Velarde, *Historia*, 17–18; Costa, *Jesuits*, 315.

48. Díaz, *Conquistas*, 517; Costa, *Jesuits*, 412–413.

49. Warren, *Sulu Zone, 1768–1898*, 166–168; Owen, "Kabikolan," 39; Cruikshank, "Moro Impact," 152.

50. Murillo Velarde, *Historia*, 48; Junker, "Trade Competition," 249.

51. Cruikshank, "Moro Impact," 153.

52. Yepes, *Etnografía*, lib. 3 cap. 10: 67; Combés, *Historia*, 62; Scott, *Barangay*, 63, and *Cracks*, 79.

53. Warren, *Sulu Zone, 1768–1898*, 208. See also Appendix B.

54. Majul, *Muslims*, 121.

55. Colin, *Labor evangélica*, 1: 207n Gregorio López June 1607.

56. AGI AF 20 and Colin, *Labor evangélica*, 3: 168 Juan Manuel de la Vega 28 Aug. 1608.

57. Jesús, *Historia general*, 31.

58. NL Ayer 1300 fol. 152 and BR 19: 264 Fernando de los Ríos Coronel 1621. They were employed as domestic servants, agricultural laborers, and to enhance Magindanao's military power (Majul, *Muslims*, 123, 166).

59. Cummins, *Travels and Controversies*, 123.

60. AGI AF 8-82 and BR 27: 346 Sebastián Hurtado de Corcuera 20 Aug. 1637.

61. Torrubia, *Dissertación*, 49, refers to Bishop Miguel García Serrano, but since the date is 1635 it should be Hernando Guerrero. See Barrantes, *Guerras piráticas*, 232–233; Montero y Vidal, *Piratería*, 1: 71, 2:166.

62. NL Ayer MS 1300 VA I: 551–607 Relación . . . desde el mes de Julio hasta el de 1628.

63. Barrantes, *Guerras piráticas*, 233.

64. Warren, *Sulu Zone, 1768–1898*, 208.

65. Barrantes, *Guerras pirácticas*, 161; Montero y Vidal, *Piratería*, 2: 358; Saleeby, *History of Sulu*, 191.

66. Forrest, *Voyage*, 330.

67. Montero y Vidal, *Piratería*, 1: 172. See also Pagès (*Travels*, 1: 219).

68. Warren, *Sulu Zone, 1768–1898*, 170–171, refers to letter of the provincial of the Recollects in AGI AF 627 18 May 1772.

69. Cruikshank, "Moro Impact," 154.

70. Barrantes, *Guerras piráticas*, 43–44.

71. Cruikshank, "Moro Impact," 159–160.

72. Colin, *Labor evangélica*, 1: 207.

73. ARSI Phil 10 fols. 26–27 Diego García 7 July 1600.

74. ARSI Phil 10 fols. 65–68 Diego García 25 June 1601; Colin, *Labor evangélica*, 1: 207; Montero y Vidal, *Historia general*, 1: 518; Cruikshank, *Samar*, 89–90.

75. Cruikshank, *Samar*, 92.

76. NL Ayer 1300 VA I: 403–405 Valerio de Ledesma 20 Aug. 1616; Colin, *Labor evangélica*, 3: 563; Pagès, *Travels*, 1: 192.

77. Barrantes, *Guerras piráticas*, 132.

78. PNA Patronatos Unclassified (Bound vol.) Thomás de Aquino 19 Oct. 1785.

79. ARSI Phil 5 fols. 1–33 letra anua 1595 and 1596 Diego Sánchez 27 June 1597; Costa, *Jesuits*, 134.

80. AGI AF 18B and BR 9: 193–194 Gómez Pérez Dasmariñas 6 Dec. 1595.

81. Colin, *Labor evangélica*, 2: 134–140n; Chirino, *Relación*, 79, 316–317; Costa, *Jesuits*, 160–61.

82. Colin, *Labor evangélica*, 2: 133n Francisco Váez, carta anua for 1598–1599.

83. ARSI Phil 5 fols. 1–33 Diego Sánchez 27 June 1597; Colin, *Labor evangélica*, 2: 143n; Chirino, *Relación*, 83–84, 323.

84. Colin, *Labor evangélica*, 2: 144–145; Chirino, *Relación*, 85–86, 324–325; Costa, *Jesuits*, 290.

85. ARSI Phil 5 fols.1–33 Diego Sánchez 27 June 1597; Costa, *Jesuits*, 164–165; Chirino, *Relación*, 177–186, 428–437.

86. ARSI Phil 10 fols. 26–27 Diego García 7 July 1600.

87. ARSI Phil 9 fols. 372–375 Diego García 10 July 1599. See also Phil 12 fols. 138–148 Alejo López 1690.

88. ARSI Phil 10 fols. 104–107 Mateo Sánchez 12 Apr. 1603.

89. Costa, *Jesuits*, 171.

90. ARSI Phil 10 fols. 5–12 Diego García 8 June 1600; Costa, *Jesuits*, 184–187. Palo and Dulag were merged at Dulag, and Carigara, Alangalang and Ogmuc at Alangalang.

91. ARSI Phil 11 fols. 19–22 Adriano Cortés 16 May 1612.

92. Costa, *Jesuits*, 264.

93. ARSI Phil 12 fols. 1–12 Ignacio Alcina 24 June 1660.

94. Costa, *Jesuits*, 242 (1610–1651), 438 (1659–1696).

95. In 1617 Mateo Sánchez, one of the first Jesuits to serve in the Visayas, compiled one of the islands' earliest dictionaries—*Vocabulario de la lengua Bisaya*—while based in Dagami in Leyte.

96. Colin, *Labor evangélica*, 2: 138n–140n.

97. Colin, *Labor evangélica*, 2: 126–130; Costa, *Jesuits*, 159, 312, 316.

98. BR 17: 65–66 Annuae literae societatis Jesu (Dilingae) 1610.

99. Colin, *Labor evangélica*, 1: 27.

100. ARSI Phil 5 fols. 75–92 Juan de Ribera 1 June 1601.

101. Chirino, *Relación*, 80, 318. In the English version "dote" is translated as "dowry," whereas it was bridewealth. Chirino's comment may relate to the practice of dividing bridewealth in the case of divorce.

102. Chirino, *Relación*, 364.

103. Yepes, *Etnografía*, lib. 4 cap. 5: 184–185, cap. 8: 207.

104. Cruikshank, *Samar*, 87–88, and "Moro Impact," 148.

105. Pagès, *Travels*, 199.

106. Cruikshank, "Moro Impact," 159–160, 165–166.

107. ARSI Phil 5 fols. 75–92 Juan de Ribera 1 June 1601, Phil 14 fols. 23–24 Valerio de Ledesma 28 Apr. 1601.

108. PNA Patronatos Unclassified (Bound vol.) Thomás de Aquino 19 Oct. 1785; Luengo, *History of the Philippines*, 120–132.

109. Lilly Philippine Ms II Bishop Miguel Lino de Ezpeleta 8 Sept. 1769.

110. PNA Patronatos Unclassified (Bound vol.) Franciscan provincial 12 Sept. 1785; Díaz Arenas, *Memorias históricas*, cuaderno 5.

111. ARSI Phil 10 fols. 26–27 Diego García 7 July 1600; Phil 11 fols. 115–118 Historiae Provinciae Philippinarum 15 July 1620.

112. Colin, *Labor evangélica*, 3: 795 Razón del número de religiosos . . . 1656.

113. ARSI Phil 2 I fols. 412–415, II fols. 314–317, Phil 14 fols. 106–121 Catologus christianorum.

114. The tributary population declined from 18,895.5 to 17,232 between 1750 and 1792. See Appendix D.

115. PNA Patronatos Unclassified (Bound vol.) Provincial of Franciscans 12 Sept. 1785.

116. Colin, *Labor evangélica*, 1: 35, 3: 791.

117. ARSI Phil 14 fols. 28–29 Diego Laurencio 4 Apr. 1606

118. Colin, *Labor evangélica*, 1: 34.

119. San Antonio, *Philippine Chronicles*, 91.

120. Rodríguez, *Historia*, 15: 360nn 1672, 1675.

121. AGI AF 20 Memoria delos conventos y ministerios [1610]; Redondo y Sendino, *Breve reseña*, 29–32.

122. Rodríguez, *Historia*, 2: 72–74 Pedro de Arce July 1626.

123. Regalado and Franco, *History of Panay*, 115–116.

124. San Agustín, *Conquistas*, lib. 3 cap. 28: 734–775; Díaz, *Conquistas*, 643–644; Morales Maza, *Augustinians*, 186–187.

125. Morales Maza, *Augustinians*, 199.

126. Costa, *Jesuits*, 466–467. In the late 1660s some *mundos* wished to establish independent communities under Jesuit jurisdiction, and with official agreement an estimated 3,000 began settling near Suaraga and Bongol, where the Jesuits possessed estates. Subsequently the bishop changed his mind and the Augustinians rightly claimed they were fugitives from their administration.

127. AGI AF 71 Testimonio sobre la pretensión de los indios llamados mundos 1696.

128. AGI AF 293 Bishop of Cebu 20 Aug. 1733; Martínez Zúñiga, *Estadismo*, 2: 93.

129. Rodríguez, *Historia*, 2: 391 Sebastián de Foronda 1714.

130. Rodríguez, *Historia*, 2: 72–74 Pedro de Arce July 1626; Aragón, *Estados de la población de Filipinas*. Between 1626 and 1714 the parishes of Aklan, Ibahay, and Ajuy were secularized. In 1626 together these had had 2,400 *tributos*, or just under 20 percent of the total of 12,700 recorded.

131. AGI AF 20 Memoria delos conventos y ministerios [1610]; Rodríguez, *Historia*, 2: 72–74 Pedro de Arce July 1626; Rodríguez, *Historia*, 2: 391 Sebastián de Foronda 1714.

132. AGI AF 71 Testimonio sobre la pretensión de los indios llamados mundos 1696.

133. Díaz, *Conquistas*, 35.

134. San Agustín, *Conquistas*, lib. 2 cap. 11: 377; Redondo y Sendino, *Breve reseña*, 138. These sources do not indicate whether this population was in Augustinian parishes only, but the figures are consistent with those contained in other Augustinian sources.

135. NL Ayer 1449 (Box) Razón de los pueblos . . . Pedro Velasco 1760 and BL Additional Mss. 13,976 Lista de los conventos y ministerios . . . Valladolid 1765. Since only children of non-tributary age are included, the ratio is not indicative of completed family size.

136. PNA Erección de pueblos Antique 1783–1897 Book 1 Nicolás de la Concepción 17 Oct. 1797.

137. Montero y Vidal, *Piratería*, 1: 355–356; Regalado and Franco, *History of Panay*, 134.

138. PNA Erección de pueblos Antique 1783–1897 Book 1 Nicolás de la Concepción 17 Oct. 1797.

139. Martínez de Zúñiga, *Estadismo*, 2: 96–97.

140. Morales Maza, *Augustinians*, 237.

141. Díaz Arenas, *Memoria históricas*, cuaderno 5. In 1870 there were 15,845 *almas* belonging to independent tribes in Antique and 4,700 in Capiz; the number in Iloilo was not recorded (Cavada y Méndez de Vigo, *Historia geográfica*, 2: 88, 97).

142. Cordoniu y Nieto, *Topografía médica*, 321–322.

143. PNA Memorias medicas. Memoria sanitaria . . . 1895. See also Cavada y Méndez de Vigo, *Historia geográfica*, 2: 88, 97, 110.

144. De Bevoise, *Agents*, 102–104.

145. Corpuz, *Roots*, 542.

146. ARSI Phil 10 fols. 26–27 Diego García 7 July 1600; Medina, *Historia*, 137; Cullinane and Xenos, "Growth of Population," 91–92.

147. Colin, *Labor evangélica*, 2: 406–411; San Agustín, *Conquistas*, lib. 3 cap. 20: 688.

148. VanderMeer, "Population Patterns," 324–325.

149. Bayle, "Informe sobre los naturales," 391.

150. Cullinane and Xenos, "Growth of Population."

151. VanderMeer, "Population Patterns," 325–329, 335.

152. VanderMeer, "Population Patterns," 324; Cullinane and Xenos, "Growth of Population," 110, 138n64.

153. For the population of 23,000 in 1600 see chapter 5. The estimate of about 60,000 for 1800 is derived from the rate of increase between 41,480 in 1770 and 79,755 in 1818, and taking into account that the increase was greater in the latter part of the period.

154. San Agustín, *Conquistas*, lib. 2 cap. 36: 535.

155. AGN (Mexico City) Filipinas vol. 3 fols. 257–280 Francisco Xavier de Pisson 1755.

156. AUST Libros 171 and 229 Censo del archipelago 1815. The parishes of the city, Lutaos, San Nicolas, Opon, Talamban, Sogor, and Mandawe had 3,789, and there were 654 *mestizos*.

157. VanderMeer, "Population Patterns," 325.

158. Díaz, *Conquistas*, 271.

159. VanderMeer, "Population Patterns," 323–325, 333–334.

160. Aragón, *Estados de la población.*

161. Bayle, "Informe sobre los naturales," 393–394.

162. San Agustín, *Conquistas*, lib. 2 cap. 22: 438; Martínez Cuesta, *History of Negros*, 34–35. The convent at Binalbagan, established in 1575, had dependencies at Ilog, Bago, and Teggauan.

163. Rodríguez, *Historia*, 1: 168, 300; AGI AF 74 Salazar 25 June 1588.

164. AGI AF 79 and BR 9: 95–119 Francisco de Ortega 1594.

165. Costa, *Jesuits*, 186–187.

166. Martínez Cuesta, *History of Negros*, 69–70.

167. The Recollects had charge of this parish between 1626 and 1638 (Martínez Cuesta, *History of Negros*, 37, 71). See also Rodríguez, *Historia*, 2: 72–74 Pedro de Arce July 1626. There are typographical errors in the dates provided by Martínez Cuesta.

168. ARSI Phil 2 1 fols. 412–415, 2 II fols. 314–317, Phil 14 fols. 106–109 Catologus christianorum 1659, 1675, 1696.

169. Costa, *Jesuits*, 538–539.

170. ARSI Phil 14 fols. 118–121 Catologus christianorum 1755.

171. APSR Sección Visayas Tomo 1 Diego Garrido 21 Mar. 1770.

172. Díaz, *Conquistas*, 34–35. The account was written in 1718.

173. Díaz Arenas, *Memorias históricas*, cuaderno 5. The 735 are described as "reducidos."

174. Aragón, *Estados de la población*. Of 14,713 tributos, 4,284 were in the regions of Ilog, Himamaylan, and Silay.

175. That reassessments were irregular is suggested by the fact that figures for individual towns were similar over long periods. See Martínez Cuesta, *History of Negros*, 105–106.

176. Martínez Cuesta, *History of Negros*, 53.

177. Martínez Cuesta, *History of Negros*, 44.

178. ARSI Phil 2 II fols. 314–317 Catologus christianorum 1659; ARSI Phil 14 fols. 106–109. Catologus christianorum 1696. Martínez Cuesta, *History of Negros*, 74, gives slightly different figures, especially for 1675, where he gives 2,019 instead of 2,557. These figures have been checked in the original documents in the Jesuits' archive in Rome. The difficulty of deciphering some figures may account for some differences, especially those for 1737, but Martínez Cuesta incorrectly translates the names of the categories.

179. Martínez Cuesta, *History of Negros*, 108.

180. Calculated from ARSI Phil 2 II fols. 314–317, 412–415 Catologus christianorum 1659 and 1675, ARSI Phil 14 fols. 106–121 Catologus christianorum 1696, 1737, 1743, 1755. The sex of adults is not given, so it has been necessary to assume balanced sex ratios. The sex ratios for youths and children are highly variable between villages and some are so low as to suggest there were errors in recording.

181. Martínez Cuesta, *History of Negros*, 109.

182. Martínez Cuesta, *History of Negros*, 110, 119n13.

183. Cavada y Méndez de Vigo, *Historia geográfica*, 2: 171.

184. Martínez Cuesta, *History of Negros*, 155.

185. Díaz Arenas, *Memorias históricas*, cuaderno 5.

186. For a graphic description of Negros in the nineteenth century, see Azcarraga y Palmero, *Libertad de comercio*, 168–169.

187. Although Alcina describes the causes and nature of warfare in the Visayas in some detail he uses the past tense (Yepes, *Etnografía*, lib. 4 caps. 10–11: 218–230).

188. Colin, *Labor evangélica*, 2: 134–136, 156.

189. Chirino, *Relación*, 93. It reads "una pestilencia que con dolor de estomago y cabeza los acababa."

190. ARSI Phil 5 fols. 1–33 Diego Sánchez 27 June 1597; Colin, *Labor evangélica*, 2: 143n.

191. Colin, *Labor evangélica*, 3: 795. He refers to them as "las pestes que a tiempos los afligen."

192. NL Ayer 1300 and VA I: 523–145 Relación del estado . . . 1626. It reads "viruelas genero de peste."

193. Murillo Velarde, *Historia*, 252.

194. AGI AF 9–51 Diego Salcedo 25 June 1668, AF 23–32 Audiencia June 1668.

195. The outbreak of smallpox in the Manila Bay region in 1706 had not reached the Visayas by the following year (ARSI Phil 8 fols.74–133 Succio 25 Jan. 1707).

196. Díaz, *Conquistas*, 271.

197. ARSI Phil 8 fols. 26–47 Magino Sola 11 June 1696. It reads "una epidemia maligna de frios y calenturas acompañadas de cámaras de sangre."

198. Cavada y Méndez de Vigo, *Historia geográfica*, 2: 61–62, 73, 142.

199. ARSI Phil 7 fols. 83–134 Juan de Bueras 4 Aug. 1634; Colin, *Labor evangélica*, 1: 256, 387; Murillo Velarde, *Historia*, 27, 252.

200. Boomgaard, "Bridewealth and Birth Control," 200–211.

201. Hidalgo Nuchera, *Encomienda*, 208. In the nineteenth century single men became liable for tribute at age eighteen and women at twenty (Moreno y Díaz, *Manual*, 33).

202. Reid, "Low Population Growth," 39–41; Krzywicki, *Primitive Society*, 201–202; Hern, "Polygyny and Fertility," 53–64.

203. Yepes, *Etnografía*, lib. 4 cap. 13: 242, cap. 15: 253–255; Colin, *Labor evangélica*, 1: 74.

204. Bayle, "Informe sobre los naturales," 393.

205. AGI PAT 23-9 and BR 5: 144–145, 154–155 Miguel de Loarca [1582].

206. Hidalgo Nuchera, *Encomienda*, 166–169, 191; AGI AF 296 Oficiales reales 13 July 1709.

207. Yepes, *Etnografía*, lib. 4 cap. 23: 144.

208. Alcina, *Historia*, lib. 1 cap. 4: 13.

209. Henley, *Food, Fertility and Fever*, 370–373; Henley, "Population and Means of Subsistence," 365–368. See also Boomgaard, "Human Capital, Slavery and Low Rates of Economic and Population Growth," 92.

210. Yepes, *Etnografía*, lib. 4 cap. 14: 246.

211. Calculated from Table 6.2. There were 86 to 95 boys for every 100 girls in the missions in Bohol.

212. Yepes, *Etnografía*, lib. 4 cap. 12: 233.

213. The ratios are calculated by summing the number of married persons (uxorati) and single persons (soluti) indicated in Table 6.2 and dividing by two.

214. Figures provided by the provincial of the Augustinian Recollects in 1785 also give a ratio of 2.41 for Bohol (PNA Patronatos Unclassified (Bound vol.) Thomás de Aquino 19 Oct. 1785). Three villages are omitted from the calculation because of obvious clerical errors by the scribe.

215. San Antonio, *Philippine Chronicles*, 91.

216. AGI AF 22-7-20 fols. 10–12 Oficiales reales 16 June 1655.

217. AGI AF 82-57 Bishop of Cebu 25 Feb. 1667.

218. Reid, *Southeast Asia*, 2: 285–298, and "South-East Asian Population History," 49.

219. Reid, "Age of Commerce," 291–294; Boomgaard, "Crisis Mortality," 197–203.

220. Reid, "Low Population Growth," 35. This coincides with Norman Owen's view noted by Reid in "South-East Asian Population History," 58.

221. Owen, "Towards a History of Health," 9.

222. San Antonio, *Philippine Chronicles*, 91.

223. Cullinane and Xenos, "Growth of Population," 130; McCoy, "The Queen Dies Slowly," 300.

Chapter 7: Manila and Tondo

1. Reed, *Colonial Manila*, 21–22.

2. AGI AF 59-2 Petición y interrogatorio . . . Martín de Goiti 20 June 1572.

3. AGI PAT 24-17 número 1 fols. 9 and 11 and BR 3: 93–97, 101 Relación de lo subcedido en el viaje que se hizo a Luzon 8 May 1570.

4. AGI PAT 24-25 and BR 3: 157–158 No author 20 Apr. 1572, AF 59-2 Petición y interrogatorio . . . Martín de Goiti 20 June 1572; San Agustín, *Conquistas*, lib. 2 cap. 3: 332–333, cap. 4: 335–338.

5. San Agustín, *Conquistas*, lib. 2 cap. 5: 341–343.

6. San Agustín, *Conquistas*, lib. 2 cap. 10: 36; Díaz-Trechuelo, "The Role of the Chinese," 176, gives the alternative meaning of the Chinese term as "to deal or contract."

7. AGI AF 18B Luis Pérez Dasmariñas 9 June 1595.

8. Cushner, *Landed Estates*, 5–6. Its jurisdiction extended north to the Maysilo River, south to Las Pinas, and east to the San Mateo Mountains and the north shore of Laguna de Bay.

9. According to Bishop Serrano in 1622 these three secular benefices were ministering to 20,000 souls (AGI AF 74 and BR 20: 228–230 Miguel García Serrano 31 July 1622).

10. Wernstedt and Spencer, *Philippine Island World*, 56–57, 372; Cushner, *Landed Estates*, 5.

11. Chirino, *Relación*, 255–256.

12. AGI PAT 23-9 and BR 5: 85 Miguel de Loarca [1582].

13. Morga, *Sucesos*, 270.

14. Scott, *Barangay*, 199–200.

15. Doeppers, "Hispanic Influences," 29–30.

16. Morga, *Sucesos*, 258–259. The description suggests the betel was from the areca tree rather than the betel palm. Betel was used in ceremonies and chewed for medicinal purposes and personal pleasure.

17. Morga, *Sucesos*, 264; San Agustín, *Conquistas*, lib 3. cap. 8: 621.

18. Scott, *Barangay*, 190.

19. Morga, *Sucesos*, 258–259.

20. Quirino and García, "Manners," 371, 424.

21. Quirino and García, "Manners," 371–372, 424.

22. AGI PAT 24-17 número 1 fols. 7 and 9 and BR 3: 93–97 Relación de lo subcedido en el viaje que se hizo a Luzon 8 May 1570.

23. Morga, *Sucesos*, 270; Quirino and García, "Manners," 370–371 423, 425; AGI AF 6 and BR 4: 68 Francisco de Sande 7 June 1576.

24. Plasencia, "Relación del culto," 598.

25. AGI PAT 25-60 fol. 42 Juan de Plasencia 24 Oct. 1589; ARSI Phil 5 fols. 44–55 Raimundo de Prado 25 July 1599.

26. AGI PAT 24-17 número 1 fol. 7 and BR 3: 94 Relación de lo subcedido en el viaje que se hizo a Luzon 8 May 1570; Morga, *Sucesos*, 280; Scott, *Barangay*, 192.

27. Morga, *Sucesos*, 280; Nicholl, "Brunei Rediscovered," 45; Bellwood and Omar, "Trade Patterns," 158–160; Reed, *Colonial Manila*, 3.

28. AGI AF 6 and BR 4: 80 Francisco de Sande 7 June 1576; San Agustín, *Conquistas*, lib. 2 cap. 4: 337.

29. See, for example, AGI AF 6 and BR 3:181 Guido de Lavezaris 29 June 1573; AGI PAT 23-9 and BR 5: 82–83, 90–91 Miguel de Loarca [1582].

30. AGI AF 84 and BR 34: 232–233 Diego de Herrera 25 July 1570; AGI PAT 24-25 ramo 2 fol. 1 and BR 3: 141 Relación del descubrimiento 20 Apr. 1572; Quirino and García, "Manners," 366, 371, 419, 425.

31. AGI PAT 24-17 número 1 fol. 7 and BR 3: 94 Relación de lo subcedido en el viaje que se hizo a Luzon 8 May 1570.

32. AGI PAT 24-25 ramo 2 fol. 6 and BR 3: 148 Relación del descubrimiento 20 Apr. 1572.

33. AGI AF 74, Rodríguez, *Historia*, 15: 346, and BR 7: 32 Domingo de Salazar 25 June 1588.

34. AGI PAT 25-38 Relación punctual de las encomiendas 31 May 1591.

35. Reed, *Colonial Manila*, 33.

36. AGI PAT 24-25-2 fol. 9 Miguel de Legazpi 20 Apr. 1572.

37. AGI AF 74, Rodríguez, *Historia*, 15: 347–348, BR 7: 29–51 Domingo de Salazar 25 June 1588.

38. AGI PAT 25-38 fol.1 Relación punctual de las encomiendas 31 May 1591; AGI AF 7 Francisco Tello 6 July 1601.

39. Reed, *Colonial Manila*, 25.

40. BR 3: 211–216 Martín Enríquez 5 Dec. 1573, AGI AF 34 Díaz de Ceballos 4 June 1576.

41. AGI AF 7-3-38 Rodrigo de Vivero 8 July 1608.

42. AGI AF 18 Santiago de Vera 13 July 1589.

43. Schurz, *Manila Galleon*, 193–194.

44. AGI AF 7-65 and BR 20: 139–140 Alonso Fajardo 10 Dec. 1621.

45. Cushner, *Landed Estates*, 36.

46. Merino, *Cabildo Secular*, opposite p. 60. Of the 238, which excludes 45 widows, 141 were soldiers, 17 *cabildo* officials, 8 held Audiencia posts, 12 were actuaries, 2 were doctors, and 58 were ordinary citizens.

47. Merino, *Cabildo Secular*, 35.

48. AGI AF 34 Díaz de Ceballos 4 June 1576. See also AGI AF 34–112 Santiago de Vera 26 June 1587.

49. Merino, *Cabildo Secular*, 33. Similarly, more than one hundred died attempting to dislodge the Moros from Maluku in the 1580s (AGI PAT 25-1 Relación de toda la gente y armas, no date; Merino, *Cabildo Secular*, 34).

50. Merino, *Cabildo Secular*, opposite p. 60. The sex ratio in 1634 was 386 men to 240 women.

51. AGI PAT 24-19 R19 fol. 41 Hernando Riquel 2 June 1576 assigned 16 Jan. 1571.

52. These were allocated to Captain Juan de Isla ("río desta ciudad"), Antonio Álvarez ("río de Manila"), and Pedro Valenciano (Taytay and Zapa). They included the towns of Pasig, Tagui, and Zapa (AGI PAT 24-19 fols. 18r–18v Hernando Riquel 2 June 1576).

53. AGI AF 74, Rodríguez, *Historia*, 15: 346, and BR 7: 32 Domingo de Salazar 25 June 1588.

54. AGI AF 6 and BR 4: 68 Francisco de Sande 7 June 1576.

55. AGI AF 84-44 Pedimiento de ciertos indios principales 15 June 1582; see also AGI AF 74 and BR 5: 188–189 Domingo de Salazar 20 June 1582.

56. AGI AF 18B Luis Pérez Dasmariñas 9 June 1595.

57. Hidalgo Nuchera, *Encomienda*, 169–200.

58. AGI AF 19-7 Testimonio sobre la tasación . . . 28 Sept. 1604. The towns of Pasig, Taytay, Taguig, and Tabuco were grouped with other towns in Laguna de Bay and required to pay fifty-five *gantas de arroz*, valued at one *tostón*, and one *gallina*. However, by the beginning of the eighteenth century they were paying the equivalent of ten reals, four reals for fifteen *gantas de arroz limpio*, one for a *gallina*, and the rest in cash (AGI AF 296 Certificación 13 July 1709).

59. AGI AF 8-7 and BR 23: 36–38 Juan Niño de Tavora 1 Aug. 1629.

60. Phelan, "Free Versus Compulsory Labor," 193.

61. AGI AF 34-52 Diego de Zarate 10 June 1581.

62. Reed, *Colonial Manila*, 41–51.

63. NL Ayer 1440 fols. 110–114 Memorial de los indios del pueblo de Taytay 8 Mar. 1719. See also AGI AF 80 and BR 19: 72 Pedro de San Pablo 7 Aug. 1620.

64. Díaz, *Conquistas*, 542.

65. Taytay and Antipolo were originally administered by the Franciscans, but were ceded to the Jesuits because of the shortage of priests (Costa, *Jesuits*, 137).

66. ARSI Phil 9 fols. 313–314 Francisco Almerique 23 June 1597; Phil 5 fols. 1–33 Diego Sánchez 27 June 1597; ARSI Phil 9 fols. 372–375 Diego García 10 July 1599; Phil 10 fols. 5–12 Diego García 8 June 1600; ARSI Phil 5 fols. 75–92 Juan de Ribera 1 June 1601.

67. ARSI Phil 5 fols. 62–73 Raimundo de Prado 16 June 1600; Chirino, *Relación*, 174, 423.

68. ARSI Phil 9 fols. 372–375 Diego García 10 July 1599. See also Phil 12 fols. 138–148 Alejo López 1690; Costa, *Jesuits*, 469–471.

69. Cushner, *Landed Estates*, 10–11.

70. Roth, "Church Lands," 43, 46, 135.

71. AGI AF 18B and BR 10: 88 Antonio de Morga 8 June 1598; see also BR 10: 149 Ignacio de Santibáñez 26 June 1598.

72. AGI AF 19 Rodrigo Díaz Guiral 30 June 1606.

73. Cushner, *Landed Estates*, 30.

74. PNA Cedulario 1679–1687 pp. 333–376 1685. They included those of Quiapo, Malate, Dilao, San Sebastián, San Miguel, Binondo and Santa Cruz, Rosario, San Jacinto.

75. Cushner, *Landed Estates*, 57.

76. Cushner, *Landed Estates*, 47; Cushner, "Meysapan," 42.

77. Cushner, *Landed Estates*, 42, 50; Roth, "Church Lands," 137–138.
78. Cushner, "Meysapan," 41–42.
79. Roth, "*Casas de reservas*," 117.
80. Roth, "Church Lands," 137.
81. Roth, "*Casas de reservas*," 119, 122–123.
82. AF 19 and BR 14: 169 Rodrigo Díaz Guiral 30 June 1606.
83. AGI AF 27 and BR 18: 297–298 Hernando de los Ríos Coronel 1619–1620; AGI AF 8-7 and BR 23: 36 Juan Niño de Tavora 1 Aug. 1629; Morga, *Sucesos*, 314.
84. Colin, *Labor evangélica*, 1: 20.
85. BR 35: 194 Sebastián Cavallero 1644.
86. AGI PAT 24-25 fol. 2 and BR 3: 154–156 Juan Pacheco Maldonado 20 Apr. 1572; AGI PAT 25-36 Santiago de Vera 26 June 1587; AGI AF 34–112 Santiago de Vera 26 June 1587; AGI AF 18A Licenciado Ayala 20 June 1588; AGI AF 29-51 Francisco de Lasmissas 31 May 1595; see also Morga, *Sucesos*, 305; Schurz, *Manila Galleon*, 71.
87. BR 7: 220, 230 and Retana, *Archivo del bibliófilo filipino*, 3: 24 Domingo de Salazar 24 June 1590.
88. AGI PAT 25-38 fol.1 Relación punctual de las encomiendas 1 Nov. 1591.
89. Chirino, *Relación*, 11, 243.
90. BR 7: 224–228, and Retana, *Archivo del bibliófilo filipino*, 3: 13–25 Domingo de Salazar 24 June 1590.
91. AGI AF 29-51 Francisco de Lasmissas 31 May 1595, AF 84 Bernardo de Santa Catalina 15 Dec. 1603.
92. AGI AF 35 Juan Núñez 24 June 1595; AF 6 and BR 10: 259 Francisco Tello 12 July 1599; AGI AF 329 libro 1 fols. 27v–37r Real cédula 16 Feb. 1602.
93. BR 10: 149–150 Ignacio de Santibáñez 26 June 1598; Morga, *Sucesos*, 314–316; Díaz-Trechuelo, "Domestic Economy," 186.
94. AGI AF 6 and BR 10: 289 Francisco Tello 12 July 1599; BR 10: 149 Ignacio de Santibáñez 26 June 1598; AGI AF 329 libro 1 fols. 27v–37r Real cédula 16 Feb. 1602.
95. AGI AF 18B Apuntamientos tocantes as los sangleis 1597; BR 9: 315–325 Luis Pérez Dasmariñas 28 June 1597; AGI AF 67 Real cédula 17 June 1679; Morga, *Sucesos*, 317; Díaz-Trechuelo, "The Role of the Chinese," 193–194.
96. AGI AF 84 and BR 12: 138–140 Cabildo eclesiástico de Manila 11 Dec. 1603; AF 19 and BR 12: 145 Audiencia 12 Dec. 1603; AGI AF 19 and BR 14: 51 Manuel de Madrid y Luna 5 July 1605; AGI AF 19 Rodrigo Díaz Guiral 30 June 1606; Morga, *Sucesos*, 217–226; Guerrero, "The Chinese," 25. Schurz, *Manila Galleon*, 83, cites a report by Governor Anda that up to 1768 there were fourteen Chinese uprisings.
97. Díaz, *Conquistas*, 403; BR 29: 249 Relation of the Insurrection of Chinese 1640; BR 36: 200 Father Letona 1662.
98. Morga, *Sucesos*, 225.
99. BR 35: 185–194 Sebastián Cavallero 1644; Díaz-Trechuelo, "The Role of the Chinese," 185–186; Merino, *Cabildo Secular*, 207, 210–212, 234n35, refers to AGI AF 28 12 June 1683, 24 June 1683. For a discussion of the taxes paid by the Chinese, see also BR 22: 287 Crown to Juan Niño de Tavora 27 Mar. 1629; AGI AF 8 and BR 26: 139 Sebastián Hurtado de Corcuera 30 June 1636; AF 330 libro 4 fols. 52r–54r Real cédula 2 Sept. 1638.
100. Díaz-Trechuelo, "The Role of the Chinese," 191.
101. Gemelli Careri, *Voyage Around the World*, 420.

102. AGI AF 202 Bermúdez de Castro 23 June 1729 quoted in Díaz-Trechuelo, "The Role of the Chinese," 192.

103. AGI AF 27 Gómez Pérez Dasmariñas 20 Mar. 1591; BR 10: 149 Ignacio de Santibáñez 26 June 1598.

104. AGI AF 6 and BR 8: 78–95 Gómez Pérez Dasmariñas 13 Apr. 1591; AGI AF 27 Cabildo of Manila 22 June 1591.

105. Díaz-Trechuelo, "The Role of the Chinese," 97.

106. Morga, *Sucesos*, 308.

107. AGI PAT 25-36 Santiago de Vera 26 June 1587; AGI AF 34-112 Santiago de Vera 26 June 1587; Reid, *Southeast Asia*, 2: 18–19. Between 1604 and 1635, 54 of the 355 Japanese vessels licensed to trade in Southeast Asia were destined for Manila (Reid, "An 'Age of Commerce,'" 10).

108. AGI AF 29-51 Francisco de Lasmissas 31 May 1595; Reed, *Colonial Manila*, 53.

109. Paske-Smith, "Japanese Trade," 700–708; Schurz, *Manila Galleon*, 103.

110. AGI AF 27 and BR 18: 308 Hernando de los Ríos Coronel 1619–1620; BR 20: 97 Miguel García Serrano 30 July 1621.

111. Reid, "An 'Age of Commerce,'" 10.

112. AGI AF 84-4, Rodríguez, *Historia*, 14: 185, and BR 34: 289 Martín de Rada 30 June 1574.

113. The Spanish reads "enfermedad peligrosa de calenturas malignas y contagiosas" (Colin, *Labor evangélica*, 1: 561–563).

114. AGI AF 18B Vecinos de la ciudad de Manila 31 May 1592; AGI AF 18B and BR 8: 237 Gómez Pérez Dasmariñas 31 May 1592.

115. AGI AF 35 Juan Núñez 24 June 1595; Chirino, *Relación*, 128–132, 373–375.

116. ARSI Phil 9 fols. 313–314 Francisco Almerique 23 June 1597; Phil 10 fols. 5–12 Diego García 8 June 1600.

117. Díaz, *Conquistas*, 255; Murillo Velarde, *Historia*, 252; ARSI Phil 8 fols. 74–133 Antonio Succio 25 Jan. 1707.

118. AGI AF 9-51 Diego Salcedo 25 June 1668; AF 23-32 Audiencia June 1668.

119. Lilly Philippine Ms II Diego García Herreros 7 June 1786.

120. AGI AF 340 libro 3 N950–951 fols. 259v–260r Real cédula 30 Sept. 1633.

121. AGI AF 34-112 Santiago de Vera 26 June 1587; AF 340 libro 3 N810–811 fols.189v–190r Real cédula 4 Aug. 1626.

122. AGI AF 339 libro 1 fol. 58v Real cédula 7 Nov. 1574. For the history of hospitals in colonial Manila see Casero Nieto, "Hospitales en Manila," 217–258.

123. AGI AF 18A Santiago de Vera 30 June 1584.

124. AGI AF 18A Audiencia 25 June 1588; AGI AF 74 and BR 7: 268 Expediente sobre la cobranza de los tributos 1591; AGI AF 59-31 Hernando de los Ríos 16 Feb. 1594, AGI AF 35 Juan Núñez 24 June 1595; Morga, *Sucesos*, 285; Alcobendas, "Religiosos médico-cirujanos (Part II)," 238–239 ; Guerra, *El hospital*, 537.

125. AGI AF 18A Fiscal Ayala 20 June 1585, 15 July 1589; Guerra, *El hospital*, 539.

126. Alcobendas, "Religiosos médico-cirujanos" (Part II), 238–239.

127. Guerra, *El hospital*, 546; Abad, "Los franciscanos," 429. For defensive reasons it was demolished in 1662, but rebuilt between Dilao and Balete (AGI AF 82-289 Juan de Vargas Urtado 29 May 1679, 10 Apr. 1682; Martínez, *Compendio histórico*, 29–30; Casero Nieto, "Hospitales en Manila," 235–236).

128. Retana, *Archivo del bibliófilo filipino*, 3: 32 Domingo de Salazar 24 June 1590; Guerra, *El hospital*, 542–543.

129. AGI AF 84-90 Bernardo Navarro, Diego de Soria, and Juan de Hermaça 30 June 1596, 24 June 1597; Fernández, "Dominican Apostolate," 182–184; Morga, *Sucesos*, 316; Casero Nieto, "Hospitales en Manila," 250–252.

130. AGI AF 340 libro 3 N871–74 fols. 220r–221v Real cédula 6 Nov. 1630.

131. AGI AF 82-8 Francisco de Herrera 2 Aug. 1639. The total number entering the hospital between 1632 and 1639 was 3,256, of which 1,016 recovered.

132. AGI AF 297 Juan de Astudillo 14 July 1719.

133. AGI AF 84-108 Juan de Garrovillas 12 July 1597. The hospital is not named, but the other three are, so by deduction it must have been that of the Santa Hermandad de Misericordia.

134. AGI AF 35-77 Veedor y hermanos de la Mesa de Misericordia 1620; Guerra, *El hospital*, 546–547.

135. Guerra, *El hospital*, 546–547, 552; Casero Nieto, "Hospitales en Manila," 245–246.

136. AGI AF 340 libro 3 N810–11 fols. 198v–190r Real cédula 4 Aug. 1626.

137. Morga, *Sucesos*, 285–286.

138. AGI AF 35 and BR 11: 82–85 Domingo de Santiago 3 July 1599, Antonio Valerio, n.d., AF 80 Andrés de Alcaras, Manuel de Madrid y Luna and Manuel de Vega 20 June 1617.

139. Alcobendas, "Religiosos médico-cirujanos," (Part I) 53–60, 63, (Part II) 237; Casero Nieto, "Hospitales en Manila," 257–258.

140. Cushner, *Landed Estates*, 99, which refers to fiscal accounts in AGI CO 1205.

141. ARSI Phil 5 fols. 62–73 Raimundo de Prado 16 June 1600.

142. BR 27: 82 Juan Grau y Monfalcón 1637.

143. BR 18: 130 and AF 7-5-33 Alonso Faxardo de Tença 10 Aug. 1618; AGI AF 80 and BR 19: 71-76 Pedro de San Pablo 7 Aug. 1620; AF 74 and BR 20: 245 Miguel García Serrano 31 July 1622; Cummins, *Travels and Controversies*, 1: 92, and BR 38: 43 Domingo Fernández Navarrete ca. 1650.

144. NL Ayer 1300 Provincials to Governor Cruzat y Góngora 7 Oct. 1701; NL Ayer 1440 fols. 110–114 Memorial de los indios del pubelo de Taytay 8 Mar. 1719.

145. AGI AF 254 Pedro Calderón Enríquez 11 July 1741.

146. AGI CO 1266 fols. 130–146 Oficiales reales 1735.

147. Retana, *Archivo del bibliófilo filipino* 1: 4–5 Entrada de la seráphica religión 1649; San Antonio, *Philippine Chronicles*, 77.

148. ARSI Phil 2 II fols. 314–317v Catologus christianorum quos colit 1659 and Phil 14 fols.118–121 Catologus christianorum quos colit 1755.

149. There are considerable variations between the towns and over time ranging from 1:0.66 to 1:2.91.

150. PNA Patronatos Resumen del estado . . . 4 July 1798. In 1784 the five parishes of Sampaloc, San Miguel, Dilao, Santa Ana, and Pandacan contained 11,760 almas (AAM Padrones 1760–1796 Plan de tributos de almas . . . 1784).

151. NL Ayer Ms 1449 (Box) Razón de los pueblos . . . 1760; Mapa General de las Almas . . . Diez 1820. The parishes were Tondo, Tambobos, Pasig, Pateras, Taguig, Malate, and Parañaque.

152. Fradera, *Colonia más peculiar*, 75–77.

153. See Appendix D Tondo.

154. Díaz, *Conquistas*, 28.

155. San Antonio, *Philippine Chronicles*, 77.

156. AUST Libro 229 no. 1 Estatística [*sic*] de las islas Filipinas 1815. The 1815 Census (AUST Libro 229 Censo del archepelago 1815) shows that *mestizos* accounted for more than 40 percent of the tributary population in some parishes and were totally absent in others.

157. NL Ayer 1334 (Shelf) Descripción histórica y política . . . ca. 1825.

Chapter 8: Southwest Luzon

1. In the early 1580s there was a *corregidor* of Balayan and an *alcalde mayor* of Bonbón, whose jurisdiction encompassed Batangas, while Calilaya was under the *alcalde mayor* of Mindoro (AGI PAT 23-9 and BR 5: 91–93 Miguel de Loarca [1582]). Subsequently in 1591 Calilaya was made a separate *alcaldía mayor* and later became known as Tayabas (*Census of the Philippine Islands*, 1: 172). Meanwhile the province of Balayan came to embrace Bonbón, Batangas, and Balayan.

2. Alcalá, *Chrónica*, 59; AGI PAT 23-9 and BR 5: 111–113 Miguel de Loarca [1582]; San Antonio, *Philippine Chronicles*, 105.

3. AGI CO 1197 fols. 282–286 Pliego de tributos . . . en la real corona 1572.

4. AGI PAT 24-25 and BR 3: 141–143 Relación del descubrimiento 20 Apr. 1572; San Agustín, *Conquistas*, lib. 2 cap. 1: 321.

5. San Agustín, *Conquistas*, lib. 2 cap. 2: 322–325; Reed, *Colonial Manila*, 21.

6. San Agustín, *Conquistas*, lib. 2 cap. 4: 338, cap. 5: 340–343, cap. 6: 345–346.

7. AGI PAT 24-19 N41-45 Hernando Riquel 2 June 1576.

8. San Agustín, *Conquistas*, lib. 2 cap. 30: 492–493, cap. 32: 499; Galende, "Augustinians," 54, though Juan de Grijalva suggests that it was founded in 1572 (*Crónica*, 149–150).

9. The town declined with a decrease in trade and the center of the province of Bay was moved to Santa Cruz (San Agustín, *Conquistas*, lib. 2 cap. 11: 373).

10. San Agustín, *Conquistas*, lib. 2 cap. 32: 611, lib. 3 cap. 24: 713–714. This convent was subsequently joined to that at Bay.

11. Martínez, *Compendio histórico*, 30; Huerta, *Estado geográfico*, 575–576.

12. Pérez, "Origen de las misiones franciscanos," 1: 115.

13. Alcalá, *Chrónica*, 68–72. They also had 2,500 *tributos* in Tayabas and 700 at Silang.

14. AGI AF 74 Domingo de Salazar 25 June 1588, AF 20-4-34 Memoria de los conventos . . . 1610.

15. San Agustín, *Conquistas*, lib. 2 cap. 36: 535; lib. 3 cap. 3: 589; lib. 3 cap. 25: 718; AGI AF 20-4-34 Memoria de los conventos . . . 1610.

16. AGI PAT 25-59 Gerónimo de Alcaraz 28 July 1599; Medina, *Cavite*, 41–42. By 1655 they had five priests working in Cavite, Silang, Indang, and Maragondon (NL Ayer 1300 VA II: 391–399 Miguel Solana 30 June 1655).

17. Wernstedt and Spencer, *Philippine Island World*, 394.

18. Cushner, *Landed Estates*, 6–7.

19. AGI PAT 25-60 fols. 41–42 Juan de Plasencia 4 Oct. 1589; Yepes, *Etnografía*, lib. 3 cap. 5: 30–32; Scott, *Barangay*, 229.

20. Cushner, *Landed Estates*, 8–10.

21. AGI PAT 23-7 and BR 3: 201 Juan de la Isla (Diego de Artieda), n.d., PAT 23-9 and BR 5: 82–83, 90–91 Miguel de Loarca [1582]; Morga, *Sucesos*, 254.

22. It is possible that sweet potatoes arrived in the Philippines from Polynesia in pre-Spanish times.

23. Morga, *Sucesos*, 258, 264; Doeppers, "Hispanic Influences," 28–29.

24. Wernstedt and Spencer, *Philippine Island World*, 397.

25. Fox, "Calatagan Excavations," 326, 332, 341; Junker, *Raiding*, 176–178, 398n15.

26. AGI PAT 25-60 fols. 41–46 Juan de Plasencia 24 Oct. 1589. See also AGI PAT 23-9 and BR 5: 171–187 Miguel de Loarca [1582]; Morga, *Sucesos*, 172–177; Quirino and García, "Manners," 382–388, 438–441.

27. AGI PAT 25-60 fols. 41–46 Juan de Plasencia 24 Oct. 1589; Plasencia, "Relación del culto," 598–603; Pérez, "Origen de las misiones franciscanos," 3: 379.

28. Scott, "Filipino Class Structure," 96–101; Rafael, *Contracting Colonialism*, 138.

29. AGI 24-25 and BR 3: 155 No author 20 Apr. 1572.

30. AGI PAT 23-9 and BR 5: 140–141, 179 Miguel de Loarca [1582]; Morga, *Sucesos*, 271; Chirino, *Relación*, 121, 363–364; Fox, "Philippines in Prehistoric Times," 56.

31. AGI PAT 24-38 and BR 3: 55 Miguel de Legazpi no date.

32. Fox, "Calatagan Excavations," 348; Junker, *Raiding*, 362–365.

33. Colin, *Labor evangélica*, 1: 75–77.

34. AGI PAT 24-38 and BR 3: 54 Miguel de Legazpi, no date.

35. Rafael, *Contracting Colonialism*, 146.

36. AGI PAT 25-60 fol. 41 Juan de Plasencia 24 Oct. 1589.

37. Scott, *Barangay*, 222–224.

38. AGI PAT 25-60 fol. 41 Juan de Plasencia 24 Oct. 1589.

39. Scott, "Filipino Class Structure," 105–106, 119, 126.

40. AGI PAT 25-60 fol. 42 Juan de Plasencia 24 Oct. 1589; Quirino and Garcia, "Manners," 383, 439–440; Scott, "Filipino Class Structure," 107.

41. AGI AF 6 and BR 3: 286 Guido de Lavezaris, no date [post 1572]; Quirino and Garcia, "Manners," 384–385, 440–441.

42. AGI PAT 24-38 and BR 3: 54 Miguel de Legazpi, n.d. See also AGI PAT 24-25 and BR 3: 154–155 No author, no date AF 84-2 No author, n.d.

43. Scott, "Filipino Class Structure," 126.

44. Quirino and García, "Manners," 373, 427.

45. Morga, *Sucesos*, 274–275.

46. Quirino and García, "Manners," 373, 427.

47. Chirino, *Relación*, 81, 319; Morga, *Sucesos*, 277.

48. Pagès, *Travels*, 1: 235.

49. Quirino and García, "Manners," 373, 427.

50. Quirino and García, "Manners," 387, 444.

51. Quirino and García, "Manners," 377–378, 434. It is not clear precisely which native groups held these superstitions.

52. Quirino and García, "Manners," 386, 442.

53. Plasencia, "Relación del culto," n.d.

54. Quirino and García, "Manners," 386, 443.

55. Cummins, *Travels and Controversies*, 1: 94, and BR 38: 47 Domingo Fernández Navarrete ca. 1650; Postma, "Mindoro Missions Revisited," 253.

56. AGI PAT 24-17 and BR 3: 74, 78 Relación de lo subcedido en el viaje 8 May 1570.

57. Junker, *Raiding*, 99–105; Lopez, "Culture Contact and Ethnogenesis," 2–6; Scott, *Filipinos in China*, 1–2.

58. AGI PAT 24-17 and BR 3: 76 Relación de lo subcedido en el viaje 8 May 1570; Junker, *Raiding*, 195.

59. AGI PAT 23-9 BR 5: 111–113 Loarca [1582]; Alcalá, *Chrónica*, 59.

60. Gardner and Maliwanag, *Indic Writings*, 1: 9–12; Lopez, *Mangyans*, 47–51, and "Culture Contact and Ethnogenesis," 26–36; Barbian, "Tribal Distribution," 5–11. Today the groups include the Iraya, Alangan, Tadyawan, Buhid, Batangan, Hanunóo, and Ratagnon.

61. Murillo Velarde, *Historia*, 63.

62. Gardner and Maliwanag, *Indic Writings*, 1: 11, 2: 36.

63. Gardner and Maliwanag, *Indic Writings*, 1: 10; Conklin, *Hanunóo Agriculture*, 11.

64. Gardner and Maliwanag, *Indic Writings*, 2: 6.

65. AGI PAT 23-8 and BR 5: 202–204, Report on saleable offices, no date. A comparison with the total population of 48,400 *almas* for Laguna de Bay in 1591 (see Appendix D) suggests that these figure must have referred to tributary populations.

66. AGI PAT 23-9 and BR 5: 87–91 Miguel de Loarca [1582].

67. AGI CO 1200 fols. 1188v–1191v Cargo de dinero de tributos 1588, fols. 1272v–1276r Alcance que resuelto contra . . . Luis de Vivanco 1589. The numbers of *tributos* in "la costa y Cavite" were 1863.5 and 1,699.5 *tributos* respectively for 1588 and 1589.

68. AGI PAT 23-9 and BR: 87–89 Miguel de Loarca [1582]. No figure is given for Tabuc(o).

69. AGI PAT 23-38 fols. 14–15 and BR 8: 115–117 Relación punctual de las encomiendas 31 May 1591.

70. Abad, "Los franciscanos," 418–419, Alonso de Montemayor 16 July 1622.

71. AGI AF 82-4 No author [1572]. See also AGI PAT 24-25 and BR3: 141 Relación del descubrimiento 20 Apr. 1572.

72. AGI CO 1200 fols. 118v–119v Cargo de dinero de tributos 1588, CO 1202 fols. 2r–16v Cargo de tributos 1591.

73. AGI PAT 24-25 and BR 3: 141 Relación del descubrimiento 20 Apr. 1572.

74. AGI AF 74 and Rodríguez, *Historia*, 1: 368, and BR 7: 50 Domingo de Salazar 25 June 1588.

75. Murillo Velarde, *Historia*, 63

76. AGI PAT 23-8 and BR5: 202–204, Report on saleable offices, no date.

77. AGI AF18B and BR 10: 308 Autos para el buen gobierno . . . 7 Dec. 1598.

78. AGI AF 25-31 Audiencia 2 June 1689.

79. BR 41: 34 Juan de Zarzuela 19 June 1691.

80. NL Ayer 1300 VA V: 201–230 and BR 44: 133–134 Provincials to Governor Cruzat y Góngora 7 Oct. 1701.

81. Roth, "Church Lands," 131, 133; Borromeo, "Cadiz Filipino," 68.

82. Roth, *Friar Estates*, 41.

83. Roth, "Casas de Reservas," 117. For example, AUST Libro 10 fols. 216–223 no. 9 Reservas concedidas a la hacienda de Biñan 26 Nov. 1695, Libro 10 fols. 310–316 no. 23 Informe por parte del colegio de Santo Tomás, n.d., Libro 10 fols. 246–266 no. 16 Reservas de las haciendas 9 Mar. 1731.

84. AUST Libro 10 fols. 310–316 no. 23 Informe por parte del colegio de Santo Tomás, n.d.

85. AUST Libro 10 fols. 317–341 no. 23 Padrón of Biñan 10 Dec. 1752.

86. The right of the *gobernadorcillo* to designate *casas de reservas* was banned in 1691, but the order was ineffective (Cushner, *Landed Estates*, 52–53).

87. Roth, "Church Lands," 138–142.

88. NL Ayer 1300 VA V: 201–230 Provincials of the religious orders 7 Oct. 1701.

89. Cushner, *Landed Estates*, 58–64, and "Meysapan," 46–47.

90. Roth, "Casas de Reservas," 120–121.

91. BR 29: 224, 249 Relation of the insurrection of Chinese 1640; AGI AF 28-44 Juan Grau y Monfalcón 16 June 1642.

92. Borromeo-Buehler, "Inquilinos of Cavite," 75; Roth, "Church Lands," 143; Wickberg, "Chinese Mestizo," 74–77.

93. AUST Libro 229 no. 1 Estatística de las Yslas 1815.

94. AGI PAT 23-9 and BR 5: 82–83 Miguel de Loarca [1582].

95. Prieto Lucena, *Manrique de Lara*, 97.

96. Borromeo, "Cadiz Filipino," 43.

97. AGI AF 74 and BR 20: 229, 233 Miguel García Serrano 31 July 1622.

98. AGI AF 12-57 Gabriel Curuzeláegui 15 May 1688. For the eighteenth century, see San Antonio, *Philippine Chronicles*, 82.

99. AGI AF 30 Oficiales reales 7 Sept. 1627.

100. AGI AF 8-45 Sebastián de Hurtado de Corcuera 4 Sept. 1635.

101. NL Ayer 1300 VA V: 201–230 Provincials of the religious orders 7 Oct. 1701.

102. AGI AF 38-1 and BR 18: 174–175 Sebastián de Pineda 26 May 1619.

103. AGI AF 38-1 and BR 18: 174–175 Sebastián de Pineda 26 May 1619.

104. AGI AF 9-7 Diego Fajardo 31 July 1649. In 1649 the Dominicans refused to send 300 *pandayes* (blacksmiths) to work in the Cavite shipyard.

105. AGI AF 8-104 Baltasar Ruiz Escalona 31 Aug. 1638; Lilly Lot 513 fols. 328–334 Francisco Combés, no date.

106. Lilly Lot 513 fols. 328–334 Francisco Combés, no date; Díaz, *Conquistas*, 517, 542.

107. AGI AF 9-13 Diego Fajardo 4 Aug. 1650.

108. NL Ayer 1300 VA V: 60 summary in BR 19: 183–197 Hernando de los Ríos Coronel 1621; Cummins, *Travels and Controversies*, 1: 92; and BR 38: 43 Domingo Fernández Navarrete ca 1650.

109. AGI AF 340 lib. 3 fols. 26r–26v Real cédula 6 Mar. 1608, AF 27 and BR 18: 316 Hernando Ríos Coronel 1619–1620; AF 9-6 Diego Fajardo 31 July 1649.

110. NL Ayer 1300 VA V: 60 Hernando de los Ríos Coronel 1621.

111. AGI AF 20 Bernardo de Santa Catalina 9 July 1616, AF 27 and BR 18: 316 Hernando de los Ríos Coronel 1619–1620, AF 9-6 Diego Fajardo 31 July 1649; Lilly Lot 514 fols. 105–106 No author, no date.

112. AGI AF 329 lib. 2 fols. 301v–313v Real cédula 10 Aug. 1619; see also AGI AF 7 and BR 18: 130 Alonso Fajardo de Tença 10 Aug. 1618; AF 9-13 Diego Fajardo 4 Aug. 1650.

113. Lilly Lot 514 fols. 105–106 No author, n.d. Although undated, most likely it refers to the seventeenth century, when the greatest impact of shipbuilding activities was felt.

114. AGI AF 340 lib. 3 fols. 414r–441v Real cédula 1 May 1608, AF 20 Juan de Espinosa 18 Aug. 1617, AF 7-53 Alonso Fajardo 10 Aug. 1618, AF 38-1 Sebastián de Pineda 26 May 1619, AF 329 lib. 2 fols. 301v– 313v Real cédula 10 Aug. 1619, AF 27 and BR 18: 327 Hernando de los Ríos Coronel 1619–1620, AF 80 and BR 19: 72–77 Pedro de San Pablo 7 Aug. 1620, AG 340 lib. 4 fols. 181v–182v Real cédula 8 Dec. 1628, AF 9-6 Diego Fajardo 13 July 1649.

115. Lilly Lot 514 fols. 105–106 No author, n.d.

116. AGI AF 38-1 Sebastián de Pineda 26 May 1619; Medina, *Historia*, 283.

117. AGI AF 20 Bernardo de Santa Catalina 9 July 1616; NL Ayer 1300 VA V: 201–230 Provincials of the religious orders 7 Oct. 1701.

118. PNA Cedulario 1645–1649 pp. 359–366 Real cédula 18 Dec. 1646.

119. Cummins, *Travels and Controversies*, 1: 85 and BR 38: 34 Domingo Fernández Navarrete [ca. 1650]; Costa, *Jesuits*, 473.

120. ARSI Phil 7 I fols. 181–276 Anua de la provincia, Juan de Bueras 26 May 1636.

121. BR 41: 159 San Francisco de Assis 1756; San Agustín, *Conquistas*, lib. 3 cap. 9: 364.

122. Postma, "Mindoro Missions Revisited," 254–255; Galende, "Augustinians," 53.

123. AGI AF 74, Rodríguez, *Historia*, 1: 368, and BR 7: 50 Domingo de Salazar 25 June 1588.

124. Alcalá, *Chrónica*, 59.

125. Costa, *Jesuits*, 375–376. The Jesuits had been granted the island of Marinduque in 1621.

126. Postma, "Mindoro Missions Revisited," 257.

127. AGI AF 11-13 Bishop Felipe Pardo 4 June 1680; AGI EC 404B Thomás de San Gerónimo, Provincial of the Recollects 23 May 1681; San Agustín, *Conquistas*, lib. 2 cap. 9: 364, lib. 3 cap. 20: 690, cap. 26: 725; Postma, "Mindoro Missions Revisited," 258–260.

128. BR 41: 173, 174, 180–181 San Francisco de Assis 1756.

129. Postma, "Mindoro Missions Revisited," 259–260.

130. Calvo, *Joseph Calvo*, 5; Majul, "'Moro' Wars," 1084.

131. *Census of the Philippine Islands*, 1: 101.

132. AGI AF 38-1 Sebastián de Pineda 26 May 1619; Montero y Vidal, *Piratería*, 1: 153; Saleeby, *History of Sulu*, 175.

133. AGI AF 30 Juan Niño de Tavora 4 Aug. 1628.

134. PNA Cedulario (1633) [*sic*] Comission to Sargento Major Don Juan de Carabeo 10 May 1635; Torrubia, *Dissertación*, 32; Montero y Vidal, *Piratería*, 1: 156.

135. *Census of the Philippine Islands*, 1: 101.

136. PNA Cedulario (1645–1649) Order to Alcalde Mayor of Tayabas 18 Dec. 1646.

137. NL Ayer 1300 VA V: 201–230 Provincials to Governor Cruzat y Góngora 7 Oct. 1701.

138. PNA Erección de pueblos Tayabas 1755–1794 Roberto Moxica 12 Dec. 1771, PNA Erección de pueblos Tayabas 1768–1896 Francisco de San Juan 20 Dec. 1768.

139. PNA Erección de pueblos Tayabas 1768–1896 Cuenta de los reales tributos 13 Dec. 1771. In 1768, the thirteen settlements had 5,172 tributary Filipinos.

140. PNA Erección de pueblos Tayabas 1768–1896 Alcalde Mayor of Tayabas 6 Nov. 1781.

141. NL Ayer 1325 (shelf) Andrés de Castro y Amoedo 1790.

142. PNA Erección de pueblos Tayabas 1755–1794 Mariano Valero 25 Dec. 1788.

143. Morga, *Sucesos*, 202; San Agustín, *Conquistas*, lib 3 cap. 24: 706–707; Costa, *Jesuits*, 284.

144. BR 27: 215–226 No author, n.d. [1637].

145. BR 36: 177–180 Diego de Santa Theresa 1743; Herce, "Recollects," 237; Postma, "Mindoro Missions Revisited," 258–259.

146. AGN Mexico City Ramo Filipinas tomo 3 exp. 14 fols. 257–280 Xavier de Pisson 1755.

147. Lopez, "Culture Contact and Ethnogenesis," 23–24; Montero y Vidal, *Historia general*, 2: 231–232.

148. ARSI Phil 2 II fols. 314–317 Catologus christianorum 1659.

149. AGI AF 74 and BR 20: 229, 233 Miguel García Serrano 31 July 1622.

150. PNA Cedulario 1636–1656 pp. 121–127 Real cédula 26 June 1653, Cedulario 1659–1664 pp. 348–357 Reales cédulas 13 Mar. 1658, 16 June 1659.

151. AGI CO 1253 fols. 111–120 Oficiales de la real hacienda 1700.

152. In 1735, the figures provided by San Antonio suggest that there was a total population of about 85,000. This is calculated from San Antonio's figures for Laguna, Balayan, and Tayabas, plus 4,844 estimated from 1,211 *tributos* for Cavite (San Antonio, *Philippine Chronicles*, 68, 79, 81). These figures are associated with a total tributary population of 14,488, which compared to about 50,000 suggests a 17 percent increase from 1700. Assuming that the total population increased by a similar percentage would suggest a total population in 1700 of about 70,550. However, this figure would have included a significant number of persons of other races, especially in Cavite; in 1785 they accounted for about 7 percent of the population (AGI IG 1527 Extracto del número de habitantes . . . 1785), though this figure is for the archbishopric of Manila and therefore does not include Tayabas.

153. This is interpolated from the number of *almas* in 1792 of 193,612 and in 1805 of 225,419 assuming geometric growth (AUST Libro 229 no. 1 Estatística de las islas Filipinas 1815).

154. Murillo Velarde, *Historia*, 63.

155. BR 41: 181 San Francisco de Assis 1756.

156. BR 36: 181 Diego de Santa Theresa 1743.

157. Herce, "Recollects," 238–239.

158. *Census of the Philippine Islands*, 2: 123.

159. Gardner and Maliwanag, *Indic Writings*, 1: 5.

160. Schuldt, *Mindoro-Sozialgeschichte*, 41, 43, 243. In 1939 the island of Mindoro had a population of 118,893.

161. Abad, "Los franciscanos," 418–419, Alonso de Montemayor 16 July 1622; Retana, *Archivo del bibliófilo filipino*, 1: 1–13 Entrada de la seráfica religión 1649.

162. AGI AF 19 and BR 12: 142–146 Pedro de Acuña 12 Dec. 1603; Wernstedt and Spencer, *Philippine Island World*, 399.

163. PNA Cedulario 1636–1656 pp. 121–127 Commission to the Alcalde Mayor of Tayabas 27 June 1653, Cedulario 1659–1664 pp. 27–31 Commission to the Alcalde Mayor of Laguna 13 Mar. 1658.

164. ARSI Phil 8 fols. 74–133 Antonio Succio 25 Jan. 1707.

165. PNA Erección de pueblos Laguna 1755–1886 Governor Arandía Santísteban 24 Mar. 1756, Fernández de Guevara 27 July 1756, 24 Mar. 1756.

166. PNA Erección de pueblos Laguna 1755–1886 Fernández de Guevara 27 July 1756, 24 Mar. 1756. These calculations exclude three out of the thirty-one villages for which information is incomplete.

167. Gardner and Maliwanag, *Indic Writings*, 2: 5.

168. Gardner and Maliwanag, *Indic Writings*, 1: 12.

169. Cordoniu y Nieto, *Topografía médica*, 321–322.

170. Martínez, *Compendio histórico*, 30; Abad, "Los franciscanos," 430–431.

171. Retana, *Archivo del bibliófilo filipino*, 1: 17 Entrada de la seráfica religión 1649.

172. Huerta, *Estado geográfico*, 559; Pastrana, "Franciscans," 105; Medina, *Cavite*, 174; Guerra, *El hospital*, 541, 550. It catered to sixteen to twenty patients.

173. Martínez, *Compendio histórico*, 30; Huerta, *Estado geográfico*, 559; Abad, "Los franciscanos, 431. The hospital was demolished in 1662 because it was in the line of fire from a battery that defended Cavite, but it was rebuilt four times before being abandoned in the nineteenth century.

174. Montero y Vidal, *Historia*, 2: 531. Another eruption occurred in 1716, destroying several towns (*Census of the Philippine Islands*, 1: 101).

175. Xenos and Ng, "Nagcarlan," 204–205. Owen, "Life, Death and the Sacraments," 229, also hints at a similar pattern at Tigaon.

Chapter 9: Bikol

1. Schurz, *Manila Galleon*, 221–222.

2. AGI AF 59-2 Información de Martín de Goiti 1573; *CDIU* 2: 213 Relación mui circumstanciada 1567; Colin, *Labor evangélica*, 1: 132; Noone, *Discovery and Conquest*, 412.

3. San Agustín, *Conquistas*, lib. 2 cap. 1: 316, 319, lib. 3 cap. 25: 718; Abella, *Bikol Annals*, 3–4; Goyena del Prado, *Ibalon*, 122.

4. Goyena del Prado, *Ibalon*, 122.

5. San Agustín, *Conquistas*, lib. 2 cap. 32: 504.

6. AGI PAT 24-1 and Rodríguez, *Historia*, 14: 66 Diego de Herrera 31 July 1570.

7. AGI PAT 23-7 Juan de la Isla, no date.

8. AGI PAT 24-9 Juan de Alva 20 July 1570.

9. AGI PAT 24-19 fols. 20r–20v Hernando Riquel 2 June 1576.

10. Abella, *Bikol Annals*, 5–6.

11. San Agustín, *Conquistas*, lib. 2 cap. 6: 346–347, cap. 7: 353–355; Noone, *Discovery and Conquest*, 411–412.

12. AGI PAT 24-25 N16 and BR 3: 161, 171 Juan Pacheco Maldonado 20 Apr. 1572; San Agustín, *Conquistas*, lib. 2 cap. 7: 355.

13. Abella, *Bikol Annals*, 5.

14. AGI AF 6 Guido de Lavezaris 16 July 1574; San Agustín, *Conquistas*, lib. 2 cap. 15: 398; Goyena del Prado, *Ibalon*, 128–129; Noone, *Discovery and Conquest*, 420.

15. San Agustín, *Conquistas*, lib. 2 cap. 30: 490; Goyena del Prado, *Ibalon*, 5–10; Abella, *Bikol Annals*, 5–6.

16. AGI AF 6 Guido de Lavezaris 17 July 1574.

17. The back coast or the east coast of Luzon.

18. AGI PAT 24-19 fols. 20r–20v, 24v–27r Hernando Riquel 2 June 1576.

19. AGI PAT 23-9 and BR 5: 52–53, 93–101 Miguel de Loarca [1582].

20. AGI PAT 24-19 fol. 30r Hernando Riquel 2 June 1576.

21. AGI AF 74 and BR 7: 269–272 Expediente sobre la cobranza de los tributos 12 Jan. 1591.

22. San Agustín, *Conquistas*, lib. 2 cap. 7: 353.

23. AGI AF 28-230 Diego de Villatoro 19 May 1679; Ribadeneyra, *Historia*, part 1 lib. 1 cap. 12: 60, cap. 14: 69; Retana, *Archivo del bibliófilo filipino*, 1: 4 José Castaño 1895.

24. AGI AF 84-4 and BR 34: 286–287 Martín de Rada 30 June 1574.

25. AGI PAT 23-21 Relación de la orden 17 Sept. 1574; Colin, *Labor evangélica*, 2: 663–664 Diego de Herrera 1570.

26. Wernstedt and Spencer, *Philippine Island World*, 409–413; Owen, "Kabikolan," 8–33; San Antonio, *Philippine Chronicles*, 62–65.

27. Owen, "Kabikolan," 433, 433n38.

28. Retana, *Archivo del bibliófilo filipino*, 1: 10–18 José Castaño 1895.

29. PNA Patronato (Bound) Bishop of Nueva Caceres 23 Sept. 1785.

30. Owen, "Kabikolan," 23.

31. Blumentritt, *Philippine Ethnography*, 114; Abad, "Los franciscanos," 423; Owen, "Kabikolan," 430n27.

32. Owen, "Kabikolan," 30.

33. AGI AF 6 Guido de Lavezaris 17 July 1574; AGI PAT 23-9 and BR 5: 94–97 Miguel de Loarca [1582]; Morga, *Sucesos*, 288.

34. Hembd, "Political Economy," 102; Owen, "Kabikolan," 187–188.

35. Scott, *Cracks*, 88.

36. AGI AF 6 Guido de Lavezaris 17 July 1574 ; San Agustín, *Conquistas*, lib. 2 cap. 7: 355; Goyena del Prado, *Ibalon*, 25–26.

37. AGI PAT 23-7 and BR 3: 195 Juan de la Isla (Diego de Artieda) no date, AF 84-2 Diego de Herrera, no date, PAT 23-9 and BR 5: 94–95, 98–99 Miguel de Loarca [1582]; *CDIU* 2: 213 Relación mui circumstanciada 1567; Morga, *Sucesos*, 261; Tegengren, "Gold," 586–588, 591–592.

38. Scott, *Cracks*, 89.

39. AGI PAT 24-9 Juan de Alva 20 July 1570. It is not clear that Ibalon actually referred to Bikol; in the years before Manila was established, the name was sometimes used to refer to the island of Luzon as a whole. For example, AGI PAT 23-7 and BR 3: 195 Juan de la Isla (Diego de Artieda) no date.

40. San Agustín, *Conquistas*, lib. 2 cap. 7: 355.

41. AGI AF 84-2 no author, no date [ca. 1572].

42. AGI AF 6 Guido de Lavezaris 17 July 1574, PAT 23-9 and BR 5: 52–53, 93–101 Miguel de Loarca [1582].

43. Abad, "Los franciscanos," 418–419, Alonso de Montemayor 16 July 1622.

44. Owen, "Kabikolan," 30. Norman Owen (*Prosperity*, 23) suggests that the maximum number of those living in the hills of all races in the nineteenth century was between 20,000 and 30,000.

45. For example, AGI PAT 24-9 Juan de Alva 20 July 1570, PAT 24-25 N16 and BR 3: 161, 171 Juan Pacheco Maldonado 20 Apr. 1572, AF 74 Domingo de Salazar 25 June 1588.

46. Colin, *Labor evangélica*, 2: 22.

47. Owen, *Prosperity*, 33.

48. AGI AF 74 Domingo de Salazar 25 June 1588; Morga, *Sucesos*, 288; Owen, "Kabikolan," 49.

49. Owen, "Kabikolan," 441n68.

50. San Antonio, *Philippine Chronicles*, 65.

51. AUST Libro 229 no. 1 Estatística [*sic*] de las Yslas 1815.

52. Owen, "Kabikolan," 51–52, 441n68.

53. AGI PAT 23-7 and BR 3: 195 Juan de la Isla (Diego de Artieda), no date, AF 84-2 Diego de Herrera, no date, PAT 23-9 and BR 5: 94–95, 98–99 Miguel de Loarca [1582]; Morga, *Sucesos*, 261.

54. Owen, "Kabikolan," 253–254; Goyena del Prado, *Ibalon*, 164; Tegengren, "Gold," 555, 586–588.

55. BR 18: 94 Pedro de Bivero 1618.

56. AGI AF 25-32 Bishop of Nueva Caceres 16 Dec. 1688; Retana, *Archivo del bibliófilo filipino*, 1: 40 Entrada de la seráfica religión 1649.

57. Mallari, *Ibalon*, 5. This allegation was denied by the bishop.

58. AGI AF 163 Audiencia 20 June 1700.

59. AGI AF 25-32 Bishop of Nueva Caceres 16 Dec. 1688.

60. Owen, "Kabikolan," 252.

61. Diaz-Trechuelo, "Eighteenth Century Philippine Economy," 790–797; Tegengren, "Gold," 566–571.

62. AGI AF 38-1 and BR 18: 173 Sebastián de Pineda 26 May 1619, AF 30 Oficiales reales 7 Sept. 1627; Colin, *Labor evangélica*, 1: 21; Schurz, *Manila Galleon*, 195.

63. Mallari, *Ibalon*, 17–19.

64. Patanñe, "To Launch a Sea Giant," 1041; Mallari, *Ibalon*, 13; Schurz, *Manila Galleon*, 195–198.

65. Owen, "Kabikolan," 281; Mallari, *Ibalon*, 13.

66. BR 27: 195 Juan Grau y Malfalcón 1637; Mallari, *Ibalon*, 32.

67. AGI AF 25-32 Bishop of Nueva Caceres 16 Dec. 1688.

68. Owen, "Kabikolan," 146–147.

69. Owen, "Kabikolan," 283, 533n8.

70. AGI AF 293 Manuel de Matos 13 June 1759.

71. AGI PAT 23-9 and BR 5: 94–95 Miguel de Loarca [1582].

72. AGI AF 296 Andrés González 15 May 1686, AF 122–123 Audiencia 20 June 1700.

73. AGI AF 85-211 Relación de las muchas mieses, no date; AGI AF 296 Andrés González 15 May 1686.

74. AGI AF 59-7 N10 Información que tuvo el obispo 19 Mar. 1582.

75. Huerta, *Estado geográfico*, 181.

76. Abella, *Bikol Annals*, 241n3. Masbate remained under Augustinian control until 1609.

77. AGI AF 74 and BR 20: 235 Miguel García Serrano 31 July 1622, AF 74 and BR 22: 87 Miguel García Serrano 25 July 1626. See also Abad, "Los franciscanos," 418–419 Alonso de Montemayor 16 July 1622.

78. Retana, *Archivo del bibliófilo filipino*, 1: 10–13; AGI AF 296 Razón de la gente administrada en esta provincia de San Gregorio 1709; San Antonio, *Philippine Chronicles*, 63; Huerta, *Estado geográfico*, 590.

79. The precise places were Mount Isarog (Tigaon, Goa, Manguirin, Mabatobato, Pili, and Sangay), in the forests of Camarines Norte and west Bikol (Lupi, Sipocot, and Ragay), and on the sparsely populated northeastern coast along San Miguel Bay and the Caramoan Peninsula (Caramoan, Siruma, and Tinambac) (Huerta, *Estado geográfico*, 200–222; Pérez, "Labor patriótica," 22–23; Abad, "Los franciscanos," 423; Owen, "Kabikolan," 27, and "Problems in Partido," 423–426).

80. AGI AF 83-136 Pablo Gomda and Gaspar Hadapon 30 Sept. 1690.

81. AGI AF 12-8 Andrés Gonzales 12 Dec. 1683, Gabriel de Curuzeláegui 20 May 1685.

82. AGI AF 296 Razón de la gente adminstrada en esta provincia de San Gregorio 1709, AF 296 Cristóbal de Jesús 21 May 1710.

83. San Antonio, *Philippine Chronicles*, 217–218.

84. Pérez, "Labor patriótica," 23–27; Sánchez Fuertes, "Estado de las misiones," 146–151.

85. AGI IG 1527 Plan general de todas las almas . . . obispado de Nueva Caceres 1780; PNA Patronatos Unclassified (Bound vol.) Bishop of Nueva Caceres 23 Sept. 1785.

86. PNA Patronatos Unclassified (Bound vol.) Bishop of Nueva Caceres 23 Sept. 1785.

87. Montero y Vidal, *Piratería*, 1: 72; Mallari, *Ibalon*, 30. Mallari, "Muslim Raids," provides a detailed chronology of Moro raids on Bikol, which is reproduced in *Ibalon*.

88. Owen, *Prosperity*, 27.

89. AGI AF 84-2 Diego de Herrera, no date.

90. AGI AF 38-1 and BR 18: 185 Sebastián de Pineda 26 June 1619; BR 27: 195 Juan Grau y Monfalcón 1637; Saleeby, *History of Sulu*, 175; Owen, "Kabikolan," 37, Mallari, *Ibalon*, 31.

91. Mallari, *Ibalon*, 31.

92. Costa, *Jesuits*, 322–323.

93. Montero y Vidal, *Piratería*, 1: 157; Mallari, *Ibalon*, 32.

94. Huerta, *Estado geográfico*, 589; Pérez, "Labor patriótica," 3: 303.

95. Retana, *Archivo del bibliófilo filipino*, 1–13 Entrada de la seráfica religión 1649.

96. Saleeby, *History of Sulu*, 185; Mallari, *Ibalon*, 37–40.

97. Mallari, *Ibalon*, 55n63.

98. AGI AF 293 Bishop of Nueva Caceres 29 June 1758; Abella, *Bikol Annals*, 105–106.

99. Saleeby, *History of Sulu*, 191.

100. Owen, "Kabikolan," 39–43, 436n51; Cruikshank, "Moro Impact," 152.

101. Abad, "Los franciscanos," 418–419 Alonso de Montemayor 16 July 1622.

102. AGI AF 222-7-20 fol. 11 Jueces oficiales de la real hacienda 16 June 1655, CO 1253 Oficiales reales 1700.

103. AGI AF 296 Cristóbal de Jesús 21 May 1710; see also Owen, *Prosperity*, 39.

104. San Antonio, *Philippine Chronicles*, 65.

105. AGI AF 296 Razón de la gente adminstrada en esta provincia de San Gregorio 1709. This was also noted by Owen, "Life, Death and the Sacraments," 232, for nineteenth-century Tigaon in Bikol.

106. Owen, *Prosperity*, 35–38.

107. Ribadeneyra, *Historia*, part 1 lib. 12: 59; see also AGI AF 74, BR 7: 678, and Rodríguez, *Historia*, 15: 357 Domingo de Salazar 25 June 1588.

108. San Agustín, *Conquistas*, lib. 2 cap. 7: 355.

109. San Antonio, *Philippine Chronicles*, 65; Huerta, *Estado geográfico*, 203.

110. Retana, *Archivo del bibliófilo filipino*, 1: 15–16; Huerta, *Estado geográfico*, 182–183; Martínez, *Compendio histórico*, 30.

111. Ribadeneyra, *Historia*, part 1 lib. 1 cap. 14: 68.

112. Owen, "Life, Death and the Sacraments," 233–234.

113. San Antonio, *Philippine Chronicles*, 63.

114. Owen, "Measuring Mortality," 97–101, 112n30.

115. Cordoniu y Nieto, *Topografía médica*, 321–322.

116. Owen, "Life, Death and the Sacraments," 228–229.

Chapter 10: Pampanga and Bulacan

1. Phelan, *Hispanization*, 100.

2. AGI PAT 24-25 and BR 3: 157–158 No author 20 Apr. 1572, AF 59-2 Petición y interrogatorio . . . Martín de Goiti 20 June 1572; San Agustín, *Conquistas*, lib. 2 cap. 3: 332–333, cap 4: 335–338, cap. 6: 348, cap. 7: 351–352.

3. AGI AF 84-3 and BR 34: 276 Memoria de los religiosos [Augustinians], no date [1573].

4. AGI PAT 24-19 fols. 41–42, 45, 46. Colin, *Labor evangélica*, 1: 158, erroneously gives the date as 15 April. Castilla and Caluya were assigned on 17 May and Vinto on 4 November 1572.

5. AGI PAT 23-9 and BR 5: 84–85 Miguel de Loarca [1582].

6. Wernstedt and Spencer, *Philippine Island World*, 371–372; Larkin, *Pampangans*, 2; McLennan, *Central Luzon Plain*, 9.

7. Larkin, *Pampangans*, 6, 45–47. The line follows inland from Lubao through San Fernando to Arayat.

8. AGI AF 6 and BR 4: 68 Francisco de Sande 7 June 1576; Medina, *Historia*, 82.

9. AGI AF 6 and BR 4: 80 Francisco de Sande 7 June 1576.

10. San Agustín, *Conquistas*, lib. 3 cap. 15: 658–660; Larkin, *Pampangans*, 18, 74.

11. AGI AF 6 and BR 4: 80 Francisco de Sande 7 June 1576, AF 84-2 No author, no date [1582]; San Agustín, *Conquistas*, lib. 2 cap. 32: 500, lib. 3 cap. 9: 626–627; Medina, *Historia*, 127–128; Doeppers, "Hispanic Influences," 28.

12. Morga, *Sucesos*, 265.

13. Doeppers, "Hispanic Influences," 28. See also Morga, *Sucesos*, 257.

14. AGI AF 84-2 No author, no date [1572].

15. Larkin, *Pampangans*, 21; Scott, "Filipino Class Structure," 105–106.

16. AGI PAT 24-25 and BR 3: 155 Relación del descubrimiento 20 Apr. 1572, PAT 23-9 and BR 5: 141 Miguel de Loarca [1582].

17. AGI PAT 25-60 fols. 47–51 and BR 16: 322, 329 Juan de Plasencia 31 Jan. 1599.

18. Larkin, *Pampangans*, 10.

19. AGI PAT 23-8 and BR 5: 202–204 Report on saleable offices, no date.

20. AGI AF 74 and Rodríguez, *Historia*, 15: 351 Domingo de Salazar 25 June 1588.

21. AGI AF 79 and BR 9: 103 Francisco Ortega, no date [1594].

22. AGI AF 18B Luis Pérez Dasmariñas 23 June 1594.

23. One *fanega* was equivalent to one *cavan* of twenty-four or twenty-five *gantas* of husked rice but two *cavanes* of unhusked rice. One *ganta* was equivalent to half a *celemín* (San Antonio, *Philippine Chronicles*, 165).

24. PNA Cedulario 1675–1685: 18–21 Auto to the *alcalde mayor* of Pampanga 11 Mar. 1681. In 1681 Pampangans had not been reassessed for thirteen years.

25. AGI AF 6 and Retana, *Archivo del bibliófilo filipino*, 3: 3–45 Domingo de Salazar, no date [1583], AF 80 and BR 19: 71–76 Pedro de San Pablo 7 Aug. 1620; Cummins, *Travels and Controversies*, 1: 55, and BR 37: 293–294 Domingo Fernández Navarrete ca. 1650.

26. AGI AF 18B and BR 10: 308 Autos para el buen gobierno 7 Dec. 1598.

27. AGI AF 20 Vicente de Sepúlveda 13 Aug. 1616.

28. In 1655 Pampangans were still being required to provide 24,000 *cavanes* unhusked rice a year for Cavite (AGI AF 22-50 Oficiales reales 4 July 1658; Cummins, *Travels and Controversies*, 1: 55 and BR 37: 293 Domingo Fernández Navarrete ca. 1650).

29. Phelan, *Hispanization*, 146.

30. AGI AF 28-225 Indice de cartas de oficiales reales 14 June 1670, AF 11-3 Juan de Vargas 20 June 1679, AF 23-59 Diego Antonio de Viga 25 June 1679, AF 75 Ginés de Troyas 26 May 1683.

31. AGI AF 6 and Retana, *Archivo del bibliófilo filipino*, 3: 3–45 Domingo de Salazar, no date [1583].

32. McLennan, *Central Luzon Plain*, 35–36.

33. PNA Cedulario Rare 1632–1649 [*sic*] Real cédula 10 Dec. 1709.

34. Roth, "Church Lands," 132–140.

35. Cushner, *Landed Estates*, 62–64; Roth, "Church Lands," 140–142.

36. *Recopilacíon* lib. 6 tit. 12 ley 40 Real cédula 26 May 1609.

37. PNA Cedulario 1716–1718 Informe del alcalde mayor de Pampanga 16 Mar. 1716.

38. AGI AF 34-52 Diego de Zarate 10 June 1581, AF 59-12 Amador de Arriarán 7 May 1586.

39. Cummins, *Travels and Controversies*, 1: 92 and BR 38: 43 Domingo Fernández Navarrete ca. 1650.

40. PNA Cedulario 1645–1649: 349–354 Real cédula 14 Dec. 1646.

41. AGI AF 38-1 and BR 18: 174 Sebastián de Pineda 26 May 1619.

42. AGI AF 9-30 Sabiniano Manrique de Lara 20 July 1661 describes the course of the rebellion. See Díaz, *Conquistas*, 571–572; Santa Cruz, *Historia*, 2: 383; Prieto Lucena, *Manrique de Lara*, 61–73.

43. Prieto Lucena, *Manrique de Lara*, 82–83.

44. PNA Cedulario 1716–1718: 99–102 Informe del alcalde mayor de Pampanga 16 Mar. 1716, Cedulario 1764: 171–177 Real cédula, no date [1764].

45. AGI AF 6 Domingo de Salazar, no date [1583], AF 8-104 Baltasar Ruiz de Escalona 31 Aug. 1638, AF 9-44 Diego Salcedo 25 June 1665.

46. AGI AF 12-57 Gabriel Curuzeláegui 15 May 1688.

47. AGI AF 19 and BR 14: 169 Rodrigo Díaz Guiral 30 June 1606, AF 26-25 Autos de la visita . . . Abella Fuertes 10 June 1695.

48. AGI AF 28-323 Diego de Villatoro [1679].

49. Morga, *Sucesos*, 225; Larkin, *Pampangans*, 27. A long list of the occasions on which the Pampangans rendered military service may be found in Henson, *Province of Pampanga*, 27–35.

50. Morga, *Sucesos*, 232–237.

51. AGI AF 38-1 and BR 18: 182 Sebastián de Pineda 26 May 1619; Schurz, *Manila Galleon*, 346.

52. AGI AF 7-52 Mapa de la real armada 15 June 1617.

53. BR 35: 264, 267 Relación de los sucesos 1647.

54. AGI AF 11 and BR 25: 148–150 Real cédula 13 June 1636, AF 8-104 and BR 29: 55 Baltasar Ruiz de Escalona 31 Aug. 1638; BR 35: 264, 267 Relación de los sucesos 1647; AGI AF 22-34 Audiencia 13 July 1656; Medina, *Historia*, 128.

55. AGI AF 22-21 Juan de Bolivar y Cruz 19 July 1655.

56. BR 47: 96–127 Fernando Valdés Tamón 1739.

57. AGI AF 7-3-45 Relación . . . provincia de Tuy, Manuel de la Vega 3 July 1609.

58. AGI AF 18A and BR 8: 213 Parecer de los augustinos 19 Jan. 1592; Medina, *Historia*, 158; Doeppers, "Hispanic Influences," 31.

59. AGI AF 18B and BR 34: 408 Gómez Pérez Dasmariñas 21 June 1591, AF 18B and BR8: 241 Gómez Pérez Dasmariñas 31 May 1592.

60. AGI AF 9-44 Diego Salcedo 25 June 1665, AF 9-43 Resumen de la carta . . . Diego Salcedo 4 Aug. 1665, AF 10-48 Sabiniano Manrique de Lara 8 Oct. 1666.

61. AGI AF 330 lib. 6 fols. 204r–205r Real cédula 26 Mar. 1670, AF 9-43 Resumen de la carta . . . Diego Salcedo 4 Aug. 1667, 26 Mar. 1670; Mozo, *Noticia*, 70–71; Díaz, *Conquistas*, 654–655; Scott, *Discovery of the Igorots*, 58–60; Antolín, *Notices*, 184–193.

62. AGI EC 404B Juan de la Madre de Dios 3 June 1680; Salazar, *Historia*, 141.

63. AGI AF 6 and BR 10: 213 Francisco Tello 12 July 1599, AF 19 and BR 157 Rodrigo Díaz Guiral 30 June 1606; NL Ayer 1300 VA V fols. 152, 173 Hernando de los Ríos Coronel 1621; AGI AF 24-28 Audiencia 22 June 1684.

64. AGI AF 18B Autos para el buen gobierno 2 Oct. 1598, AF 21-17 Juan Quesada Hurtado de Mendoza 24 Nov. 1630.

65. AGI PAT 23-9 and BR 34: 377 Relación de las islas filipinas, no date; see also AGI AF 27 and BR 18: 341 Hernando de los Ríos Coronel 1619–1620, AF 10-31 Manuel de León 31 May 1674, AF 28-320 Diego de Villatoro 19 May 1679.

66. Phelan, *Hispanization*, 146; Larkin, *Pampangans*, 31.

67. AGI AF 8-104 Baltasar Ruiz de Escalona 31 Aug. 1638.

68. AGI AF 18A Fiscal Ayala 2 June 1585; Díaz, *Conquistas*, 542.

69. AGI AF 59-7 Información que hizo el obispo 19 Mar. 1582; San Agustín, *Conquistas*, lib. 2 cap. 9: 363–364; Galende, "Augustinians," 40.

70. AGI AF 20-4-34 Memoria de los conventos 1610.

71. AGI AF 59-7 Información que hizo el obispo 19 Mar. 1593.

72. San Agustín, *Conquistas*, lib. 3 cap. 15: 658, cap. 25: 718; Larkin, *Pampangans*, 23.

73. McLennan, *Central Luzon Plain*, 43–44; Doeppers, "Hispanic Influences," 55.

74. Martínez de Zúñiga, *Estadismo*, 1: 479; Larkin, *Pampangans*, 58.

75. Pastrana, "Franciscans," 85.

76. Lilly Lot 511 vol. 2 fols. 267–268 Antolín de Alzaga 26 Aug. 1702; AGI AF 296 Domingo de Labalburu 13 June 1703; PNA Cedulario 1696–1705: 621–633 Juan Bautista de Olarte 1 June 1705; AGI AF 297-38 El Conde de Lizárraga 15 June 1714; AF 140 Márquez de Torrecampo 30 June 1725; Lopez Memorial Museum. Cédulas y autos 1707–1713 Augustinian Provincial Joseph López 24 June 1712; Mozo, *Noticia*, 19–28; Keesing, *Ethnohistory*, 73–76.

77. Pérez, *Relaciones augustinianas*, 301–321 Sebastián Foronda 20 June 1704.

78. AGI AF 140 Márquez de Torrecampo 30 June 1725.

79. Keesing, *Ethnohistory*, 77; Galende, "Augustinians," 58. Keesing gives the date as 1753.

80. Larkin, *Pampangans*, 24; McLennan, *Central Luzon Plain*, 44–45.

81. Mozo, *Noticia*, 28; NL Ayer 1499 (Box) Pedro Velasco 16 Apr. 1760; Doeppers, "Hispanic Influences," 81–82.

82. AGI AF 84-3 and BR 34: 276 Memoria de los religiosos [Augustinians].

83. AGI AF 6 and Retana, *Archivo del bibliófilo filipino*, 3: 3–45 Domingo de Salazar no date [1583].

84. AGI AF 84-3 and BR 34: 281 Memoria de los religiosos [Augustinians].

85. AGI AF 29-87 Memoria y lista de las encomiendas 1606.

86. Medina, *Historia*, 82, 128, 139, 156.

87. AGI AF 79 and BR 9: 103 Francisco de Ortega, no date [1594].

88. Díaz, *Conquistas*, 31.

89. PNA Cedulario 1764 pp. 171–177 Real cédula, no date [1764].

90. Lilly Lot 514 fols. 105–106 No author, no date.

91. AGI AF 26-25 Audiencia 10 June 1695.

92. NL Ayer 1301 Joseph Ignacio de Arzadún y Rebolledo 28 Mar. 1743.

93. AGI CO 1253 Oficiales reales 1700.

94. In 1700 there were 12,304.75 *tributos*, which suggests a total population of about 50,000, to which a few thousand need to be added for those outside Spanish administration.

95. Doeppers, "Hispanic Influences," 85–86.

96. McLennan, "Changing Human Ecology," 62.

97. AGI AF 6 and BR 4: 68 Francisco de Sande 7 June 1576; San Agustín, *Conquistas*, lib. 2 cap. 9: 364, lib. 3 cap. 18: 675.

98. Based on the geometric growth rate in the number of *almas* between 1792 and 1805.

99. AGI IG 1527 Extracto del número de habitantes 1785.

Chapter 11: Ilocos and Pangasinan

1. In fact, southern Ilocos alternated between Dominican and Augustinian control.

2. Doeppers, "Hispanic Influences," 78.

3. Morga, *Sucesos*, 59.

4. San Agustín, *Conquistas*, lib. 2 cap. 12: 379–380.

5. AGI PAT 24-14 Juan Pacheco Maldonado, no date, PAT 24-25 fol. 16 and BR 3: 171 Anon. 20 Apr. 1572; Reyes y Florentino, *Historia de Ilocos*, 2: 12–20; San Agustín, *Conquistas*, lib. 2 cap. 13: 385–390; Keesing, *Ethnohistory*, 14–15.

6. San Agustín (*Conquistas*, lib. 2 cap. 13: 385–386) later claimed that Vigan had 1,500 houses.

7. AGI PAT 24-27 and BR 34: 257–259 Francisco de Ortega 6 June 1573.

8. A *tae* or *tael* was a Chinese measure equivalent to about 31.1 grams or about 1.1 ounces avoirdupois (Tegengren, "Gold," 595).

9. AGI PAT 24-21 Martín de Goiti no date, 1570s, AF 59-2 Martín de Goiti 1573; see also Colin, *Labor evangélica*, 1: 135, but Colin's transcription is full of errors.

10. AGI PAT 24-27 fols. 3–4 and BR 34: 259–262 Francisco de Ortega 6 June 1573, AF 339 lib. I fols. 187r–190v Real cédula 24 Apr. 1580.

11. AGI PAT 24-19 and BR 3: 253–256 Martín de Rada 21 June 1574.

12. AGI AF 84-3 and BR 34: 277 Memorial de los religiosos de las Islas del Poniente, no date (1573?).

13. San Agustín, *Conquistas*, lib. 2 cap. 18: 417, cap. 20: 426.

14. San Agustín, *Conquistas*, lib. 3 cap. 2: 586.

15. AGI AF 18A and BR6: 185 Memorial of the citizens of Manila 26 July 1586.

16. AGI AF 6 Guido de Lavezaris 16 July 1574, AF 6 and BR 3: 276 Guido de Lavezaris 17 July 1574.

17. San Agustín, *Conquistas*, lib. 2 cap. 16: 401.

18. AGI PAT 24-19 fols. 48, 50–54 Hernando Riquel 2 June 1576.

19. AGI PAT 24-21 fols. 10–12 Martín de Goiti, no date [1570s].

20. Doeppers, "Hispanic Influences," 17; McLennan, *Central Luzon Plain*, 27.

21. AGI PAT 23-9 and BR 5: 104–107 Miguel de Loarca [1582].

22. Wernstedt and Spencer, *Philippine Island World*, 20, 368–372; San Agustín, *Conquistas*, lib. 3 cap. 25: 718.

23. McLennan, *Central Luzon Plain*, 17.

24. Cortes, *Pangasinan*, 12; McLennan, *Central Luzon Plain*, 23, 28.

25. Wernstedt and Spencer, *Philippine Island World*, 328–332; Jocano, *Ilocanos*, 1–2.

26. AGI PAT 23-9 and BR 34: 382 Miguel de Loarca, no date. See also Colin, *Labor evangélica*, 1: 23.

27. AGI PAT 24-21 Martín de Goiti no date, 1570s, AF 59-2 Martín de Goiti 1573, PAT 24-27 and BR 34: 257 Francisco de Ortega 6 June 1573, PAT 23-9 and BR 5: 107–111 Miguel de Loarca [1582].

28. AGI PAT 23-9 and BR 5: 107 Miguel de Loarca [1582]; Morga, *Sucesos*, 265; Cortes, *Pangasinan*, 12.

29. AGI PAT 24-21 Martín de Goiti 3 Mar. 1573.

30. Cortes, *Pangasinan*, 25–26.

31. AGI PAT 24-21 Martín de Goiti 3 Mar. 1573.

32. Lewis, *Ilocano Rice Farmers*, 83; Fox, "Philippines in Prehistoric Times," 57; Jocano, *Ilocanos*, 97–98.

33. AGI PAT 23-9 and BR 5: 105–107, 118–119 Miguel de Loarca [1582].

34. AGI PAT 24-27 and BR 34: 257 Francisco de Ortega 6 June 1573.

35. Cortes, *Pangasinan*, 34–39.

36. AGI PAT 23-9 and BR 5: 110–111 Miguel de Loarca [1582].

37. AGI PAT 23-9 and BR 5: 106 Miguel de Loarca [1582].

38. Keesing, *Ethnohistory*, 305–307; Lewis, *Ilocano Rice Farmers*, 128–129; Jocano, *Ilocanos*, 28–29.

39. Cummins, *Travels and Controversies*, 1: 95, and BR 38: 48 Domingo Fernández Navarrete, ca. 1650.

40. Keesing, *Ethnohistory*, 95, 122.

41. Wernstedt and Spencer, *Philippine Island World*, 372.

42. AGI PAT 24-14 Juan Pacheco Maldonado, no date, PAT 24-25 fol. 16 and BR 3: 171 Anon 20 Apr. 1572; Medina, *Historia*, 150; San Agustín, *Conquistas*, XLII.

43. Wernstedt and Spencer, *Philippine Island World*, 331–332.

44. AGI 24-29 and BR 3: 257–258 Martín de Rada 21 June 1574. It is not clear whether this observation applied to just Ilocos or Luzon as a whole.

45. This could refer to the more extensive use of the plow or the sickle, since the method of harvesting in Ilocos was by cutting the rice stalk by stalk using a hand knife (Lewis, *Ilocano Rice Farmers*, 58–61).

46. AGI AF 18B Francisco Tello 12 July 1599; Cummins, *Travels and Controversies*, 1: 55, and BR 37: 294 Domingo Fernández Navarrete, ca. 1650; Reyes y Florentino, *Historia de Ilocos*, 2: 141.

47. AGI PAT 24-29 Guido de Lavezaris, no date and BR 3: 265–70, AF 34-15 Guido de Lavezaris 17 July 1574.

48. Cole, *Tinguian*, 395–396; Keesing, *Ethnohistory*, 136–137, 143.

49. Reyes y Florentino, *Historia de Ilocos*, 2: 81.

50. Jocano, *Ilocanos*, 51–55, 82.

51. AGI PAT 23-9 and BR 5: 104–105 Miguel de Loarca [1582]; San Agustín, *Conquistas*, XLII and cap. 2: 379–380, cap. 18: 417.

52. APSR Pangasinan 1 doc. 1 Alonso Jiménez et al. 11 Aug. 1593; AGI AF 7 and BR 14: 302 Juan Manuel de la Vega 3 July 1609; AGI AF 30 Gasto fecho en el descubrimiento 29 Apr. 1624; Morga, *Sucesos*, 261; Medina, *Historia*, 150.

53. BR 18: 96 Pedro de Bivero 1618; Morga, *Sucesos*, 308; APSR Pangasinan 12 Gerónimo Hernández 9 Dec. 1810.

54. Scott, *Filipinos in China*, 7.

55. AGI PAT 23-9 and BR 5: 104–105 Miguel de Loarca [1582].

56. Medina, *Historia*, 150; San Agustín, *Conquistas*, XLII; Routledge, *Diego Silang*, 6.

57. AGI PAT 24-19 fols. 51–54 Hernando Riquel 2 June 1576.

58. AGI AF 74 and Rodríguez, *Historia*, 15: 351 Domingo de Salazar 25 June 1588.

59. AGI PAT 25-38 and BR 8: 104–105 Relación punctual de las encomiendas 31 May 1591. The two paying tribute to the Crown were Lingayen and Labaya (Binalatongan) (See AGI AF 29-87 Memorial y lista de las encomiendas 1606).

60. Cortes, *Pangasinan*, 26–28.

61. AGI PAT 24-27 fols. 3–4 and BR 34: 259–262 Francisco de Ortega 6 June 1573, AF 339 lib. 1 fols. 187r–190v Real cédula 24 Apr. 1580. The original document refers to 400,000 *men*.

62. AGI PAT 24-19 fols. 50–54 Hernando Riquel 2 June 1576.

63. AGI PAT 24-21 fols. 5, 8–9 Martín de Goiti [1570s].

64. AGI AF 84-2 No author, no date [1570s].

65. AGI PAT 23-9 and BR 5: 107–111 Miguel de Loarca [1582]. Only 1,000 Indians have been included out of the 2,000 Loarca assigned to Alinguey and Baratao, the former being included in Pangasinan.

66. AGI AF 74 and Domingo de Salazar 25 June 1588.

67. AGI AF 34 Captains of Manila 1577, AF 339 lib. 1 fols. 187r–190v Real cédula 24 Apr. 1580.

68. AGI AF 84-3 and BR 34: 277 Memoria de los religiosos, no date (1573?).

69. This uses Loarca's figure of 27,100 in 1582 and adds 3,000 for those outside Spanish control.

70. Schmitz, *Abra Mission*, 17.

71. San Agustín, *Conquistas*, lib. 2 cap. 12: 382.

72. AGI PAT 24-12 and BR 3: 23–229 Andrés de Mirandola 8 Jan. 1574.

73. AGI AF 7 and BR 14: 302 Juan Manuel de la Vega 3 July 1609, AF 30 Gasto fecho en el descubrimiento 29 Apr. 1624; Morga, *Sucesos*, 261; Medina, *Historia*, 150; San Agustín, *Conquistas*, lib. 2 cap. 15: 398; Noone, *Discovery and Conquest*, 420.

74. AGI AF 29-27 Oficiales reales 6 June 1576, AF 6-3-26 Francisco de Sande 7 June 1576; Scott, *Discovery of the Igorots*, 10.

75. AGI AF 7 and BR 14: 292 Juan Manuel de la Vega 3 July 1609.

76. Scott, *Discovery of the Igorots*, 13–14.

77. Antolín, *Notices*, 124–126, Real cédula 19 Dec. 1618.

78. AGI AF 30 Gasto fecho en el descubrimiento de las minas 29 Apr. 1624.

79. AGI AF 7-59 García de Aldana Cabrera 20 May 1620.

80. AGI AF 30 and BR 20: 263 Alonso Martín Quirante 1624, AF 30 Gasto fecho en el descubrimiento de las minas 29 Apr. 1624; Scott, *Discovery of the Igorots*, 30–38; Antolín, *Notices*, 158–159, Real cédula 6 Dec. 1624.

81. AGI AF 30 Gasto fecho en el descubrimiento de las minas 29 Apr. 1624; Antolín, *Notices*, 159–160.

82. AGI AF 9-43 Resumen de la carta . . . Diego de Salcedo escribió 4 Aug. 1667, AF 330 lib. 6 fols. 204r–205r Real cédula 26 Mar. 1670; Mozo, *Noticia*, 70–71; Díaz, *Conquistas*, 654–655; Antolín, *Notices*, 184–193; Scott, *Discovery of the Igorots*, 58–60.

83. AGI PAT 24-27 and BR 34: 258 Francisco de Ortega 6 June 1573.

84. AGI AF 59-23 Servicios . . . Francisco Morante 8 June 1595.

85. San Agustín, *Conquistas*, lib. 2: cap. 25: 462–463; Reyes y Florentino, *Historia de Ilocos*, 2: 33.

86. Motulsky et al, “Glucose-6-phosphate dehydrogenase,” 102, 106.

87. De Bevoise, *Agents*, 142.

88. BR 32: 65n Pedro de Alfaro to Juan de Ayora 13 Oct. 1579.

89. AGI PAT 23-8 and BR 5: 202–204 Report on saleable offices, no date.

90. AGI PAT 25-38 fol.6 and BR 8: 105 Relación punctual de las encomiendas 28 May 1591.

91. Morga, *Sucesos*, 289.

92. San Agustín, *Conquistas*, lib. 2 cap. 12: 382; Medina, *Historia*, 150.

93. BR 4: 23–46 Francisco de Sande 7 June 1576; San Agustín, *Conquistas*, lib 2 cap. 16–21: 404–436; Boxer, *South China*, xliii–xliv.

94. Pérez, *Relaciones augustinianas*, 115; Reyes y Florentino, *Historia de Ilocos*, 2: 61.

95. San Agustín, *Conquistas*, lib. 3 cap. 6: 610–611; Reyes y Florentino, *Historia de Ilocos*, 2: 42–45, 57; Foronda and Foronda, *Samtoy*, 11–12.

96. AGI AF 20-4-34 Memoria de los conventos de la orden de nuestro padre San Agustín, no date; Reyes y Florentino, *Historia de Ilocos*, 2: 82.

97. Aduarte, *Historia*, lib. 1 cap. 21: 75–76.

98. AGI AF 59-7 Información que hizo el obispo 19 Mar. 1582; Cortes, *Pangasinan*, 71. The Franciscans arrived in 1576 and, although they established a church at Agoo, they retired from the province in 1591. The Augustinians, who arrived in 1575, established a monastery at Lingayen in 1587 and a *visita* at Manaoag (Aduarte, *Historia*, lib. 1 cap. 21: 75–76; San Agustín, *Conquistas*, lib. 3 cap. 6: 610). Galende, “Augustinians,” 56, equates this with Silac de los Reyes. This is credible given that Lingayen was the major town paying tribute to the Crown, but it is not mentioned in the allocation of *encomiendas* in 1574, whereas Silac is included. Lingayen was also referred to as the *convento* de los Reyes de Pangasinan (San Agustín, *Conquistas*, lib. 3 cap. 8: 622).

99. Aduarte, *Historia*, lib. 1 cap. 21: 75–78, lib. 1 cap. 71: 389.

100. AGI AF 84 Bernardo Navarro et al. 30 June 1596. See also AGI AF 20 Baltasar Fort 1610.

101. San Agustín, *Conquistas*, lib. 3 cap. 8: 622; Aduarte, *Historia*, lib. 1 cap. 65: 342.

102. BR 9: 216–217 Real cédula 15 May 1596; Reyes y Florentino, *Historia de Ilocos*, 2: 66.

103. Reyes y Florentino, *Historia de Ilocos*, 2: 73–74, 168.

104. Foronda and Foronda, *Samtoy*, 53n170. The see was not formally transferred to Vigan until 1758.

105. Medina, *Historia*, 150; Keesing, *Ethnohistory*, 27; Doeppers, "Hispanic Influences," 57–58; Cullinane, "Accounting for Souls," 289–291.

106. Cortes, *Pangasinan*, 80–81; Phelan, *Hispanization*, 47, 75.

107. Reyes y Florentino, *Historia de Ilocos*, 2: 142–144.

108. Díaz, *Conquistas*, 653–656; Keesing, *Ethnohistory*, 102–103. See also PNA Cedulario 1633 (Bound vol.) pp. 52–55 Real cédula 30 Jan. 1634.

109. NL Ayer Ms 1449 (Box) and BR 48: 53–57 Razón de los pueblos, Pedro Velasco 16 Apr. 1760.

110. Reyes y Florentino, *Historia de Ilocos*, 2: 67, 75; Foronda and Foronda, *Samtoy*, 22–23.

111. Díaz, *Conquistas*, 251; Reyes y Florentino, *Historia de Ilocos*, 2: 82; Antolín, *Notices*, 174–175; Schmitz, *Abra Mission*, 43–47.

112. Retana, *Archivo del bibliófilo filipino*, 1: 3, Juan Sánchez 15 June 1683; AGI AF 297-38 El Conde de Lizárraga 15 June 1714.

113. AGI AF 293 Juan de la Fuente Yepez 20 June 1756.

114. Keesing, *Ethnohistory*, 137.

115. PNA EP Ilocos Sur 1794–1890 Plano topográfico que comprehende de una parte de la provincia de Ilocos Sur, no date, EP Ilocos Sur y Norte 1807–1897 Juan de Cuellar 16 July 1798; Keesing, *Ethnohistory*, 128.

116. Foronda and Foronda, *Samtoy*, 18–20, 27–29.

117. Reyes y Florentino, *Historia de Ilocos*, 2: 59.

118. AGI AF 20-4-24 Memoria de los conventos 1610.

119. Mozo, *Noticia*, 73–75; Pérez, *Relaciones augustinianas*, 114, 120–121, Manuel Carrillo 27 June 1755, 20 Mar. 1758.

120. NL Ayer Ms 1449 (Box) and BR 48: 53–57 Razón de los pueblos, Pedro Velasco 16 Apr. 1760.

121. Reyes y Florentino, *Historia de Ilocos*, 2: 80.

122. Díaz, *Conquistas*, 651–653; Reyes y Florentino, *Historia de Ilocos*, 2: 129, 151.

123. AGI AF 297-38 El Conde de Lizárraga 15 June 1714, AF 297-39 Ciudad de Manila 13 July 1714; Mozo, *Noticia*, 73.

124. Pérez, *Relaciones augustinianas*, 115, Manuel Carrillo 27 June 1755.

125. Pérez, *Relaciones augustinianas*, 122, Manuel Carrillo 20 Mar. 1758.

126. AUST Libro de Becerro 37 fols. 250r and v Discurso sobre el gentio . . . Francisco Antolín 1789.

127. Reyes y Florentino, *Historia de Ilocos*, 2: 143–144.

128. BR 18: 97 Pedro de Bivero 1618.

129. Cortes, *Pangasinan*, 73–74.

130. AGI AF 74 and BR 20: 230 Miguel García Serrano 31 July 1622.

131. AGI AF 83-82 Bartolomé Marrón 8 Feb. 1690; Collantes, *Historia*, 586; Cortes, *Pangasinan*, 107; Doeppers, "Hispanic Influences," 83–84.

132. Cortes, *Pangasinan*, 113, 119–125. The Spanish often used the term "despoblado" to refer to an area that might not be completely devoid of human settlement but sparsely settled by unconverted peoples.

133. McLennan, *Central Luzon Plain*, 45; Doeppers, "Hispanic Influences," 82.

134. AGI AF 296 Certificación jurídica de los oficiales reales 21 June 1708; Fernández, "Dominican Apostolate," 178–179. In 1800 those formerly administered by the Augustinians contained 24,644 souls.

135. De Bevoise, *Agents*, 24.

136. AGI CO 1200 fols. 1188v–1191v Cargo de dinero de tributos 1588, AF 74 and BR 7: 274 Domingo de Salazar 12 Jan. 1591.

137. AGI AF 74 and BR 8: 28 Gómez Pérez Dasmariñas 28 Feb. 1591.

138. AGI PAT 24-21 Martín de Goiti 1573; APSR Pangasinan 1 doc. 1 Alonso Jiménez et al. 11 Aug. 1593. A slightly modified version appears in Antolín, *Notices*, 112–113.

139. AGI AF 18B Luis Pérez Dasmariñas 23 June 1594; Hidalgo Nuchera, *Encomienda*, 175.

140. AGI AF 60-11 Cargos y sentencia . . . contra Francisco Salgado 1597.

141. Reyes y Florentino, *Historia de Ilocos*, 2: 59.

142. AGI AF 18B Tello 12 July 1599, AF 329 lib. 1 fols. 40v–41r Real cédula 16 Feb. 1602.

143. AGI AF 22-50 Oficiales reales 4 July 1658. The *cestos* were to be of fifteen *gantas* each.

144. NL Ayer 1300 Informe . . . plaza de Zamboanga 4 Feb. 1738. The levy was 10,896.5 *gantas* of rice.

145. APSR Pangasinan 2 doc. 22 Indians of Pangasinan 18 Dec. 1782.

146. Schurz, *Manila Galleon*, 195–196.

147. McLennan, *Central Luzon Plain*, 19.

148. AGI AF 83-82 Bartolomé Marrón 8 Feb. 1690.

149. AGI AF 9-7 Diego Fajardo 31 July 1649. Unfortunately there are no more details of this interesting incident.

150. Schurz, *Manila Galleon*, 198.

151. AGI AF 38-1 and BR 18: 178 Relación hecha . . . Sebastián de Pineda 26 May 1619; Reyes y Florentino, *Historia de Ilocos*, 2: 94.

152. AGI AF 20 Bernardo de Santa Catalina 9 July 1616, Vicente de Sepúlveda 13 Aug. 1616, AF 330 lib. 6 fols. 166v–167r Real cédula 18 Oct. 1667.

153. AGI AF 9-13 Información hecha de los tratos y contratos 1650, AF 330 lib. 5 fols. 249v–250r Real cédula 19 June 1661.

154. Cummins, *Travels and Controversies*, 1: 56, and BR 37: 294 Domingo Fernández Navarrete ca. 1650.

155. Phelan, *Hispanization*, 146–147; Cortes, *Pangasinan*, 145–168; Prieto Lucena, *Manrique de Lara*, 73–83.

156. AGI AF 9-3-45 Ivan de Polanco, no date [1655]. Other sources put the figure higher at 9,000 or 11,000 (see Cortes, *Pangasinan*, 155–156).

157. AGI AF 9-29, 9-30 Sabiniano Manrique de Lara 20 July 1661; Prieto Lucena, *Manrique de Lara*, 73–83.

158. AGI AF 14-25 Fausto Cruzat y Góngora 16 Dec. 1690, AF 16-1 Fausto Cruzat y Góngora 8 June 1692, AF 26-25 Audiencia 10 June 1695.

159. NL Ayer 1301 Visitas a las provincias 28 Mar. 1743; Cortes, *Pangasinan*, 170–176.

160. Routledge, *Diego Silang*, 16–40; Scott, *Discovery of the Igorots*, 132–136; Schmitz, *Abra Mission*, 53.

161. Collantes, *Historia de la provincia*, 444.

162. Cortes, *Pangasinan*, 212–216.

163. Cortes, *Pangasinan*, 231.

164. Cortes, *Pangasinan*, 63.

165. Herce, "Recollects," 225–226.

166 . Keesing, *Ethnohistory*, 326–330, 342–343.

167. AGI PAT 25-38 fols. 6–9 and BR 8: 105 Relación punctual de las encomiendas 31 May 1591. The total given in the manuscript is an error; it should read 17,230.

168. AGI PAT 29-87 Memoria y lista de las encomiendas 1606.

169. AGI PAT 20-4-34 Memoria de los conventos y ministerios 1610. The figures exclude Alingayen and Agoo.

170. AGI PAT 25-45 Breve sumario . . . en esto año 1593; PAT 25-52 and BR 9: 61 Gómez Pérez Dasmariñas 20 June 1593; PAT 25-47 Información sobre los castigos de los indios Zambales 1593.

171. AGI PAT 24-29 and BR 3: 257 Martín de Rada 21 June 1574.

172. AGI PAT 24-27 fols. 3–4 and BR 34: 259–262 Francisco de Ortega 6 June 1573, PAT 24-19 and BR 3: 253–256 Martín de Rada 21 June 1574, AF 339 lib. 1 fols. 187r–190v Real cédula 24 Apr. 1580.

173. AGI PAT 24-38 and BR 3: 57, 60 Miguel de Legazpi, no date, AF 84-3 and BR 34: 279 Memoria de los religiosos, no date [1570s], AF 18B Fancisco Tello 12 July 1599, AF 329 lib. 1 fols. 40v–41r Real cédula 16 Feb. 1602.

174. AGI AF 6 Guido de Lavezaris 16 July 1574.

175. Aduarte, *Historia*, libro 1 cap. 71: 390.

176. A *pariancillo* (small Chinese quarter) developed at Lingayen and there were many merchants at Binmaley who traded in Chinese goods (Cortes, *Pangasinan*, 134–136).

177. BR 36: 97 Ignacio de Paz ca. 1658.

178. Reyes y Florentino, *Historia de Ilocos*, 2: 83, 87, 96, 141; PNA Cedulario (1626–1630) Mandamiento 26 Aug. 1628.

179. See chapter 3.

180. See Lamb, *Climate*, 2: 603–604.

181. Reyes y Florentino, *Historia de Ilocos*, 2: 142–143.

182. PNA Cedulario (1626–1630) Mandamiento 26 Aug. 1628.

183. See chapter 7.

184. Reyes y Florentino, *Historia de Ilocos*, 2: 96, 141.

185. See Appendix A.

186. BR 19: 66–67 Relation of events in the Filipinas, no author, 14 June 1620; Reyes y Florentino, *Historia de Ilocos*, 2: 87, 90; Saderra Masó, *Violent and Destructive Earthquakes*, 7–11.

187. Aduarte, *Historia*, lib. 1: cap. 65: 343, lib. 2 cap. 44: 284–285.

188. AGI AF 9-3-45 and AF 22-7-20 Oficiales reales 16 June 1655.

189. APSR Cagayan 18 Número de almas el obsipado de Nueva Segovia 1800. Also in Fernández, "Dominican Apostolate," opposite p. 178.

190. In 1792 there were 15,072 *almas* in Zambales (AUST Libro 229 no. 1 Estatística [*sic*] de las Yslas 1815).

191. Keesing, *Ethnohistory*, 40, 77–82, 105, 156–158.

192. NL Ayer 1333 (shelf) Descripción de la provincia de Ilocos ca. 1794. This figure excluded Ilocanos who were living outside the province, such as those in Manila.

193. AGI AF 293 Bishop of Nueva Segovia 20 June 1756.

194 . AUST Libro 17 fol. 2 and APSR Pangasinan 12 Mapa de los que han muerto . . . 1789. This figure includes settlements in southern Ilocos formerly administered by the Augustinians, where 965 died.

195. NL Ayer 1333 (shelf) Descripción de la provincia de Ilocos ca. 1794; PNL Historical Data Papers, Ilocos Norte–Batac.

196. APSR Pangasinan 2 doc. 10 Joachín del Rosario 30 May 1766, APSR Pangasinan 5 fols. 23–54 Andrés Meléndez 7 July 1766; Keesing, *Ethnohistory*, 40–42.

197. De Bevoise, *Agents*, 22.

198. AGI PAT 23-9 and BR 5: 105–107, 118–119 Miguel de Loarca [1582].

199. De Bevoise, *Agents*, 22.

200. PNA EP Ilocos Sur y Norte 1807–1897 Juan de Cuellar 16 July 1798.

201. McLennan, *Central Luzon Plain*, 106–111.

202. Xenos, "Ilocos Coast," 47, 73; McLennan, "Changing Human Ecology," 63–66.

203. PNA EP Zambales 1757–1824 vol. 2 *alcalde mayor* of Zambales, Manuel de Cendain 9 Sept. 1802.

204. McLennan, *Central Luzon Plain*, 105–116; Xenos, "Ilocos Coast," 47–49.

Chapter 12: Cagayan

1. AGI AF 18A and BR 7: 124 Fiscal Ayala 15 July 1589; San Agustín, *Conquistas*, lib. 2 cap. 37: 543.

2. BR 6: 204–206 Santiago de Vera et al. 26 July 1586, BR 9: 39 Gómez Pérez Dasmariñas 1593; San Agustín, *Conquistas*, lib. 2 cap. 16: 401; Costa, *Jesuits*, 50–57, 130–131.

3. AGI PAT 24-27 and BR 34: 257 Francisco de Ortega 6 June 1573. See also chapter 11.

4. BR 4: 25 Francisco de Sande 7 June 1576; AGI AF 34 Captains of Manila 1577.

5. AGI AF 6 Francisco de Sande 30 May 1580.

6. Ferrando and Fonseca, *Historia*, 1: 327–335.

7. AGI PAT 24-19 fols. 51–52, 58–64 Hernando Riquel 2 June 1576.

8. AGI AF 74 and Rodríguez, *Historia*, 15: 352, Domingo de Salazar 25 June 1588.

9. AGI PAT 25-38 fols. 9–14 Relación punctual de las encomiendas 31 May 1591.

10. AGI AF 74 and Rodríguez, *Historia*, 15: 353, Domingo de Salazar 25 June 1588.

11. AGI CO 1200 fols. 118v–91v Cargo de dinero de tributos 1588.

12. AGI AF 18A Fiscal Ayala 15 July 1589, AF 18B Gómez Pérez Dasmariñas 21 June 1591, PAT 25-44 Interrogatorio . . . Gabriel de Mercado 5 Feb. 1593.

13. AGI PAT 25-44 Interrogatorio . . . Gabriel de Mercado 5 Feb. 1593.

14. AGI PAT 25-44 Interrogatorio . . . Gabriel de Mercado 5 Feb. 1593.

15. CO 1202 fols. 182v–183v Cargo de tributos . . . 1594.

16. See chapter 13.

17. AGI AF 7-3-N45 Relación . . . de Tuy, Juan Manuel de la Vega 3 July 1609; Fernandez and Juan, "Nueva Vizcaya," 73–79. The fort was at old Cabagan, now San Pablo.

18. Wernstedt and Spencer, *Philippine Island World*, 18, 314–317; Keesing, *Ethnohistory*, 168–169.

19. San Agustín, *Conquistas*, lib. 2 cap. 14: 392.

20. De Jesus, "Control and Compromise," 22.

21. Keesing, *Ethnohistory*, 170.

22. AGI PAT 23-9 and BR 5: 99–101 Miguel de Loarca [1582]; AGI AF 74 Domingo de Salazar 25 June 1588; Quirino and García, "Manners," 389–390; Scott, *Barangay*, 266–267.

23. AGI AF 18B Luis Pérez Dasmariñas 9 June 1595.

24. Scott, *Barangay*, 264.

25. Quirino and Garcia, "Manners," 392.

26 San Agustín, *Conquistas*, lib. 2 cap. 37: 543–545.

27. Scott, *Barangay*, 268.

28. AGI PAT 25-1 Gonzalo Ronquillo 26 Sept. 1582.

29. Keesing, *Ethnohistory*, 224

30. Aduarte, *Historia*, lib. 1 cap. 59: 302–303.

31. Keesing, *Ethnohistory*, 224–225, 333.

32. Keesing, *Ethnohistory*, 238–239.

33. Malumbres, *Isabela*, 14.

34. Aduarte, *Historia*, lib. 2 cap. 17:108.

35. AGI AF 18B Luis Pérez Dasmariñas 9 June 1595.

36. Wallace, *Hill and Valley Farmers*, 124.

37. Wallace, *Hill and Valley Farmers*, 17–18.

38. AUST Libro de Becerro 37 Discurso sobre el gentió . . . Francisco Antolín 1789.

3. San Agustín, *Conquistas*, lib. 2 cap. 13: 386.

40. San Agustín, *Conquistas*, lib. 2 cap. 14: 391–393.

41. AGI PAT 23-9 and BR 5: 99–101 Miguel de Loarca [1582].

42. The regions listed were: "la provincia de potol (Fotol) y pueblos de catayuran y poblaciones del valle de sinabanga y río y provincia de dumon y río y pueblos de gatara y talapa y provincias de lobo y pueblos del río de nabunga y calabatan río de maquila y sus poblaciones y pueblos de tubigarao y caporagua y río de lulu y bato y sus poblaciones y ríos y provincia de zinbuey y con sus poblaciones y río de nalaguangan con sus poblaciones y pueblos de lulutan y batagua y pueblos del río de balisi y pueblo de purrao y culi e provincia de yugan con todas las poblaciones de los dichos ríos y provincias" (AGI PAT 25-44 Interrogatorio . . . Gabriel de Mercado 5 Feb. 1593).

43. Alonso Sánchez came to possess a portion of four *encomiendas* in the middle Cagayan Valley that in 1591 together possessed a total of 9,400 people and 2,350 *tributos*.

44. AGI PAT 25-38 fols. 9–14 Relación punctual de las encomiendas 31 May 1591.

45. AGI AF 18B Luis Pérez Dasmariñas 6 Dec. 1595.

46. AGI AF 6 Francisco Tello 17 June 1598, 12 July 1599.

47. BR 18: 101 Pedro de Bivero 1618.

48. AGI AF 20 and BR 17: 211 Baltasar Fort 1610. BR 17: 211 gives the date as 1612. However, the document is undated and supporting correspondence in the AGI suggests that more likely it was 1610.

49. BR 18: 100 Pedro de Bivero 1618; NL Ayer 1300 VA I: 551–607 Relación . . . hasta el de 1628.

50. AGI AF 7-83 and BR 22: 95 Fernando de Silva 30 July 1626.

51. NL Ayer 1300 VA I: 551–607 Relación . . . hasta el de 1628.

52. San Agustín, *Conquistas*, lib. 2 cap. 17: 544.

53. Salazar, *Historia*, 158. Father Antolín later computed their number at 10,000 *almas* (AUST Libro de Becerro 37 Discurso sobre el gentió . . . Francisco Antolín 1789).

54. Aduarte, *Historia*, lib. 2 cap. 17: 107–113; Salazar, *Historia*, 158; Malumbres, *Cagayan*, 28.

55. Malumbres, *Isabela*, 15.

56. APSR 110 Aditamento, Francisco Antolín, 1788; AUST Libro de Becerro 37 fols. 256r Discurso sobre el gentió . . . Francisco Antolín 1789; AGI AF 83-82 Bartolomé Marrón 8 Feb. 1690.

57. Salazar, *Historia*, 160. Santa Rosa was located at the site of former mission of Batavag.

58. AGI AF 75 Francisco de Olmedo 30 Jan. 1688, AF 83-82 Bartolomé Marrón 8 Feb. 1690.

59. De Jesus, *Tobacco Monopoly*, 111–113.

60. De Jesus, *Tobacco Monopoly*, 113–114.

61. AGI AF 75 Archbishop Felipe Pardo 10 June 1686.

62. AGI AF 82 Principales . . . de Cagayan 1 Mar. 1691.

63. APSR Cagayan 16 doc. 1 Miguel Ruiz 17 July 1624.

64. AGI AF 83 Principales . . . de Cagayan 1 Mar. 1591; AF 75 Francisco de Olmedo 30 Jan. 1688.

65. APSR Cagayan 16 doc. 1 Miguel Ruiz 17 July 1624.

66. AGI AF 75 Archbishop Felipe Pardo 10 June 1686.

67. AGI AF 75 Francisco de Olmedo 30 Jan. 1688, AF 83-82 Bartolomé Marrón 8 Feb. 1690; Salazar, *Historia*, 158.

68. BR 50: 214 Fausto Cruzat y Góngora 1696; Scott, *Discovery of the Igorots*, 69.

69. AGI AF 83-82 Bartolomé Marrón 8 Feb. 1690.

70. AGI AF 75 Francisco de Olmedo 30 Jan. 1688, AF 83 Principales . . . de Cagayan 1 Mar. 1691.

71. AGI AF 83-58 and AF 75 Various Dominicans 9 May 1686.

72. For example, AGI AF 7-83 Fernando de Silva 4 Aug. 1625.

73. De Jesus, *Tobacco Monopoly*, 116.

74. AGI AF 23-35 Francisco de Montemayor y Mansilla 12 July 1678.

75. AGI AF 83 Dominican Provincial 8 Sept. 1690.

76. BR 48: 130 Bernardo Ustariz [1745].

77. See chapter 13.

78. AGI AF 296 Juan Martínez ca. 1711.

79. APSR Cagayan 1 doc. 2 No author, 13 July 1741.

80. Collantes, *Historia*, 586; Malumbres, *Isabela*, 57.

81. AGI AF 83 Principales of Cagayan 1 Mar. 1691. In 1743 people were banned from being absent from their villages for more than forty days (NL Ayer 1301 Visita a las provincias de Cagayan 28 Mar. 1743).

82. Malumbres, *Cagayan*, 33–39.

83. AGI AF 83-82 Bartolomé Marrón 8 Feb. 1690, AF 83-203 Juan de Santo Domingo February 1695; Salazar, *Historia*, 395.

84. See chapter 13; APSR Cagayan 1 doc. 2 No author, 13 July 1741.

85. Aduarte, *Historia*, lib. 1 cap. 37: 158–159; Malumbres, *Cagayan*, 32–33.

86. AGI AF 35 Juan Núñez 24 June 1595.

87. APSR Cagayan 16 no. 12 Manuel Vélez 15 Mar. 1757. This was probably the same disease that struck missions in the Chico Valley in the same year (see chapter 13).

88. Wallace, *Hill and Valley Farmers*, 97.

89. Wallace, *Hill and Valley Farmers*, 97.

90. Russell, *Malaria*, 9; De Bevoise, *Agents*, 143–144.

91. AGI AF 293 Bishop of Nueva Segovia 12 July 1733; AGI AF 293 Manuel de Arandia 7 July 1756.

92. De Bevoise, *Agents*, 148–149.

93. AGI AF 7-55 Memoria . . . sobre el hospital de Manila 1618; Malumbres, *Cagayan*, 356.

94. Quirino and García, "Manners," 395; Scott, *Barangay*, 270.

95. APSR Cagayan 18 doc. 1 Mapa de los pueblos y almas . . . 1758.

96. The ratio for the Middle Cagayan and Kalinga/Apayao territory was 1:1.3 and for the province of Irraya 1:15.

97. In 1591 there were 1,400 *tributos* in the Babuyan Islands.

98. AGI AF 75 Francisco de Olmedo 30 Jan. 1688.

99. AGI AF 23-35 Francisco de Montemayor y Mansilla 12 July 1678.

100. Malumbres, *Cagayan*, 298–315, Juan de Varona y Velásquez 3 Mar. 1746.

101. AGI CO 1266 Oficiales reales 1750.

102. APSR Cagayan 1 doc. 2 No author, 13 July 1741; APSR Cagayan 10 doc. 4 Padrón de los Babuyanes 1741.

103. APSR Cagayan 18 doc. 3 Estadísticas ó planes de almas 1758–1805.

104. Malumbres, *Cagayan*, 298–315, Juan de Varona y Velásquez 3 Mar. 1746; PNA EP Cagayan 1749–1926 Joseph de Figueroa 30 Sept. 1787.

105. See especially APSR Cagayan 18 doc. 3 Estadísticas ó estados de almas 1758–1805 and Cagayan 26 doc. 7 Estadísticas ó estados de almas 1758–1800.

106. De Jesus, *Tobacco Monopoly*, 130–132.

Chapter 13: Interior Luzon

1. Wernstedt and Spencer, *Philippine Island World*, 342–346.

2. Keesing, *Ethnohistory*, 11.

3. Scott, *Discovery of the Igorots*, 2.

4. Scott, "A Preliminary Report of Upland Rice," 87–94; Dozier, *Mountain Arbiters*, 242; Keesing, *Ethnohistory*, 314.

5. See Bodner, "Evolution of Agriculture," 10–44; Keesing, *Ethnohistory*, 319–324.

6. Beyer, "The Origin and History of the Philippine Rice Terraces."

7. Keesing, *Ethnohistory*, 304, 320–324.

8. Lambrecht, "Hudhud," cited in Bodner, "Evolution of Agriculture," 17–18.

9. Conklin, *Ethnographic Atlas*, 38; Maher, "Archaeological Investigations" and "Great Ifugao War"; Bodner, "Evolution of Agriculture," 421–422.

10. Vanoverbergh, *Dress and Adornment*, 240–241; Dozier, *Mountain Arbiters*, 239–242.

11. The Tinguian of Abra who were encountered by expeditions from the west coast are discussed in chapter 11.

12. AGI PAT 25-38 and BR 8: 113–114 Relación punctual de las encomiendas 31 May 1591. According to Keesing (*Ethnohistory*, 271) the six *encomiendas* were Bataguan and Sugarro; Balissi, Mayot and Camiguil; Purrao and Culit; Taotao; Yoguan; and Pugao.

13. AGI AF 7-3-45 Relación . . . de Tuy, Manuel de la Vega 3 July 1609.

14. AGI AF 7-3-45 Relación . . . de Tuy, Manuel de la Vega 3 July 1609.

15. APSR Cagayan 28 doc. 31 Antolín 20 Aug. 1788; AUST Libro 37 fols. 245v–246v Discurso sobre el gentió y población, Francisco Antolín, 1787; Keesing, *Ethnohistory*, 270. As noted in chapter 12, the Yogad and Gaddang may not have lived there in pre-Spanish times, but retreated upvalley in the colonial period.

16. AGI AF 7-3-45 Relación . . . de Tuy, Manuel de la Vega 3 July 1609, AF 34-138 Diligencias . . . Pedro Sid, no date.

17. PNA Cedulario 1696–1705 pp. 621–633 Juan Bautista de Olarte 1 June 1705; APSR Cagayan 1 doc. 2 No author, 13 July 1741, Cagayan 28 doc. 13 Josef Herrera 18 July 1743, Cagayan 29 no doc. number Vicente Salazar 8 July 1747.

18. AGI AF 34-138 Diligencias . . . Pedro Sid, no date; BR 8: 250–251 Gómez Pérez Dasmariñas 1 June 1592; AGI AF 7-3-45 and BR 14: 280–311 Relación . . . de Tuy, Manuel de la Vega 3 July 1609.

19. Keesing, *Ethnohistory*, 277–279; Fernández and Juan, "Social and Economic Development," 70–85.

20. AGI AF 7-3-45 and BR 14: 295–296 Relación . . . de Tuy, Manuel de la Vega 3 July 1609.

21. AGI AF 7-3-45 and BR 14: 284–297 Relación . . . de Tuy, Manuel de la Vega 3 July 1609.

22. This assumes the two settlements had similar populations to Sicat and Marangui.

23. Retana, *Archivo del bibliófilo filipino*, 1: 55, Entrada de la seráfica religión, 1649.

24. Pérez, *Relaciones augustinianas*, 97, Alejandro Cacho 1717.

25. The average size of settlement was 82.3 and the total number of houses recorded was 971.

26. AGI AF 7-3-45 and BR 14: 295–296 Relación . . . de Tuy, Manuel de la Vega 3 July 1609.

27. Retana, *Archivo del bibliófilo filipino*, 2: 185, Manuel del Río 1739.

28. AGI PAT 25-52 Gómez Pérez Dasmariñas 20 June 1593.

29. AGI AF 7-3-45 and BR 14: 306 Relación . . . de Tuy, Manuel de la Vega 3 July 1609.

30. AGI AF 79 and BR9: 102 Francisco de Ortega, no date.

31. AGI AF 7-59 García Aldana y Cabrera 20 May 1620.

32. AUST Libro Becerro 37 Discurso sobre el gentió, Francisco Antolín, 1787. See chapter 4 for a discussion of Antolín.

33. AUST Libro Becerro 37 fols. 250r–250v Discurso sobre el gentió, Francisco Antolín, 1787.

34. BR 8: 250–251 Gómez Pérez Dasmariñas 1 June 1592; AGI AF 7-59 García Aldana y Cabrera 20 May 1620.

35. Pérez, *Relaciones augustinianas*, 69 Alejandro Cacho 1717.

36. AGI AF 7-3-45 fol. 13 and BR 14: 300 Relación . . . de Tuy, Manuel de la Vega 3 July 1609.

37. Aduarte, *Historia*, lib. 2 cap. 43: 280.

38. BR 8: 250–251 Gómez Pérez Dasmariñas 1 June 1592.

39. APSR Cagayan 29 no doc. number Manuel Paredes 1740. See also APSR Cagayan 28 doc. 31 Francisco Antolín 20 Aug. 1788.

40. Fernández and Juan, "Social and Economic Development," 97.

41. Aduarte, *Historia*, lib. 2 cap. 43: 279–281; Retana, *Archivo del bibliófilo filipino*, 1:55, Entrada de la seráfica religión, 1649; AUST Libro Becerro 37 fol. 255r Discurso

sobre el gentió, Francisco Antolín, 1787; APSR Cagayan 110 Aditamento Francisco Antolín, 1787; Malumbres, *Nueva Vizcaya*, 18, 412; Fernández and Juan, "Social and Economic Development," 89–90.

42. AGI AF 296 Francisco Ximénez 12 June 1703; AGI AF 296 Certificación . . . para hacer entrada a los indios Ituyes 13 June 1703; APSR Cagayan 110 Aditamento, Francisco Antolín, 1787; Fernández and Juan, "Social and Economic Development," 97.

43. AGI AF 14 R3 N35 fol. 1 Fausto Cruzat y Góngora 17 June 1691; AUST Libro 79 fols. 4v–9r Francisco Ximénez 26 Jan. 1704.

44. Retana, *Archivo del bibliófilo filipino*, 2: 177–205, Manuel del Río 1739; Keesing, *Ethnohistory*, 285–286.

45. APSR Cagayan 110 Aditamento, Francisco Antolín, 1787; Fernández and Juan, "Social and Economic Development," 102, 113–115.

46. AGI AF 140 Márquez de Torrecampo 30 June 1725; Pérez, *Relaciones augustinianas*, 329–335, Vivas no date; Mozo, *Noticia*, 63.

47. Pérez, *Relaciones augustinianas*, 331, Miguel Vivas, no date; Mozo, *Noticia*, 41–45. The settlements were at Buhay, Dupax, Meuba, Mayon, Diangan, Limanab, Batu, Paitan and Bayombong.

48. APSR Cagayan 28 doc. 8 Entrega de la mision de Ituy . . . 1740; Mozo, *Noticia*, 38–52. This was finally approved by the Crown in 1742.

49. The five Dominican missions contained 2,032 Christians and 552 *infieles*, while there were 400 Christians in Bayombong, Gapan, and Bagabag. Two other missions had been established at Carig and Lapao with 400 *infieles* and 43 families respectively (APSR Cagayan 1 doc. 2 No author 13 July 1741).

50. AUST Libro 79 fols. 50–51 Juan Ormaza 7 Dec. 1740; APSR Cagayan 29 Juan Ormaza 19 Mar. 1741.

51. Ustariz, *Relación*, no page; BR 48: 123–130 Bernardo Ustariz 1745.

52. Malumbres, *Nueva Vizcaya*, 27–29; Scott, *Discovery of the Igorots*, 86–89; Salgado, *Ilongots*, 86–89.

53. APSR Cagayan 30 fol. 226 Bernardo Ustariz n.d. and *Relación*, no page; Malumbres, *Nueva Vizcaya*, 29.

54. APSR Cagayan 28 doc. 14 Vicente Salazar 8 July 1747, APSR Cagayan 29 no doc. number Vicente Salazar 8 July 1747 and APSR Cagayan 30 fols. 111 and 114 Compendio cronológico, Francisco Antolín. Dupax and Meuba had been aggregated, Santa María had been formed of Batu and Paitan, and Bambang had been formed of the *rancherías* or *pueblecillos* of Limanab, Diangan, and Mayon.

55. Scott, *Discovery of the Igorots*, 157–158.

56. Malumbres, *Nueva Vizcaya*, 47; Scott, *Discovery of the Igorots*, 148.

57. AUST Libro 79 fols. 122v–124v Lista del P. Campo, no date.

58. Retana, *Archivo del bibliófilo filipino*, 2: 185, Manuel del Río 1739.

59. APSR 29 No document number, P. Río 13 May 1741.

60. Retana, *Archivo del bibliófilo filipino*, 2: 177–205, Manuel del Río 1739.

61. APSR Cagayan 1 doc. 2 No author 13 July 1741.

62. APSR Cagayan 28 doc. 13 Josef Herrera 18 July 1743.

63. APSR Cagayan 29 no doc. number Vicente Salazar 8 July 1747 and APSR Cagayan 30 fols. 111 and 114 Compendio cronológico, Francisco Antolín.

64. BR 48: 126–127 Bernardo Ustariz 1745; Malumbres, *Nueva Vizcaya*, 55.

65. PNA EP Cagayan 1749–1926 Bishop Miguel García San Esteban 20 Sept. 1774.

66. APSR Cagayan 28 doc. 28 Juan Crespo 25 Oct. 1778; Scott, *Discovery of the Igorots*, 161–163.

67. APSR Cagayan 18 doc. 3 Estadísticas ó estados de Almas 1758–1800.

68. PNA Erección de pueblos Cagayan 1749–1926 Joseph de Figueroa 20 Oct. 1787.

69. APSR Cagayan 28 doc. 31 Francisco Antolín, no date 20 Aug. 1788; Antolín, *Notices*, 25.

70. Pérez, *Relaciones augustinianas*, 306 José López, no date.

71. Lilly Lot 511 fols. 267–268 Antolín de Alzaga 26 Aug. 1702; PNA Cedulario 1696–1705 pp. 621–623 Juan Bautista de Olarte 1 June 1705; Mozo, *Noticia*, 18–22; Keesing, *Ethnohistory*, 73.

72. AGI AF 296 Governor Domingo de Labalburu 13 June 1703; AF 296 Augustinian Provincial 24 May 1704; PNA Cedulario 1696–1705 pp. 621–623 Juan Bautista de Olarte 1 June 1705; Pérez, *Relaciones augustinianas*, 302, Sebastián Foronda 20 June 1704; Abad Pérez, "Nueva primavera de las misiones," 126–127.

73. Pérez, *Relaciones augustinianas*, 65, Alejandro Cacho 1717.

74. Pérez, *Relaciones augustinianas*, 309, Certificación, no date; see also PNA Cedulario 1696–1705 pp. 621–623 Juan Bautista de Olarte 1 June 1705.

75. Pérez, *Relaciones augustinianas*, 324–327, Francisco de Zamora 12 June 1707. They were founded at San Juan Sahagún, San Bartolomé (Lupao), San Sebastián (Dimala), San Juan Bautista, and San Guillermo.

76. AGI AF 140 Márquez de Torrecampo 30 June 1725; Pérez, *Relaciones augustinianas*, 328–335, Instancia del P. Miguel Vivas, no date. This included 695 in the province of Ituy. See also Abad Pérez, "Nueva primavera de las misiones," 126–129.

77. Pérez, *Relaciones augustinianas*, 333, Instancia del P. Miguel Vivas, no date; Mozo, *Noticia*, 48–49.

78. Keesing, *Ethnohistory*, 77, 87.

79. The best known is his "Noticias de los infieles Igorotes en lo interior de la isla de Manila, de sus minas de oro cobre y su comercio." The original is to be found in APSR Cagayan 35 fols. 1–123 and has been edited and translated by William Henry Scott in *Asian Folklore Studies*, vols. 29–30 (1970–1971) and in Antolín, *Notices*. A similar manuscript is located in AUST Libro Becerro 37 fols. 1–57. Other long accounts are unpublished: "Discurso sobre el gentió y población de esta misión de Ituy y Paniqui" (AUST Libro Becerro 37 fols. 245–271 and APSR Cagayan 30 fols. 182–235) and "Misiones de Ituy y Paniqui en lo interior de esta isla de Manila" (APSR Cagayan 28 doc. 29 fols. 449–462 No date).

80. Pérez, *Relaciones augustinianas*, 99–116, Manuel Carrillo 1756; Scott, *Discovery of the Igorots*, 170.

81. These same crops were noted as being grown in the seventeenth century. See AGI AF 7-59 García de Aldana y Cabrera 20 May 1620; AGI AF 30-36 and BR 20: 262–294 Alonso Martín Quirante 1624; Scott, *Discovery of the Igorots*, 43–46.

82. Pérez, *Relaciones augustinianas*, 136, Pedro de Vivar 1755–1756.

83. APSR Pangasinan 1 doc. 1 Priests of Pangasinan 12 Aug. 1593; Antolín, *Notices*, 24–25, 30–35; Pérez, *Relaciones augustinianas*, 237, Benito Herosa 1780.

84. Mas y Sans, *Informe*, 1: 48.

85. Malumbres, *Nueva Vizcaya*, 236, 240.

86. Keesing, *Ethnohistory*, 85–86.

87. *Census of the Philippine Islands*, 1: 539.

88. AGI AF 30-36 and BR 20: 275–276 Alonso Martín Quirante 1624.

89. Antolín, *Notices*, 56–57.

90. AGI AF 30-36 and BR 20: 269 Alonso Martín Quirante 1624.

91. Father Carrillo (Pérez, *Relaciones augustinianas*, 113) gives 1,772 persons in twenty-six settlements and Father Vivar (Pérez, *Relaciones augustinianas*, 148) gives 2,304 in thirty settlements. Estimates of the number of houses assume a household size of four.

92. Antolín, *Notices*, 78; Scott, *Discovery of the Igorots*, 174.

93. Pérez, *Relaciones augustinianas*, 147, Pedro de Vivar 1756.

94. Malumbres, *Nueva Vizcaya*, 236.

95. AUST Libro Becerro 37 fol. 8v. Noticias . . . no date.

96. Antolín, *Notices*, 40–43; Pérez, *Relaciones augustinianas*, 237, 241, Benito Herosa 1780.

97. Pérez, *Relaciones augustinianas*, 241–242, Benito Herosa 1780; Antolín, *Notices*, 20–23; Scott, *Discovery of the Igorots*, 189.

98. Antolín, *Notices*, 23.

99. *Census of the Philippine Islands*, 1: 537.

100. Reid, "Low Population Growth," 39–41; Reid, *Southeast Asia*, 1: 161–162.

101. AGI AF 7-3-45 and BR 14: 301–307 Relación . . . de Tuy, Manuel de la Vega 3 July 1609.

102. AGI AF 7-59 García de Aldana y Cabrera 20 May 1620.

103. AGI AF 30 and BR 20: 263 Alonso Martín Quirante 1624, AF 30 Gasto fecho en el descubrimiento de las minas 29 Apr. 1624; Antolín, *Notices*, 158–159, Real cédula 6 Dec. 1624; Scott, *Discovery of the Igorots*, 30–38.

104. AGI AF 7-59 García de Aldana y Cabrera 20 May 1620.

105. Scott, *Discovery of the Igorots*, 42.

106. The Alaguet, who were considered more docile than the Igorot, lived a seminomadic existence in the mountains on the southern fringe of Mountain Province between Pangasinan and Nueva Vizcaya (Keesing, *Ethnohistory*, 283; Scott, *Discovery of the Igorots*, 63).

107. AGI AF 296 Francisco Ximénez 12 June 1703. Father Ximénez refers to the mission San Francisco de Agno, which may have been a *visita* of San Bartolomé. It was clearly located in the same region.

108. Salazar, *Historia*, 448–449; Scott, *Discovery of the Igorots*, 63.

109. Antolín, *Notices*, 197; De Jesus, "Control and Compromise," 27; Corpuz, *Roots*, 169.

110. AGI AF 83-82 Bartolomé Morrón 8 Feb. 1690.

111. AGI AF 297-38 El Conde de Lizárraga 15 June 1714.

112. AGI AF140 Márquez de Torrecampo 30 June 1725. During the 1740s small numbers of Igorot settled in the Ituy missions and in a small Igorot settlement called San Pablo de Balit (APSR Cagayan 28 doc. 13 Joseph Herrera 18 July 1743, doc. 14 Vicente Salazar 8 July 1747; Ustariz, *Relación*, no page).

113. Salazar, *Historia*, 449; Keesing, *Ethnohistory*, 283.

114. Fernández and Juan, "Social and Economic Development," 116–119. In the event no permanent road was built. The trail was washed out by heavy rains and difficult to maintain in the face of native hostility.

115. AUST Lib. 79 fols. 122v–124v Lista del P. Campo, no date; Antolín, *Notices*, 54–57.

116. Antolín, *Notices*, 62–63.

117. Mozo, *Noticia*, 81–83; Scott, *Discovery of the Igorots*, 83.

118. Geeroms, "Former Spanish Missions I," 437–454.

119. Pérez, *Relaciones augustinianas*, 113, Manuel Carrillo 26 June 1755.

120. Pérez, *Relaciones augustinianas*, 147, Pedro de Vivar 1756. Only fourteen names of villages are included in both lists, which suggests an unstable settlement pattern.

121. Keesing, *Ethnohistory*, 81.

122. Pérez, *Relaciones augustinianas*, 123, Breve y verdadera relación, Manuel Carrillo 20 Mar. 1758.

123. Pérez, *Relaciones augustinianas*, 147, Pedro de Vivar 1756.

124. Antolín, *Notices*, 58–65; Scott, *Discovery of the Igorots*, 82–83.

125. Concepción, *Historia general*, 14 cap. 11: 371; Reyes y Florentino, *Historia de Ilocos*, 168–171; Geeroms, "Former Spanish Missions II," 454–466; Keesing, *Ethnohistory*, 82–83; Scott, *Discovery of the Igorots*, 130–131.

126. Scott, *Igorots*, 139.

127. Reyes y Florentino, *Historia de Ilocos*, 2: 55; Scott, *Discovery of the Igorots*, 15–16.

128. AGI A9-43 Resumen de la carta que el gobernador Diego de Salcedo escribió 4 Aug. 1667, AF 330 lib. 6 fols. 204r–205r Real cédula 26 Mar. 1670; Mozo, *Noticia*, 70–71; Díaz, *Conquistas*, 654–655; Malumbres, *Nueva Vizcaya*, 220–225; Scott, *Discovery of the Igorots*, 58–60; Antolín, *Notices*, 184–193. See also chapter 11.

129. Díaz, *Conquistas*, 654–655; Antolín, *Notices*, 186–187.

130. Keesing, *Ethnohistory*, 102.

131. Malumbres, *Nueva Vizcaya*, 224.

132. Scott, *Discovery of the Igorots*, 126. See also NL Ayer Ms 1449 (Box) and BR 48-52-58 Razón de los pueblos, Pedro de Velasco 16 Apr. 1760.

133. Scott, *Discovery of the Igorots*, 126.

134. Pérez, *Igorrotes*, 15; Geeroms, "Former Spanish Missions II," 377.

135. Malumbres, *Nueva Vizcaya*, 243–244; Keesing, *Ethnohistory*, 107.

136. Mas y Sans, *Informe*, 1: 25–26; Buzeta and Bravo, *Diccionario*, 1: 53.

137. Fernández and Juan, "Social and Economic Development," 111; Conklin, *Ethnographic Atlas*, 37.

138. Collantes, *Historia*, 13; Mas y Sans, *Informe*, 1: 27.

139. For example, against the Ifugao inhabitants of Quiangan in 1767 (Antolín, *Notices*, 96–97).

140. APSR Cagayan 28 doc. 28 Juan Crespo 25 Oct. 1778; Malumbres, *Nueva Vizcaya*, 77–78; Scott, *Discovery of the Igorots*, 161–163.

141. Malumbres, *Nueva Vizcaya*, 91–94; Molano, "Description of Kiangan," 137; Scott, *Discovery of the Igorots*, 199–200.

142. Malumbres, *Nueva Vizcaya*, 238; Mas y Sans, *Informe*, 1: 27; Scott, *Discovery of the Igorots*, 223.

143. Malumbres, *Nueva Vizcaya*, 248. In 1865 the Ifugao were said to number 21,000 (AUST Libro 229 Nomenclator de los grupos de población 1865) and in 1889 Father Julián Malumbres estimated that there were 29,800 souls in the district of Quiangan (Malumbres, "Carta a la provincial," 462).

144. AUST Libro Becerro 37 fols. 250r and v Discurso sobre el gentió, Francisco Antolín 1787; Antolín, *Notices*, 18–23.

145. AUST Libro Becerro 37 fols. 250r and v Discurso sobre el gentió, Francisco Antolín 1787.

146. Malumbres, *Nueva Vizcaya*, 403. A large number of figures are available for different regions and *comandancias* during the nineteenth century, many published in Mas y Sans, *Informe*; Malumbres, *Nueva Vizcaya*; *Census of Philippine Islands*, 2: 123–132, and Keesing, *Ethnohistory*, 292–300. However, it is difficult to establish overall demographic trends from these figures since they often refer to individual groups and the boundaries of *comandancias* are not consistent over time.

147. Scott, "Spanish Occupation," 52–55.

148. AGI AF 7-3-45 and BR 14: 302 Relación . . . de Tuy, Manuel de la Vega 3 July 1609. The Blair and Robertson translation reads: "It is reported that about eighteen to twenty thousand Indians use lance and shield." However, the original is more ambiguous, reading "abra 18,000 a 20,000 yndios usan de lanza y coraza." The reference to "yndios" rather than "hombres" suggests it referred to the total population.

149. AGI AF 7-59 García Aldana y Cabrera 20 May 1620. It is not clear what categories of persons he was including in this figure, but the term "chusma," may have embraced women, children, or old men. If it did, then the figure of 7,000 adult males may have been exaggerated.

150. AUST Libro 79 fols. 122v–124v Lista del P. Campo, no date; Antolín, *Notices*, 57.

151. Antolín, *Notices*, 20, 23.

152. AUST Libro Becerro 37 fols. 248r and v, Discurso sobre el gentió, Francisco Antolín 1787.

153. Antolín, *Notices*, 92–95.

154. APSR Cagayan 29 no number Father Campo 26 Feb. 1741, APSR Cagayan 29 no number Juan Ormaza 19 Mar. 1741, APSR Cagayan 1 no. 2 No author, 13 July 1741.

155. Díaz, *Conquistas*, 556.

156. AUST Libro Becerro 37 fols. 253r and v Discurso sobre el gentió, Francisco Antolín 1787.

157. Díaz, *Conquistas*, 556.

158. Mas y Sans, *Informe*, 1: 20.

159. AUST Libro Becerro 37 fols. 254v Discurso sobre el gentió, Francisco Antolín 1787.

160. AUST Libro Becerro 37 fols. 254r Discurso sobre el gentió, Francisco Antolín 1787.

161. AUST Libro Becerro 37 fols. 258v Discurso sobre el gentió, Francisco Antolín 1787.

162. Newson, "Historical-Ecologic Perspective," 52.

163. AGI PAT 25-38 fols. 9–14 Relación punctual de las encomiendas 31 May 1591.

164. Reynolds and Grant, *Isneg*, 12–14.

165. Aduarte, *Historia*, lib. 1 cap. 68: 362.

166. Reynolds and Keyes, "Isneg Family," 81–85.

167. Malumbres, *Cagayan*, 244–245; Malumbres, *Nueva Vizcaya*, 365; Vanoverbergh, *Isneg*, 28.

168. Aduarte, *Historia*, lib. 2 cap. 28: 183–184.

169. AF 7-83 Fernando de Silva 4 Aug. 1625, 30 July 1626.

170. Aduarte, *Historia*, lib. 2 cap. 48: 318–322; Geeroms, "Former Spanish Missions I," 21–23.

171. BR 35: 47–48 B. de Santa Cruz 1693; Keesing, *Ethnohistory*, 196.

172. Salazar, *Historia*, 384–385.

173. AGI AF 83-82 Bartolomé Marrón 8 Feb. 1690, AF 83-203 Juan de Santo Domingo February 1695.

174. Malumbres, *Nueva Vizcaya*, 370.

175. AGI AF 83-203 Juan de Santo Domingo February 1695; Salazar, *Historia*, 395–397.

176. AGI AF 296 Certificación jurídica del los oficiales reales 21 June 1708; Malumbres, *Cagayan*, 298–315.

177. APSR Cagayan 10 doc. 4 Joseph Thomás Marín 2 Mar. 1741, vol. 18 doc. 6 Joseph Thomás Marín no date; Geeroms, "Former Spanish Missions I," 28.

178. APSR Cagayan 1 doc. 6 José de Figueroa 20 Oct. 1787; Vanoverbergh, *Isneg*, 33–34.

179. APSR Cagayan 11 doc. 12 Antonio de Feixas 20 Apr. 1778; also in Malumbres, *Nueva Vizcaya*, 391.

180. Reynolds and Keyes, "Isneg Family," 84.

181. Keesing, *Ethnohistory*, 155–156. See chapter 11.

182. Mozo, *Noticia*, 62; see also Pérez, *Relaciones augustinianas*, 115 Manuel Carrillo 27 June 1755.

183. Keesing, *Ethnohistory*, 203.

184. Malumbres, *Nueva Vizcaya*, 403.

185. Vanoverbergh, *Isneg*, 59.

186. Barton, *Kalingas*, 6–7, 97; Dozier, *Kalinga*, 4; Scott, "Economic and Material Culture," 318–319.

187. Dozier, *Mountain Arbiters*, 25, 242, 247; Scott, "A Preliminary Report of Upland Rice," 89–90.

188. Aduarte, *Historia*, lib. 1 cap. 59: 303; Keesing, *Ethnohistory*, 225.

189. Dozier, *Mountain Arbiters*, 12–13.

190. Dozier, *Kalinga*, 68–72.

191. Aduarte, *Historia*, lib. 1 cap. 59: 302–303.

192. AGI AF 83-82 Bartolomé Marrón 8 Feb. 1690; Salazar, *Historia*, 514–516.

193. AGI AF 296 Francisco Ximénez 12 June 1703.

194. Salazar, *Historia*, 393–394; Keesing, *Ethnohistory*, 227–228; Geeroms, "Former Spanish Missions I," 31–32.

195. AGI AF 297-175 Infante de Amaya 3 June 1718.

196. APSR Cagayan 11 doc. 12 Tomás de Anibarra 20 Mar. 1773; Geeroms, "Former Spanish Missions I," 34.

197. APSR Cagayan 1 doc. 2 No author, 13 July 1741.

198. APSR Cagayan 14 doc. 9 Tomás Marín 1743. In 1739 the mission had contained 244 *personas*, excluding children (APSR Cagayan 29 no number Domingo de Posada 30 Apr. 1739).

199. APSR Cagayan 14 doc. 10 Francisco Ximénez 1743. In addition in Tabang there were 120 "de adviento."

200. APSR Cagayan 10 doc. 17 No author 30 Mar. 1752.

201. APSR Cagayan 10 doc. 24 Alonso Amado 2 Mar. 1758; APSR Cagayan 18 doc. 3 No author, December 1764.

202. APSR Cagayan 11 doc. 12 Tomás de Anibarra 20 Mar. 1773.

203. APSR Cagayan 18 Estadísticas ó estados de almas 1758–1805.

204. Orag continued to exist but its population was included in that for Tuao.

205. APSR Cagayan 1 doc. 2 No author 13 July 1741; APSR Cagayan 14 doc. 7 Razón del estado de las casas . . . 1743.

206. APSR Cagayan 14 doc. 10 Francisco Ximénez 1743.

207. APSR Cagayan 11 doc. 12 Antonio Feixas 20 Apr. 1778.

208. APSR Cagayan 11 doc. 12 Tomás de Anibarra 20 Mar. 1773.

Chapter 14: Demographic Change in the Early Spanish Philippines

1. Newson, "Demographic Impact of Colonization," 165–167.

2. Owen, "Towards a History of Health," 9–10, and "Paradox of Nineteenth-Century Population Growth."

3. Reid, "Low Population Growth," 36, and *Southeast Asia*, 1: 14.

4. The area of Ilocos may be estimated at about 6,300 square kilometers (*Census of the Philippine Islands*, 2: 28), which, given an estimated population of about 172,000 in 1570, would give a population density of about twenty-seven persons per square kilometer.

5. Reid, "Low Population Growth," 37–43, and *Southeast Asia*, 1: 15–18. Henley, "Population and the Means of Subsistence," 357–358, has shown that continuous war among rival groups in Sulawesi resulted in relatively low mortality.

6. Boomgaard, "Bridewealth and Birth Control."

7. Henley, *Food, Fertility and Fever*, 370–373, and "Population and Means of Subsistence," 365–368. See also Boomgaard, "Human Capital, Slavery and Low Rates of Economic and Population Growth," 92.

8. Boomgaard, *Southeast Asia*, 119.

9. Reid, *Southeast Asia*, 1: 45–61.

10. Dobson, "Mortality Gradients," 288; McKeown, *Modern Rise of Population*, 69.

11. Boomgaard, "Crisis Mortality"; Camara Dery, *Pestilence in the Philippines*.

12. Henley, "Population and Means of Subsistence."

13. De Bevoise, *Agents*, 27.

14. See Appendix E.

15. The long passage across the Pacific and the small number of ships involved in the galleon trade meant that in the early colonial period Mexico was an unlikely source of infection.

16. Grau y Figueras, *Memoria sobre la población*, 9; Mas y Sans, *Población*, 20.

17. For 1565 see Table 14.1 and for 1655 Appendix E.

18. Dobyns, "Estimating Aboriginal American Population," 415.

19. Newson, "Demographic Collapse," 247–254.

20. Newson, "Indian Population Patterns," 49–62.

21. Using figures contained in the following studies, the following ratios can be calculated: 3.9:1 for Peru from 1520 to 1630 (Cook, *Demographic Collapse*, 94); 3.4:1 for the Central Andes for 1520 to 1571 (Smith, "Depopulation in the Central Andes," 459;

5.2:1 for highland Ecuador for 1520 to 1600 (Newson, *Life and Death*, 341); and 5.5:1 for 1520–1580 for the Cuchumatán region of highland Guatemala (Lovell, "The Demography of the Cuchumatán Highlands," 204).

22. Reid, "Seventeenth-Century Crisis," 49–50, and "South-East Asian Population History," 46–49.

23. Reid, "Seventeenth-Century Crisis," 49–52.

24. Reid, *Southeast Asia*, 2: 274.

25. Knaap, "Demography of Ambon," 238.

26. Reid, "South-East Asian Population History," 49.

27. Owen, "Towards a History of Health," 9–10; "Paradox of Nineteenth-Century Population Growth."

28. Reid, "South-East Asian Population History," 50–53.

29. See Appendix E.

30. Owen, "Towards a History of Health," 13.

31. Owen, " Paradox of Nineteenth-Century Population Growth," 51–53.

32. Boomgaard, *Southeast Asia*, 131–139.

33. Reid, "Low Population Growth," 39–40; Boomgaard, *Southeast Asia*, 132–134.

34. Henley, "From Low to High Fertility."

Glossary

Words

aguardiente	spirit (alcoholic)
ahogamiento de la madre	a nervous illness affecting reproductive functioning
alcalde mayor	magistrate
alcaldía	jurisdiction of an *alcalde mayor*
alférez	standard-bearer
alguacil	constable, police officer
aliping namamahay	serf in Tagalog society
aliping sagigilid	slave in Tagalog society
alma	soul
alma de confesión	soul or person who has been confirmed, generally over the age of seven or eight
ánima	soul
anitero/a	shaman
arroz limpio	husked rice
arroz sucio	unhusked rice
Audiencia	high judicial court and by extension the region under its jurisdiction
babaylan	shaman
barangay (boat)	an edge-pegged, plank-built boat constructed on a keel with an outrigger
barangay (social unit)	a pre-Hispanic social and political unit or community
behetría	community without a hereditary leader
biroco	large outrigger
botica	pharmacy
bubas	swelling, bubo, syphilis
búfano	buffalo
cabecera	central village or settlement of a municipality
cabeza de barangay	head of a *barangay*
cabildo	town council
caingin	swidden or shifting cultivation
camotes	sweet potatoes (*Ipomoea batatas* (L.))
cantor	singer, member of a choir
carabao	Asian buffalo
caracoa	large outrigger with an elevated fighting deck designed for war
carta anua	annual letter
casa de reserva	estate worker who is exempt from the *polo* and other services
casería	hamlet

catecúmeno	catechumen
cédula	decree
champán	a flat-bottomed boat used for river navigation
cimarrón	runaway, fugitive
comandancia	territory under a military commander
congregación	congregation of a dispersed population into a nucleated settlement
cordonería	cordage works
corregidor	royal official with judicial and administrative authority
derrama	financial contribution made for a common purpose
diwata	spirit (object of worship)
doctrina	mission or parish where the residents were undergoing Christian instruction
encomendero	owner of an *encomienda*
encomienda	an allocation of Indians to an individual who was then entitled to exact tribute and labor from them in return for Christian instruction
enfermedad	illness
entrada	military or missionary expedition into unexplored or unpacified territory
estado de almas	summary of the population of a parish
estancia	ranch
fiscal	attorney general
gallina	chicken or, more precisely, a hen
gobernadorcillo	political post created by the Spanish that oversaw the *cabezas de barangay*
hacendero	owner of a hacienda
hidalgo	nobleman, gentleman
hombre	man
indio	Indian, but in the Philippine context a native Filipino.
infieles	pagans
inquilino	tenant farmer
joanga	small junk
maginoo	village elite in Tagalog society
maharlika	commoner in Tagalog society
manicipia	slave (Latin)
manta	blanket or shawl
medriñaque	textile made from abaca or palm fiber
mestizo	a person of mixed white and native ancestry. A Chinese *mestizo* was of mixed Chinese and native ancestry
ministerio	ministry
mita	rotational forced labor system used in Spanish America
montes	hills, mountains
morador	inhabitant
mundo	fugitive from Spanish rule in Panay
nipa	type of palm tree
nono	ancestor or tutelary spirit

oidor	judge
oripun	indebted dependent or slave in the Visayas
pacificación	peaceful subjugation
padrón	detailed list or census
parao	a boat with a deep keel and single sail
parian	neighborhood where the Chinese lived or were confined
peso	monetary unit equal to eight reals
peste	disease
plan de almas	summary of total population (souls)
polo	forced labor system
presidio	garrison
principal	native leader
principalia	native elite, including the *cabezas de barangay* and *gobernadorcillo*
procurador	representative, solicitor, attorney
ranchería	small rural settlement, hamlet
rancho	hut
real	monetary unit equal to one-eighth of a peso
reducción	reduction or settlement formed by the amalgamation of smaller settlements or created by drawing together unconverted people
remontados	apostates
repartimiento	rotational draft labor system
república de españoles	Spanish republic
república de indios	Indian republic
requerimiento	document used during the Spanish conquest that called upon natives to recognize the authority of the king and pope and to justify any Spanish action against them if they refused
reservado/a	person exempt from tribute and other services
sangley	Chinese
sementera	land that has been sown
situado	contribution, subsidy
tasación	official tribute assessment
timagua	freeman or common person (Visayan)
timawa	freeman or common person (Tagalog)
tingues	hills or mountains
tostón	half a peso or four *reals*
trapiche	sugar mill
tributante	equivalent to two tribute payers, normally a married couple
tributario	tribute payer, tributary
tributo	tribute, tribute payer
tributo entero	equivalent to two tribute payers, normally a married couple
vagamundo	vagabond; some one living outside his or her natal community
vandala	forced sales to the government
vecino	citizen, householder
viruela	smallpox
visita	a subordinate or outlying village; an official inspection
zangjera	type of irrigation system in Ilocos

Weights and Measures

cavan	a box of 24 or 25 *gantas*
celemín	dry measure, about 4.6 dry liters (1.04 dry gallons)
chinanta	measure of weight, 6.3 kilograms (13.9 lbs.)
fanega	measure of capacity, about 1.3 bushels
ganta	half a *celemín* or about 2.31 dry liters (0.5 dry gallons)
league	about 3.5 miles
cuartillo	quarter of a *celemín* or about 1.16 dry liters (1 dry quart)
mae	a Chinese measure equivalent to one-tenth of a *tae* or about 3.1 grams (about one-tenth of an ounce)
tae	a Chinese measure equivalent to about 31.1 grams (1.1 oz.)

Bibliography

Archival Sources

Research for this book was undertaken on three continents. For the sixteenth and seventeenth centuries by far the most important sources were located in the Archivo General de Indias (AGI) in Seville. This archive contains correspondence to and from governors, royal officials, bishops, priests, members of the religious orders, and private individuals in the Philippines. The most important sections researched for this study were the Audiencia de Filipinas and Patronato. Information on tribute records was obtained from the Contaduría section, and eighteenth-century censuses were found in Indiferente General. It is worth noting that although the eighteenth century is not the focus of this study, the amount of documentation for that period is immense and has not been consulted extensively by researchers.

A significant number of sixteenth- and early seventeenth-century documents in the AGI have been translated and published by Emma Blair and James Robertson in their fifty-five-volume collection *The Philippine Islands, 1493–1803* (Cleveland: A. H. Clark, 1903–1909). The collection also contains partial translations of some of the chronicles of the religious orders. Translated more than one hundred years ago, the English now seems a little dated. Also, for the precise terms used, particularly for population categories, it is better to consult the original sources if possible. However, these volumes constitute a readily accessible source for those unable to visit Spain, and the first twenty-four volumes are available free of charge as part of Project Gutenberg at http://www.gutenberg.org/etext/13255. The only drawback with the electronic edition is that the pagination does not follow that in the printed volumes. Meanwhile, some documents from the Patronato and Audiencia de Filipinas sections of the AGI have been digitized as part of their ongoing digitalization project. Some documents referring to the Philippines, particularly from the early colonial period, can be read remotely through the "Archivos españoles en red" website at http://aer.mcu.es/.

Of particular importance for research on the Philippines were the archives of the four main religious orders that worked there in colonial times. Two series of Dominican records exist in the Philippines at the University of Santo Tomas in Manila. The first is the Archivo de la Provincia del Santísimo Rosario (APSR), which is the main archive for the Dominican order and has outstanding records on their activities in Cagayan, Pangasinan, and interior Luzon. Very few of these documents have been published. The other is the archive of the University of Santo Tomas itself, which apart from containing many useful documents houses many early printed books and pamphlets.

The records of the Jesuit order were consulted in the Archivum Romanum Societatis Iesu (ARSI) in Rome. The most important section researched was that dealing with the Philippine province. Most of these documents are in Spanish, but some are in Latin. While they have not been published, these documents formed the basis of Horacio de la Costa's study *The Jesuits in the Philippines, 1581–1768* (Cambridge, Mass.: Harvard University Press, 1961). A microfilm copy of some of these documents is available at Saint Louis University in Saint Louis in the United States. Some transcriptions may also be found in Pablo Pastells' edition of Francisco Colín's *Labor Evangélica* (Heinrich y Compañía: Barcelona, 1900–1902), but they contain some errors.

Documents relating to the activities of the Augustinians in the Philippines are to be found in the archive of the Augustinian order in Valladolid, Spain. It contains few early colonial documents, but sources relevant to the Augustinian Philippine province found in this and other archives have been published in twenty volumes by Isacio Rodríguez, *Historia de la provincia Agustiniana del smo. nombre de Jésus de Filipinas* (Manila: Arnoldus, 1965–1988).

For the Franciscan order, research was conducted in the Archivio Generale dell'Ordine dei Frati Minori in Rome, but little of relevance was found. More important for the Philippines is the Archivo Franciscano Ibero-Oriental in Madrid, though its strength is in the eighteenth century. It was not researched for this study.

Apart from the religious orders, research was also conducted in the Philippine National Archives. The strength of this archive lies in the late eighteenth century and nineteenth centuries; it contains relatively few documents relating to the early colonial period. However, documents referring to the creation of new towns (Erección de pueblos) contained useful geographical information, including some maps. Other sections that proved of value were Cabezas de Barangay, Cedulario, and Patronatos. Finally, research was also conducted in the Archdiocesan Archives of Manila, which contained a large number of ecclesiastical censuses that proved invaluable for charting demographic trends at the end of the eighteenth and beginning of the nineteenth centuries.

The author was fortunate to be awarded two fellowships at the Newberry Library, Chicago. This private foundation has a small collection of Philippine documents, some in native Filipino languages, but also transcripts in Spanish made by Ventura del Arco in the Real Academia de la Historia in Madrid in the mid-nineteenth century. There is a guide to the collection by Paul Lietz titled *Calendar of Philippine Documents in the Ayer Collection of the Newberry Library* (Chicago: The Newberry Library, 1956). Research was also conducted in the Lilly Library at the University of Indiana, which contains the collections of Charles Boxer, including the Boxer Codex.

Apart from the edited collections of documents discussed above, other important volumes used were the *Archivo del bibliófilo filipino*, compiled by Wenceslao E. Retana, which contains transcripts of a few early colonial documents, and Angel Pérez' *Relaciones agustinianas de las razas del norte de Luzon*, which was important for the study of societies in interior Luzon. As with most studies of the early Spanish colonial period, the two major unedited Spanish collections of early colonial documents (*CDI* and *CDIU*) contained some essential materials, particularly on Legazpi's expedition and the late sixteenth century.

Printed Sources

Abad, Antolín. Los franciscanos en Filipinas (1578–1898). *Revista de Indias* 24 (1964): 411–444.

Abad Pérez, Antolín. Nueva primavera de las misiones católicas en Filipinas. *Missionalia hispánica* 40 (1983): 121–129.

Abella, Domingo. *Bikol Annals: A Collection of Vignettes of Philippine History*. Manila: No publisher given, 1954.

Aduarte, Diego. *Historia de la provincia del sancto rosario de la orden de predicadores en Filipinas, Iapón y China*. Madrid: L. Beltran, 1640.

Aguilar, Filomeno V. *Clash of Spirits: The History of Power and Sugar Planter Hegemony on a Visayan Island*. Honolulu: University of Hawai'i Press, 1998.

Alcalá, Marcos de. *Chrónica de la santa provincia de San Joseph de religiosos descalzos*. Madrid: Manuel Fernández, 1738.

Alcina, Francisco Ignacio. *La historia de las islas e indios del padre Alcina 1668*. Edited by María Luisa Martín-Meras and María Dolores Higueras. Madrid: Instituto Histórico de Marina, 1974.

Alconbendas, Severiano. Religiosos médico-cirujanos de la provincia de San Gregorio Magno de Filipinas. *Archivo Ibero-Americano* 34 (1934): 48–74 (Part I), 234–265 (Part II), 35 (1935): 50–71 (Part III), 36 (1936): 145–171 (Part IV).

Andaya, Barbara W., and Yoneo Ishii. Religious Developments in Southeast Asia, c.1500–1800. In *The Cambridge History of Southeast Asia: vol. 1 From Early Times to c. 1800*, edited by Nicholas Tarling, 508–571. Cambridge: Cambridge University Press, 1992.

Anderson, Roy M., and Robert M. May. Population Biology of Infectious Diseases: Part I. *Nature* 280 (1979): 361–367.

Antolín, Francisco. *Notices of the Pagan Igorots in the Interior of the Island of Manila*. Translated by William H. Scott. Manila: Orientalia Dominicana, University of Santo Tomas Press, 1988.

Appell, George. N. The Penis Pin at the Peabody Museum, Harvard University. *Journal of the Malaysian Branch Royal Asiatic Society* 41 (1968): 203–205.

Aragón, Yldefonso de. *Estados de la población de Filipinas correspondiente a el año de 1818*. Manila: Imp. de D. Manuel Memije, 1919.

Azcarraga y Palmero, Manuel. *La libertad de comercio en las islas Filipinas*. Madrid: Imp. José Noguera, 1872.

Bamber, Scott. Diseases of Antiquity and the Premodern Period in Southeast Asia. In *The Cambridge World History of Human Disease*, edited by Kenneth Kiple, 425–440. Cambridge: Cambridge University Press, 1993.

Barbian, Karl Josef. The Tribal Distribution of the Mangyans. *Philippine Quarterly of Culture and Society* 5 (1977): 5–11.

Barrantes, Vicente. *Guerras piráticas de Filipinas*. Madrid: Manuel G. Fernández, 1878.

Barrows, David P. The Governor-General of the Philippines under Spain and the United States. In *The Pacific Ocean in History*, edited by H. Morse Stephens and Hubert E. Bolton. New York: The Macmillan Company, 1917.

———. History of the Population. In *Census of the Philippine Islands*, 1: 411–490. Washington D.C.: U.S. Bureau of the Census, 1905.

Bartlett, M. S. The Critical Community Size for Measles in the United States. *Journal of the Royal Statistical Society, Series A* 123 (1960): 37–49.

———. Measles Periodicity and Community Size. *Journal of the Royal Statistical Society, Series A* 120 (1957): 48–70.

Barton, Roy F. *The Kalingas: Their Institutions and Custom Law*. Chicago: University of Chicago Press, 1949.

Bauzon, Leslie E. *Deficit Government: Mexico and the Philippine Situado 1606–1804*. Tokyo: Centre for East Asian Cultural Studies, 1981.

Bayle, Constantino. Informe sobre los naturales de la diócesis de Cebu. *Archivo Missionalia Hispánica* 6 (1949): 389–398.

Bellwood, Peter. Southeast Asia before History. In *The Cambridge History of Southeast Asia: Vol. 1 From Early Times to c. 1800*, edited by Nicholas Tarling, 55–136. Cambridge: Cambridge University Press, 1992.

Bellwood, Peter, and Matussin Omar. Trade Patterns and Political Developments in Brunei and Adjacent Areas, AD 700–1500. *Brunei Museum Journal* 4 (4)(1980): 155–179.

Beyer, Otley J. The Origin and History of the Philippine Rice Terraces. *Proceedings of the Eighth Pacific Science Congress* 1 (1955): 387–398.

Black, Francis L. Infectious Diseases in Primitive Societies. *Science* 187 (1975): 515–518.

———. Measles Endemicity in Insular Populations: Critical Community Size and its Evolutionary Implications. *Journal of Theoretical Biology* 11 (1966): 207–211.

———. Modern Isolated Pre-agricultural Populations as a Source of Information on Prehistoric Epidemic Patterns. In *Changing Disease Patterns and Human Behaviour*, edited by N. F. Stanley and R. A. Joske, 37–54. New York: Academic Press, 1980.

Blair, Emma H., and James A. Robertson. *The Philippine Islands, 1493–1803*. 55 vols. Cleveland: A. H. Clark, 1903–1909.

Blumentritt, Ferdinand. *Ataques de los holandeses en los siglos XVI, XVII y XVIII: Bosquejo histórico*. Madrid: Imp. de Fortanet, 1882.

———. *An Attempt at Writing a Philippine Ethnography*. Translated by Marcelino N. Maceda. Marawi City: University Research Center, Mindanao State University, 1980.

Bodner, Connie C. The Evolution of Agriculture in Central Bontoc. PhD dissertation, University of Missouri, 1986.

Boomgaard, Peter. Bridewealth and Birth Control: Low Fertility in the Indonesian Archipelago, 1500–1900. *Population and Development Review* 29 (2) (2003): 197–214.

———. *Children of the Colonial State: Population Growth and Economic Development in Java, 1795–1880*. Amsterdam: Free University Press, 1989.

———. Crisis Mortality in Seventeenth Century Indonesia. In *Asian Population History*, edited by Ts'ui-jung Liu, James Lee, David Sven Reher, Osamu Saito, and Wang Feng, 191–220. Oxford: Oxford University Press, 2001.

———. Human Capital, Slavery and Low Rates of Economic and Population Growth in Indonesia, 1600–1910. *Slavery and Abolition* 24 (2) (2003): 83–96.

———. Morbidity and Mortality in Java 1820–1880: Changing Patterns of Disease and Death. In *Death and Disease in Southeast Asia: Explorations in Social, Medical and Demographic History*, edited by Norman G. Owen, 48–69. Oxford: Oxford University Press, 1987.

———. *Southeast Asia: An Environmental History*. Santa Barbara: ABC-CLIO Inc., 2007.

Borah, Woodrow. *Early Colonial Trade and Navigation Between Mexico and Peru*, Ibero-Americana 38. Berkeley and Los Angeles: University of California Press, 1954.

———. The Historical Demography of Aboriginal and Colonial America: An Attempt at Perspective. In *The Native Population of the Americas in 1492*, edited by William M. Denevan, 13–34. Madison: University of Wisconsin Press, 1992.

———. The Historical Demography of Latin America: Sources, Techniques, Controversies, Yields. In *Population and Economics*, Proceedings of Section V of the Fourth Congress of the International Economic History Association, 1968, edited by Paul Deprez, 175–205. Winnipeg: University of Manitoba Press, 1970.

Borromeo, Soledad. El Cadiz Filipino: Colonial Cavite, 1571–1896. PhD dissertation. Berkeley, University of California Press, 1973.

Borromeo-Buehler, Soledad. The Inquilinos of Cavite: A Social Class in the Nineteenth-Century Philippines. *Journal of South East Asian Studies* 16 (1) (1975): 69–98.

Boserup, Esther. *The Conditions of Agricultural Growth: The Economics of Agrarian Population Change under Pressure*. Chicago: Aldine Publishing Co., 1965.

Boxer, Charles R. *The Dutch Seaborne Empire 1600–1800*. London: Hutchinson, 1965.

———. Plata es Sangre: Sidelights on the Drain of Spanish American Silver in the Far East, 1550–1700. *Philippine Studies* 18 (1970): 457–478.

———. Portuguese and Spanish Projects for the Conquest of Southeast Asia, 1580–1600. *Journal of Asian History* 3 (2) (1969): 118–136.

———, ed. *South China in the Sixteenth Century*. London: Hakluyt Society, 1953.

Brewer, I. W. Tuberculosis in the Philippines. *Philippine Journal of Science* 5 (1910): 331–333.

Brown, Donald E., James W. Edwards, and Ruth P. Moore. *The Penis Inserts of Southeast Asia: An Annotated Bibliography with an Overview and Comparative Perspectives*. Center for Southeast Asia Studies Occasional Paper number 15. Berkeley: University of California Press, 1988.

Browning, David. Preliminary Comments on the 1776 Population Census of the Spanish Empire. *Bulletin of the Society for Latin American Studies* 19 (1974): 5–13.

Buzeta, Manuel, and Felipe Bravo. *Diccionario geográfico, estadístico, histórico de las islas Filipinas*. 2 vols. Madrid: D. José de la Peña, 1850.

Cadeliña , Rowe V. Adaptive Strategies to Deforestation: The Case of the Ata of Negros Island, Philippines. *Silliman Journal* 27 (1980): 93–112.

Calvo, José. *Joseph Calvo de la Compañía de Jesús, procurador general de Philippinas, puesto a los reales pies de V. Mag*. Madrid, 1744.

Camara Dery, Luis. *Pestilence in the Philippines: A Social History of the Filipino People, 1571–1800*. Quezon City: New Day Pub., 2006.

Carletti, Francesco. *My Voyage around the World*. Translated by Herbert Weinstock. London: Methuen and Co. Ltd., 1965.

Casero Nieto, Juan Antonio. Los hospitales en Manila durante la colonización española. *Missionalia hispánica* 40 (1983): 217–258.

Casiño, Eric S. Two Kingdoms: Early Brunei-Sulu Relations. In *Filipino Heritage*. vol. 3, edited by Alfredo R. Roces, 738–741. Manila: Lahing Pilipino Publishing Inc., 1977.

Cavada y Méndez de Vigo, Agustín de. *Historia geográfica, geológica y estadística de Filipinas*. Manila: Imp. Ramires y Giraudier, 1876.

Cavendish, Thomas. The Admirable and Prosperous Voyage of the Worshipful Master Written by Master Francis Pretty 1586–1588. In *The Principal Navigations, Voyages, Traffiques and Discoveries of the English Nation*, collected by Richard Hakluyt and edited by E. Goldsmid, 5–84. London: E and G. Goldsmid, 1890.

Census of the Philippine Islands. 4 vols. Washington D.C.: U.S. Bureau of the Census, 1905.

Chang, T'ien-tse. *Sino-Portuguese Trade from 1514 to 1614: A Synthesis of Portuguese and Chinese Sources*. Leiden: E. J. Brill Ltd., 1934.

Chau Ju-Kua. Chau Ju-Kua's Description of the Philippines in the Thirteenth Century: A New Translation. *Historical Bulletin* 11 (1967): 69–72.

Chaunu, Pierre. *Les Philippines et le Pacifique des Ibériques (XVIe, XVIIe, XVIIIe Siècles) Introduction Méthodologique et Indices d'Activité*. Paris: S.E.V.P.E.N., 1960.

Chirino, Pedro de. *Relación de las islas filipinas*. Manila: Historical Conservation Society, [1604] 1969.

Clark, Hugh R. *Community, Trade and Networks: Southern Fujian Province from the Third to the Thirteenth Century*. Cambridge: Cambridge University Press, 1991.

Cliff, Andrew, and Peter Haggett. *Atlas of Disease Distributions*. Oxford: Blackwell, 1988.

Cockburn, T. Aidan. Infectious Diseases in Ancient Populations. *Current Anthropology* 12 (1971): 45–62.

Cole, Fay C. *The Tinguian: Social, Religious and Economic Life of a Philippine Tribe*. Anthropological Series vol. 14 no. 2. Chicago: Field Museum of Natural History Publications, 1922.

Colección de documentos inéditos relativos al descubrimiento, conquista y organización de las antiguas posesiones españoles de América y Oceanía. 42 vols. Madrid, 1864–1884.

Colección de documentos inéditos relativos al descubrimiento, conquista y organización de las antiguas posesiones españoles de ultramar. 25 vols. 2nd Series. Madrid: Real Academia de la Historia, 1885–1932.

Colin, Pedro. *Labor evangélica*, 3 vols. Edited by Pablo Pastells. Barcelona: Heinrich y Compañía, 1900–1902.

Collantes, Domingo. *Historia de la provincia del santísimo rosario de Filipinas, China y Tunquin, orden de predicadores, Quarta parte, desde año 1700 hasta el de 1765*. Manila: Colegio de Santo Tomas, 1783.

Combés, Francisco. *Historia de las islas de Mindanao y Ioló* [1657]. Madrid, 1867.

Comyn, Tomás de. *Estado de las Islas Filipinas en 1810*. Manila: Imprenta de Repullés, 1820.

Concepción, Juan de la. *Historia general de Philipinas*. 14 vols. Manila: Por A. de la Rosa y Balagtas, 1788–1792.

Conklin, Harold C. *Ethnographic Atlas of the Ifugao*. New Haven, Conn.: Yale University Press, 1980.

———. *Hanunóo Agriculture*. Rome: FAO, 1957.

Cook, N. David. *Born to Die: Disease and New World Conquests, 1492–1650*. Cambridge: Cambridge University Press, 1998.

———. *Demographic Collapse: Indian Peru, 1520–1620*. Cambridge: Cambridge University Press, 1980.

Cook, N. David, and W. George Lovell, eds. *'Secret Judgments of God': Old World Disease in Colonial Spanish America*. Norman: University of Oklahoma Press, 1992.

Cook, Sherburne F., and Lesley Byrd Simpson. *The Population of Central Mexico in the Sixteenth Century*, Ibero-Americana 31. Berkeley: University of California Press, 1948.

Cordoniu y Nieto, Antonio. *Topografía médica de las islas filipinas*. Madrid: Imp. Alejandro Gómez Fuentenebro, 1857.

Corpuz, Onofre D. *The Bureaucracy in the Philippines*. Quezon City: University of the Philippines, 1957.

———. *The Roots of the Filipino Nation*, vol. 1. Quezon City: AKLAHI Foundation, 1988.

Cortes, Rosario M. *Pangasinan 1572–1820*. Quezon City: University of the Philippines, 1974.

Cortesão, Armando. *The Suma Oriental of Tomé Pires*. 2 vols. London: Hakluyt Society, 1944.

Costa, Horacio de la. Church and State in the Philippines during the Administration of Bishop Salazar, 1581–1594. *Hispanic American Historical Review* 30 (3) (1950): 314–335.

———. *The Jesuits in the Philippines, 1581–1768*. Cambridge, Mass.: Harvard University Press, 1961.

Crosby, Alfred W. Virgin Soil Epidemics as a Factor in the Aboriginal Depopulation in America. *William and Mary Quarterly* 33 (1976): 289–299.

Cruikshank, Bruce. The Moro Impact on Samar Island, the Philippines. *Philippine Quarterly of Culture and Society* 7 (3) (1979): 141–185.

———. *Samar: 1768–1898*. Manila: Historical Conservation Society, 1985.

Cullinane, Michael. Accounting for Souls: Ecclesiastical Sources for the Study of Philippine Demographic History. In *Population and History: The Demographic Origins of the Modern Philippines*, edited by Daniel F. Doeppers and Peter Xenos, 281–346. Madison: University of Wisconsin Press, 1998.

———. The Changing Nature of the Cebu Urban Elite in the Nineteenth Century. In *Philippine Social History: Global Trade and Local Transformations*, edited by Alfred J. McCoy and Ed. C. de Jesus, 251–296. Quezon City: Ateneo de Manila University Press, 1982.

Cullinane, Michael, and Peter Xenos. The Growth of Population in Cebu during the Spanish Era: Constructing a Regional Demography from Local Sources. In *Population and History: The Demographic Origins of the Modern Philippines*, edited by Daniel F. Doeppers and Peter Xenos, 71–138. Madison: University of Wisconsin Press, 1998.

Cummins, James S., ed. *The Travels and Controversies of Friar Domingo de Navarrete, 1618–1686*. 2 vols. Cambridge: Cambridge University Press, 1962.

Cunningham, Charles H. *The Audiencia in the Spanish Colonies: As Illustrated by the Audiencia de Manila (1583–1810)*. University of California Publications in History, vol. 9. Berkeley: University of California Press, 1919.

Cushner, Nicholas P. *The Isles of the West: Early Spanish Voyages to the Philippines, 1521–1564*. Quezon City: Ateneo de Manila University Press, 1966.

———. *Landed Estates in the Colonial Philippines*. Yale University Southeast Asia Studies 20. New Haven, Conn.: Yale University Press, 1976.

———. Meysapan: The Formation and Social Effects of a Landed Estate in the Philippines. *Journal of Asian History* 7 (1973): 30–53.

———. *Spain in the Philippines: From Conquest to Revolution*. Quezon City: Ateneo de Manila University Press, 1971.

Cushner, Nicholas P., and John A. Larkin. Royal Land Grants in the Colonial Philippines (1571–1626): Implications for the Formation of a Social Elite. *Philippines Studies* 26 (1978): 102–111.

De Bevoise, Ken. *Agents of the Apocalypse: Epidemic Disease in the Colonial Philippines*. Princeton, N.J.: Princeton University Press, 1995.

———. Until God Knows When: Smallpox in the Late Colonial Philippines. *Pacific Historical Review* 59 (1990): 149–185.

De Jesus, Ed. C. Control and Compromise in the Cagayan Valley. In *Philippine Social History: Global Trade and Local Transformations*, edited by Alfred J. McCoy and Ed. C. de Jesus, 21–37. Quezon City: Ateneo de Manila University Press, 1982.

———. *The Tobacco Monopoly in the Philippines: Bureaucratic Enterprise and Social Change, 1766–1880.* Quezon City: Ateneo de Manila University Press, 1980.

Denevan, William M., ed. *Native Population of the Americas in 1492.* Madison: University of Wisconsin Press, 1992.

Díaz, Casimiro. OSA *Conquistas de las Islas filipinas.* Valladolid: Luis N. de Gaviria, 1890.

Díaz Arenas, Rafael *Memorias históricas y estadísticas de Filipinas.* Manila: Imp. Del Diario de Manila, 1850.

Díaz-Trechuelo, María Lourdes. Eighteenth Century Philippine Economy: Mining. *Philippine Studies* 11 (1965): 763–797.

———. The Role of the Chinese in the Philippine Domestic Economy (1570–1770). In *The Chinese in the Philippines*, vol. 1, edited by A. Felix, 175–210. Manila: Solidaridad Publication House, 1966.

Dobson, Mary J. Mortality Gradients and Disease Exchanges: Comparisons from Old England and Colonial America. *Social History of Medicine* 2 (1989): 259–295.

Dobyns, Henry F. Estimating Aboriginal American Population: An Appraisal of Techniques with a New Hemispheric Estimate. *Current Anthropology* 7 (1966): 395–416.

Doeppers, Daniel F. Evidence from the Grave: The Changing Social Composition of the Populations of Metropolitan Manila and Molo, Iloilo, during the Later Nineteenth Century. In *Population and History: The Demographic Origins of the Modern Philippines*, edited by Daniel F. Doeppers and Peter Xenos, 265–277. Madison: University of Wisconsin Press, 1998.

———. Hispanic Influences on Demographic Patterns in the Central Plain of Luzon, 1565–1780. *University of Manila Journal of East Asiatic Studies* 12 (1968): 11–96.

Dozier, Edward P. *The Kalinga of Northern Luzon, Philippines.* New York: Holt, Rinehart and Winston, 1967.

———. *Mountain Arbiters: The Changing Life of a Philippine Hill People.* Tucson: University of Arizona Press, 1966.

Dunstan, Helen. The Late Ming Epidemics: A Preliminary Survey. *Ch'ing-shih wen-t'i* 3 (3) (1975): 1–59.

Echevarría, Ramón. *Rediscovery in Southern Cebu.* Cebu City: Historical Conservation Society, 1974.

Farley, John. *Bilharzia: A History of Imperial Tropical Medicine.* Cambridge: Cambridge University Press, 1991.

Farris, William W. Diseases of the Premodern Period in Japan. In *The Cambridge World History of Human Disease*, edited by Kenneth Kiple, 376–385. Cambridge: Cambridge University Press, 1993.

———. *Population, Disease and Land in Early Japan: 645–900.* Cambridge: Cambridge University Press, 1985.

Fenner, Bruce L. *Cebu Under the Spanish Flag, 1521–1896.* Cebu City: San Carlos Publications, 1985.

Fenner, Frank L. The Effects of Changing Social Organisation on the Infectious Diseases of Man. In *The Impact of Civilisation on the Biology of Man*, edited by S. Boyden, 48–76. Canberra: Australian National University Press, 1970.

———. Smallpox in Southeast Asia. *Crossroads: An Interdisciplinary Journal of Southeast Asian Studies* 3 (2–3) (1987): 34–48.

Fenner, Frank, Donald A. Henderson, Isao Arita, Zdeněk Ježek, and Ivan D. Ladnyi. *Smallpox and its Eradication*. Geneva: World Health Organization, 1988.

Fernández Arias, Evaristo. *El paralelo entre la conquista y dominación de América y el descubrimiento y pacificación de Filipinas*. Madrid: W. E. Retana, 1893.

Fernández, Pablo. Dominican Apostolate in the Philippines. *Boletin eclesiástico de Filipinas* 39 (1965): 148–181.

———. *History of the Church in the Philippines, 1521–1898*. Manila: National Bookstore, 1979.

Fernández, Pablo, and Jesús de Juan. Social and Economic Development of the Province of Nueva Vizcaya, Philippines 1571–1898. *Acta Manilana* 1 (8) (1969): 59–134.

Ferrando, Juan, and Joaquín Fonseca. *Historia de los PP dominicos en las islas Filipinas y en sus misiones del Japón, China, Tun-kin y Formosa*. 6 vols. Madrid: M. Rivadeneyra, 1870–1872.

Foronda, Marcelino A., and Juan A. Foronda. *Samtoy: Essays on Iloko History and Culture*. Manila: United Publishing Co., 1972.

Forrest, Thomas. *A Voyage to New Guinea and the Moluccas*. London: G. Scott, 1779.

Fox, Robert B. The Archaeological Record of Chinese Influences in the Philippines. *Philippine Studies* 15 (1) (1967): 51–62.

———. The Calatagan Excavations: Burial Sites in Batangas. *Philippine Studies* 7 (1959): 325–390.

———. The Philippines in Prehistoric Times. In *Readings in Philippine Prehistory*, edited by Mauro García, 35–61. Manila: Filipiana Book Guild, 1979.

Fradera, Josep M. *Filipinas, colonia más peculiar: la hacienda pública en la definición de la política colonial, 1762–1868*. Madrid: Consejo Superior de Investigaciones Científicas, 1999.

Galende, Pedro. The Augustinians in the Philippines (1565–1890). *Boletín eclesiástico de Filipinas* 39 (1965): 35–79.

Gardner, Fletcher, and Ildefonso Maliwanag. *Indic Writings of the Mindoro-Palawan Axis*. 3 vols. San Antonio, Tex.: Witte Memorial Museum, 1939–1940.

Garruto, Ralph M. Disease Patterns of Isolated Groups. In *Biocultural Aspects of Disease*, edited by Henry Rothschild, 557–597. New York: Academic Press, 1981.

Gayo Aragón, Jesús. Ideas jurídico-teológicos de los religiosos de Filipinas en el siglo XVI sobre la conquista de las islas. Manila: Universidad de Santo Tomas, 1950.

Geeroms, Henry. Former Spanish Missions in the Cordillera (N. Luzon) I. *Saint Louis Quarterly* 3 (1965): 17–56.

———. Former Spanish Missions in the Cordillera (N. Luzon) II. *Saint Louis Quarterly* 3 (1965): 437–480.

———. Former Spanish Missions in the Cordillera (N. Luzon) III. *Saint Louis Quarterly* 4 (1966): 373–434.

Gemelli Careri, John Francis. *A Voyage around the World*. In *A Collection of Voyage and Travels*. vol. 4 part V: The Philippines, 416–500. London: Awnsham and John Churchill, 1704.

Glover, Ian C., and Charles F. W. Higham. New Evidence for Early Rice Cultivation in South, Southeast and East Asia. In *The Origins and Spread of Agriculture and Pastoralism in Eurasia*, edited by David R. Harris, 413–441. London: UCL Press, 1996.

Goodman, Alan H., and Debra L. Martin. Reconstructing Health Profiles from Skeletal Remains. In *The Backbone of History: Health and Nutrition in the Western Hemisphere*, edited by Richard H. Steckel and Jerome C. Rose, 11–60. Cambridge: Cambridge University Press, 2002.

González, E. R., and R. Mellafe. La función de la familia en la historia social hispanoamericana colonial. *Anuario del Instituto de Investigaciones Históricas* 8 (1965): 57–71.

Goyena del Prado, Mariano. *Ibalon: Ethnohistory of the Bikol Region*. Translated by M. L. F. Realubit. Legazpi City: AMS Press, 1981.

Grau y Figueras, Casimiro de. *Memoria sobre la población y riqueza de las islas Filipinas*. Barcelona: Imp. Ramírez, 1855.

Grau y Monfalcón, Juan. *Memorial informatorio*. Madrid, 1637.

Grijalva, Juan de. *Crónica de la orden de nuestro padre San Agustín*. Mexico, 1624.

Guerra, Francisco. *El hospital en Hispanoamérica y Filipinas, 1492–1898*. Madrid: Ministerio de Sanidad y Consumo, 1994.

Guerrero, Milagros C. The Chinese in the Philippines, 1570–1770. In *The Chinese in the Philippines*, vol. 1, edited by Alfonso Felix, 15–39. Manila: Solidaridad Publication House, 1966.

Gwei-Djen, Lu, and Joseph Needham. Diseases of Antiquity in China. In *The Cambridge World History of Human Disease*, edited by Kenneth Kiple, 345–354. Cambridge: Cambridge University Press, 1993.

Haggett, Peter. Prediction and Predictability in Geographic Systems. *Transactions of the Institute of British Geographers NS* 19 (1994): 6–20.

Hall, Kenneth R. Economic History of Southeast Asia. In *The Cambridge History of Southeast Asia* vol. 1, edited by Nicholas Tarling, 183–275. Cambridge: Cambridge University Press, 1992.

Hanke, Lewis. *Aristotle and the American Indians: A Study in Race Prejudice in the Modern World*. London: Hollis and Carter, 1959.

———. *The Spanish Struggle for Justice in the Conquest of America*. Boston: Little Brown, 1965.

Hanke, Lewis, and Agustín Millares Carlo, eds. *Cuerpo de documentos del siglo XVI sobre los derechos de España en las Indias y las Filipinas*. Mexico, D.F.: Fondo de Cultura Económica, 1943.

Harden, Victoria A. Typhus, Epidemic. In *The Cambridge World History of Human Disease*, edited by Kenneth Kiple, 1080–1084. Cambridge: Cambridge University Press, 1993.

Haring, Clarence H. *The Spanish Empire in America*. New York: Harcourt, Brace and World, 1963.

Hart, Donn V. *Bisayan Filipino and Malayan Humoral Pathologies: Folk Medicine and Ethnohistory in Southeast Asia*, Southeast Asia Program, Data Paper 76. Ithaca, N.Y.: Cornell University, 1969.

Hayes, C., C. Mamiloto, T. O'Rourke, G. Schultz, V. Basaca-Sevilla, A. Gonzales, C. Ranoa, and J. Cross. Dengue Studies in the Philippines. In *Arbovirus Research in Australia*. Proceedings of the 4th symposium, Brisbane, 43–44. CSIRO: no place of publication given, 1986.

Headley, John M. Spain's Asian Presence, 1565–1590. *Hispanic American Historical Review* 75 (1995): 623–646.
Hembd, Jerry. The Political Economy of Uneven Regional Development in the Philippines: The Case of Bikol. PhD dissertation, Stanford University, 1984.
Henige, David. *Numbers from Nowhere: The American Indian Contact Population Debate*. Norman: University of Oklahoma Press, 1998.
Henley, David. *Fertility, Food and Fever: Population, Economic and Environment in North and Central Sulawesi, 1600–1930*. Leiden: KILV Press, 2005.
———. From Low to High Fertility on Sulawesi (Indonesia) During the Colonial Period: Explaining the 'First Fertility Transition.' *Population Studies* 60 (3): 309–327.
———. Population and the Means of Subsistence: Explaining the Historical Demography of Island Southeast Asia, with Particular Reference to Sulawesi. *Journal of Southeast Asian Studies* 36 (3): 337–372.
Henson, Mariano A. *The Province of Pampanga and its Towns AD 1300–1955*. Manila: Villanueva Bookstore, 1955.
Herce, Pedro. Recollects in the Philippines. *Boletín eclesiástico de Filipinas* 39 (1965): 220–253.
Hern, Warren M. Polygyny and Fertility Among the Shipibo of the Peruvian Amazon, *Population Studies* 46 (1) (1992): 53–64.
Hidalgo Nuchera, Patricio. *Encomienda, tributo y trabajo en Filipinas*. Madrid: Universidad Autónoma de Madrid, 1995.
———. *Recta administración. Primeros tiempos de la colonización hispana en Filipinas: la situación de la población nativa*. Madrid: Ediciones Polifemo, 2001.
Hopkins, David R. *Princes and Peasants: Smallpox in History*. Chicago: University of Chicago Press, 1983.
Huerta, Felix de. *Estado geográfico, topográfico, estadístico, histórico-religioso de la santa y apostólica provincia de S. Gregorio Magno*. Binondo: M. Sánchez y Compania, 1865.
Hutterer, Karl L. *An Archaeological Picture of a Pre-Spanish Cebuano Community*. Cebu City: University of San Carlos Publications, 1973.
———. The Evolution of Philippine Lowland Societies. *Mankind* 9 (1974): 287–299.
———. Prehistoric Trade and the Evolution of Philippine Societies: A Reconsideration. In *Economic Exchange and Social Interaction in Southeast Asia: Perspectives from Prehistory, History and Ethnography*, edited by Karl L. Hutterer, 177–196. Ann Arbor: Center for South and Southeast Asian Studies, The University of Michigan, 1977.
Ileto, Reynaldo C. *Magindanao, 1860–1888: The Career of Datu Uto of Buayan*. Marawi City: Mindanao State University, no date [1971].
Jannetta, Ann B. Diseases of the Premodern Period in Japan. In *The Cambridge World History of Human Disease*, edited by Kenneth Kiple, 385–389. Cambridge: Cambridge University Press, 1993.
———. *Epidemics and Mortality in Early Modern Japan*. Princeton, N.J.: Princeton University Press, 1987.
Jesús, Luis de. *Historia general de los descalzos del orden de los ermitaños del gran padre San Agustín de la congregación de España y de las Indias*. Madrid: Lucas Antonio de Bedmar, 1681.
Jocano, F. Landa. *The Ilocanos*. Quezon City: University of the Philippines, 1982.
———. *The Philippines at the Spanish Contact*. Manila: MCS Enterprises, Inc., 1975.

Johnston, William D. Tuberculosis. In *The Cambridge World History of Human Disease*, edited by Kenneth Kiple, 1059–1068. Cambridge: Cambridge University Press, 1993.

Junker, Laura L. *Raiding, Trading and Feasting: The Political Economy of Philippine Chiefdoms*. Honolulu: University of Hawai'i Press, 1999.

———. Trade Competition, Conflict and Political Transformations in Sixteenth-Century Philippine Chiefdoms. *Asian Perspectives* 33 (2) (1994): 229–260.

Keesing, Felix M. *The Ethnohistory of Northern Luzon*. Stanford, Calif.: Stanford University Press, 1962.

Knaap, Gerrit. The Demography of Ambon in the Seventeenth Century: Evidence from Colonial Proto-Censuses. *Journal of Southeast Asian Studies* 26 (2) (1995): 227–241.

Kroeber, Alfred L. *Cultural and Natural Areas of Native North America*. University of California Publications in American Archaeology and Ethnology 38. Berkeley: University of California Press, 1939.

Krzywicki, Ludwik. *Primitive Society and its Vital Statistics*. London: Macmillan and Co., 1934.

Lamb, Hubert H. *Climate: Present, Past and Future*, vol. 2. London: Methuen, 1977.

Lambrecht, Francis. The Hudhud of Dinulawan and Bugan at Gonhadan. *Saint Louis Quarterly* 5 (1967): 267–313.

Larkin, John A. *The Pampangans: Colonial Society in a Philippine Province*. Berkeley and Los Angeles: University of California Press, 1972.

Le Gentil de la Galaisière, Guillaume J. H. J. B. *Voyage dans les mers de l'Inde*. Paris: Imprimerie Royale, 1781.

Leung, Angela K. C. Diseases of the Premodern Period in China. In *The Cambridge World History of Human Disease*, edited by Kenneth Kiple, 354–362. Cambridge: Cambridge University Press, 1993.

Lewis, Henry T. *Ilocano Rice Farmers: A Comparative Study of Two Philippine Barrios*. Honolulu: University of Hawai'i Press, 1971.

Lilienfeld, A. M., and D. E. Lilienfeld. *Foundations of Epidemiology*. 2nd ed. New York: Oxford University Press, 1980.

Lim, Aurora R. *The Evidence of Ceramics as an Aid in Understanding the Pattern of Trade in the Philippines and Southeast Asia*. Asian Studies Monograph 36. Bangkok: Institute of Asian Studies, 1987.

Lisboa, Marcos de. *Vocabulario de la lengua Bikol* [comp. 1628]. Manila: Colegio de Santo Tomás, 1865.

Livingstone, Frank B. *Frequencies of Hemoglobin Variants*. New York: Oxford University Press, 1985.

López, Francisco. *Vocabulario de la lengua Iloca*. Ms Marsden Collection M2, King's College London, ca. 1627.

Lopez, Violeta B. Culture Contact and Ethnogenesis in Mindoro up to the End of the Spanish Rule, *Asian Studies* 12 (1974): 1–38.

———. *The Mangyans of Mindoro*. Quezon City: University of the Philippines, 1976.

Lovell, W. George. The Demography of the Cuchumatán Highlands, Guatemala, 1500–1821. In *Studies in Spanish American Population History*, edited by David J. Robinson, 195–216. Boulder, Colo.: Westview Press, 1981.

Luengo, Josemaría. *A History of the Philippines: A Focus on the Christianization of Bohol, 1521–1991*. Tubigon, Bohol: Mater Dei Publications, 1992.

Magner, Lois N. Diseases of the Premodern Period in Korea. In *The Cambridge World History of Human Disease*, edited by Kenneth Kiple, 393–400. Cambridge: Cambridge University Press, 1993.

Maher, Robert F. Archaeological Investigations in Central Ifugao. *Asian Perspectives* 16 (1973): 39–70.

———. The Great Ifugao War: A Study in Archaeology and Oral History. *Asian Perspectives* 18 (1975): 64–74.

Majul, Cesar A. Islamic and Arab Cultural Influences in the South of the Philippines. *Journal of Southeast Asian History* 7 (1966): 61–73.

———. The 'Moro' Wars. In *Filipino Heritage*, vol. 4, edited by Alfredo R. Roces, 1080–1086. Manila: Lahing Pilipino Publishing Inc., 1977.

———. *Muslims in the Philippines*. 2nd ed. Quezon City: University of the Philippines Press, 1973.

Mallari, Francisco. *Ibalon Under Storm and Siege: Essays on Bicol History: 1565–1860*. Cagayan del Oro: Xavier University, 1990.

———. Muslim Raids in Bicol, 1580–1792. *Philippine Studies* 34 (1986): 257–286.

Malumbres, Julián. Carta a la provincial. *Correo Sino-Annamita* 23 (1889): 417–463.

———. *Historia de Cagayan*. Manila: Colegio de Santo Tomás, 1918.

———. *Historia de Isabela*. Manila: Colegio de Santo Tomás, 1918.

———. *Historia de Nueva Viscaya y provincia montañosa*. Manila: Colegio de Santo Tomás, 1919.

Manguin, Pierre-Yves. The Southeast Asian Ship: An Historical Approach. *Journal of Southeast Asian Studies* 11 (2) (1980): 266–276.

Mapa general de las almas que administran los Padres Agustinos calzados sacado en el año de 1820. Madrid: Imprenta que fue de García, 1820.

Marcy, Peter T. Factors Affecting the Fecundity and Fertility of Historical Populations. *Journal of Family History* 6 (1981): 309–326.

Martínez Cuesta, Angel. *History of Negros*. Manila: Historical Conservation Society, 1980.

Martínez de Zúñiga, Joaquin. *Estadismo de las islas Filipinas ó mis viajes por este país*. Madrid: Imp. Viuda de M. Minuesa de los Ríos, 1893.

———. *Historia de las islas Filipinas*. Sampaloc: Imp. Concepción Religioso Franciscano, 1803.

Martínez, Domingo. *Compendio histórico de la apostólica provincia de San Gregorio de Philipinas de religiosos menores descalzos de N.P. San Francisco*. Madrid: Imp. Viuda de Manuel Fernández, 1756.

Mas y Sans, Sinibaldo de. *Informe sobre le estado de las islas Filipinas en 1842*. 2 vols. Madrid, 1843.

McCoy, Alfred W. The Queen Dies Slowly: The Rise and Decline of Iloilo City. In *Philippine Social History: Global Trade and Local Transformations*, edited by Alfred J. McCoy and Ed. C. de Jesus, 297–358. Quezon City: Ateneo de Manila University Press, 1982.

McKeown, Thomas. *The Modern Rise of Population*. London: Edward Arnold, 1976.

———. *The Origins of Human Disease*. Oxford: Basil Blackwell, 1988.

McLennan, Marshall S. *The Central Luzon Plain: Land and Society on the Inland Frontier*. Manila: Alemar-Phoenix Publishing House, Inc., 1980.

———. Changing Human Ecology on the Central Luzon Plain: Nueva Ecija, 1705–1939. In *Philippine Social History: Global Trade and Local Transformations*, edited by Alfred J. McCoy and Ed. C. de Jesus, 57–90. Quezon City: Ateneo de Manila University Press, 1982.

McNeill, William H. *Plagues and Peoples*. New York: Oxford University Press, 1976.

Medina, Isagani R. *Cavite Before the Revolution, 1571–1896*. Quezon City: University of the Philippines Press, 1994.

Medina, Juan de. *Historia de los sucesos de la orden de N. Gran P. S. Agustín de estas Islas Filipinas* [1630] Manila: Chofrey y Comp, 1893.

Mentrida, Alonso de. *Diccionario de la lengua Bisaya, Hiligueina y Haraya de la isla de Panay* [comp. 1637]. Manila: D. Manuela y D. Felis Dayot, 1841.

Merino, Luis. *The Cabildo Secular, or Municipal Government of Manila: A Social Component, Organization, Economics*. Iloilo: Research Center, University of San Agustin, 1980.

Molano, Juan. Description of Kiangan in 1801. In Notes on the History of the Mountain Province – II, translated by William H. Scott, *University of Baguio Journal* 7 (1972): 133–137.

Montero y Vidal, José. *Historia general de Filipinas*. 3 vols. Madrid: M. Tello, 1887–1895.

———. *Historia de la piratería malayo-mahometana en Mindanao, Jolo y Borneo*. 2 vols. Madrid: M. Tello, 1888.

Morales Maza, Resurección. *The Augustinians in Panay*. Iloilo City: Research and Development Foundation Inc., The University of San Agustin, 1987.

Moreno y Díaz, Rafael. *Manual de cabeza de barangay*. Manila: Imprenta Amigos del Pais, 1874.

Morga, Antonio de. *Sucesos de las islas filipinas*, Hakluyt Society ser. 2 vol. 140. Edited by James S. Cummins. Cambridge: Cambridge University Press, 1971.

Mörner, Magnus. *Race Mixture in the History of Latin America*. Boston: Little, Brown and Company, 1967.

Motulsky, A.G., E. Stransky, and G. R. Fraser. Glucose-6-phosphate dehydrogenase (G6PD) Deficiency, Thalassaemia and Abnormal Haemoglobins in the Philippines. *Journal of Medical Genetics* 1 (1964): 102–106.

Mozo, Antonio. *Noticia histórico-natural de los gloriosos triumphos y felices adelantamientos*. Madrid: Andrés Ortega, 1763.

Murillo Velarde, Pedro. *Geografía histórica*. Madrid: D. Gabriel Ramírez, 1752.

———. *Historia de la provincia de Philippinas de la Compañía de Jesús*. Manila: Imp. Compañía de Jesús, 1749.

Needham, Joseph. *Science and Civilization in China. vol. 4. Physics and Physical Engineering. part III Civil Engineering and Nautics*. Cambridge: Cambridge University Press, 1971.

Neel, James V. Health and Disease in Unacculturated Amerindian Populations. In *Health and Disease in Tribal Societies*, CIBA Foundation Symposium 49, 155–168. Amsterdam: Elsevier, 1977.

Newson, Linda A. The Demographic Collapse of Native Peoples of the Americas, 1492–1650. *Proceedings of the British Academy* 81 (1993): 247–288.

———. The Demographic Impact of Colonization. In *The Cambridge Economic History of Latin America Vol. 1 The Colonial Era and the Short Nineteenth Century*, edited by Victor Bulmer-Thomas, John H. Coatsworth, and Roberto Cortés-Conde, 143–184. Cambridge: Cambridge University Press, 2006.

———. Disease and Immunity in the Pre-Spanish Philippines. *Social Science and Medicine* 48 (1999): 1833–1850.

———. A Historical-Ecological Perspective on Epidemic Disease. In *Advances in Historical Ecology*, edited by William Balée, 41–63. New York: Columbia University Press, 1998.

———. Indian Population Patterns in Colonial Spanish America. *Latin American Research Review* 20 (3) (1985): 41–74.

———. *Life and Death in Early Colonial Ecuador*. Norman: University of Oklahoma Press, 1995.

———. Old World Diseases in the Early Colonial Philippines and Spanish America. In *Population and History: The Demographic Origins of the Modern Philippines*, edited by Daniel F. Doeppers and Peter Xenos, 39–70. Madison: University of Wisconsin Press, 1998.

Nicholl, Robert. Brunei Rediscovered: A Survey of Early Times. *Journal of Southeast Asian Studies* 14 (1) (1983): 32–45.

Nishimura, Masao. Long Distance Trade and the Development of Complex Societies in the Prehistory of the Central Philippines – The Cebu Archaeological Project: Basic Concepts and First Result. *Philippine Quarterly of Culture and Society* 16 (1988): 107–157.

Noone, Martin J. *General History of the Philippines, part I, vol. I The Discovery and Conquest of the Philippines (1521–1581)*. Manila: Manila Historical Conservation Society, 1986.

Nort, Olivier de. *Description du penible voyage fait entour de l'univers ou globe terrestre par Sr. Olivier du Nort d'Utrecht*. Amsterdam: Vesve de Cornille, 1610.

Oración, Timoteo S. Notes on the Culture of Negritos on Negros Island. *Silliman Journal* 7 (1960): 201–218.

Ots Capdequí, José M. *España en América: El regimen de tierras en la época colonial*. Mexico D.F.: Fondo de Cultura Económica, 1959.

Owen, Norman G. ed. *Death and Disease in Southeast Asia: Explorations in Social, Medical and Demographic History*. Oxford: Oxford University Press, 1987.

———. Kabikolan in the Nineteenth Century: Socioeconomic Change in the Provincial Philippines. 2 vols. PhD dissertation, University of Michigan, 1976.

———. Life, Death and the Sacraments in a Nineteenth-Century Bikol Parish. In *Population and History: The Demographic Origins of the Modern Philippines*, edited by Daniel F. Doeppers and Peter Xenos, 225–252. Madison: University of Wisconsin Press, 1998.

———. Measuring Mortality in the Nineteenth Century Philippines. In *Death and Disease in Southeast Asia: Explorations in Social, Medical and Demographic History*, edited by Norman G. Owen, 94–102. Oxford: Oxford University Press, 1987.

———. The Paradox of Nineteenth-Century Population Growth in Southeast Asia: Evidence from Java and the Philippines. *Journal of Southeast Asian Studies* 18 (1) (1987): 45–57.

———. Philippine Historical Demography: Sources and Prospects. Unpublished manuscript, 1995.

———. The Principalia in Philippine History: Kabikolan 1790–1898. *Philippine Studies* 22 (1974): 297–324.

———. Problems in Partido, 1741–1810. *Philippine Studies* 38 (4) (1990): 297–324.

———. *Prosperity without Progress: Manila Hemp and Material Life in the Colonial Philippines*. Berkeley: University of California Press, 1984.

———. Towards a History of Health in Southeast Asia. In *Death and Disease in Southeast Asia: Explorations in Social, Medical and Demographic History*, edited by Norman G. Owen, 3–30. Oxford: Oxford University Press, 1987.

Pagès, Monsieur de. *Travels Round the World in the Years 1767, 1768, 1769, 1770, 1771*. 2nd ed. John Murray: London, 1793.

Parker, Geoffrey. *The Grand Strategy of Philip II*. New Haven, Conn.: Yale University Press, 1998.

Paske-Smith, M. T. The Japanese Trade and Residence in the Philippines Before and During the Spanish Occupation. *Transactions of the Asiatic Society of Japan* 42 (1914): 684–710.

Pastrana, Apolinar. The Franciscans and the Evangelisation of the Philippines (1578–1900). *Boletín eclesiástico de Filipinas* 39 (1965): 80–115.

Patañe, E. P. To Lauch a Sea Giant. In *Filipino Heritage*, vol. 4, edited by Alfredo R. Roces, 1041–1043. Manila: Lahing Pilipino Publishing Inc., 1977.

Pedrosa, Ramón. Abortion and Infanticide in the Philippines during the Spanish Contact. *Philippiniana Sacra* 18 (52) (1983): 7–37.

Pérez, Angel. *Las igorrotes: estudio geográfico y etnográfico sobre algunos distritos de norte de Luzon*. Manila: Imprenta 'El Mercantil,' 1902.

———. *Relaciones agustinianas de las razas del norte de Luzon*. Manila: Bureau of Printing, 1904.

Pérez, Lorenzo. *Labor patriótica de los franciscanos en el Extremo Oriente*. Madrid: Imp. de los hijos de Tomás Minuesa de los Ríos, 1929.

———. Origen de las misiones franciscanos en el extremo oriente. *Archivo Ibero-Americano* 1 (1914): 100–120.

Phelan, John L. Free Versus Compulsory Labor: Mexico and the Philippines 1540–1648. *Comparative Studies in Society and History* 1 (1959): 189–201.

———. *The Hispanization of the Philippines: Spanish Aims and Filipino Responses 1565–1700*. Madison: University of Wisconsin Press, 1959.

———. Some Ideological Aspects of the Conquest of the Philippines. *The Americas* 13 (1957): 221–239.

Pigafetta, Antonio. *The First Voyage Around the World: An Account of Magellan's Expedition*. Edited by Theodore J. Cachey, Jr. New York: Marsillo Publishers, 1995.

Plasencia, Juan de. Relación del culto que los Tagalogs tenían [1676]. In *Francisco de, Cronica de la provincia de San Gregorio Magno de Religiosos Descalzos de N. S. P. San Francisco en las Islas Filipinas, China, Japon, etc.*, edited by Santa Inés. Biblioteca Histórica Filipina, vol. 2 part 3. Manila: Tipo-litografía de Chofre Comp., 1892.

Postma, Antoon. Mindoro Missions Revisited, *Philippine Quarterly of Culture and Society* 5 (1977): 252–265.

Prieto Lucena, Ana María. *Filipinas durante el gobierno de Manrique de Lara, 1653–1663*. Sevilla: Escuela de Estudios Hispano-Americanos, 1984.

Quirino, Carlos, and Mauro García. The Manners, Customs and Beliefs of the Philippine Inhabitants of Long Ago. *The Philippine Journal of Science* 87 (4) (1958): 325–388.

Rabor, Dioscoro S. *Guide to the Philippine Flora and Fauna, vol. 11 Birds and Mammals*. Quezon City: Natural Resources Management Center, University of the Philippines and the Ministry of Natural Resources, 1986.

Rafael, Vicente L. *Contracting Colonialism: Translation and Christian Conversion in Tagalog Society under Early Spanish Rule*. Durham, N.C.: Duke University Press, 1993.

Rahmann, Rudolf, and Marcelino Maceda. Some Notes on the Negritos of Northern Negros. *Athropos* 50 (1958): 810–836.

———. Notes on the Negritos of Iloilo, Island of Panay. *Anthropos* 53 (1955): 864–876.

Ramenofsky, Ann F. *Vectors of Death*. Albuquerque: University of New Mexico Press, 1987.

Recopilación de los leyes de los reynos de las indias. 3 vols. Madrid: Gráficas Ultra, 1943.

Redondo y Sendino, Felipe. *Breve reseña de lo que fue y de lo que es la diócesis de Cebú*. Manila: Colegio de Santo Tomás, 1886.

Reed, Robert R. *Colonial Manila: The Context of Hispanic Urbanism and Process of Morphogenesis*. University of California Publications in Geography 22. Berkeley and Los Angeles: University of California Press, 1978.

Regalado, Felix B., and Quintin B. Franco. *History of Panay*. Iloilo City: Central Philippines University, 1973.

Reid, Anthony. An 'Age of Commerce' in Southeast Asian History. *Modern Asian Studies* 24 (1) (1990): 1–30.

———. Economic and Social Change, c.1400–1800. In *The Cambridge History of Southeast Asia*, vol. 1, edited by Nicholas Tarling, 460–507. Cambridge: Cambridge University Press, 1992.

———. Introduction: Slavery and Bondage in Southeast Asian History. In *Slavery, Bondage and Dependency in Southeast Asia*, edited by Anthony Reid, 1–43. New York: St. Martin's Press, 1983.

———. Low Population Growth and Its Causes in Pre-Colonial Southeast Asia. In *Death and Disease in Southeast Asia: Explorations in Social, Medical and Demographic History*, edited by Norman G. Owen, 33–47. Oxford: Oxford University Press, 1987.

———. The Seventeenth-Century Crisis in Southeast Asia. *Modern Asian Studies* 24 (4) (1990): 639–659.

———. *Southeast Asia in the Age of Commerce 1450–1680, vol. I: The Lands Below the Winds*. New Haven, Conn., and London: Yale University Press, 1988.

———. *Southeast Asia in the Age of Commerce 1450–1680, vol. II: Expansion and Crisis*. New Haven, Conn., and London: Yale University Press, 1993.

———. South-East Asian Population History and the Colonial Impact. In *Asian Population History*, edited by Ts'ui-jung Liu, James Lee, David Sven Reher, Osamu Saito, and Wang Feng, 45–62. Oxford: Oxford University Press, 2001.

Retana, Wenceslao E., ed. *Archivo del bibliófilo filipino*. 5 vols. Madrid: Imp. De la Viuda de M. Minuesa de los Ríos, 1895–1905.

Reyes y Florentino, Isabelo de los. *Las islas Visayas en la época de la conquista*. 2nd ed. Manila: Chofre y Compañía, 1889.

———. *Historia de Ilocos*. 2 vols. Manila: Establecimiento Tipográfio La Opinión, 1890.

Reynolds, Hubert, and Fern B. Grant, eds. *The Isneg of the Northern Philippines: A Study of Trends of Change and Development*. Dumaguete City: Anthropological Museum, Silliman University, 1973.

Reynolds, Hubert, and Lillian K. Keyes. The Isneg Family. In *The Isneg of the Northern Philippines: A Study of Trends of Change and Development*, edited by Hubert Reynolds and Fern B. Grant, 79–129. Dumaguete City: Anthropological Museum, Silliman University, 1973.

Ribadeneyra, Marcelo de. OFM. *Historia del archipelago y otros reynos*. 2 vols. Manila: Historical Conservation Society, 1970.

Ricard, Robert. *The Spiritual Conquest of Mexico*. Berkeley and Los Angeles: University of California Press, 1966.

Roberts, Leslie. Disease and Death in the New World. *Science* 246 (1989): 1245–1247.
Rodríguez, Isacio R. *Historia de la provincia Agustiniana del smo. nombre de Jésus de Filipinas.* 20 vols. Manila: Arnoldus, 1965–1988.
Roth, Dennis M. The *Casas de Reservas* in the Philippines. *Journal of South East Asian Studies* 5 (1974): 115–124.
———. Church Lands in the Agrarian History of the Tagalog Region. In *Philippine Social History: Global Trade and Local Transformations*, edited by Alfred J. McCoy and Ed. C. de Jesus, 131–153. Quezon City: Ateneo de Manila University Press, 1982.
———. *The Friar Estates of the Philippines.* Albuquerque: University of New Mexico Press, 1977.
Routledge, David. *Diego Silang.* Quezon City: Philippine Center for Advanced Studies, University of the Philippine System, 1979.
Ruiz, Miguel. *Bocabulario Tagalo.* Ms Marsden Collection M2/17, King's College London, n.d. [comp. 1580?].
Russell, P. F. *Malaria: An Account of Its Cause, Cure and Prevention.* Manila: Bureau of Printing, 1932.
Saderra Masó, Miguel. *Catalogue of Violent and Disruptive Earthquakes in the Philippines, 1599–1909.* Manila: Bureau of Printing, 1910.
Salazar, Nelia P., Mary Elizabeth G. Miranda, Maximino N. Santos, and Lilian A. de Llagas. The Malaria Situation in the Philippines with Special Reference to Mosquito Vectors. *Southeast Asian Journal of Tropical Medicine and Public Health* 19 (4) (1988): 709–712.
Salazar, Vicente. *Historia de la provincia del santísimo rosario de Philipinas . . . tercera parte.* Manila: Colegio y Universidad de Santo Tomás, 1742.
Saleeby, Najeeb M. *The History of Sulu.* Manila: Bureau of Printing, 1908.
Salgado, Pedro V. *The Ilongots 1591–1994.* Manila: Lucky Press Limited, 1994.
Samuels, Marwyn S. *Contest for the South China Sea.* London: Methuen, 1982.
San Agustín, Gaspar de. *Conquistas de las islas filipinas.* Madrid: Consejo de Investigaciones Superiores, 1975.
San Antonio, Juan Francisco de. *The Philippine Chronicles of Fray San Antonio.* Manila: Casalinda and Historical Conservation Society, 1977.
San Buenaventura, Pedro de. *Vocabulario de lengua Tagala.* Pila: Thomas Pinpin and Domingo Loag Tagalogs, 1613.
Sánchez Fuertes, Cayetano. Estado de las misiones franciscanos en Filipinas 1751. *Missionalia hispánica* 42 (1985): 141–162.
Sánchez, Matheo. *Vocabulario de la lengua Bisaya* (comp. 1617). Manila, 1711.
Santa Cruz, Baltasar de. *Historia de la provincia del santo rosario de Filipinas, Iapón y China, de la sagrada orden de predicadores.* Zaragoza: D. Gascon, 1693.
Santos, Domingo de los. *Vocabulario de la lengua Tagala.* Manila, 1703.
Schmitz, Josef. *The Abra Mission in Northern Philippines, 1598–1955.* Manila: Arnoldus Press, 1971.
Schuldt, Volker. *Mindoro-Sozialgeschichte einer philippinischen Insel im 20. Jahrhundert: Studie eines verzögerten Entwicklungsprozesses.* Frankfurt: Peter Lang, 1990.
Schurz, William L. *The Manila Galleon.* New York: E. P. Dutton and Co., Inc., 1959.
Scott, William H. *Barangay.* Quezon City: Ateneo de Manila University Press, 1994.
———. *Cracks in the Parchment Curtain and Other Essays in Philippine History.* Quezon City: New Day Publishers, 1982.

———. *The Discovery of the Igorots: Spanish Contacts with the Pagans of Northern Luzon.* Quezon City: New Day Publishers, 1974.
———. Economic and Material Culture of the Kalingas of Madukayan. *Southwestern Journal of Anthropology* 14 (1958): 318–337.
———. Filipino Class Structure in the Sixteenth Century. In *Cracks in the Parchment Curtain and Other Essays in Philippine History*, edited by William H. Scott, 96–147. Quezon City: New Day Publishers, 1980.
———. *Filipinos in China before 1500.* Manila: De la Salle University Press, 1989.
———. Oripun and Alipin in the Sixteenth Century Philippines. In *Slavery, Bondage and Dependency in Southeast Asia*, edited by Anthony Reid, 138–155. New York: St. Martin's Press, 1983.
———. *Prehispanic Source Materials for the Study of Philippine History*. Rev. ed. Quezon City: New Day Publishers, 1984.
———. A Preliminary Report of Upland Rice. *Southwestern Journal of Anthropology* 14 (1958): 87–105.
———. *Slavery in the Spanish Philippines.* Manila: De la Salle University Press, 1991.
———. The Spanish Occupation of the Cordillera in the 19th Century. In *Philippine Social History: Global Trade and Local Transformations*, edited by Alfred J. McCoy and Ed. C. de Jesus, 39–56. Quezon City: Ateneo de Manila University Press, 1982.
Seed, Patricia. *Ceremonies of Possession in Europe's Conquest of the New World, 1492–1640.* Cambridge: Cambridge University Press, 1995.
Siler, J. F., M. W. Hall, and A. Parker Hitchens. Dengue: Its History, Epidemiology, Mechanism of Transmission, Etiology, Clinical Manifestations, Immunity and Prevention. *Philippine Journal of Science* 29 (1926): 1–304.
Smith, Clifford T. Depopulation of the Central Andes in the Sixteenth Century. *Current Anthropology* 11 (1970): 453–464.
Snow, B. E., R. Shutler, D. E. Nelson, J. S. Vogel, and J. R. Southon. Evidence for Early Rice Cultivation in the Philippines. *Philippine Quarterly of Culture and Society* 14 (1986): 3–11.
Spalding, Karen. Social Climbers: Changing Patterns of Mobility Among the Indians of Colonial Peru. *Hispanic American Historical Review* 53 (4) (1970): 645–664.
Spate, Oskar H. K. *The Spanish Lake*. London: Croom Helm, 1979.
Speilbergen, Joris van. *The East and West Indian Mirror, Being an Account of Joris van Speilbergen's Voyage Around the World.* Hakluyt Society ser. 2 vol. 18. Translated by J. A. J. de Villiers. London: Hakluyt Society, 1906.
Spencer, Joseph E. The Rise of Maize as a Major Crop Plant in the Philippines. *Journal of Historical Geography* 1 (1975): 1–16.
Tabangui, M. A., and A. M. Pasco. Studies on the Geographical Distribution, Incidence and Control of *Schistosomiasis japonica* in the Philippines. *Philippine Journal of Science* 74 (1941): 301–329.
Tantuico, Francisco S. *Leyte: The Historic Islands.* Tacloban City: The Leyte Publishing Corporation, 1964.
Tarling, Nicholas. *Piracy and Politics in the Malay World: A Study of British Imperialism in Nineteenth-Century South-East Asia*. Melbourne: F. W. Cheshire, 1963.
———. *Sulu and Sabah: A Study of British Policy Towards the Philippines and North Borneo from the Eighteenth Century*. Kuala Lumpur: Oxford University Press, 1978.

Tegengren, Felix R. A Historical Review of Gold in the Philippines, *The Philippine Journal of Science* 92 (4) (1963): 551–600.

TePaske, John J. New World Silver, Castile and the Philippines 1590–1800. In *Precious Metals in the Later Medieval and Early Modern Worlds*, edited by J. F. Richards, 425–445. Durham, N.C.: Carolina Academic Press, 1983.

Thornton, Russell, Tim Miller, and Jonathan Warren. American Indian Population Recovery Following Smallpox Epidemics. *American Anthropologist* 93 (3) (1991): 28–45.

Torrubia, José. *Dissertación histórico-política.* Madrid: D. Agustín de Gordejuela y Sierra, 1753.

Twitchett, Denis. Population and Pestilence in T'ang China. In *Studia Sino-Mongolica: Festschrift für Herbert Franke*, edited by W. Bauer, 35–69. Wiesbaden: Steiner, 1959.

Ustariz, Bernardo. *Relación de los sucesos y progresos de la misión de Santa Cruz y de Paniqui y de Ituy, medias entre las de Pangasinan, Cagayan y Pampanga. Año de 1745.* Manila, 1745.

VanderMeer, Canute. Population Patterns on the Island of Cebu, the Philippines: 1500 to 1900. *Annals of the Association of American Geographers* 57 (1967): 315–337.

Vanoverbergh, Morice. *Dress and Adornment in the Mountain Province of Luzon.* Catholic Anthropological Conference, vol. 1 no. 5: 181–244. Washington, D.C.: Catholic Anthropological Conference, 1929.

———. *Isneg.* Catholic Anthropological Conference, vol. 3 no. 1: 1–80. Washington, D.C.: Catholic Anthropological Conference, 1932.

Villiers, John. Manila and Maluku: Trade and Warfare in the Eastern Archipelago 1580–1640. *Philippine Studies* 34 (1986): 146–161.

Wallace, Ben J. *Hill and Valley Farmers: Socio-Economic Change among a Philippine People.* Cambridge, Mass.: Schenkman Publishing Co. Inc., 1970.

Warren, James. *The Sulu Zone, 1768–1898: The Dynamics of External Trade, Slavery and Ethnicity in the Transformation of a Southeast Asian Maritime State.* 2nd ed. Quezon City: New Day Publications, 1985.

———. *The Sulu Zone: The World Capitalist Economy and the Historical Imagination.* Amsterdam: VU University Press, 1998.

Wernstedt, Frederick L., and Joseph E. Spencer. *The Philippine Island World: A Physical, Human and Regional Geography.* Cambridge: Cambridge University Press, 1967.

Wheatley, Paul. Geographical Notes on Some Commodities Involved in Sung Maritime Trade. *Journal of the Malay Branch of the Royal Asiatic Society* 32 (2) (1959): 5–140.

———. *The Golden Khersonese: Studies in the Historical Geography of the Malay Peninsula before AD 1500.* Kuala Lumpur: University of Malaya Press, 1961.

———. *Nagara and Commandery: Origins of Southeast Asian Urbanism.* Chicago: University of Chicago Press, 1983.

Wickberg, Edgar. The Chinese Mestizo in Philippine History. *Journal of Southeast Asian History* 5 (1964): 62–100.

Wolters, Oliver W. *Early Indonesian Commerce.* Ithaca, N.Y.: Cornell University Press, 1967.

Wood, Frances. *Did Marco Polo Go to China?* London: Secker and Warburg, 1995.

Xenos, Peter. The Ilocos Coast since 1800: Population Pressure, the Ilocano Diaspora, and Multiphasic Response. In *Population and History: The Demographic Origins of the Modern Philippines*, edited by Daniel F. Doeppers and Peter Xenos, 39–70. Madison: University of Wisconsin Press, 1998.

Xenos, Peter, and Shui-Meng Ng. Nagcarlan, Laguna: A Nineteenth-Century Parish Demography. In *Population and History: The Demographic Origins of the Modern Philippines*, edited by Daniel F. Doeppers and Peter Xenos, 183–252. Madison: University of Wisconsin Press, 1998.
Yepes, Victoria. *Una etnografía de los indios Bisayas del siglo XVII*. Madrid: Consejo Superior de Investigaciones Científicas, 1996.
Zorc, David P. *The Bisayan Dialects of the Philippines: Subgrouping and Reconstruction*. Canberra: Australian National University Press, 1977.

Index

Page numbers in **boldface type** refer to illustrations and maps.